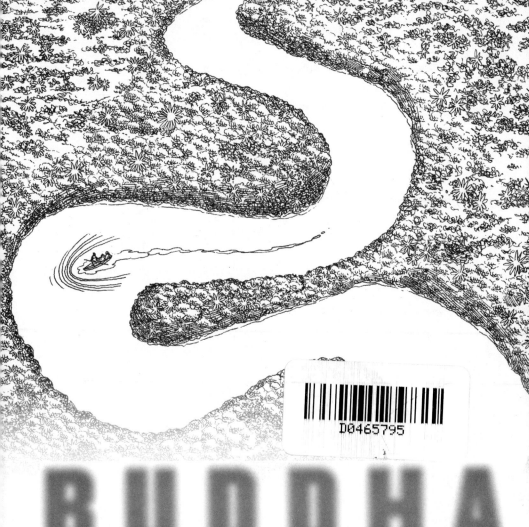

BUDDHA

OSAMU TEZUKA

VERTICAL.

2: *The Four Encounters*

THE JOURNEY

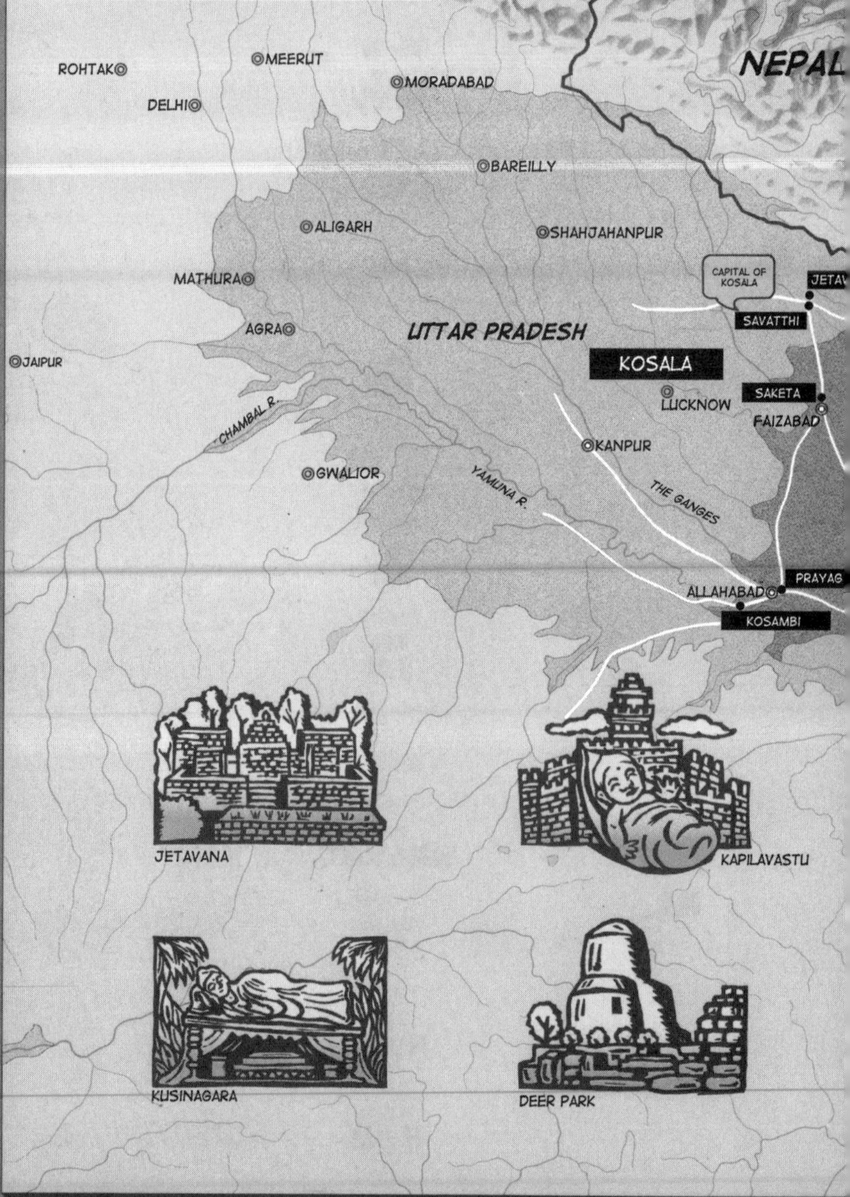

ROHTAK
MEERUT
MORADABAD
DELHI
NEPAL
BAREILLY
ALIGARH
SHAHJAHANPUR
MATHURA
CAPITAL OF KOSALA
SAVATTHI
AGRA
UTTAR PRADESH
KOSALA
JAIPUR
SAKETA
LUCKNOW
FAIZABAD
CHAMBAL R.
KANPUR
GWALIOR
YAMUNA R.
THE GANGES
PRAYAG
ALLAHABAD
KOSAMBI
JETAVANA
KAPILAVASTU
KUSINAGARA
DEER PARK

LUMBINI ANCIENT PLACE NAMES — MAJOR ROUTES ● PLACES VISITED BY THE BUDDHA

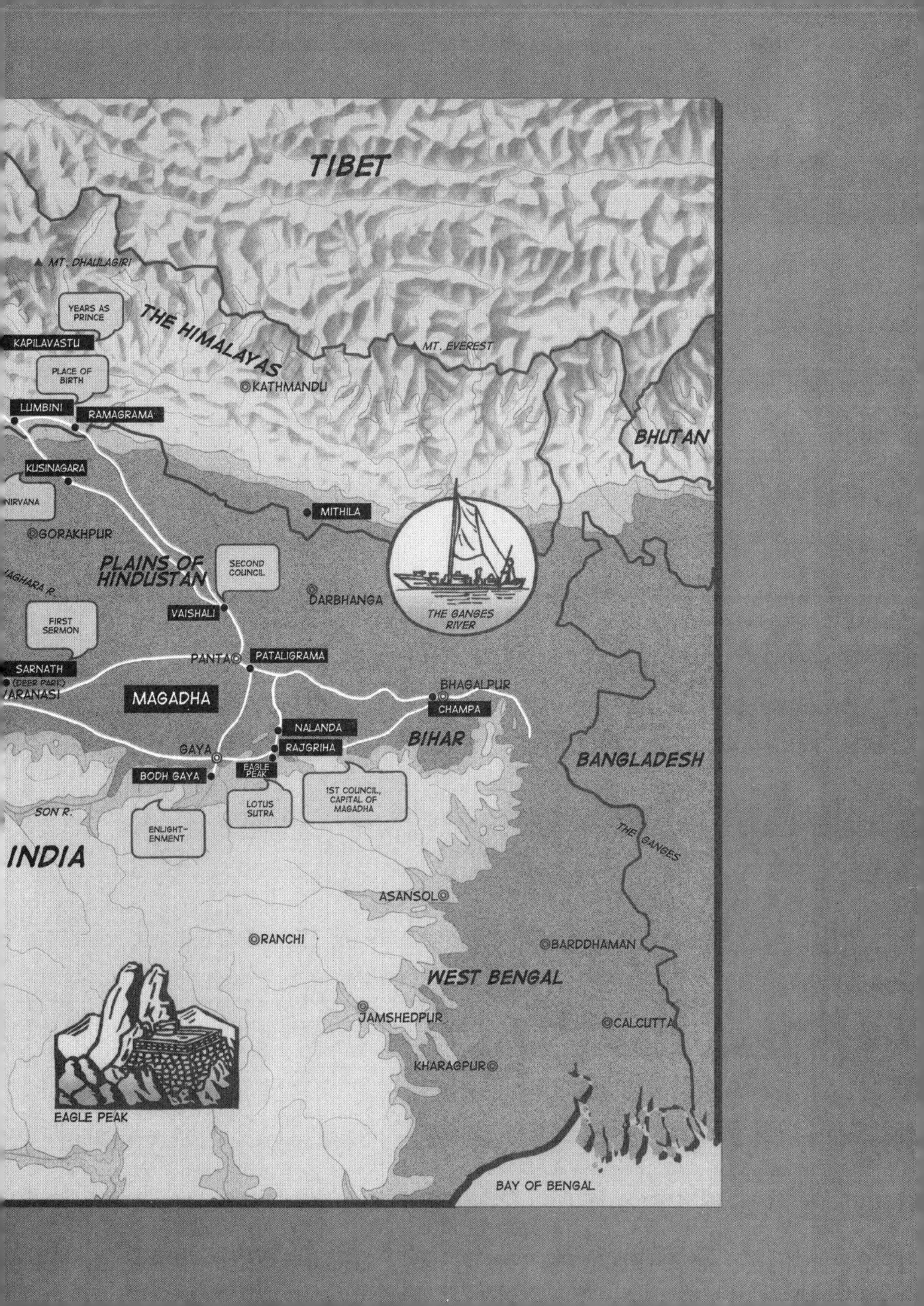

TIBET
MT. DHAULAGIRI
YEARS AS PRINCE
THE HIMALAYAS
KAPILAVASTU
MT. EVEREST
PLACE OF BIRTH
KATHMANDU
LUMBINI
RAMAGRAMA
BHUTAN
KUSINAGARA
NIRVANA
MITHILA
GORAKHPUR
PLAINS OF HINDUSTAN
SECOND COUNCIL
DARBHANGA
VAISHALI
THE GANGES RIVER
FIRST SERMON
PANTA
PATALIGRAMA
SARNATH
(DEER PARK)
VARANASI
MAGADHA
BHAGALPUR
CHAMPA
NALANDA
BIHAR
GAYA
RAJGRIHA
BANGLADESH
BODH GAYA
EAGLE PEAK
1ST COUNCIL, CAPITAL OF MAGADHA
SON R.
LOTUS SUTRA
ENLIGHT-ENMENT
INDIA
THE GANGES
ASANSOL
RANCHI
BARDDHAMAN
WEST BENGAL
JAMSHEDPUR
CALCUTTA
KHARAGPUR
EAGLE PEAK
BAY OF BENGAL

PUBLISHED BY VERTICAL, INC., NEW YORK.

ORIGINALLY PUBLISHED IN JAPANESE AS *BUDDA DAI NIKAN SHIMON SHUTSUYU* BY USHIO SHUPPANSHA, TOKYO, 1987.

ISBN 1-932234-57-8

MANUFACTURED IN THE UNITED STATES OF AMERICA

FIRST PAPERBACK EDITION. THE ARTWORK OF THE ORIGINAL HAS BEEN PRODUCED AS A MIRROR-IMAGE IN ORDER TO CONFORM WITH THE ENGLISH LANGUAGE. THIS WORK OF FICTION CONTAINS CHARACTERS AND EPISODES THAT ARE NOT PART OF THE HISTORICAL RECORD.

VERTICAL, INC.
1185 AVE. OF THE AMERICAS 32ND FLOOR
NEW YORK, NY 10036
WWW.VERTICAL-INC.COM

CONTENTS

PART TWO

1/ THE PRINCE
7

2/ THE GARDEN OF MEDITATION
49

3/ THE RAPIDS
83

4/ YASHODARA
133

5/ MIGAILA
171

6/ THE FOUR ENCOUNTERS
217

7/ RAHULA
261

8/ THE FIVE ASCETICS
299

9/ DAWN OF THE JOURNEY
341

10/ THE DEATH OF BANDAKA
369

PART TWO

CHAPTER ONE

THE PRINCE

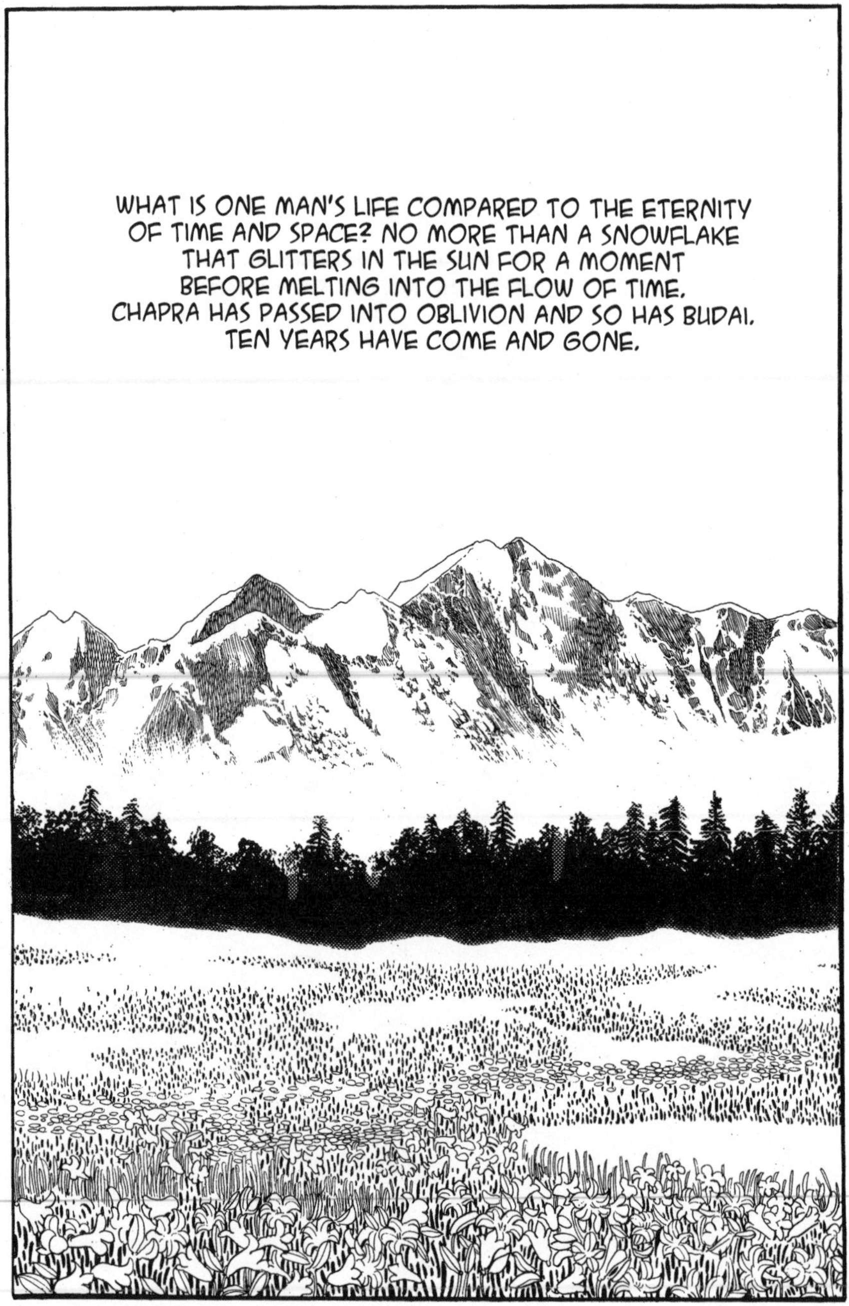
WHAT IS ONE MAN'S LIFE COMPARED TO THE ETERNITY OF TIME AND SPACE? NO MORE THAN A SNOWFLAKE THAT GLITTERS IN THE SUN FOR A MOMENT BEFORE MELTING INTO THE FLOW OF TIME. CHAPRA HAS PASSED INTO OBLIVION AND SO HAS BUDAI. TEN YEARS HAVE COME AND GONE.

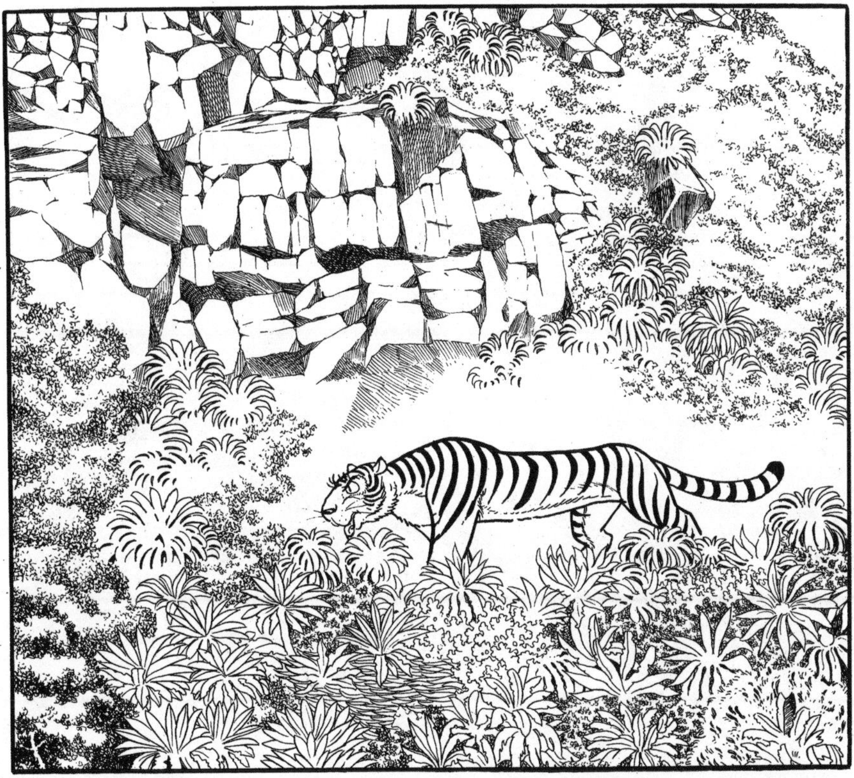

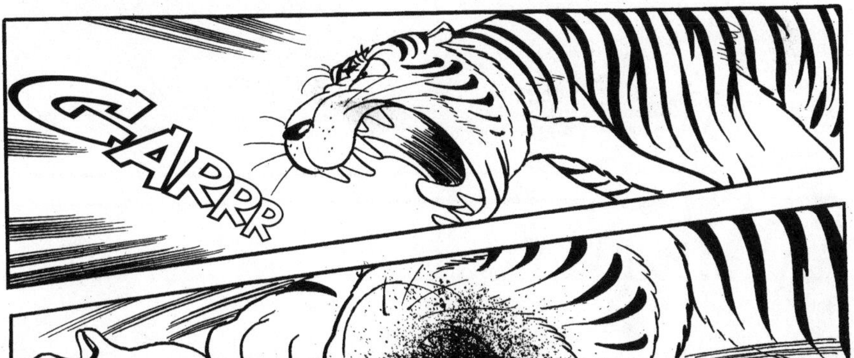
GARRR

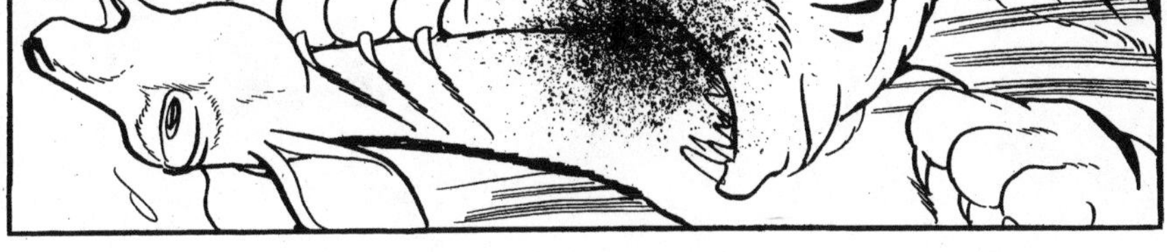

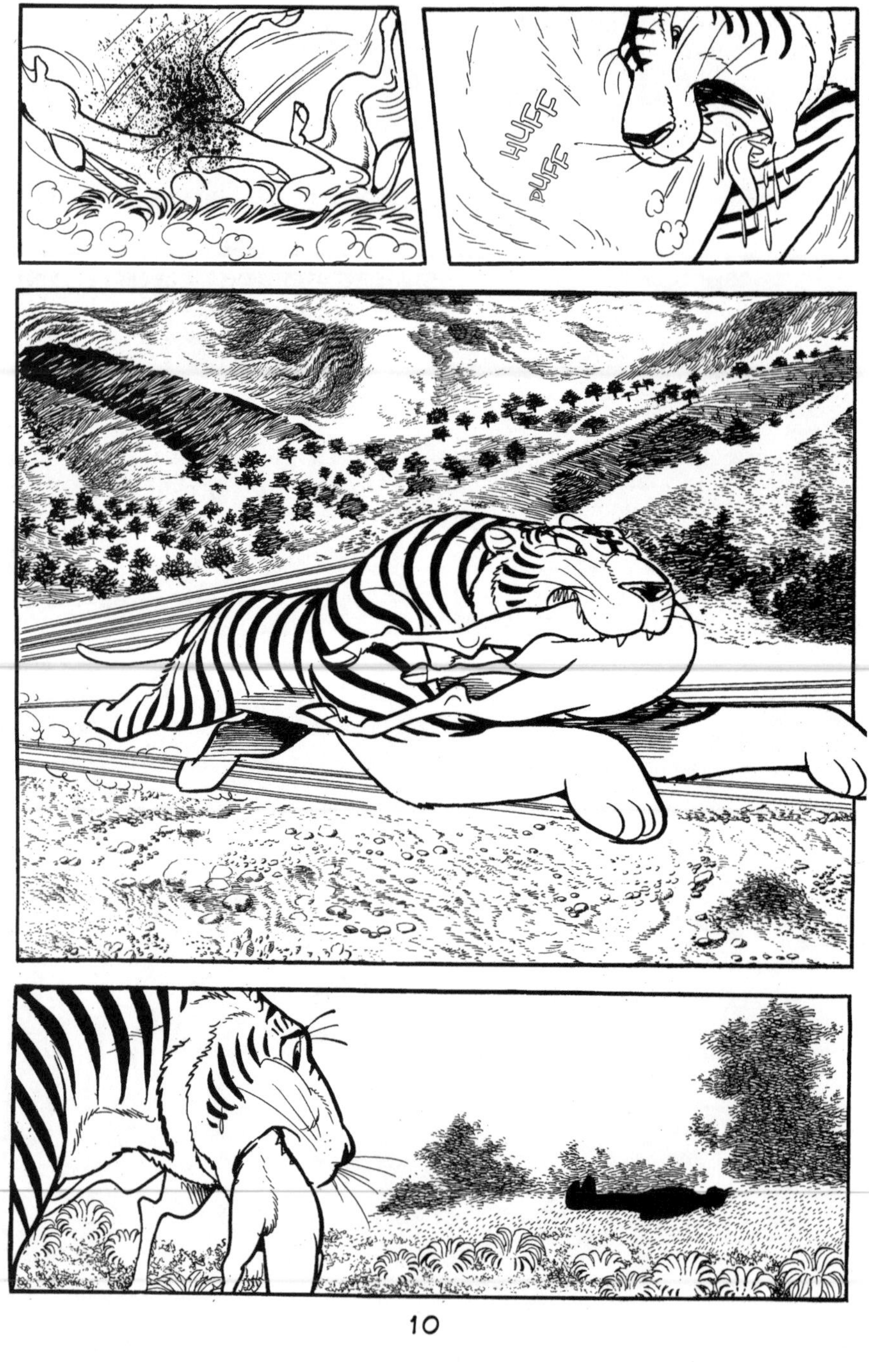
HUFF
PUFF

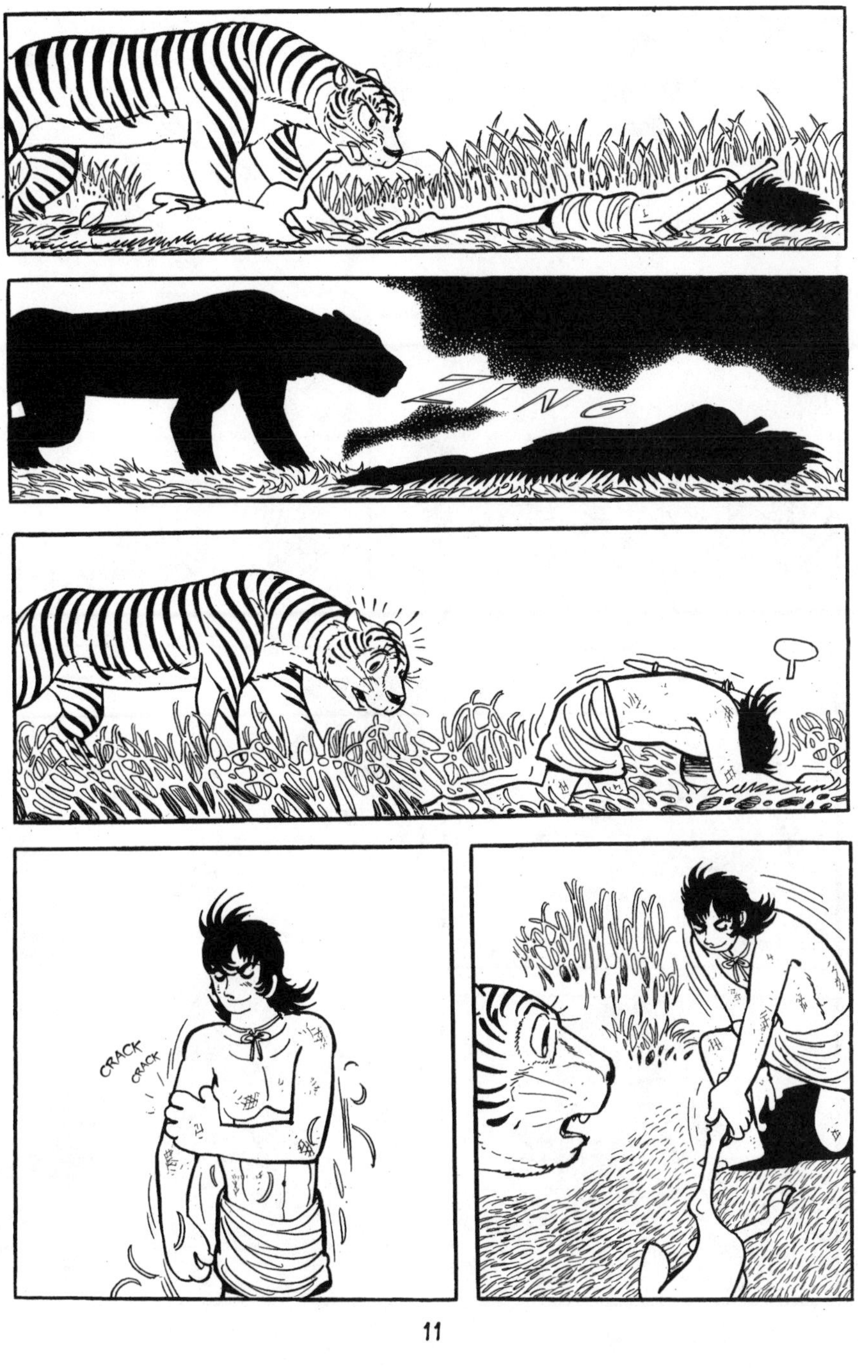
ZING
CRACK
CRACK

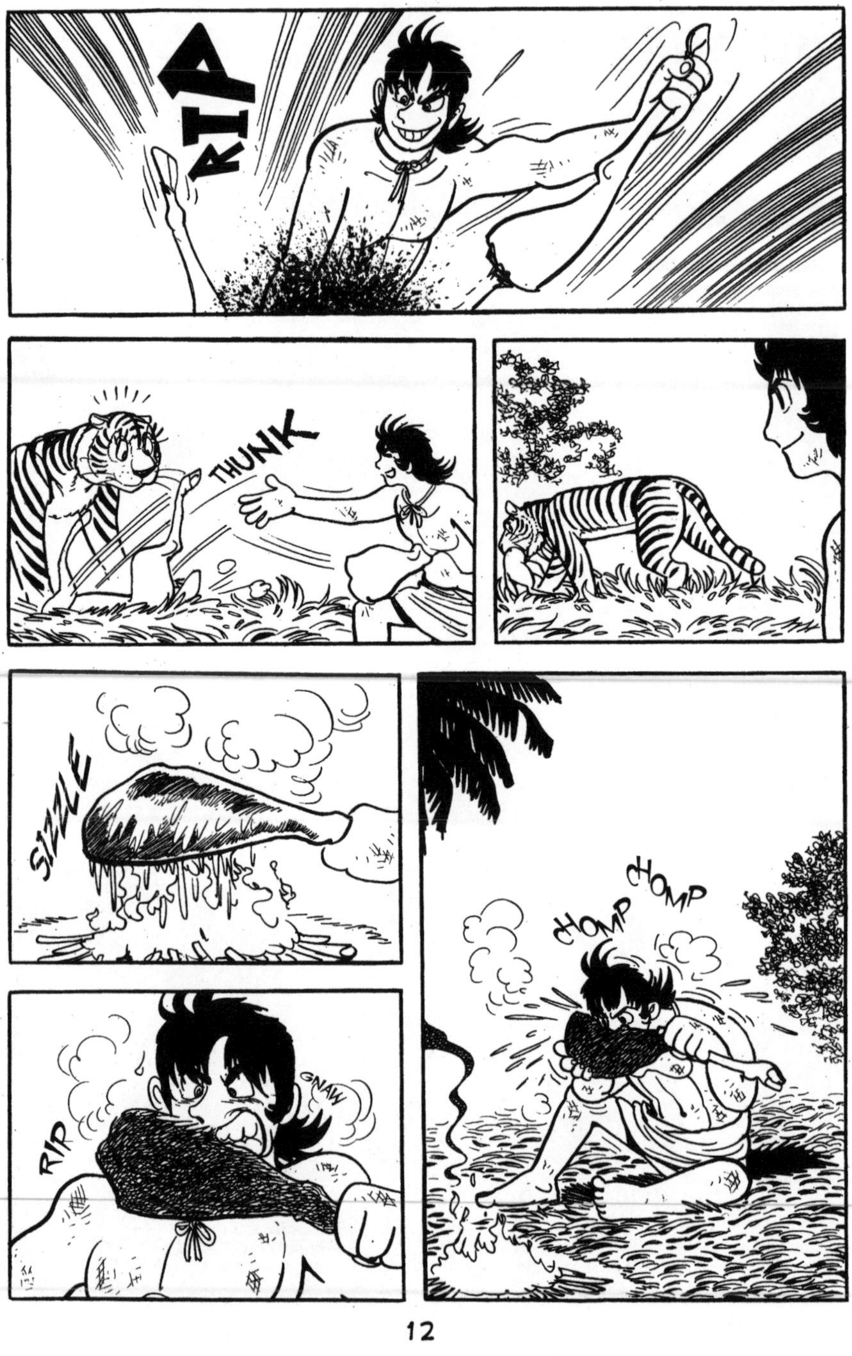
RIP
THUNK
SIZZLE
CHOMP
CHOMP
RIP
GNAW

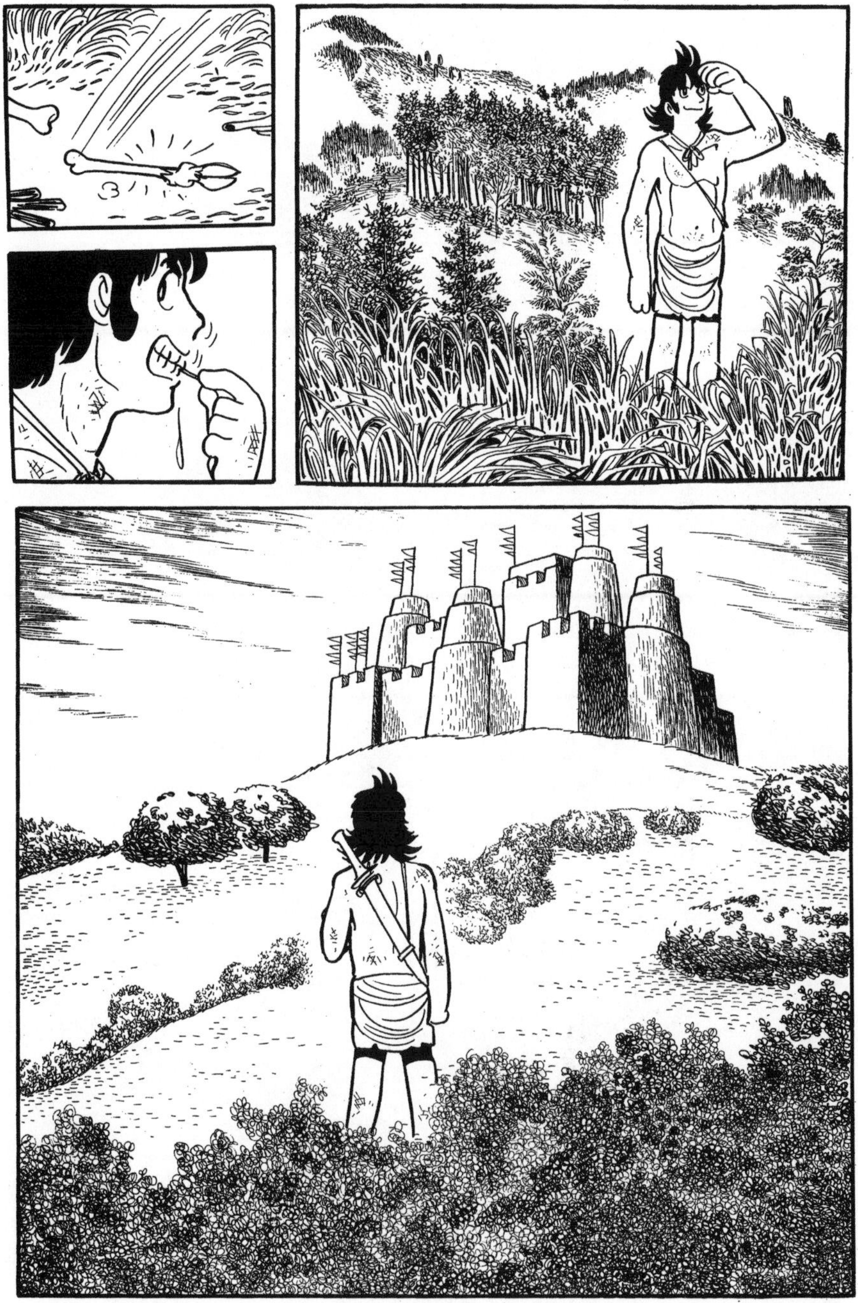

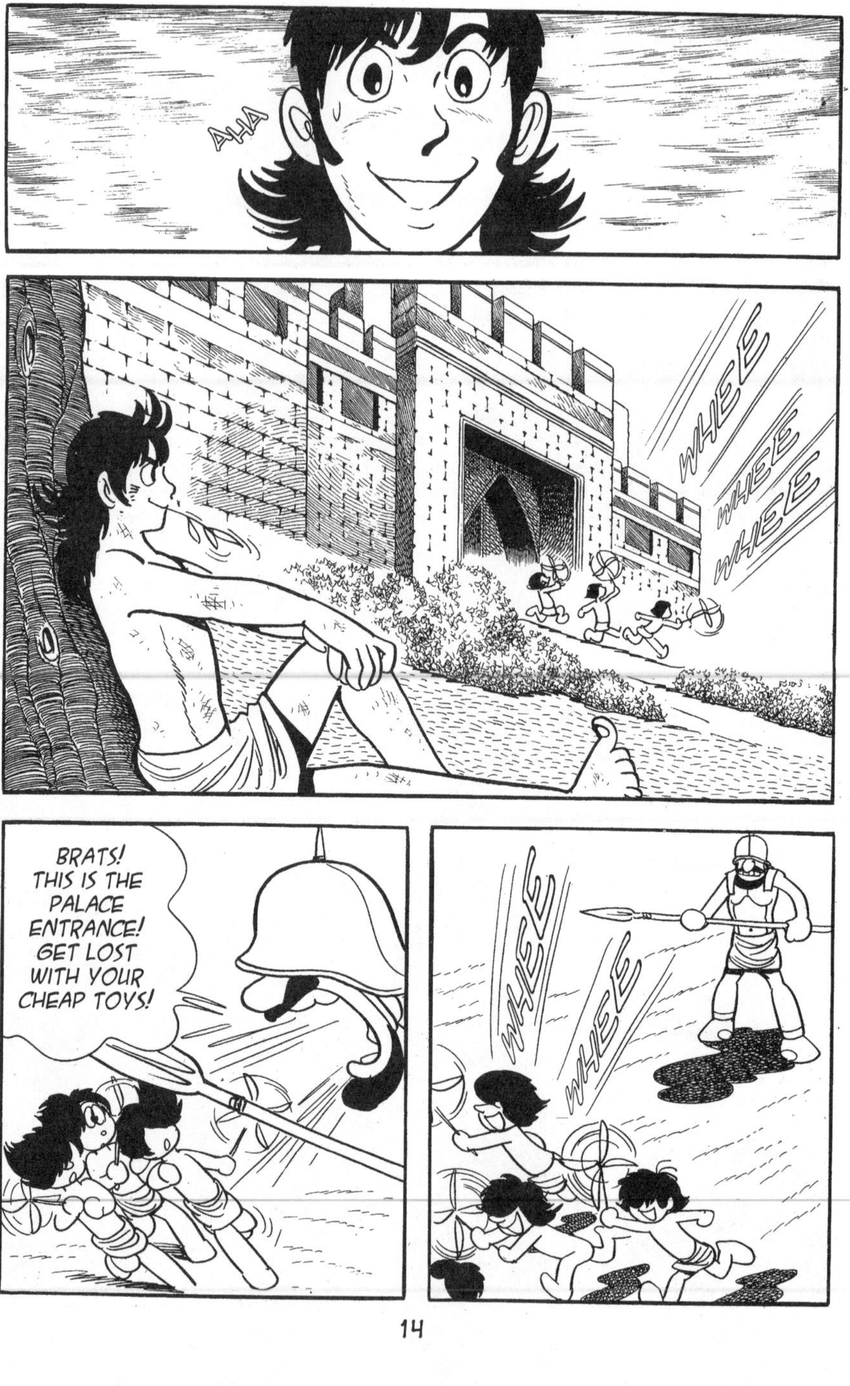
AHA
WHEE
WHEE
WHEE
BRATS! THIS IS THE PALACE ENTRANCE! GET LOST WITH YOUR CHEAP TOYS!
WHEE
WHEE

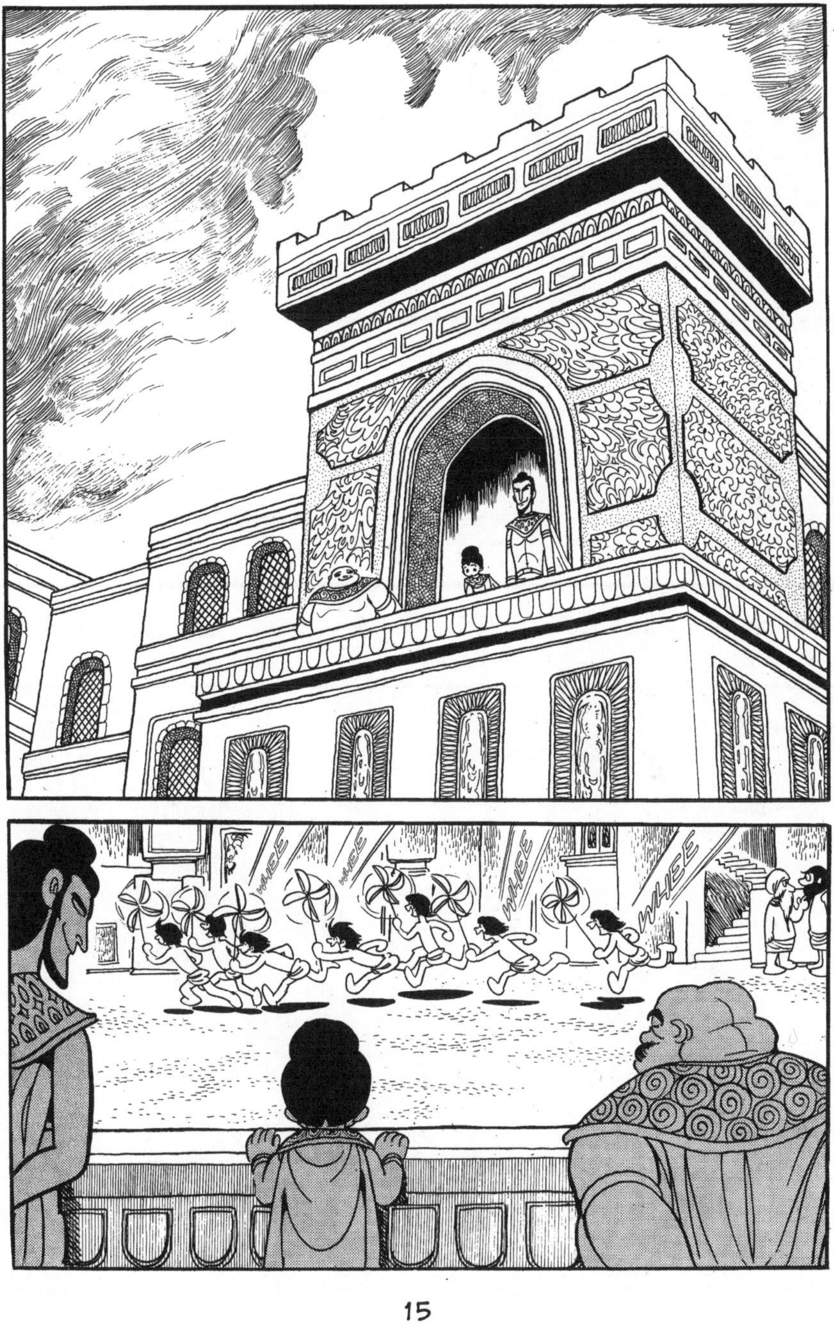
WHEE
WHEE
WHEE
WHEE

 I'D LIKE ONE OF THOSE. CAN YOU GET ME ONE?

 MY DEAR PRINCE, THOSE TOYS ARE FOR LOWLY SHUDRA.

THE SON OF A KING DOESN'T NEED SUCH JUNK.

 BUT IT LOOKS LIKE SO MUCH FUN...

 UH-UH

 ...
...

YAY
WHEE
YAY

 LOOK OVER THERE, YOUNG PRINCE.

THEY'RE BEING EXPELLED, CHASED OUT OF THE LAND.

 WHAT DID THEY DO? ARE THEY BAD?

THEY'RE LOWLIFE SHUDRA WHO GOT CAUGHT EATING VAISYA FOOD.

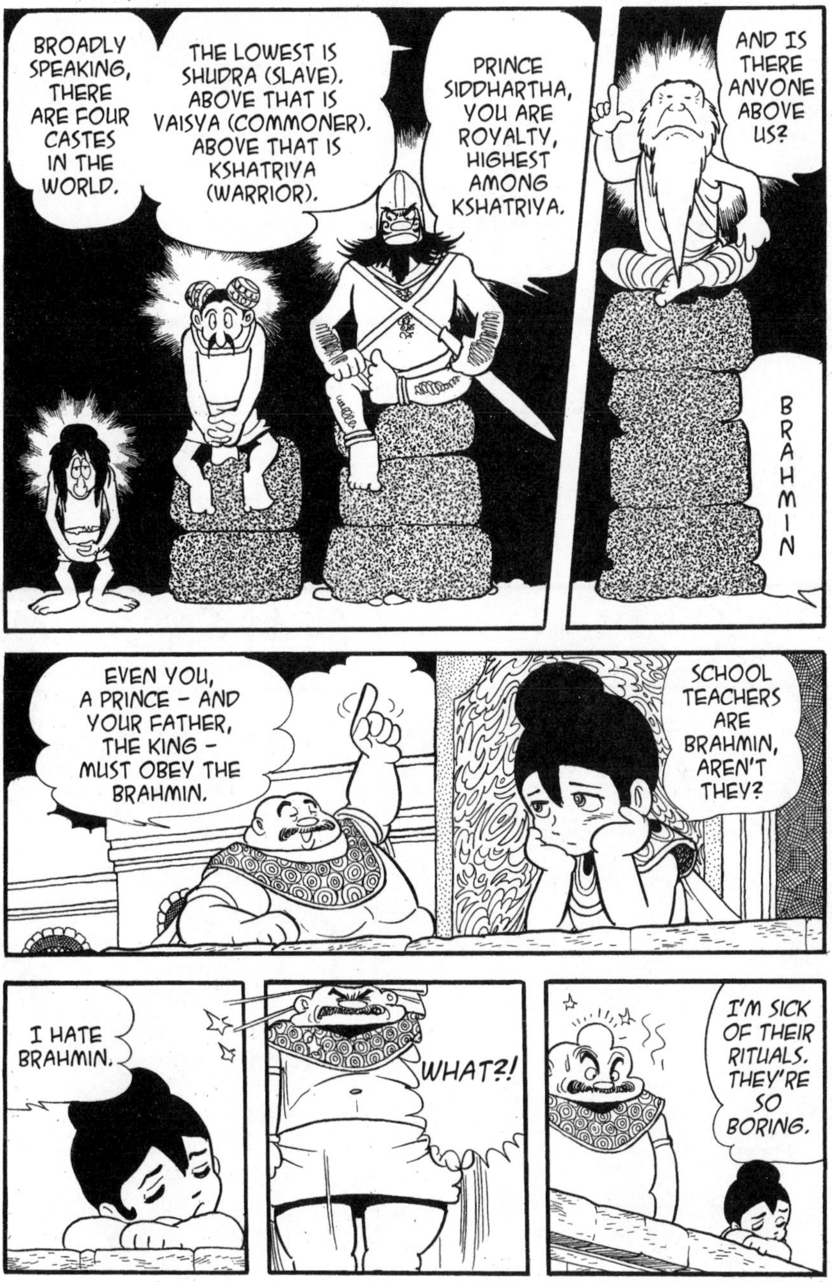
BROADLY SPEAKING, THERE ARE FOUR CASTES IN THE WORLD.
THE LOWEST IS SHUDRA (SLAVE). ABOVE THAT IS VAISYA (COMMONER). ABOVE THAT IS KSHATRIYA (WARRIOR).
PRINCE SIDDHARTHA, YOU ARE ROYALTY, HIGHEST AMONG KSHATRIYA.
AND IS THERE ANYONE ABOVE US?
BRAHMIN
EVEN YOU, A PRINCE - AND YOUR FATHER, THE KING - MUST OBEY THE BRAHMIN.
SCHOOL TEACHERS ARE BRAHMIN, AREN'T THEY?
I HATE BRAHMIN.
WHAT?!
I'M SICK OF THEIR RITUALS. THEY'RE SO BORING.

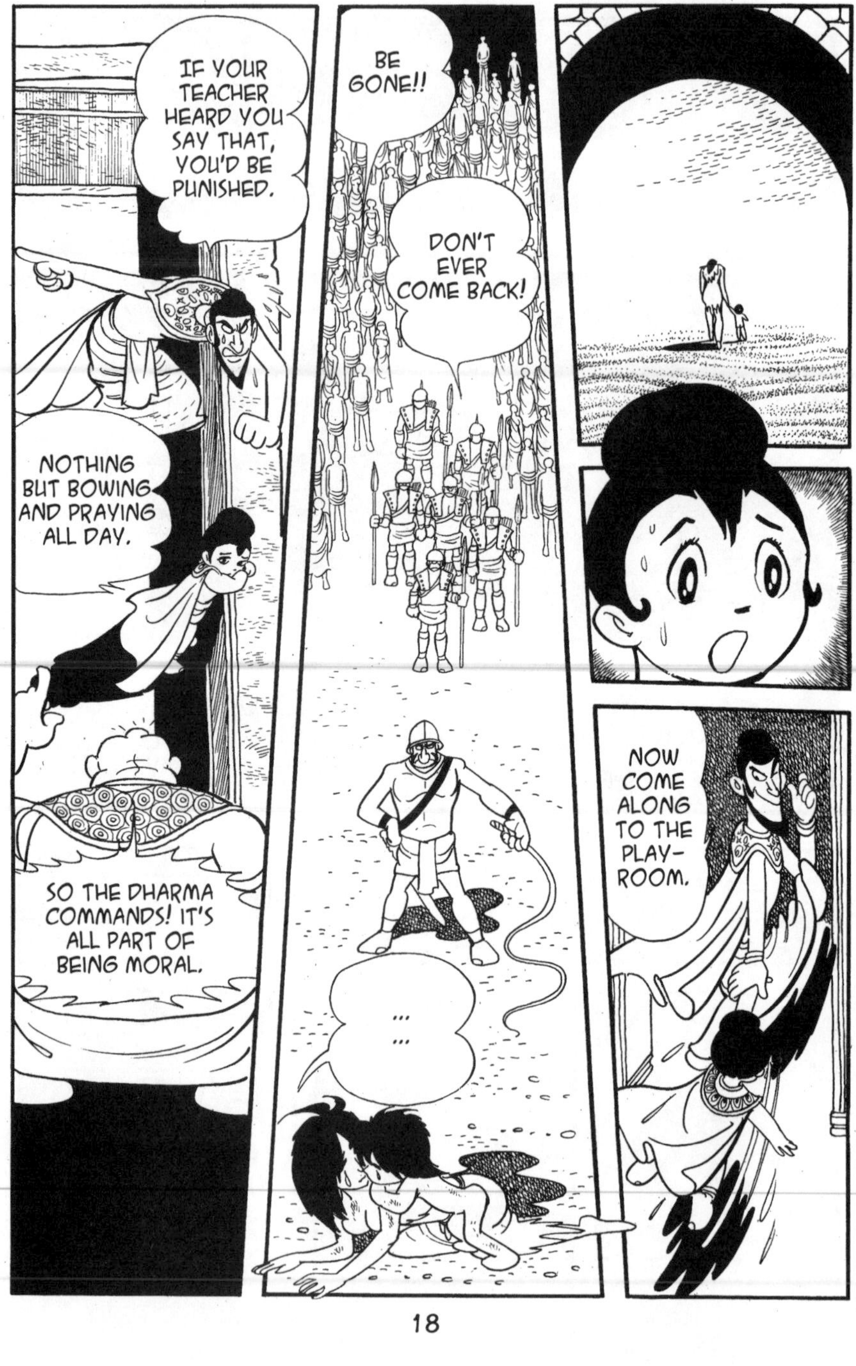
IF YOUR TEACHER HEARD YOU SAY THAT, YOU'D BE PUNISHED.
NOTHING BUT BOWING AND PRAYING ALL DAY.
SO THE DHARMA COMMANDS! IT'S ALL PART OF BEING MORAL.
BE GONE!!
DON'T EVER COME BACK!
... ...
NOW COME ALONG TO THE PLAY-ROOM.

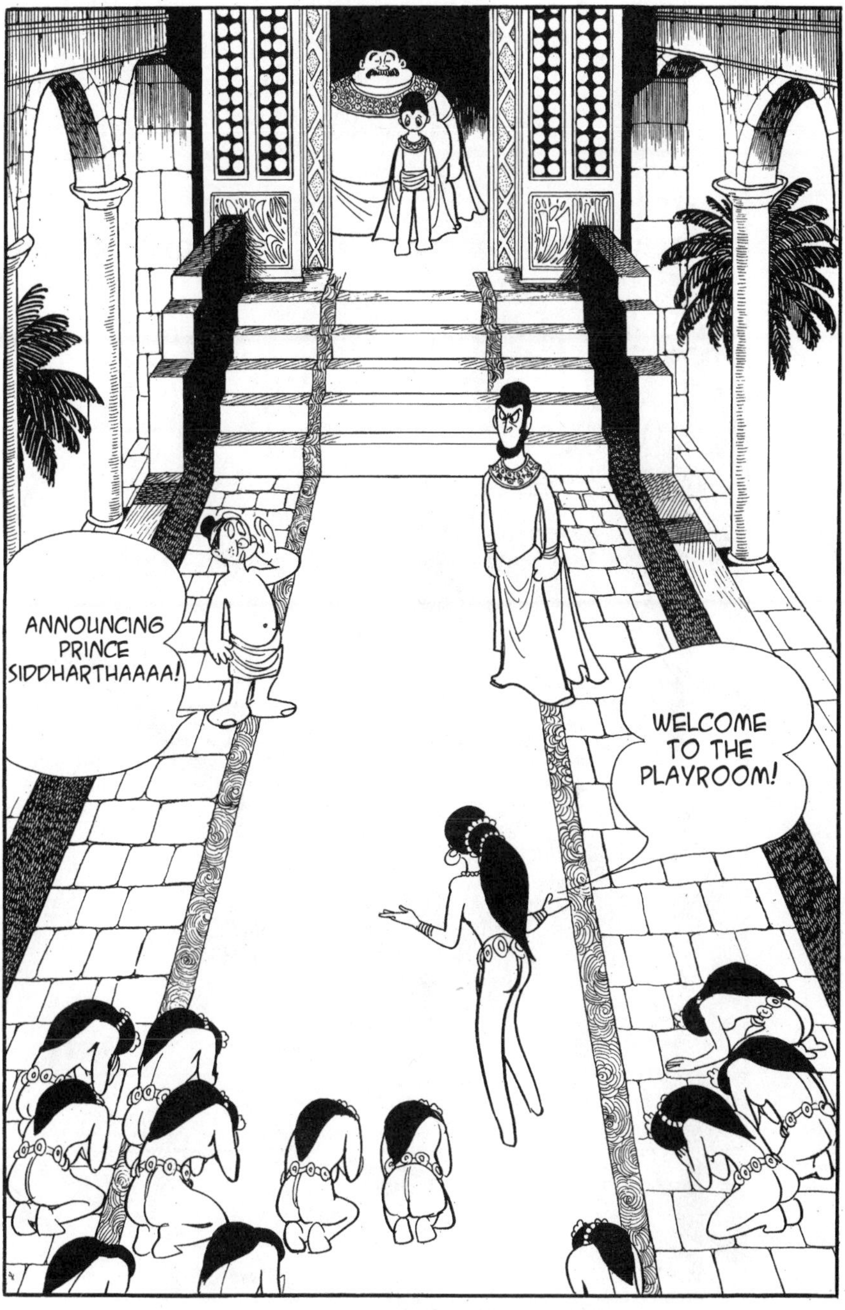
ANNOUNCING PRINCE SIDDHARTHAAAA!
WELCOME TO THE PLAYROOM!

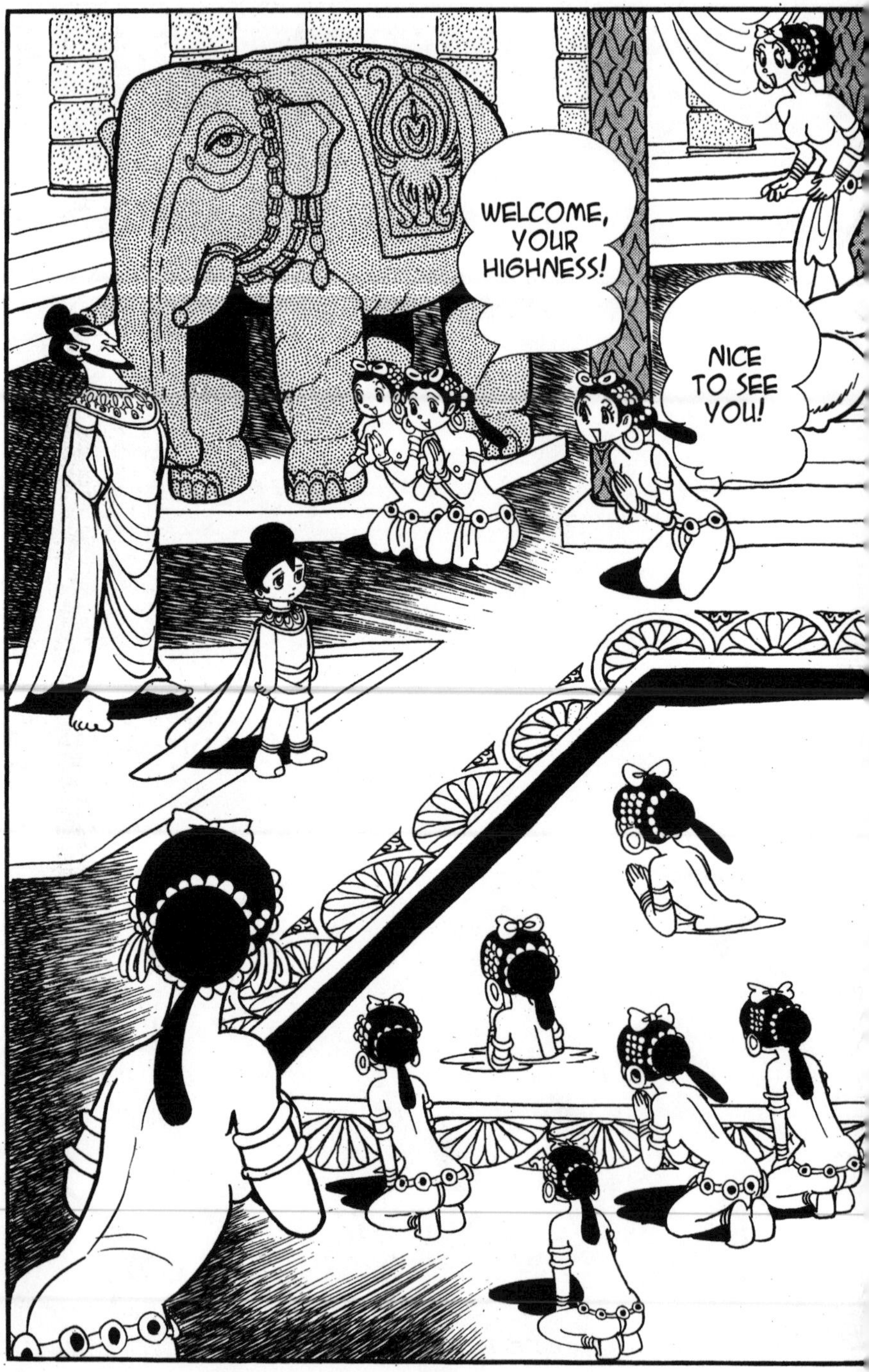
WELCOME, YOUR HIGHNESS!
NICE TO SEE YOU!

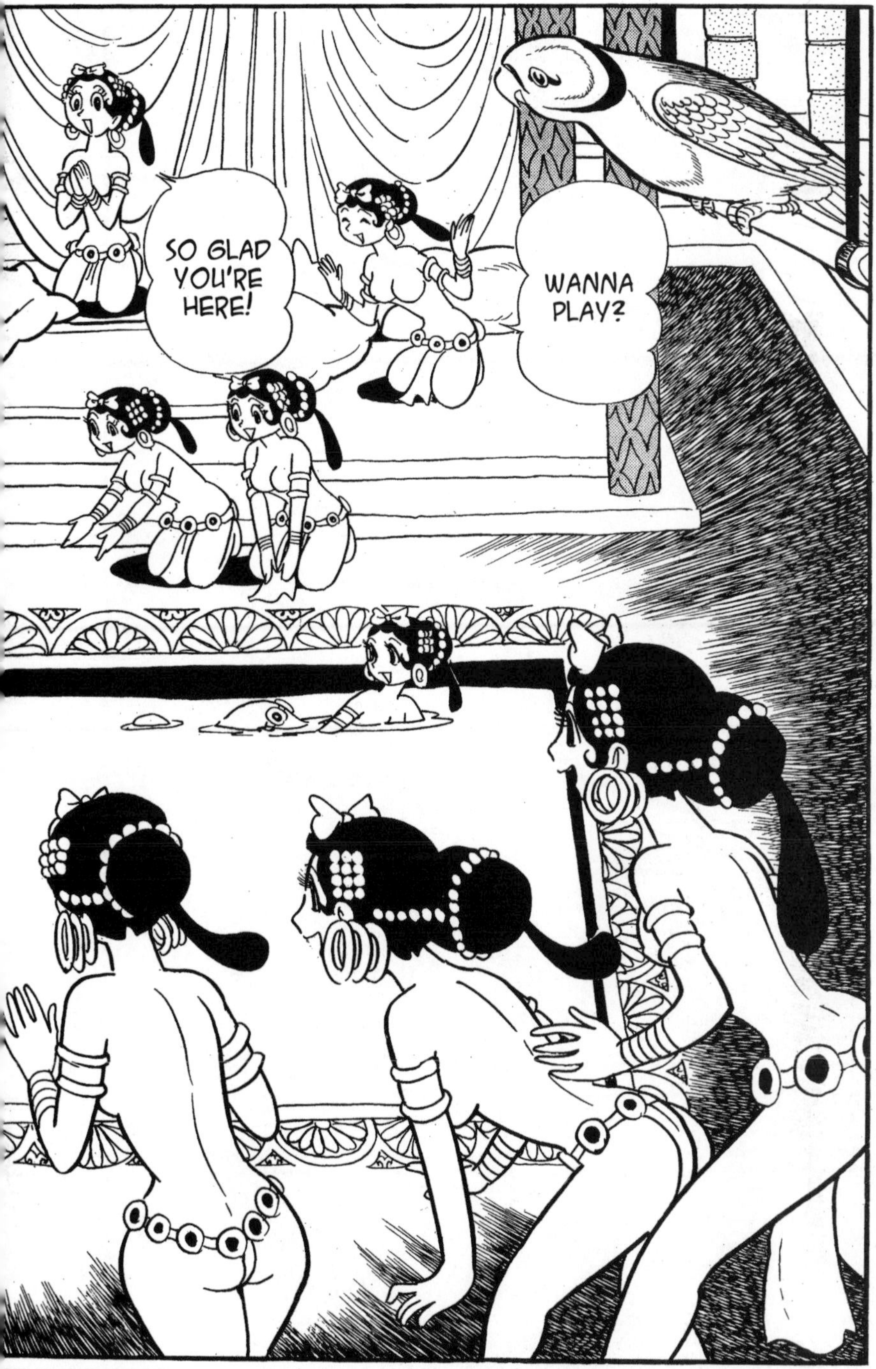
SO GLAD YOU'RE HERE!
WANNA PLAY?

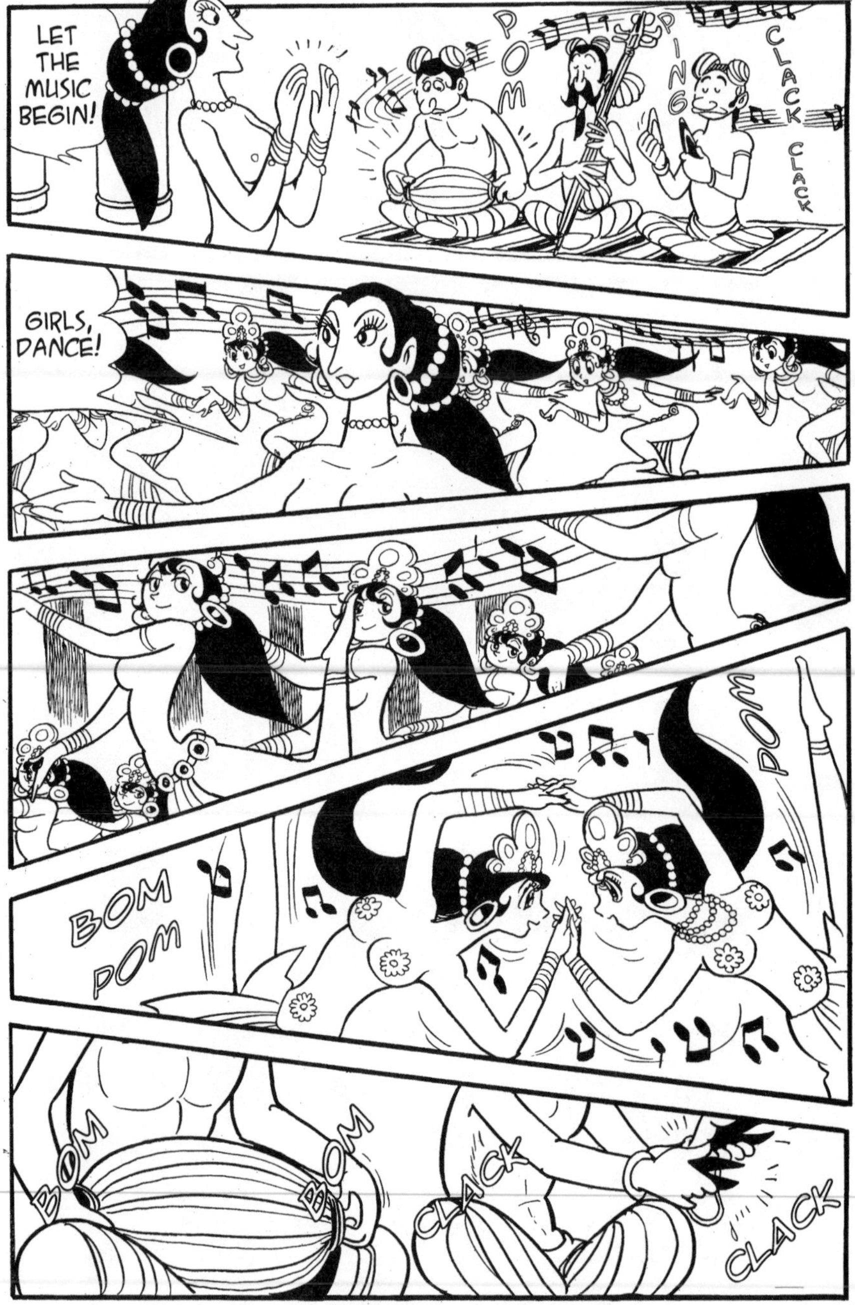
LET THE MUSIC BEGIN!
POM
PING
CLACK
CLACK CLACK
GIRLS, DANCE!
POM
BOM POM
BOM
BOM
CLACK
CLACK CLACK

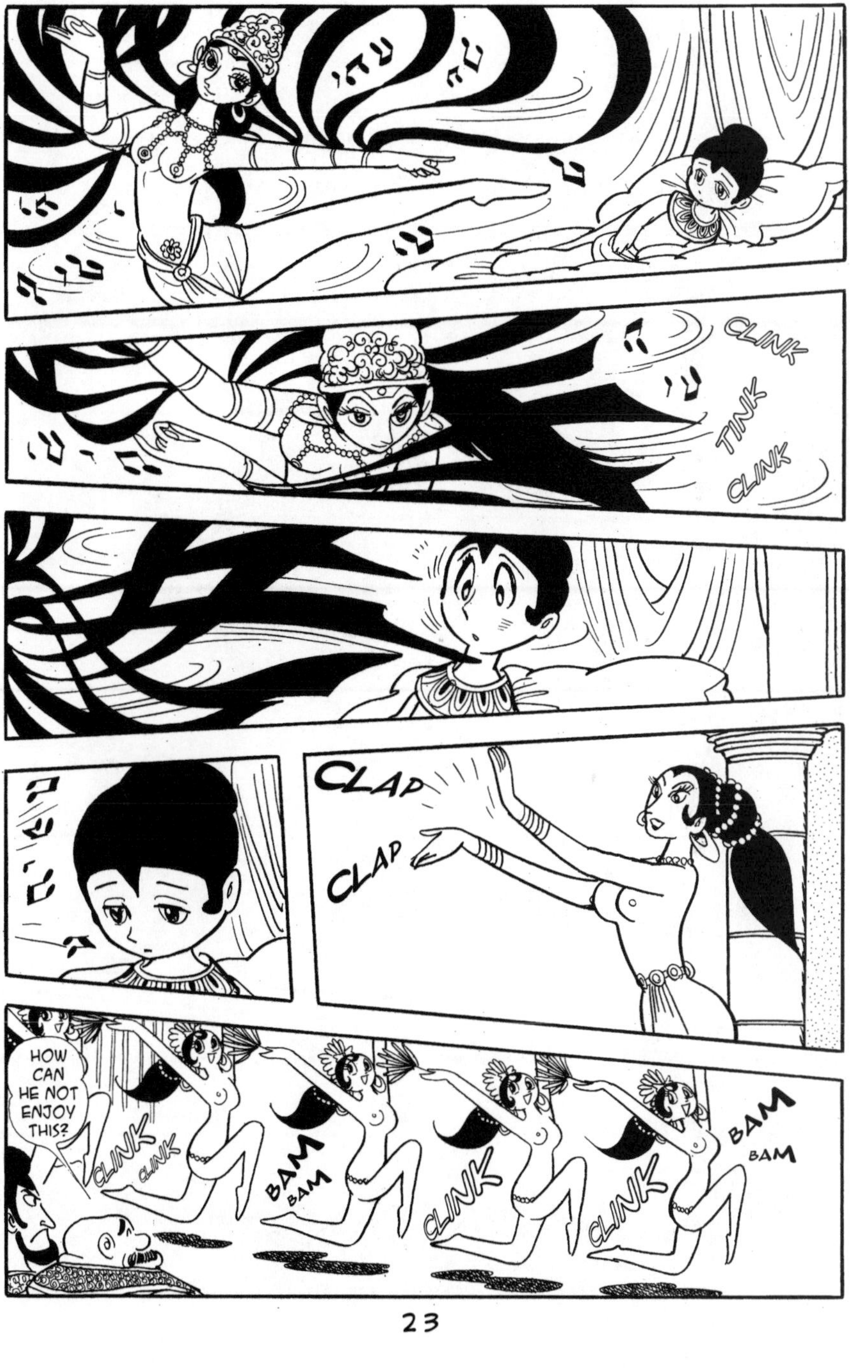

CLINK
TINK
CLINK
CLAP
CLAP
HOW CAN HE NOT ENJOY THIS?
CLINK
CLINK
BAM
BAM
CLINK
CLINK
BAM
BAM

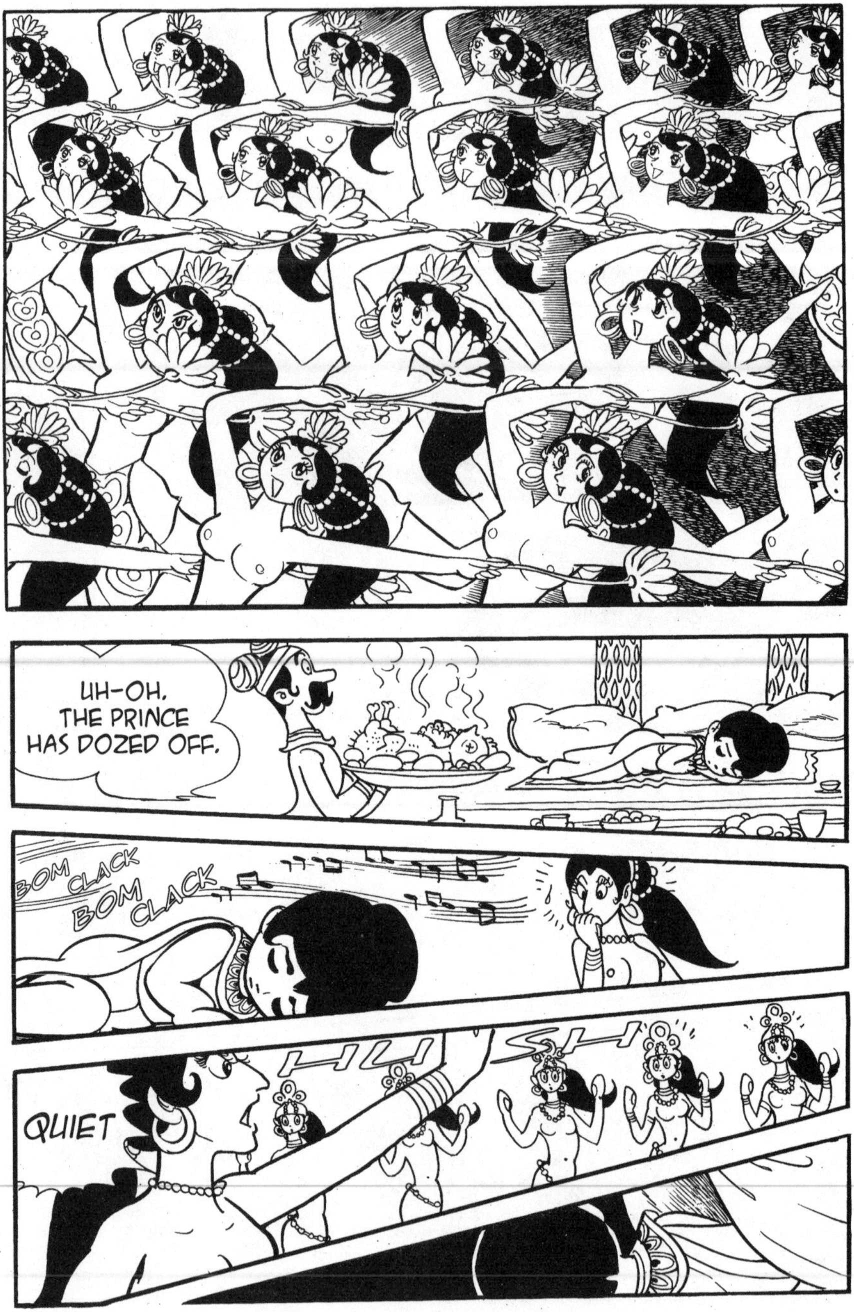
UH-OH. THE PRINCE HAS DOZED OFF.
BOM CLACK BOM CLACK
HUSH
QUIET

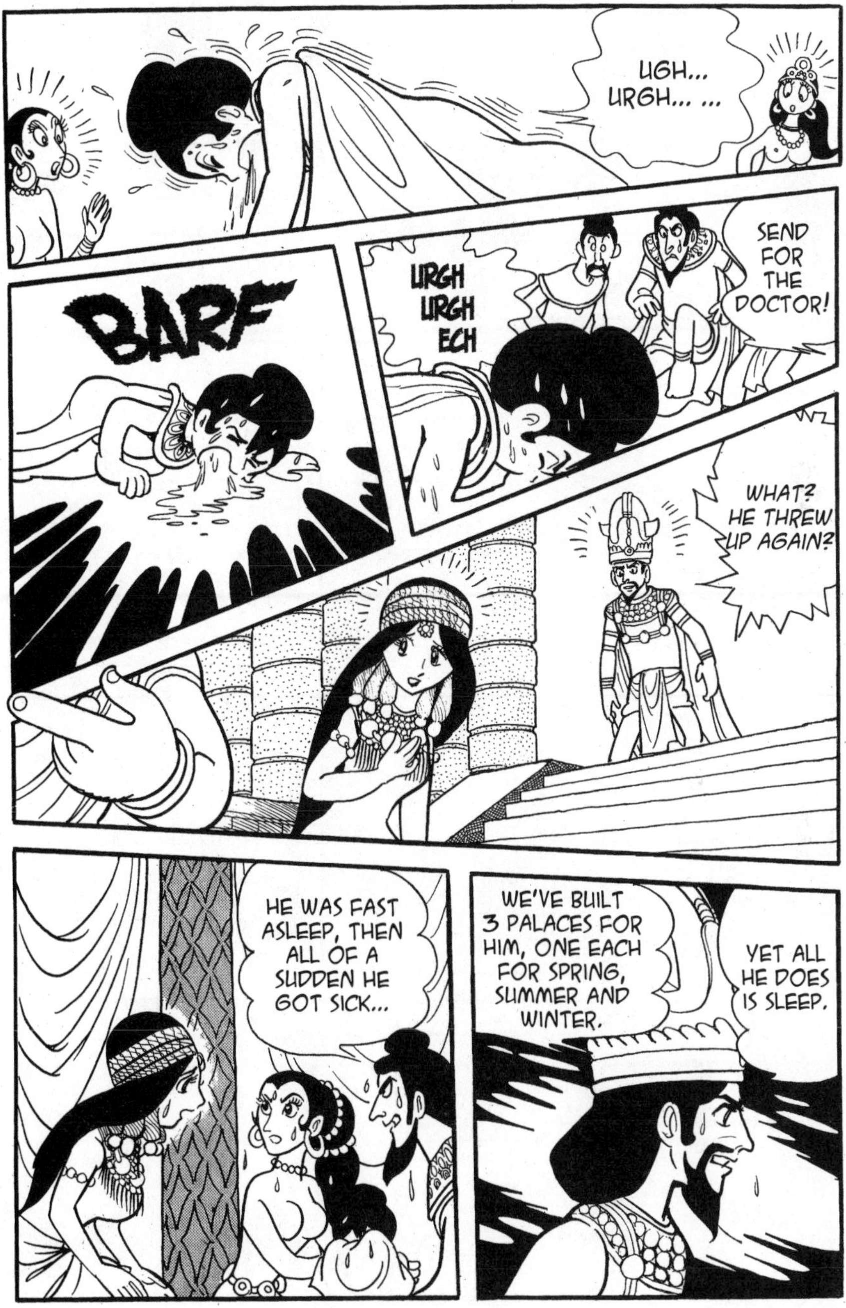
UGH... URGH... ...
BARF
URGH URGH ECH
SEND FOR THE DOCTOR!
WHAT? HE THREW UP AGAIN?
HE WAS FAST ASLEEP, THEN ALL OF A SUDDEN HE GOT SICK...
WE'VE BUILT 3 PALACES FOR HIM, ONE EACH FOR SPRING, SUMMER AND WINTER.
YET ALL HE DOES IS SLEEP.

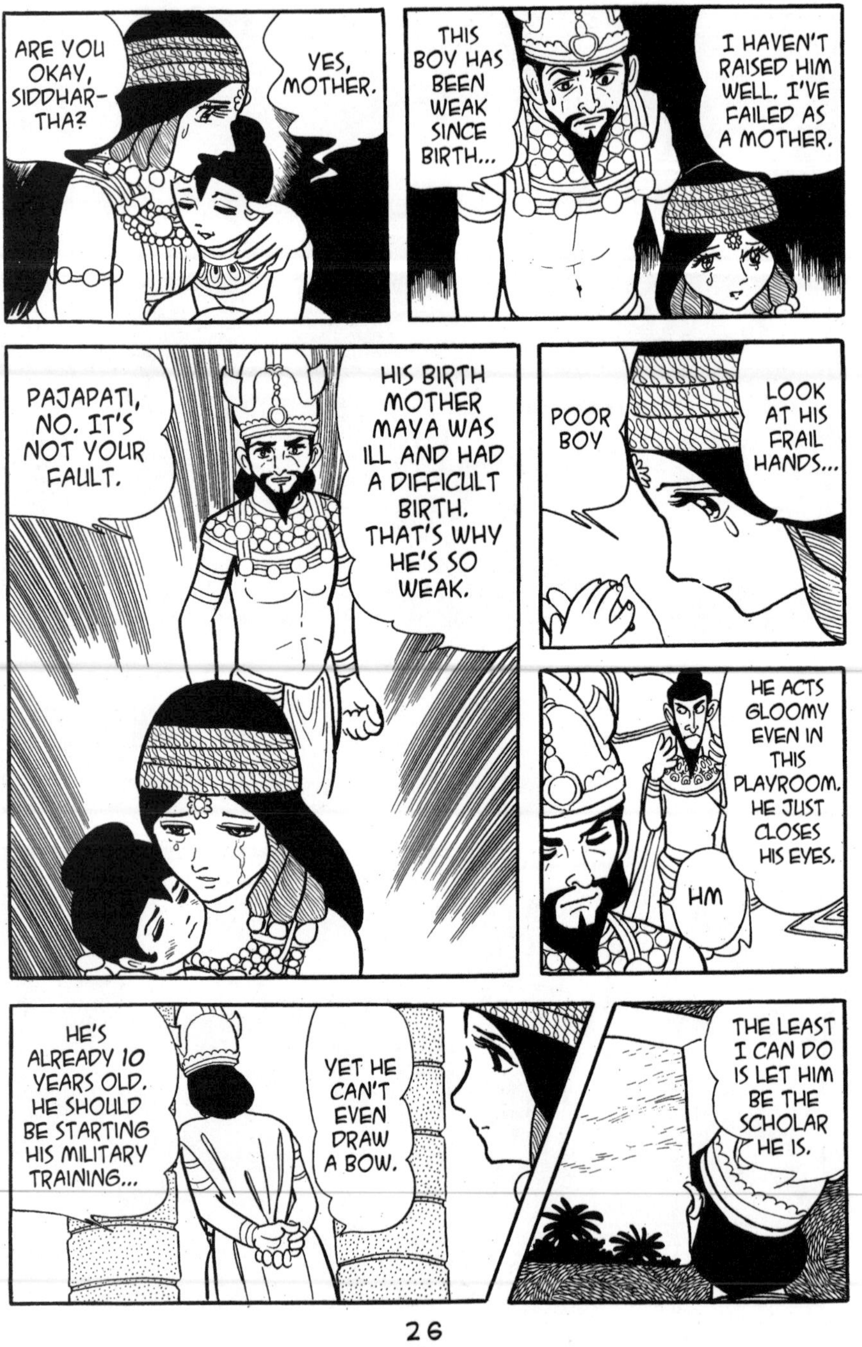
ARE YOU OKAY, SIDDHARTHA?
YES, MOTHER.
THIS BOY HAS BEEN WEAK SINCE BIRTH...
I HAVEN'T RAISED HIM WELL. I'VE FAILED AS A MOTHER.
PAJAPATI, NO. IT'S NOT YOUR FAULT.
HIS BIRTH MOTHER MAYA WAS ILL AND HAD A DIFFICULT BIRTH. THAT'S WHY HE'S SO WEAK.
POOR BOY
LOOK AT HIS FRAIL HANDS...
HE ACTS GLOOMY EVEN IN THIS PLAYROOM. HE JUST CLOSES HIS EYES.
HM
HE'S ALREADY 10 YEARS OLD. HE SHOULD BE STARTING HIS MILITARY TRAINING...
YET HE CAN'T EVEN DRAW A BOW.
THE LEAST I CAN DO IS LET HIM BE THE SCHOLAR HE IS.

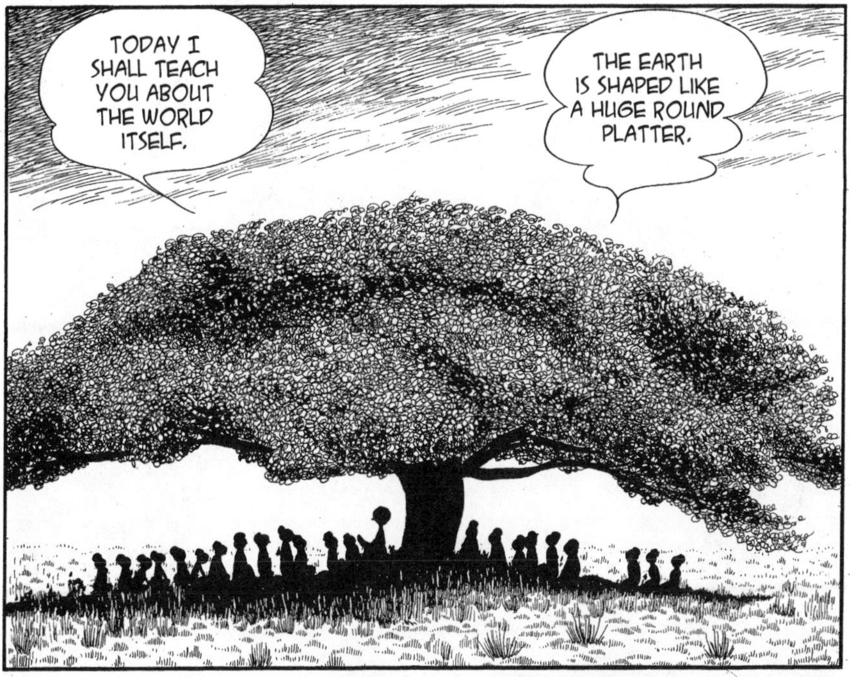
TODAY I SHALL TEACH YOU ABOUT THE WORLD ITSELF.
THE EARTH IS SHAPED LIKE A HUGE ROUND PLATTER.

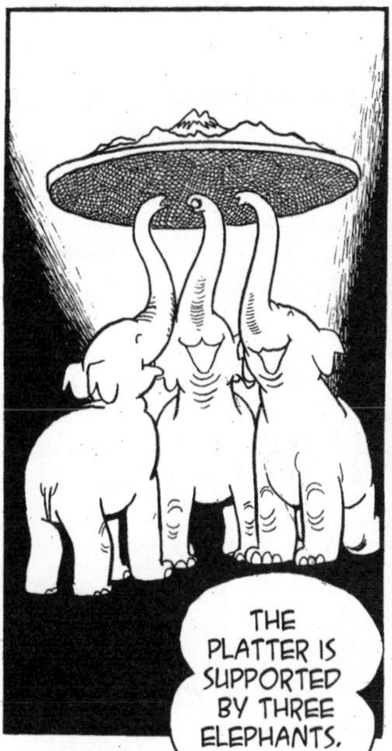
THE PLATTER IS SUPPORTED BY THREE ELEPHANTS.

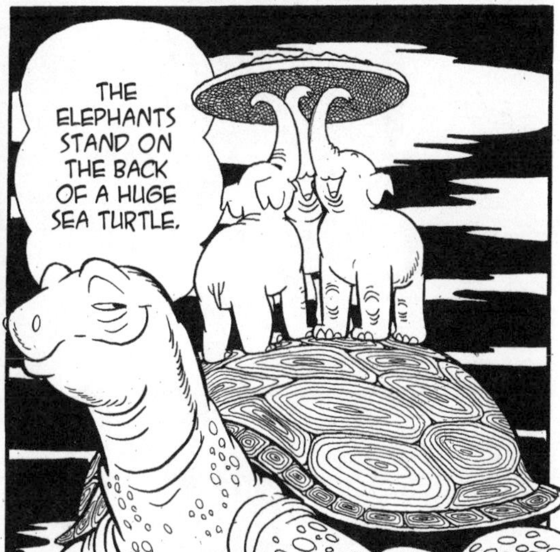
THE ELEPHANTS STAND ON THE BACK OF A HUGE SEA TURTLE.

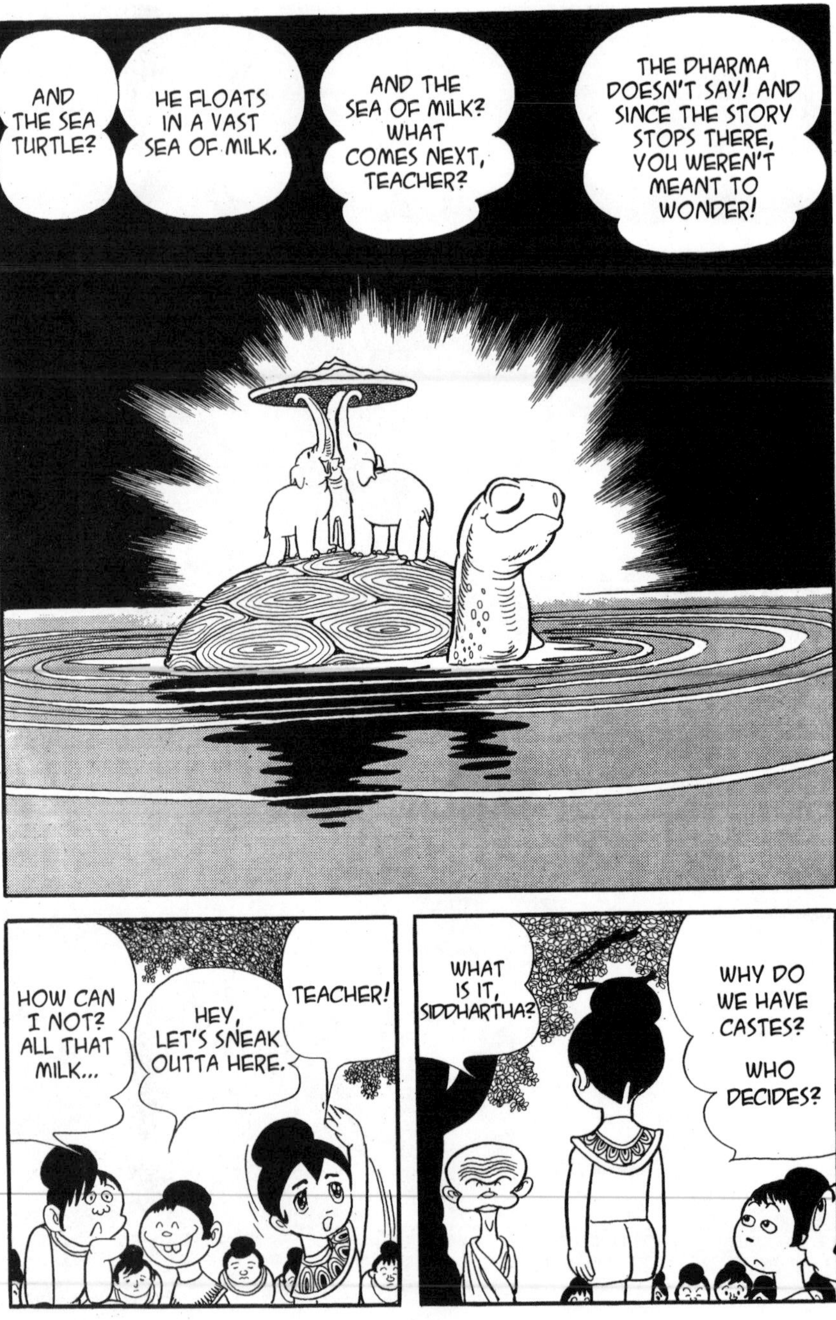
AND THE SEA TURTLE?
HE FLOATS IN A VAST SEA OF MILK.
AND THE SEA OF MILK? WHAT COMES NEXT, TEACHER?
THE DHARMA DOESN'T SAY! AND SINCE THE STORY STOPS THERE, YOU WEREN'T MEANT TO WONDER!
HOW CAN I NOT? ALL THAT MILK...
HEY, LET'S SNEAK OUTTA HERE.
TEACHER!
WHAT IS IT, SIDDHARTHA?
WHY DO WE HAVE CASTES?
WHO DECIDES?

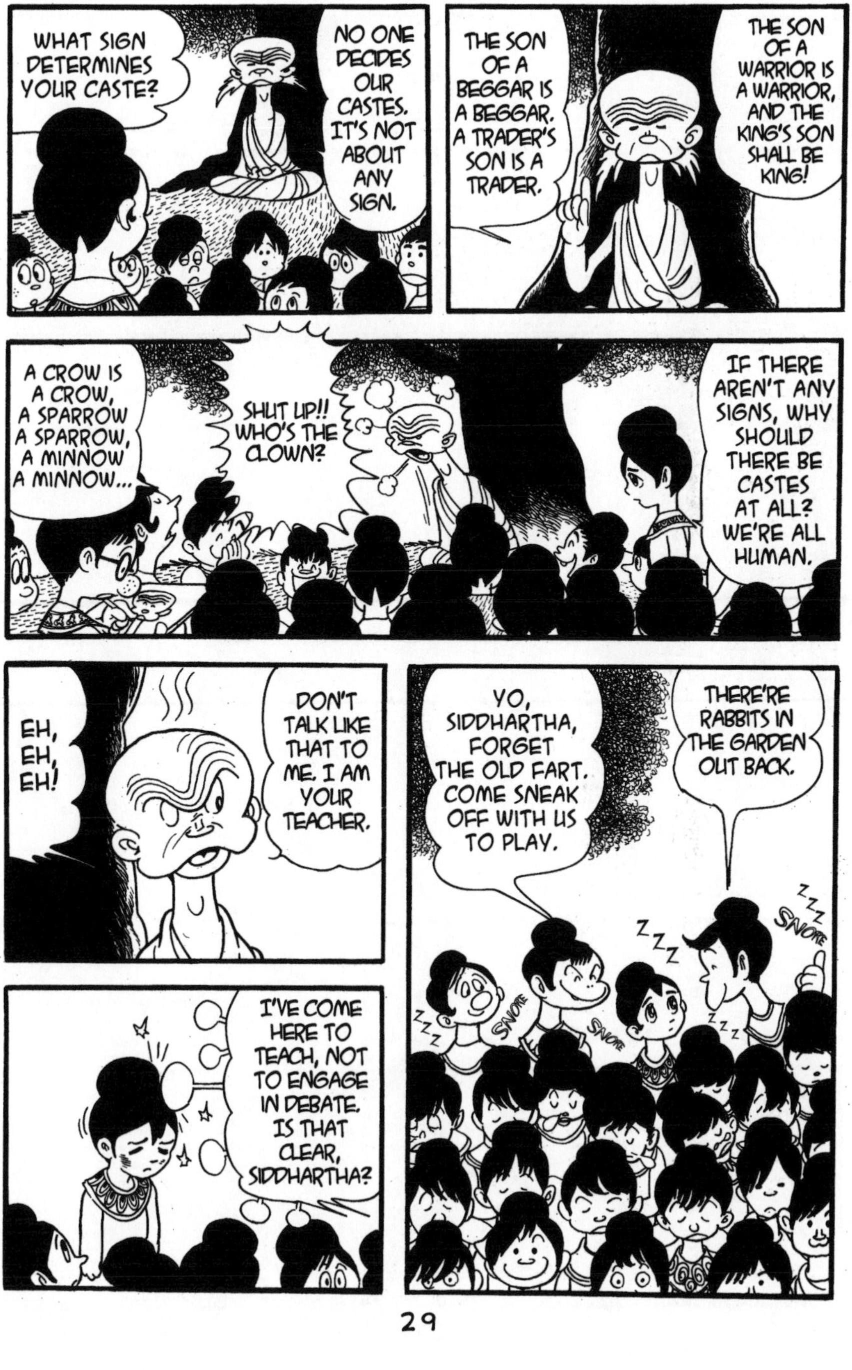

WHAT SIGN DETERMINES YOUR CASTE?
NO ONE DECIDES OUR CASTES. IT'S NOT ABOUT ANY SIGN.
THE SON OF A BEGGAR IS A BEGGAR. A TRADER'S SON IS A TRADER.
THE SON OF A WARRIOR IS A WARRIOR, AND THE KING'S SON SHALL BE KING!
A CROW IS A CROW, A SPARROW A SPARROW, A MINNOW A MINNOW...
SHUT UP!! WHO'S THE CLOWN?
IF THERE AREN'T ANY SIGNS, WHY SHOULD THERE BE CASTES AT ALL? WE'RE ALL HUMAN.
EH, EH, EH!
DON'T TALK LIKE THAT TO ME. I AM YOUR TEACHER.
I'VE COME HERE TO TEACH, NOT TO ENGAGE IN DEBATE. IS THAT CLEAR, SIDDHARTHA?
YO, SIDDHARTHA, FORGET THE OLD FART. COME SNEAK OFF WITH US TO PLAY.
THERE'RE RABBITS IN THE GARDEN OUT BACK.
ZZZ
SNORE
ZZZ
ZZZ
SNORE
SNORE
ZZZ

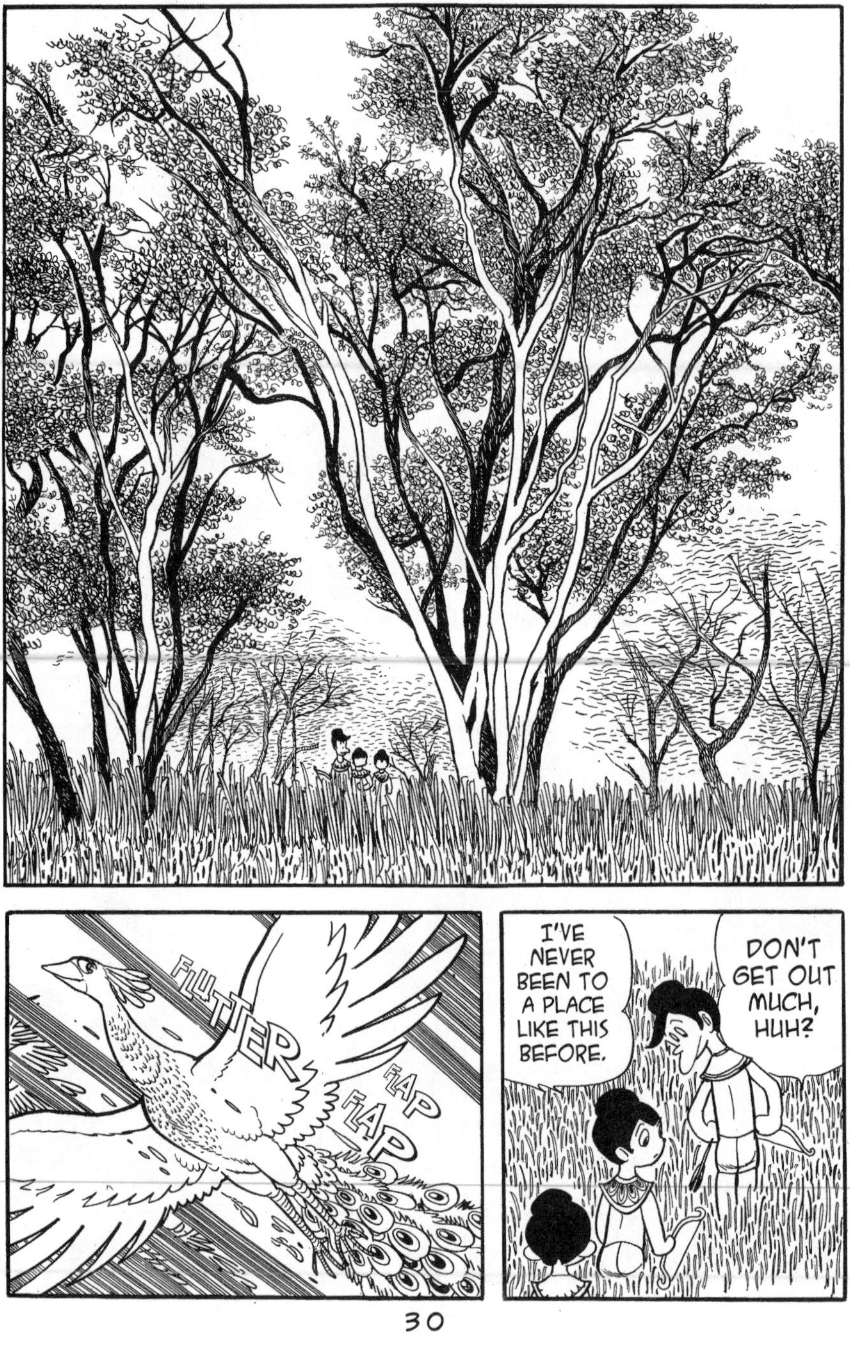
FLUTTER
FLAP
FLAP
I'VE NEVER BEEN TO A PLACE LIKE THIS BEFORE.
DON'T GET OUT MUCH, HUH?

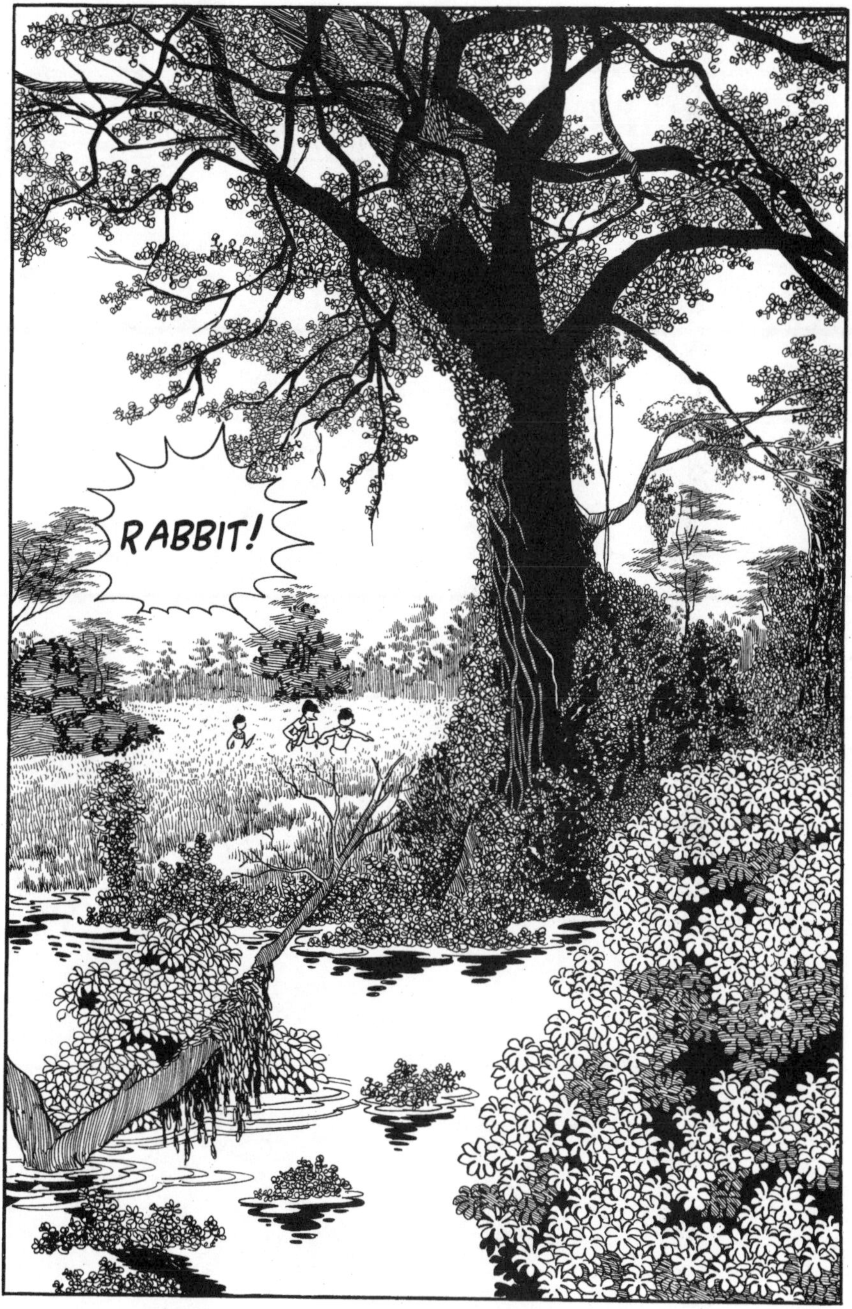
RABBIT!

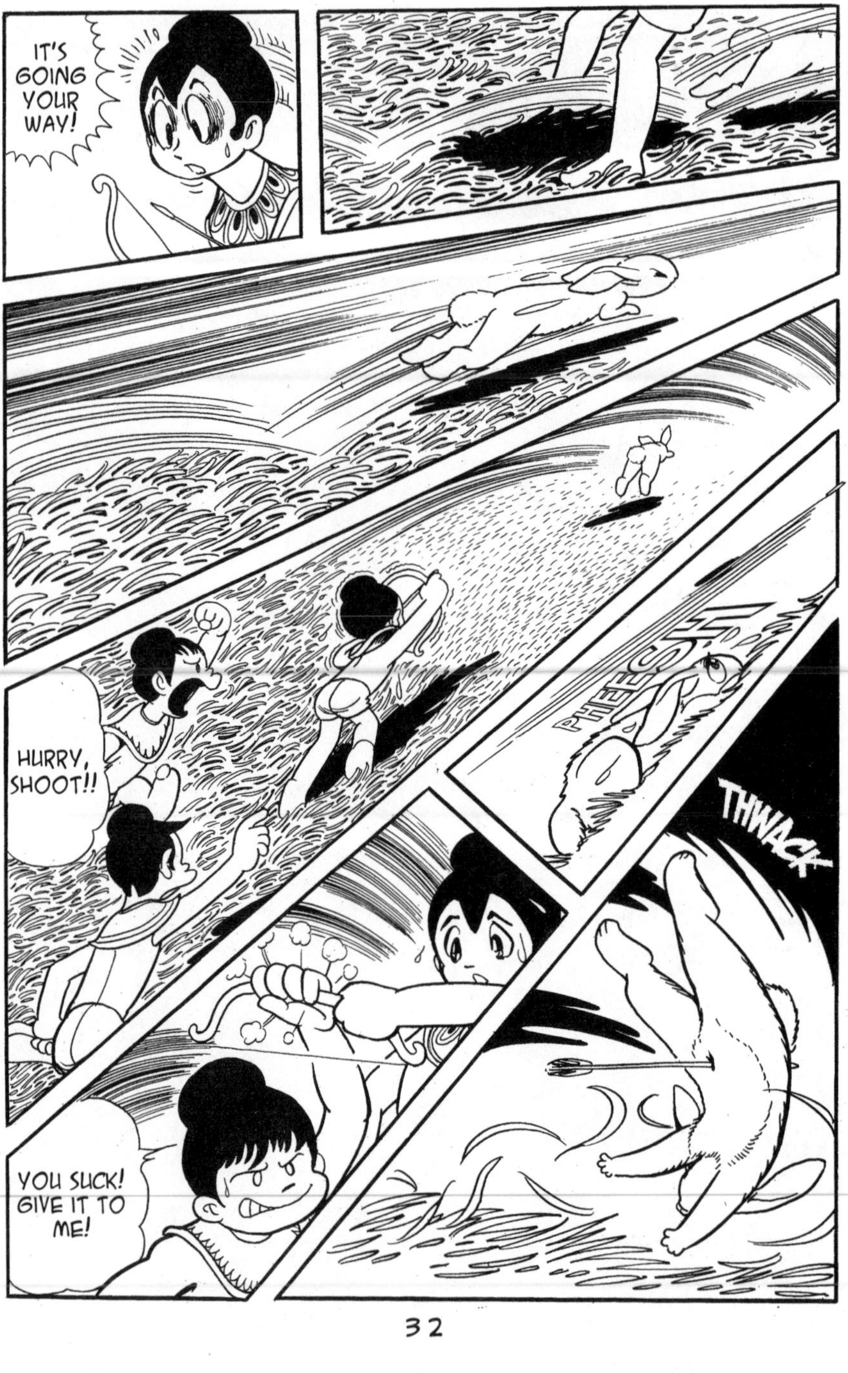
IT'S GOING YOUR WAY!
HURRY, SHOOT!!
PHEESH
THWACK
YOU SUCK! GIVE IT TO ME!

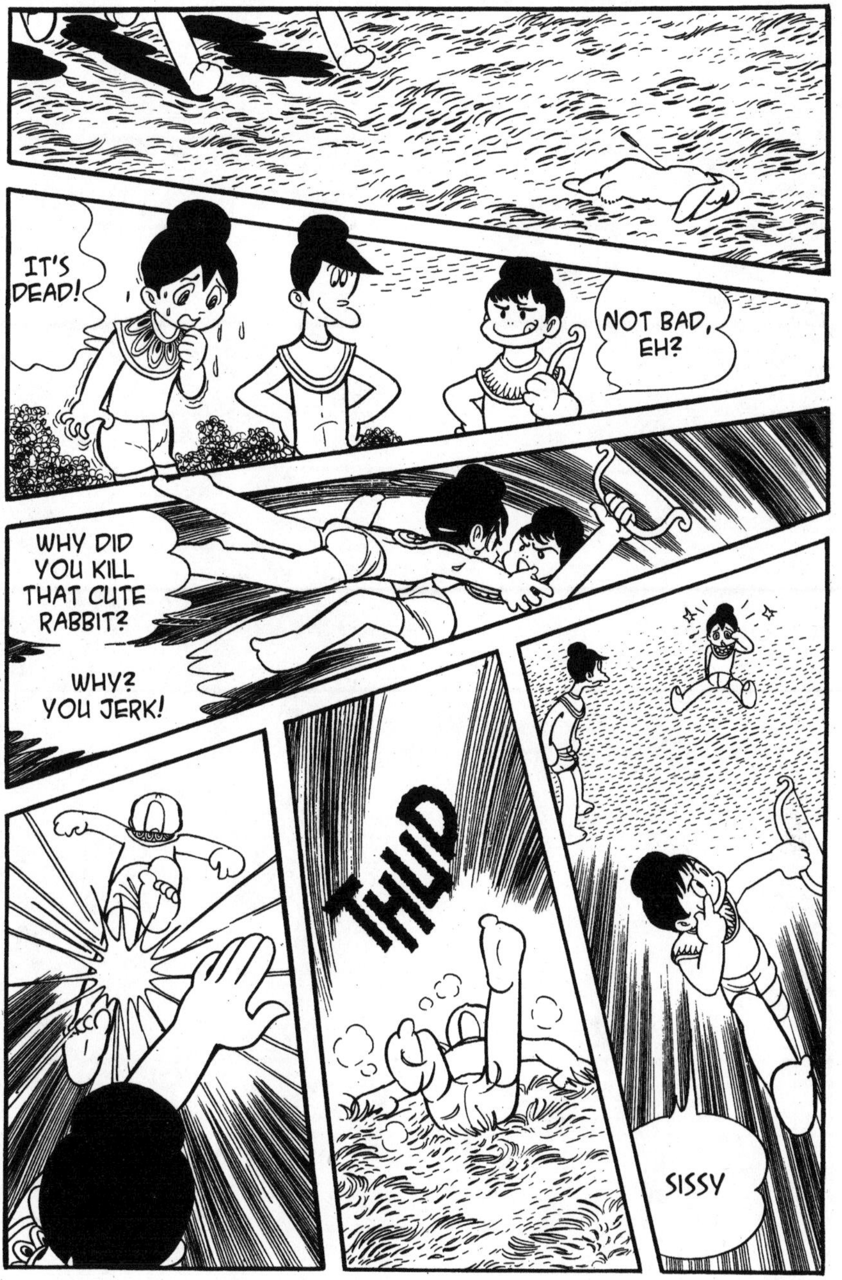
IT'S DEAD!
NOT BAD, EH?
WHY DID YOU KILL THAT CUTE RABBIT?
WHY? YOU JERK!
THUD
SISSY

slip
SLOSH
OOPS
SPLASH!!
HELP!!

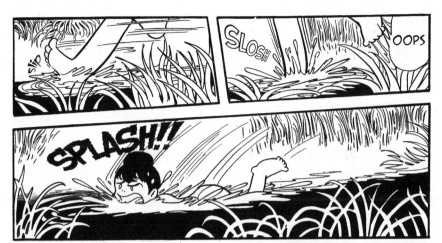

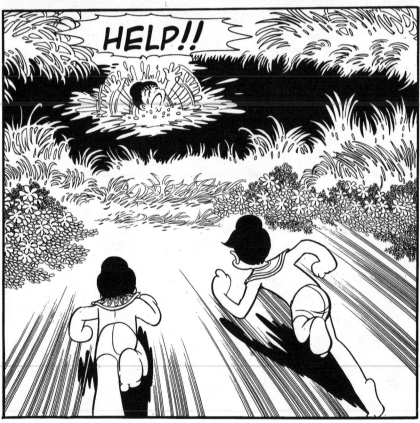

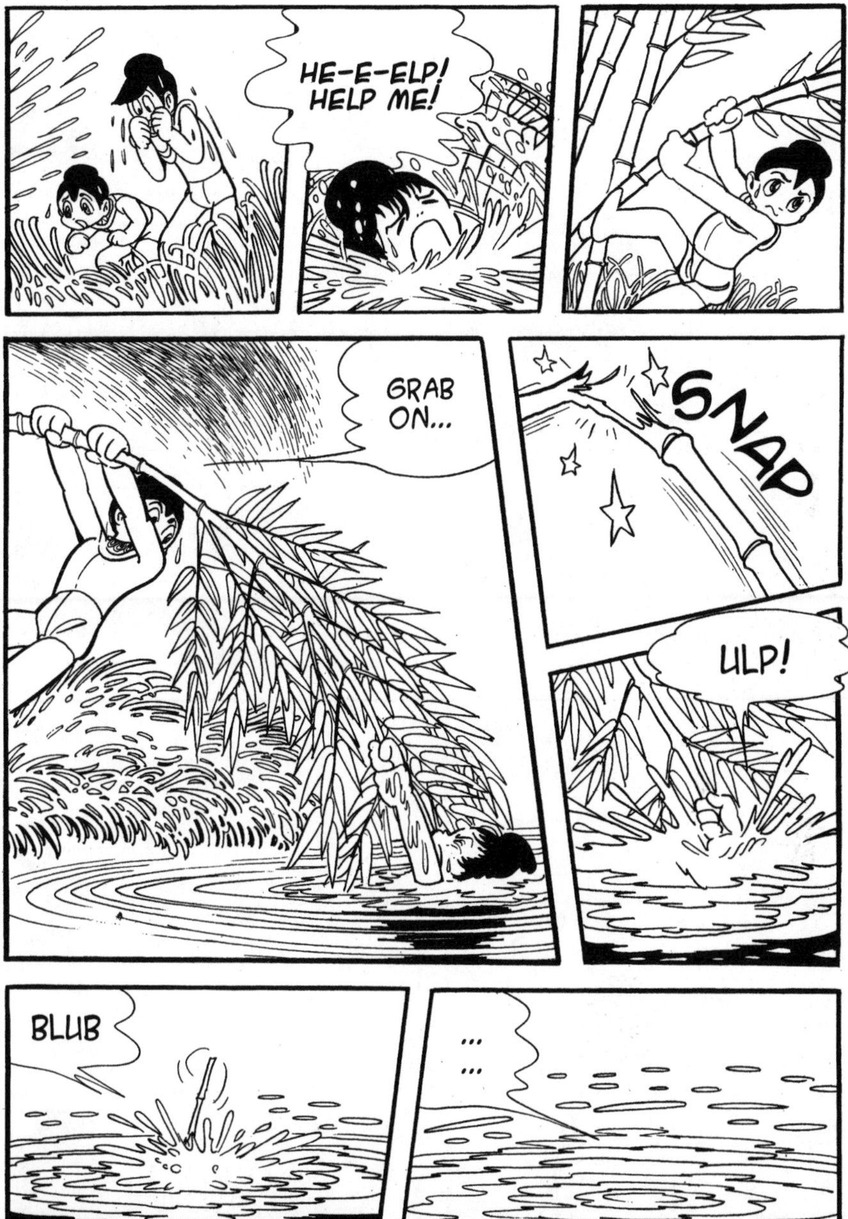
HE-E-ELP! HELP ME!
GRAB ON...
SNAP
ULP!
BLUB
...
...

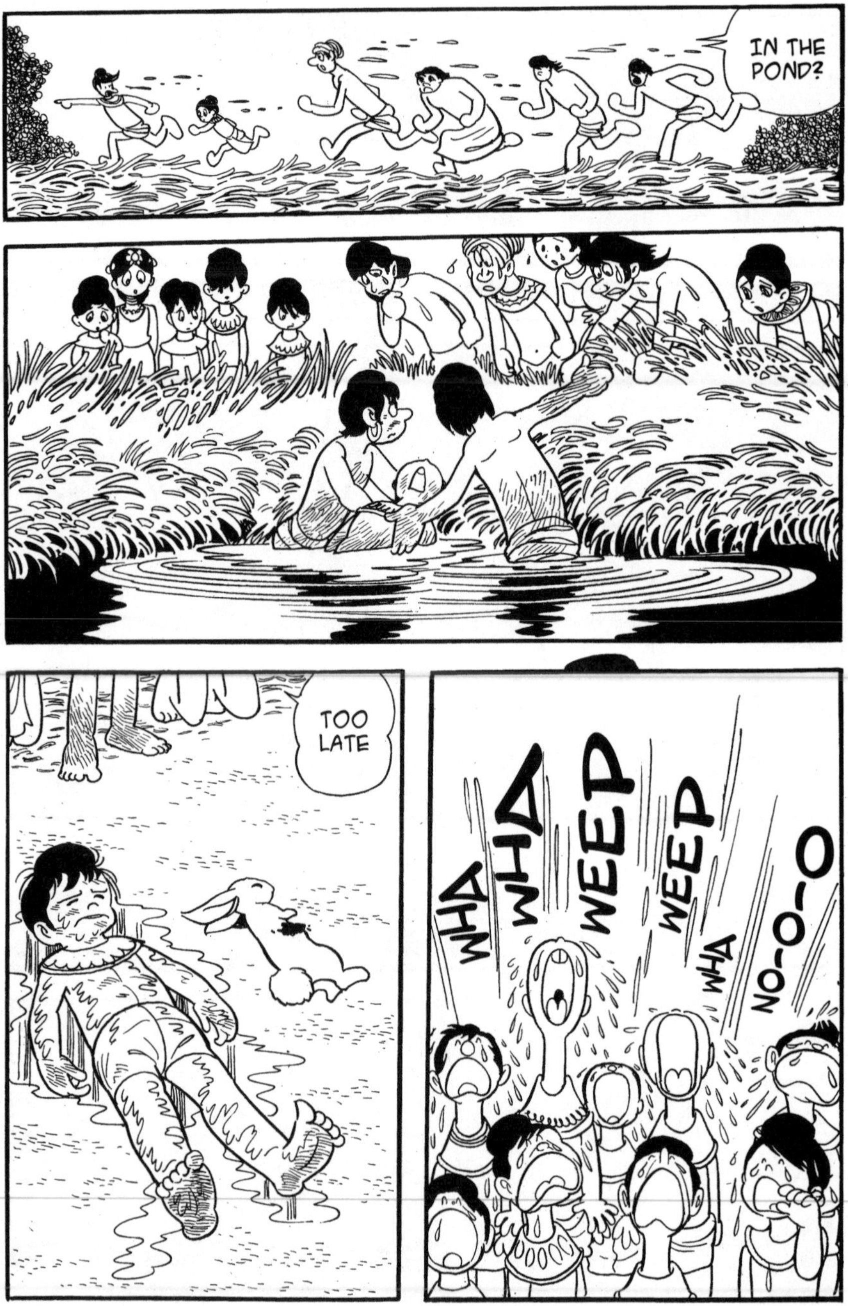
IN THE POND?
TOO LATE
WHA
WHA
WEEP
WEEP
WHA
NO-O-O-O

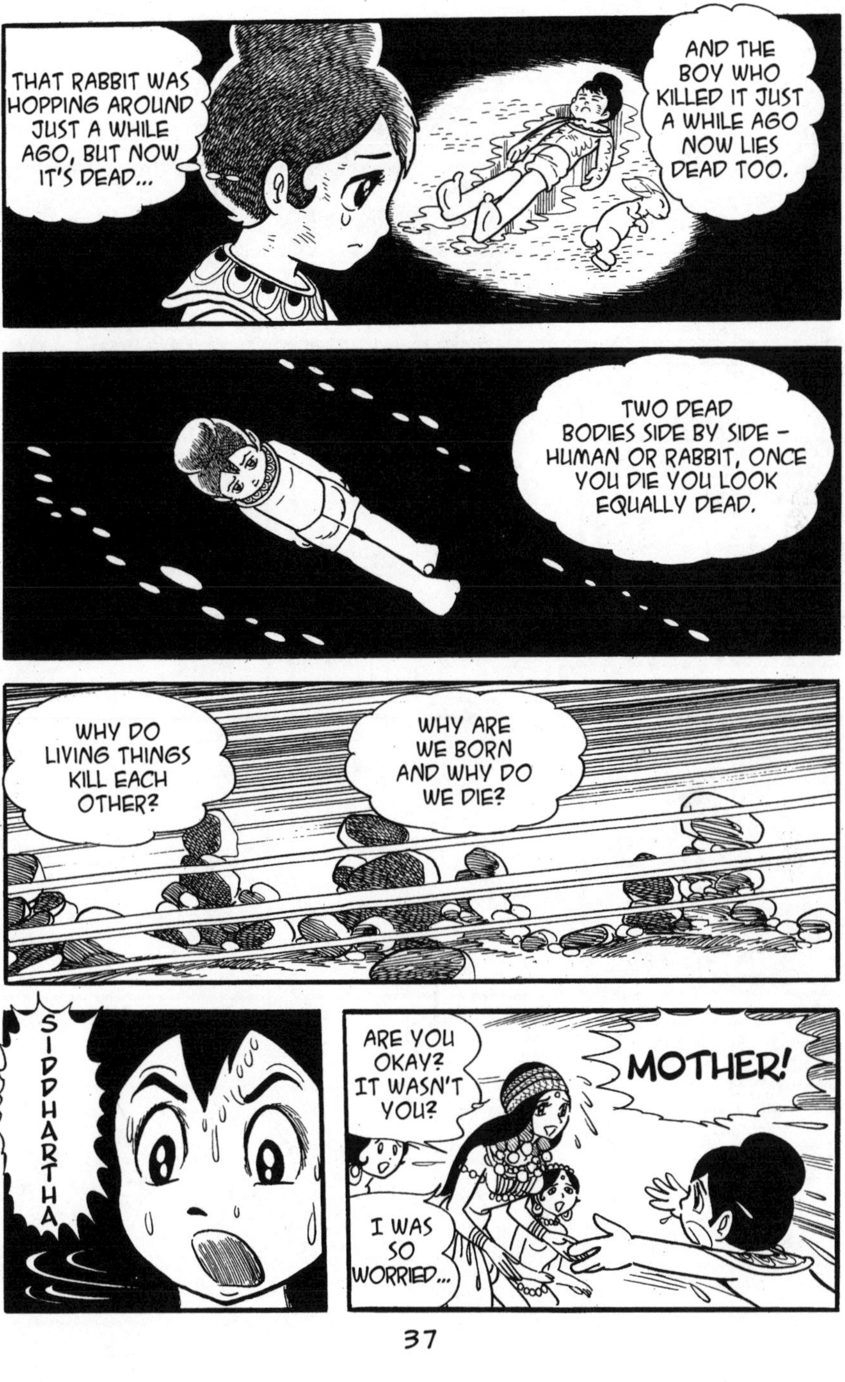
THAT RABBIT WAS HOPPING AROUND JUST A WHILE AGO, BUT NOW IT'S DEAD...
AND THE BOY WHO KILLED IT JUST A WHILE AGO NOW LIES DEAD TOO.
TWO DEAD BODIES SIDE BY SIDE - HUMAN OR RABBIT, ONCE YOU DIE YOU LOOK EQUALLY DEAD.
WHY DO LIVING THINGS KILL EACH OTHER?
WHY ARE WE BORN AND WHY DO WE DIE?
SIDDHARTHA
ARE YOU OKAY? IT WASN'T YOU?
MOTHER!
I WAS SO WORRIED...

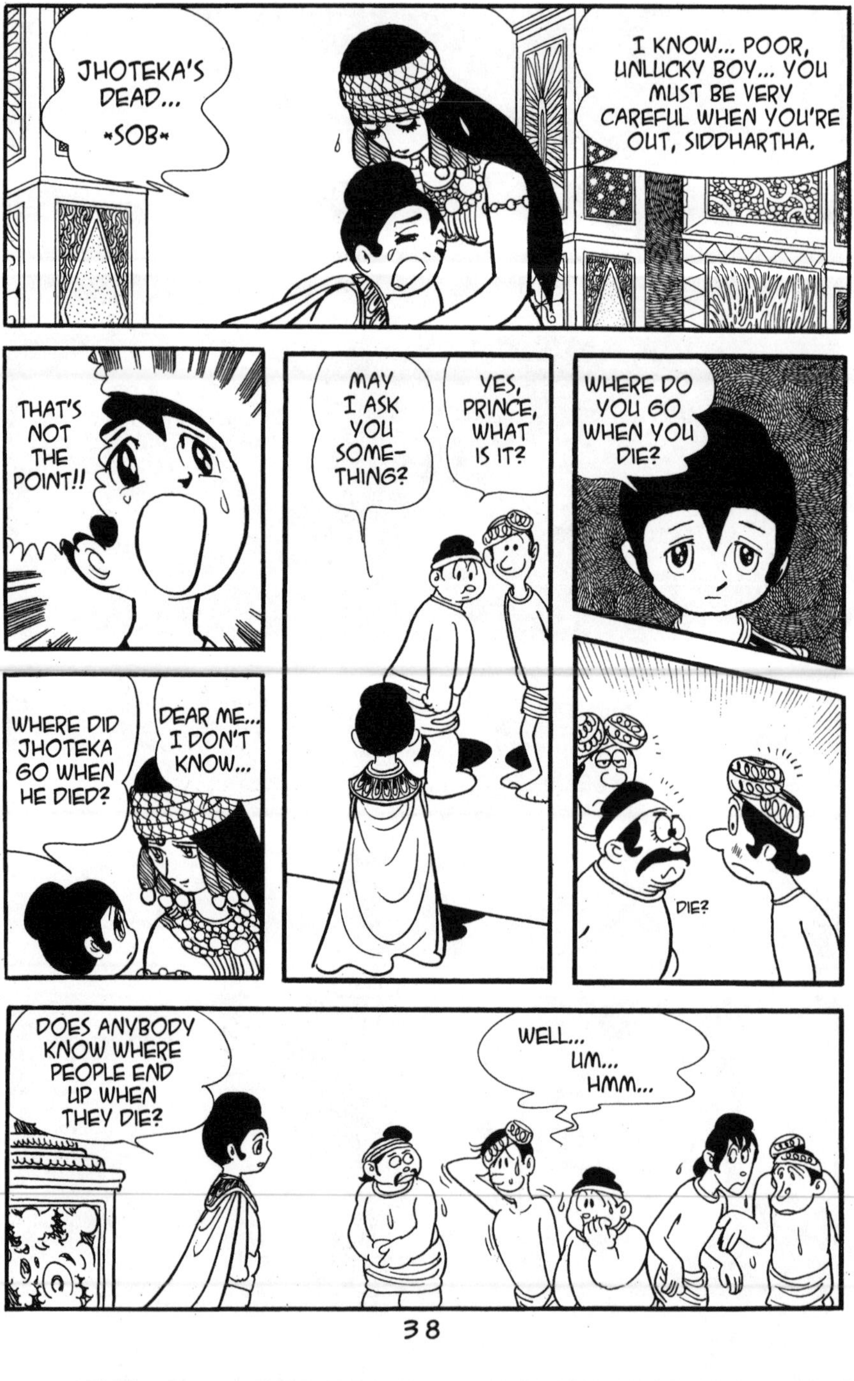
JHOTEKA'S DEAD... *SOB*
I KNOW... POOR, UNLUCKY BOY... YOU MUST BE VERY CAREFUL WHEN YOU'RE OUT, SIDDHARTHA.
THAT'S NOT THE POINT!!
WHERE DID JHOTEKA GO WHEN HE DIED?
DEAR ME... I DON'T KNOW...
MAY I ASK YOU SOME-THING?
YES, PRINCE, WHAT IS IT?
WHERE DO YOU GO WHEN YOU DIE?
DIE?
DOES ANYBODY KNOW WHERE PEOPLE END UP WHEN THEY DIE?
WELL... UM... HMM...

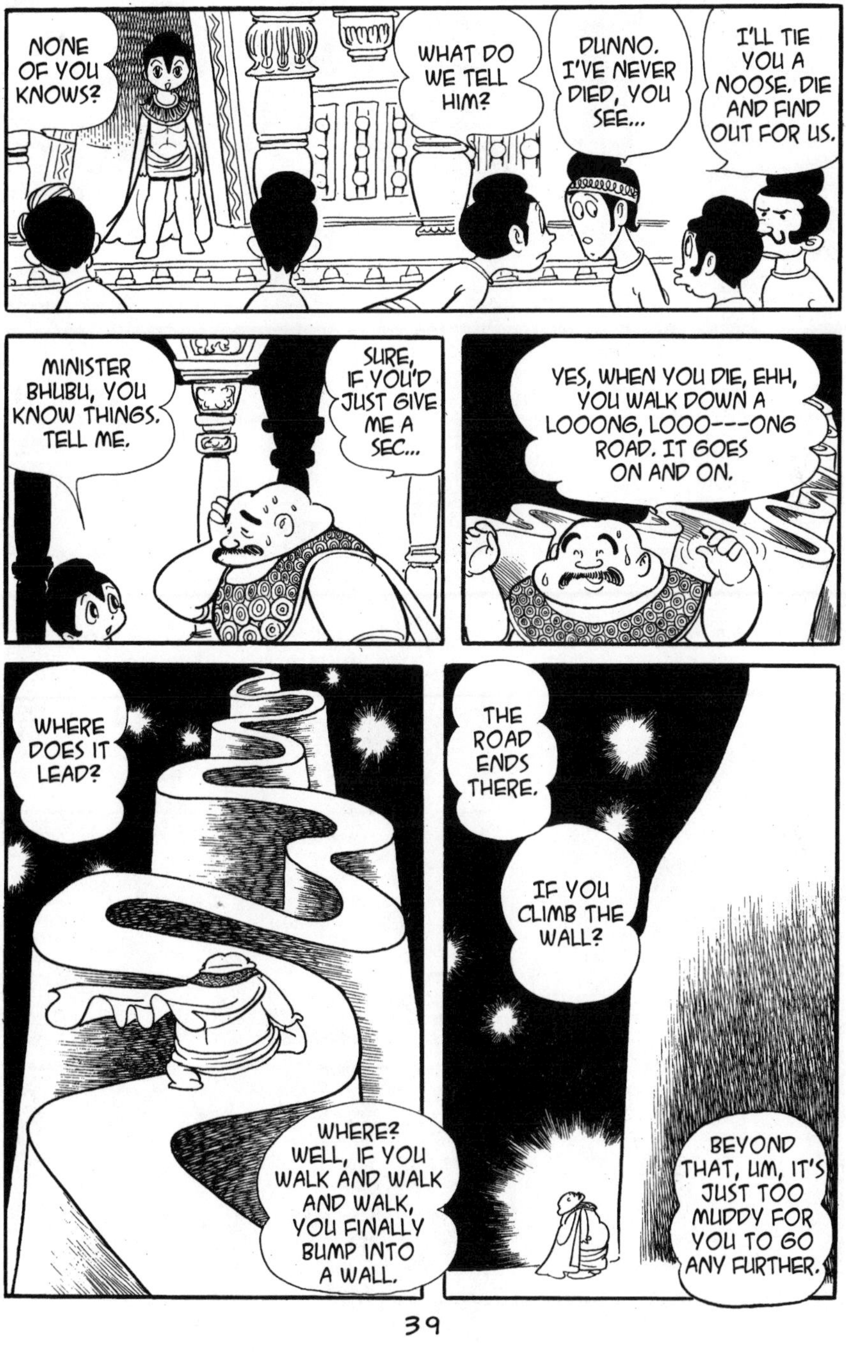
NONE OF YOU KNOWS?
WHAT DO WE TELL HIM?
DUNNO. I'VE NEVER DIED, YOU SEE...
I'LL TIE YOU A NOOSE. DIE AND FIND OUT FOR US.
MINISTER BHUBU, YOU KNOW THINGS. TELL ME.
SURE, IF YOU'D JUST GIVE ME A SEC...
YES, WHEN YOU DIE, EHH, YOU WALK DOWN A LOOONG, LOOO---ONG ROAD. IT GOES ON AND ON.
WHERE DOES IT LEAD?
WHERE? WELL, IF YOU WALK AND WALK AND WALK, YOU FINALLY BUMP INTO A WALL.
THE ROAD ENDS THERE.
IF YOU CLIMB THE WALL?
BEYOND THAT, UM, IT'S JUST TOO MUDDY FOR YOU TO GO ANY FURTHER.

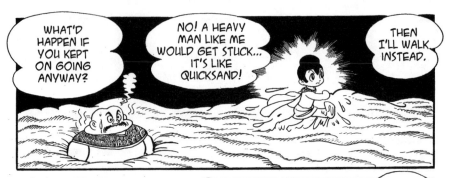

WHAT'D HAPPEN IF YOU KEPT ON GOING ANYWAY?

NO! A HEAVY MAN LIKE ME WOULD GET STUCK... IT'S LIKE QUICKSAND!

THEN I'LL WALK INSTEAD.

OH, BUT BEYOND THAT IS A FOG SO DENSE YOU WOULDN'T KNOW WHERE YOU WERE GOING!

BUT I'D STILL BE ABLE TO GO ON, RIGHT?

WHAT DO I GET TO?

AN IRON GATE WITH A SIGN THAT SAYS, "NO TRESPASSING."

I CLIMB OVER IT ANYWAY!

IF YOU DID SUCH A THING...

YOU'D GET ARRESTED. WE'D HAVE TO PAY THE FINE FOR YOU AND...

ENOUGH, MINISTER BHUBU. YOU'RE JUST MAKING THIS UP.

PHEW, HIS HIGHNESS IS MIGHTY CLEVER. SUCH A FOOL HE MADE OUT OF ME.

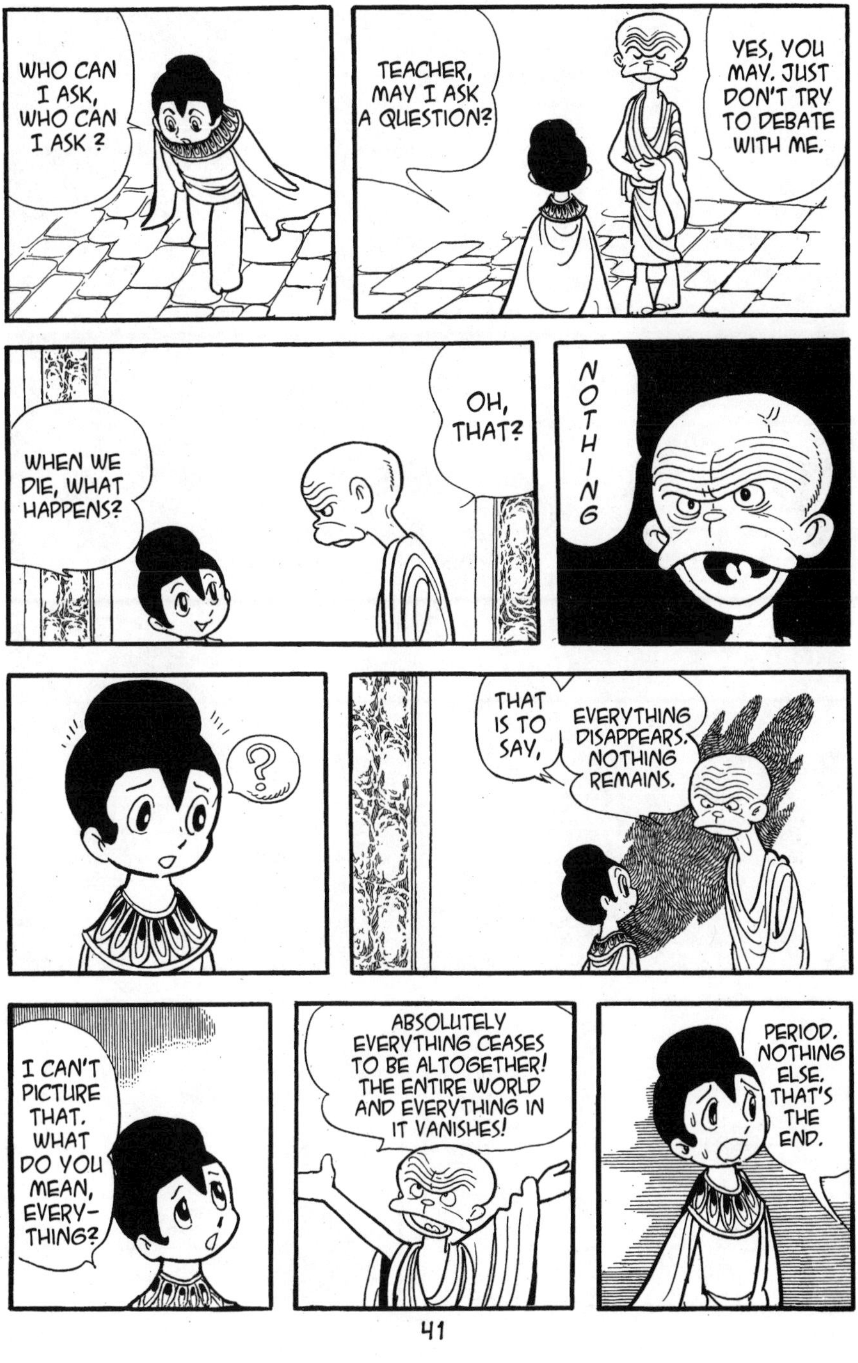
WHO CAN I ASK, WHO CAN I ASK ?
TEACHER, MAY I ASK A QUESTION?
YES, YOU MAY. JUST DON'T TRY TO DEBATE WITH ME.
WHEN WE DIE, WHAT HAPPENS?
OH, THAT?
NOTHING
?
THAT IS TO SAY,
EVERYTHING DISAPPEARS. NOTHING REMAINS.
I CAN'T PICTURE THAT. WHAT DO YOU MEAN, EVERY-THING?
ABSOLUTELY EVERYTHING CEASES TO BE ALTOGETHER! THE ENTIRE WORLD AND EVERYTHING IN IT VANISHES!
PERIOD. NOTHING ELSE. THAT'S THE END.

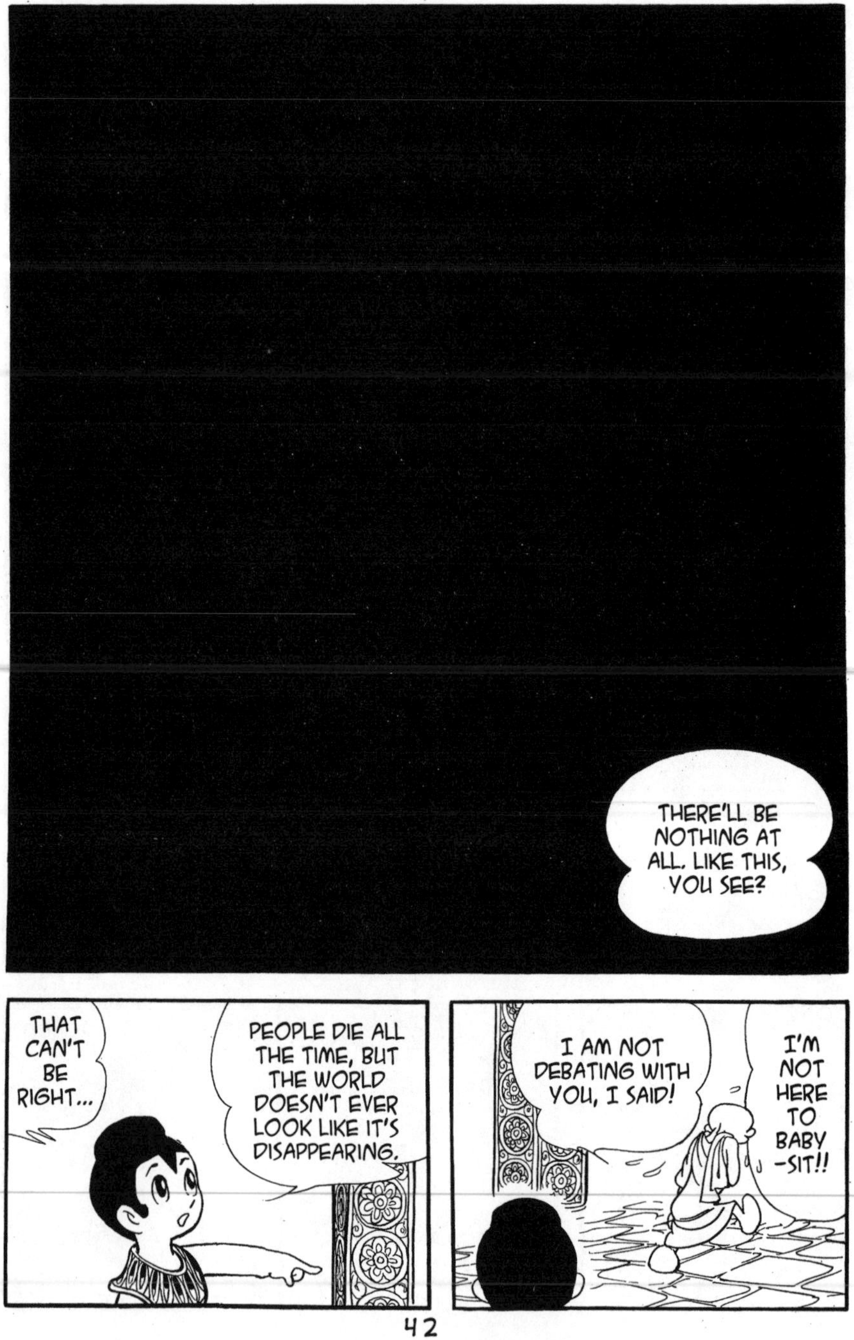
THERE'LL BE NOTHING AT ALL. LIKE THIS, YOU SEE?
THAT CAN'T BE RIGHT...
PEOPLE DIE ALL THE TIME, BUT THE WORLD DOESN'T EVER LOOK LIKE IT'S DISAPPEARING.
I AM NOT DEBATING WITH YOU, I SAID!
I'M NOT HERE TO BABY-SIT!!

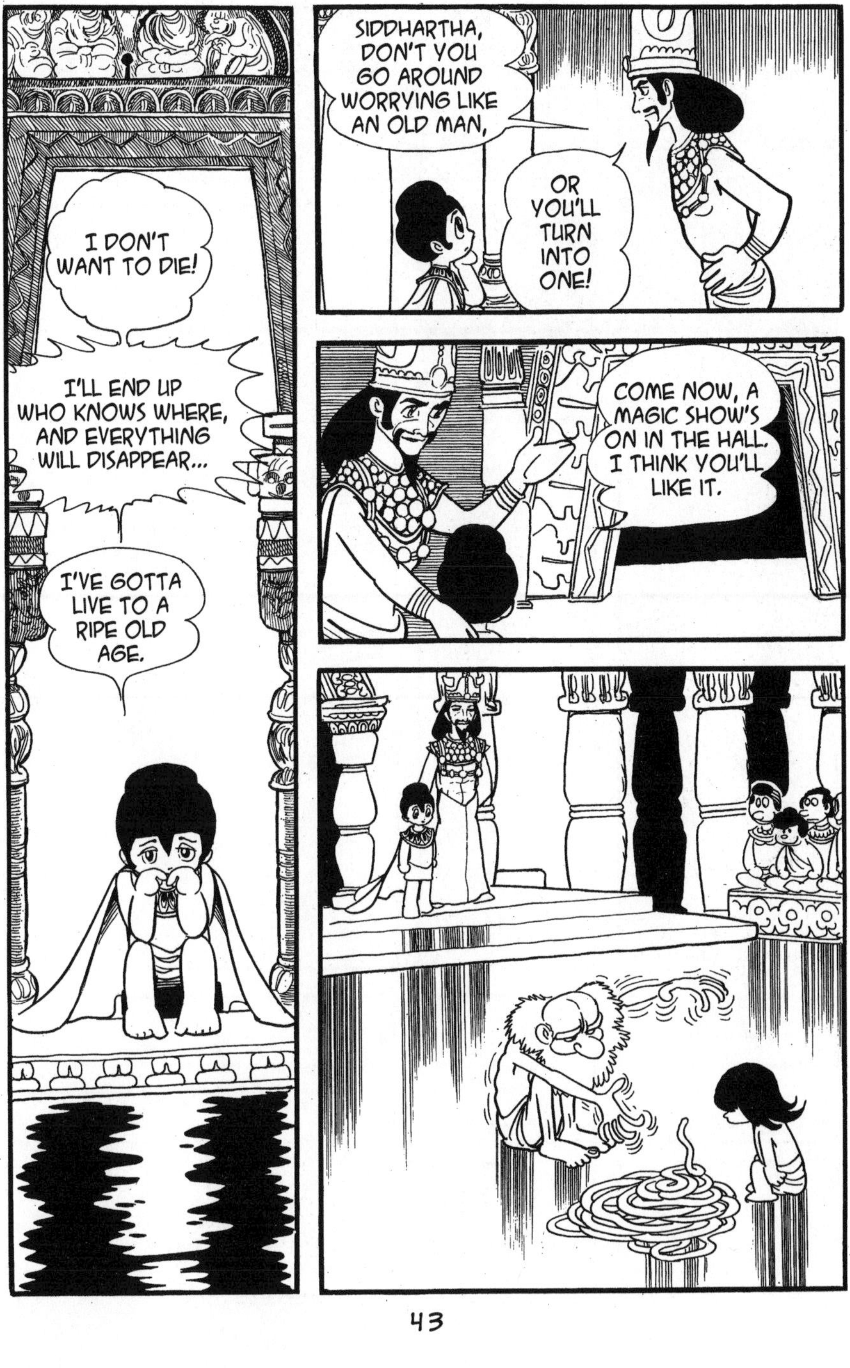
I DON'T WANT TO DIE!
I'LL END UP WHO KNOWS WHERE, AND EVERYTHING WILL DISAPPEAR...
I'VE GOTTA LIVE TO A RIPE OLD AGE.
SIDDHARTHA, DON'T YOU GO AROUND WORRYING LIKE AN OLD MAN,
OR YOU'LL TURN INTO ONE!
COME NOW, A MAGIC SHOW'S ON IN THE HALL. I THINK YOU'LL LIKE IT.

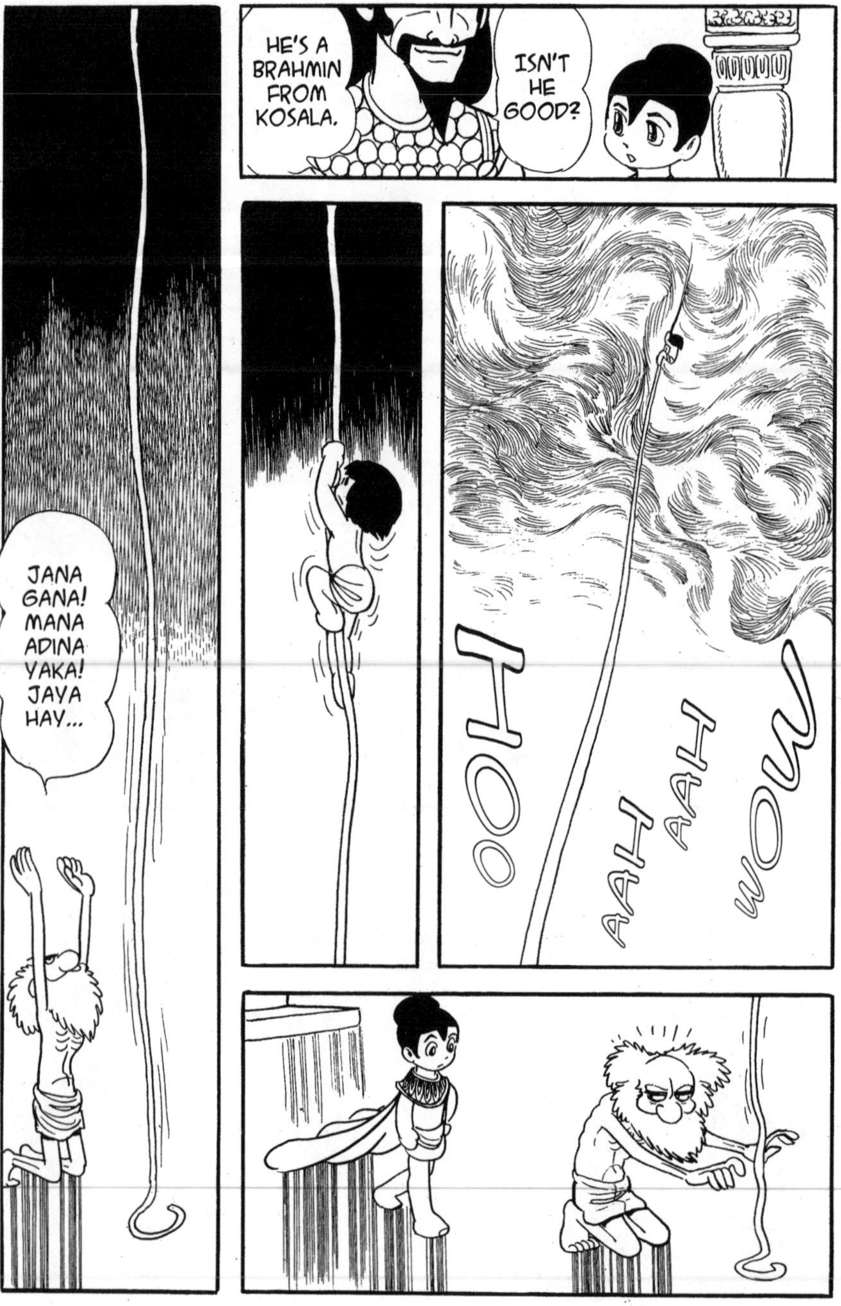
JANA GANA! MANA ADINA YAKA! JAYA HAY...
HE'S A BRAHMIN FROM KOSALA.
ISN'T HE GOOD?
HOO
AAH
AAH
WOW

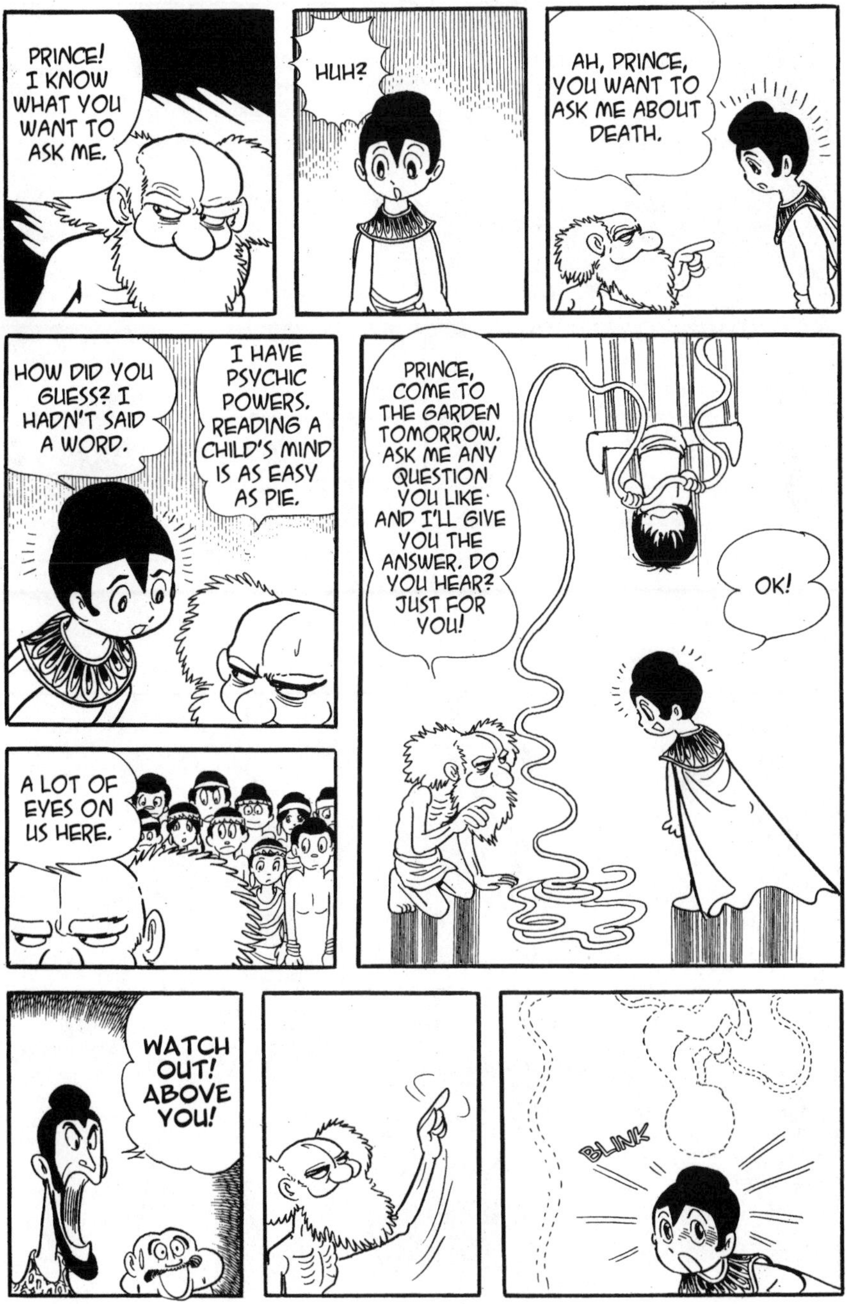
PRINCE! I KNOW WHAT YOU WANT TO ASK ME.
HUH?
AH, PRINCE, YOU WANT TO ASK ME ABOUT DEATH.
HOW DID YOU GUESS? I HADN'T SAID A WORD.
I HAVE PSYCHIC POWERS. READING A CHILD'S MIND IS AS EASY AS PIE.
A LOT OF EYES ON US HERE.
PRINCE, COME TO THE GARDEN TOMORROW. ASK ME ANY QUESTION YOU LIKE AND I'LL GIVE YOU THE ANSWER. DO YOU HEAR? JUST FOR YOU!
OK!
WATCH OUT! ABOVE YOU!
BLINK

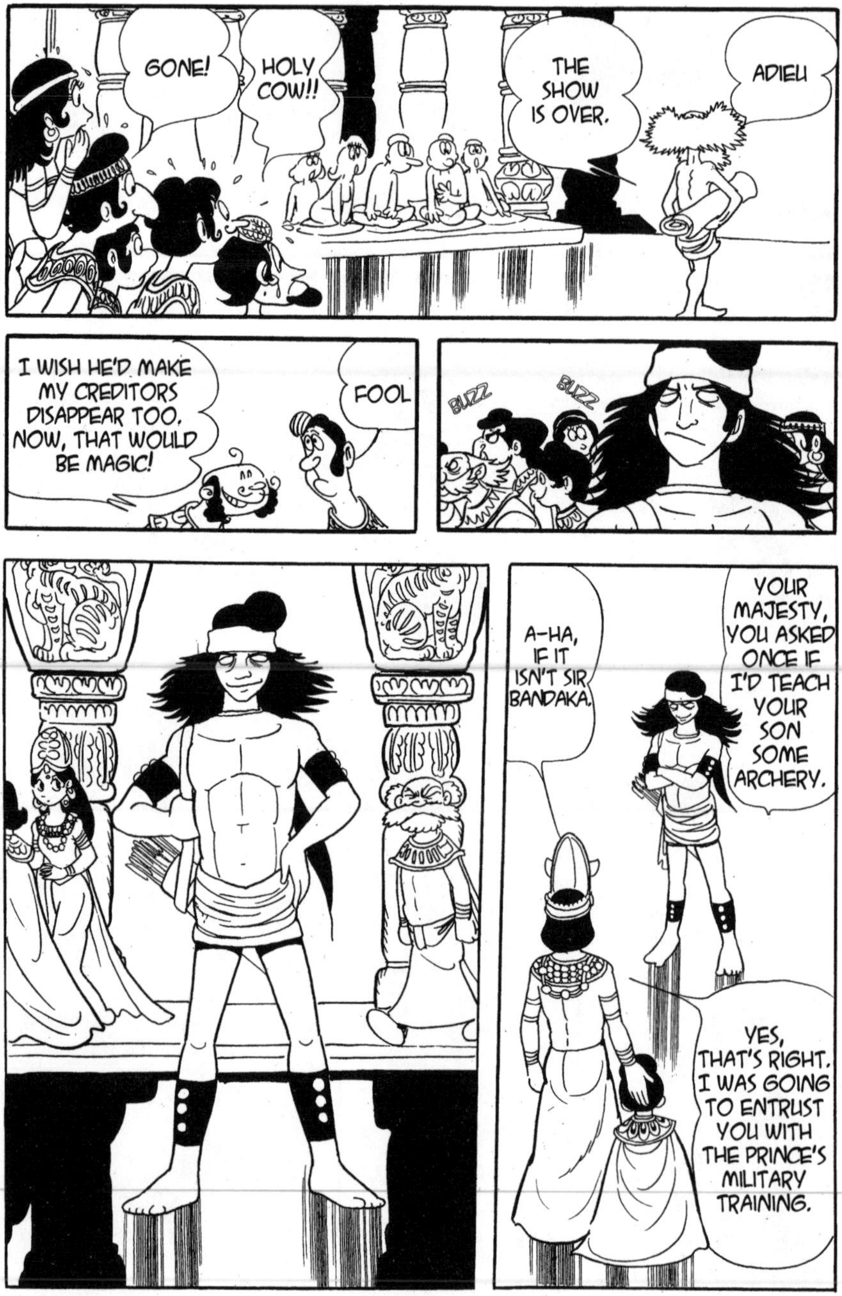
GONE!
HOLY COW!!
THE SHOW IS OVER.
ADIEU
I WISH HE'D MAKE MY CREDITORS DISAPPEAR TOO. NOW, THAT WOULD BE MAGIC!
FOOL
BUZZ
BUZZ
A-HA, IF IT ISN'T SIR BANDAKA.
YOUR MAJESTY, YOU ASKED ONCE IF I'D TEACH YOUR SON SOME ARCHERY.
YES, THAT'S RIGHT. I WAS GOING TO ENTRUST YOU WITH THE PRINCE'S MILITARY TRAINING.

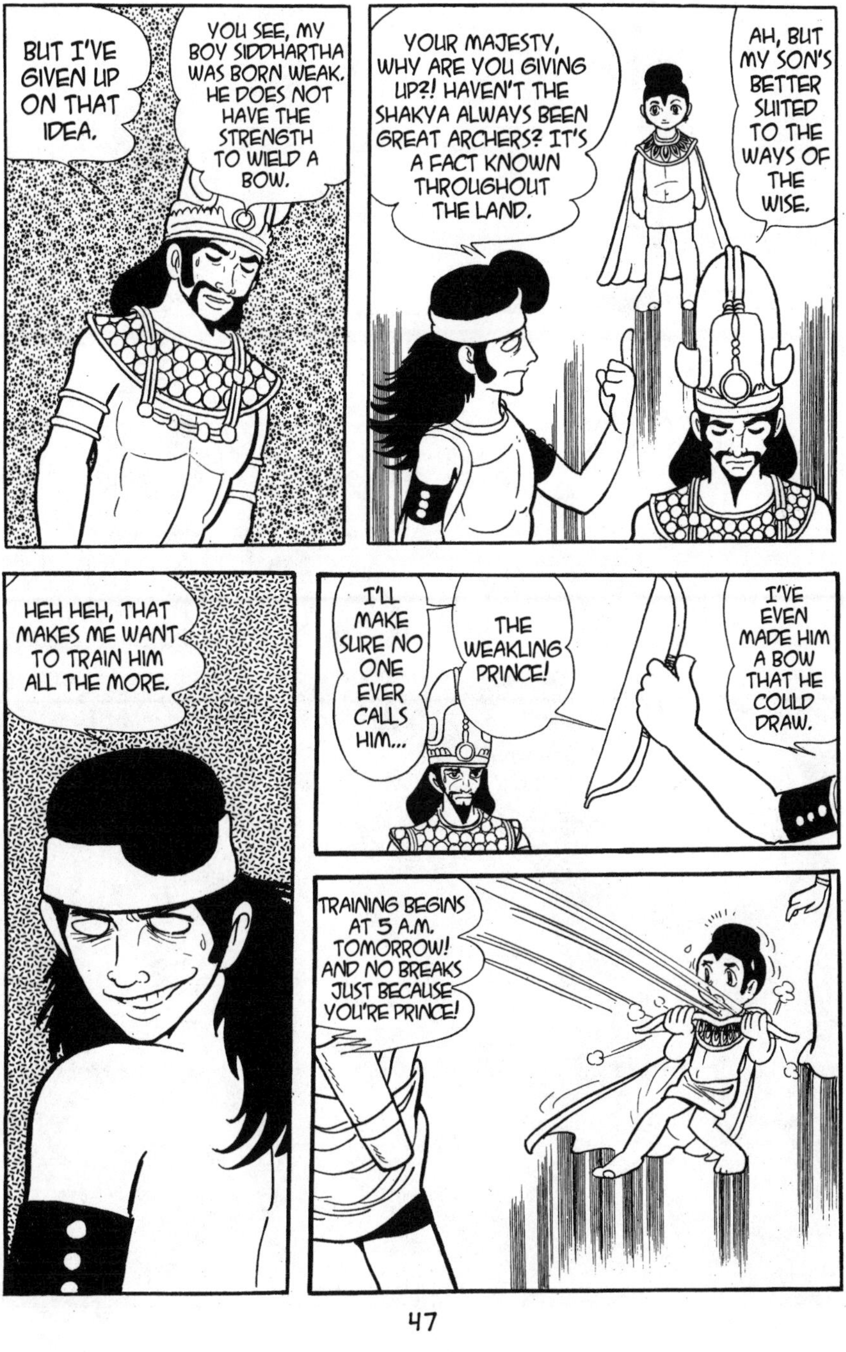

BUT I'VE GIVEN UP ON THAT IDEA.
YOU SEE, MY BOY SIDDHARTHA WAS BORN WEAK. HE DOES NOT HAVE THE STRENGTH TO WIELD A BOW.
YOUR MAJESTY, WHY ARE YOU GIVING UP?! HAVEN'T THE SHAKYA ALWAYS BEEN GREAT ARCHERS? IT'S A FACT KNOWN THROUGHOUT THE LAND.
AH, BUT MY SON'S BETTER SUITED TO THE WAYS OF THE WISE.
HEH HEH, THAT MAKES ME WANT TO TRAIN HIM ALL THE MORE.
I'LL MAKE SURE NO ONE EVER CALLS HIM...
THE WEAKLING PRINCE!
I'VE EVEN MADE HIM A BOW THAT HE COULD DRAW.
TRAINING BEGINS AT 5 A.M. TOMORROW! AND NO BREAKS JUST BECAUSE YOU'RE PRINCE!

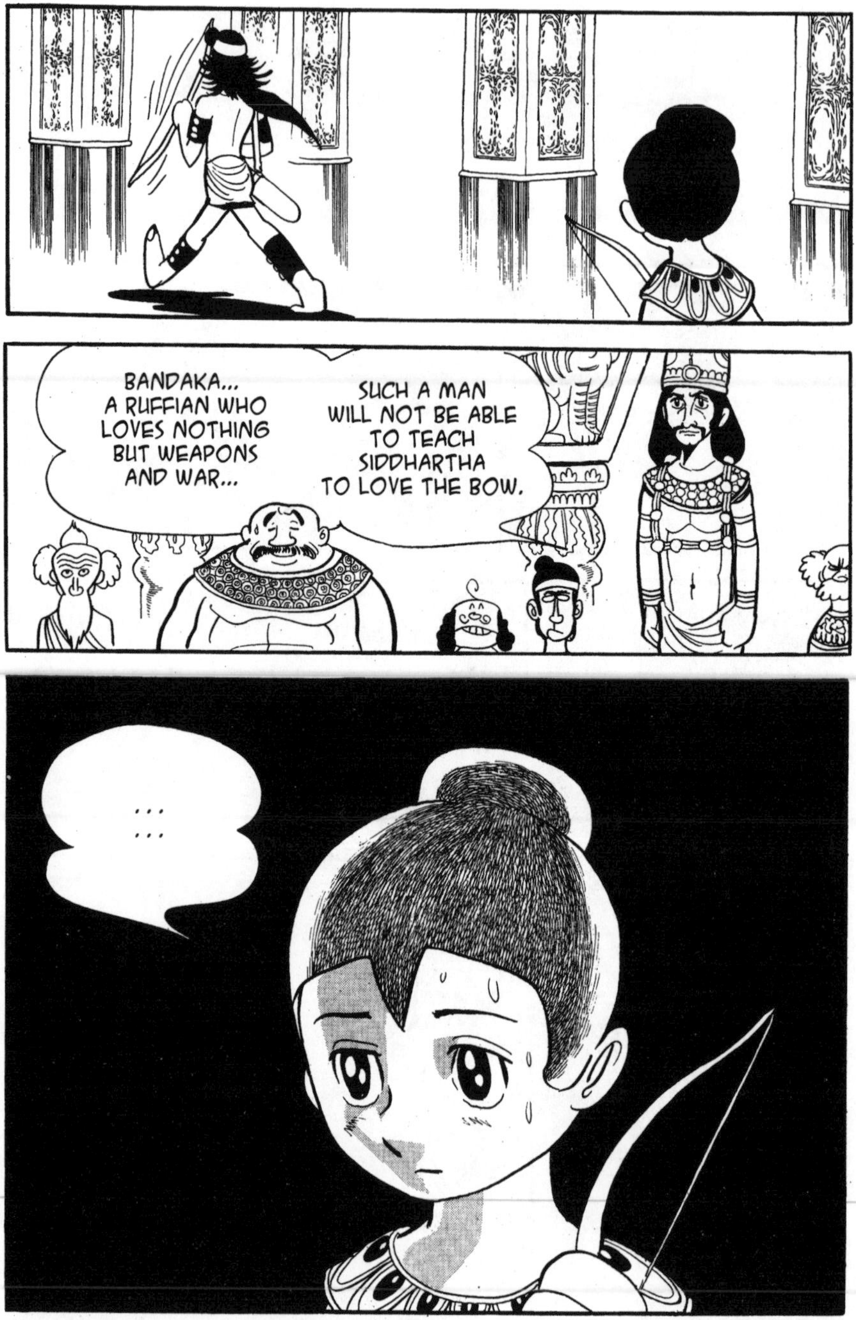
BANDAKA... A RUFFIAN WHO LOVES NOTHING BUT WEAPONS AND WAR...
SUCH A MAN WILL NOT BE ABLE TO TEACH SIDDHARTHA TO LOVE THE BOW.
... ...

CHAPTER TWO

THE GARDEN OF MEDITATION

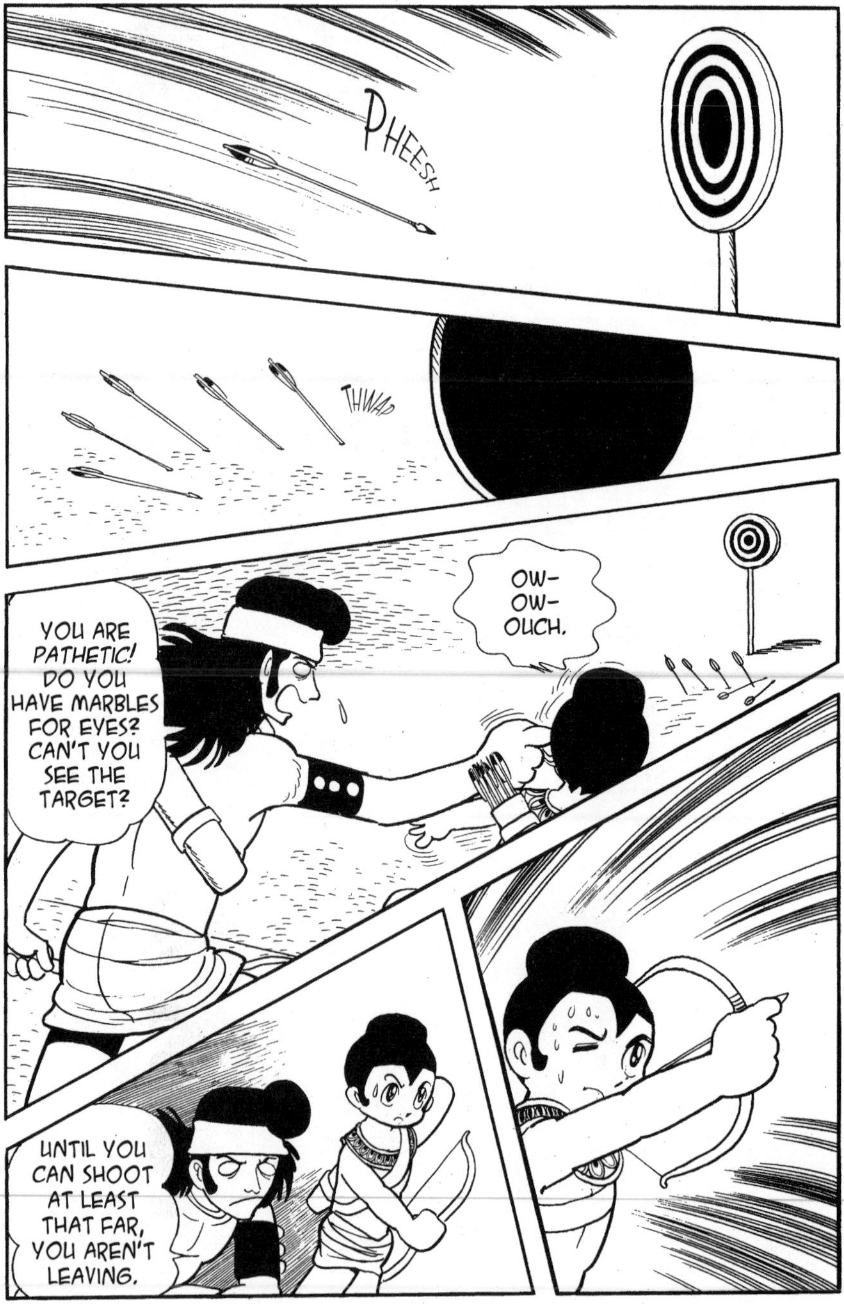
PHEESH
THWAP
YOU ARE PATHETIC! DO YOU HAVE MARBLES FOR EYES? CAN'T YOU SEE THE TARGET?
OW-OW-OUCH.
UNTIL YOU CAN SHOOT AT LEAST THAT FAR, YOU AREN'T LEAVING.

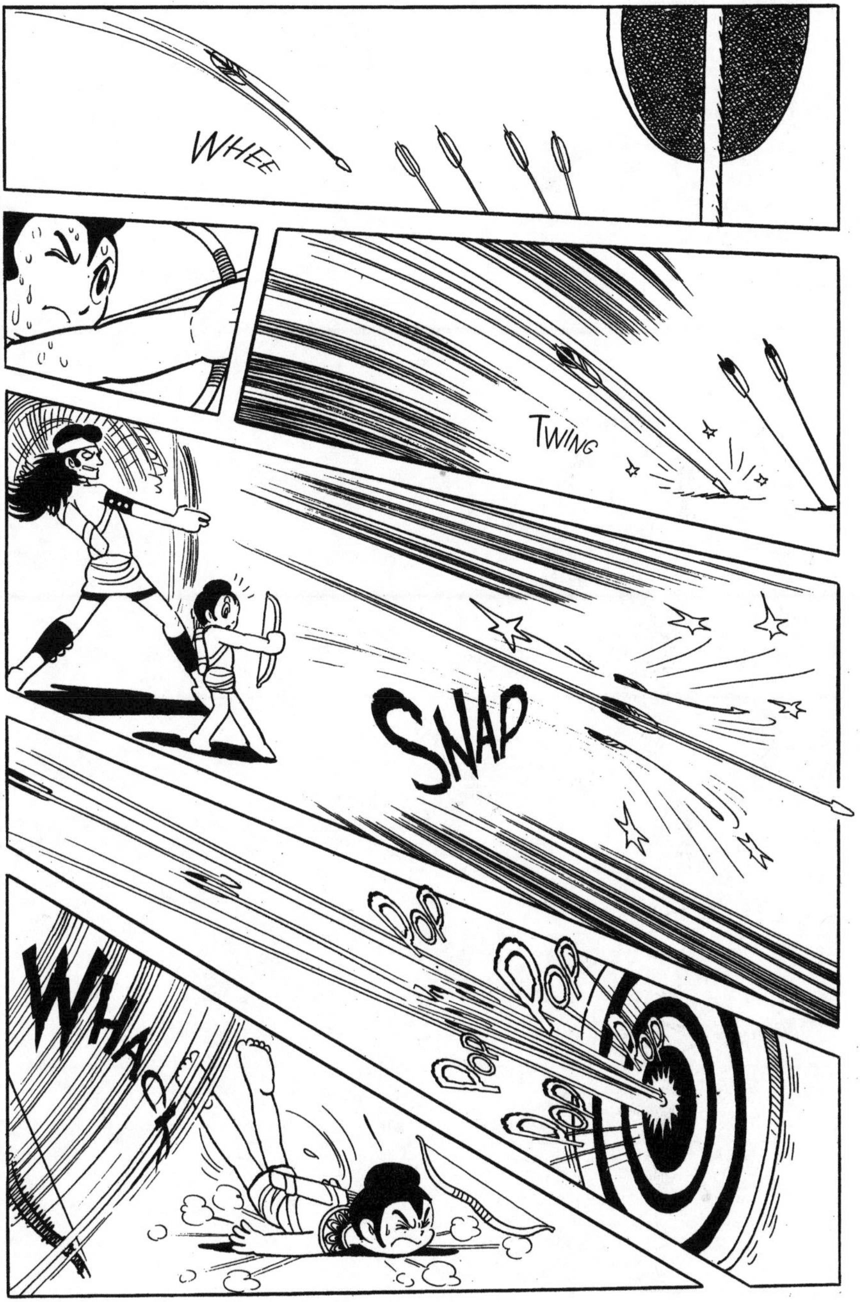
WHEE
TWING
SNAP
pop
pop
pop
pop
pop
pop
WHACK

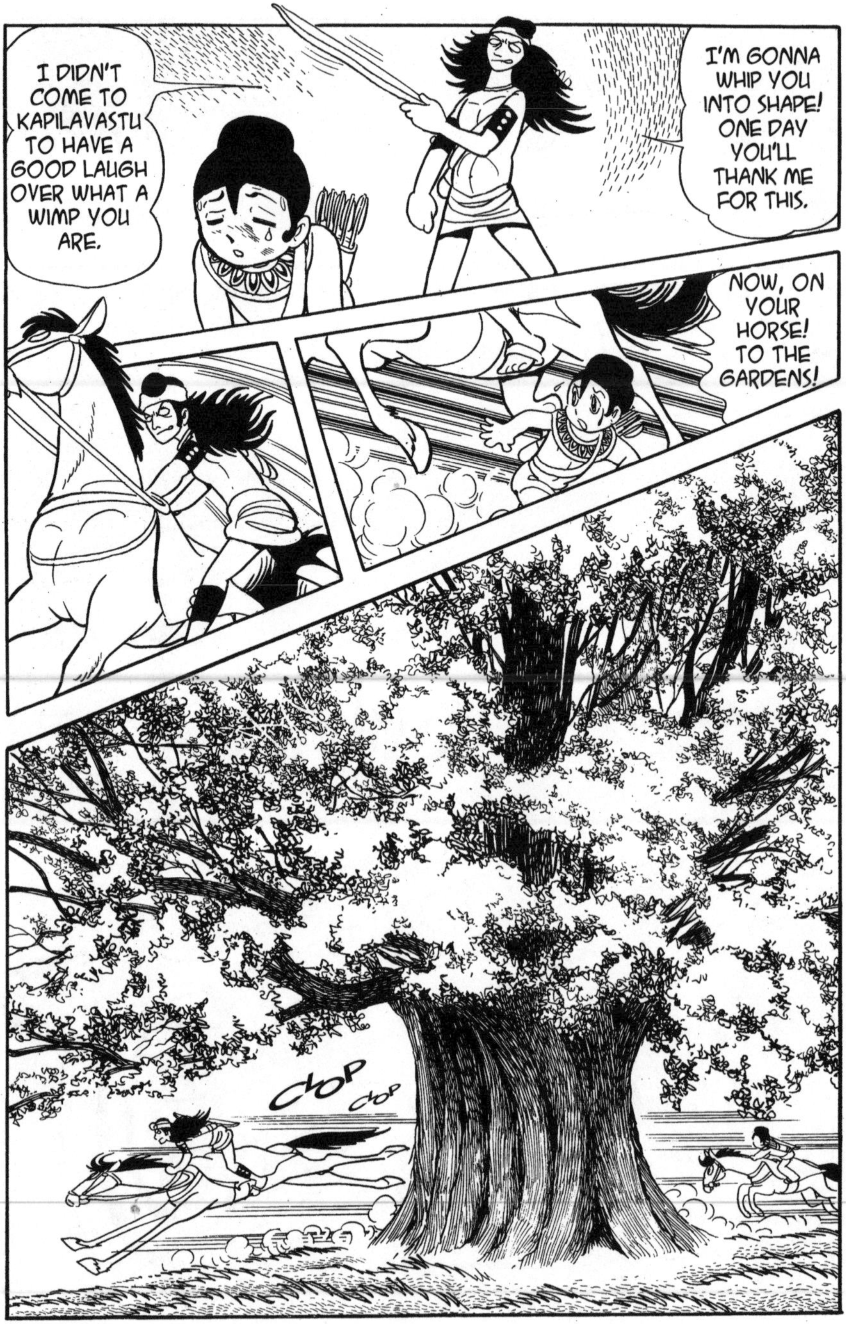
I DIDN'T COME TO KAPILAVASTU TO HAVE A GOOD LAUGH OVER WHAT A WIMP YOU ARE.
I'M GONNA WHIP YOU INTO SHAPE! ONE DAY YOU'LL THANK ME FOR THIS.
NOW, ON YOUR HORSE! TO THE GARDENS!
CLOP
CLOP

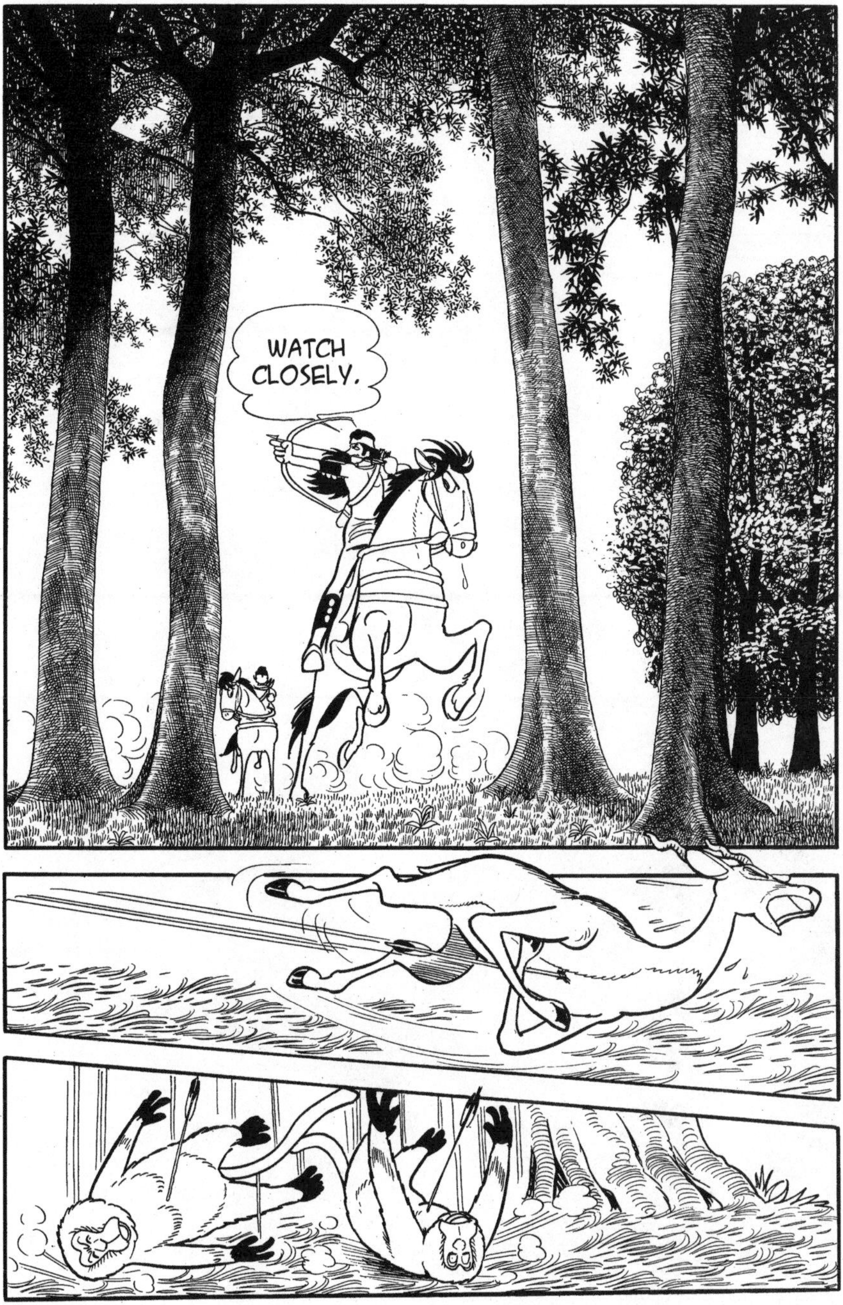
WATCH CLOSELY.

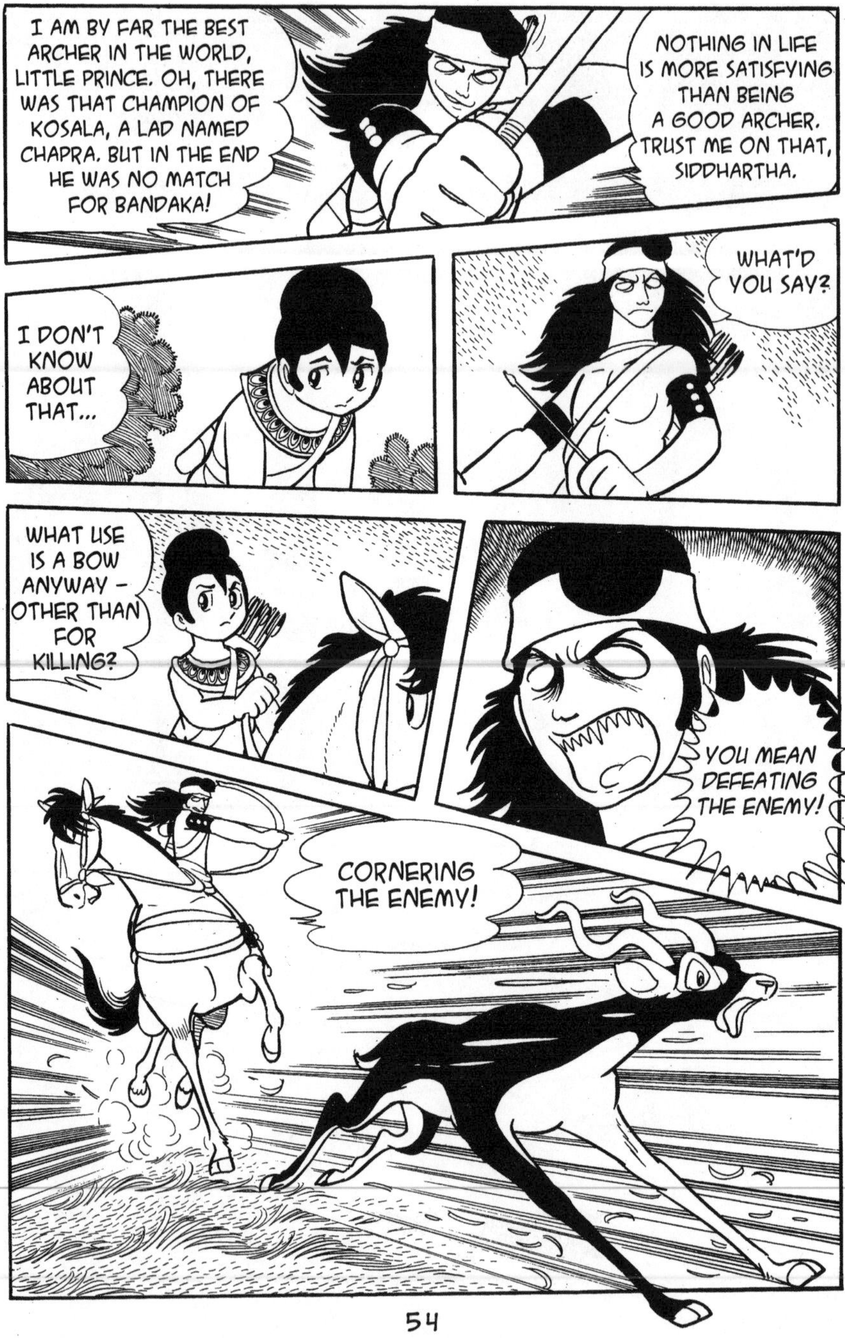
I AM BY FAR THE BEST ARCHER IN THE WORLD, LITTLE PRINCE. OH, THERE WAS THAT CHAMPION OF KOSALA, A LAD NAMED CHAPRA. BUT IN THE END HE WAS NO MATCH FOR BANDAKA!
NOTHING IN LIFE IS MORE SATISFYING THAN BEING A GOOD ARCHER. TRUST ME ON THAT, SIDDHARTHA.
I DON'T KNOW ABOUT THAT...
WHAT'D YOU SAY?
WHAT USE IS A BOW ANYWAY – OTHER THAN FOR KILLING?
YOU MEAN DEFEATING THE ENEMY!
CORNERING THE ENEMY!

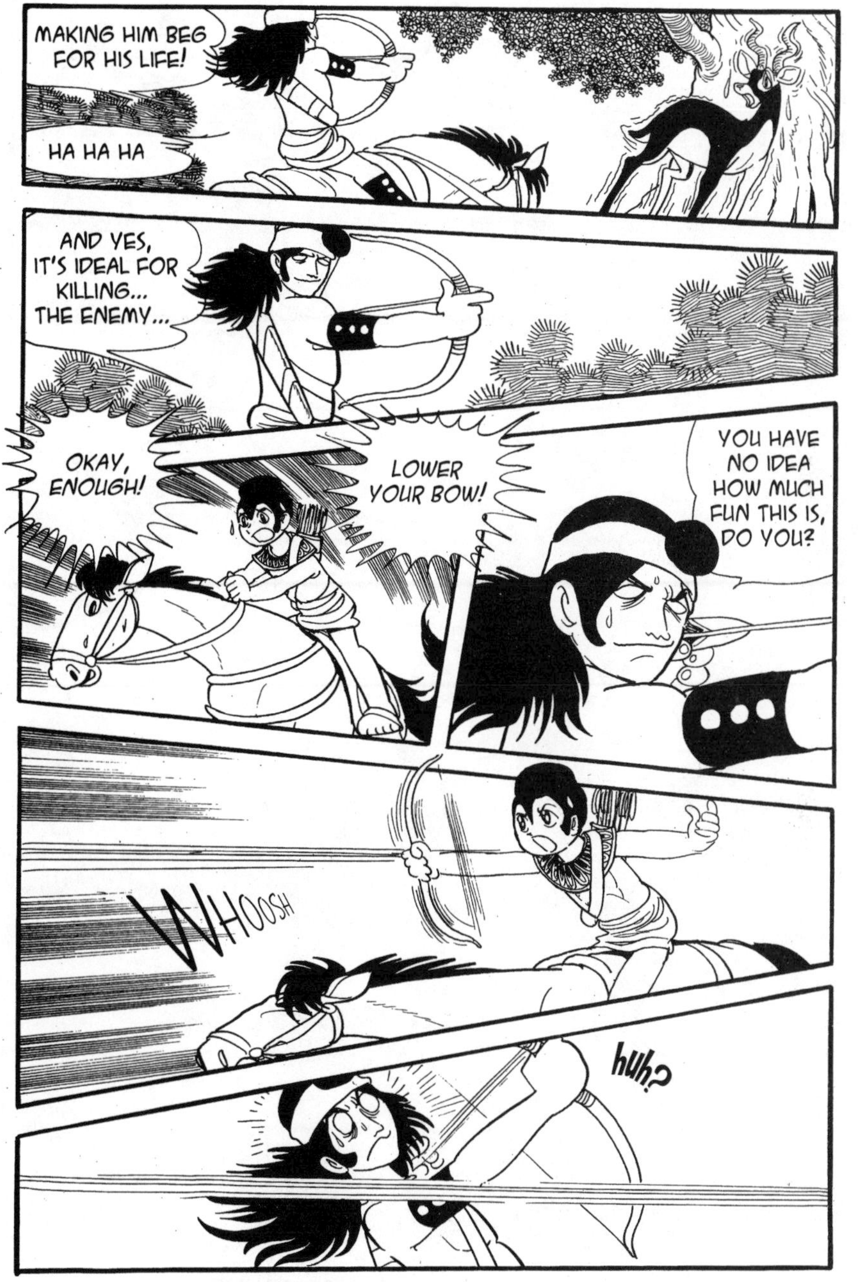

MAKING HIM BEG FOR HIS LIFE!
HA HA HA
AND YES, IT'S IDEAL FOR KILLING... THE ENEMY...
OKAY, ENOUGH!
LOWER YOUR BOW!
YOU HAVE NO IDEA HOW MUCH FUN THIS IS, DO YOU?
WHOOSH
huh?

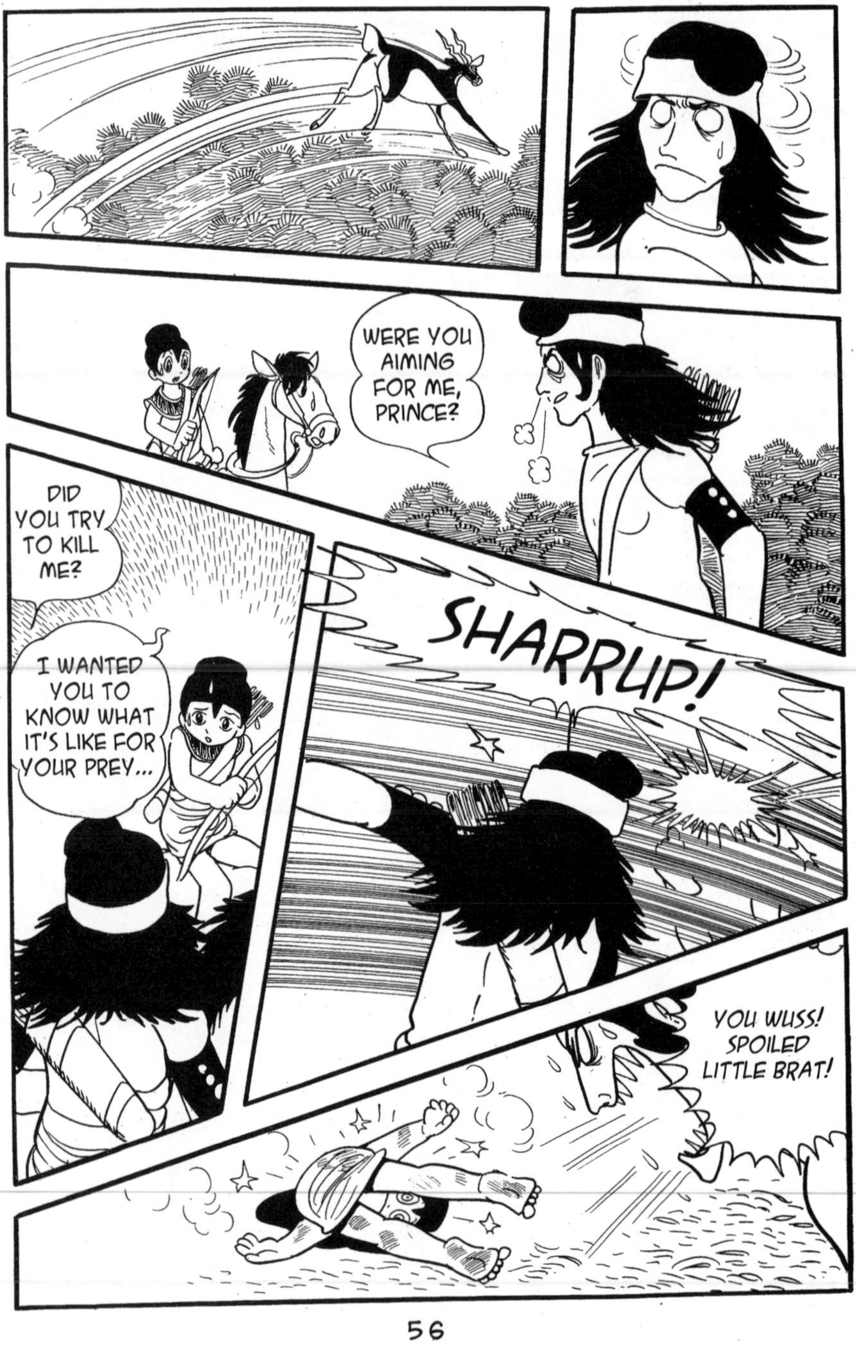
WERE YOU AIMING FOR ME, PRINCE?
DID YOU TRY TO KILL ME?
I WANTED YOU TO KNOW WHAT IT'S LIKE FOR YOUR PREY...
SHARRUP!
YOU WUSS! SPOILED LITTLE BRAT!

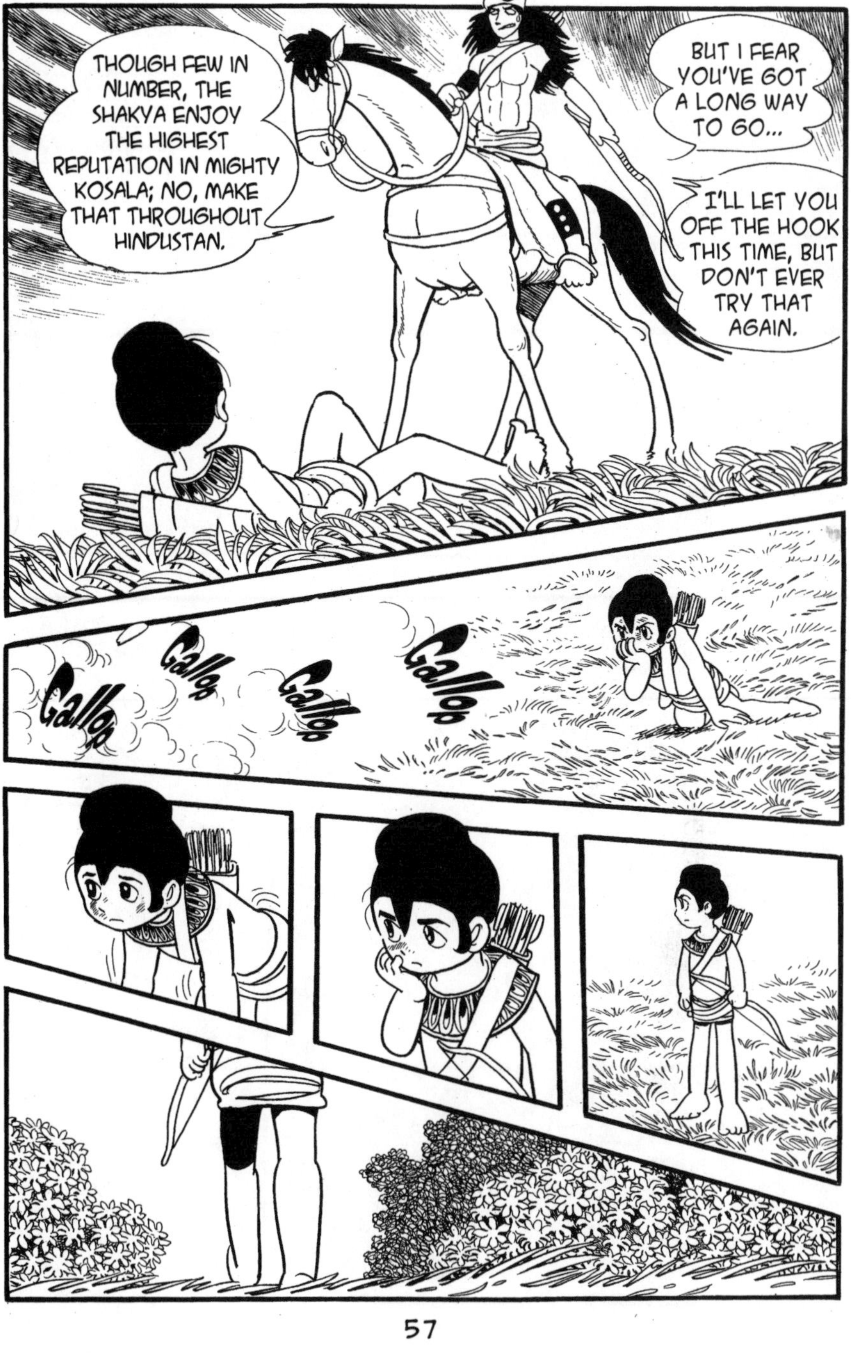
THOUGH FEW IN NUMBER, THE SHAKYA ENJOY THE HIGHEST REPUTATION IN MIGHTY KOSALA; NO, MAKE THAT THROUGHOUT HINDUSTAN.
BUT I FEAR YOU'VE GOT A LONG WAY TO GO...
I'LL LET YOU OFF THE HOOK THIS TIME, BUT DON'T EVER TRY THAT AGAIN.
Gallop
Gallop
Gallop
Gallop

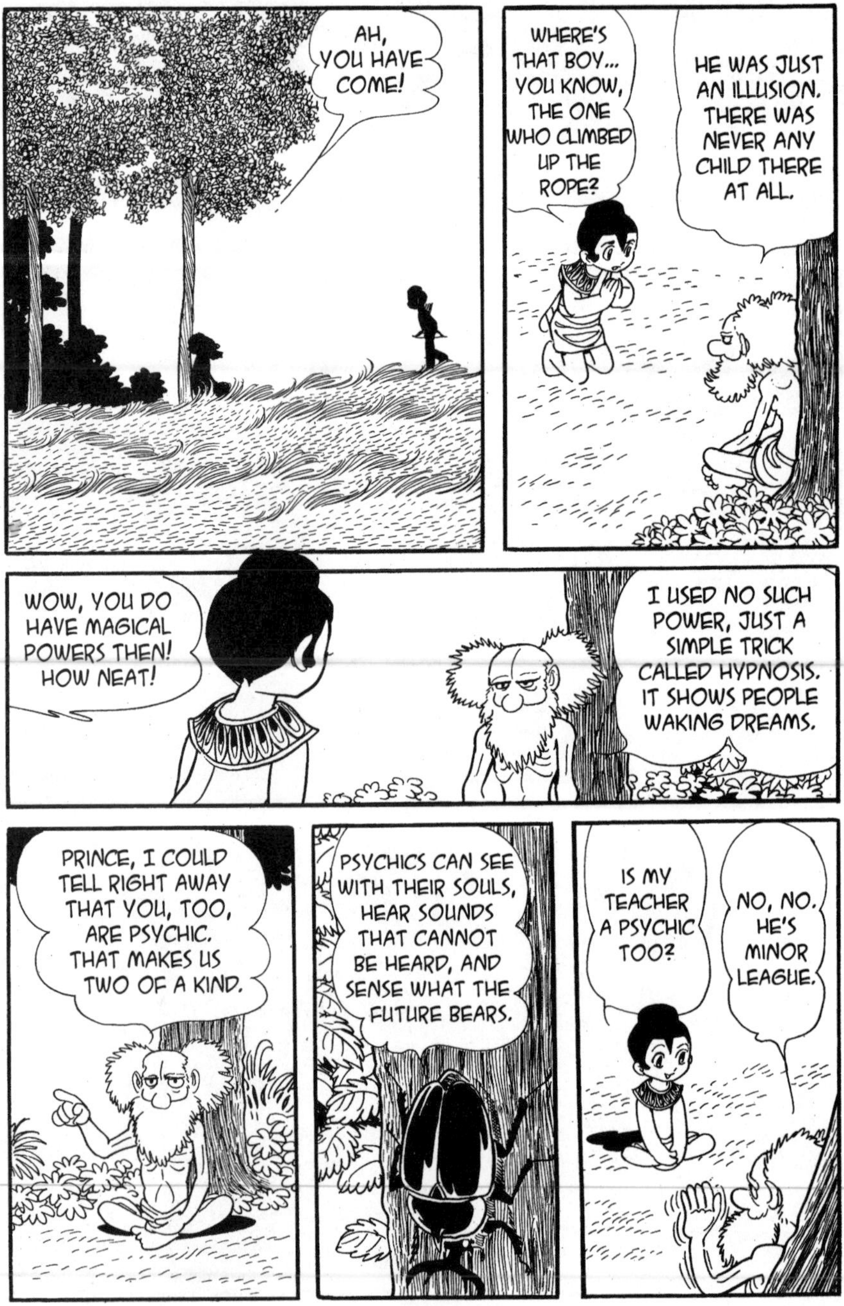
AH, YOU HAVE COME!
WHERE'S THAT BOY... YOU KNOW, THE ONE WHO CLIMBED UP THE ROPE?
HE WAS JUST AN ILLUSION. THERE WAS NEVER ANY CHILD THERE AT ALL.
WOW, YOU DO HAVE MAGICAL POWERS THEN! HOW NEAT!
I USED NO SUCH POWER, JUST A SIMPLE TRICK CALLED HYPNOSIS. IT SHOWS PEOPLE WAKING DREAMS.
PRINCE, I COULD TELL RIGHT AWAY THAT YOU, TOO, ARE PSYCHIC. THAT MAKES US TWO OF A KIND.
PSYCHICS CAN SEE WITH THEIR SOULS, HEAR SOUNDS THAT CANNOT BE HEARD, AND SENSE WHAT THE FUTURE BEARS.
IS MY TEACHER A PSYCHIC TOO?
NO, NO. HE'S MINOR LEAGUE.

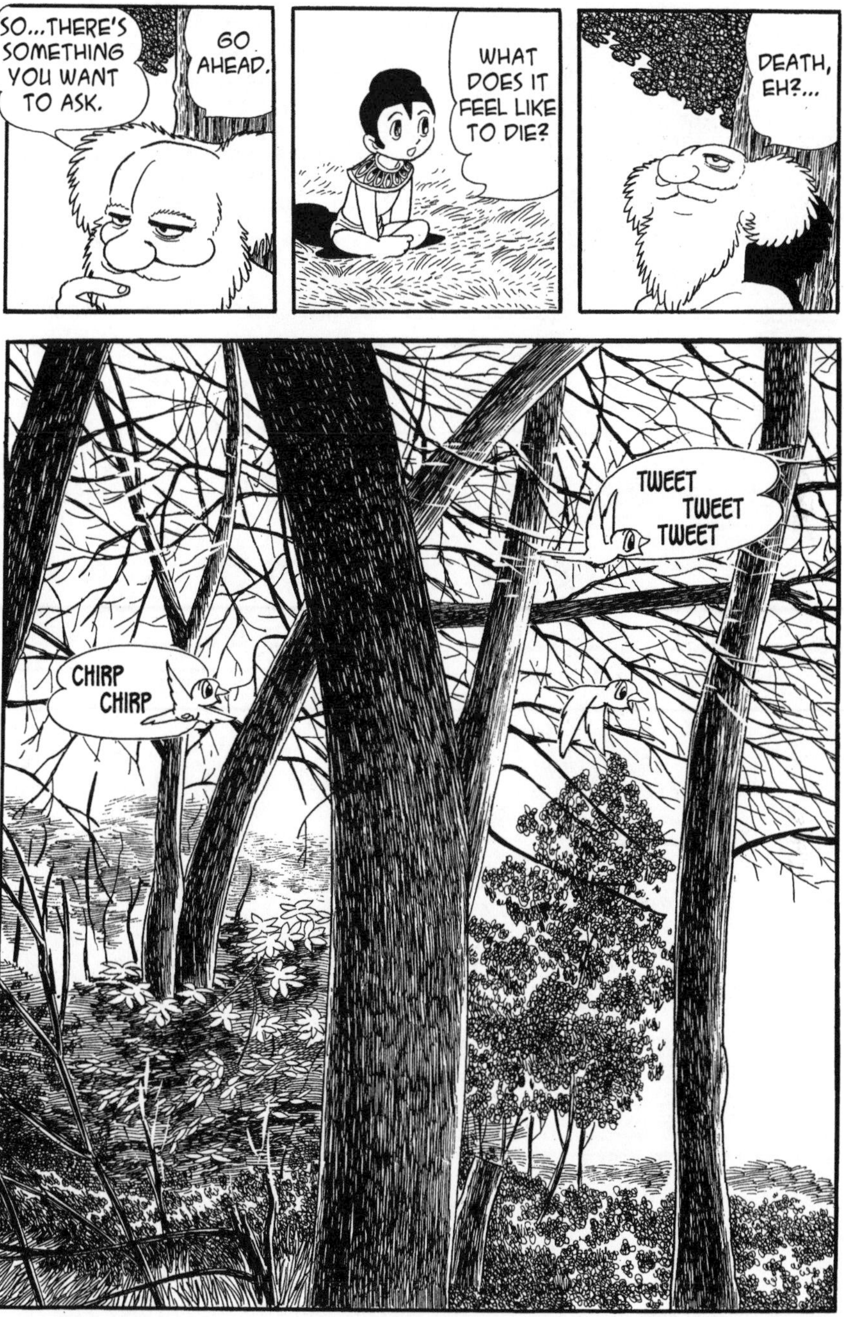
SO...THERE'S SOMETHING YOU WANT TO ASK.
GO AHEAD.
WHAT DOES IT FEEL LIKE TO DIE?
DEATH, EH?...
TWEET TWEET TWEET
CHIRP CHIRP

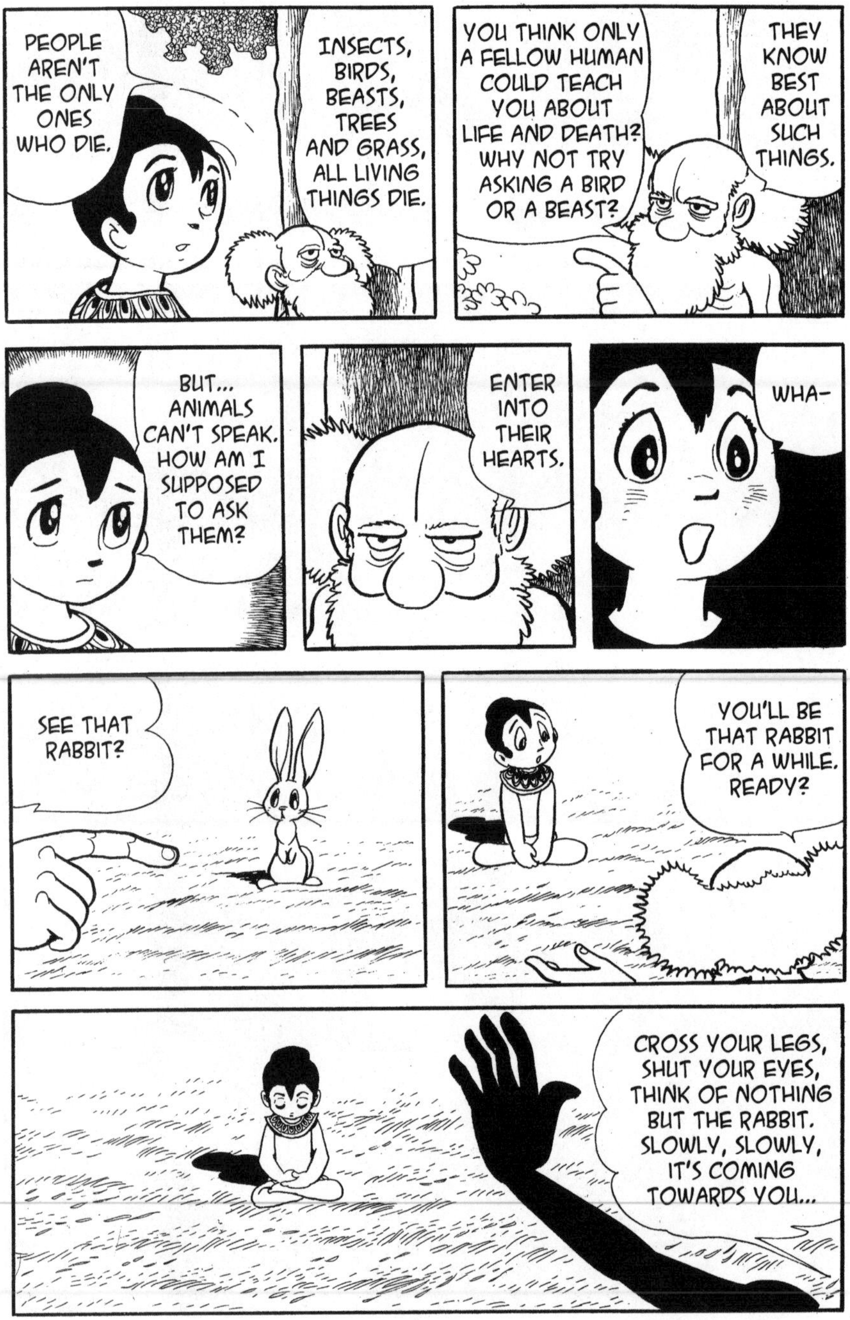
PEOPLE AREN'T THE ONLY ONES WHO DIE.
INSECTS, BIRDS, BEASTS, TREES AND GRASS, ALL LIVING THINGS DIE.
YOU THINK ONLY A FELLOW HUMAN COULD TEACH YOU ABOUT LIFE AND DEATH? WHY NOT TRY ASKING A BIRD OR A BEAST?
THEY KNOW BEST ABOUT SUCH THINGS.
BUT... ANIMALS CAN'T SPEAK. HOW AM I SUPPOSED TO ASK THEM?
ENTER INTO THEIR HEARTS.
WHA-
SEE THAT RABBIT?
YOU'LL BE THAT RABBIT FOR A WHILE. READY?
CROSS YOUR LEGS, SHUT YOUR EYES, THINK OF NOTHING BUT THE RABBIT. SLOWLY, SLOWLY, IT'S COMING TOWARDS YOU...

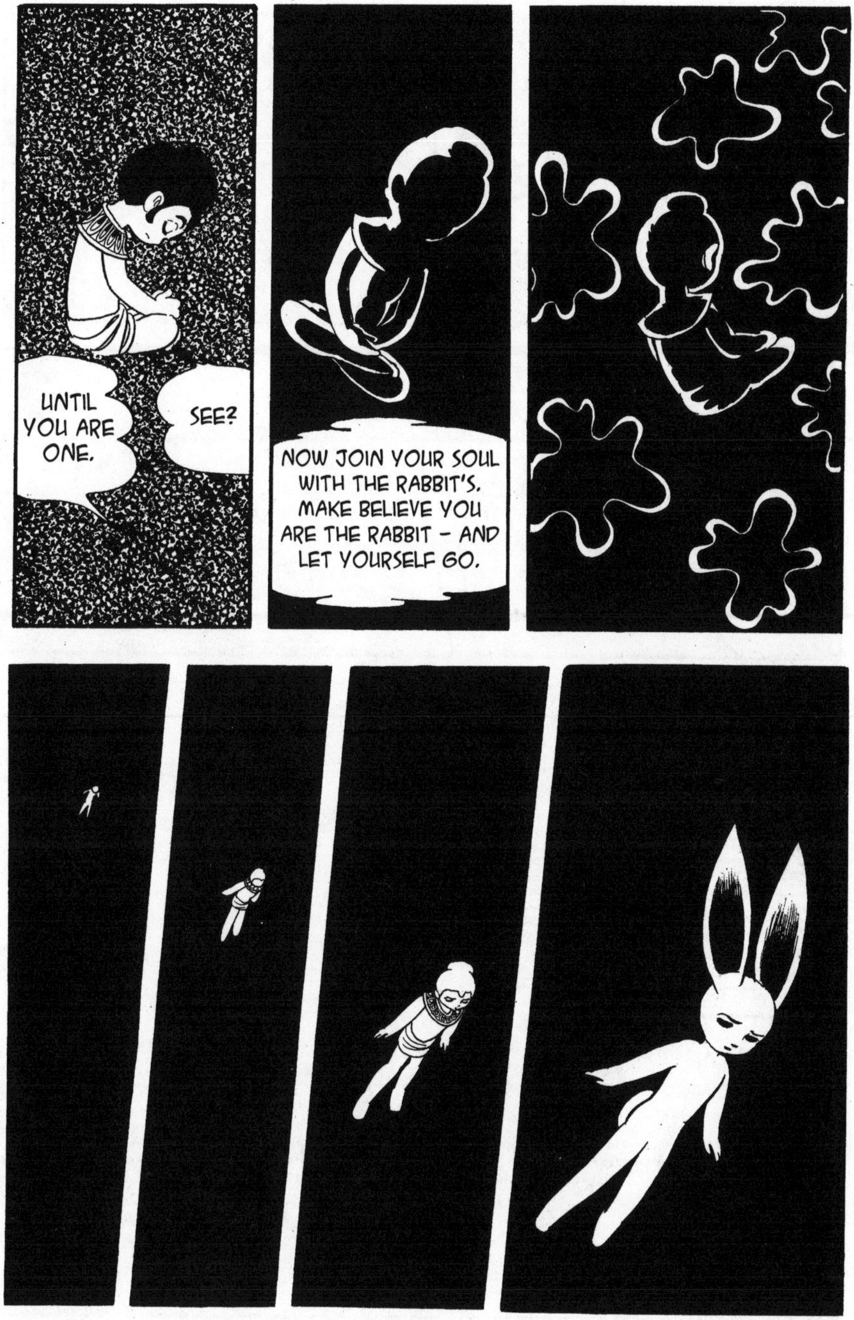
UNTIL YOU ARE ONE.
SEE?
NOW JOIN YOUR SOUL WITH THE RABBIT'S. MAKE BELIEVE YOU ARE THE RABBIT - AND LET YOURSELF GO.

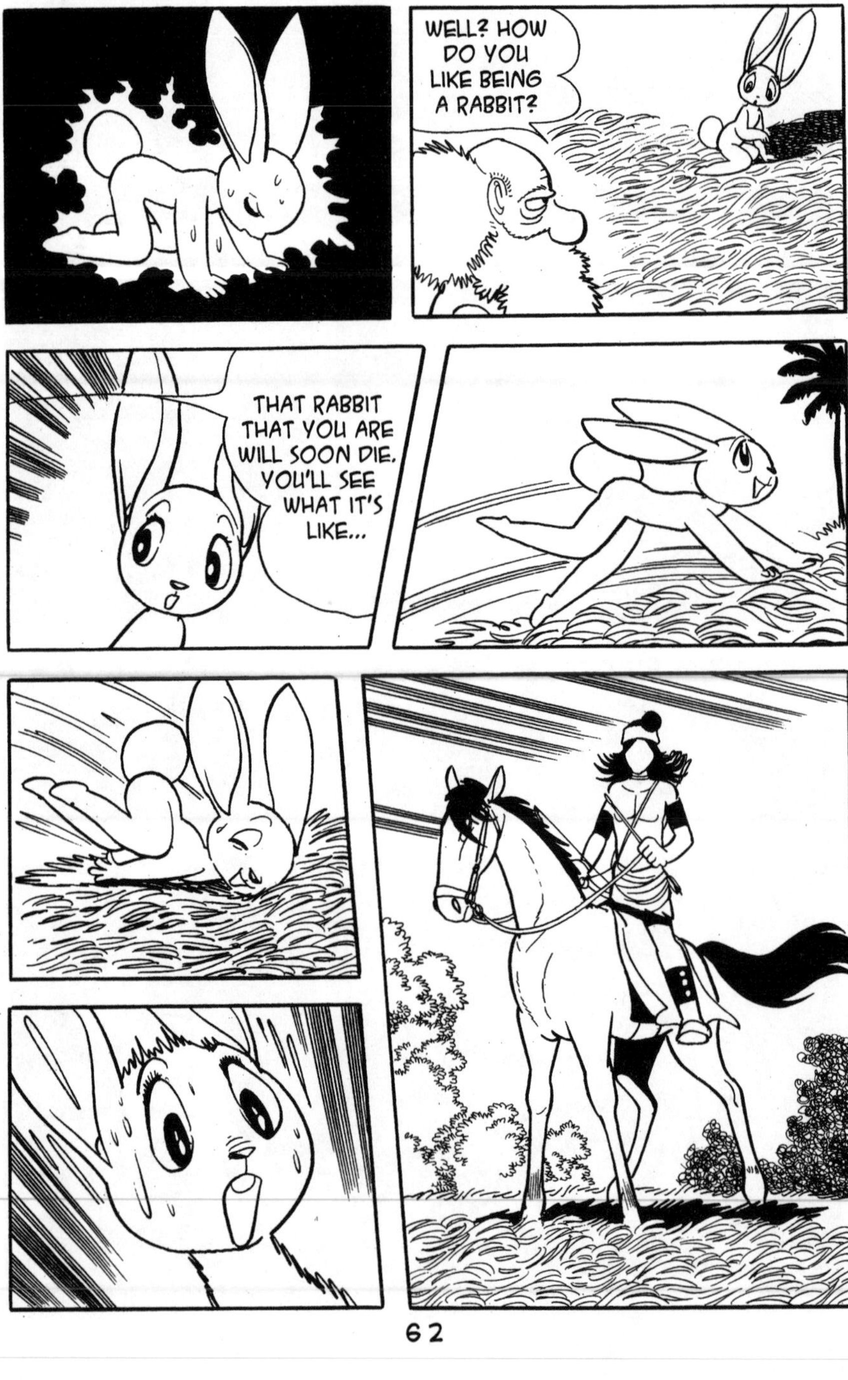
WELL? HOW DO YOU LIKE BEING A RABBIT?
THAT RABBIT THAT YOU ARE WILL SOON DIE. YOU'LL SEE WHAT IT'S LIKE...

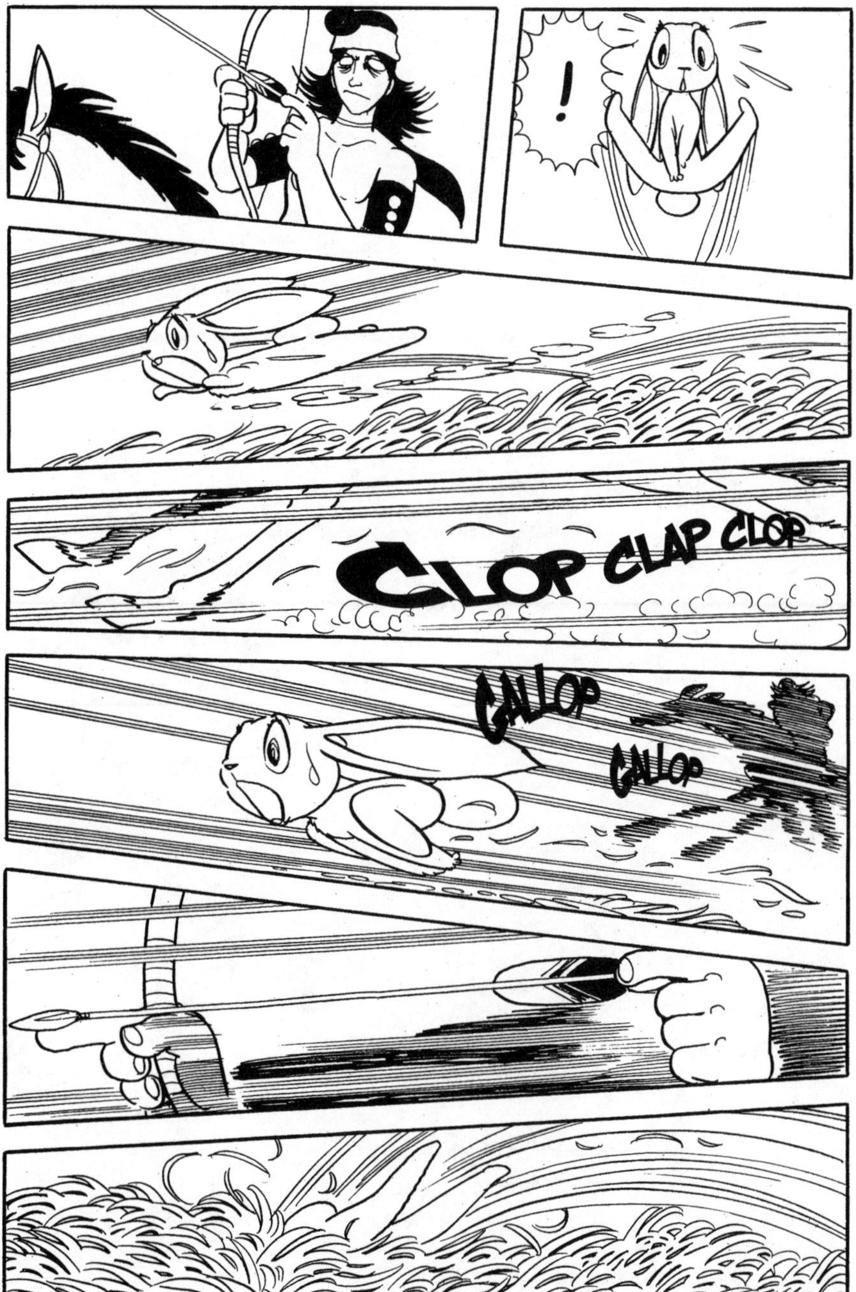
!
CLOP CLAP CLOP
GALLOP
GALLOP

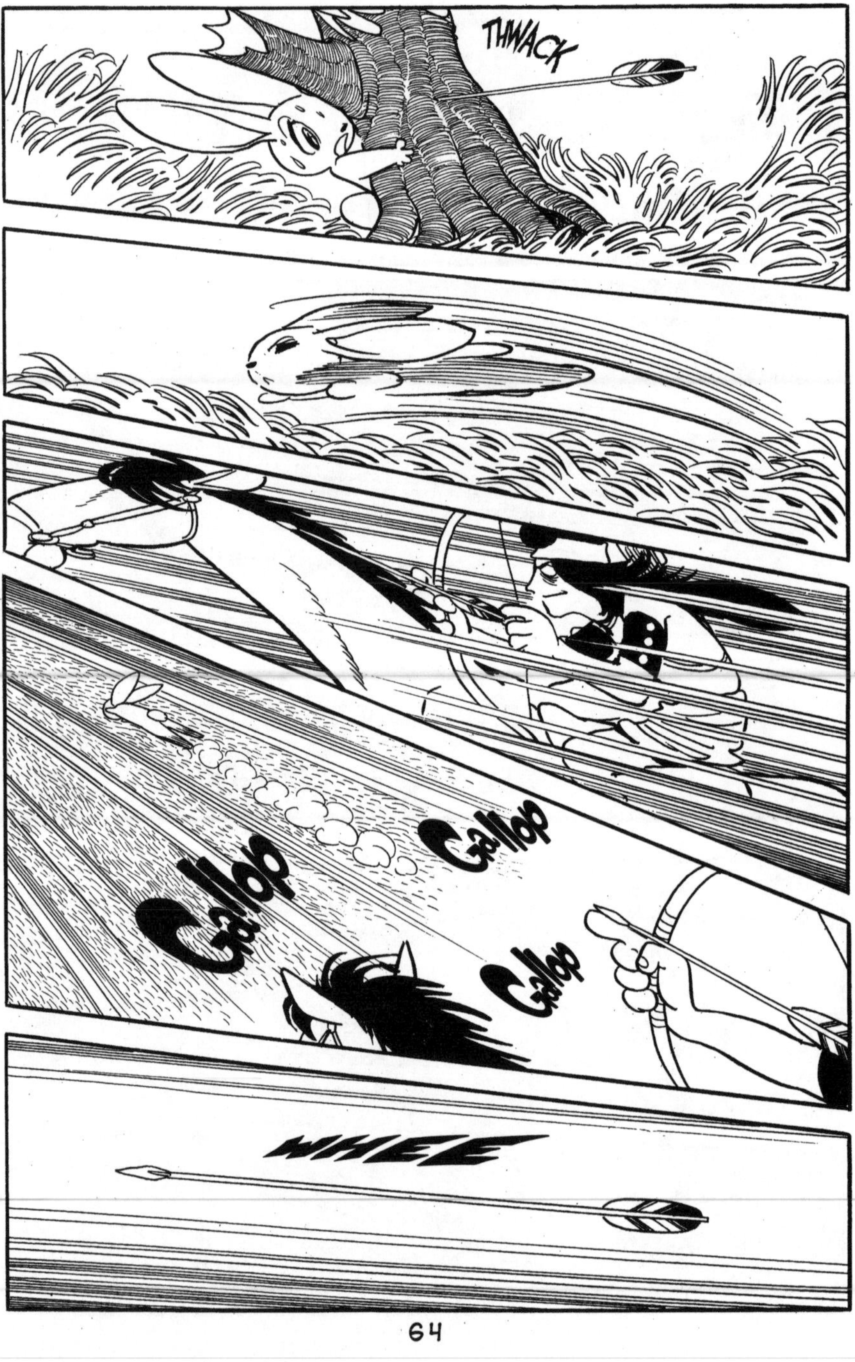
THWACK
Gallop
Gallop
Gallop
WHEE

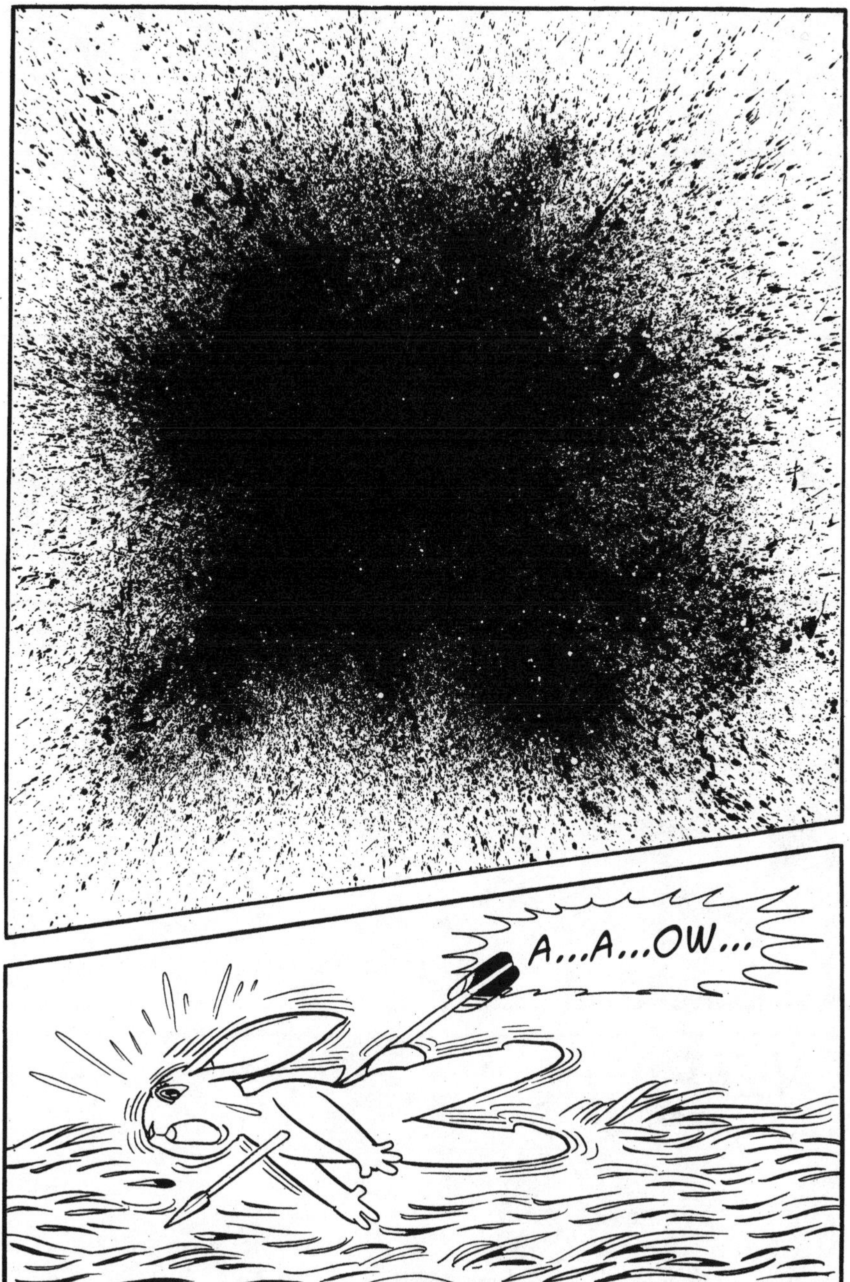
A...A...OW...

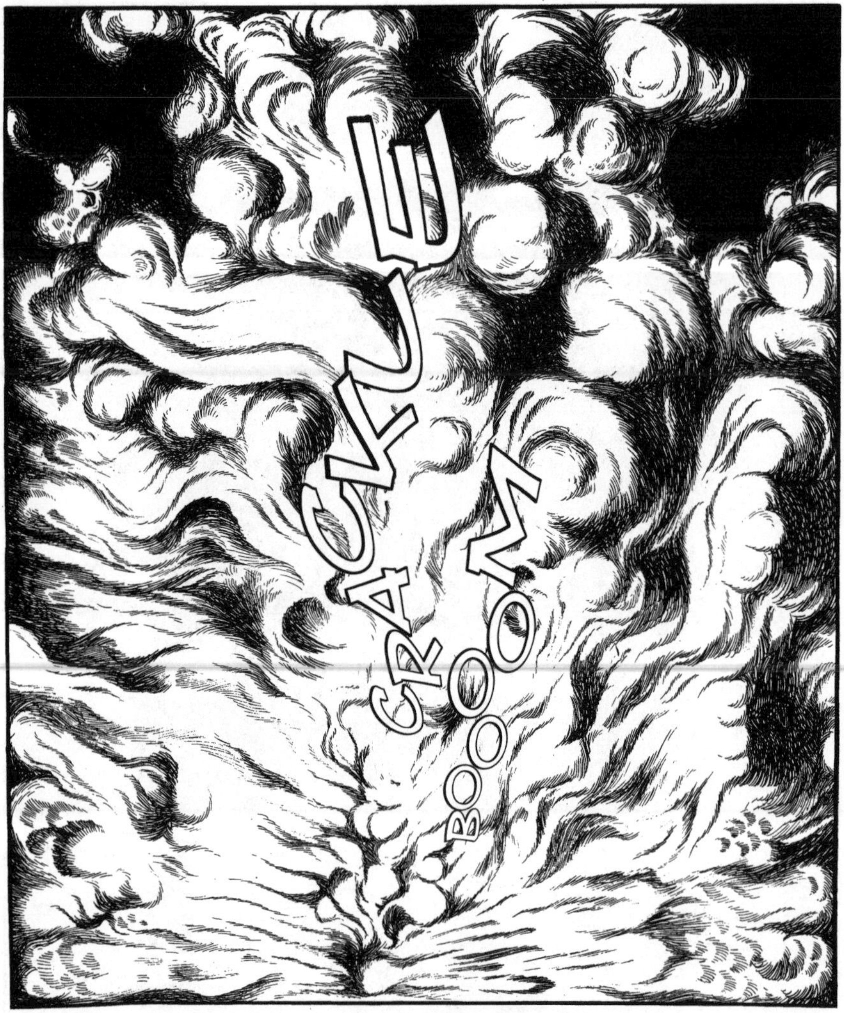
CRACKLE
BOOOOOM
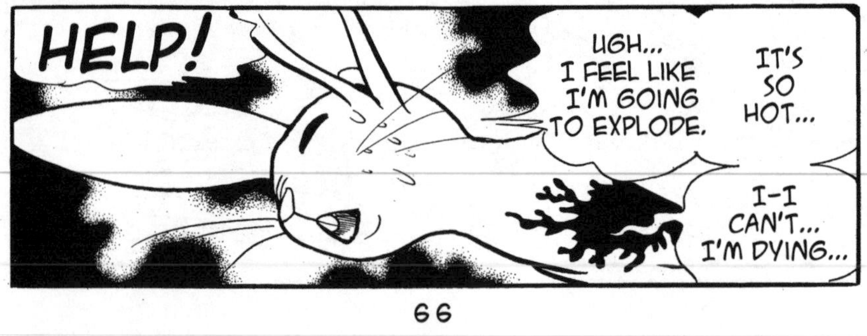
HELP!
UGH... I FEEL LIKE I'M GOING TO EXPLODE.
IT'S SO HOT...
I-I CAN'T... I'M DYING...

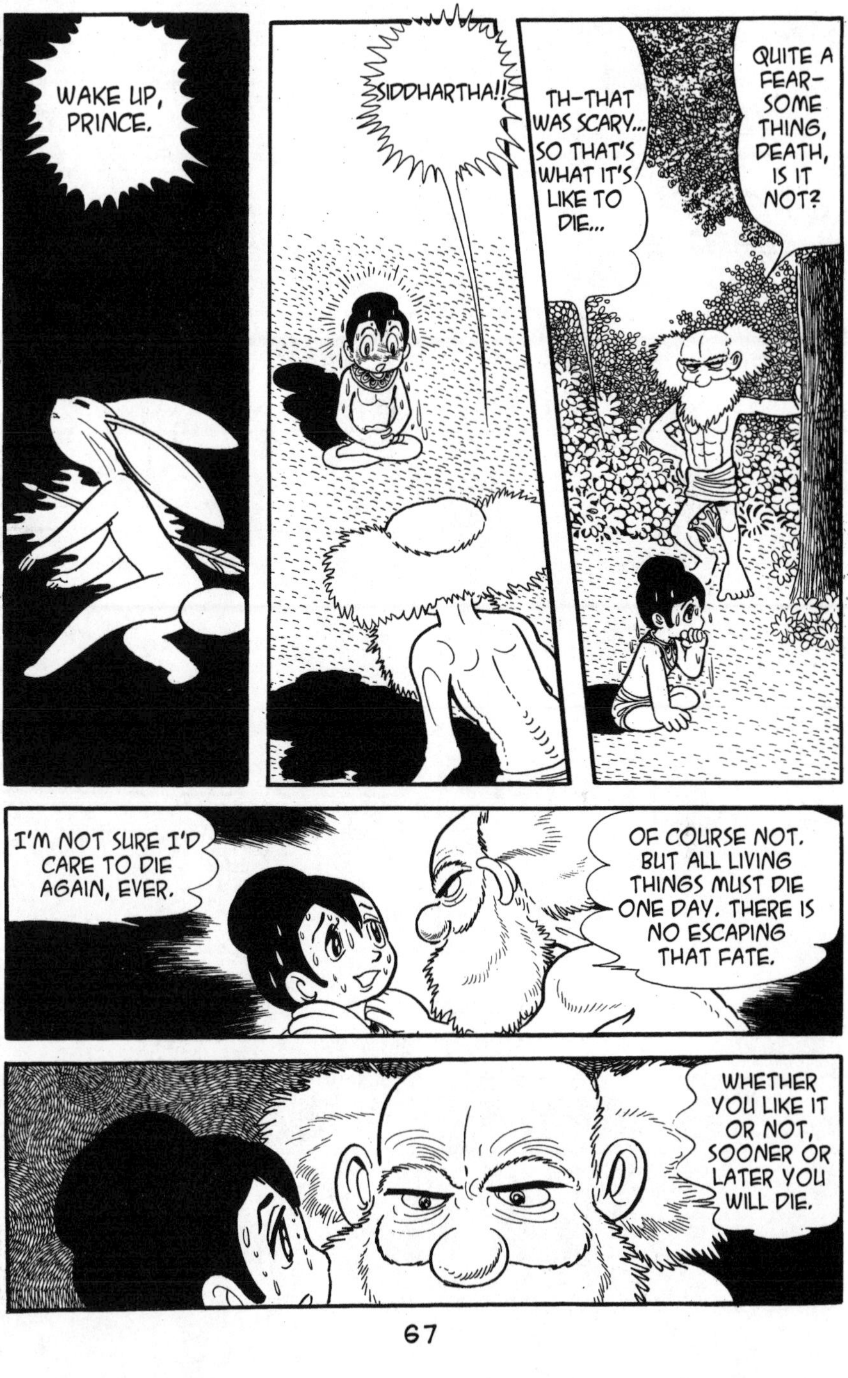
WAKE UP, PRINCE.
SIDDHARTHA!!
TH-THAT WAS SCARY... SO THAT'S WHAT IT'S LIKE TO DIE...
QUITE A FEAR-SOME THING, DEATH, IS IT NOT?
I'M NOT SURE I'D CARE TO DIE AGAIN, EVER.
OF COURSE NOT. BUT ALL LIVING THINGS MUST DIE ONE DAY. THERE IS NO ESCAPING THAT FATE.
WHETHER YOU LIKE IT OR NOT, SOONER OR LATER YOU WILL DIE.

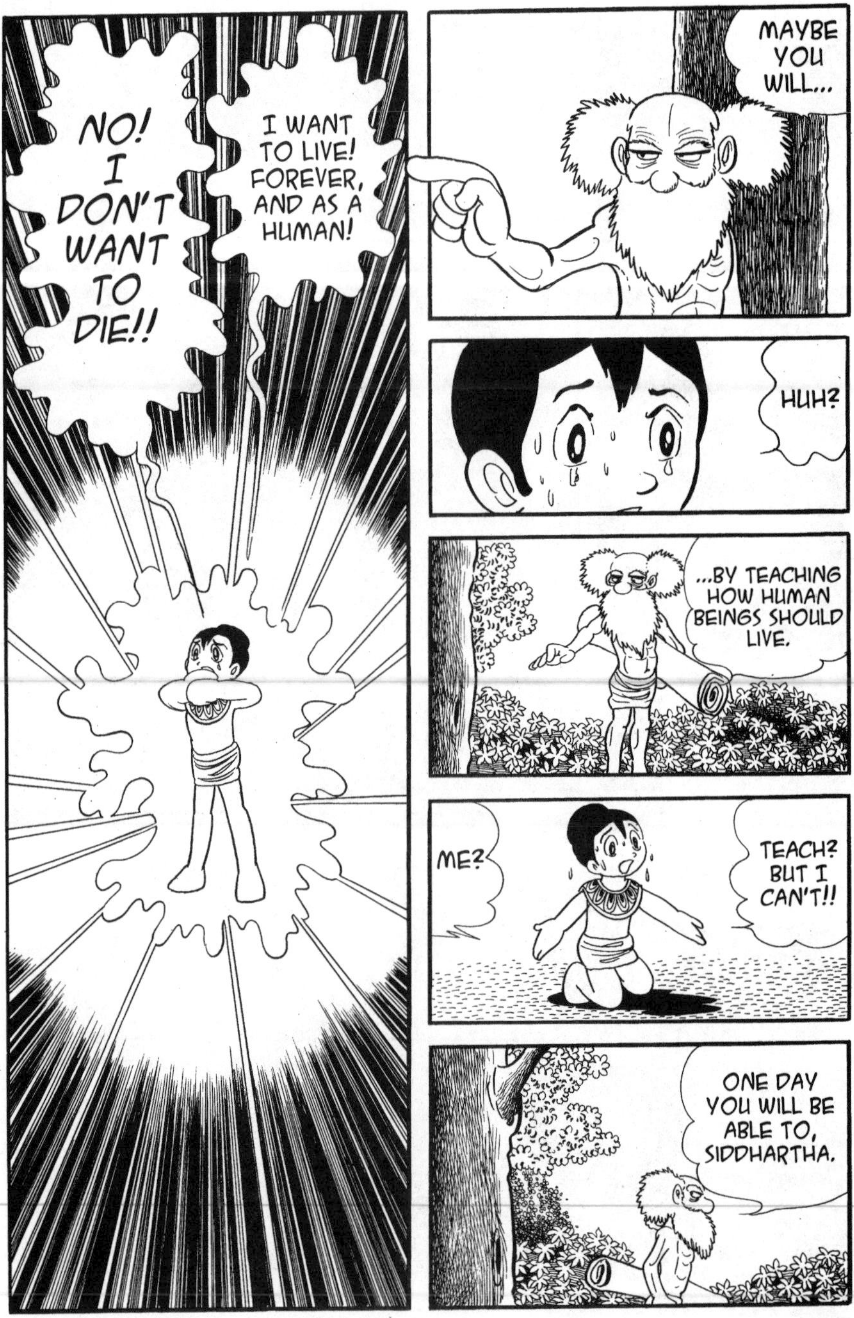
NO! I DON'T WANT TO DIE!!
I WANT TO LIVE! FOREVER, AND AS A HUMAN!
MAYBE YOU WILL...
HUH?
...BY TEACHING HOW HUMAN BEINGS SHOULD LIVE.
ME?
TEACH? BUT I CAN'T!!
ONE DAY YOU WILL BE ABLE TO, SIDDHARTHA.

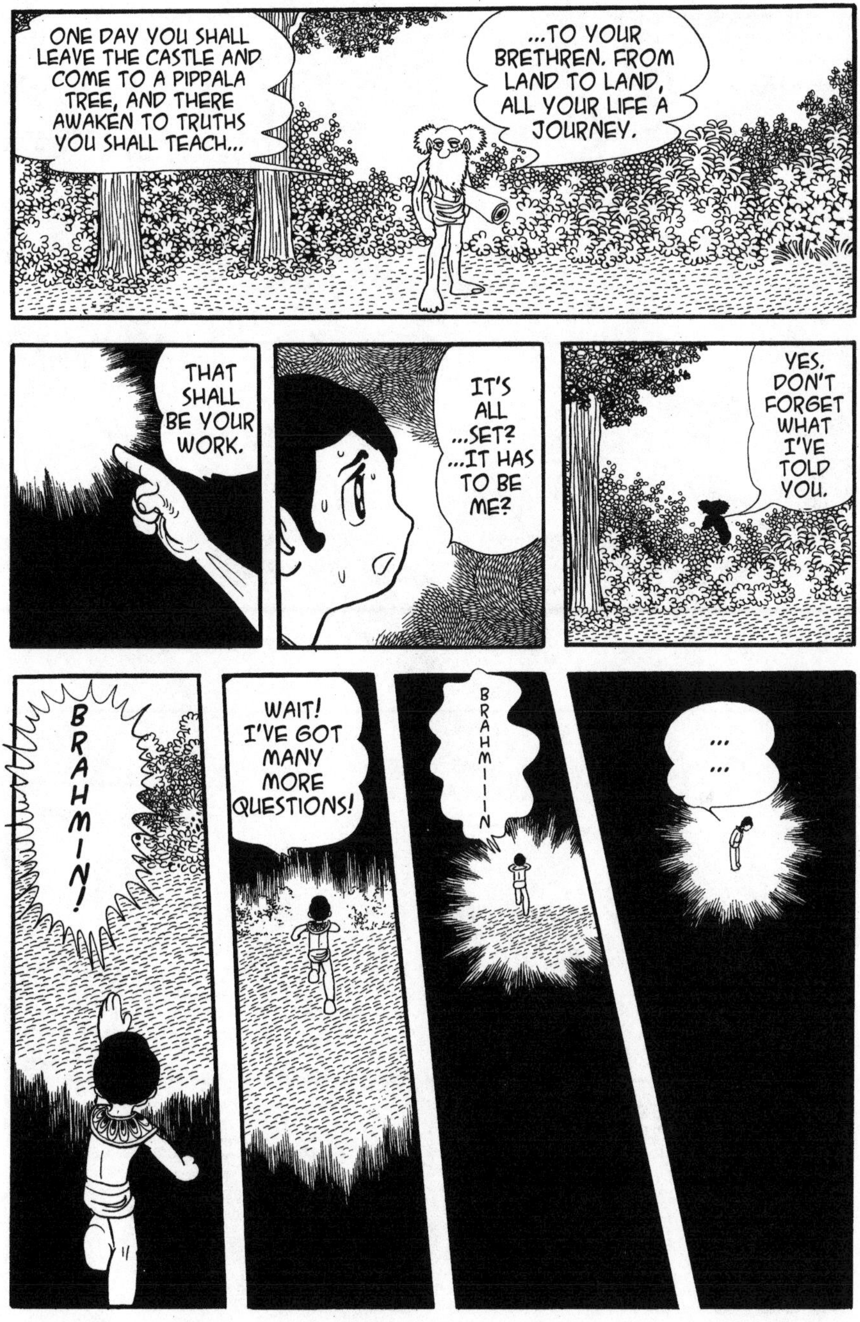

ONE DAY YOU SHALL LEAVE THE CASTLE AND COME TO A PIPPALA TREE, AND THERE AWAKEN TO TRUTHS YOU SHALL TEACH...
...TO YOUR BRETHREN. FROM LAND TO LAND, ALL YOUR LIFE A JOURNEY.
THAT SHALL BE YOUR WORK.
IT'S ALL ...SET? ...IT HAS TO BE ME?
YES. DON'T FORGET WHAT I'VE TOLD YOU.
BRAHMIN!
WAIT! I'VE GOT MANY MORE QUESTIONS!
BRAHMIIIN
...
...

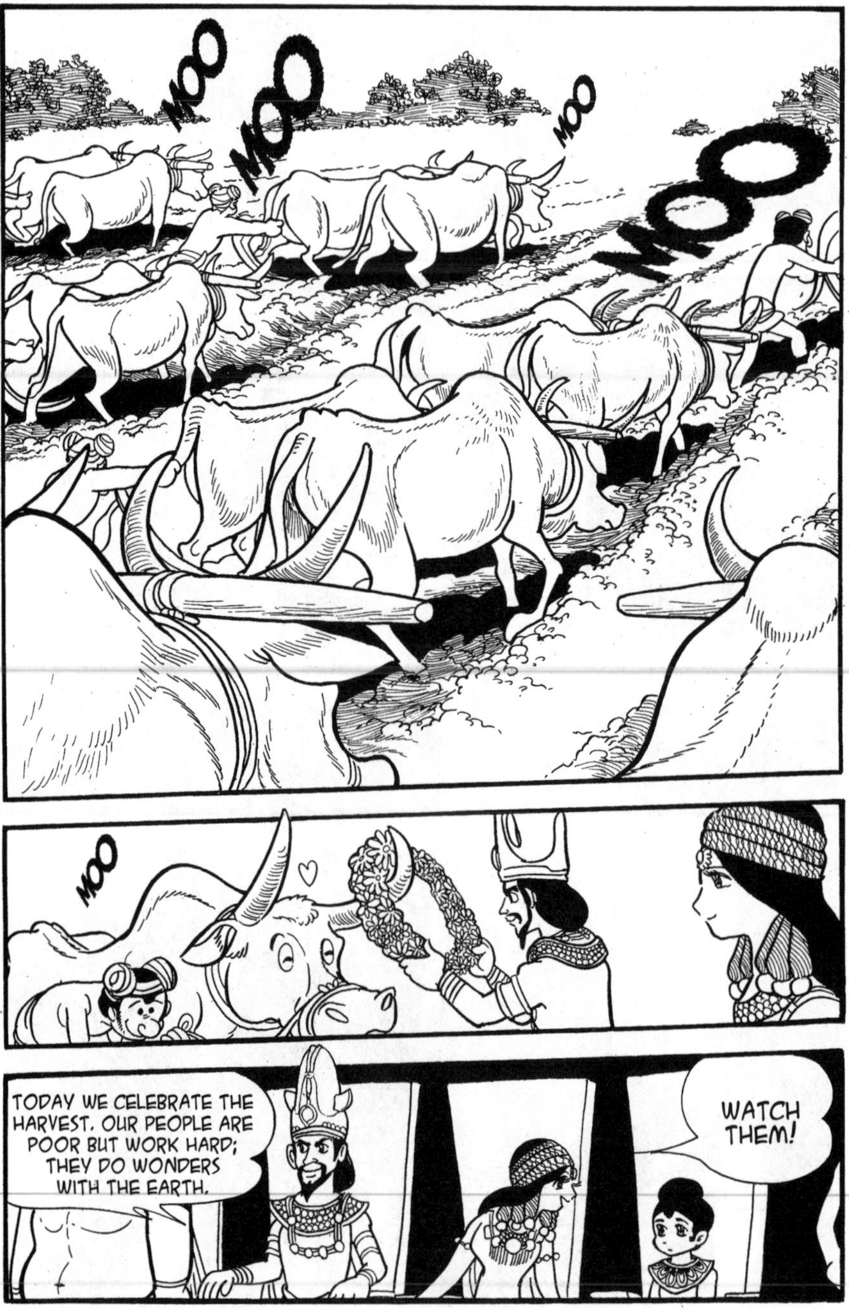
MOO
MOO
MOO
MOO
MOO
TODAY WE CELEBRATE THE HARVEST. OUR PEOPLE ARE POOR BUT WORK HARD; THEY DO WONDERS WITH THE EARTH.
WATCH THEM!

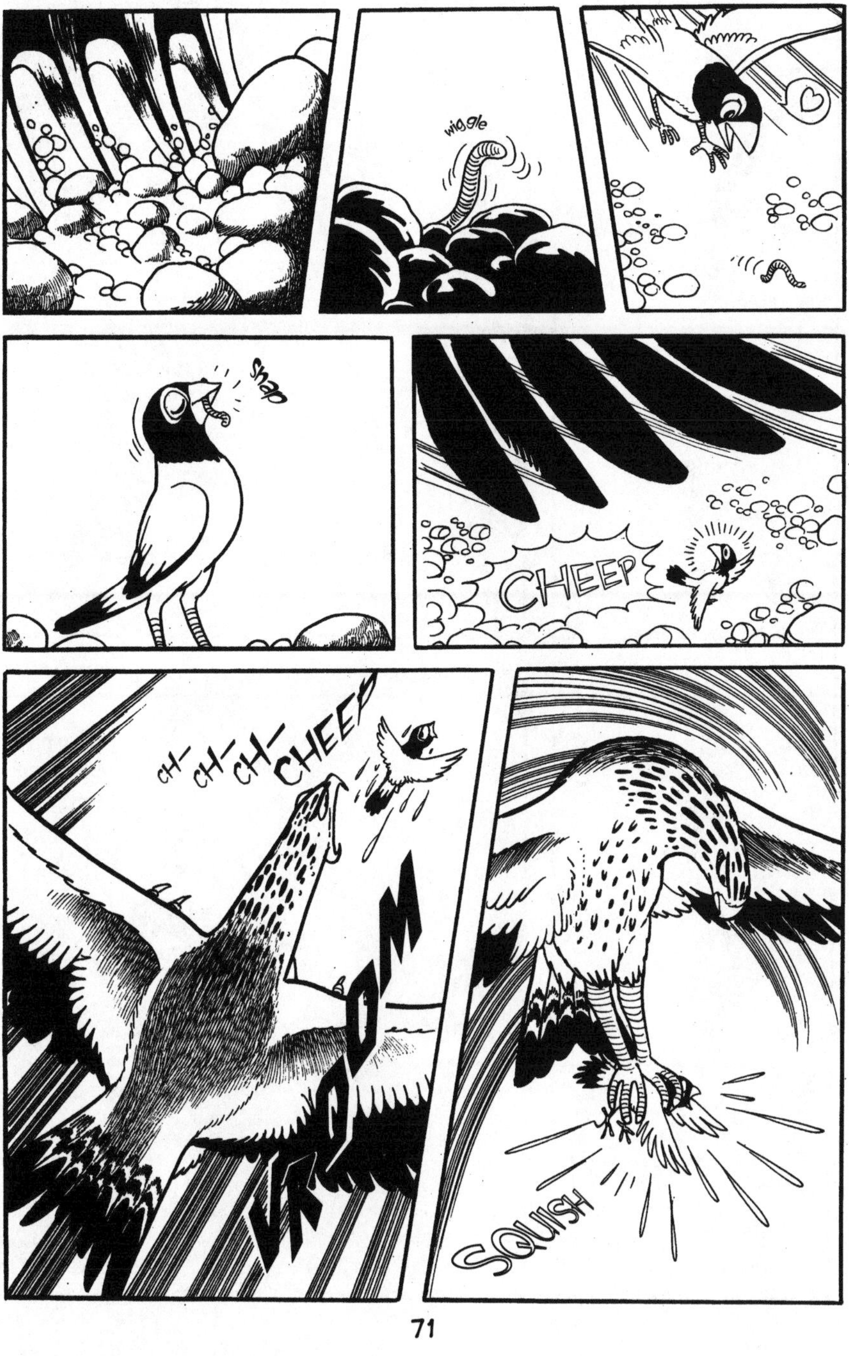
wiggle
snap
CHEEP
CH-CH-CH-CHEEP
VROOM
SQUISH

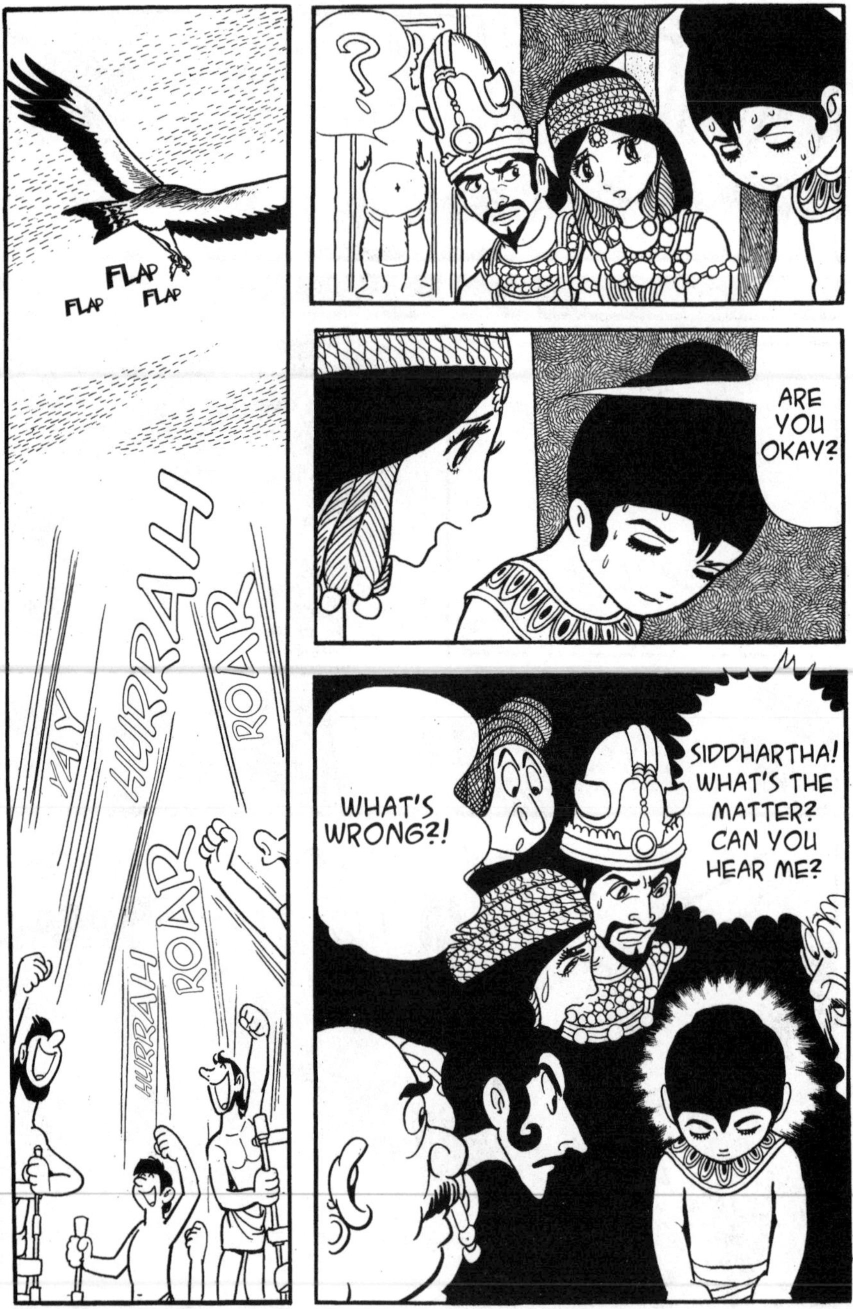
FLAP FLAP FLAP
YAY
HURRAH
ROAR
ROAR
HURRAH
ROAR
?
ARE YOU OKAY?
WHAT'S WRONG?!
SIDDHARTHA! WHAT'S THE MATTER? CAN YOU HEAR ME?

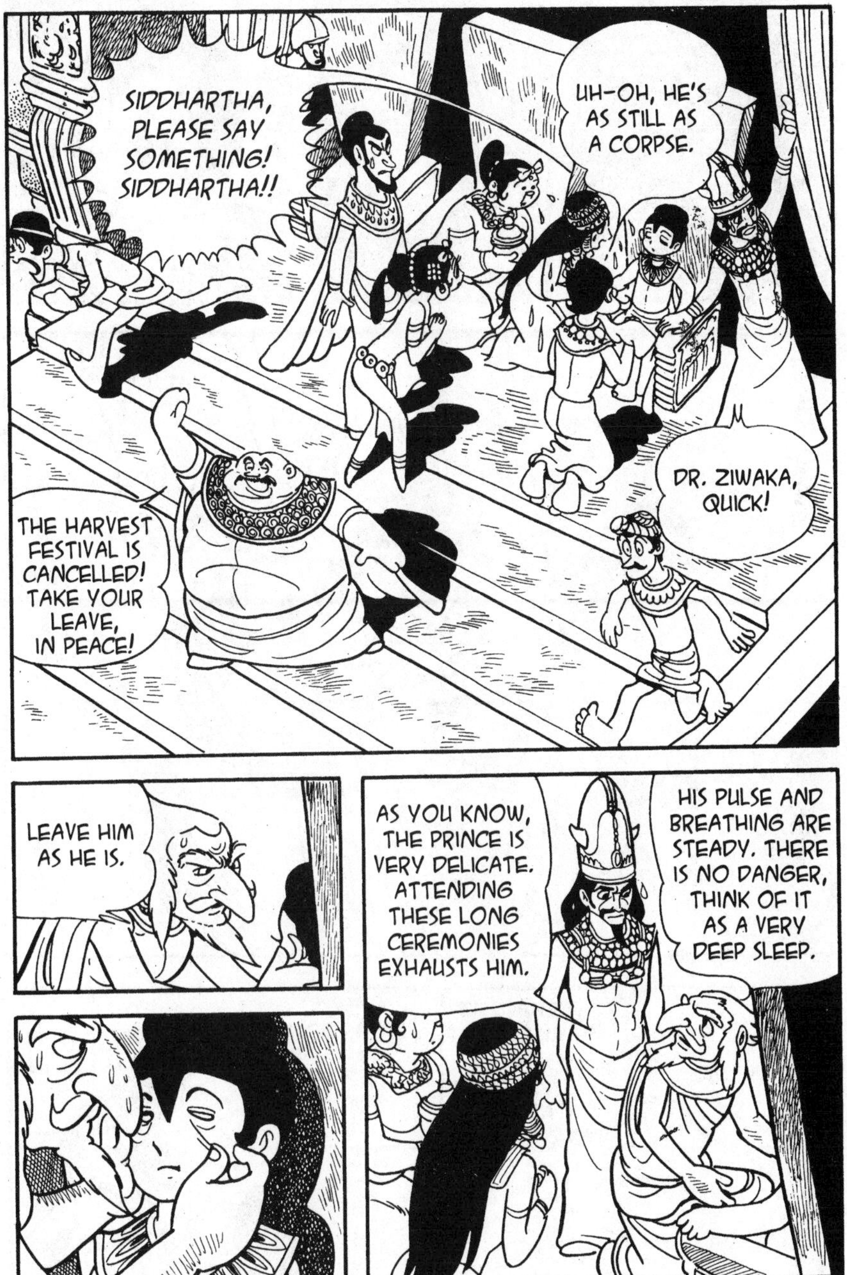
SIDDHARTHA, PLEASE SAY SOMETHING! SIDDHARTHA!!
UH-OH, HE'S AS STILL AS A CORPSE.
DR. ZIWAKA, QUICK!
THE HARVEST FESTIVAL IS CANCELLED! TAKE YOUR LEAVE, IN PEACE!
LEAVE HIM AS HE IS.
AS YOU KNOW, THE PRINCE IS VERY DELICATE. ATTENDING THESE LONG CEREMONIES EXHAUSTS HIM.
HIS PULSE AND BREATHING ARE STEADY. THERE IS NO DANGER, THINK OF IT AS A VERY DEEP SLEEP.

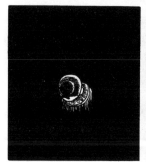

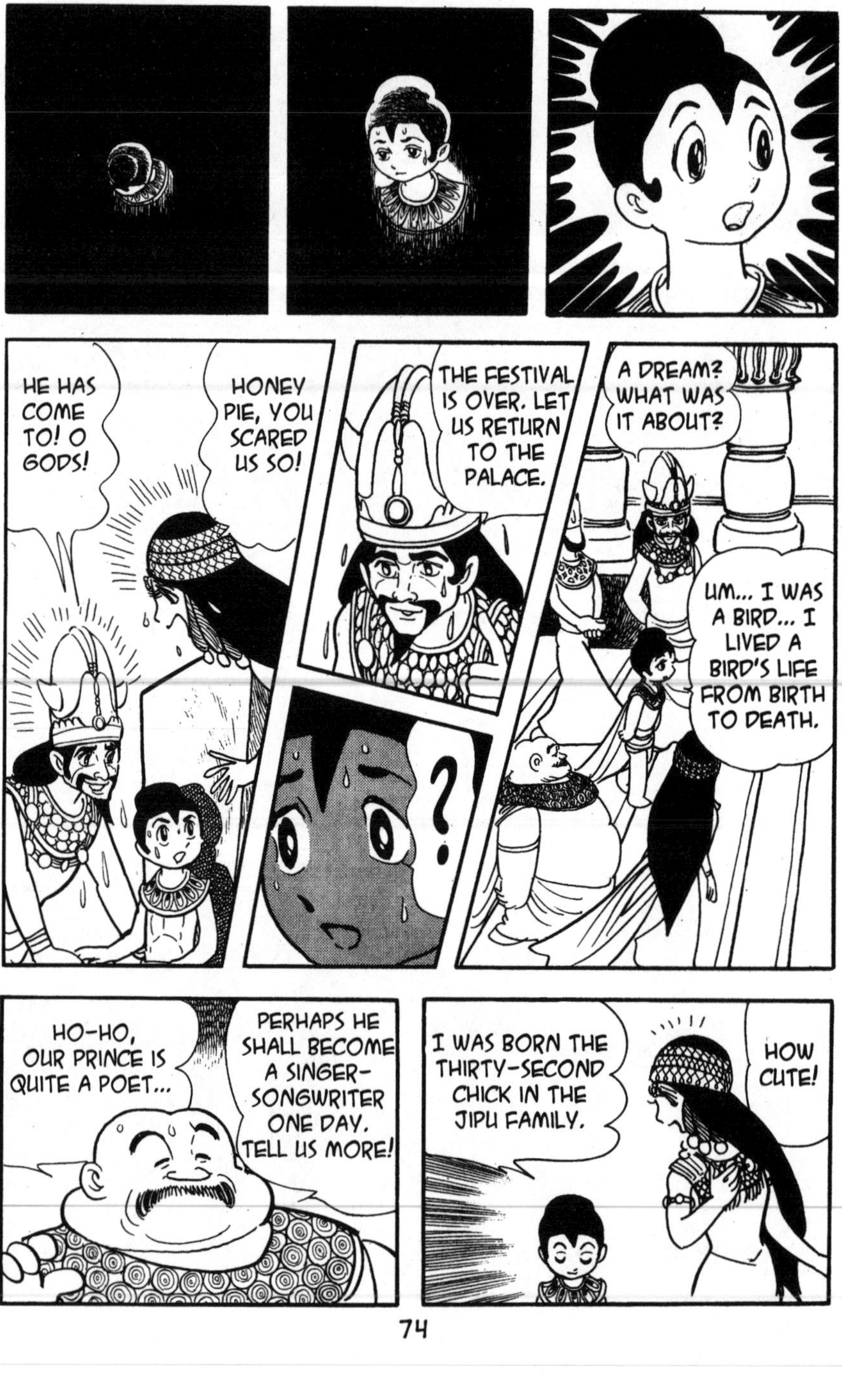
HE HAS COME TO! O GODS!
HONEY PIE, YOU SCARED US SO!
THE FESTIVAL IS OVER. LET US RETURN TO THE PALACE.
?
A DREAM? WHAT WAS IT ABOUT?
UM... I WAS A BIRD... I LIVED A BIRD'S LIFE FROM BIRTH TO DEATH.
HO-HO, OUR PRINCE IS QUITE A POET...
PERHAPS HE SHALL BECOME A SINGER-SONGWRITER ONE DAY. TELL US MORE!
I WAS BORN THE THIRTY-SECOND CHICK IN THE JIPU FAMILY.
HOW CUTE!

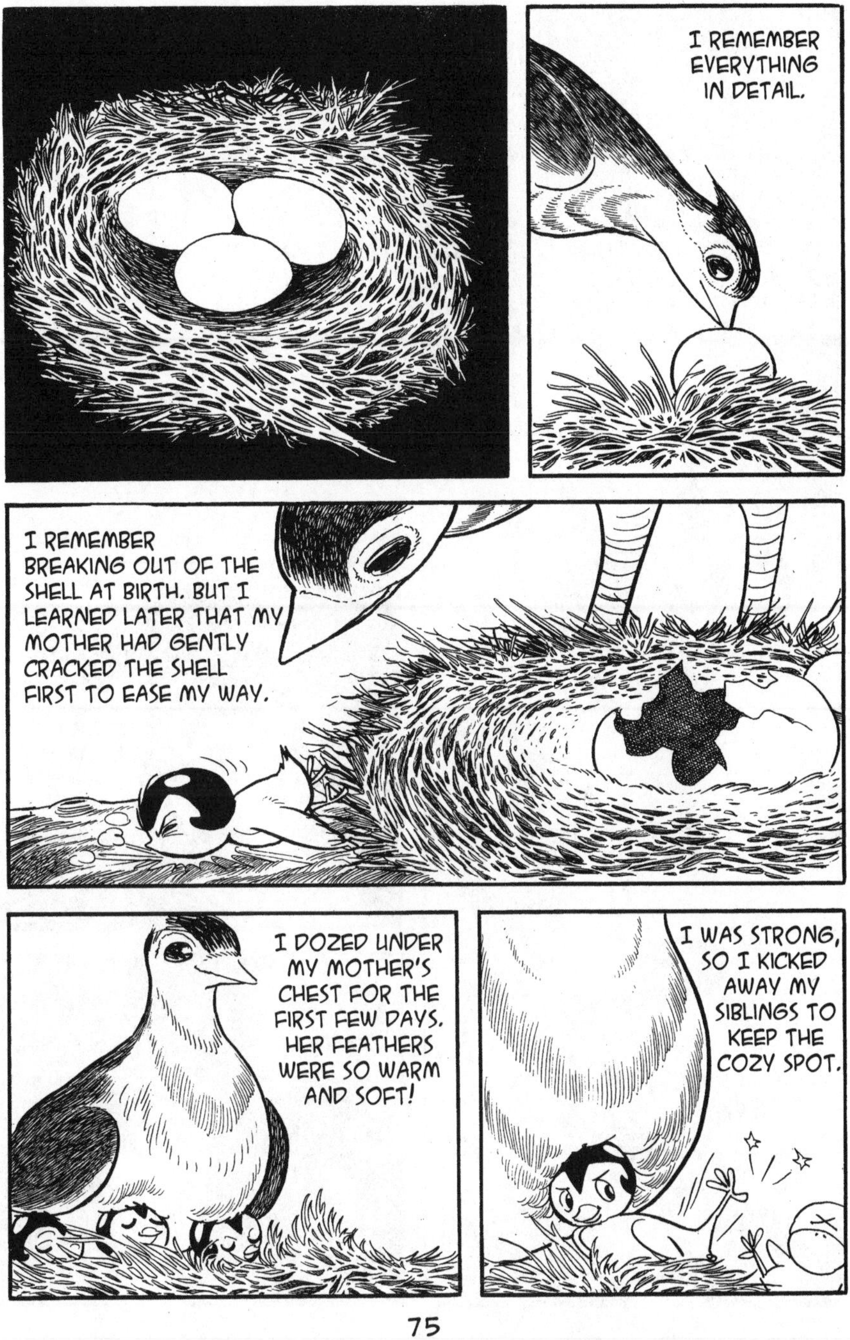
I REMEMBER EVERYTHING IN DETAIL.
I REMEMBER BREAKING OUT OF THE SHELL AT BIRTH. BUT I LEARNED LATER THAT MY MOTHER HAD GENTLY CRACKED THE SHELL FIRST TO EASE MY WAY.
I DOZED UNDER MY MOTHER'S CHEST FOR THE FIRST FEW DAYS. HER FEATHERS WERE SO WARM AND SOFT!
I WAS STRONG, SO I KICKED AWAY MY SIBLINGS TO KEEP THE COZY SPOT.

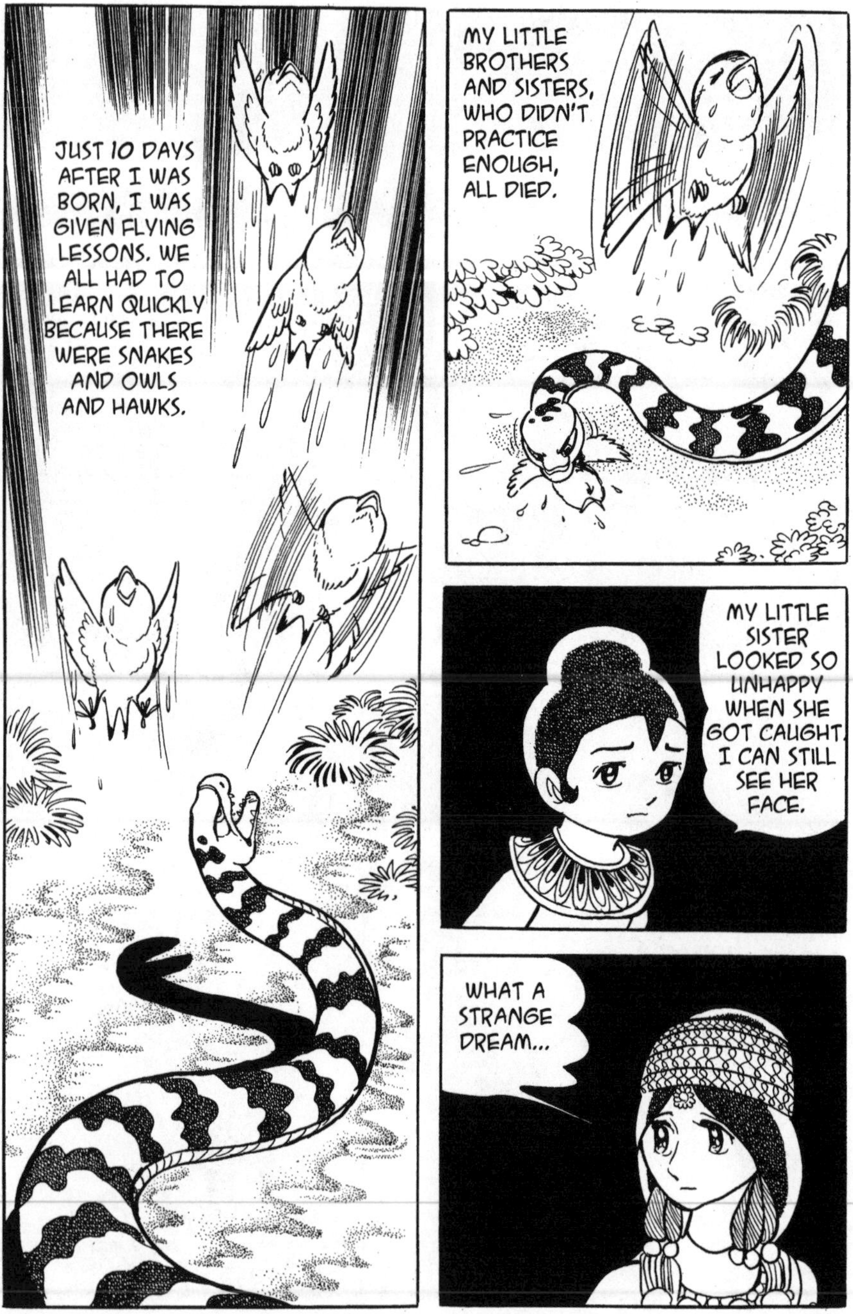
JUST 10 DAYS AFTER I WAS BORN, I WAS GIVEN FLYING LESSONS. WE ALL HAD TO LEARN QUICKLY BECAUSE THERE WERE SNAKES AND OWLS AND HAWKS.
MY LITTLE BROTHERS AND SISTERS, WHO DIDN'T PRACTICE ENOUGH, ALL DIED.
MY LITTLE SISTER LOOKED SO UNHAPPY WHEN SHE GOT CAUGHT. I CAN STILL SEE HER FACE.
WHAT A STRANGE DREAM...

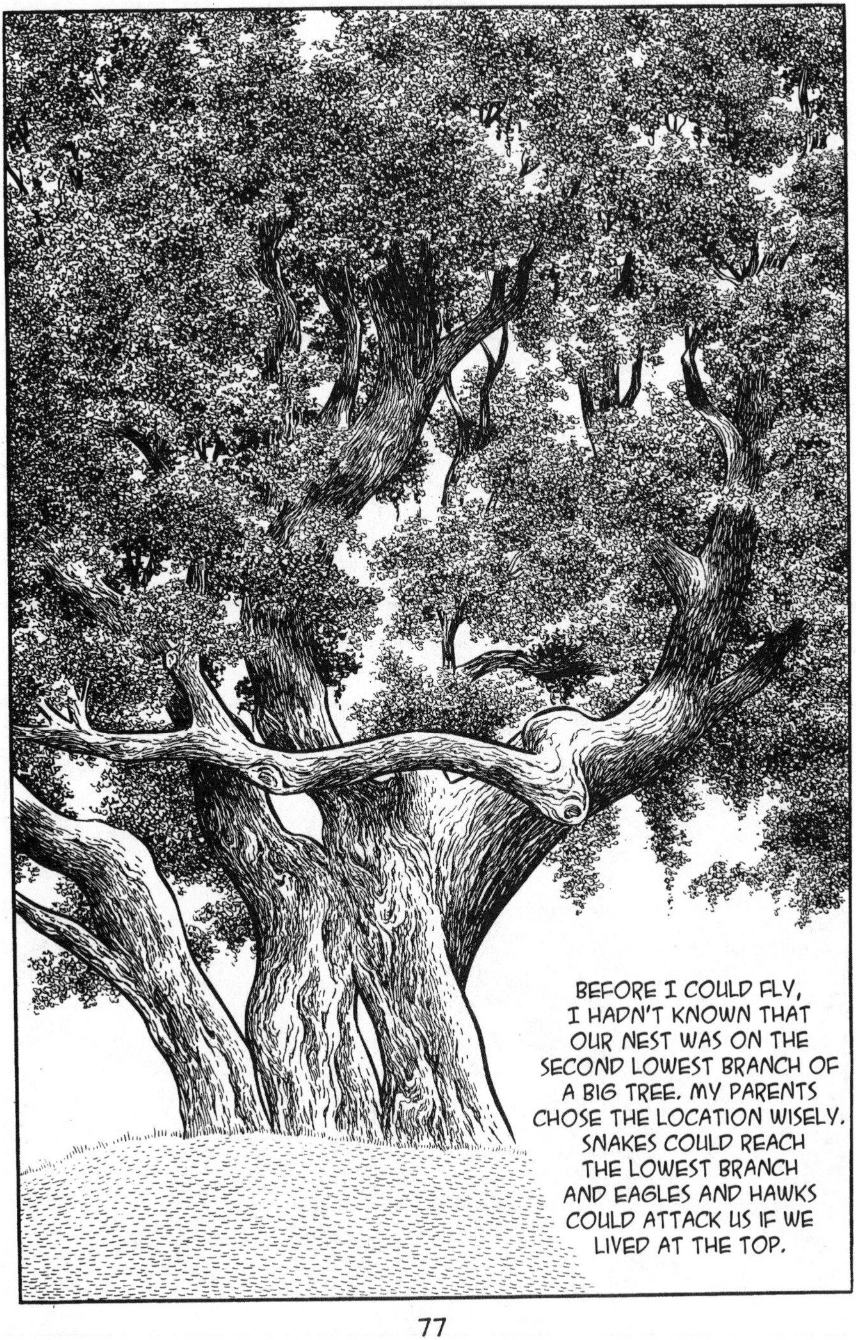
BEFORE I COULD FLY, I HADN'T KNOWN THAT OUR NEST WAS ON THE SECOND LOWEST BRANCH OF A BIG TREE. MY PARENTS CHOSE THE LOCATION WISELY. SNAKES COULD REACH THE LOWEST BRANCH AND EAGLES AND HAWKS COULD ATTACK US IF WE LIVED AT THE TOP.

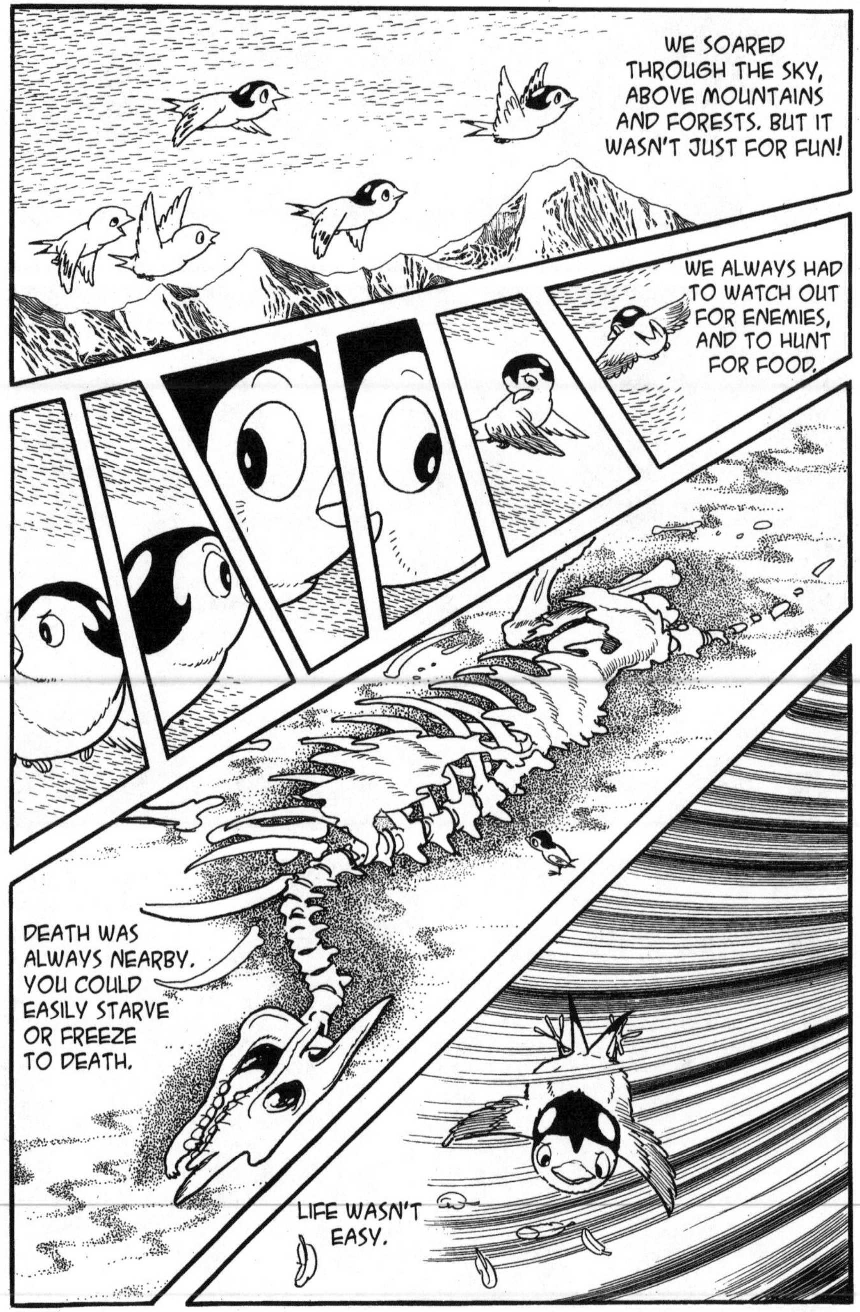
WE SOARED THROUGH THE SKY, ABOVE MOUNTAINS AND FORESTS. BUT IT WASN'T JUST FOR FUN!
WE ALWAYS HAD TO WATCH OUT FOR ENEMIES, AND TO HUNT FOR FOOD.
DEATH WAS ALWAYS NEARBY. YOU COULD EASILY STARVE OR FREEZE TO DEATH.
LIFE WASN'T EASY.

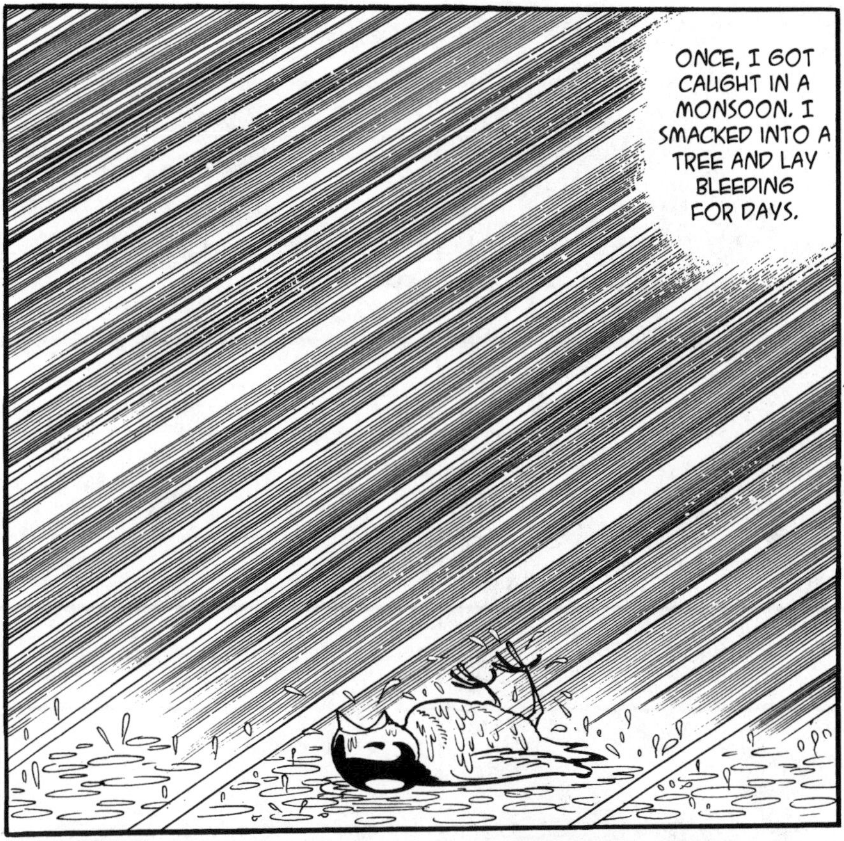
ONCE, I GOT CAUGHT IN A MONSOON. I SMACKED INTO A TREE AND LAY BLEEDING FOR DAYS.

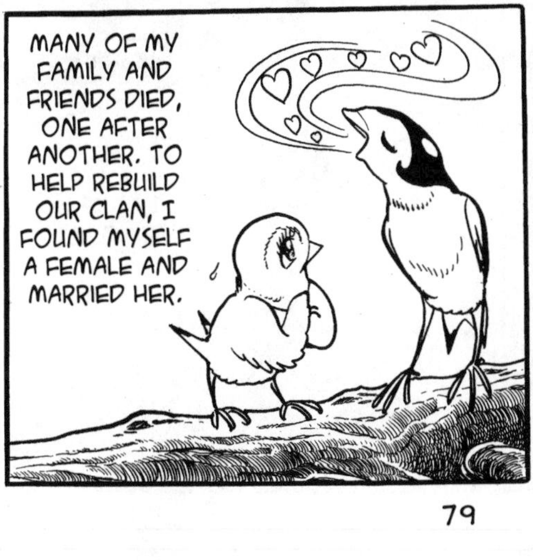
MANY OF MY FAMILY AND FRIENDS DIED, ONE AFTER ANOTHER. TO HELP REBUILD OUR CLAN, I FOUND MYSELF A FEMALE AND MARRIED HER.

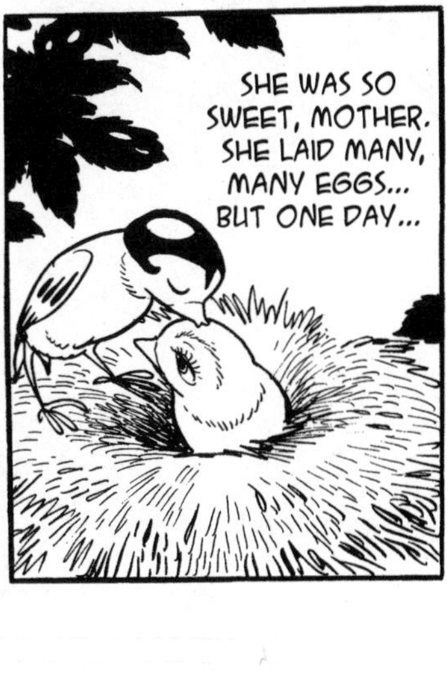
SHE WAS SO SWEET, MOTHER. SHE LAID MANY, MANY EGGS... BUT ONE DAY...

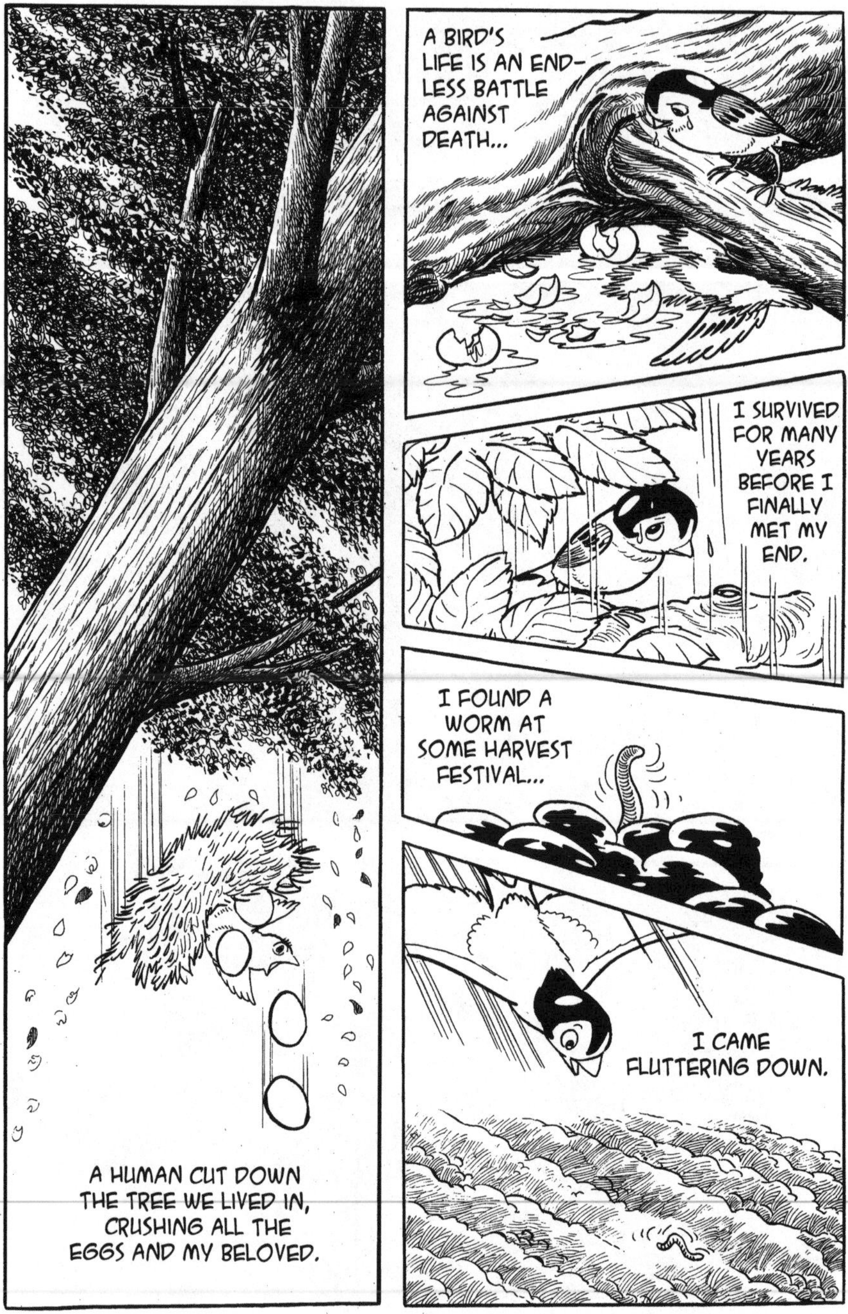
A HUMAN CUT DOWN THE TREE WE LIVED IN, CRUSHING ALL THE EGGS AND MY BELOVED.
A BIRD'S LIFE IS AN END-LESS BATTLE AGAINST DEATH...
I SURVIVED FOR MANY YEARS BEFORE I FINALLY MET MY END.
I FOUND A WORM AT SOME HARVEST FESTIVAL...
I CAME FLUTTERING DOWN.

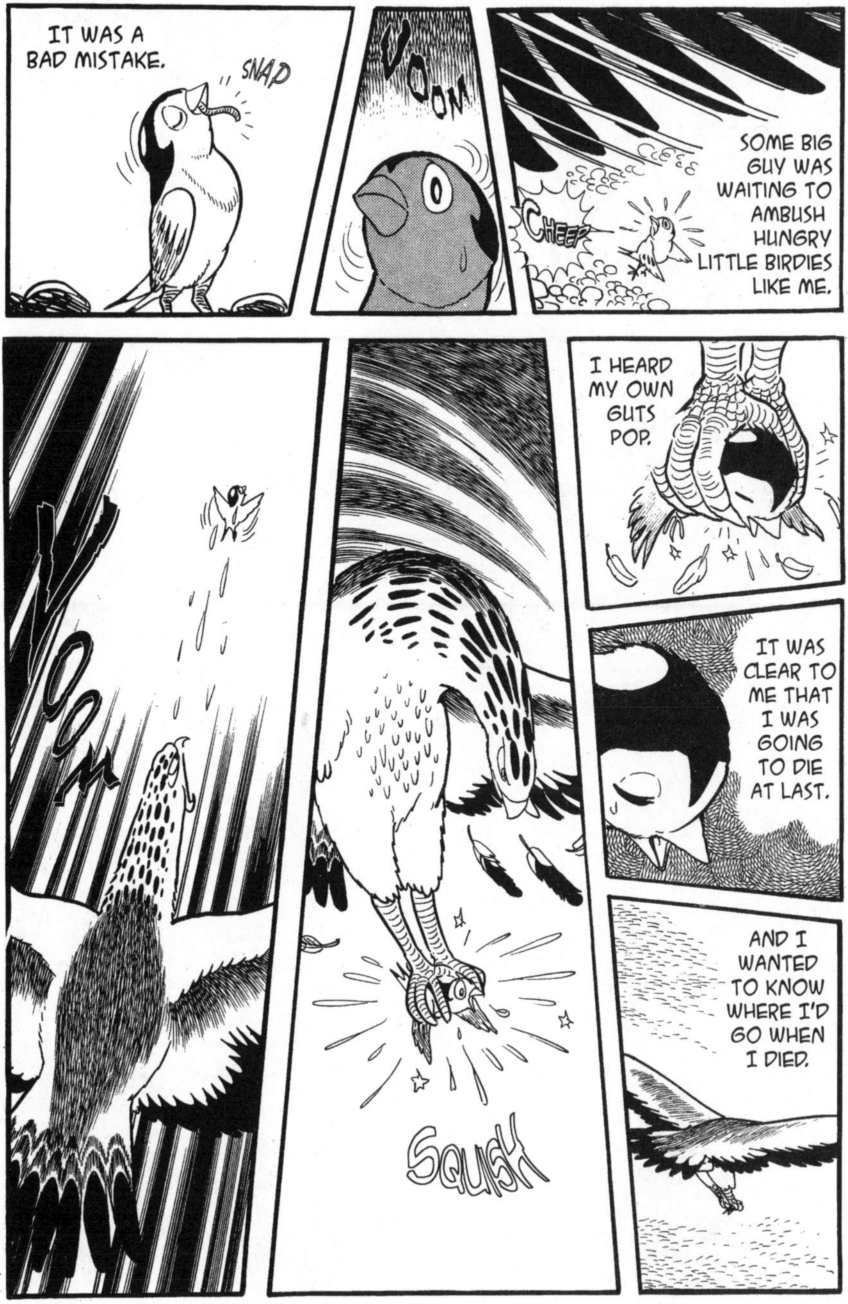
IT WAS A BAD MISTAKE.
SNAP
VOOM
SOME BIG GUY WAS WAITING TO AMBUSH HUNGRY LITTLE BIRDIES LIKE ME.
CHEEP
SQUISH
I HEARD MY OWN GUTS POP.
IT WAS CLEAR TO ME THAT I WAS GOING TO DIE AT LAST.
AND I WANTED TO KNOW WHERE I'D GO WHEN I DIED.

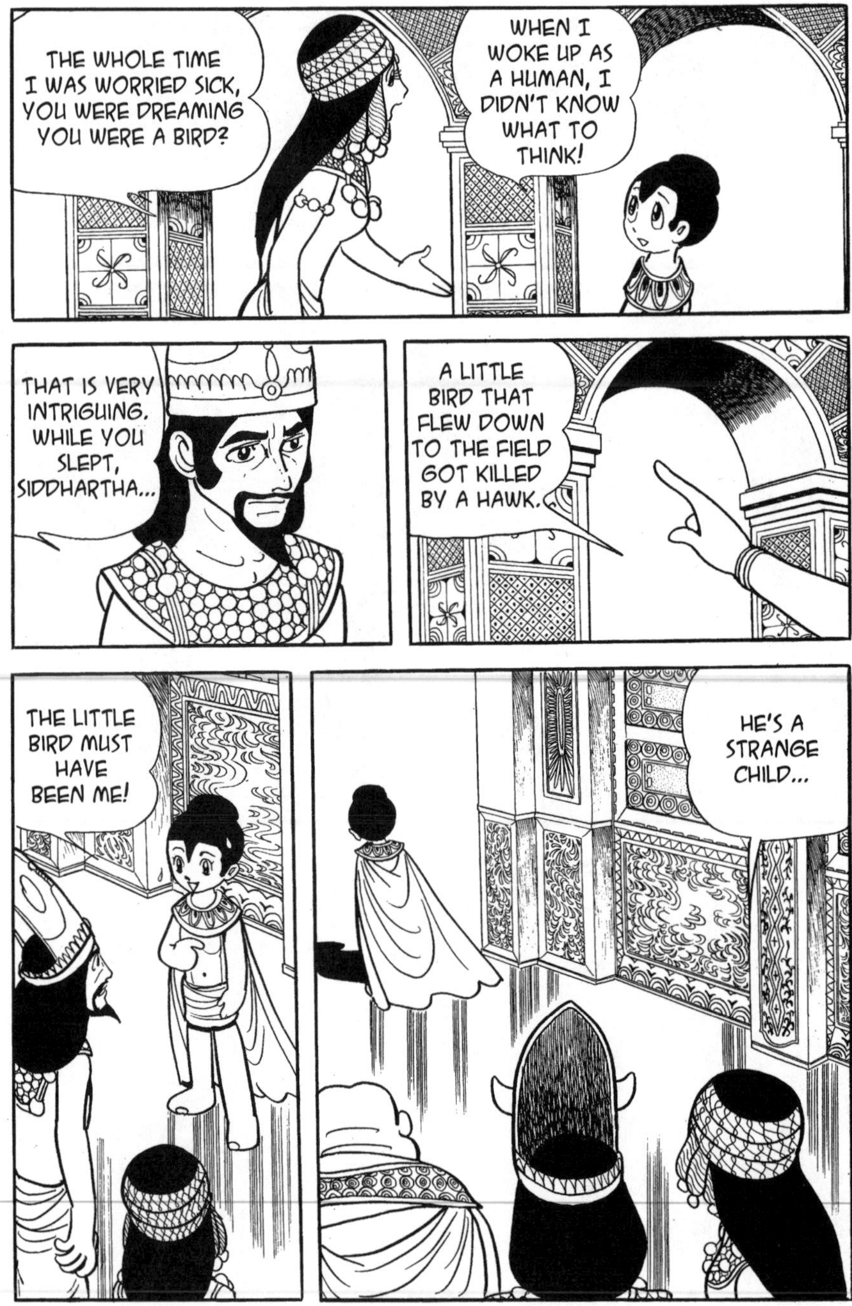
THE WHOLE TIME I WAS WORRIED SICK, YOU WERE DREAMING YOU WERE A BIRD?
WHEN I WOKE UP AS A HUMAN, I DIDN'T KNOW WHAT TO THINK!
THAT IS VERY INTRIGUING. WHILE YOU SLEPT, SIDDHARTHA...
A LITTLE BIRD THAT FLEW DOWN TO THE FIELD GOT KILLED BY A HAWK.
THE LITTLE BIRD MUST HAVE BEEN ME!
HE'S A STRANGE CHILD...

CHAPTER THREE

THE RAPIDS

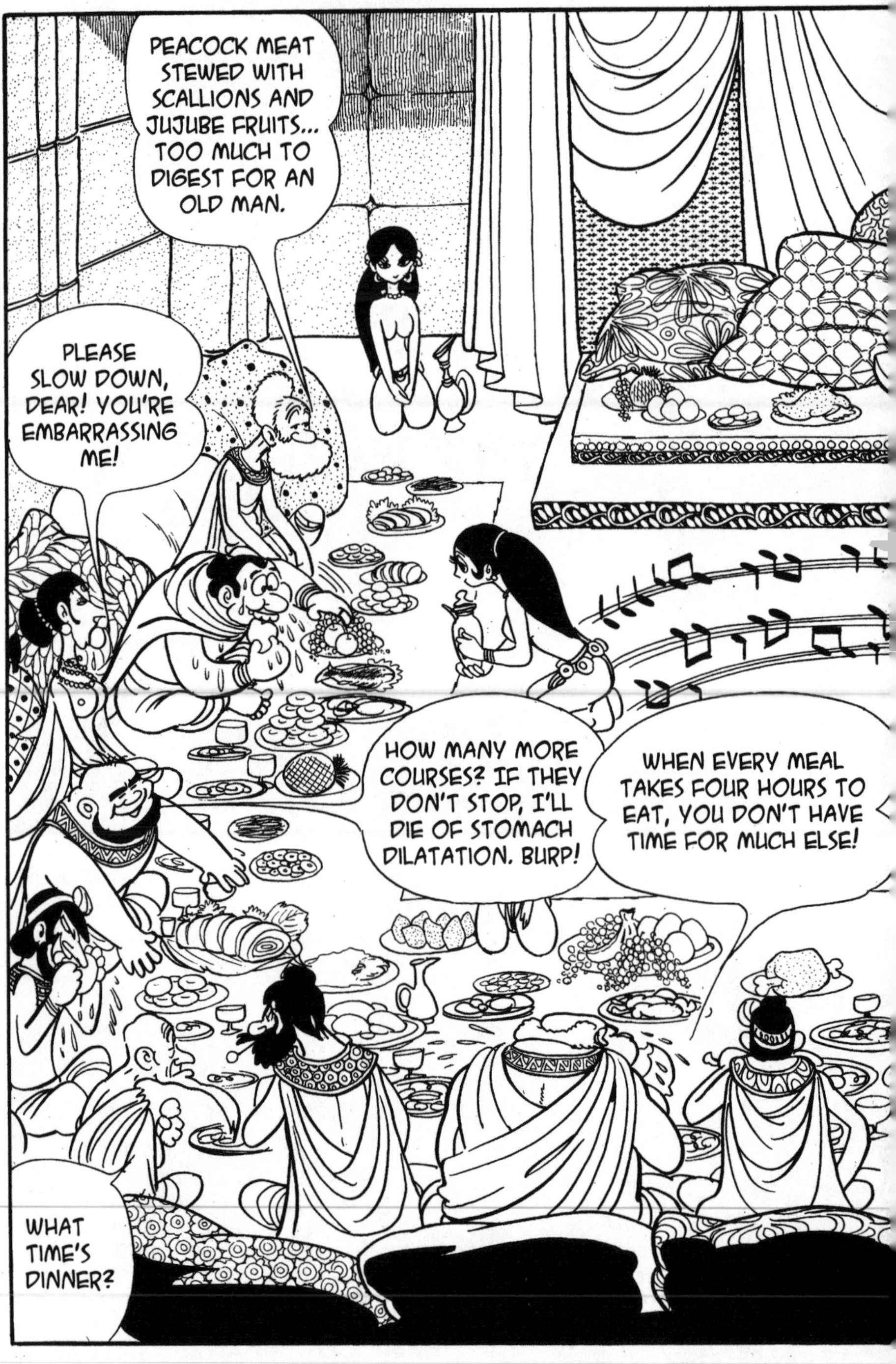
PEACOCK MEAT STEWED WITH SCALLIONS AND JUJUBE FRUITS... TOO MUCH TO DIGEST FOR AN OLD MAN.
PLEASE SLOW DOWN, DEAR! YOU'RE EMBARRASSING ME!
HOW MANY MORE COURSES? IF THEY DON'T STOP, I'LL DIE OF STOMACH DILATATION. BURP!
WHEN EVERY MEAL TAKES FOUR HOURS TO EAT, YOU DON'T HAVE TIME FOR MUCH ELSE!
WHAT TIME'S DINNER?

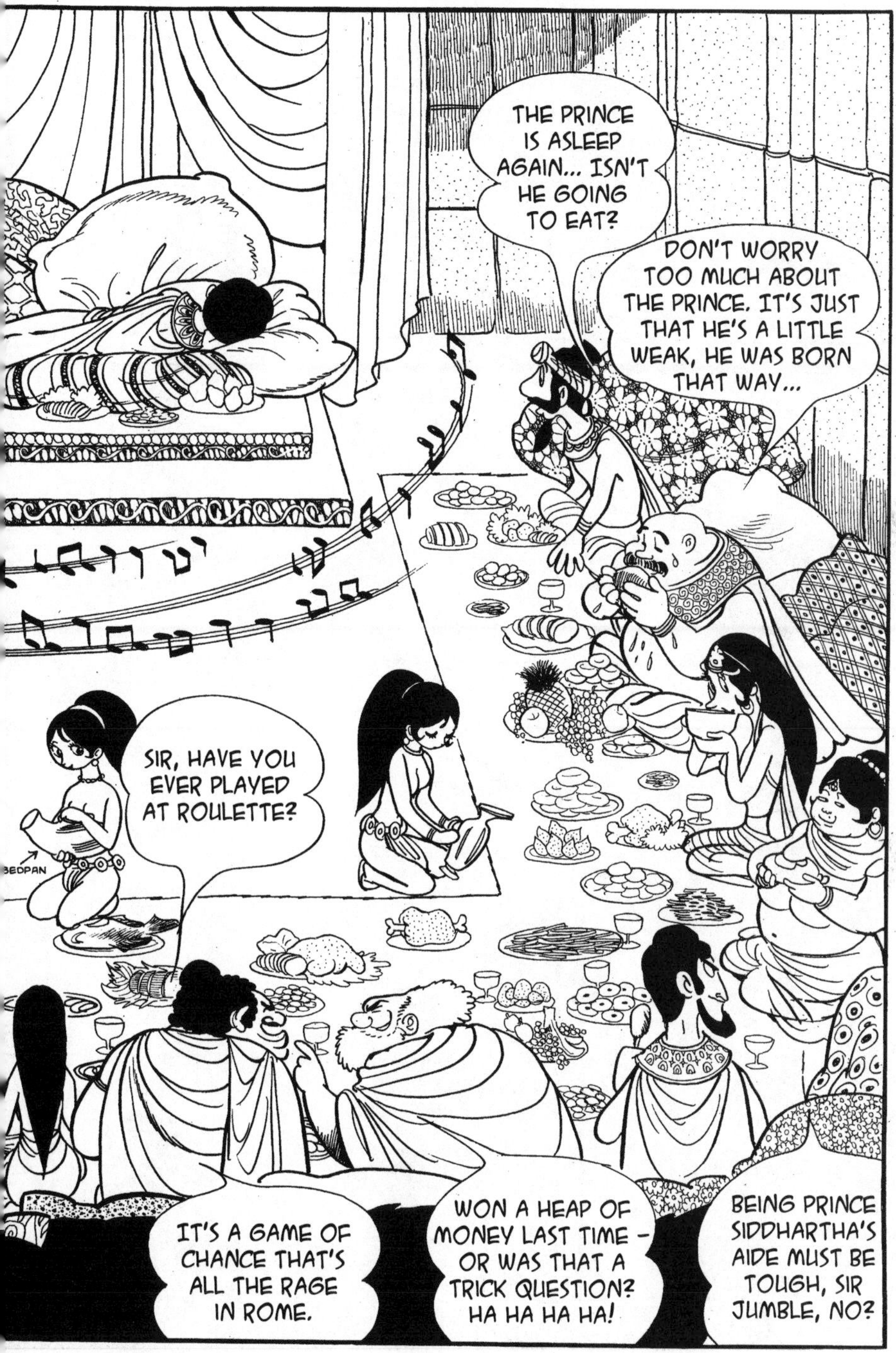
THE PRINCE IS ASLEEP AGAIN... ISN'T HE GOING TO EAT?
DON'T WORRY TOO MUCH ABOUT THE PRINCE. IT'S JUST THAT HE'S A LITTLE WEAK, HE WAS BORN THAT WAY...
SIR, HAVE YOU EVER PLAYED AT ROULETTE?
BEDPAN
IT'S A GAME OF CHANCE THAT'S ALL THE RAGE IN ROME.
WON A HEAP OF MONEY LAST TIME - OR WAS THAT A TRICK QUESTION? HA HA HA HA!
BEING PRINCE SIDDHARTHA'S AIDE MUST BE TOUGH, SIR JUMBLE, NO?

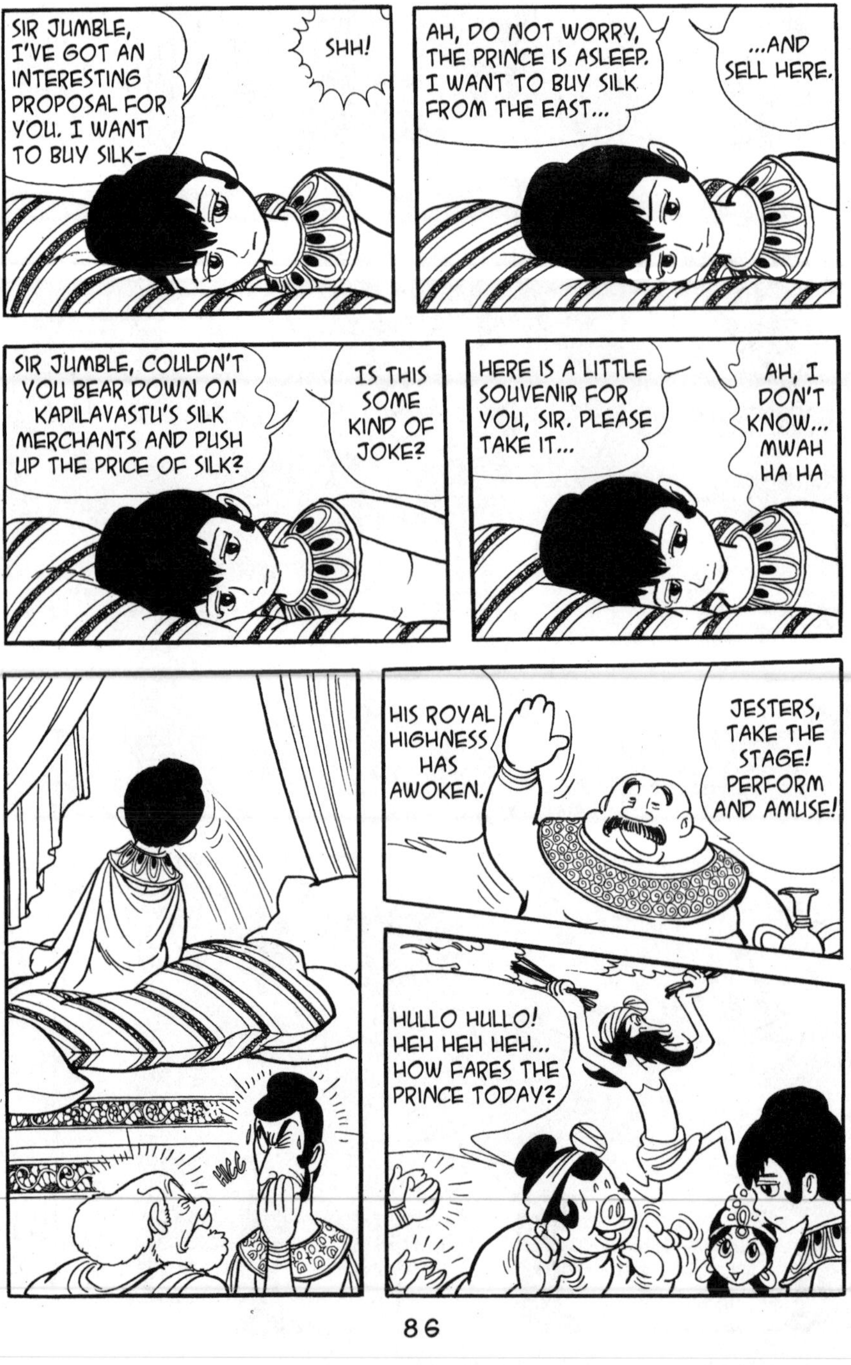
SIR JUMBLE, I'VE GOT AN INTERESTING PROPOSAL FOR YOU. I WANT TO BUY SILK-
SHH!
AH, DO NOT WORRY, THE PRINCE IS ASLEEP. I WANT TO BUY SILK FROM THE EAST...
...AND SELL HERE.
SIR JUMBLE, COULDN'T YOU BEAR DOWN ON KAPILAVASTU'S SILK MERCHANTS AND PUSH UP THE PRICE OF SILK?
IS THIS SOME KIND OF JOKE?
HERE IS A LITTLE SOUVENIR FOR YOU, SIR. PLEASE TAKE IT...
AH, I DON'T KNOW... MWAH HA HA
HUG
HIS ROYAL HIGHNESS HAS AWOKEN.
JESTERS, TAKE THE STAGE! PERFORM AND AMUSE!
HULLO HULLO! HEH HEH HEH... HOW FARES THE PRINCE TODAY?

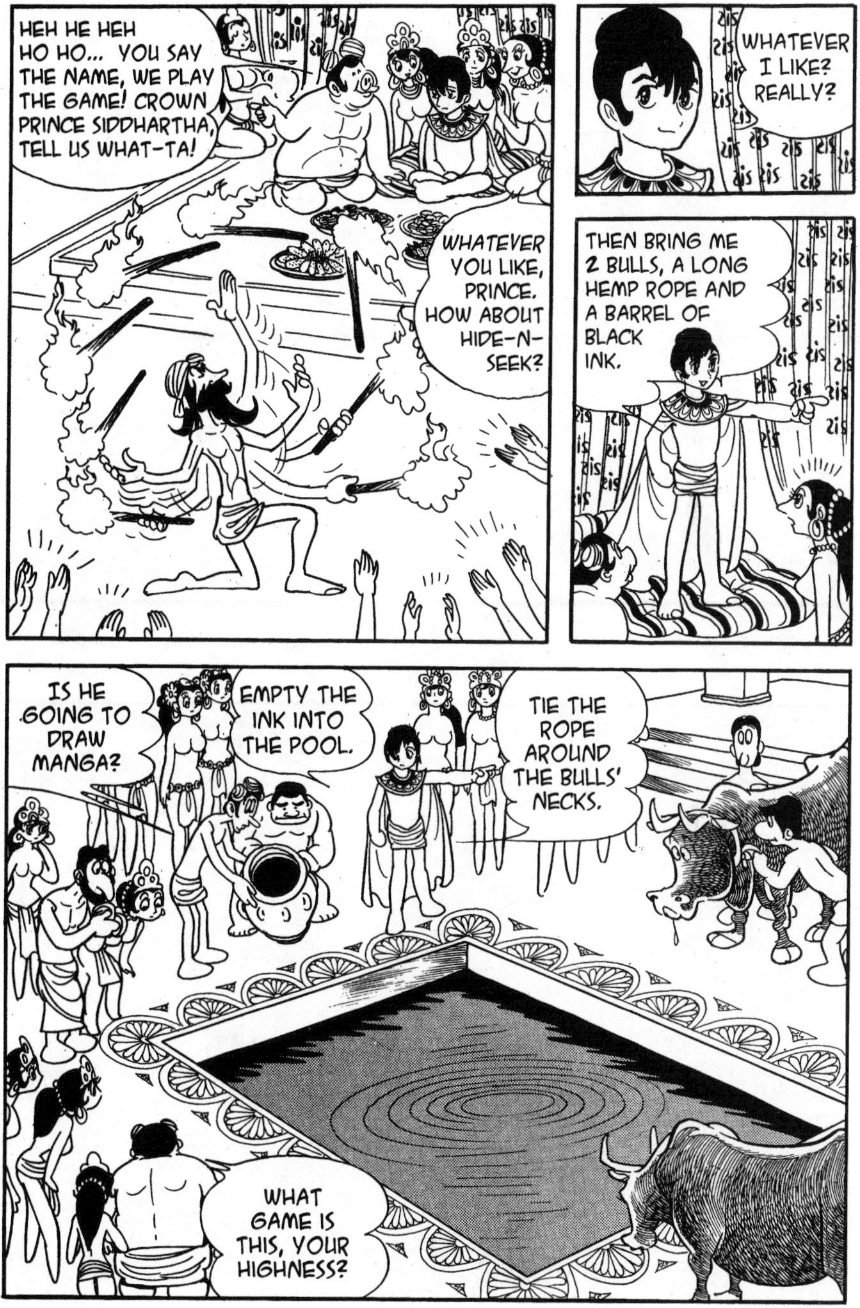
HEH HE HEH HO HO... YOU SAY THE NAME, WE PLAY THE GAME! CROWN PRINCE SIDDHARTHA, TELL US WHAT-TA!
WHATEVER YOU LIKE, PRINCE. HOW ABOUT HIDE-N-SEEK?
WHATEVER I LIKE? REALLY?
THEN BRING ME 2 BULLS, A LONG HEMP ROPE AND A BARREL OF BLACK INK.
IS HE GOING TO DRAW MANGA?
EMPTY THE INK INTO THE POOL.
TIE THE ROPE AROUND THE BULLS' NECKS.
WHAT GAME IS THIS, YOUR HIGHNESS?

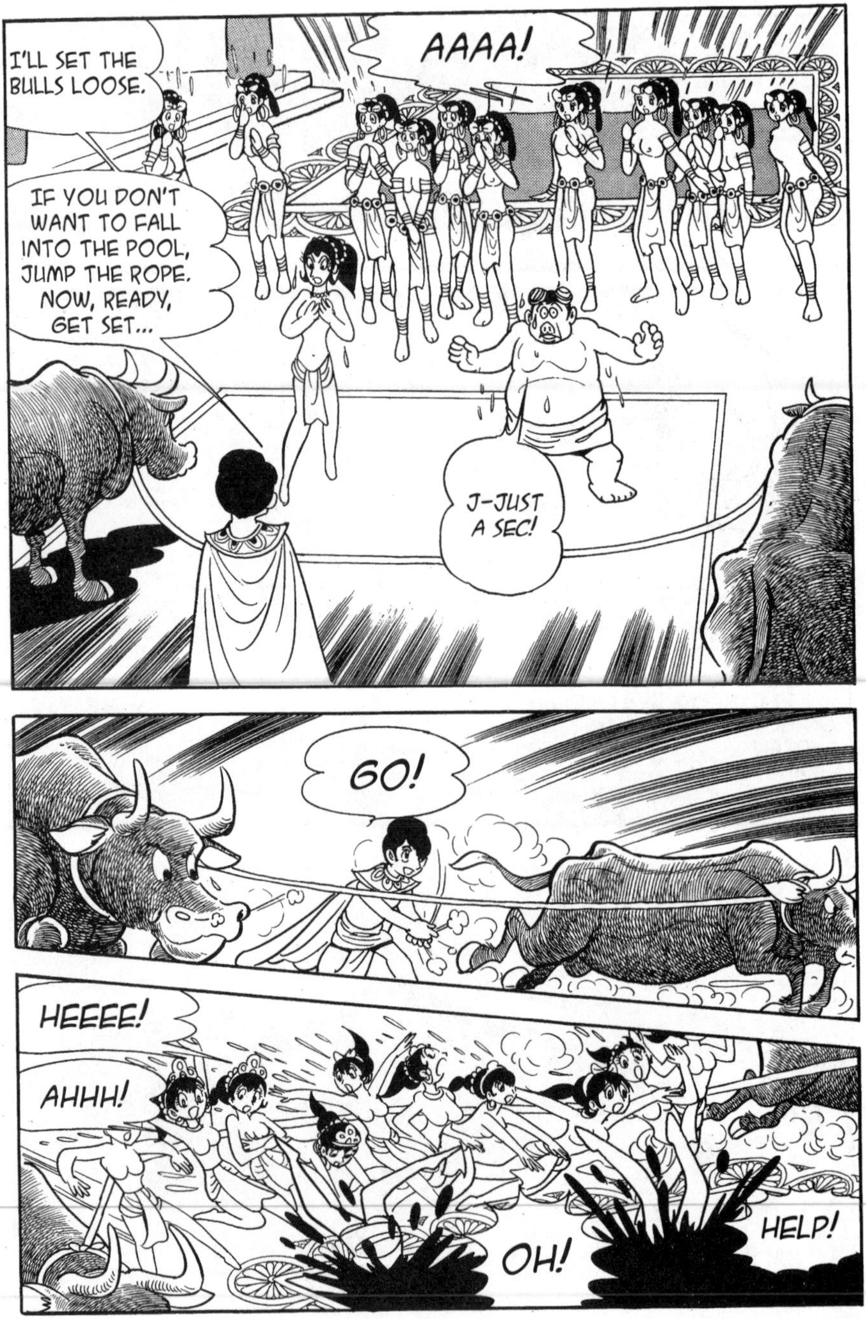
I'LL SET THE BULLS LOOSE.
AAAA!
IF YOU DON'T WANT TO FALL INTO THE POOL, JUMP THE ROPE. NOW, READY, GET SET...
J-JUST A SEC!
GO!
HEEEEE!
AHHH!
OH!
HELP!

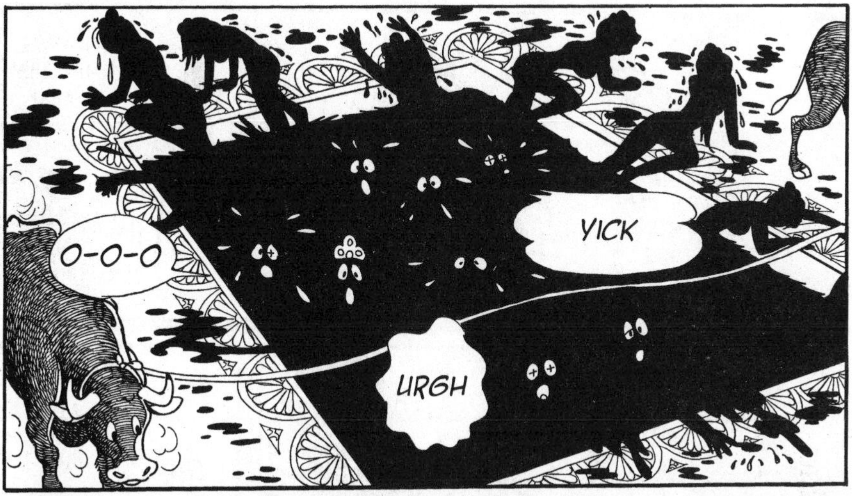
O-O-O
YICK
URGH

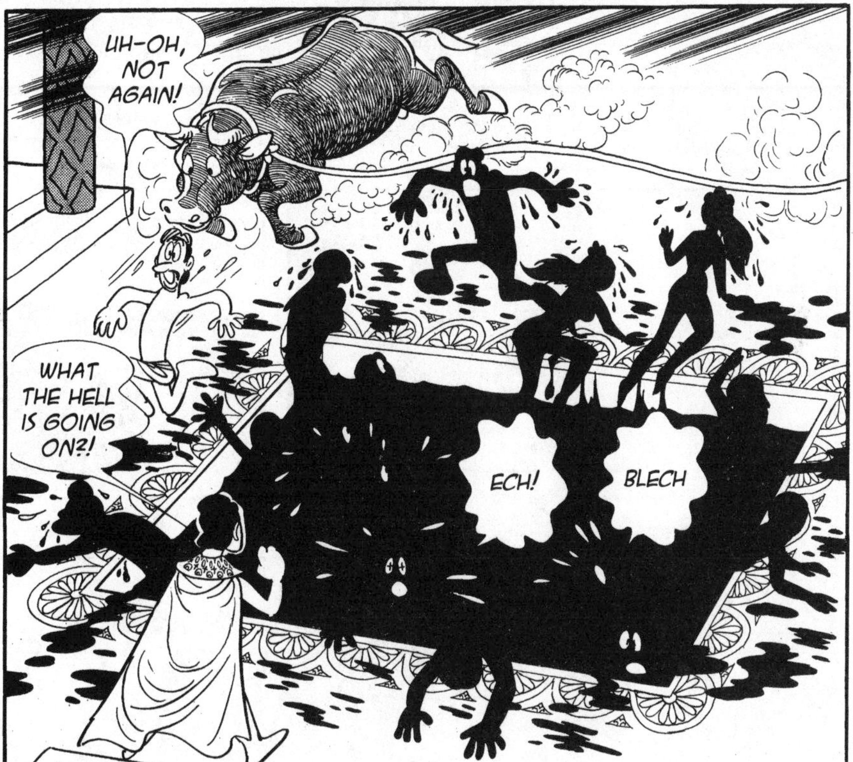
UH-OH, NOT AGAIN!
WHAT THE HELL IS GOING ON?!
ECH!
BLECH

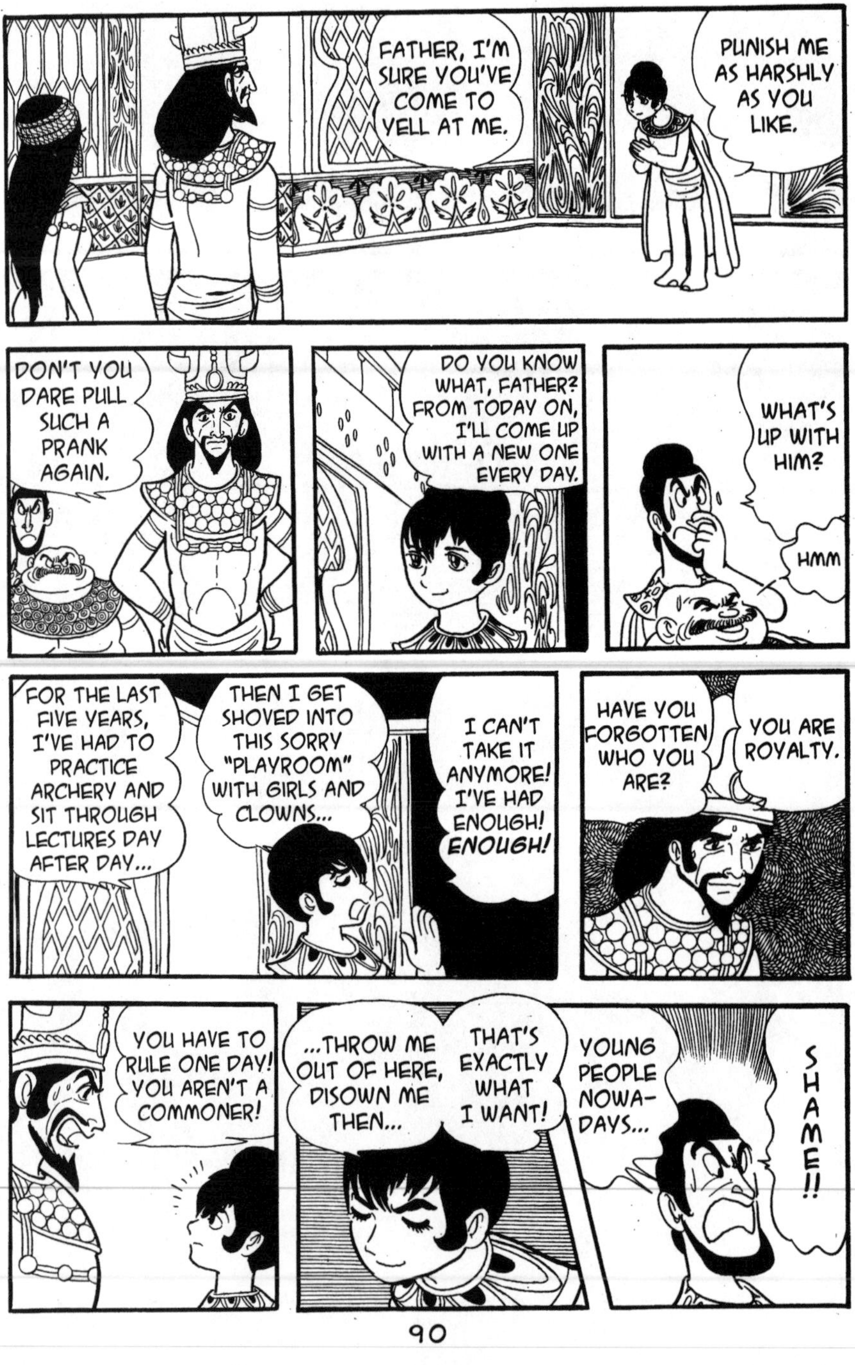
FATHER, I'M SURE YOU'VE COME TO YELL AT ME.
PUNISH ME AS HARSHLY AS YOU LIKE.
DON'T YOU DARE PULL SUCH A PRANK AGAIN.
DO YOU KNOW WHAT, FATHER? FROM TODAY ON, I'LL COME UP WITH A NEW ONE EVERY DAY.
WHAT'S UP WITH HIM?
HMM
FOR THE LAST FIVE YEARS, I'VE HAD TO PRACTICE ARCHERY AND SIT THROUGH LECTURES DAY AFTER DAY...
THEN I GET SHOVED INTO THIS SORRY "PLAYROOM" WITH GIRLS AND CLOWNS...
I CAN'T TAKE IT ANYMORE! I'VE HAD ENOUGH! ENOUGH!
HAVE YOU FORGOTTEN WHO YOU ARE?
YOU ARE ROYALTY.
YOU HAVE TO RULE ONE DAY! YOU AREN'T A COMMONER!
...THROW ME OUT OF HERE, DISOWN ME THEN...
THAT'S EXACTLY WHAT I WANT!
YOUNG PEOPLE NOWA-DAYS...
SHAME!!

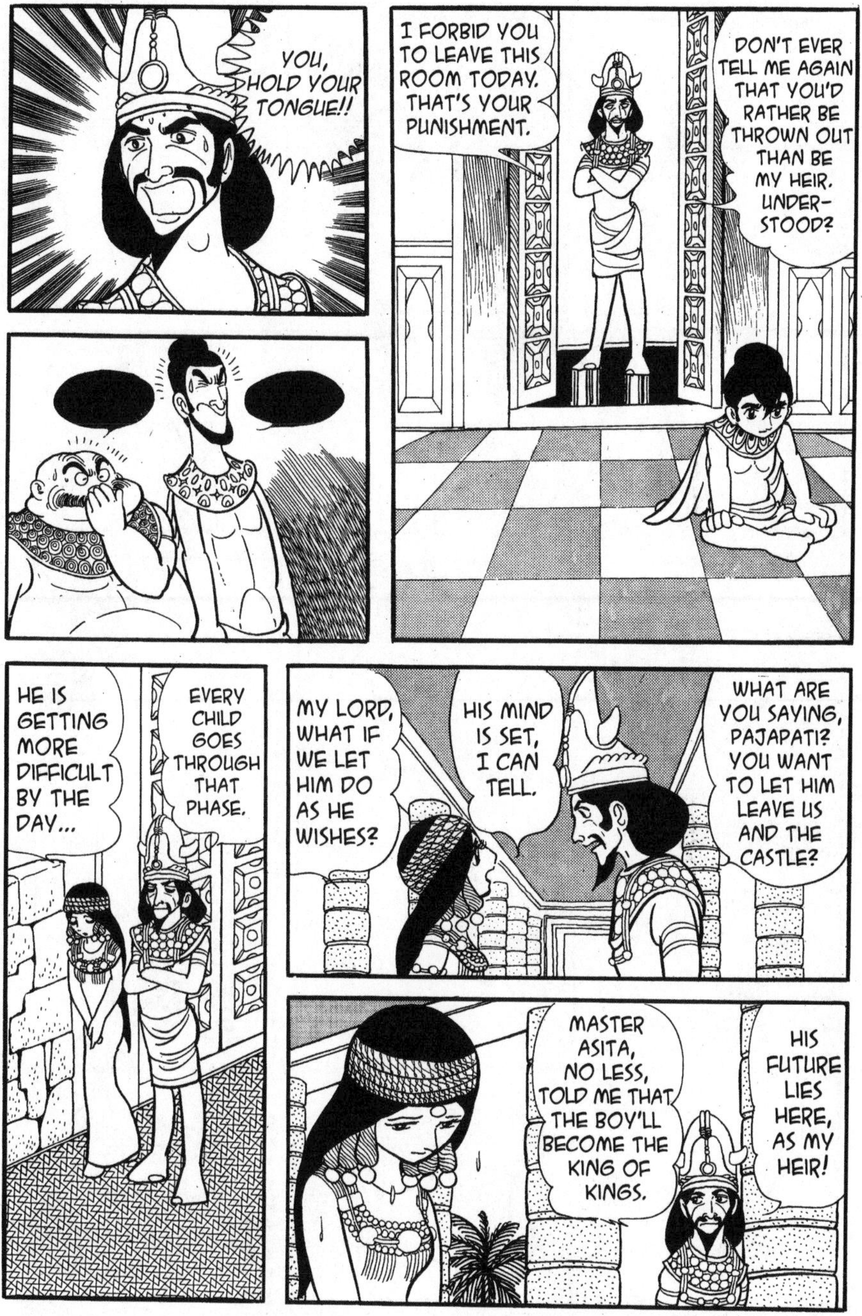
YOU, HOLD YOUR TONGUE!!
I FORBID YOU TO LEAVE THIS ROOM TODAY. THAT'S YOUR PUNISHMENT.
DON'T EVER TELL ME AGAIN THAT YOU'D RATHER BE THROWN OUT THAN BE MY HEIR. UNDER-STOOD?
HE IS GETTING MORE DIFFICULT BY THE DAY...
EVERY CHILD GOES THROUGH THAT PHASE.
MY LORD, WHAT IF WE LET HIM DO AS HE WISHES?
HIS MIND IS SET, I CAN TELL.
WHAT ARE YOU SAYING, PAJAPATI? YOU WANT TO LET HIM LEAVE US AND THE CASTLE?
MASTER ASITA, NO LESS, TOLD ME THAT THE BOY'LL BECOME THE KING OF KINGS.
HIS FUTURE LIES HERE, AS MY HEIR!

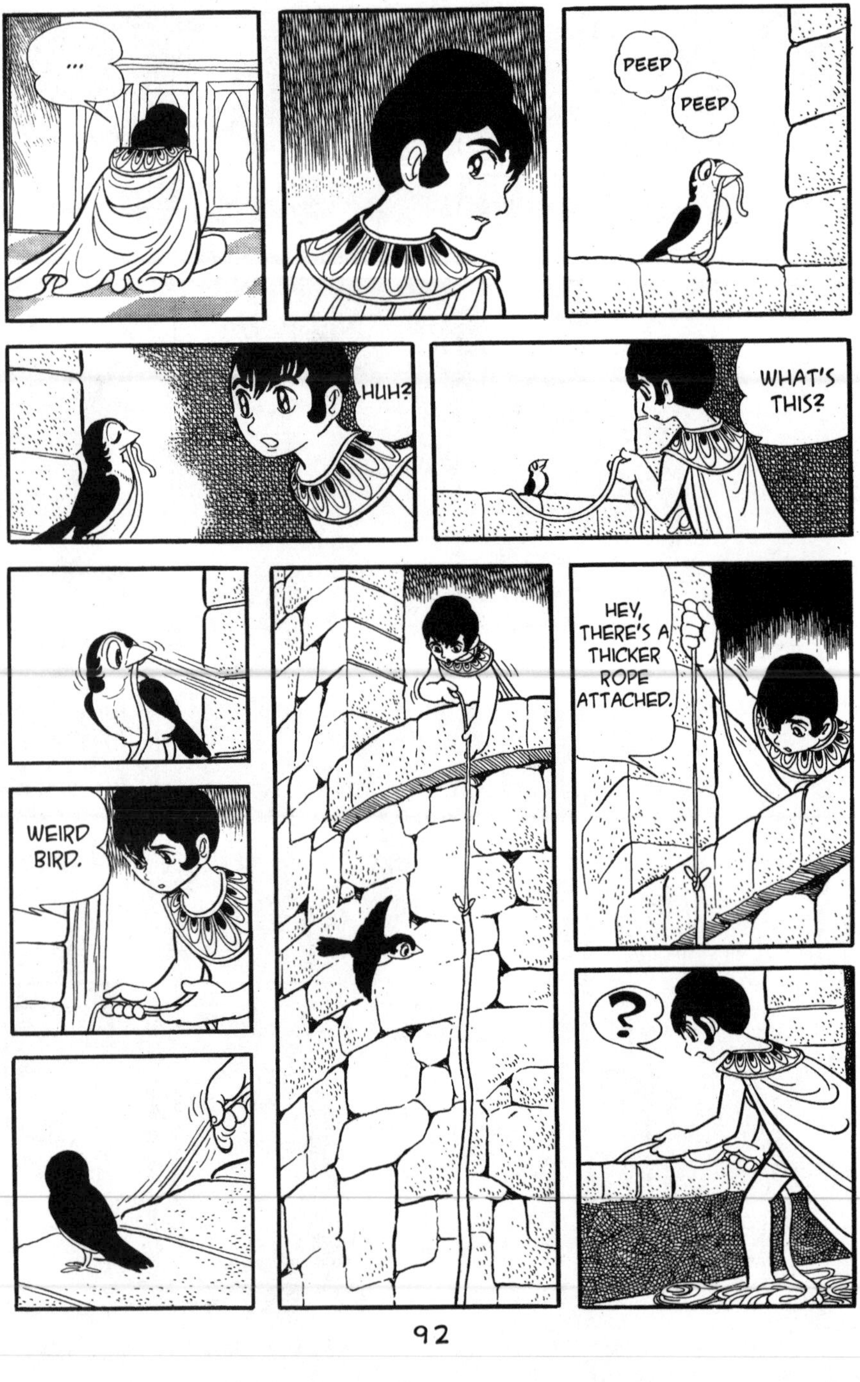
...
PEEP
PEEP
HUH?
WHAT'S THIS?
HEY, THERE'S A THICKER ROPE ATTACHED.
WEIRD BIRD.
?

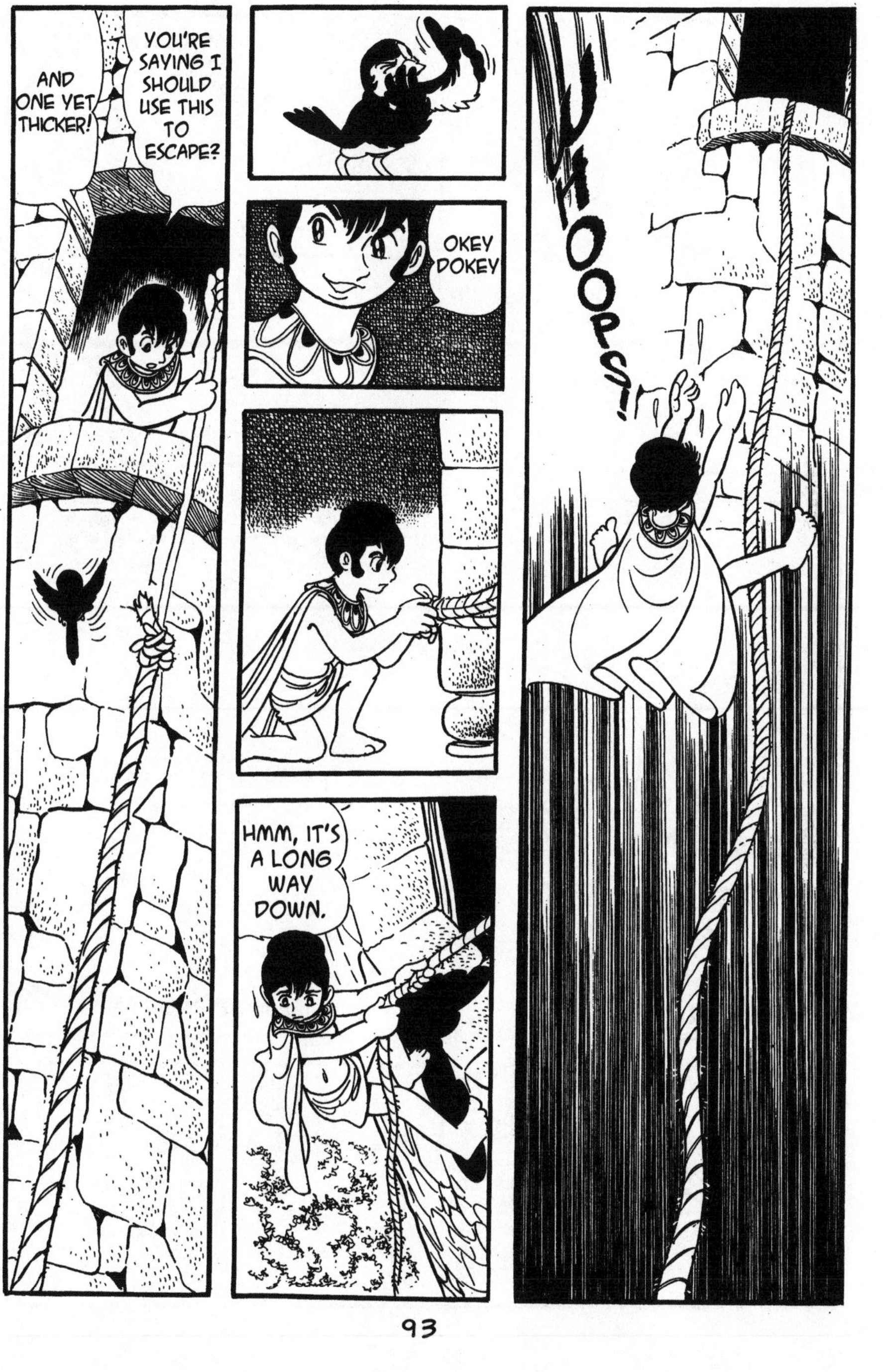
YOU'RE SAYING I SHOULD USE THIS TO ESCAPE?
AND ONE YET THICKER!
OKEY DOKEY
HMM, IT'S A LONG WAY DOWN.
WHOOPS!

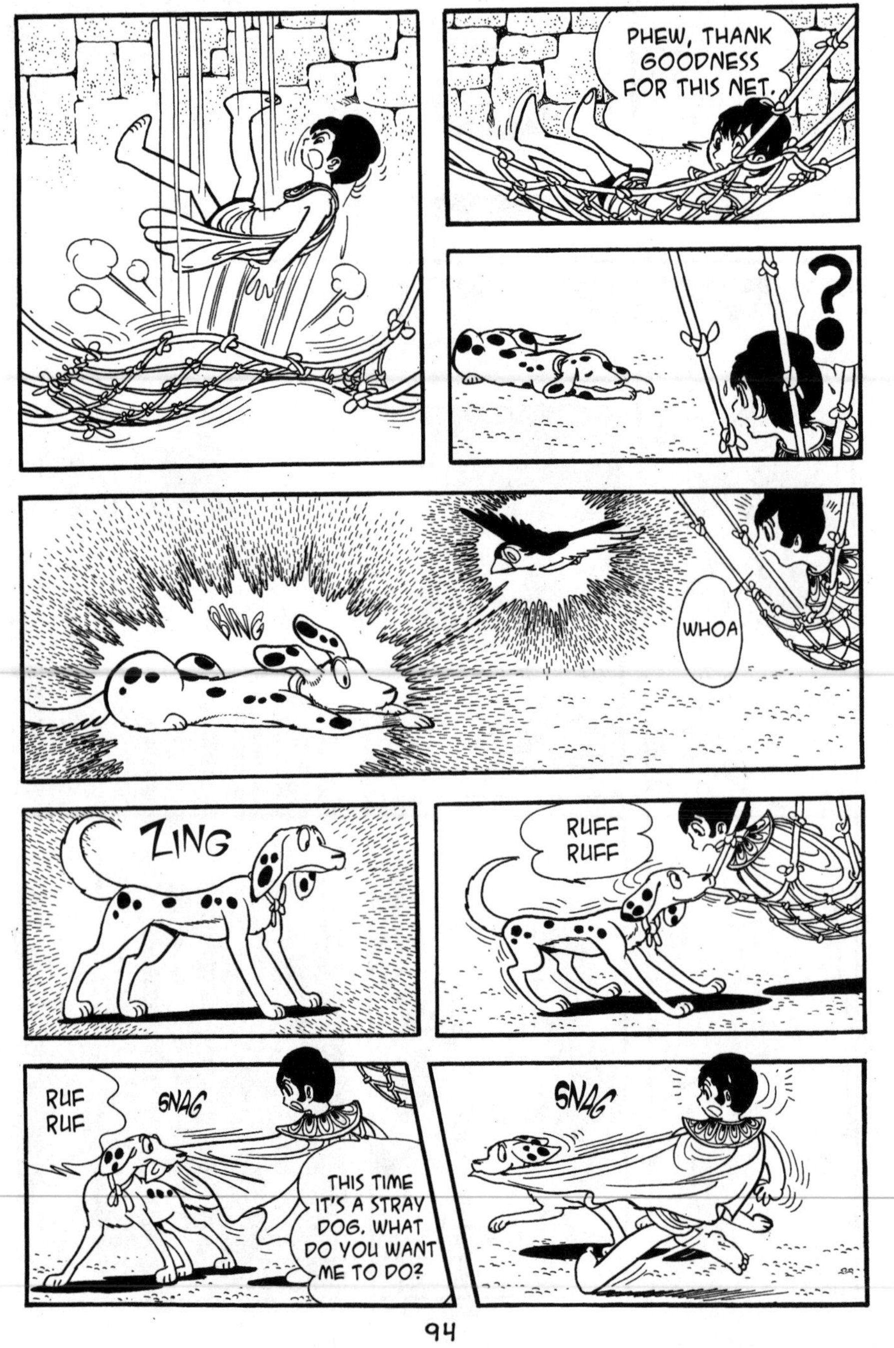
PHEW, THANK GOODNESS FOR THIS NET.
?
BING
WHOA
ZING
RUFF RUFF
RUF RUF
SNAG
THIS TIME IT'S A STRAY DOG. WHAT DO YOU WANT ME TO DO?
SNAG

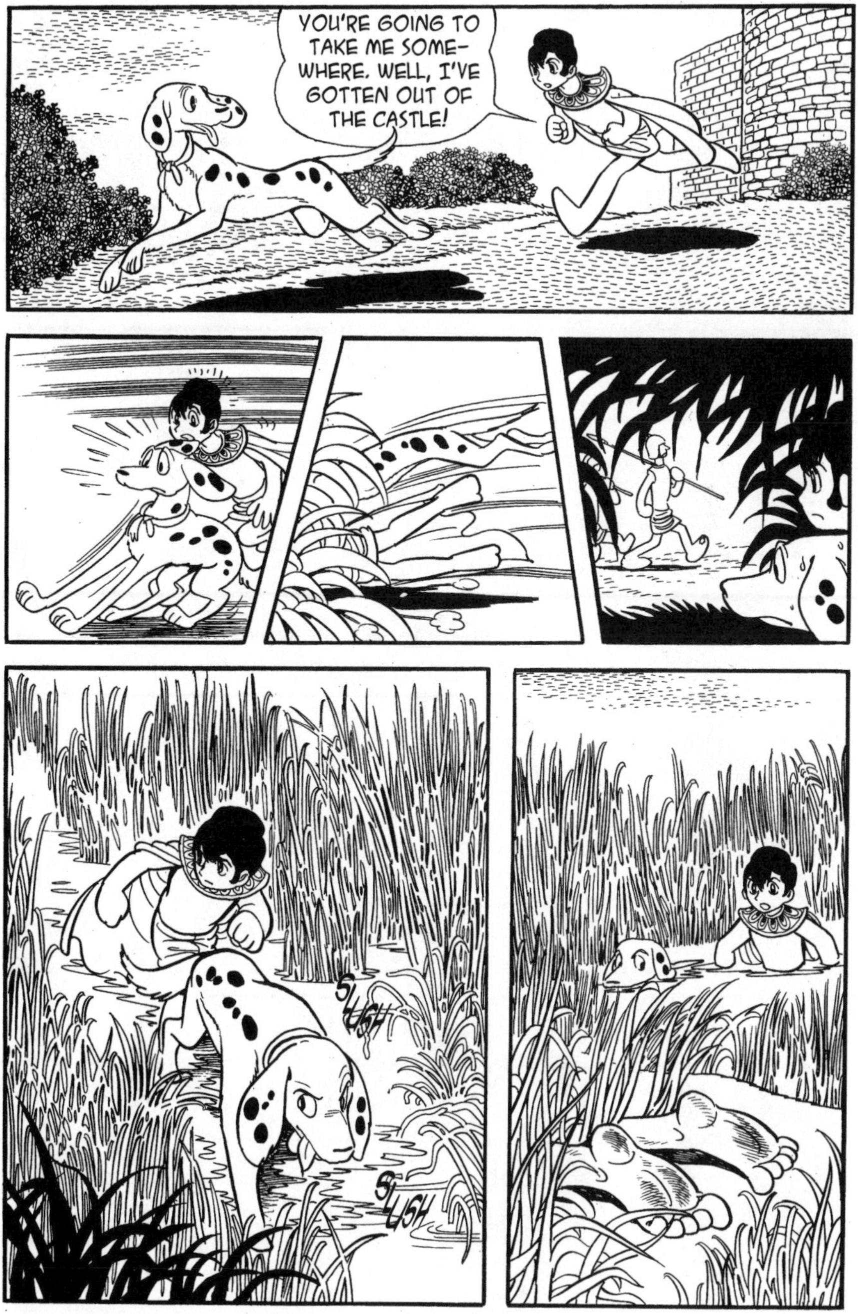
YOU'RE GOING TO TAKE ME SOME-WHERE. WELL, I'VE GOTTEN OUT OF THE CASTLE!
SLUSH
SLUSH

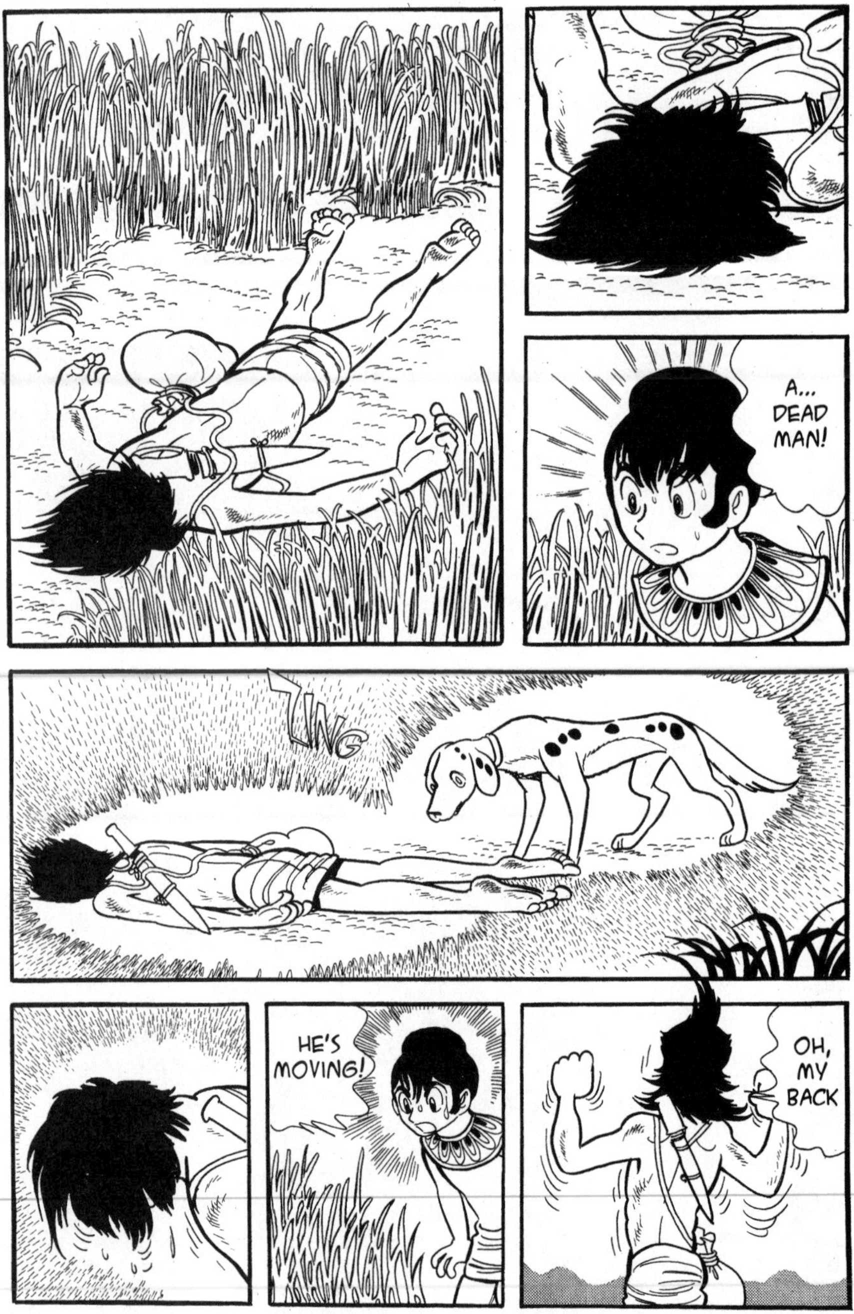
A... DEAD MAN!
ZING
HE'S MOVING!
OH, MY BACK

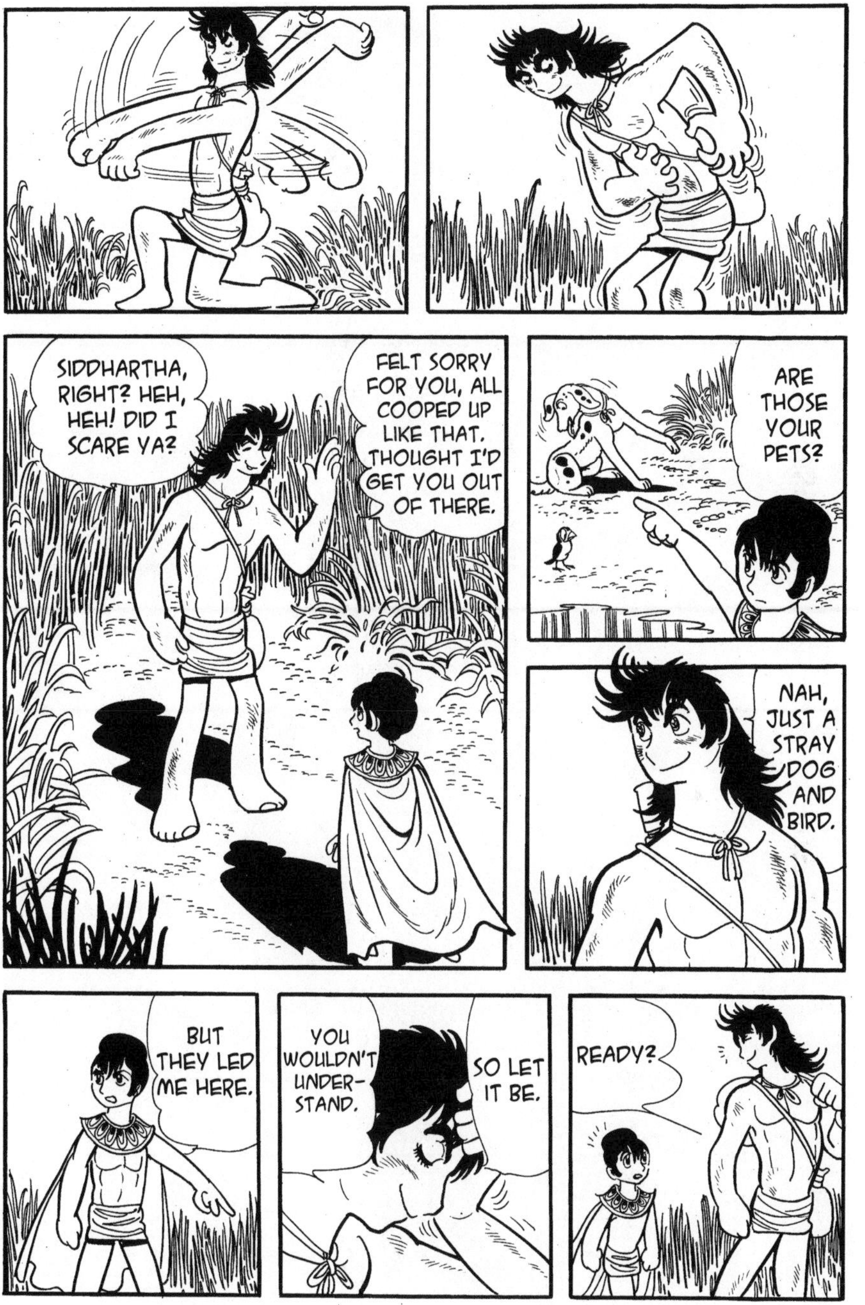
SIDDHARTHA, RIGHT? HEH, HEH! DID I SCARE YA?
FELT SORRY FOR YOU, ALL COOPED UP LIKE THAT. THOUGHT I'D GET YOU OUT OF THERE.
ARE THOSE YOUR PETS?
NAH, JUST A STRAY DOG AND BIRD.
BUT THEY LED ME HERE.
YOU WOULDN'T UNDER-STAND.
SO LET IT BE.
READY?

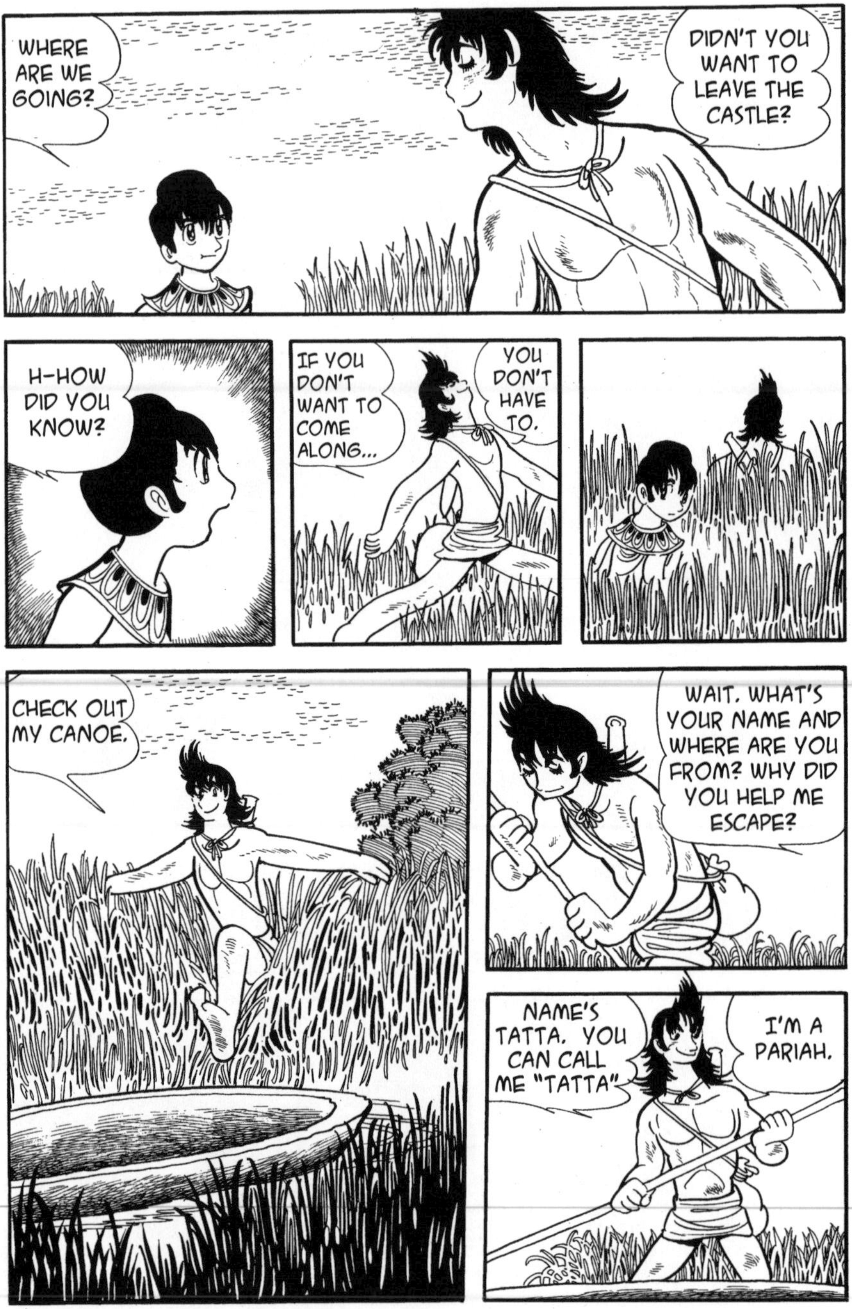
WHERE ARE WE GOING?
DIDN'T YOU WANT TO LEAVE THE CASTLE?
H-HOW DID YOU KNOW?
IF YOU DON'T WANT TO COME ALONG...
YOU DON'T HAVE TO.
CHECK OUT MY CANOE.
WAIT. WHAT'S YOUR NAME AND WHERE ARE YOU FROM? WHY DID YOU HELP ME ESCAPE?
NAME'S TATTA. YOU CAN CALL ME "TATTA"
I'M A PARIAH.

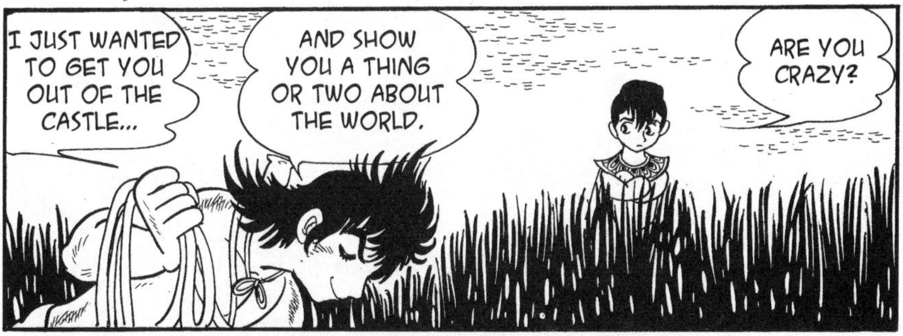
I JUST WANTED TO GET YOU OUT OF THE CASTLE...
AND SHOW YOU A THING OR TWO ABOUT THE WORLD.
ARE YOU CRAZY?

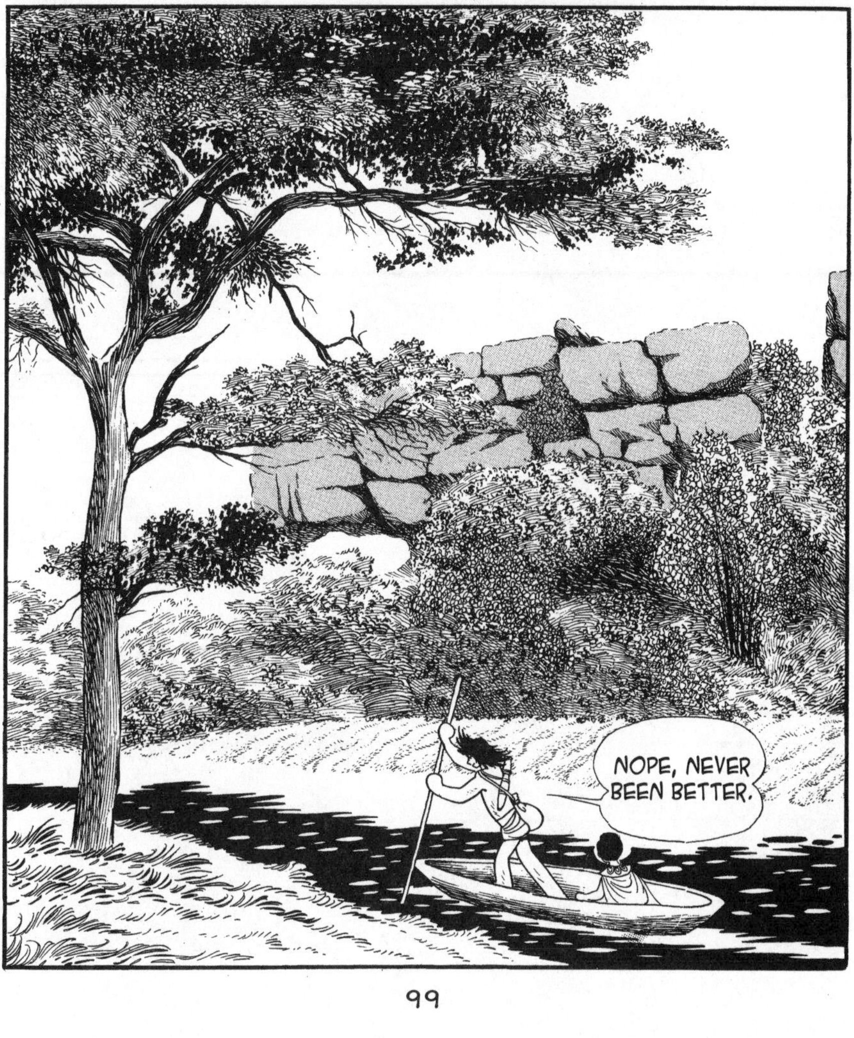
NOPE, NEVER BEEN BETTER.

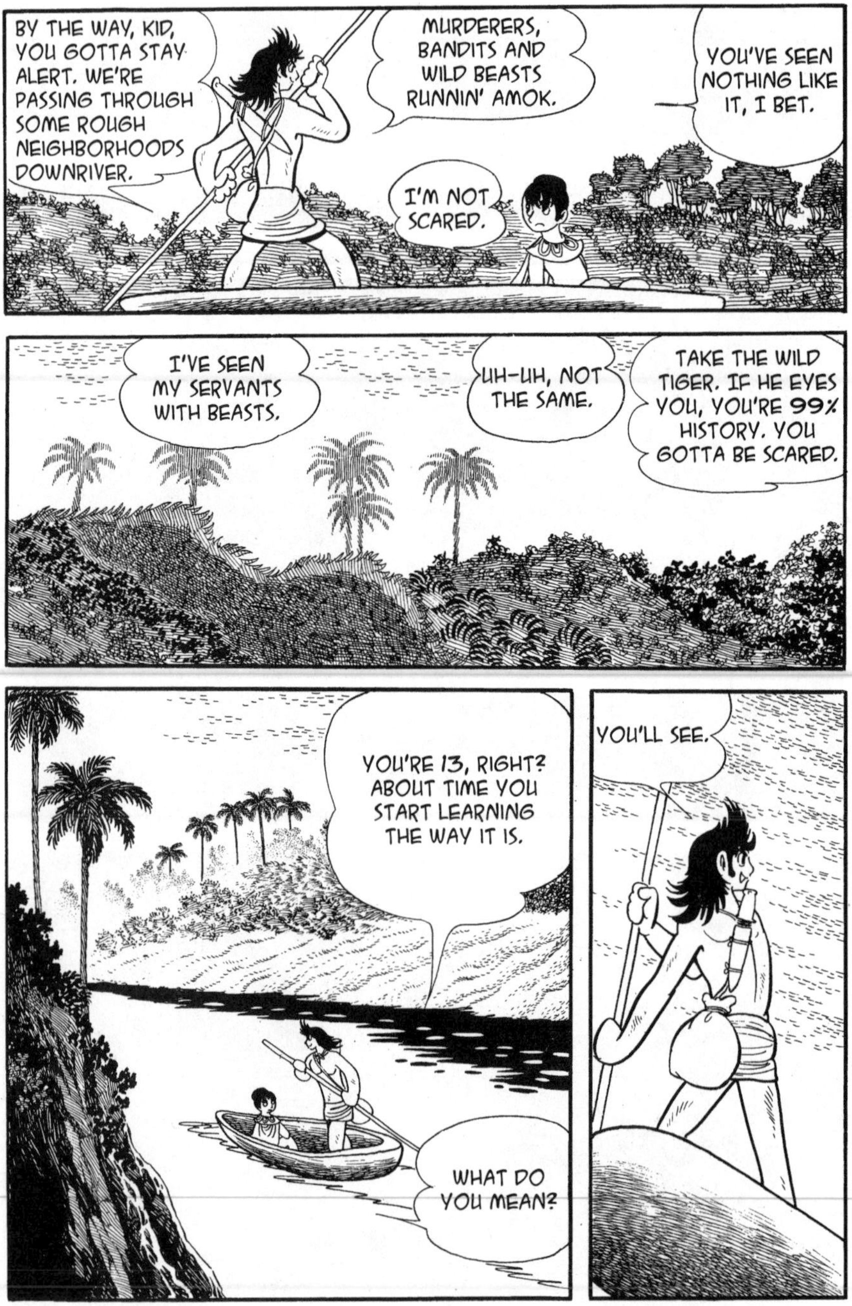

BY THE WAY, KID, YOU GOTTA STAY ALERT. WE'RE PASSING THROUGH SOME ROUGH NEIGHBORHOODS DOWNRIVER.
MURDERERS, BANDITS AND WILD BEASTS RUNNIN' AMOK.
I'M NOT SCARED.
YOU'VE SEEN NOTHING LIKE IT, I BET.
I'VE SEEN MY SERVANTS WITH BEASTS.
UH-UH, NOT THE SAME.
TAKE THE WILD TIGER. IF HE EYES YOU, YOU'RE 99% HISTORY. YOU GOTTA BE SCARED.
YOU'RE 13, RIGHT? ABOUT TIME YOU START LEARNING THE WAY IT IS.
WHAT DO YOU MEAN?
YOU'LL SEE.

PLOSH

THWACK
THWACK
THWACK

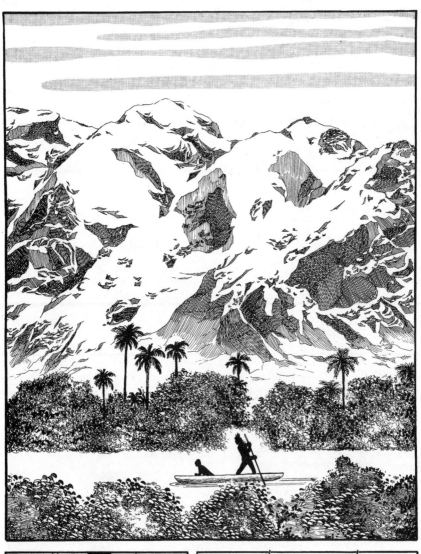

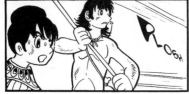

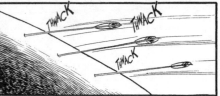

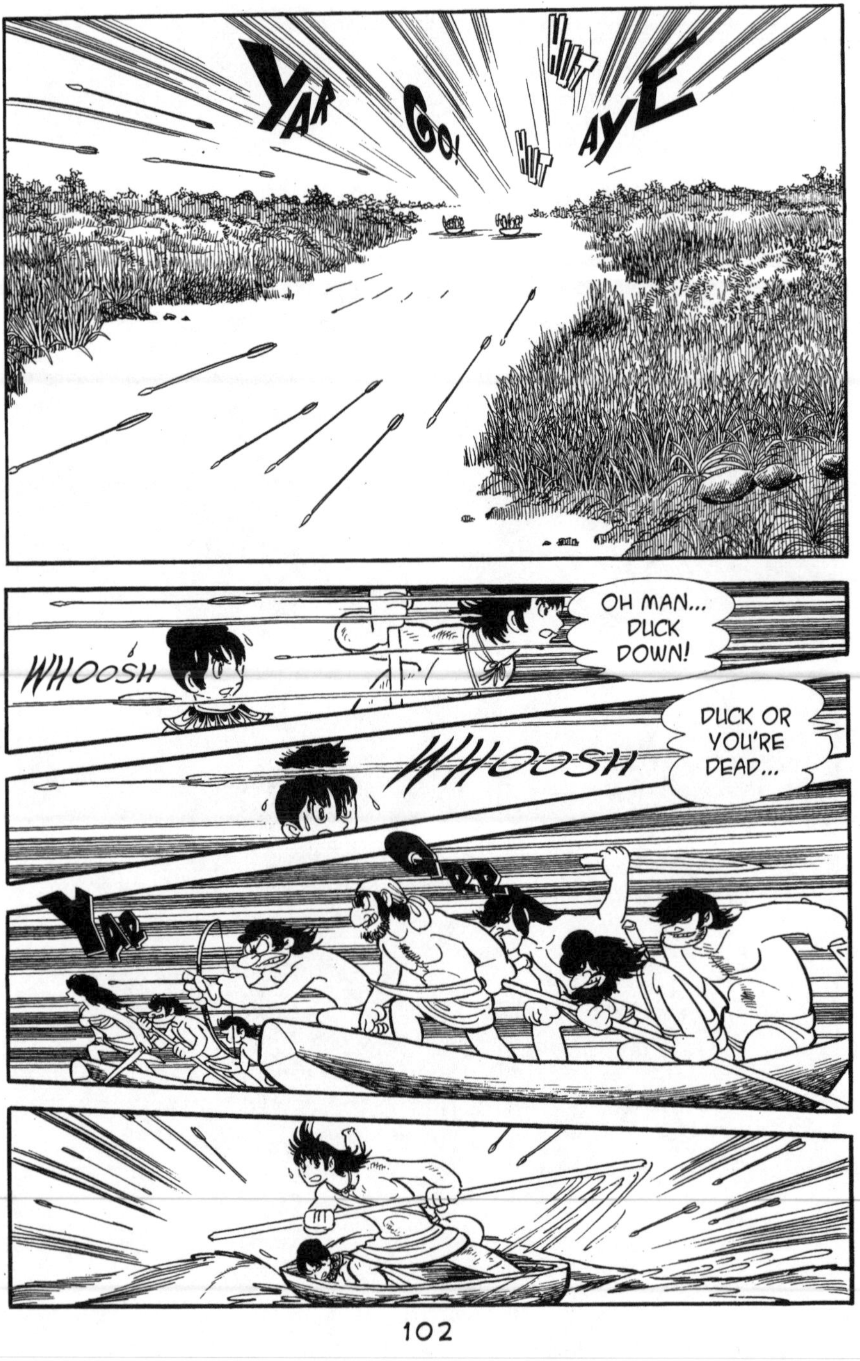
YAR
GO!
HUT
HUT
AYE
WHOOSH
OH MAN... DUCK DOWN!
WHOOSH
DUCK OR YOU'RE DEAD...
YAR

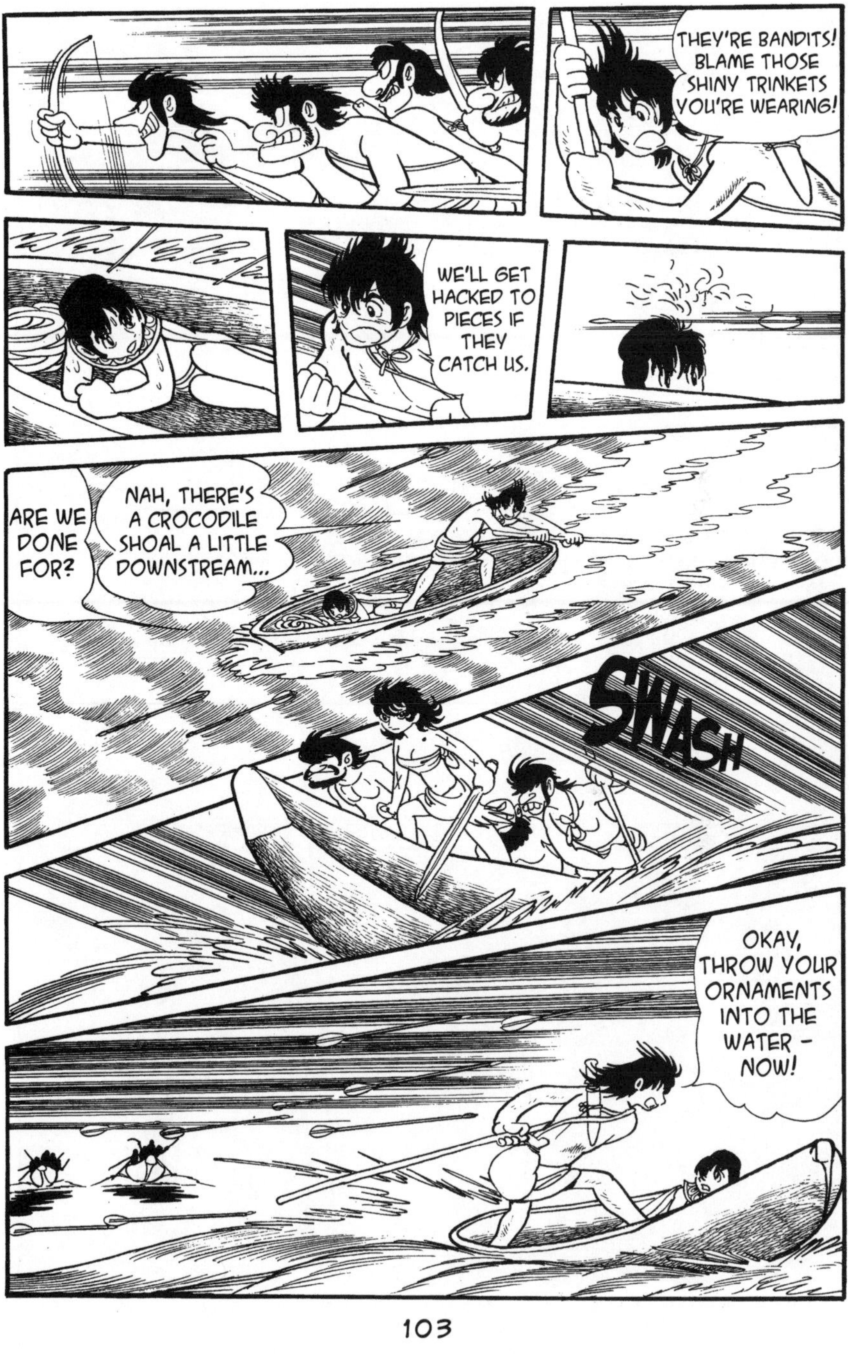
THEY'RE BANDITS! BLAME THOSE SHINY TRINKETS YOU'RE WEARING!
WE'LL GET HACKED TO PIECES IF THEY CATCH US.
ARE WE DONE FOR?
NAH, THERE'S A CROCODILE SHOAL A LITTLE DOWNSTREAM...
SWASH
OKAY, THROW YOUR ORNAMENTS INTO THE WATER - NOW!

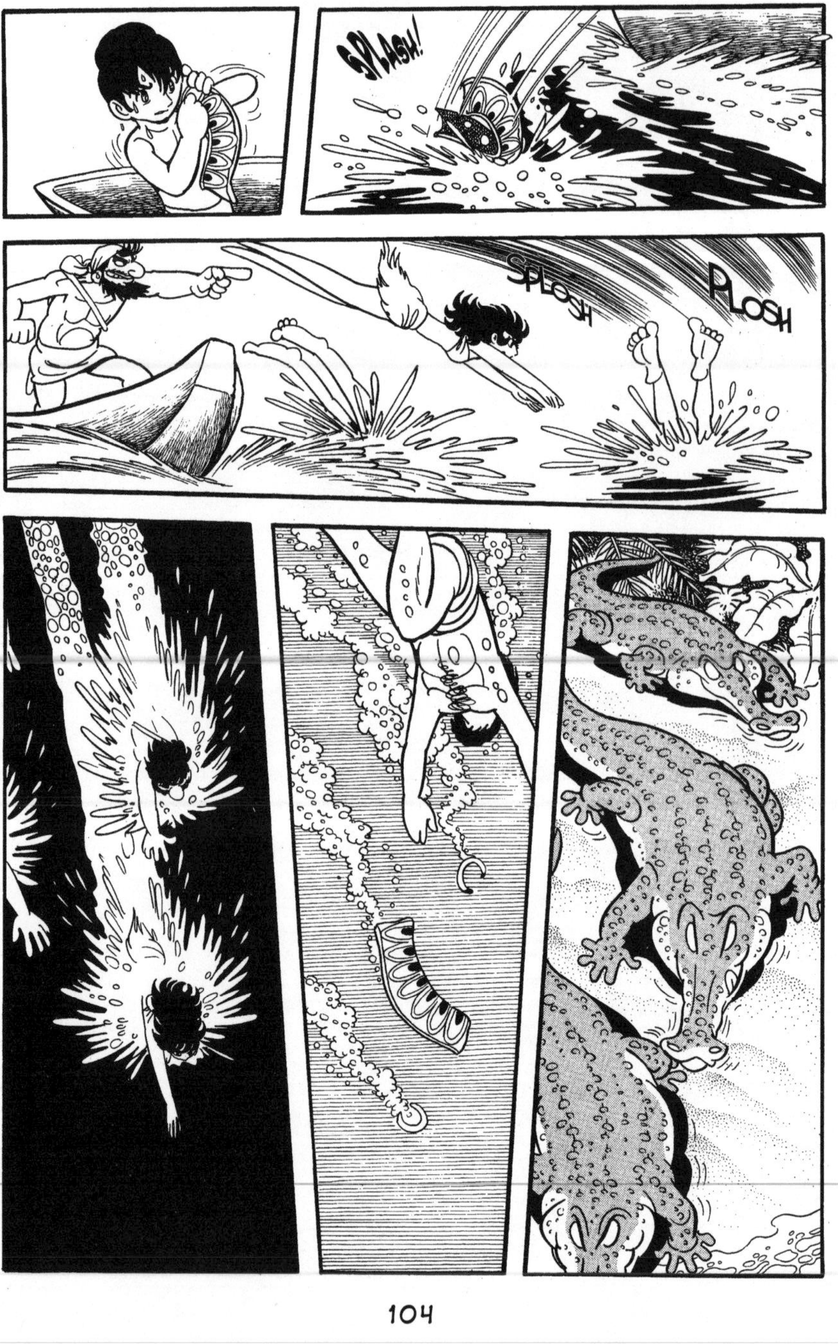
SPLASH!
SPLOSH
PLOSH

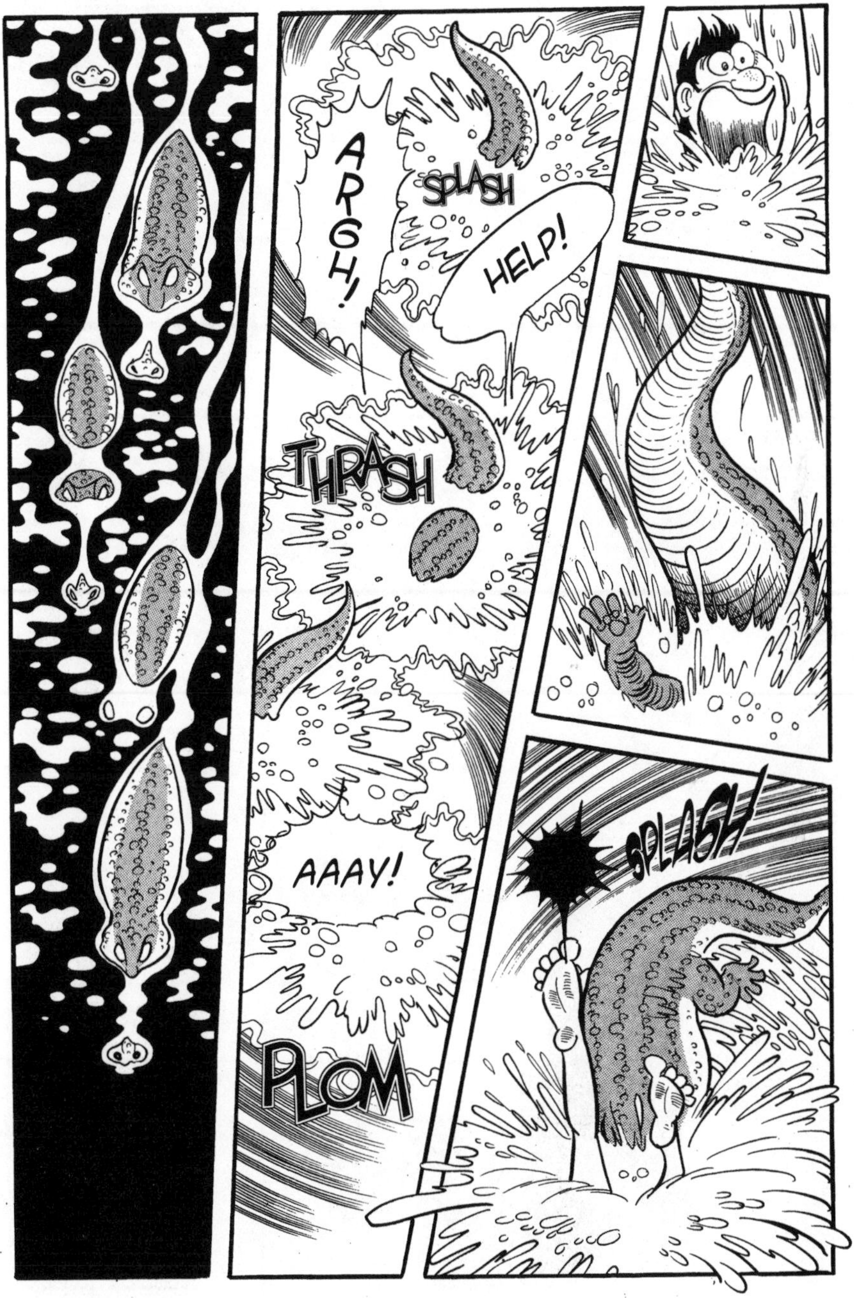
ARGH!
SPLASH
HELP!
THRASH
AAAY!
PLOM
SPLASH

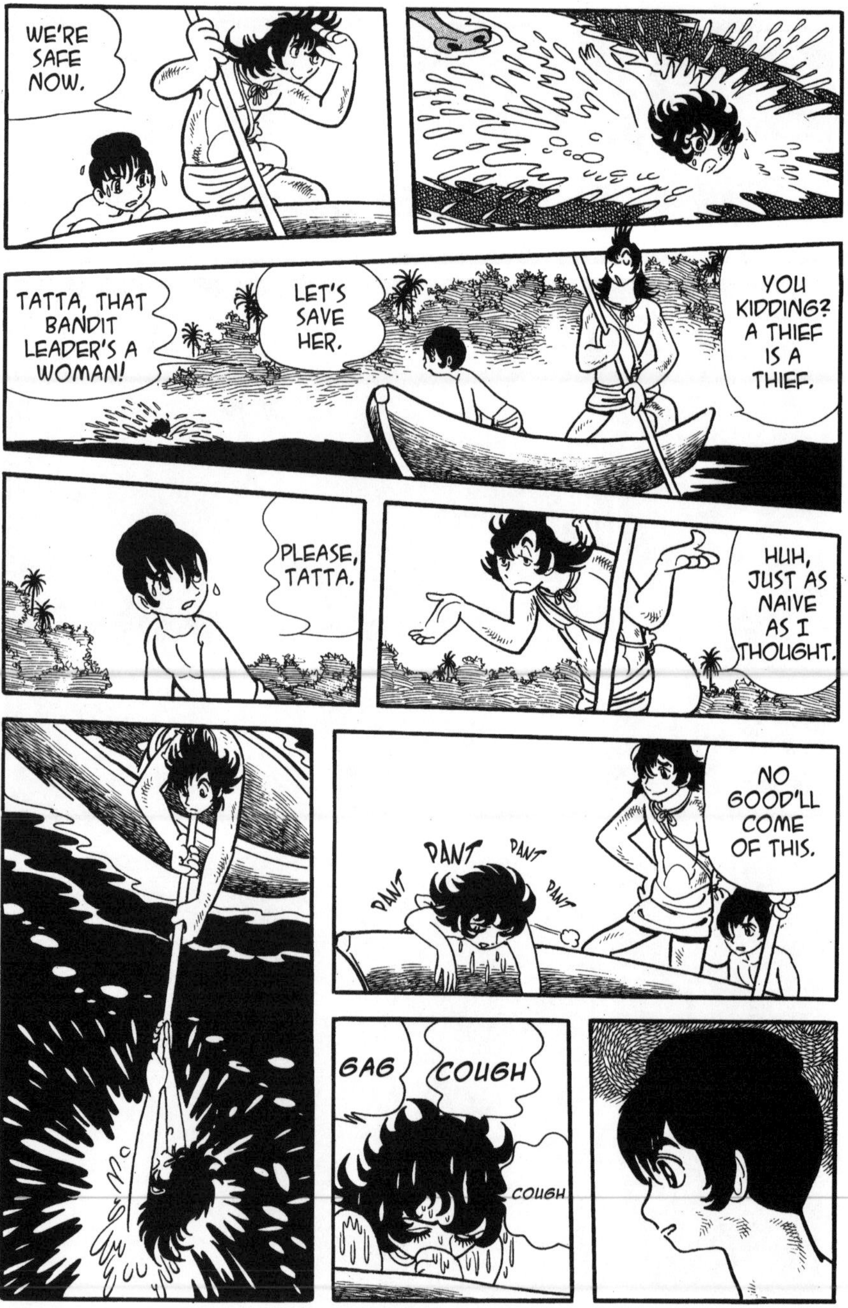

WE'RE SAFE NOW.
TATTA, THAT BANDIT LEADER'S A WOMAN!
LET'S SAVE HER.
YOU KIDDING? A THIEF IS A THIEF.
PLEASE, TATTA.
HUH, JUST AS NAIVE AS I THOUGHT.
PANT
PANT
PANT
PANT
NO GOOD'LL COME OF THIS.
GAG
COUGH
COUGH

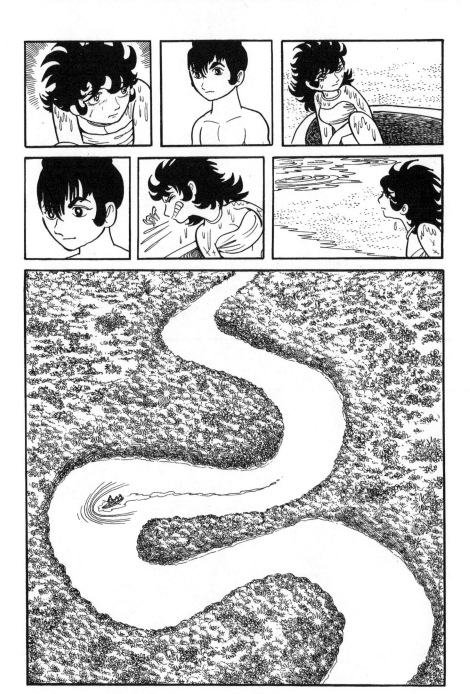

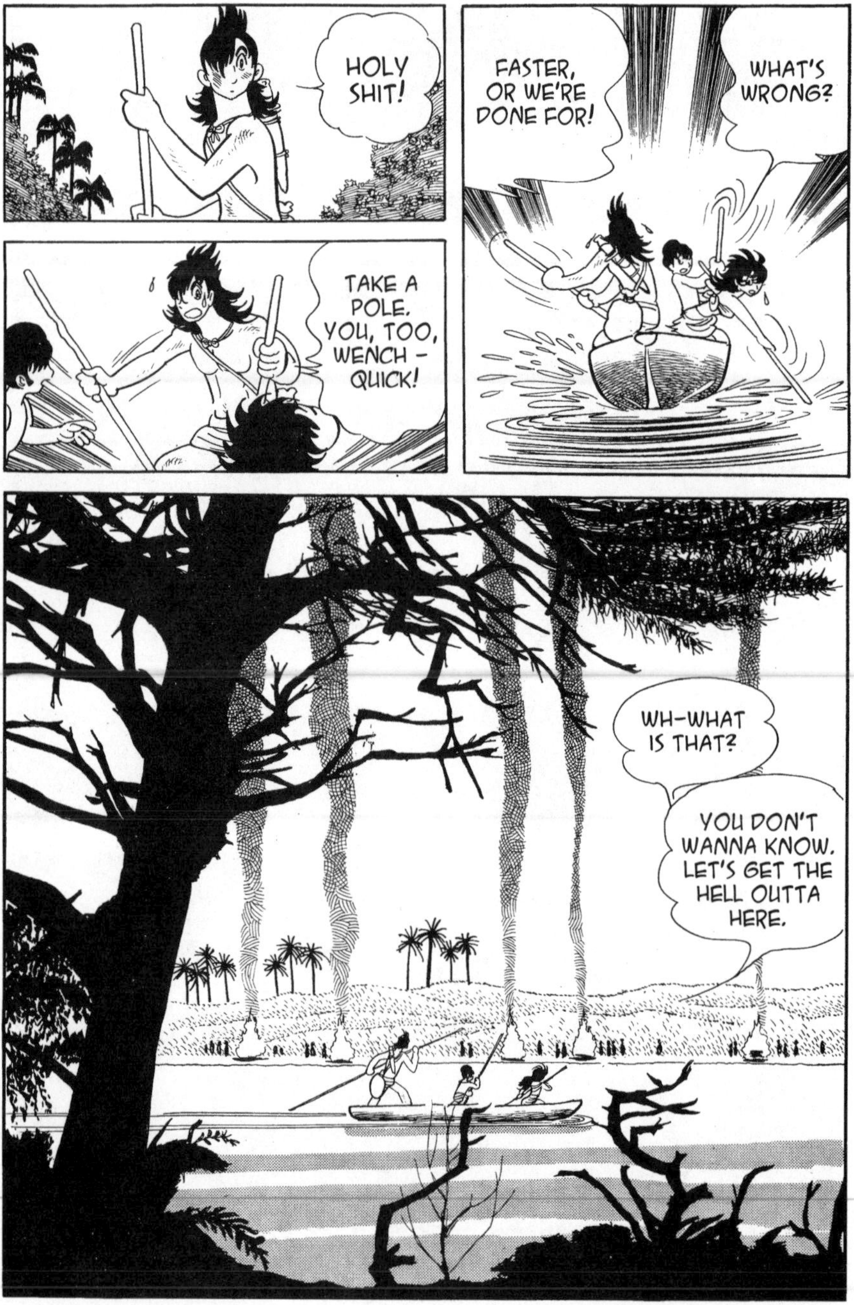
HOLY SHIT!
TAKE A POLE. YOU, TOO, WENCH - QUICK!
FASTER, OR WE'RE DONE FOR!
WHAT'S WRONG?
WH-WHAT IS THAT?
YOU DON'T WANNA KNOW. LET'S GET THE HELL OUTTA HERE.

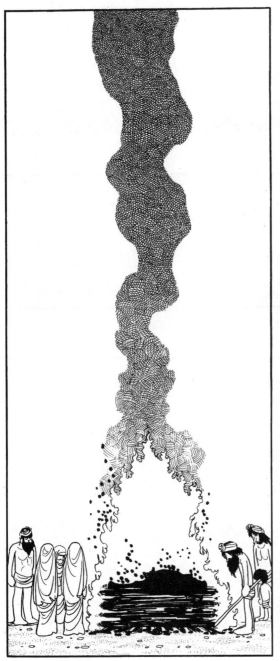

IT'S AN EPIDEMIC, THEY'RE BURNING THE CORPSES.

DON'T EVEN LOOK!

PANT

PANT

PANT

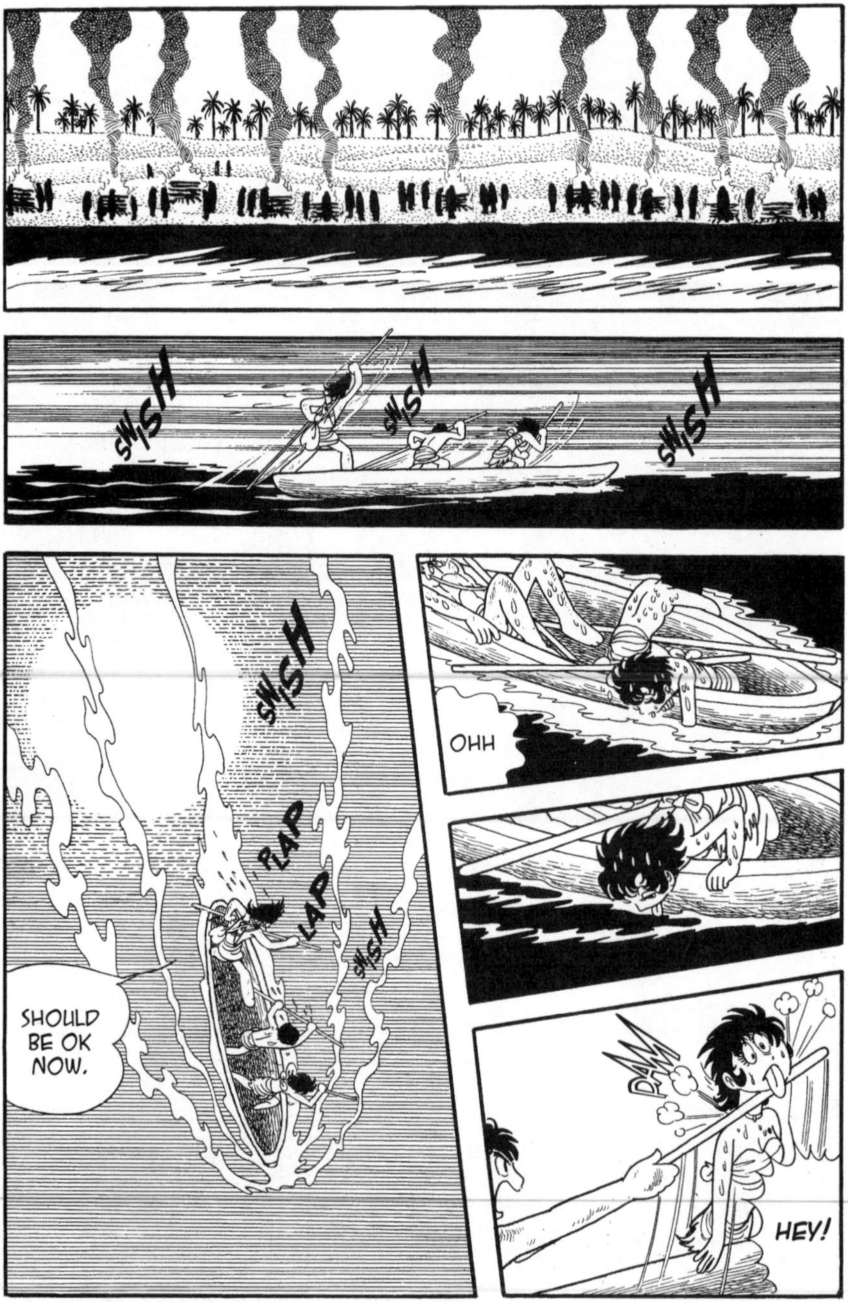
SWISH
SWISH
SWISH
SWISH
FLAP
LAP
SWISH
SHOULD BE OK NOW.
OHH
DAM
HEY!

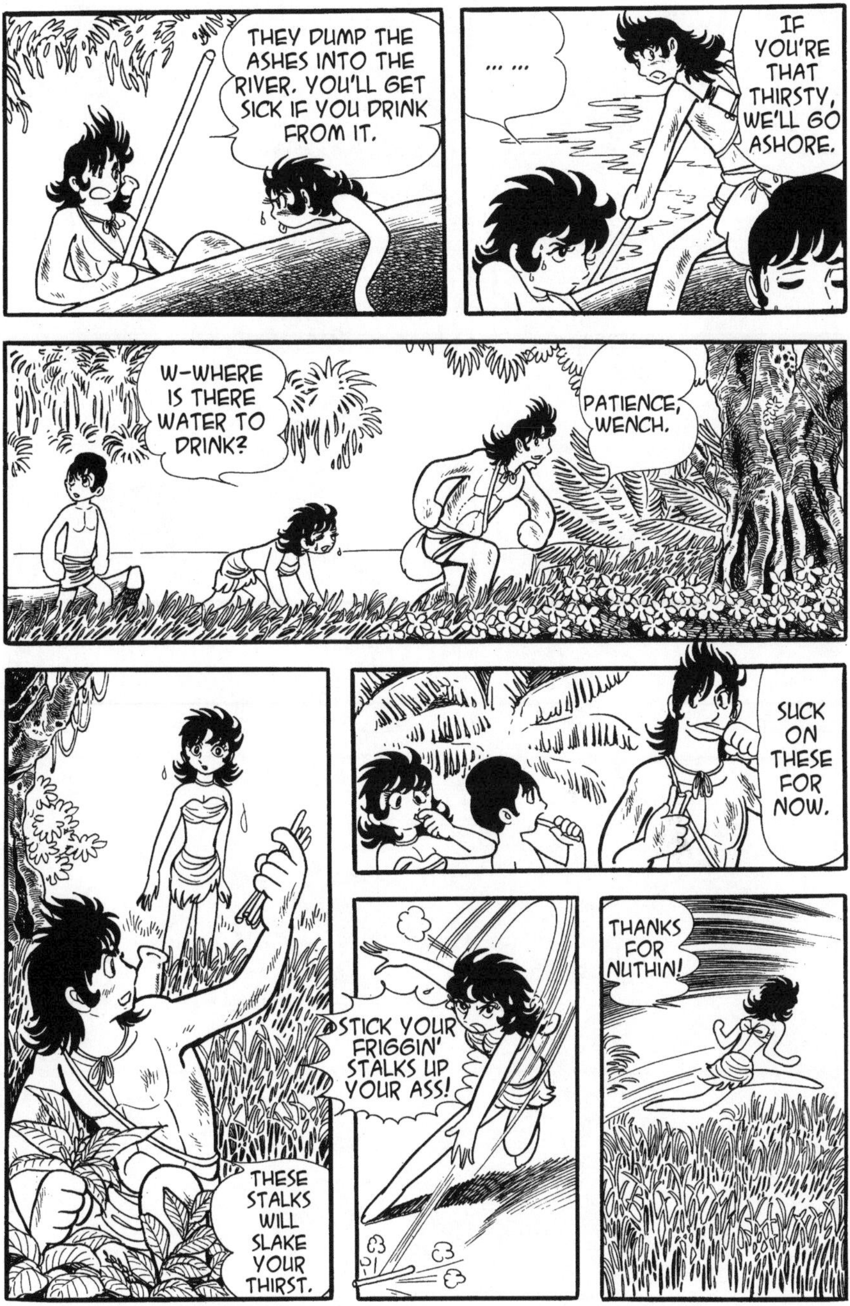
THEY DUMP THE ASHES INTO THE RIVER. YOU'LL GET SICK IF YOU DRINK FROM IT.
... ...
IF YOU'RE THAT THIRSTY, WE'LL GO ASHORE.
W-WHERE IS THERE WATER TO DRINK?
PATIENCE, WENCH.
THESE STALKS WILL SLAKE YOUR THIRST.
SUCK ON THESE FOR NOW.
STICK YOUR FRIGGIN' STALKS UP YOUR ASS!
THANKS FOR NUTHIN!

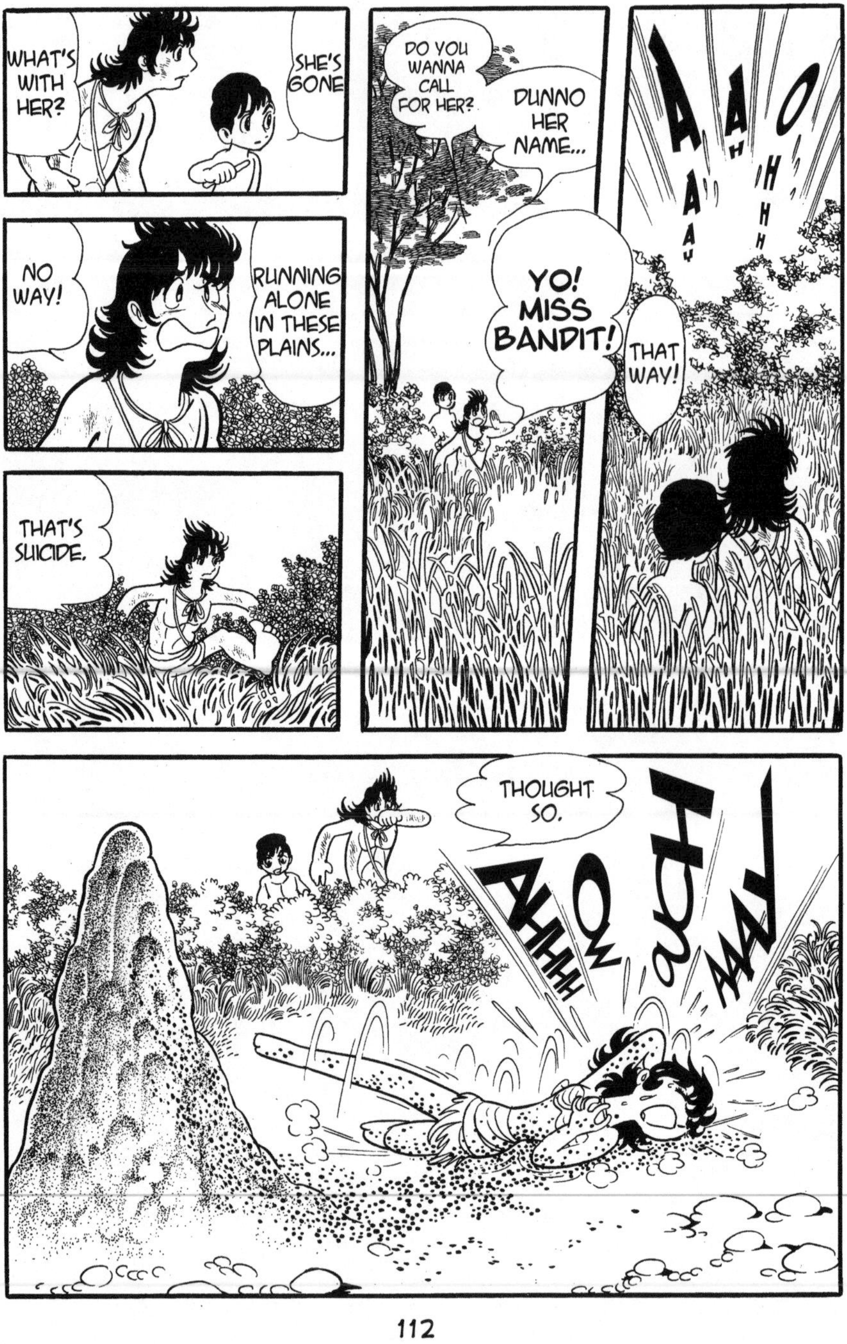
WHAT'S WITH HER?
SHE'S GONE
NO WAY!
RUNNING ALONE IN THESE PLAINS...
THAT'S SUICIDE.
DO YOU WANNA CALL FOR HER?
DUNNO HER NAME...
YO! MISS BANDIT!
AAAY
AH
OHHH
THAT WAY!
THOUGHT SO.
AHHHHH
OW
OUCH
AAAY

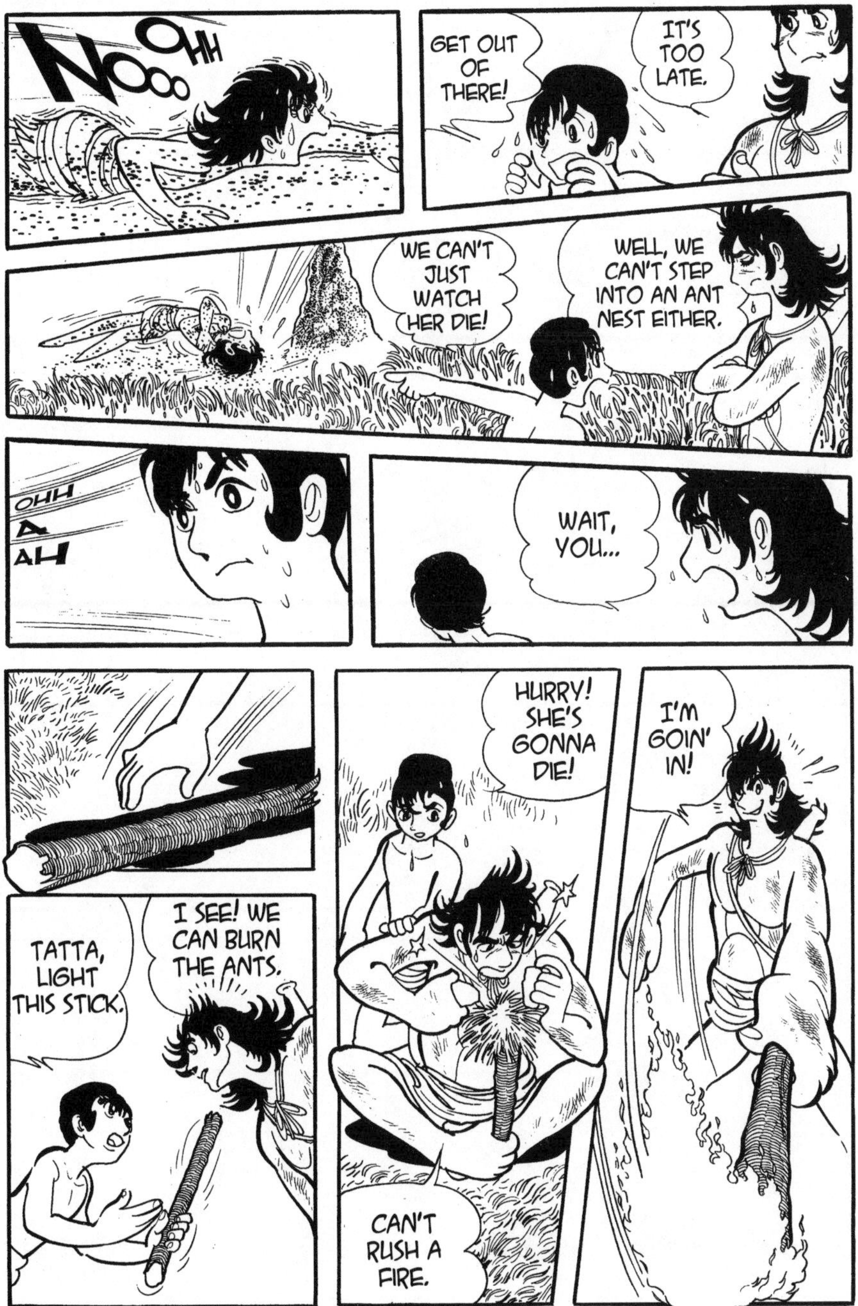
NOOOOHH
GET OUT OF THERE!
IT'S TOO LATE.
WE CAN'T JUST WATCH HER DIE!
WELL, WE CAN'T STEP INTO AN ANT NEST EITHER.
AHAOHH
WAIT, YOU...
TATTA, LIGHT THIS STICK.
I SEE! WE CAN BURN THE ANTS.
HURRY! SHE'S GONNA DIE!
CAN'T RUSH A FIRE.
I'M GOIN' IN!

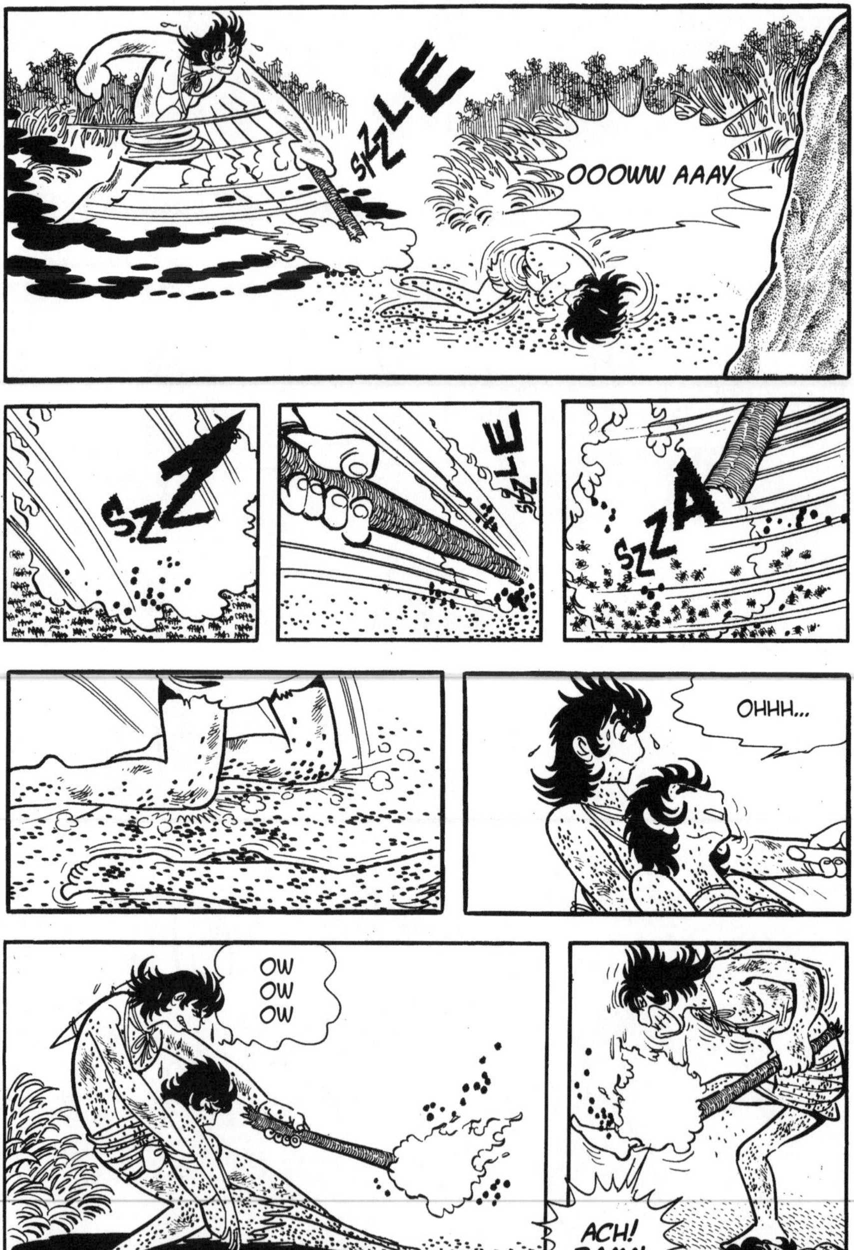
SIZZLE
OOOWW AAAY
SZZ
SIZZLE
SZZA
OHHH...
OW
OW
OW
ACH!
DAMN

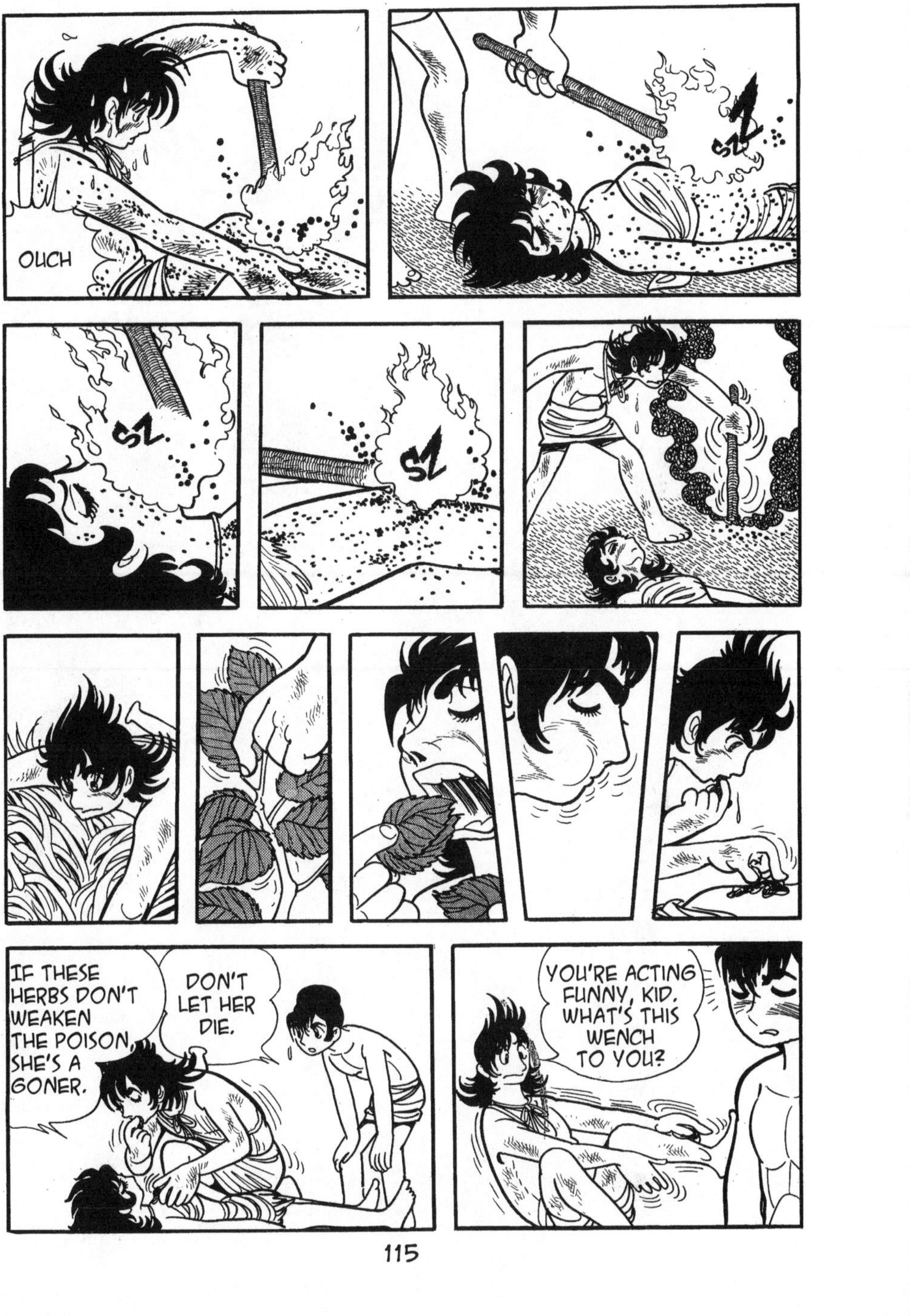

OUCH
SZ
SZ
SZ
IF THESE HERBS DON'T WEAKEN THE POISON, SHE'S A GONER.
DON'T LET HER DIE.
YOU'RE ACTING FUNNY, KID. WHAT'S THIS WENCH TO YOU?

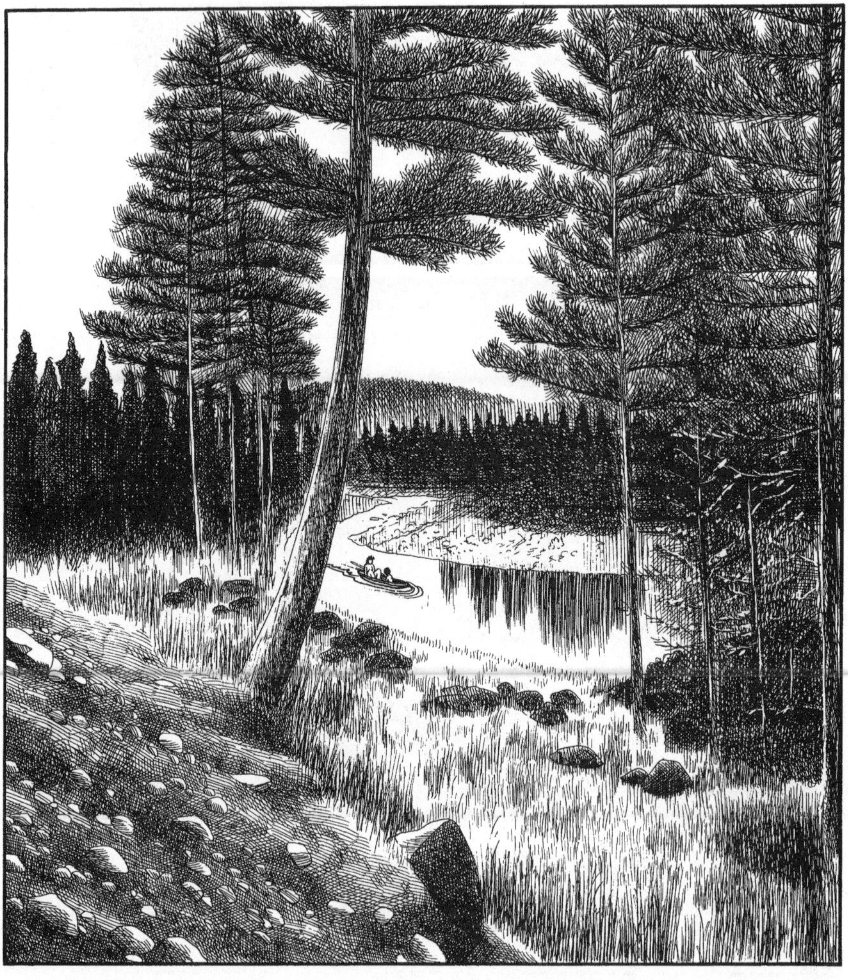

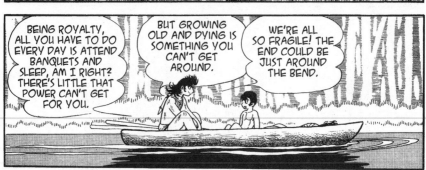

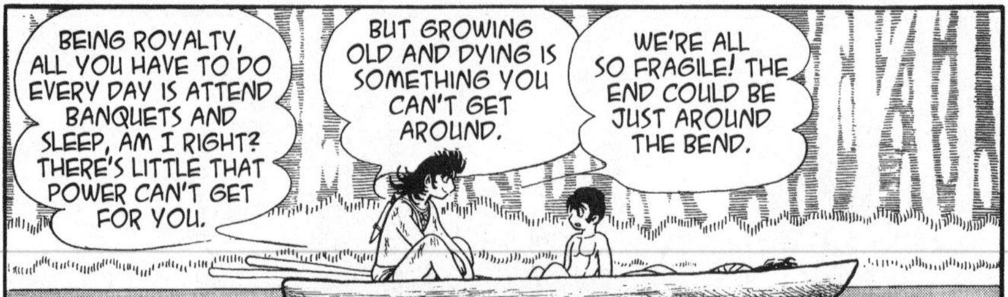
BEING ROYALTY, ALL YOU HAVE TO DO EVERY DAY IS ATTEND BANQUETS AND SLEEP, AM I RIGHT? THERE'S LITTLE THAT POWER CAN'T GET FOR YOU.
BUT GROWING OLD AND DYING IS SOMETHING YOU CAN'T GET AROUND.
WE'RE ALL SO FRAGILE! THE END COULD BE JUST AROUND THE BEND.

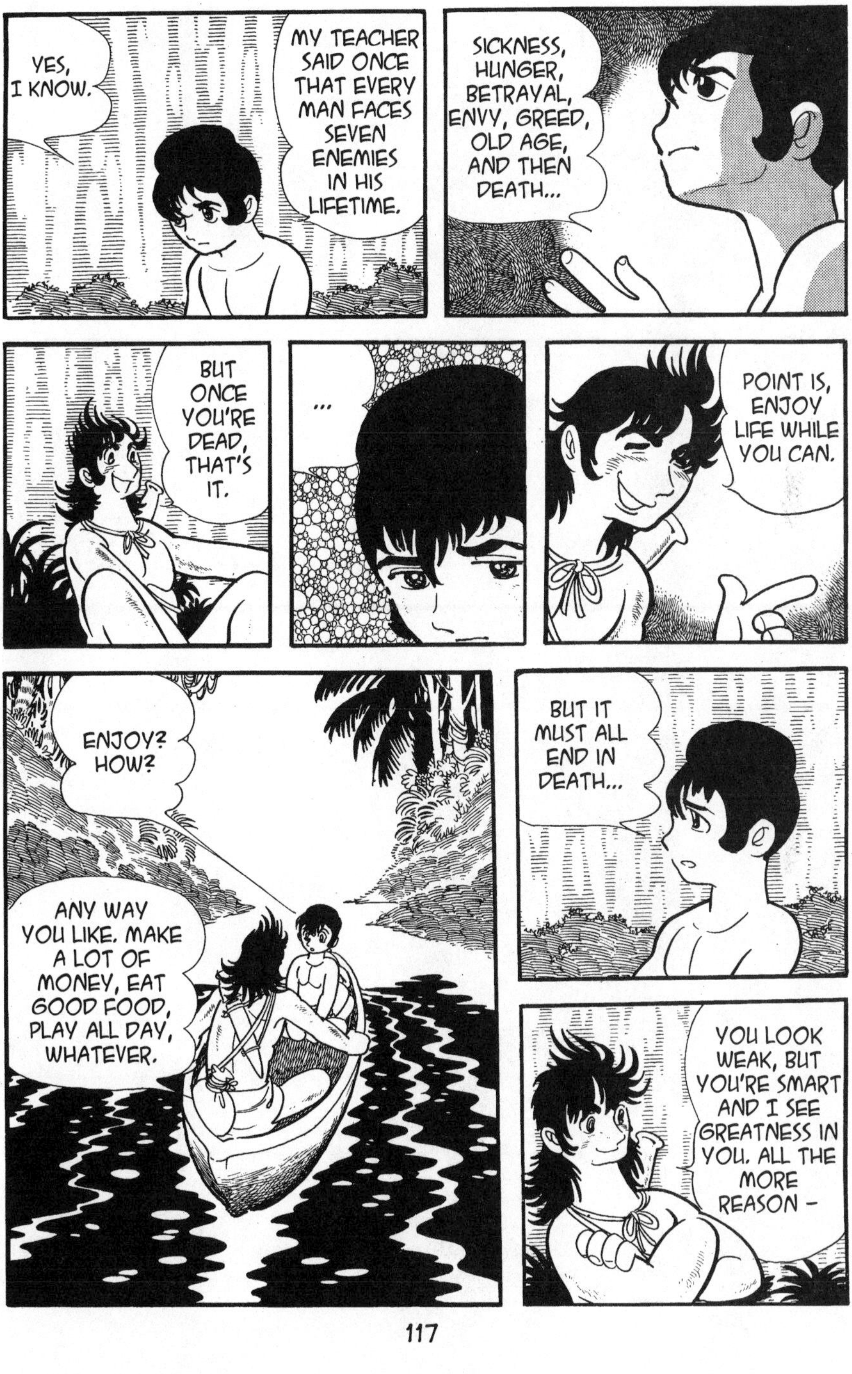
YES, I KNOW.
MY TEACHER SAID ONCE THAT EVERY MAN FACES SEVEN ENEMIES IN HIS LIFETIME.
SICKNESS, HUNGER, BETRAYAL, ENVY, GREED, OLD AGE, AND THEN DEATH...
BUT ONCE YOU'RE DEAD, THAT'S IT.
...
POINT IS, ENJOY LIFE WHILE YOU CAN.
ENJOY? HOW?
ANY WAY YOU LIKE. MAKE A LOT OF MONEY, EAT GOOD FOOD, PLAY ALL DAY, WHATEVER.
BUT IT MUST ALL END IN DEATH...
YOU LOOK WEAK, BUT YOU'RE SMART AND I SEE GREATNESS IN YOU. ALL THE MORE REASON -

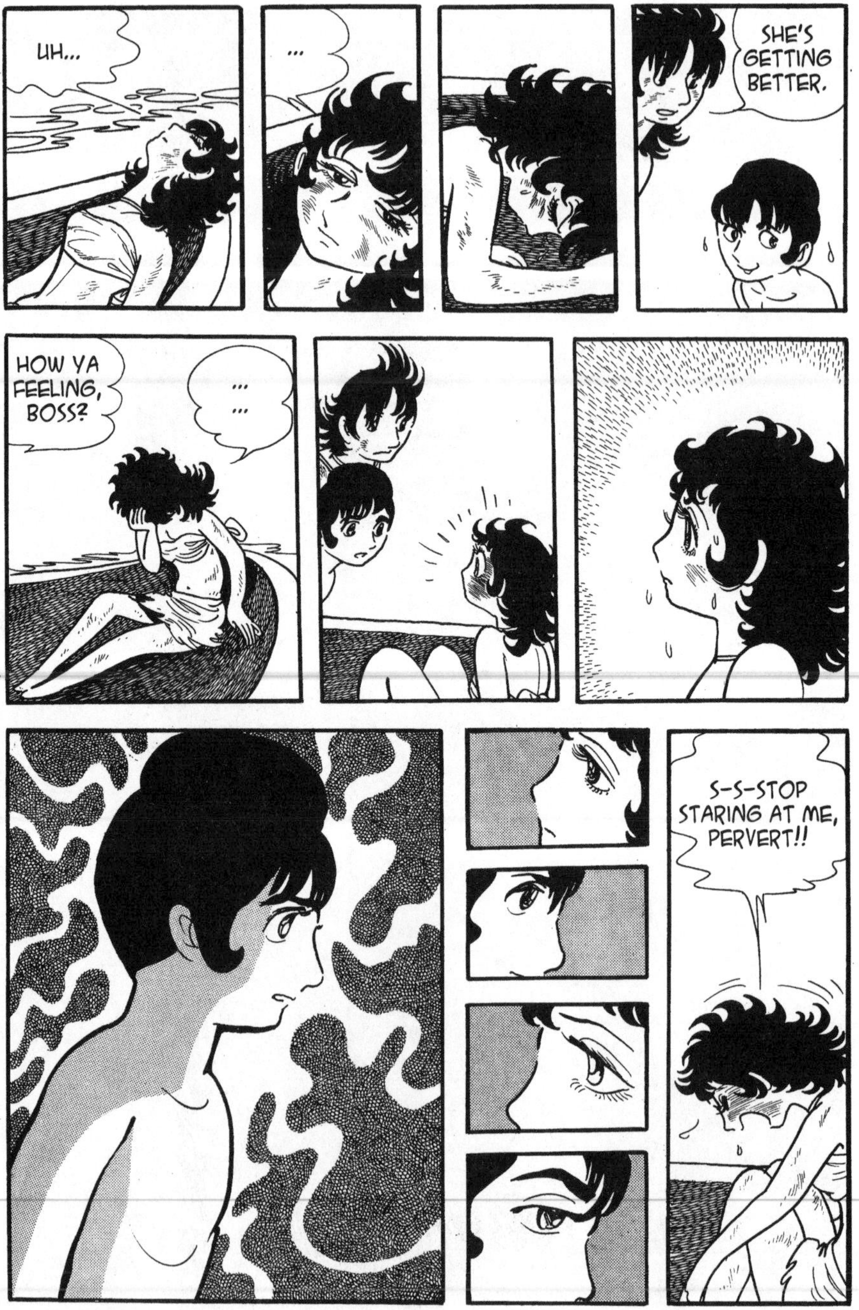
UH...
...
SHE'S GETTING BETTER.
HOW YA FEELING, BOSS?
... ...
S-S-STOP STARING AT ME, PERVERT!!

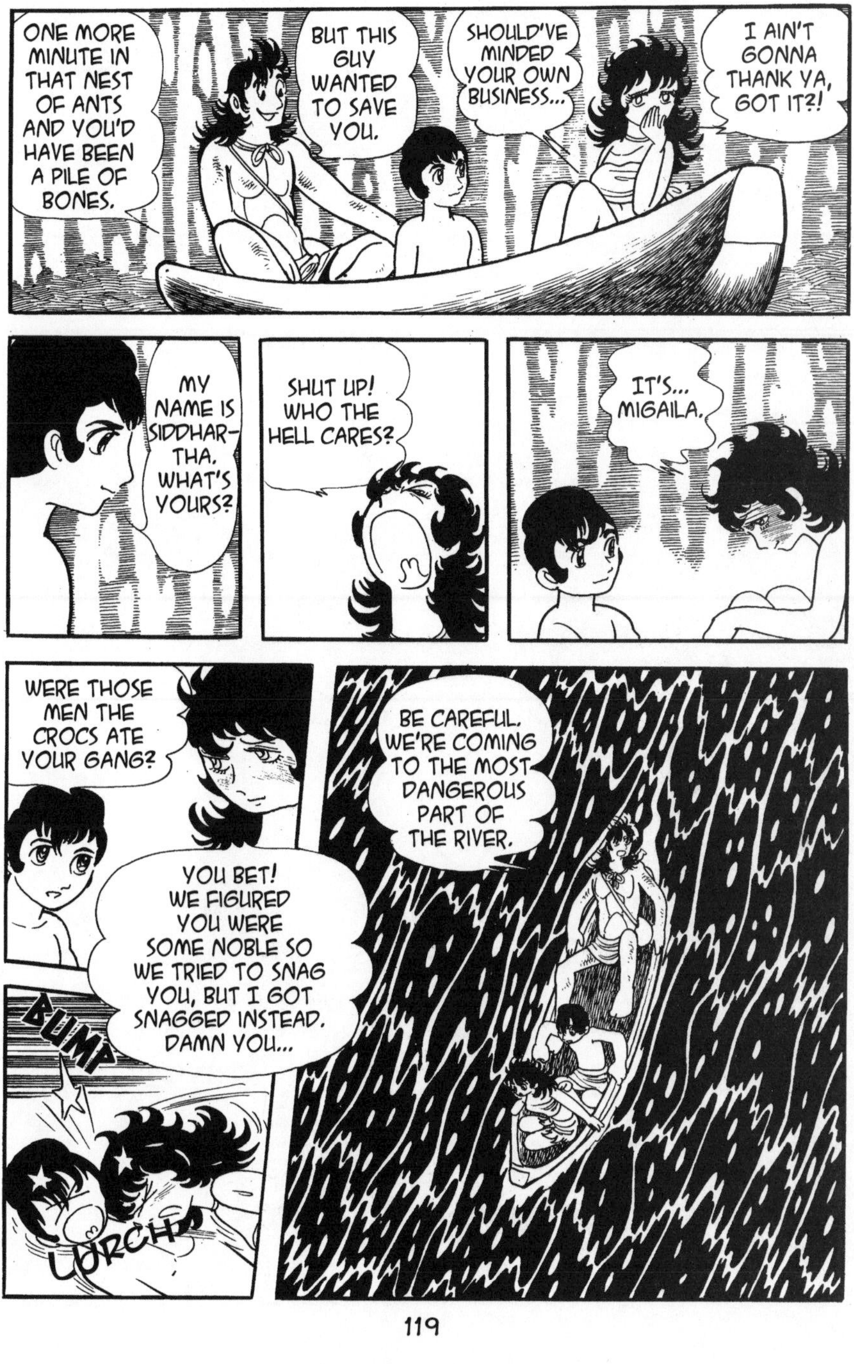
ONE MORE MINUTE IN THAT NEST OF ANTS AND YOU'D HAVE BEEN A PILE OF BONES.
BUT THIS GUY WANTED TO SAVE YOU.
SHOULD'VE MINDED YOUR OWN BUSINESS...
I AIN'T GONNA THANK YA, GOT IT?!
MY NAME IS SIDDHARTHA. WHAT'S YOURS?
SHUT UP! WHO THE HELL CARES?
IT'S... MIGAILA.
WERE THOSE MEN THE CROCS ATE YOUR GANG?
YOU BET! WE FIGURED YOU WERE SOME NOBLE SO WE TRIED TO SNAG YOU, BUT I GOT SNAGGED INSTEAD. DAMN YOU...
BUMP
LURCH
BE CAREFUL. WE'RE COMING TO THE MOST DANGEROUS PART OF THE RIVER.

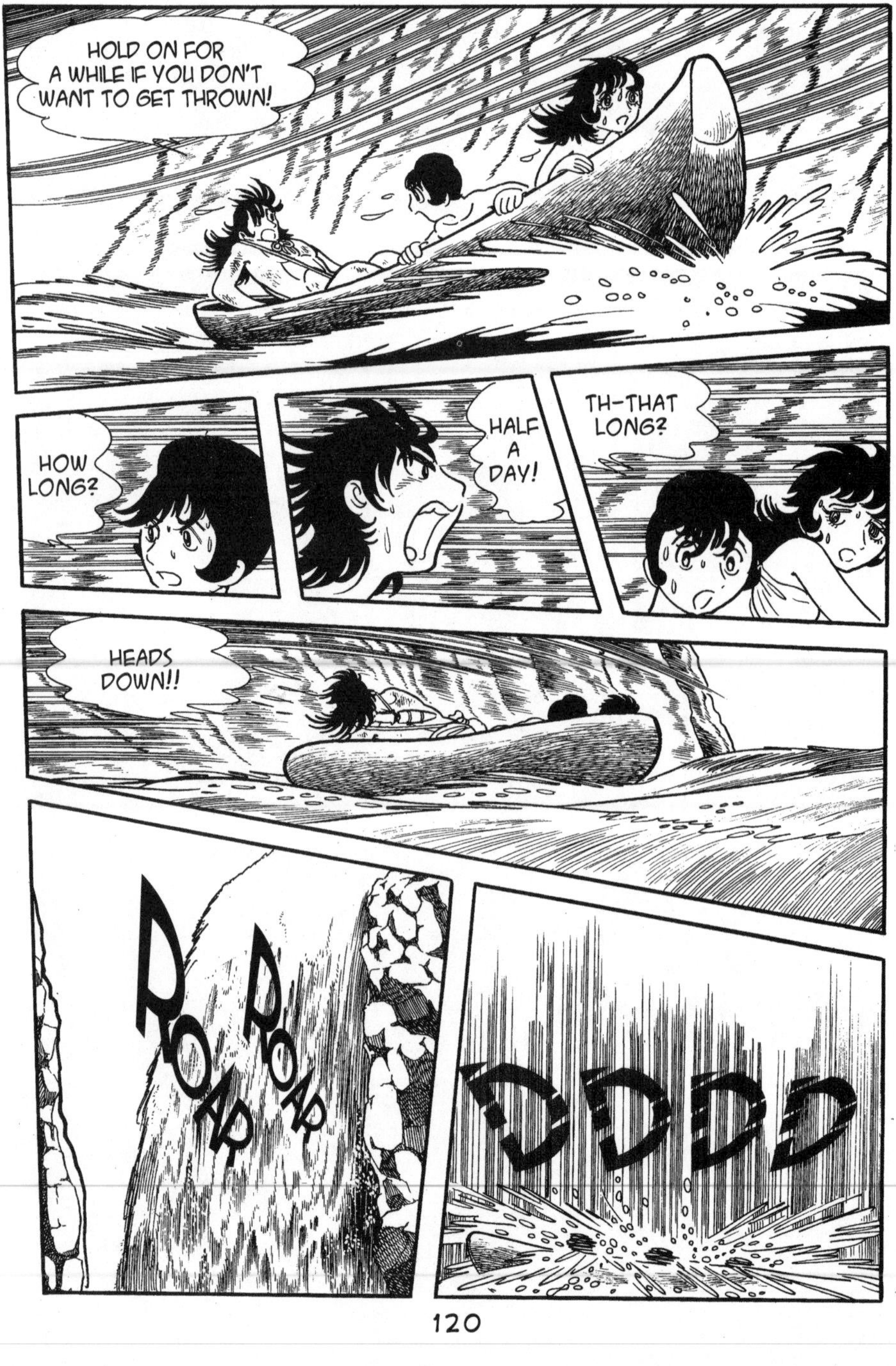
HOLD ON FOR A WHILE IF YOU DON'T WANT TO GET THROWN!
HOW LONG?
HALF A DAY!
TH-THAT LONG?
HEADS DOWN!!
ROAR ROAR
DDDDD

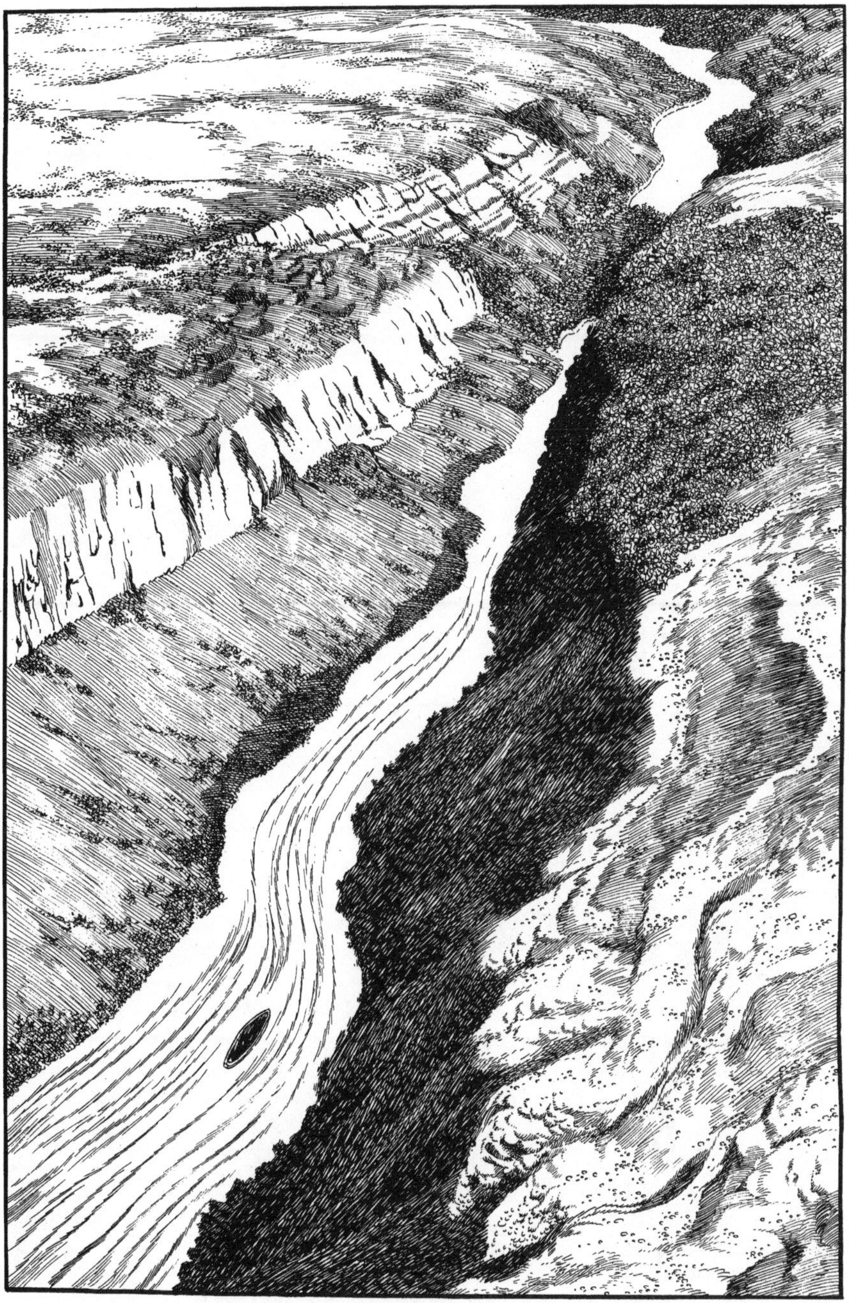

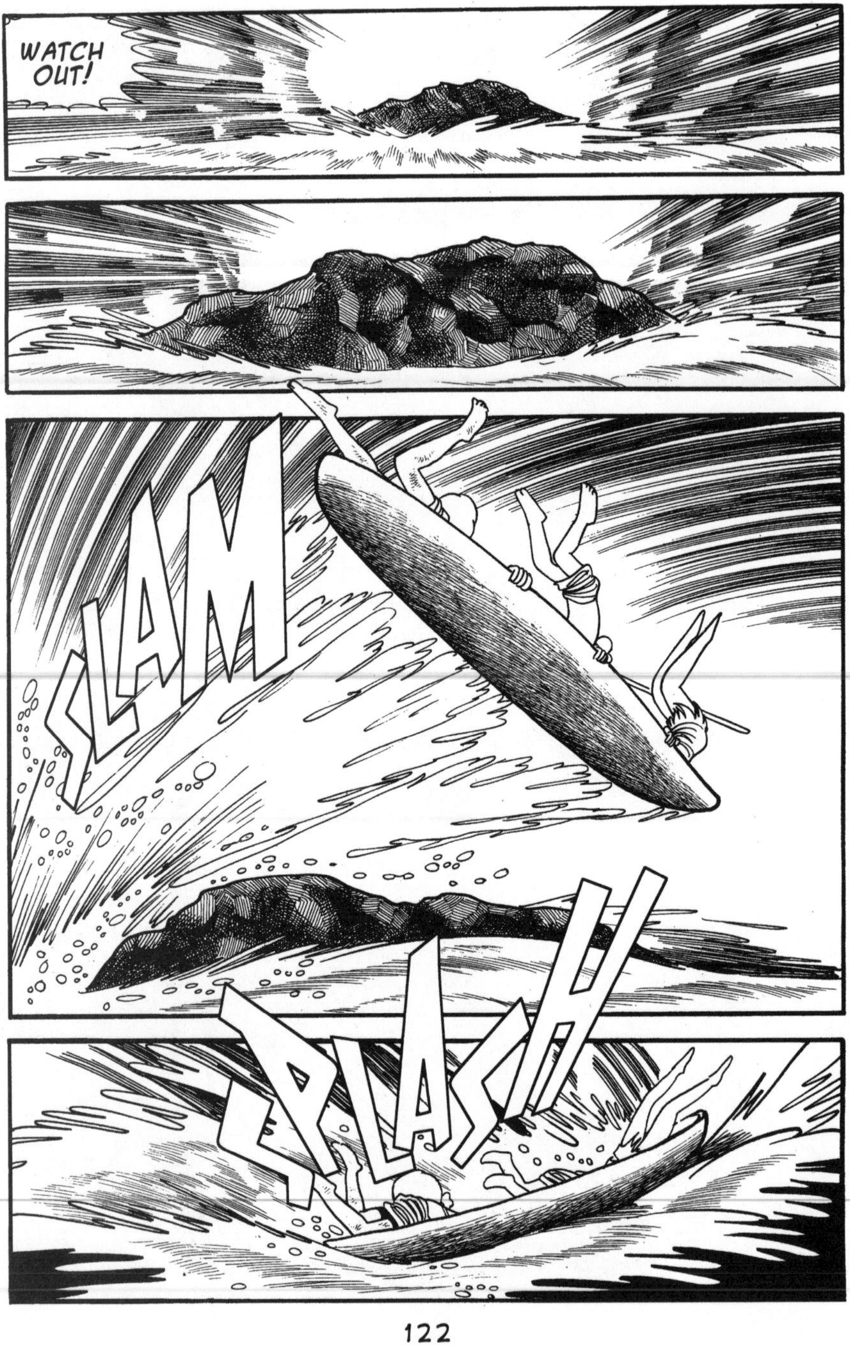
WATCH OUT!
SLAM
SPLASH

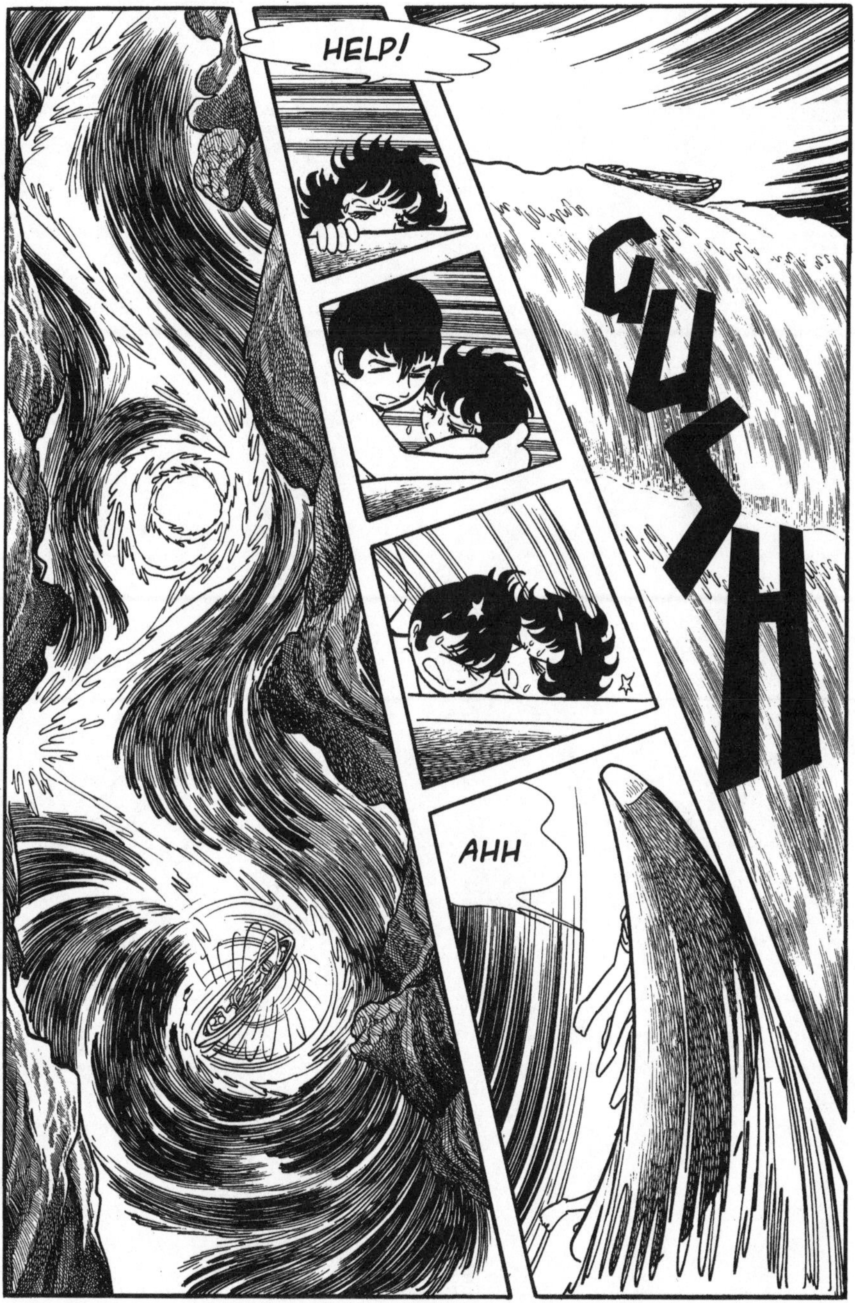
HELP!
GUSH
AHH

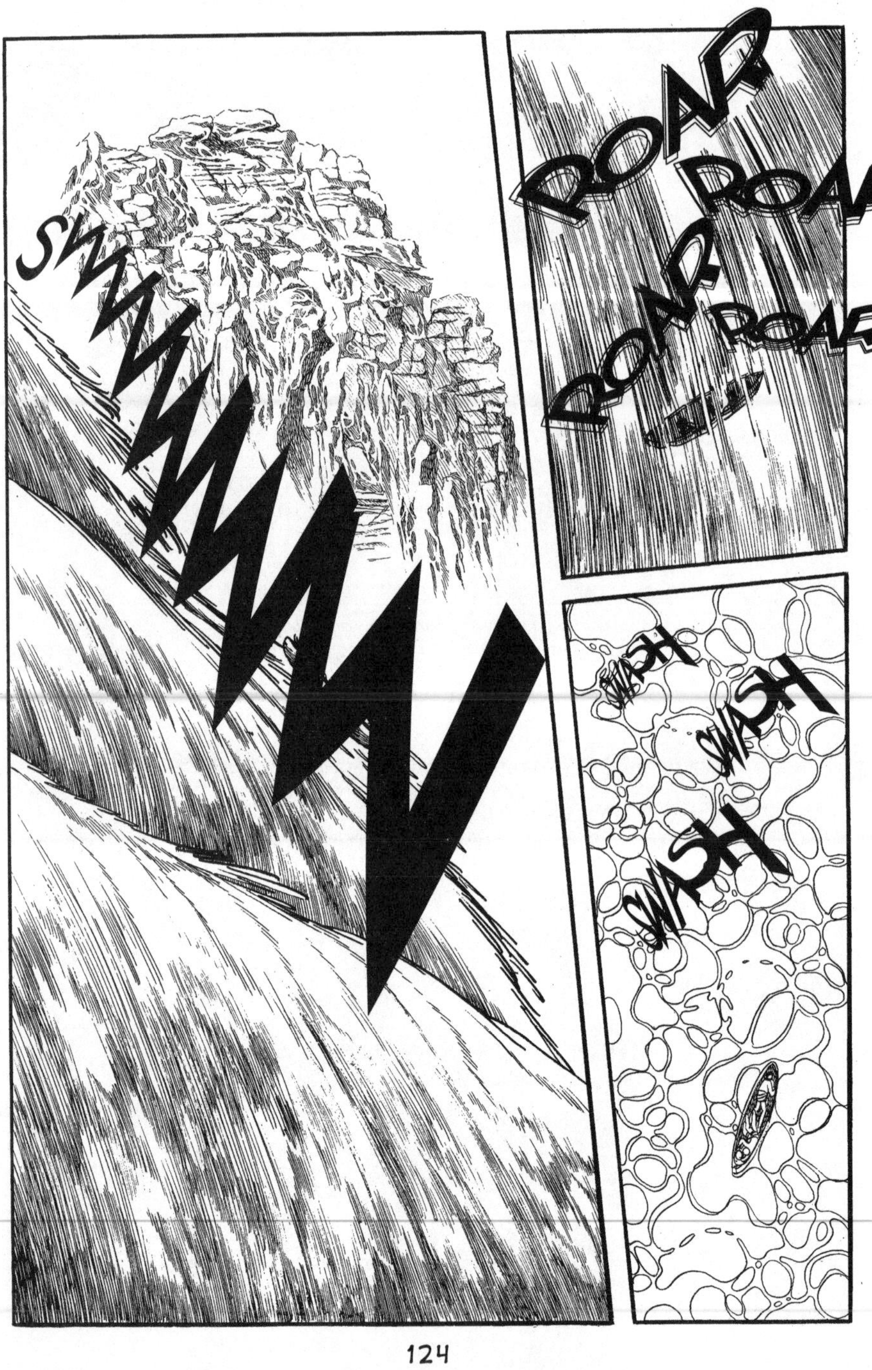
SWWWWWV
ROAR
ROAR
ROAR
ROAR
SWASH
SWASH
SWASH

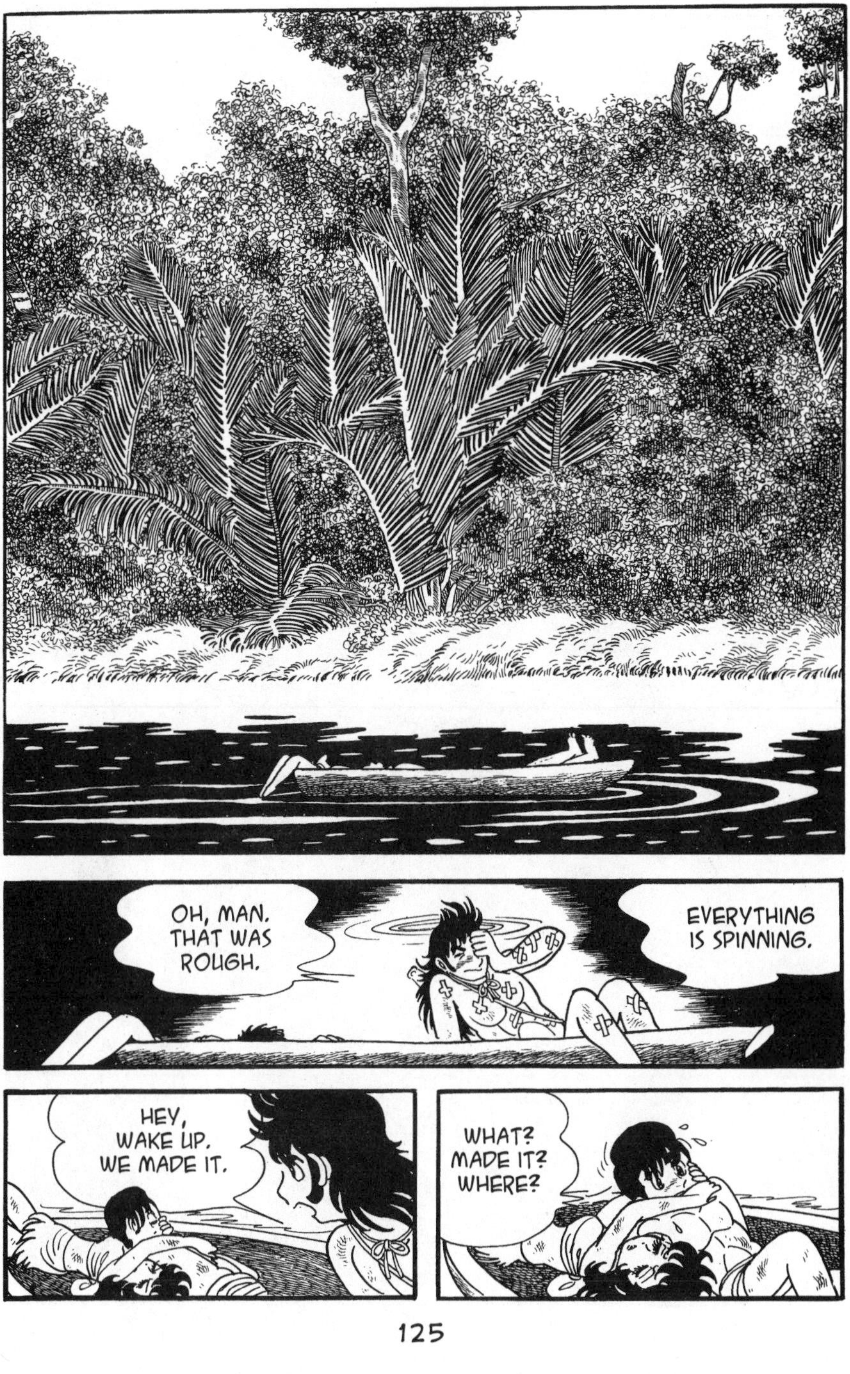

OH, MAN. THAT WAS ROUGH.
EVERYTHING IS SPINNING.
HEY, WAKE UP. WE MADE IT.
WHAT? MADE IT? WHERE?

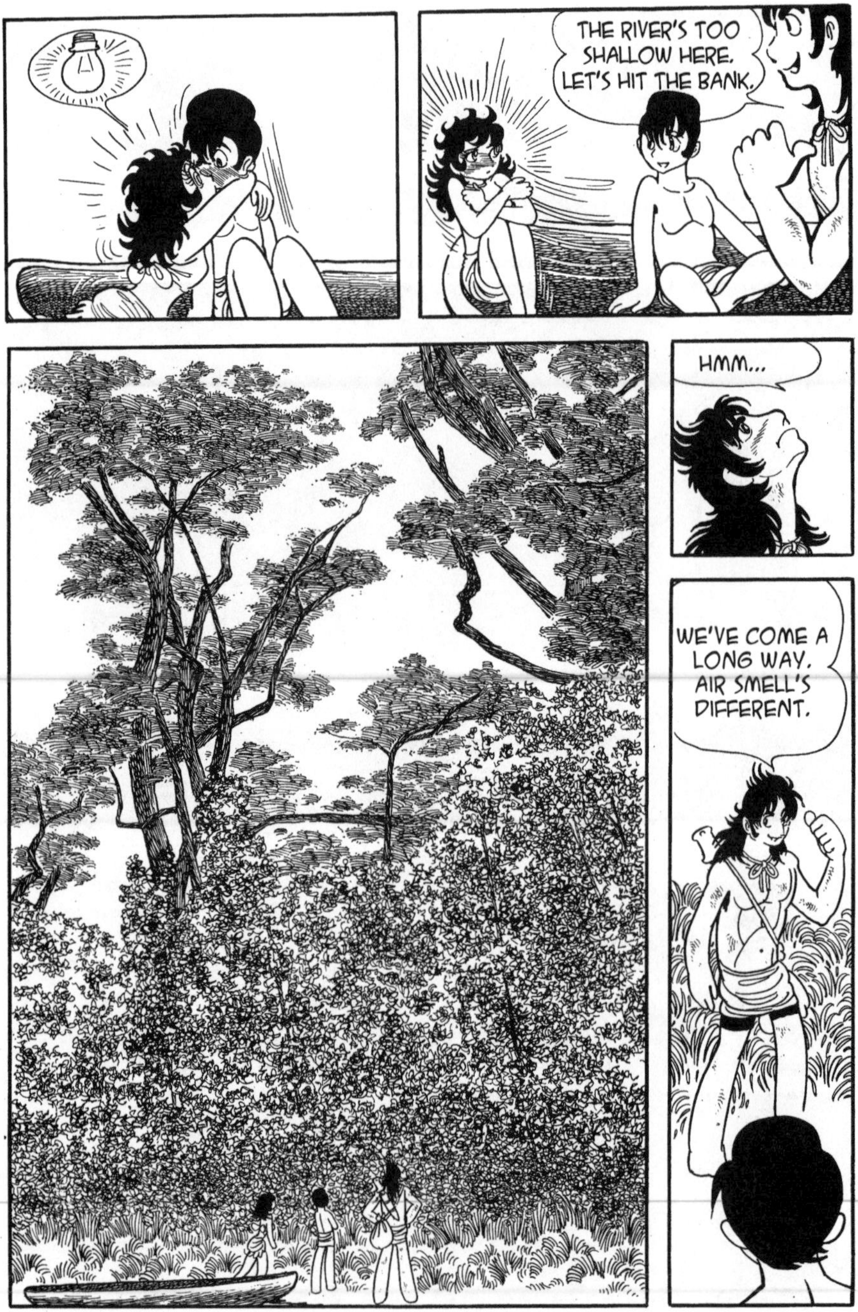
THE RIVER'S TOO SHALLOW HERE. LET'S HIT THE BANK.
HMM...
WE'VE COME A LONG WAY. AIR SMELL'S DIFFERENT.

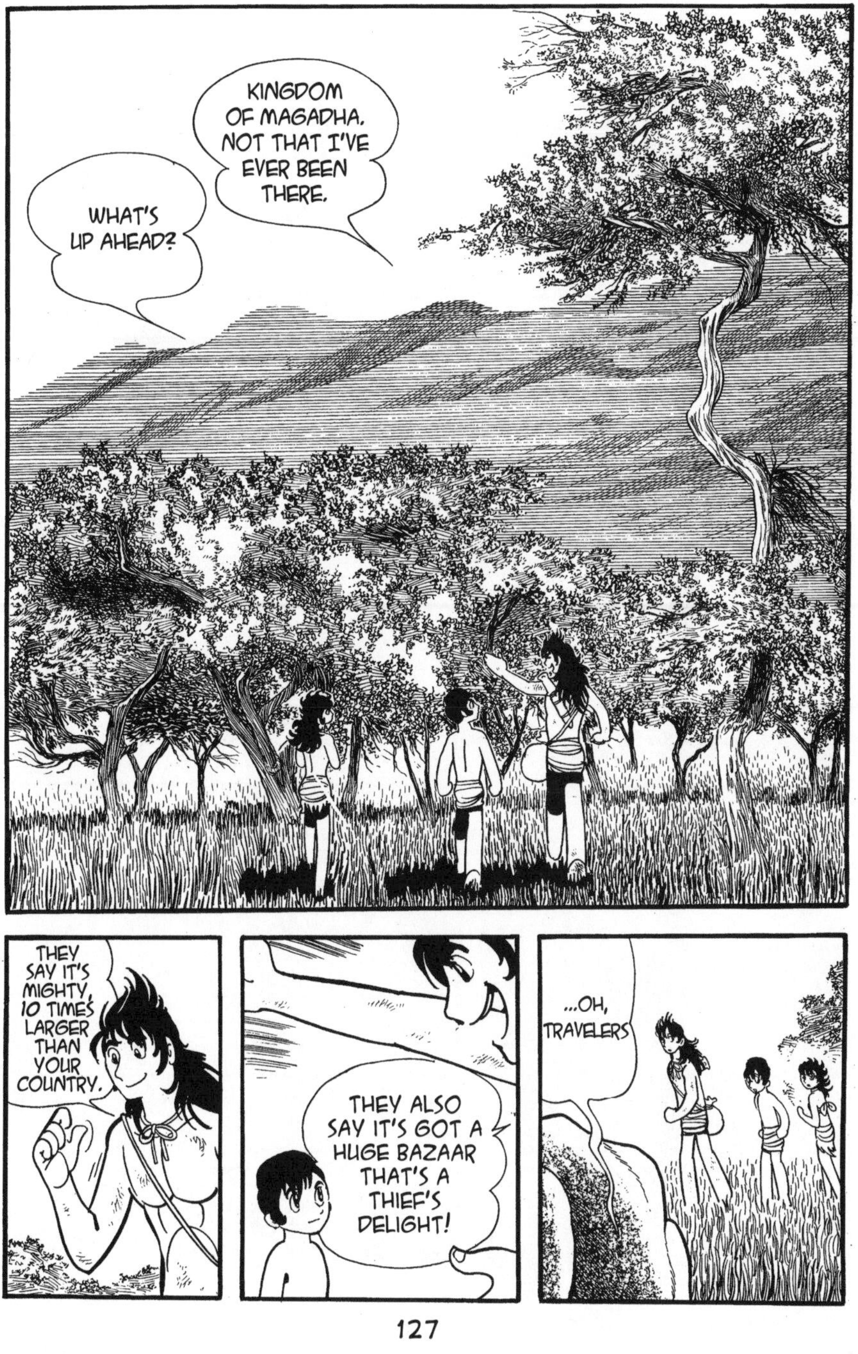
WHAT'S UP AHEAD?
KINGDOM OF MAGADHA. NOT THAT I'VE EVER BEEN THERE.
THEY SAY IT'S MIGHTY, 10 TIMES LARGER THAN YOUR COUNTRY.
THEY ALSO SAY IT'S GOT A HUGE BAZAAR THAT'S A THIEF'S DELIGHT!
...OH, TRAVELERS

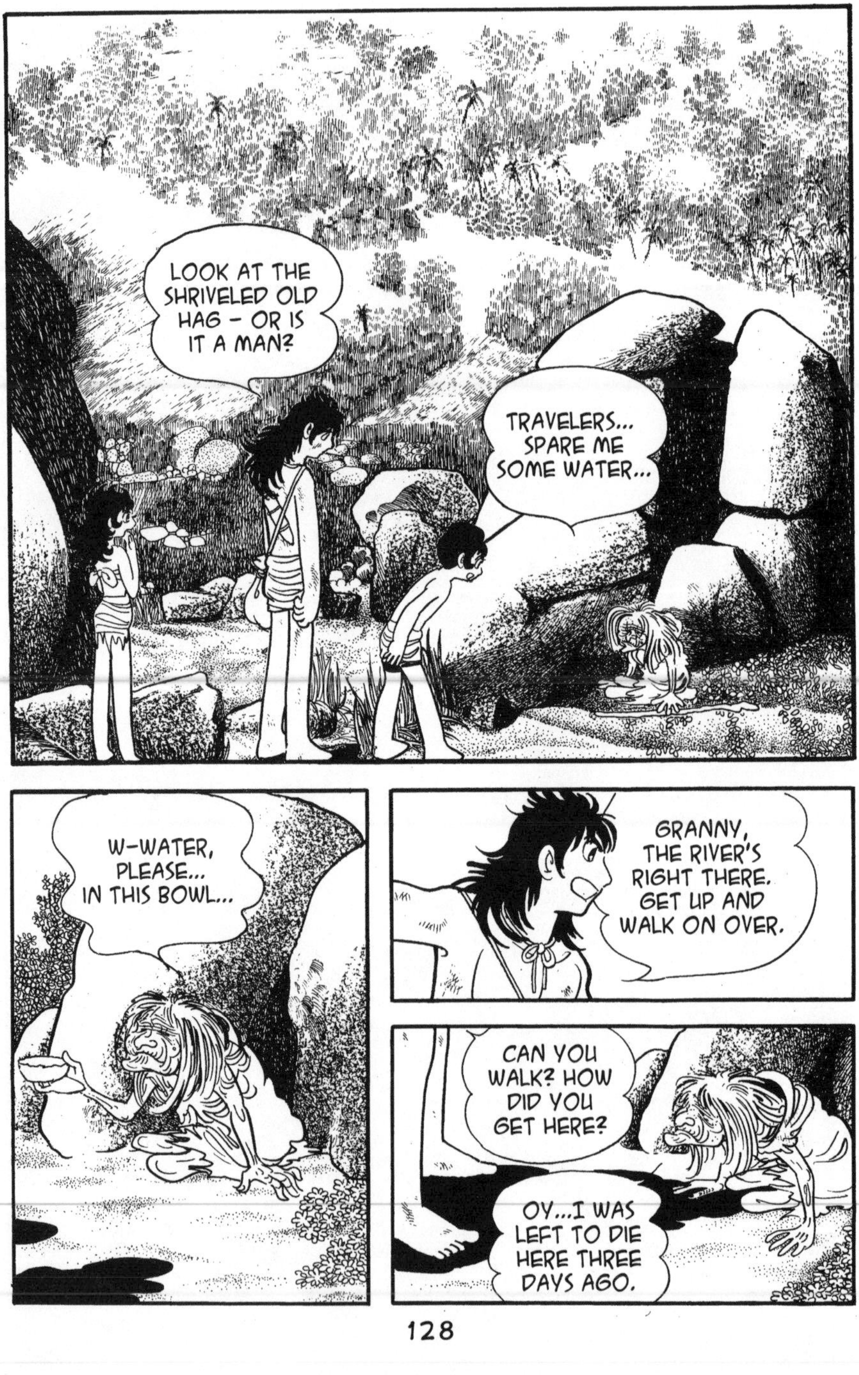
LOOK AT THE SHRIVELED OLD HAG – OR IS IT A MAN?
TRAVELERS... SPARE ME SOME WATER...
W-WATER, PLEASE... IN THIS BOWL...
GRANNY, THE RIVER'S RIGHT THERE. GET UP AND WALK ON OVER.
CAN YOU WALK? HOW DID YOU GET HERE?
OY...I WAS LEFT TO DIE HERE THREE DAYS AGO.

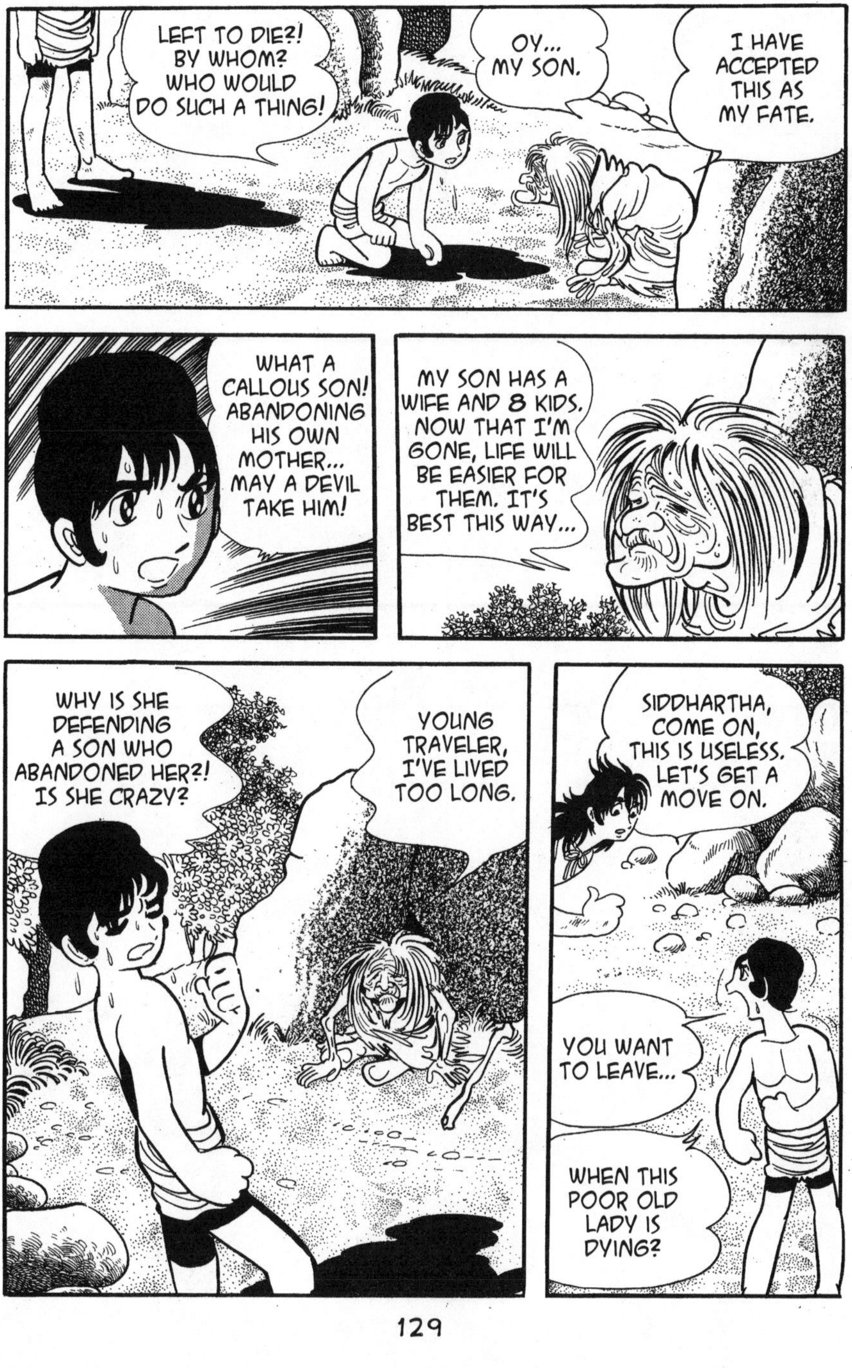
LEFT TO DIE?! BY WHOM? WHO WOULD DO SUCH A THING!
OY... MY SON.
I HAVE ACCEPTED THIS AS MY FATE.
WHAT A CALLOUS SON! ABANDONING HIS OWN MOTHER... MAY A DEVIL TAKE HIM!
MY SON HAS A WIFE AND 8 KIDS. NOW THAT I'M GONE, LIFE WILL BE EASIER FOR THEM. IT'S BEST THIS WAY...
WHY IS SHE DEFENDING A SON WHO ABANDONED HER?! IS SHE CRAZY?
YOUNG TRAVELER, I'VE LIVED TOO LONG.
SIDDHARTHA, COME ON, THIS IS USELESS. LET'S GET A MOVE ON.
YOU WANT TO LEAVE...
WHEN THIS POOR OLD LADY IS DYING?

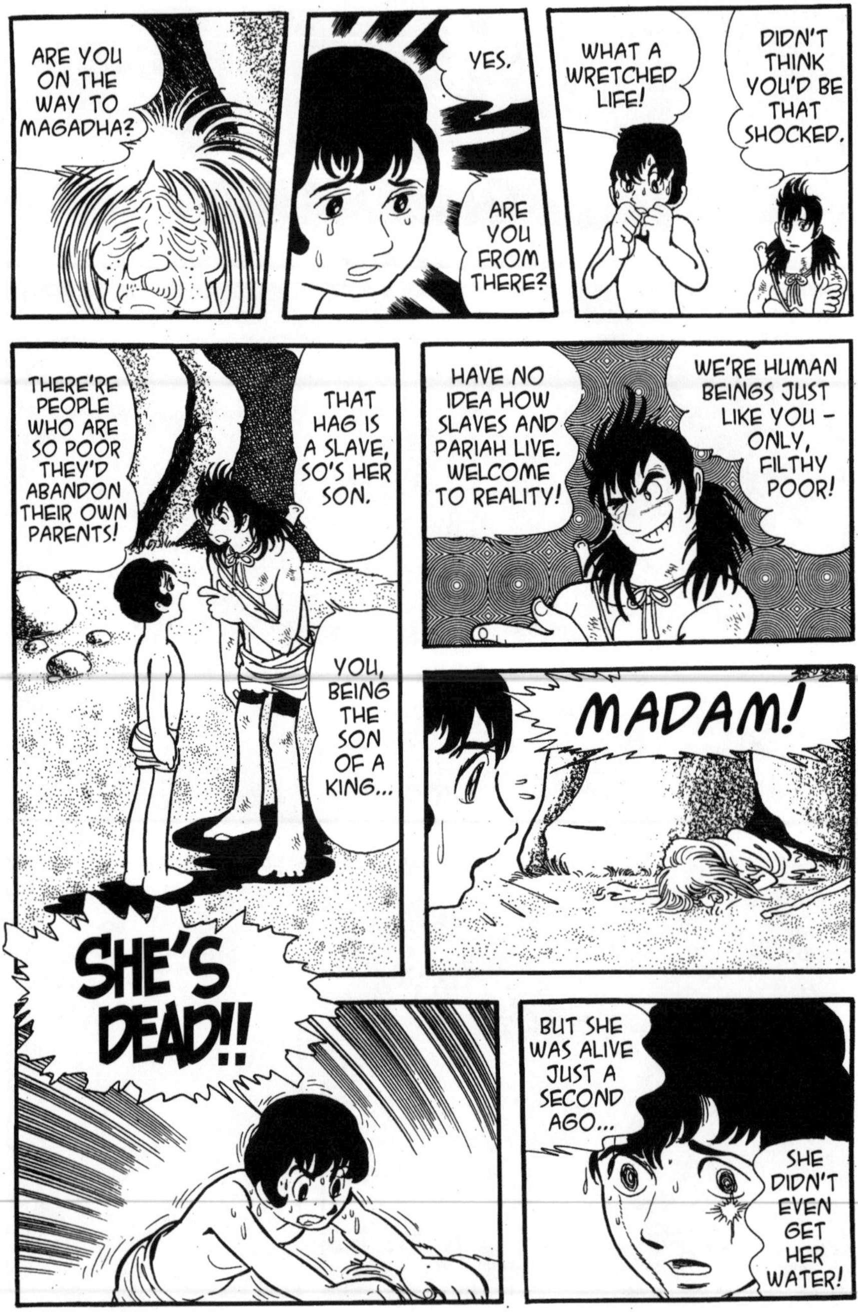
ARE YOU ON THE WAY TO MAGADHA?
YES.
ARE YOU FROM THERE?
WHAT A WRETCHED LIFE!
DIDN'T THINK YOU'D BE THAT SHOCKED.
THERE'RE PEOPLE WHO ARE SO POOR THEY'D ABANDON THEIR OWN PARENTS!
THAT HAG IS A SLAVE, SO'S HER SON.
YOU, BEING THE SON OF A KING...
HAVE NO IDEA HOW SLAVES AND PARIAH LIVE. WELCOME TO REALITY!
WE'RE HUMAN BEINGS JUST LIKE YOU - ONLY, FILTHY POOR!
MADAM!
SHE'S DEAD!!
BUT SHE WAS ALIVE JUST A SECOND AGO...
SHE DIDN'T EVEN GET HER WATER!

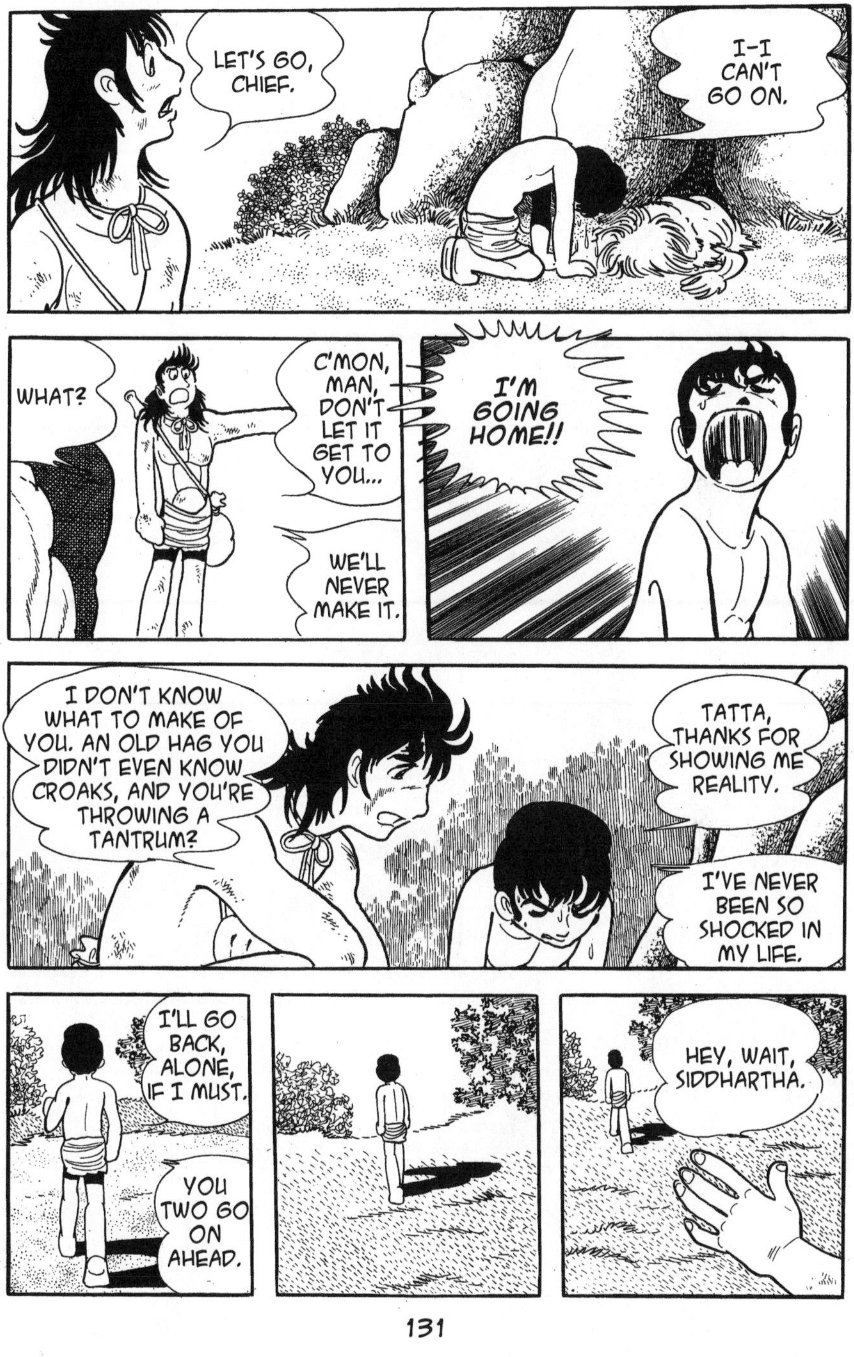
LET'S GO, CHIEF.
I-I CAN'T GO ON.
WHAT?
C'MON, MAN, DON'T LET IT GET TO YOU...
WE'LL NEVER MAKE IT.
I'M GOING HOME!!
I DON'T KNOW WHAT TO MAKE OF YOU. AN OLD HAG YOU DIDN'T EVEN KNOW CROAKS, AND YOU'RE THROWING A TANTRUM?
TATTA, THANKS FOR SHOWING ME REALITY.
I'VE NEVER BEEN SO SHOCKED IN MY LIFE.
I'LL GO BACK, ALONE, IF I MUST.
YOU TWO GO ON AHEAD.
HEY, WAIT, SIDDHARTHA.

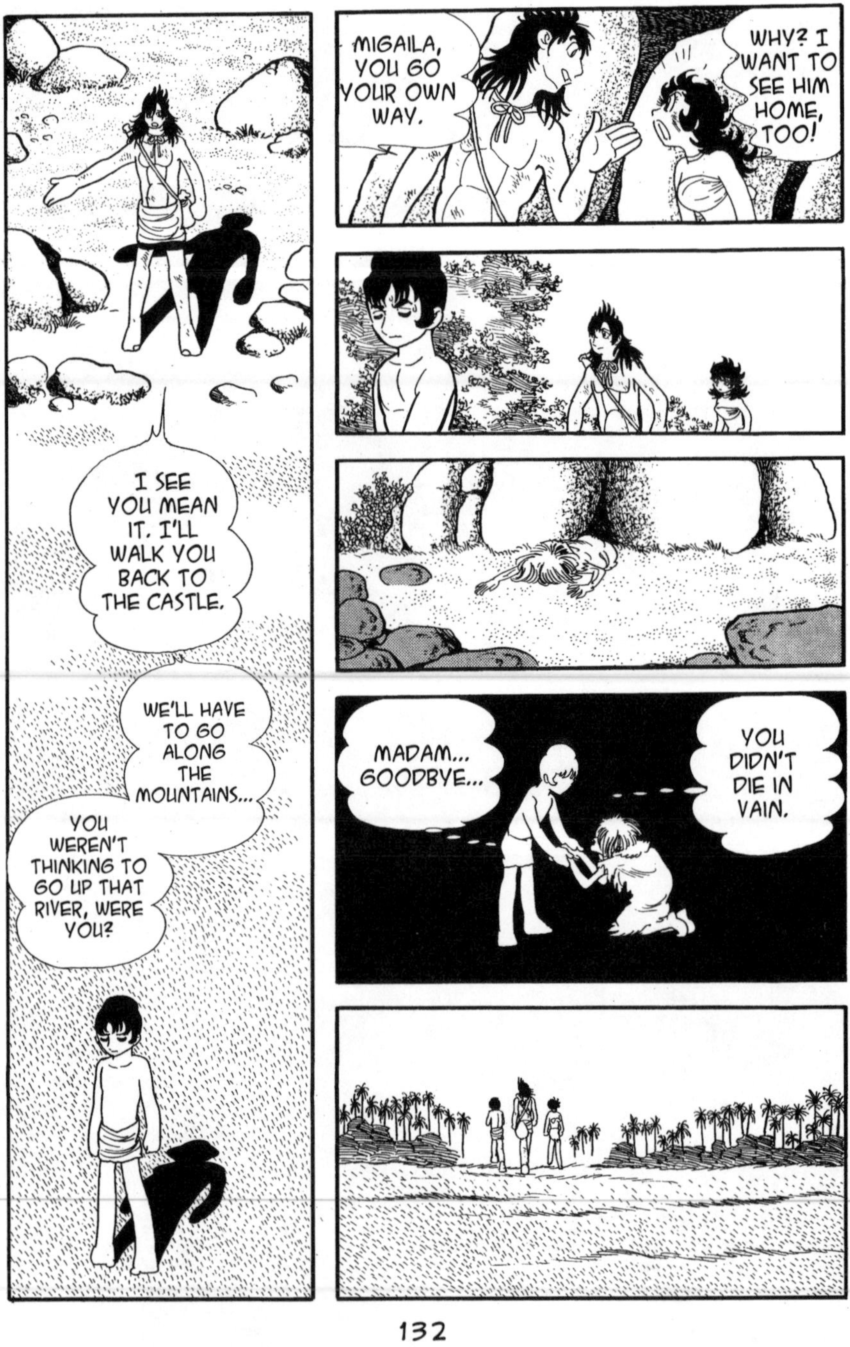
I SEE YOU MEAN IT. I'LL WALK YOU BACK TO THE CASTLE.
WE'LL HAVE TO GO ALONG THE MOUNTAINS...
YOU WEREN'T THINKING TO GO UP THAT RIVER, WERE YOU?
MIGAILA, YOU GO YOUR OWN WAY.
WHY? I WANT TO SEE HIM HOME, TOO!
MADAM... GOODBYE...
YOU DIDN'T DIE IN VAIN.

CHAPTER FOUR

YASHODARA

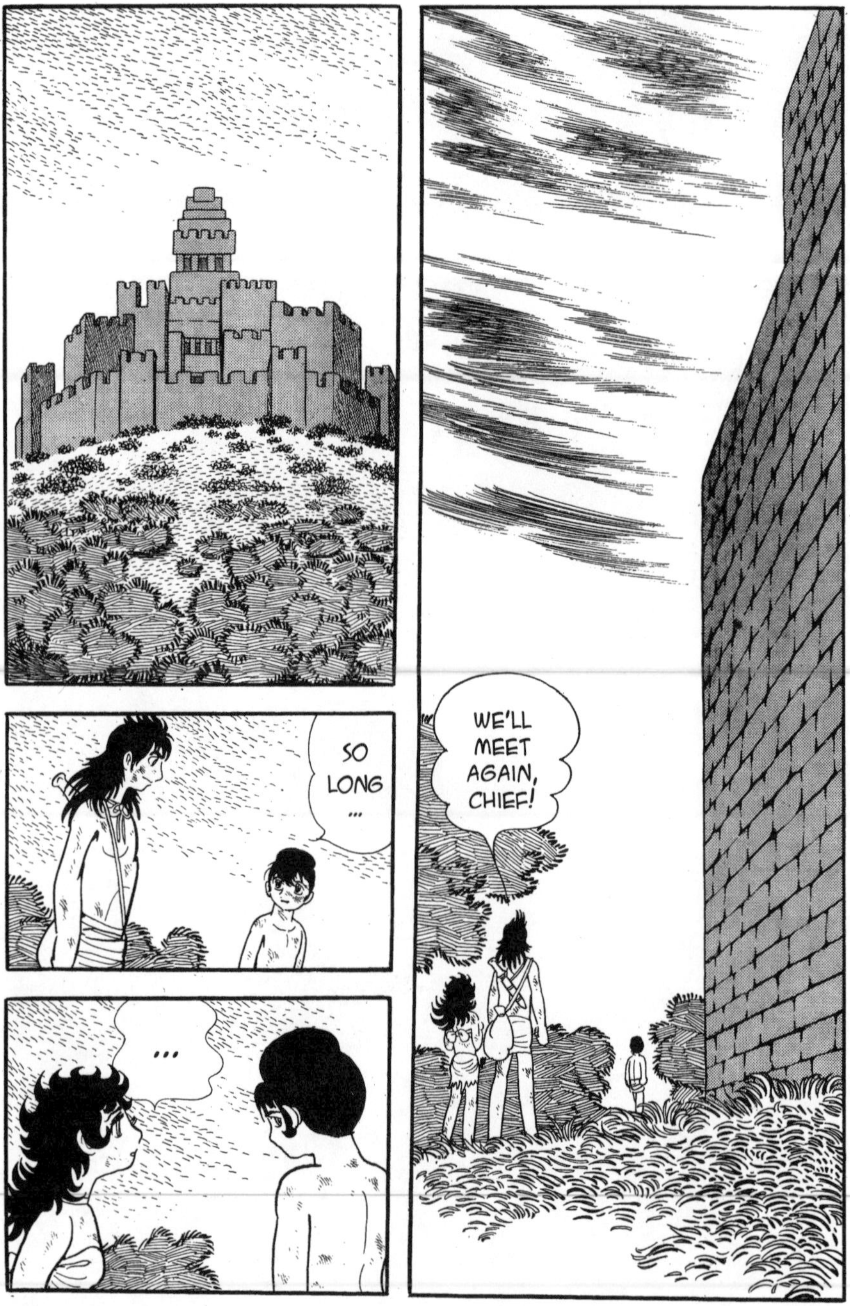
SO LONG ...
...
WE'LL MEET AGAIN, CHIEF!

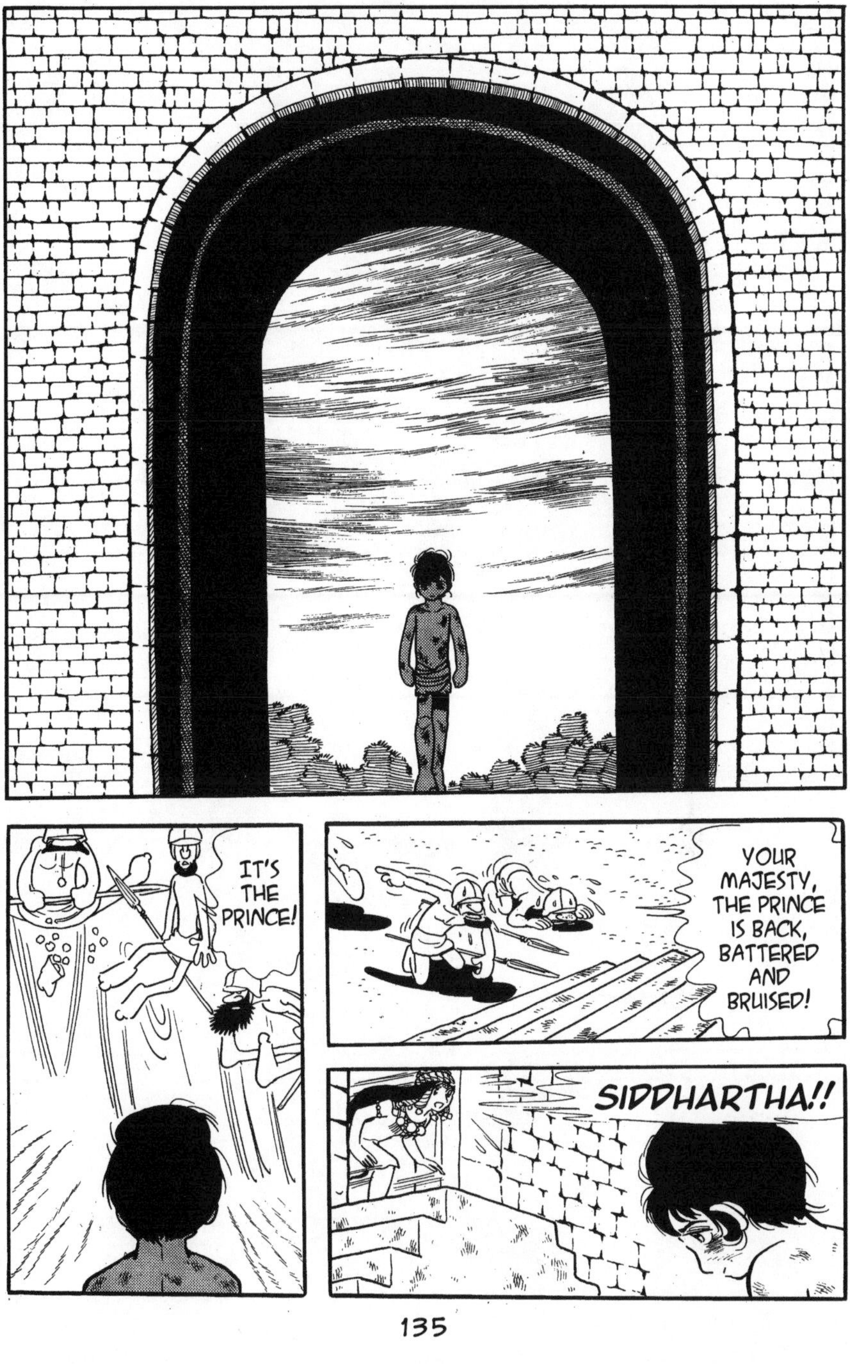
IT'S THE PRINCE!
YOUR MAJESTY, THE PRINCE IS BACK, BATTERED AND BRUISED!
SIDDHARTHA!!

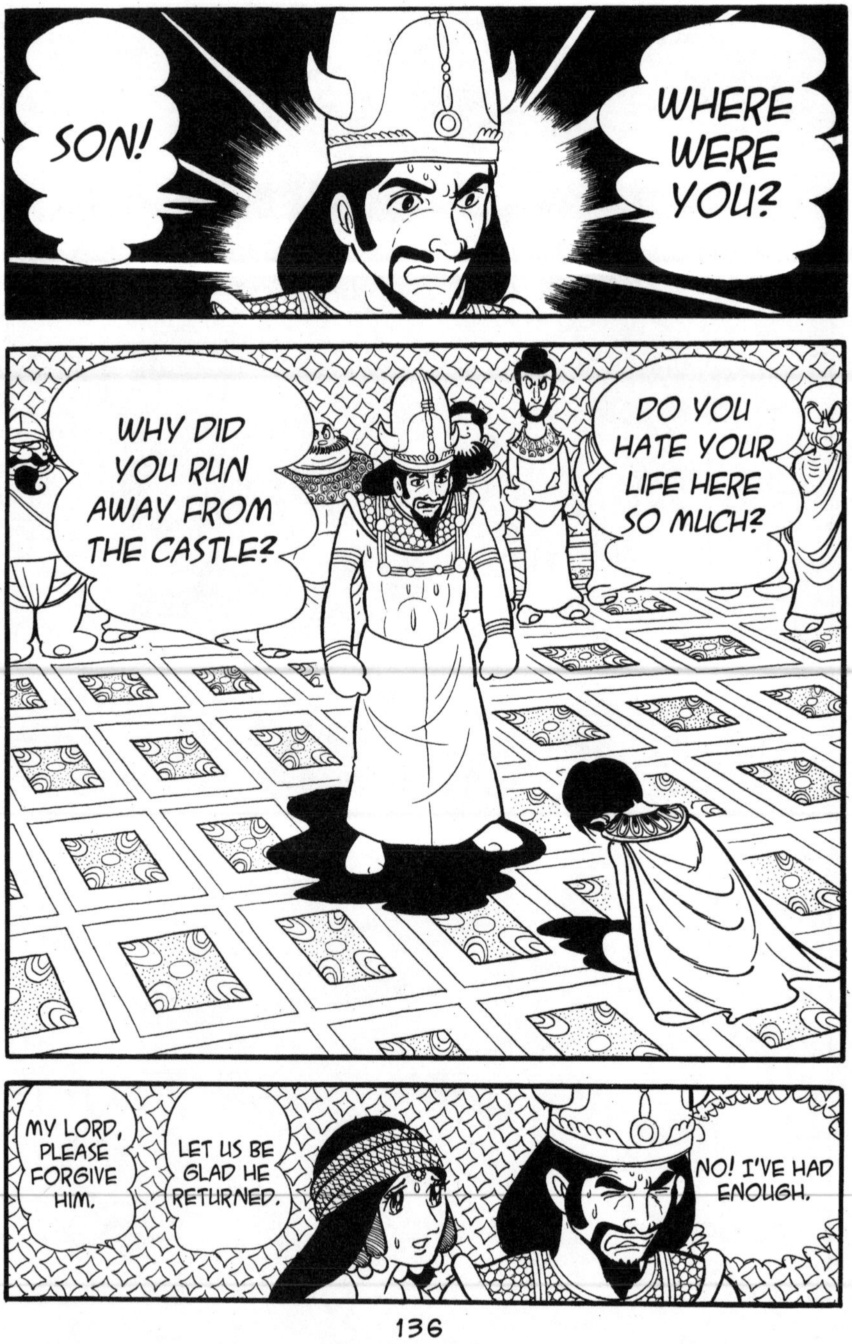
SON!
WHERE WERE YOU?
WHY DID YOU RUN AWAY FROM THE CASTLE?
DO YOU HATE YOUR LIFE HERE SO MUCH?
MY LORD, PLEASE FORGIVE HIM.
LET US BE GLAD HE RETURNED.
NO! I'VE HAD ENOUGH.

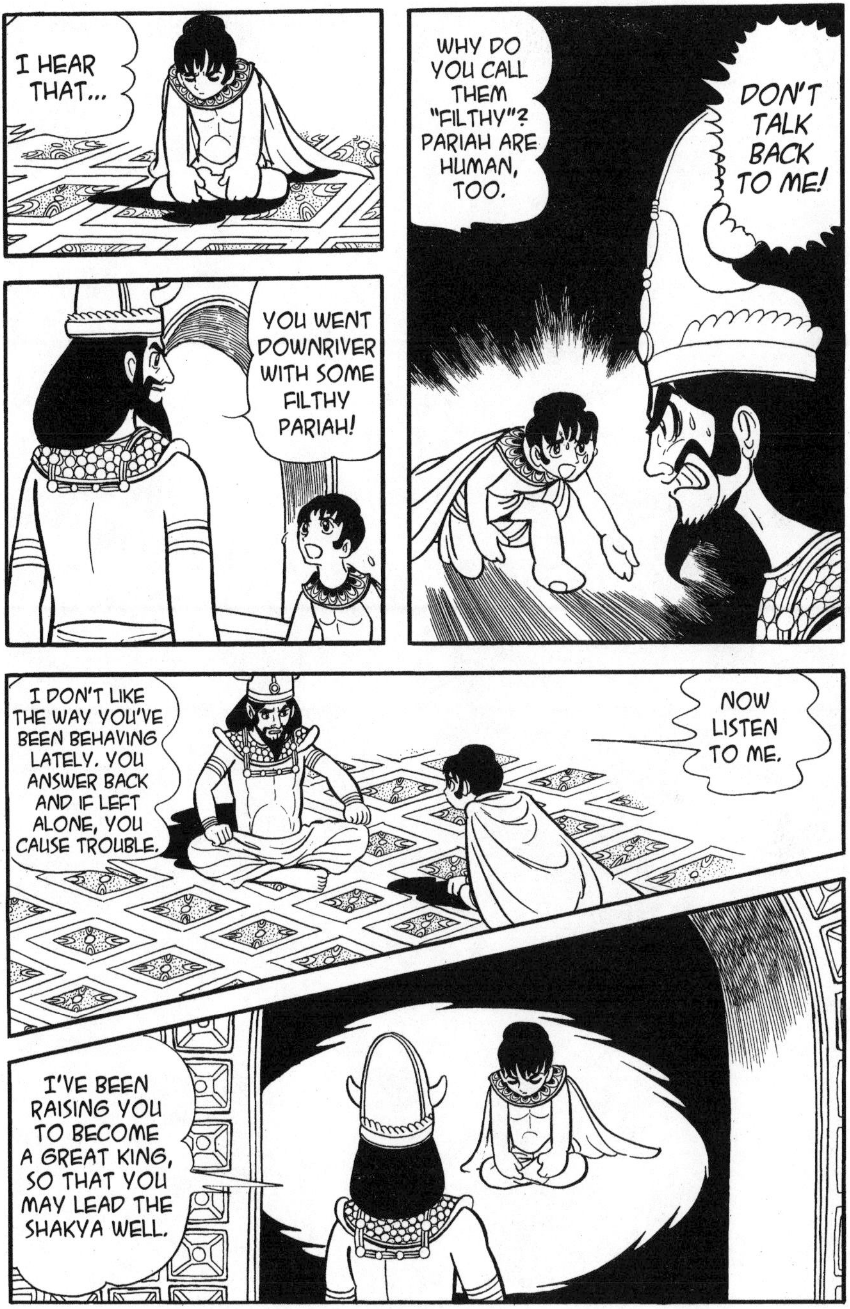
I HEAR THAT...
YOU WENT DOWNRIVER WITH SOME FILTHY PARIAH!
WHY DO YOU CALL THEM "FILTHY"? PARIAH ARE HUMAN, TOO.
DON'T TALK BACK TO ME!
I DON'T LIKE THE WAY YOU'VE BEEN BEHAVING LATELY. YOU ANSWER BACK AND IF LEFT ALONE, YOU CAUSE TROUBLE.
NOW LISTEN TO ME.
I'VE BEEN RAISING YOU TO BECOME A GREAT KING, SO THAT YOU MAY LEAD THE SHAKYA WELL.

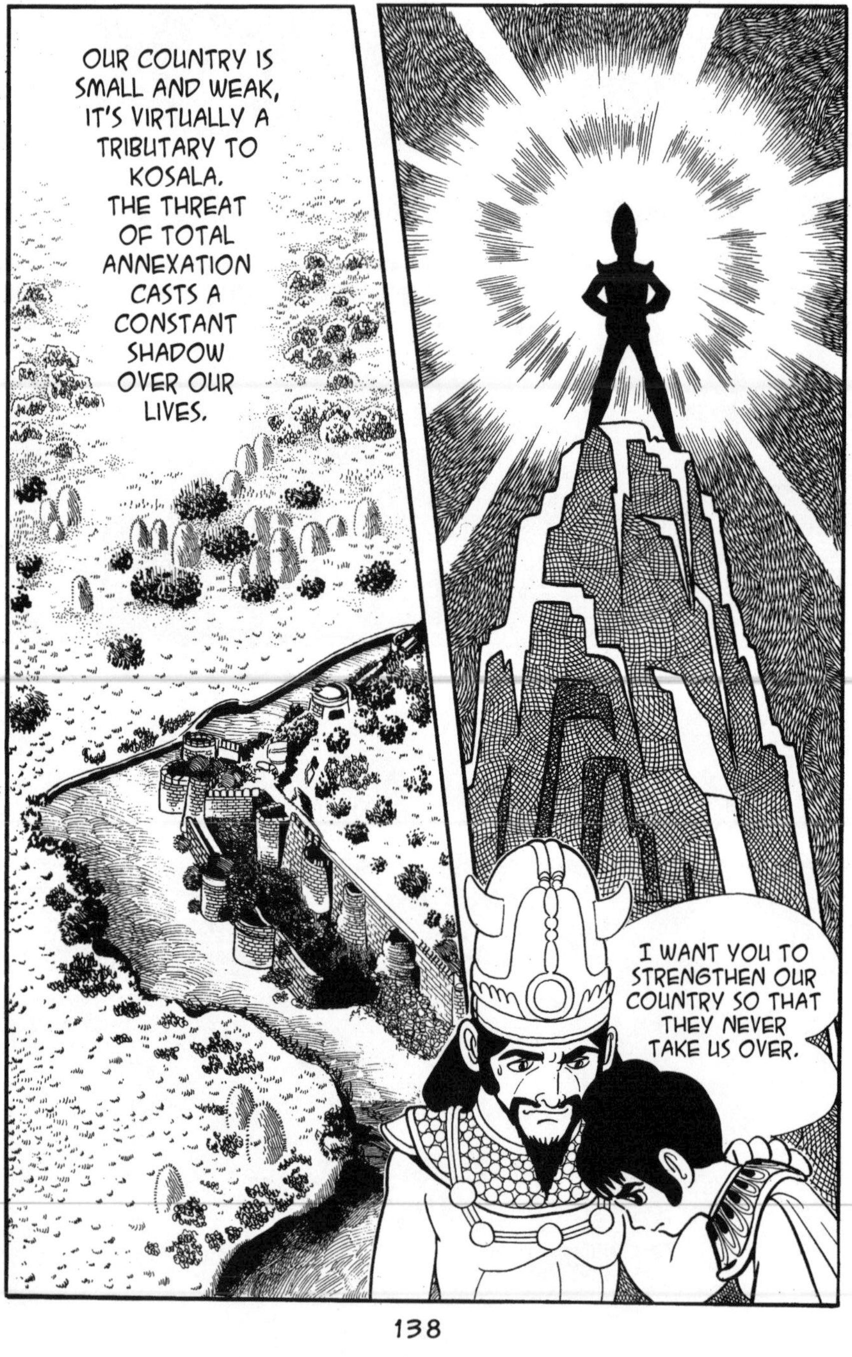
OUR COUNTRY IS SMALL AND WEAK, IT'S VIRTUALLY A TRIBUTARY TO KOSALA. THE THREAT OF TOTAL ANNEXATION CASTS A CONSTANT SHADOW OVER OUR LIVES.
I WANT YOU TO STRENGTHEN OUR COUNTRY SO THAT THEY NEVER TAKE US OVER.

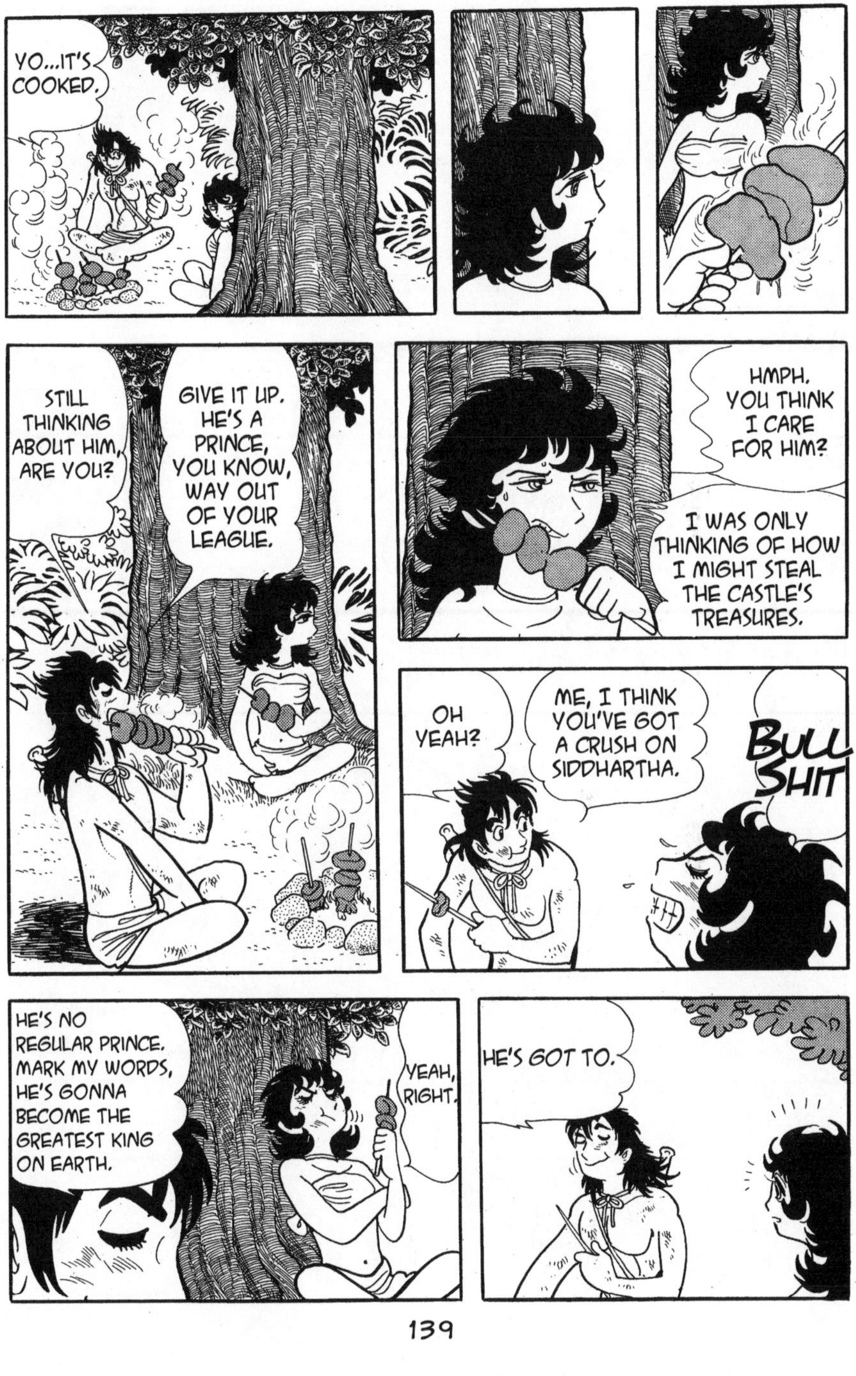
YO...IT'S COOKED.
STILL THINKING ABOUT HIM, ARE YOU?
GIVE IT UP. HE'S A PRINCE, YOU KNOW, WAY OUT OF YOUR LEAGUE.
HMPH. YOU THINK I CARE FOR HIM?
I WAS ONLY THINKING OF HOW I MIGHT STEAL THE CASTLE'S TREASURES.
OH YEAH?
ME, I THINK YOU'VE GOT A CRUSH ON SIDDHARTHA.
BULL SHIT
HE'S NO REGULAR PRINCE. MARK MY WORDS, HE'S GONNA BECOME THE GREATEST KING ON EARTH.
YEAH, RIGHT.
HE'S GOT TO.

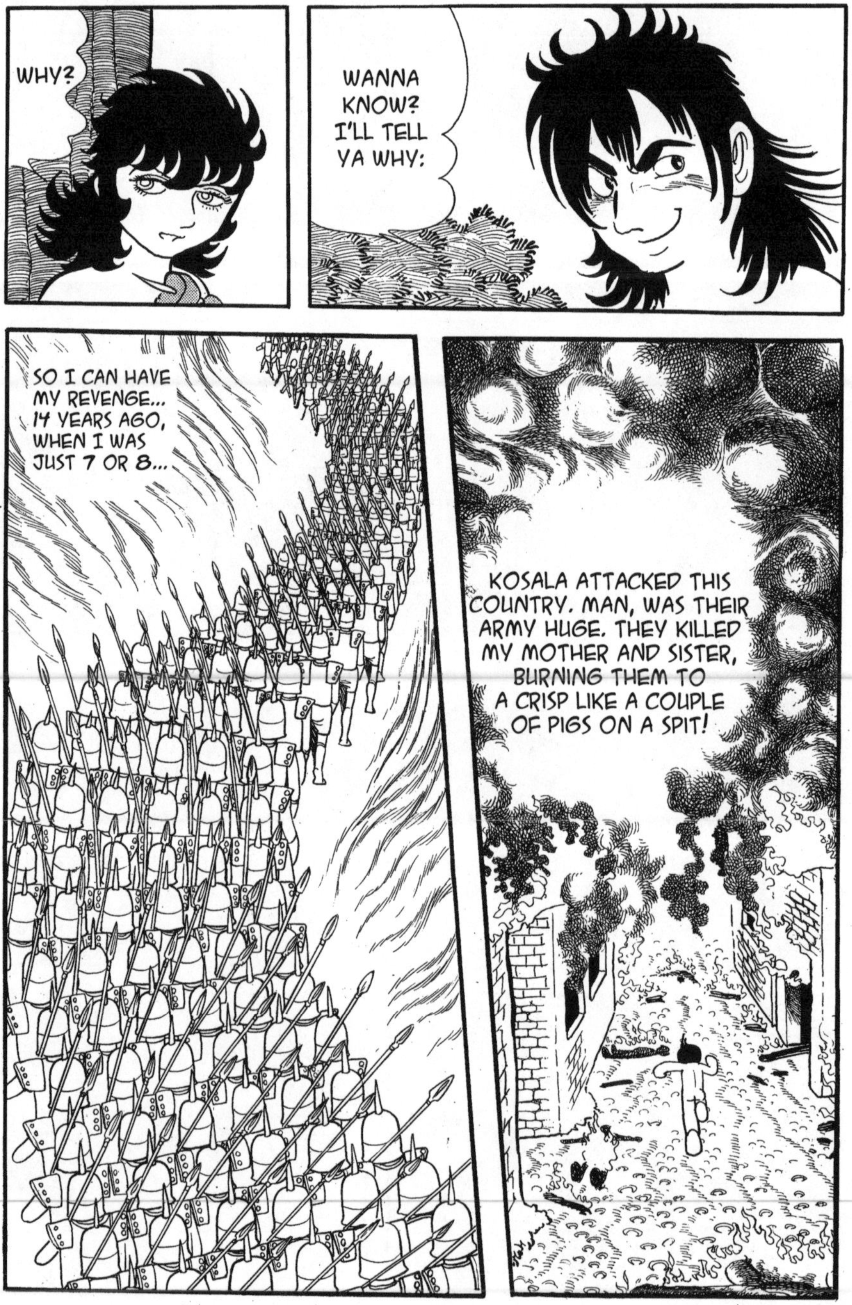
WHY?
WANNA KNOW? I'LL TELL YA WHY:
SO I CAN HAVE MY REVENGE... 14 YEARS AGO, WHEN I WAS JUST 7 OR 8...
KOSALA ATTACKED THIS COUNTRY. MAN, WAS THEIR ARMY HUGE. THEY KILLED MY MOTHER AND SISTER, BURNING THEM TO A CRISP LIKE A COUPLE OF PIGS ON A SPIT!

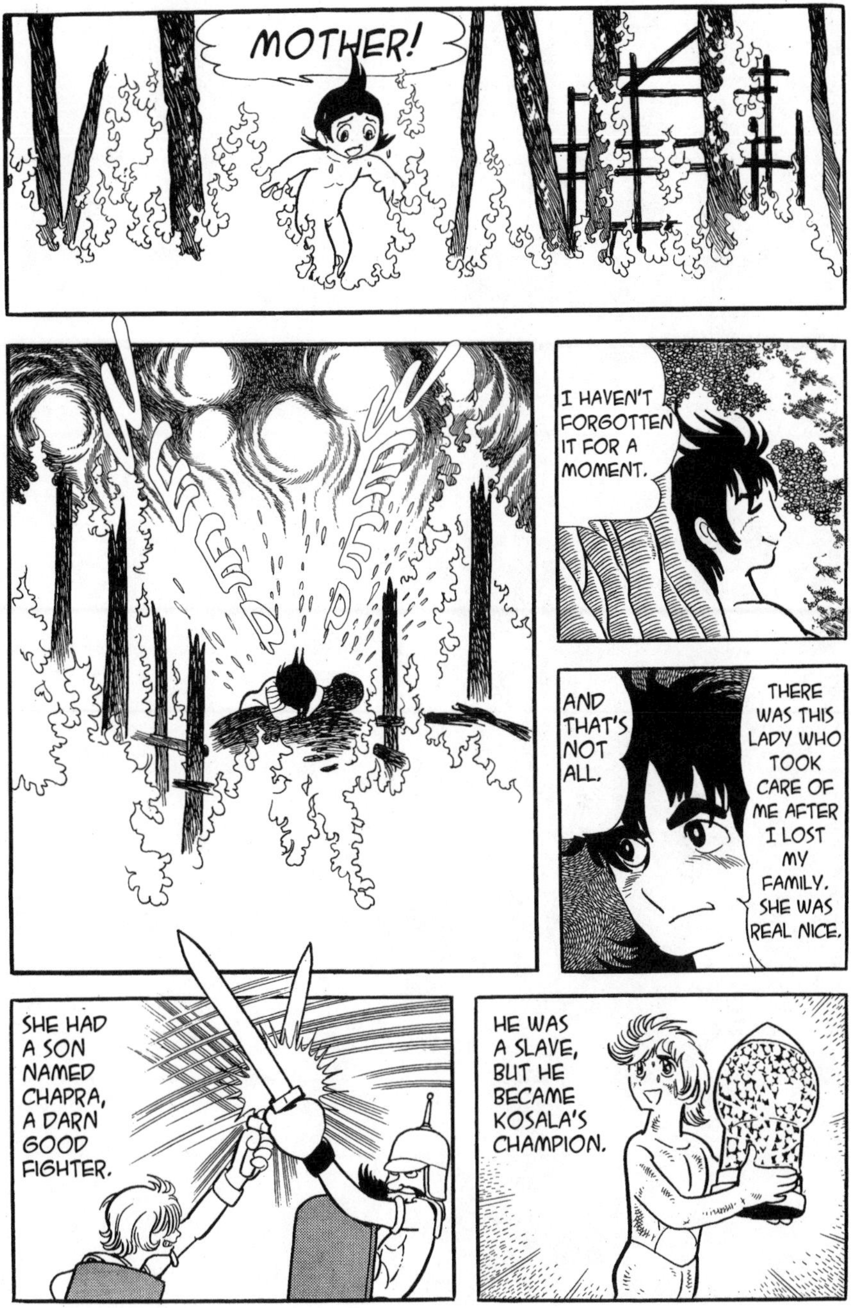
MOTHER!
I HAVEN'T FORGOTTEN IT FOR A MOMENT.
AND THAT'S NOT ALL.
THERE WAS THIS LADY WHO TOOK CARE OF ME AFTER I LOST MY FAMILY. SHE WAS REAL NICE.
SHE HAD A SON NAMED CHAPRA, A DARN GOOD FIGHTER.
HE WAS A SLAVE, BUT HE BECAME KOSALA'S CHAMPION.

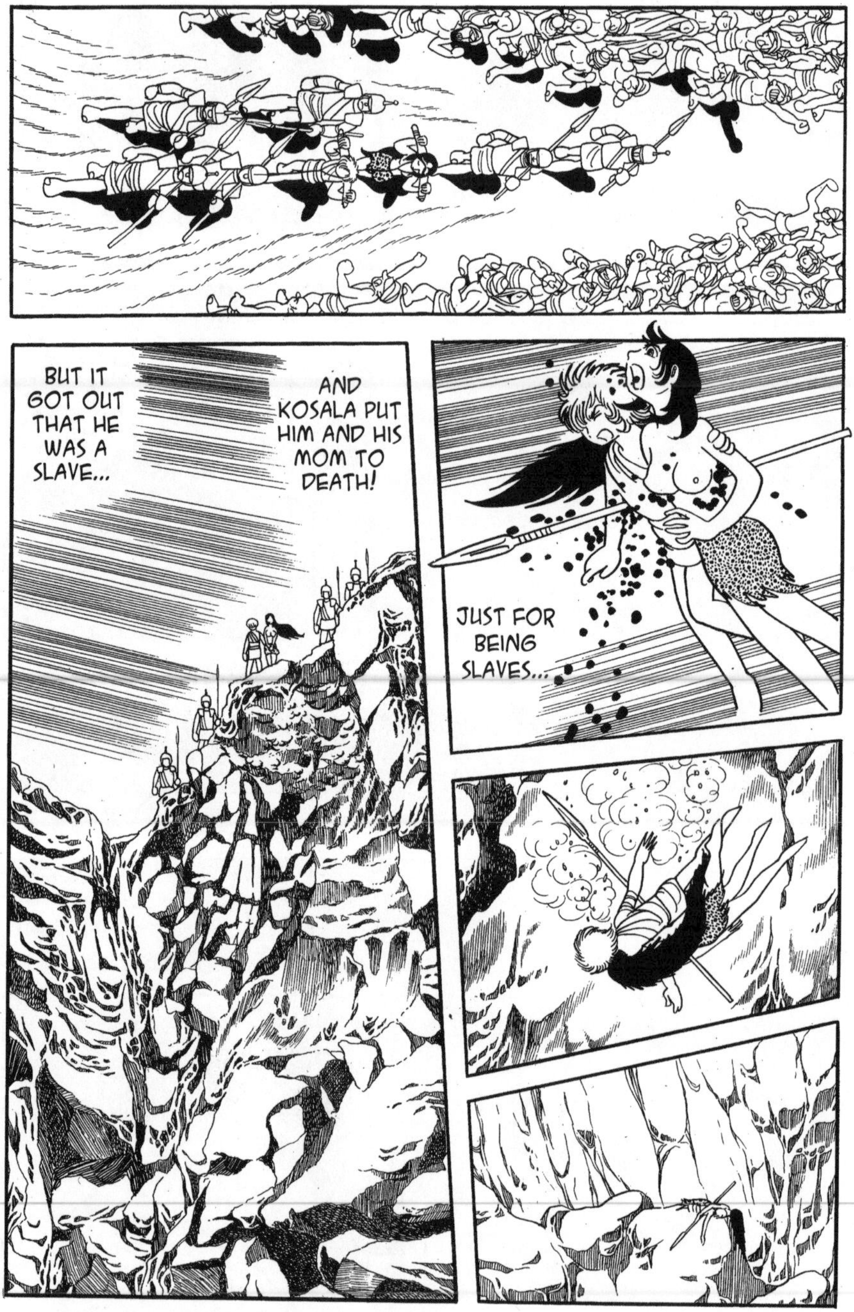
BUT IT GOT OUT THAT HE WAS A SLAVE...
AND KOSALA PUT HIM AND HIS MOM TO DEATH!
JUST FOR BEING SLAVES...

I HATE THE FUCKIN' KOSALANS!! GET IT?

...

I'M GONNA GET MY REVENGE.

THOUGHT I COULD DO IT ON MY OWN, BUT A PARIAH'S GOT NO WAY TO HANDLE SO MANY KSHATRIYA AND BRAHMIN.

SO, I THOUGHT, IT WOULD BE BEST TO SIC WARRIOR ON WARRIOR. THAT'S HOW I'D DO THEM KOSALANS IN.

AND THAT'S WHERE SIDDHAR-THA COMES IN.

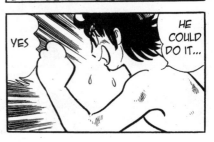

YES

HE COULD DO IT...

143

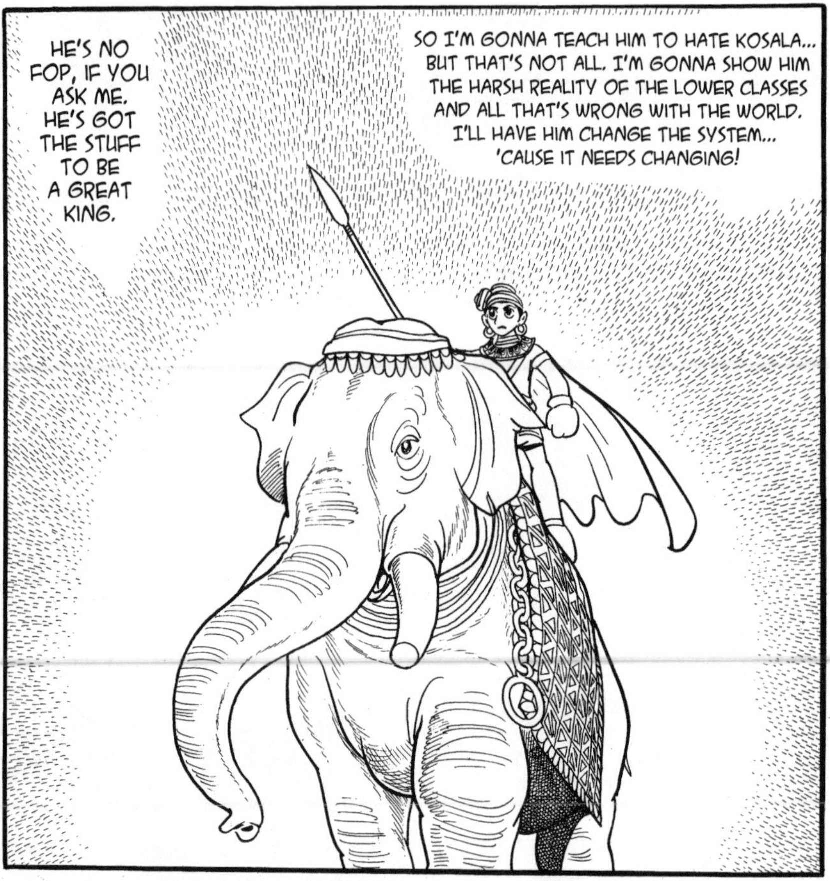
HE'S NO FOP, IF YOU ASK ME. HE'S GOT THE STUFF TO BE A GREAT KING.
SO I'M GONNA TEACH HIM TO HATE KOSALA... BUT THAT'S NOT ALL. I'M GONNA SHOW HIM THE HARSH REALITY OF THE LOWER CLASSES AND ALL THAT'S WRONG WITH THE WORLD. I'LL HAVE HIM CHANGE THE SYSTEM... 'CAUSE IT NEEDS CHANGING!

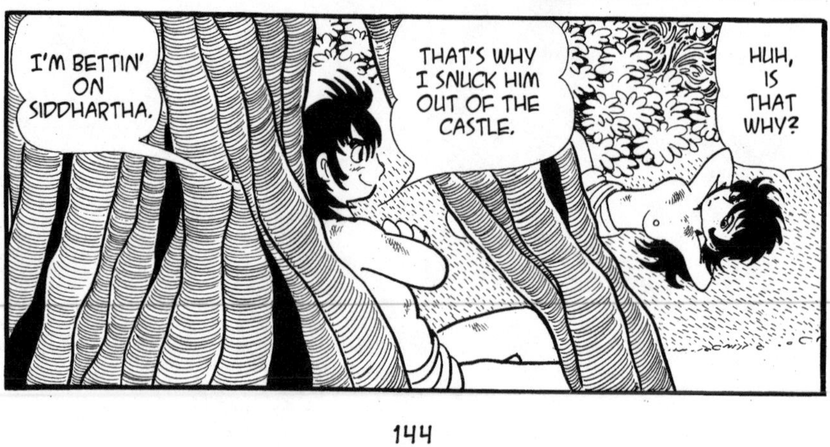
I'M BETTIN' ON SIDDHARTHA.
THAT'S WHY I SNUCK HIM OUT OF THE CASTLE.
HUH, IS THAT WHY?

I DIG YOUR STORY.

BUT SIDDHARTHA WON'T TURN OUT THAT WAY.

THAT KID'LL NEVER BE NO MIGHTY KING!

WHY NOT?

HE'S SO WEAK, SICKLY ALMOST. I DON'T THINK HE'S CUT OUT FOR WARRING.

YEAH, I'VE NOTICED, TOO.

THAT'S THE PROBLEM.

HE AIN'T NO USE IF HE DIES.

I'LL MEET WITH HIM FROM TIME TO TIME...

TAKE HIM OUT ON TRIPS...

MAKE HIM STRONG.

TATTA, I CAN TEACH HIM HOW TO STEAL.

I DUNNO ABOUT THAT.

145

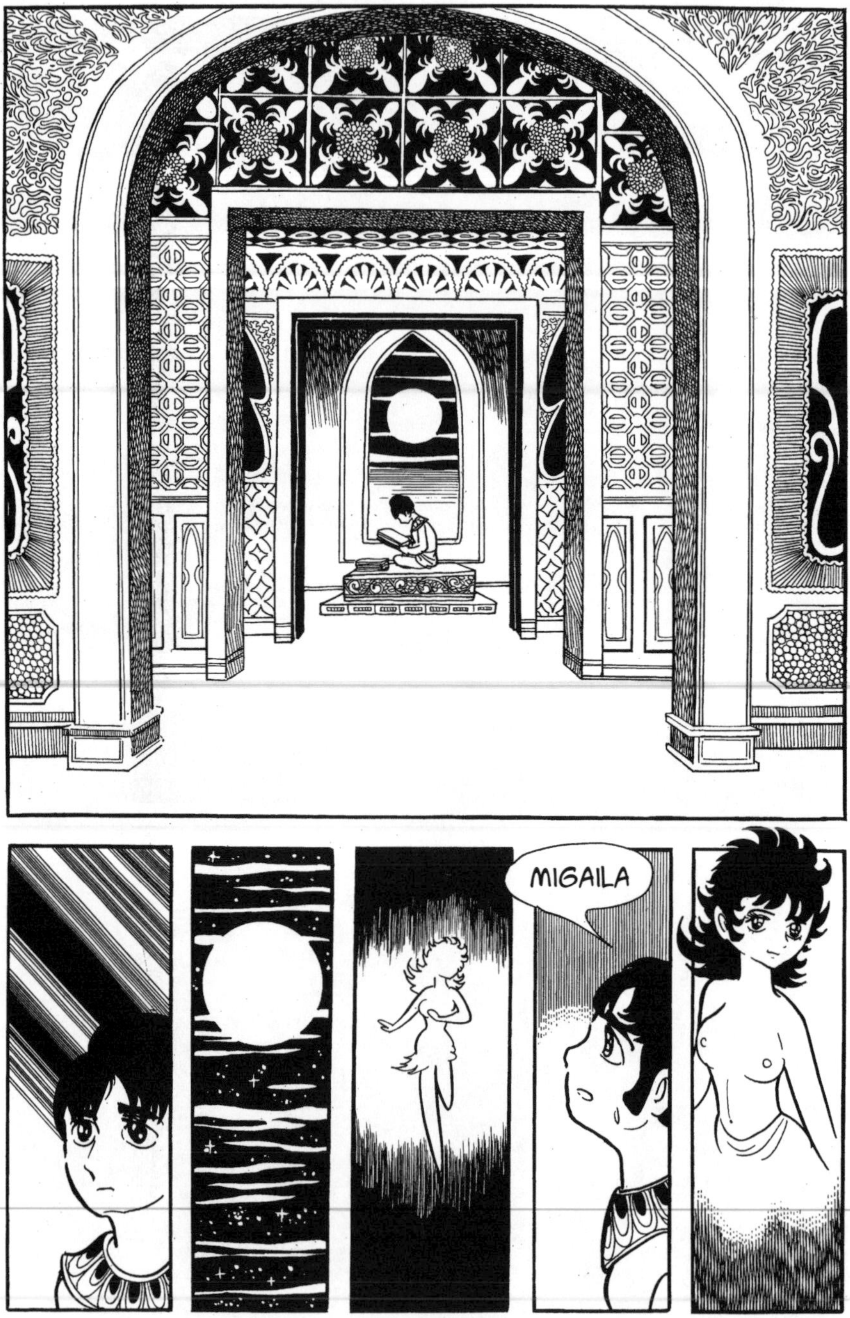
MIGAILA

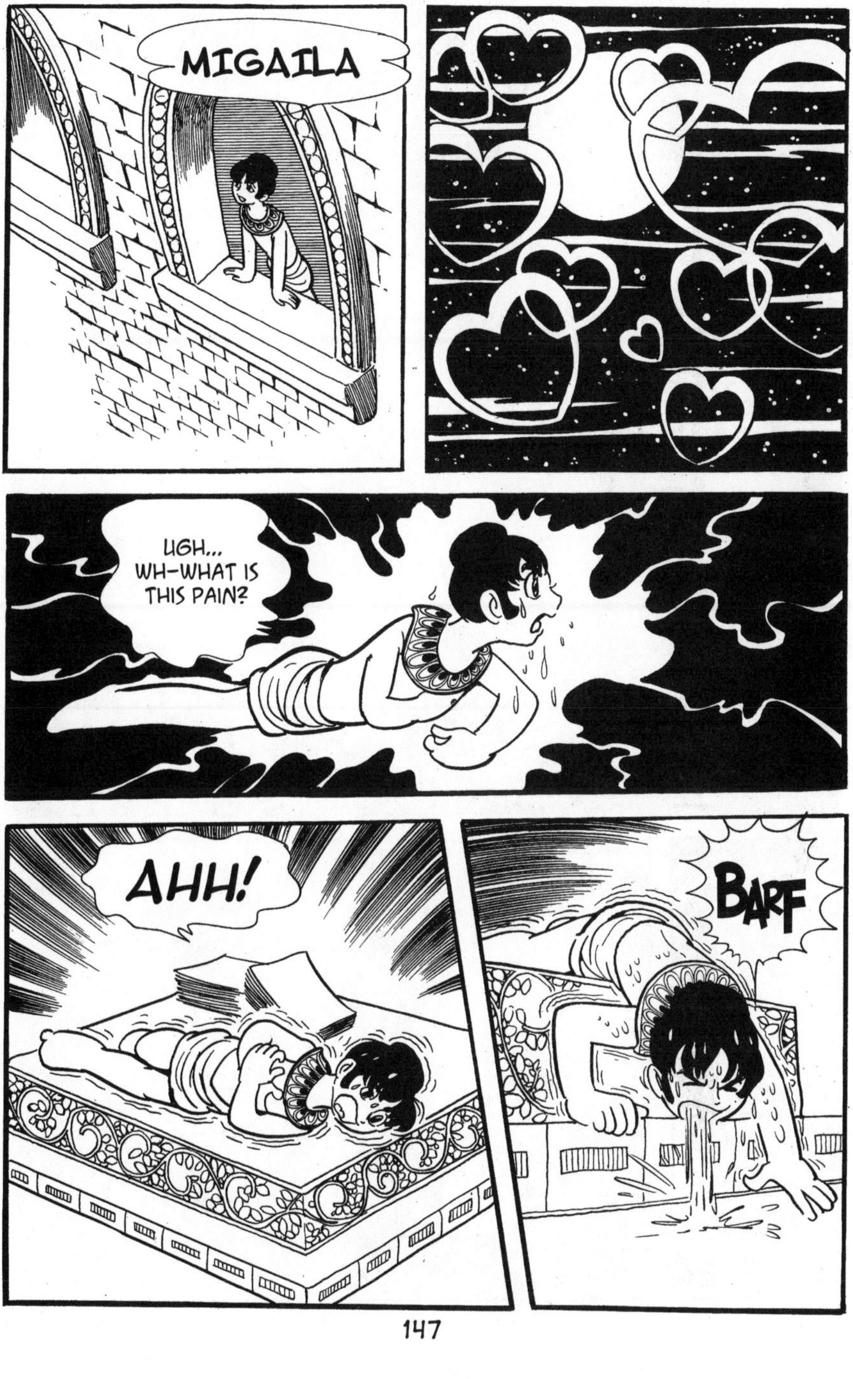
MIGAILA
UGH... WH-WHAT IS THIS PAIN?
AHH!
BARF

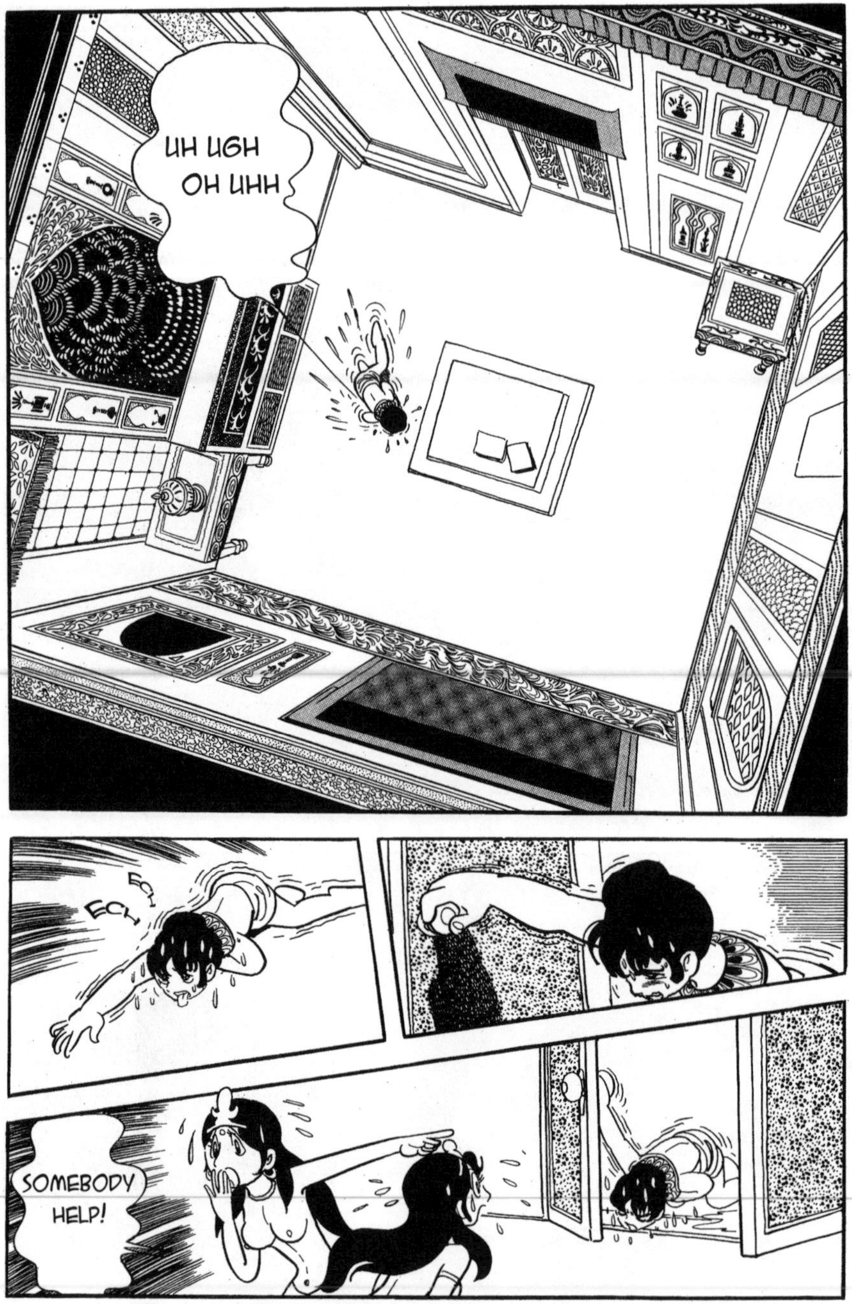
UH UGH
OH UHH
ECH ECH
SOMEBODY HELP!

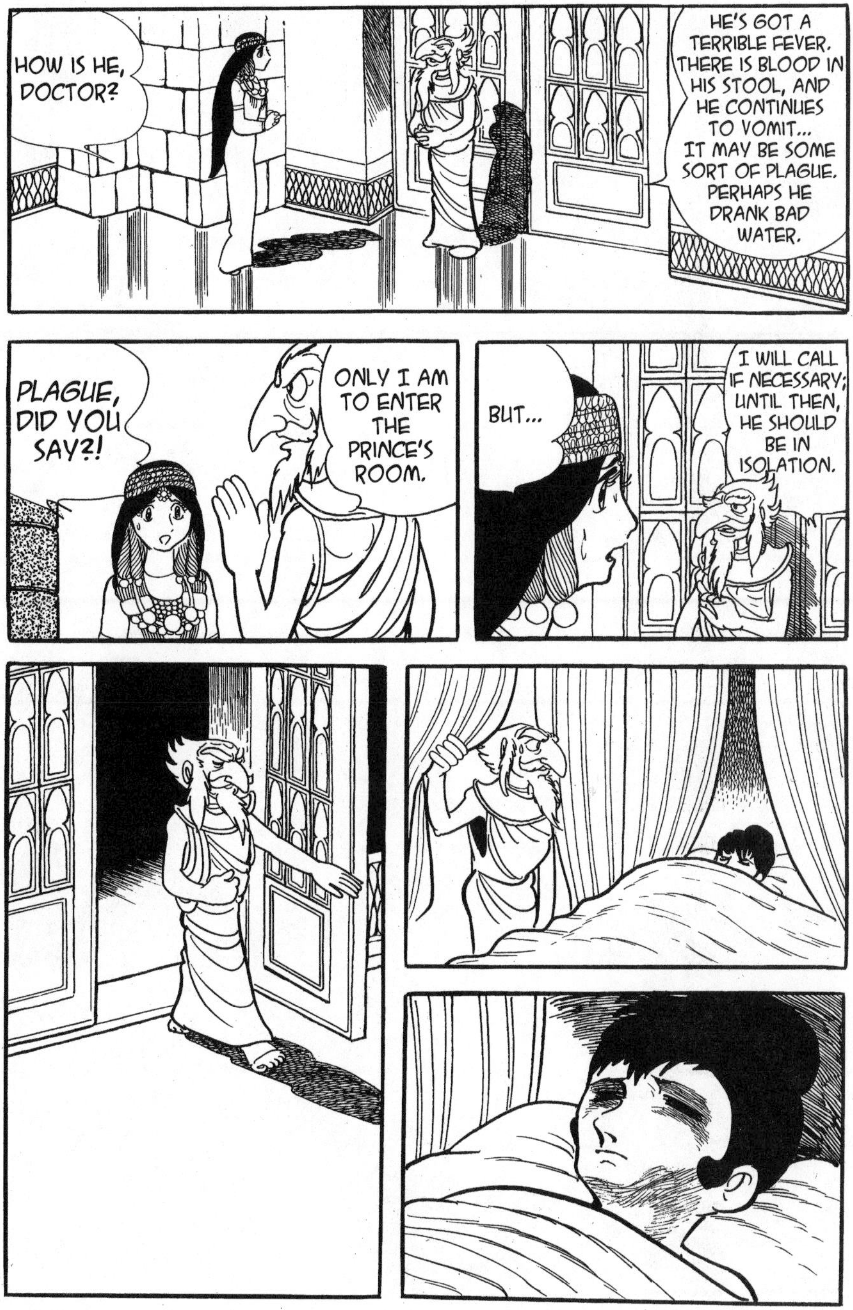
HOW IS HE, DOCTOR?
HE'S GOT A TERRIBLE FEVER. THERE IS BLOOD IN HIS STOOL, AND HE CONTINUES TO VOMIT... IT MAY BE SOME SORT OF PLAGUE. PERHAPS HE DRANK BAD WATER.
PLAGUE, DID YOU SAY?!
ONLY I AM TO ENTER THE PRINCE'S ROOM.
BUT...
I WILL CALL IF NECESSARY; UNTIL THEN, HE SHOULD BE IN ISOLATION.

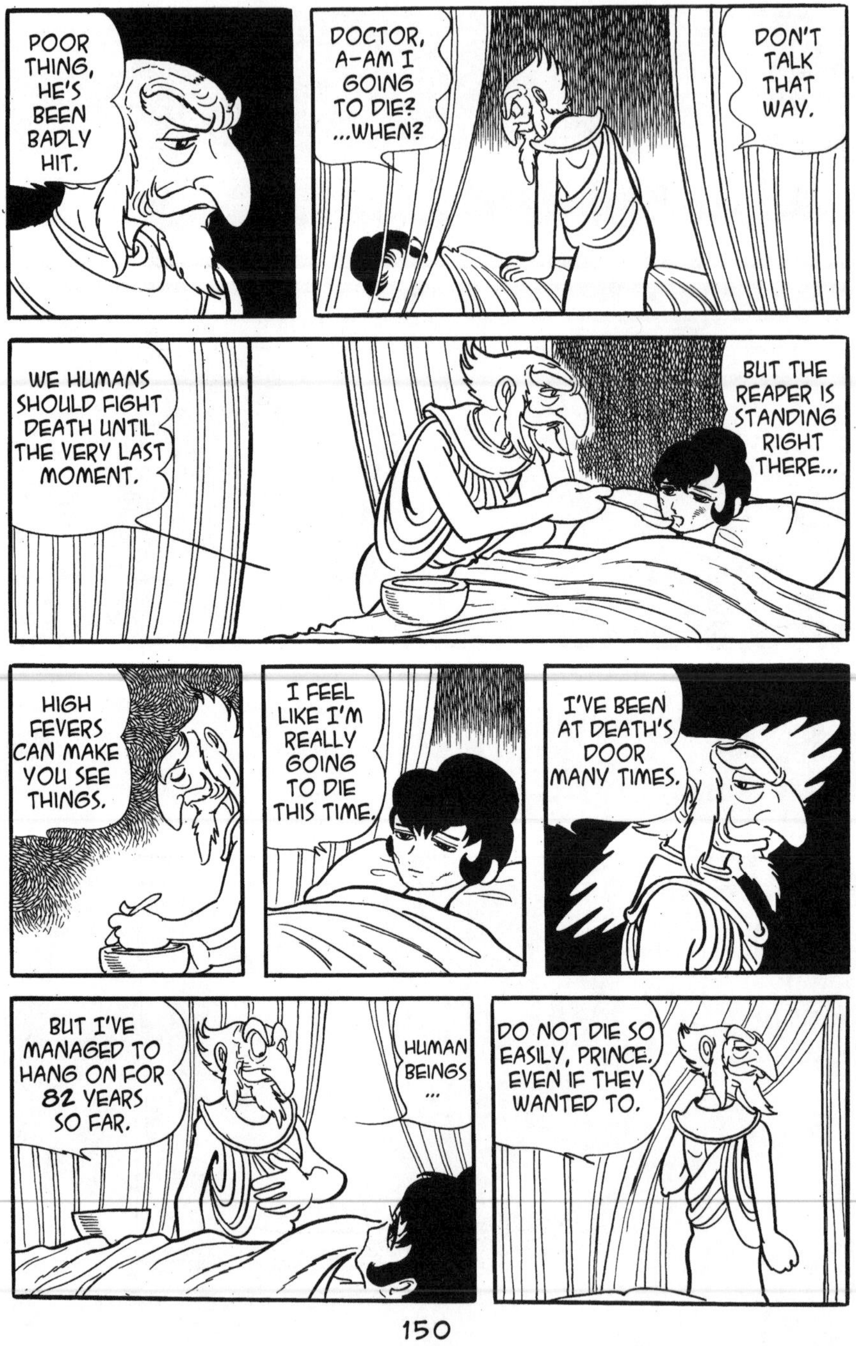
POOR THING, HE'S BEEN BADLY HIT.
DOCTOR, A-AM I GOING TO DIE? ...WHEN?
DON'T TALK THAT WAY.
WE HUMANS SHOULD FIGHT DEATH UNTIL THE VERY LAST MOMENT.
BUT THE REAPER IS STANDING RIGHT THERE...
HIGH FEVERS CAN MAKE YOU SEE THINGS.
I FEEL LIKE I'M REALLY GOING TO DIE THIS TIME.
I'VE BEEN AT DEATH'S DOOR MANY TIMES.
BUT I'VE MANAGED TO HANG ON FOR 82 YEARS SO FAR.
HUMAN BEINGS ...
DO NOT DIE SO EASILY, PRINCE. EVEN IF THEY WANTED TO.

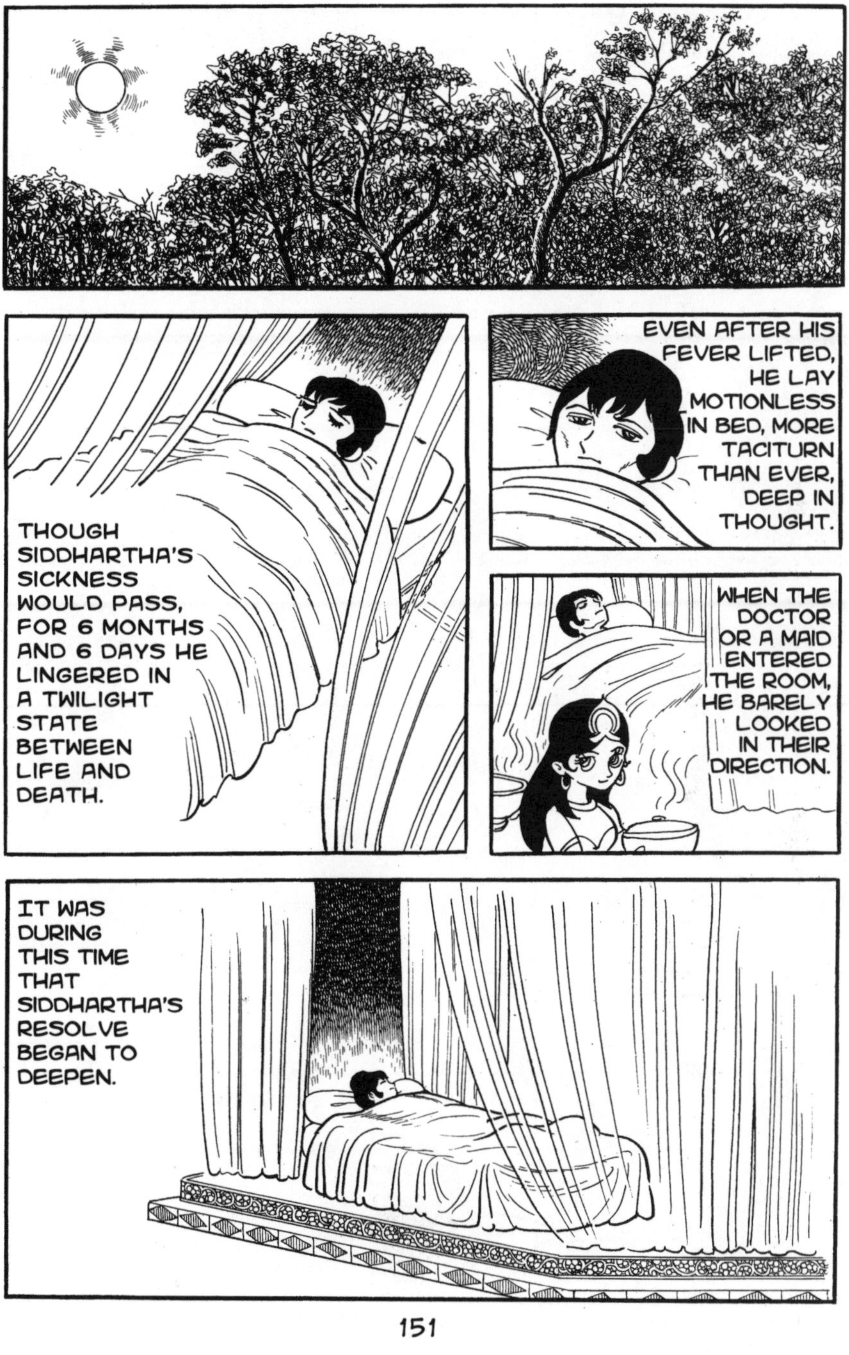
THOUGH SIDDHARTHA'S SICKNESS WOULD PASS, FOR 6 MONTHS AND 6 DAYS HE LINGERED IN A TWILIGHT STATE BETWEEN LIFE AND DEATH.
EVEN AFTER HIS FEVER LIFTED, HE LAY MOTIONLESS IN BED, MORE TACITURN THAN EVER, DEEP IN THOUGHT.
WHEN THE DOCTOR OR A MAID ENTERED THE ROOM, HE BARELY LOOKED IN THEIR DIRECTION.
IT WAS DURING THIS TIME THAT SIDDHARTHA'S RESOLVE BEGAN TO DEEPEN.

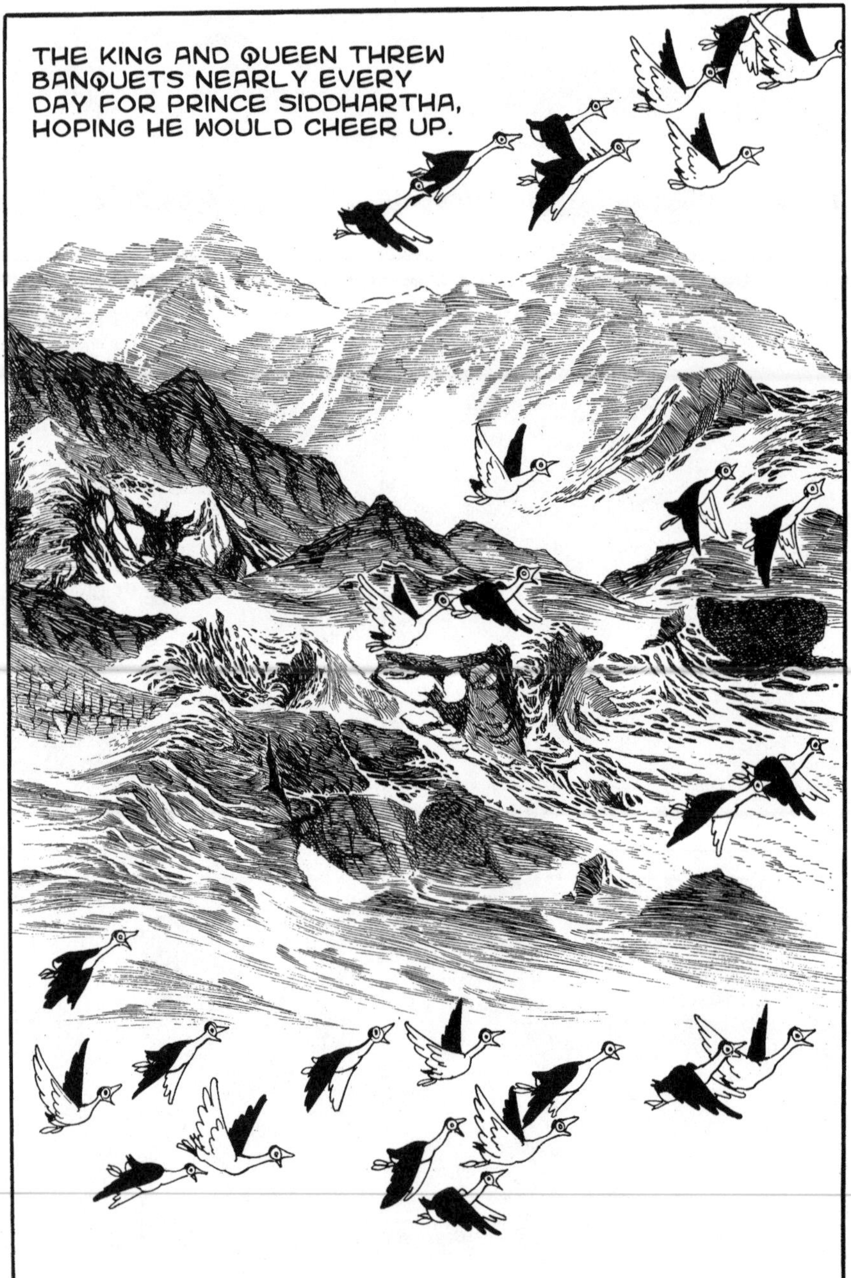
THE KING AND QUEEN THREW BANQUETS NEARLY EVERY DAY FOR PRINCE SIDDHARTHA, HOPING HE WOULD CHEER UP.

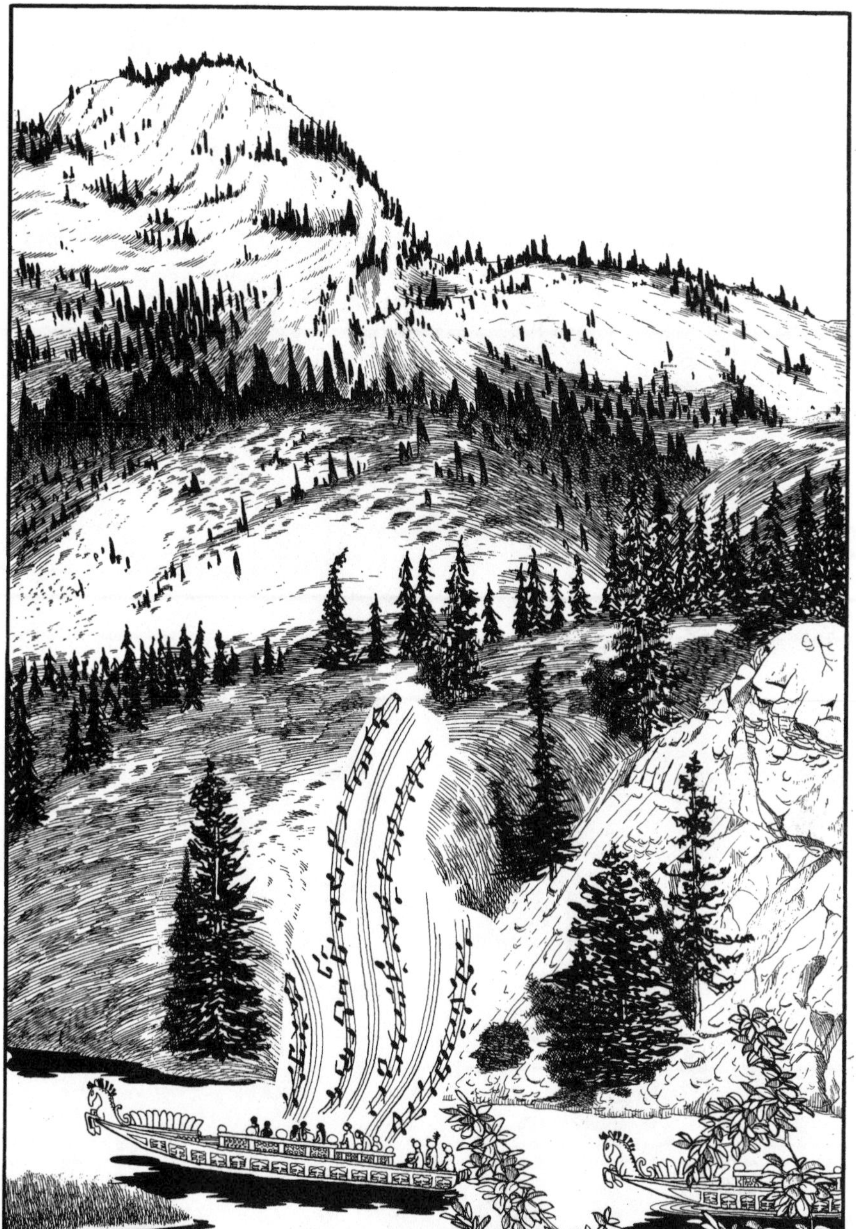

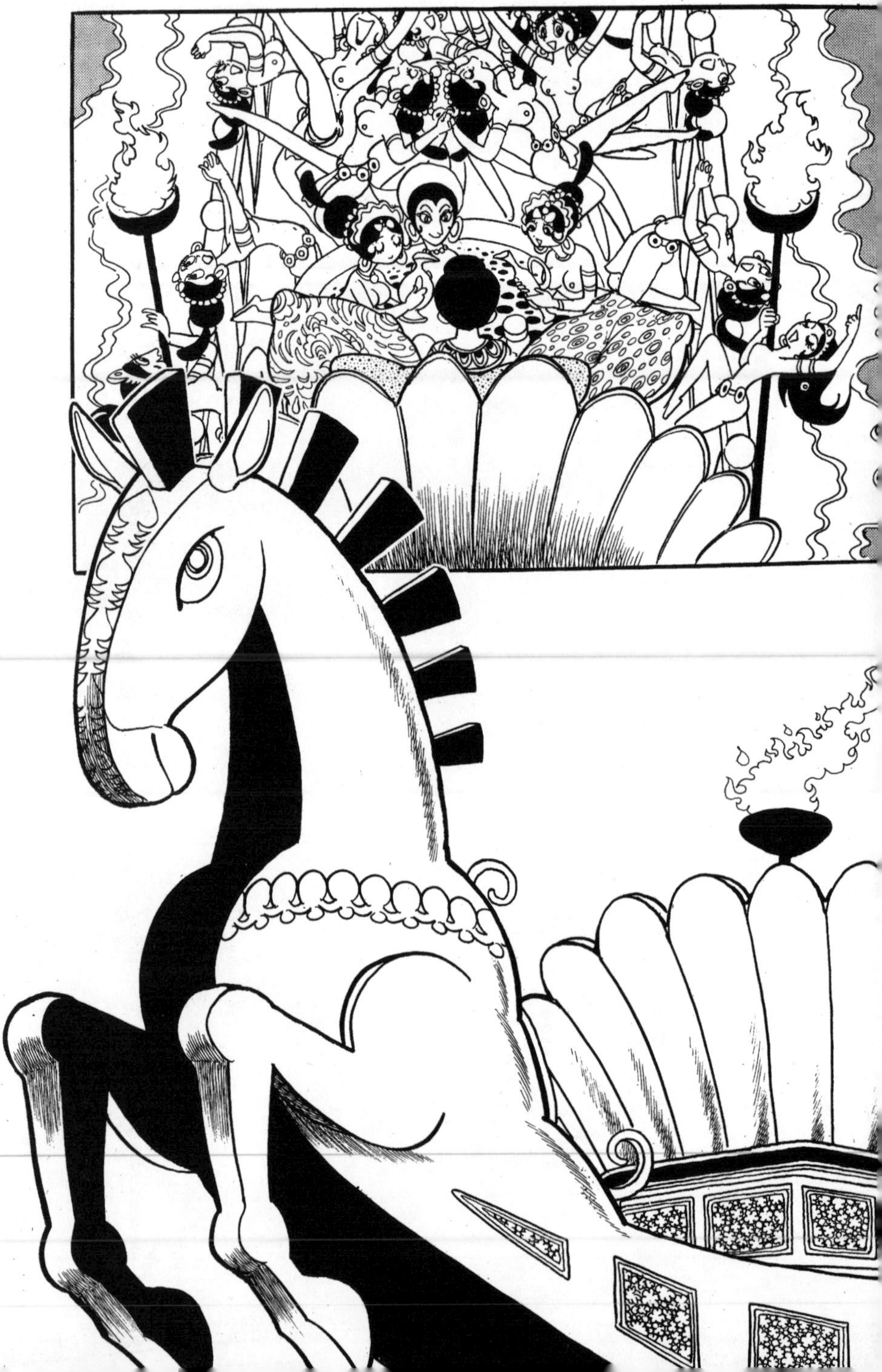

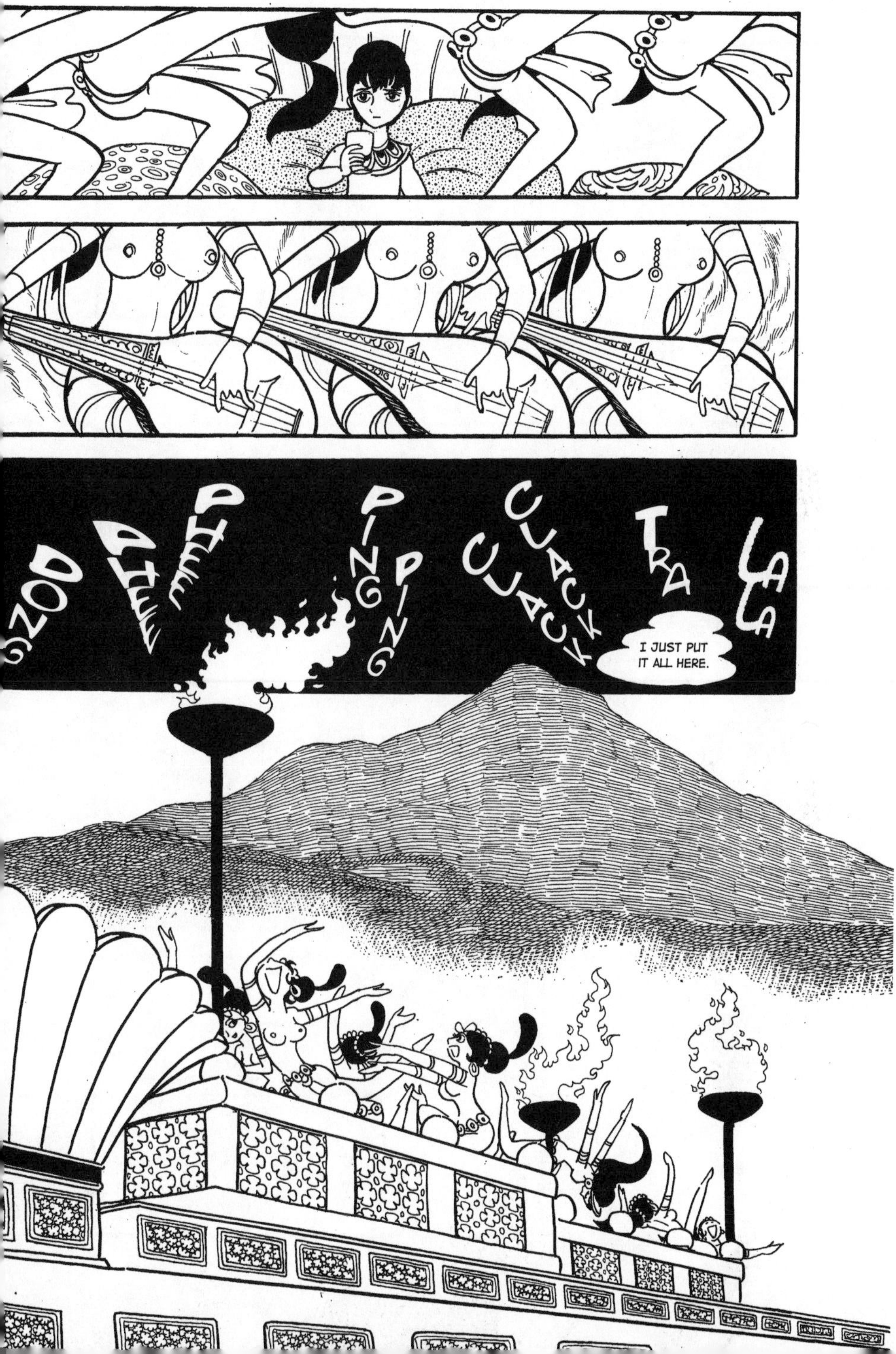
DOONG
PING
PING
TRA
LA LA
I JUST PUT IT ALL HERE.

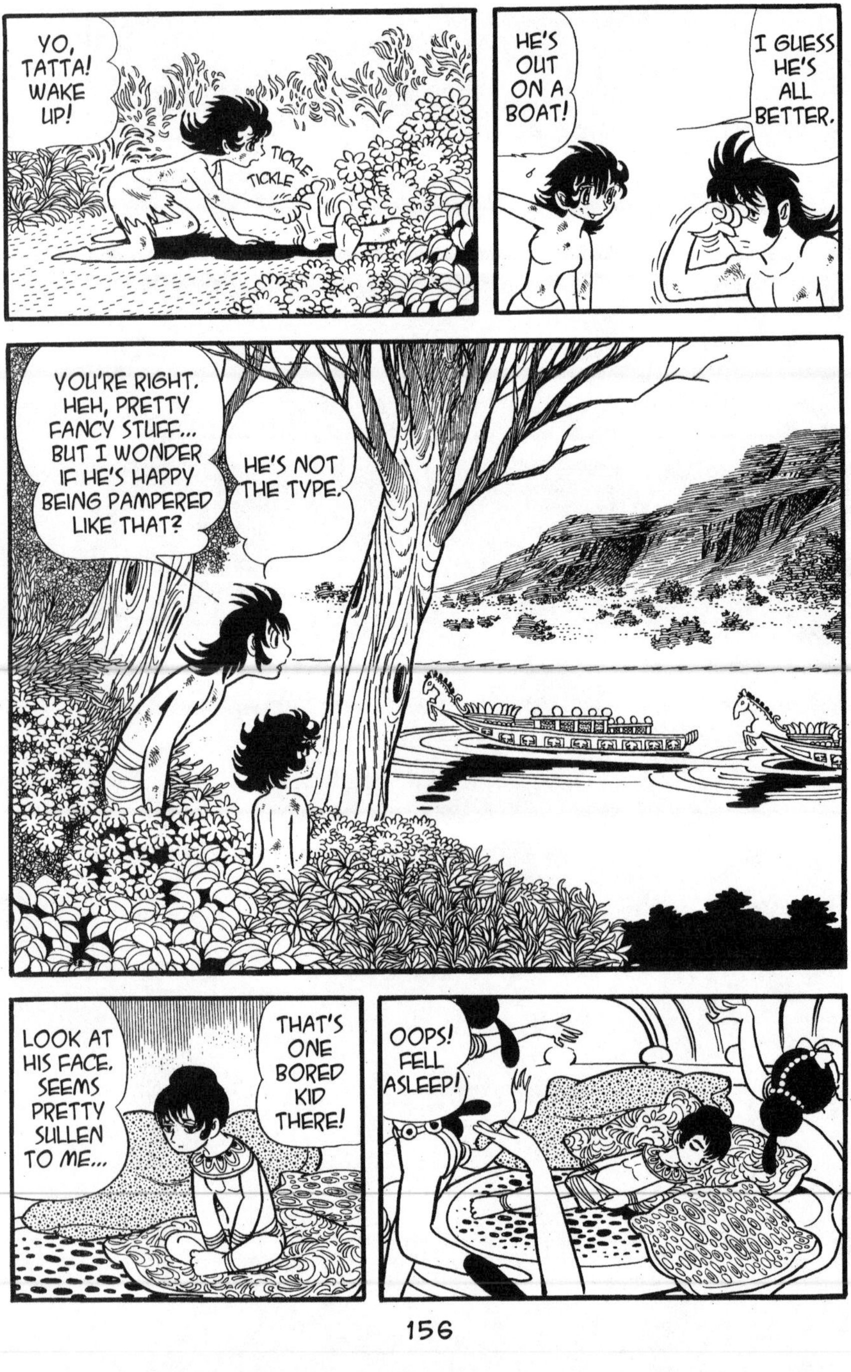

YO, TATTA! WAKE UP!
TICKLE TICKLE
HE'S OUT ON A BOAT!
I GUESS HE'S ALL BETTER.
YOU'RE RIGHT. HEH, PRETTY FANCY STUFF... BUT I WONDER IF HE'S HAPPY BEING PAMPERED LIKE THAT?
HE'S NOT THE TYPE.
LOOK AT HIS FACE. SEEMS PRETTY SULLEN TO ME...
THAT'S ONE BORED KID THERE!
OOPS! FELL ASLEEP!

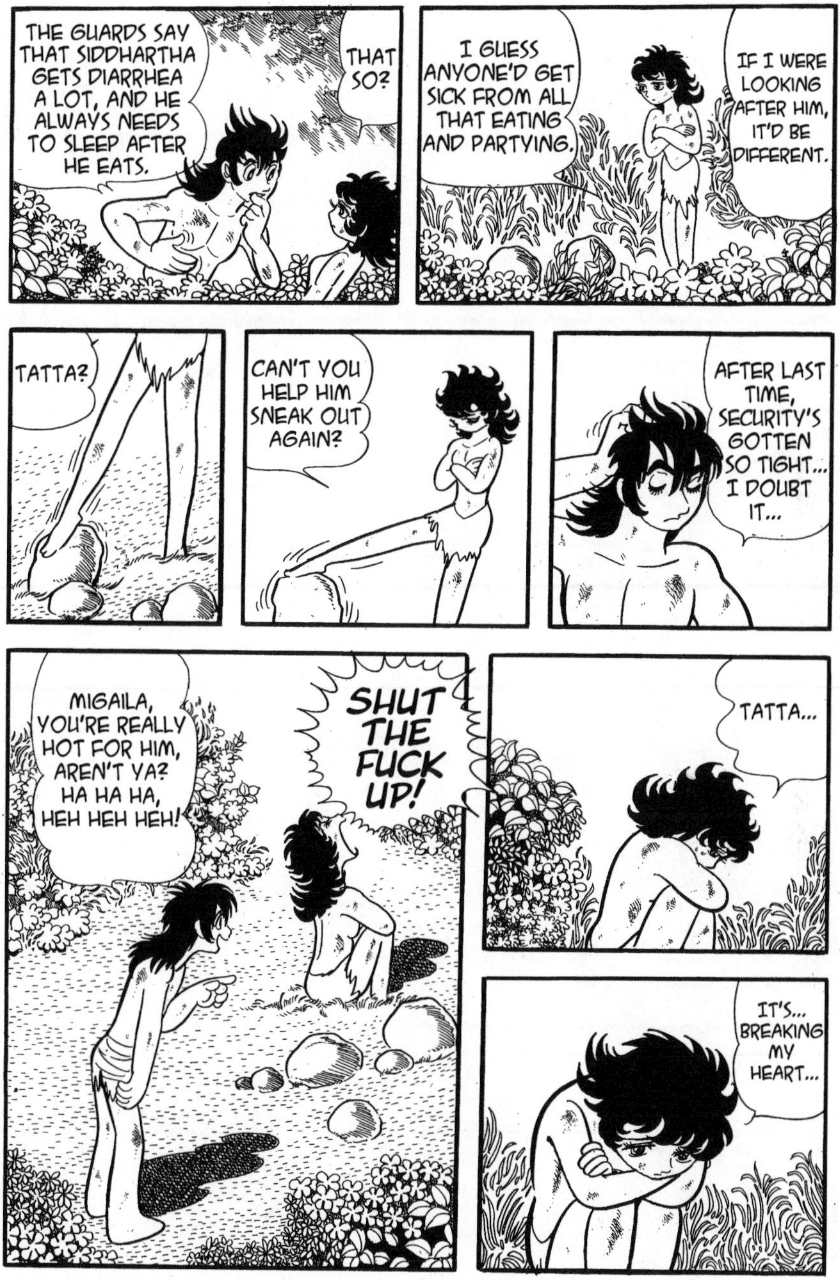
THE GUARDS SAY THAT SIDDHARTHA GETS DIARRHEA A LOT, AND HE ALWAYS NEEDS TO SLEEP AFTER HE EATS.
THAT SO?
I GUESS ANYONE'D GET SICK FROM ALL THAT EATING AND PARTYING.
IF I WERE LOOKING AFTER HIM, IT'D BE DIFFERENT.
TATTA?
CAN'T YOU HELP HIM SNEAK OUT AGAIN?
AFTER LAST TIME, SECURITY'S GOTTEN SO TIGHT... I DOUBT IT...
MIGAILA, YOU'RE REALLY HOT FOR HIM, AREN'T YA? HA HA HA, HEH HEH HEH!
SHUT THE FUCK UP!
TATTA...
IT'S... BREAKING MY HEART...

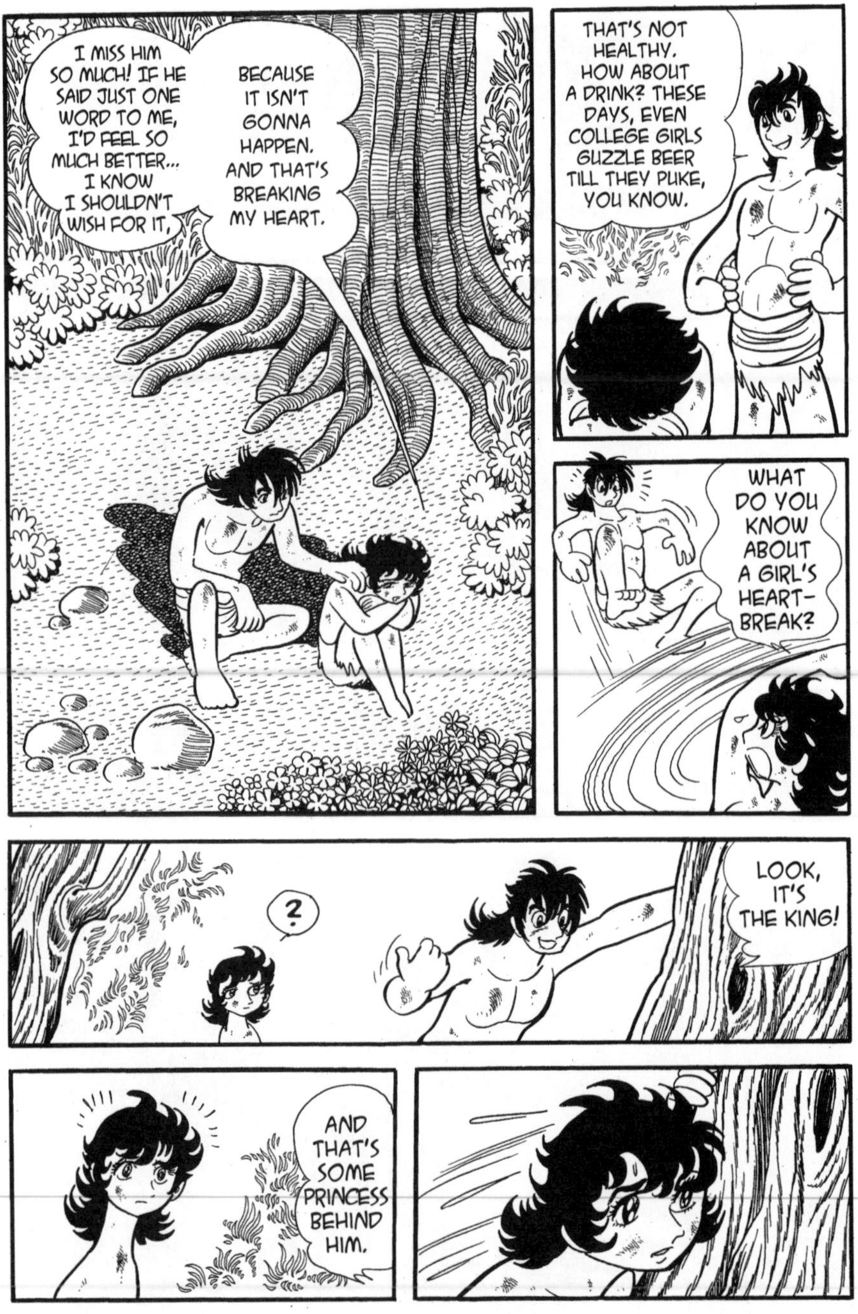
I MISS HIM SO MUCH! IF HE SAID JUST ONE WORD TO ME, I'D FEEL SO MUCH BETTER... I KNOW I SHOULDN'T WISH FOR IT,
BECAUSE IT ISN'T GONNA HAPPEN. AND THAT'S BREAKING MY HEART.
THAT'S NOT HEALTHY. HOW ABOUT A DRINK? THESE DAYS, EVEN COLLEGE GIRLS GUZZLE BEER TILL THEY PUKE, YOU KNOW.
WHAT DO YOU KNOW ABOUT A GIRL'S HEART-BREAK?
?
LOOK, IT'S THE KING!
AND THAT'S SOME PRINCESS BEHIND HIM.

MAYBE...

MAYBE WHAT?

SAY IT!

...

YOUR HEART-THROB'S GONNA MEET HIS WIFE TO BE.

SHH!

WHAT?!

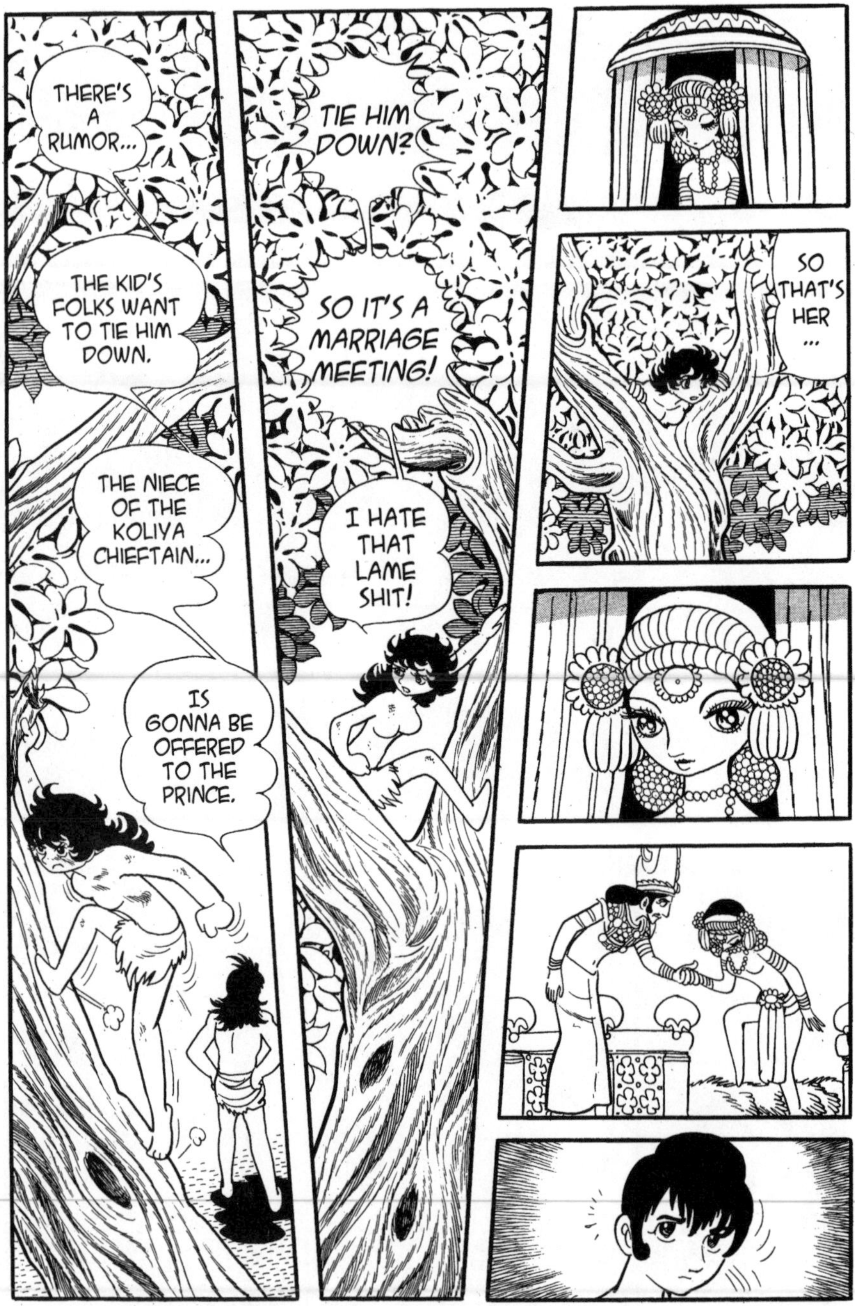
THERE'S A RUMOR...
THE KID'S FOLKS WANT TO TIE HIM DOWN.
THE NIECE OF THE KOLIYA CHIEFTAIN...
IS GONNA BE OFFERED TO THE PRINCE.
TIE HIM DOWN?
SO IT'S A MARRIAGE MEETING!
I HATE THAT LAME SHIT!
SO THAT'S HER ...

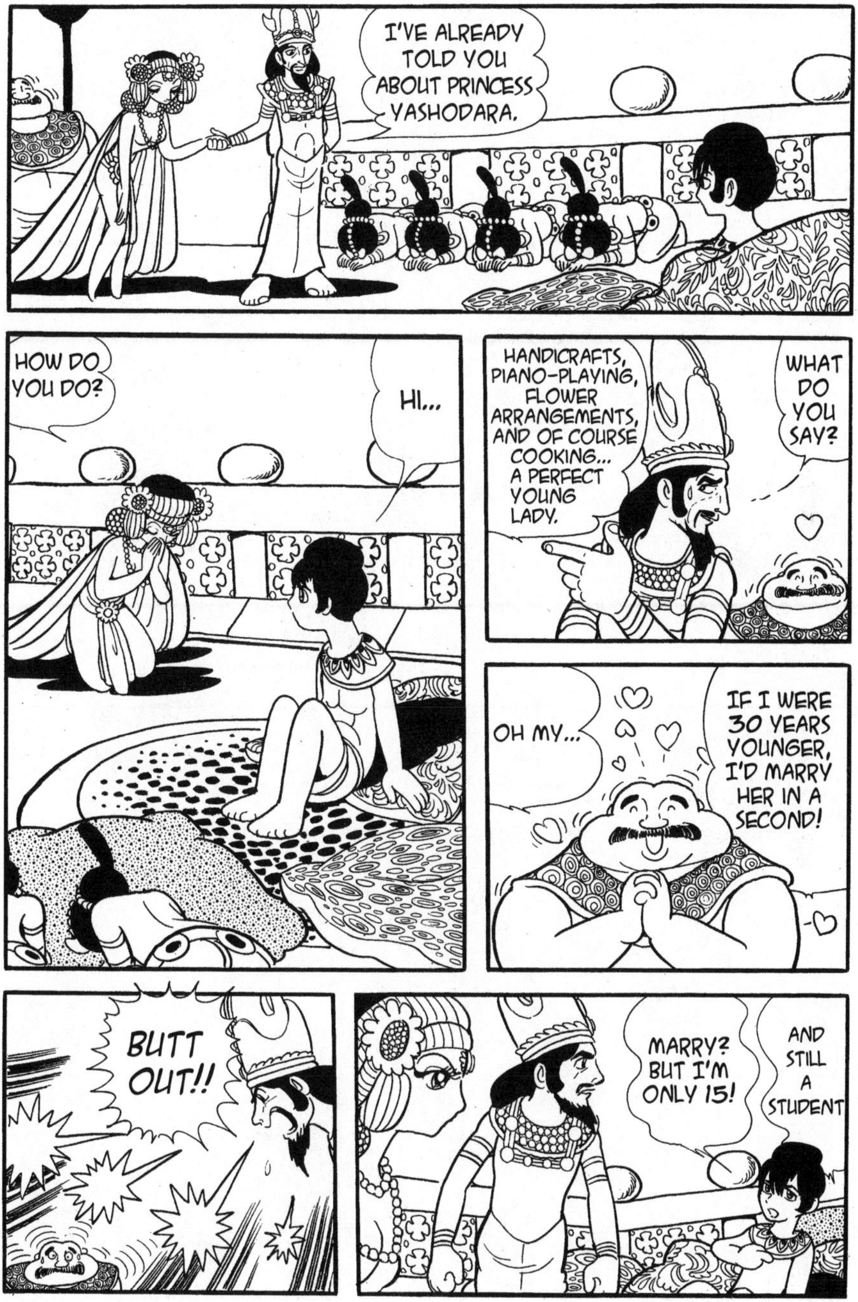
I'VE ALREADY TOLD YOU ABOUT PRINCESS YASHODARA.
HOW DO YOU DO?
HI...
HANDICRAFTS, PIANO-PLAYING, FLOWER ARRANGEMENTS, AND OF COURSE COOKING... A PERFECT YOUNG LADY.
WHAT DO YOU SAY?
OH MY...
IF I WERE 30 YEARS YOUNGER, I'D MARRY HER IN A SECOND!
BUTT OUT!!
MARRY? BUT I'M ONLY 15!
AND STILL A STUDENT

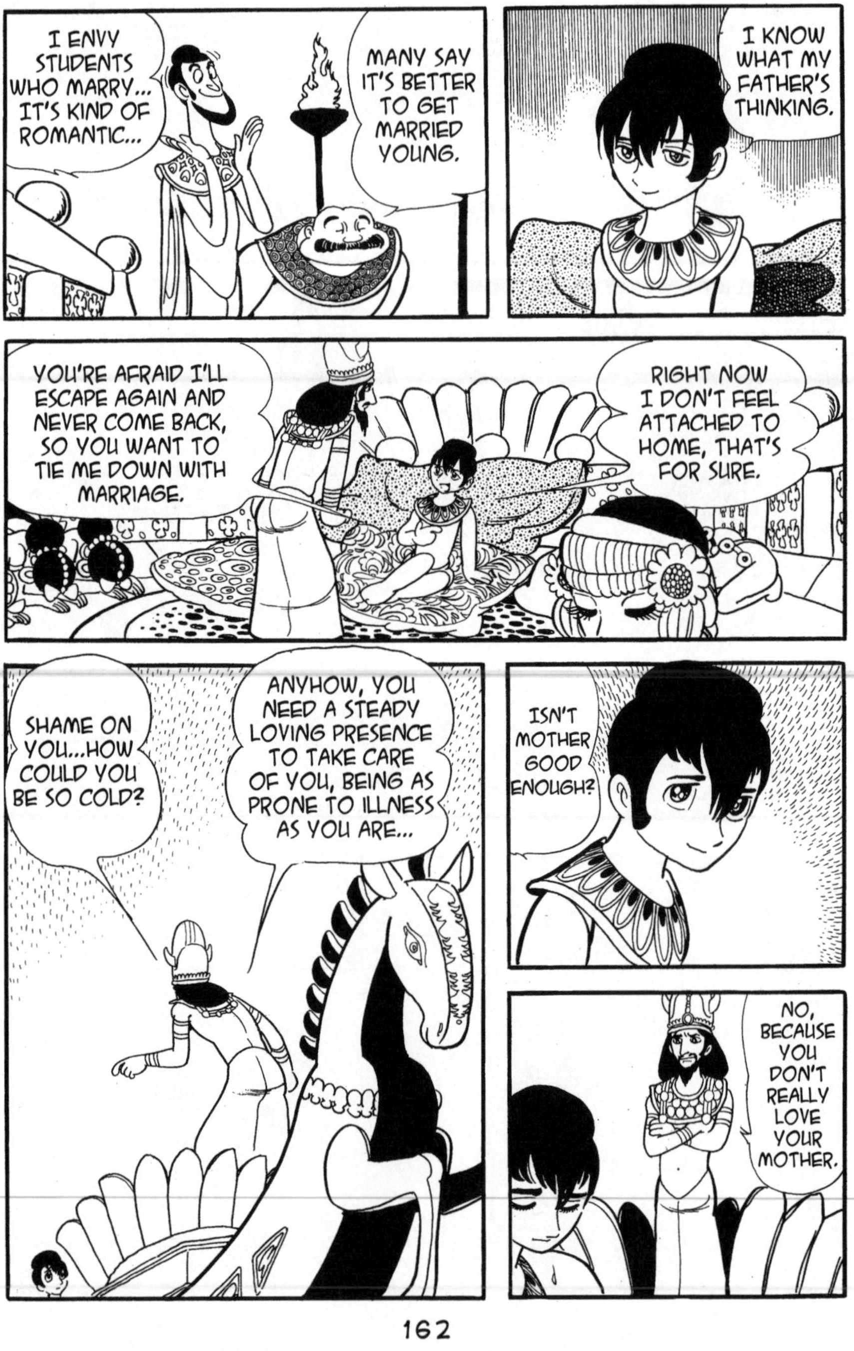
I ENVY STUDENTS WHO MARRY... IT'S KIND OF ROMANTIC...
MANY SAY IT'S BETTER TO GET MARRIED YOUNG.
I KNOW WHAT MY FATHER'S THINKING.
YOU'RE AFRAID I'LL ESCAPE AGAIN AND NEVER COME BACK, SO YOU WANT TO TIE ME DOWN WITH MARRIAGE.
RIGHT NOW I DON'T FEEL ATTACHED TO HOME, THAT'S FOR SURE.
SHAME ON YOU...HOW COULD YOU BE SO COLD?
ANYHOW, YOU NEED A STEADY LOVING PRESENCE TO TAKE CARE OF YOU, BEING AS PRONE TO ILLNESS AS YOU ARE...
ISN'T MOTHER GOOD ENOUGH?
NO, BECAUSE YOU DON'T REALLY LOVE YOUR MOTHER.

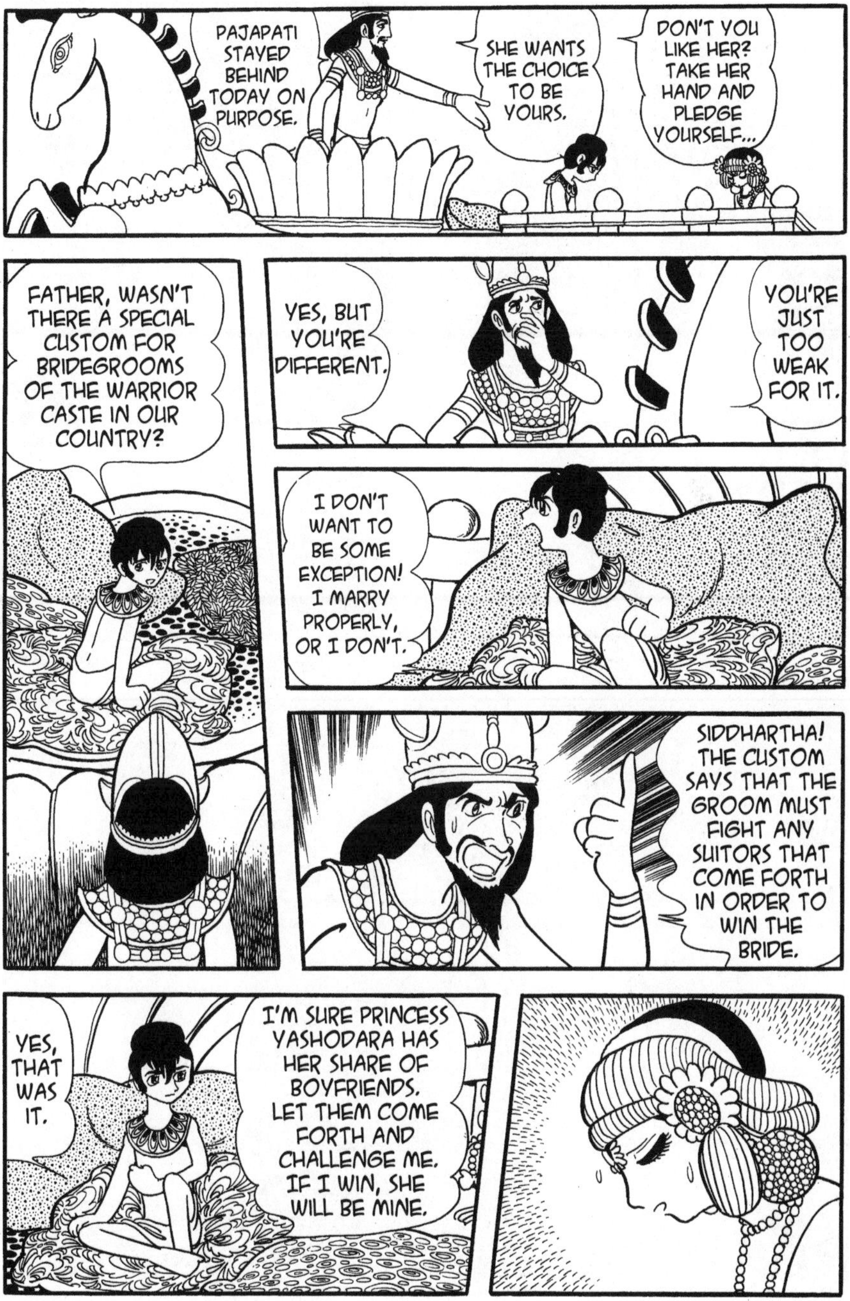
PAJAPATI STAYED BEHIND TODAY ON PURPOSE.
SHE WANTS THE CHOICE TO BE YOURS.
DON'T YOU LIKE HER? TAKE HER HAND AND PLEDGE YOURSELF...
FATHER, WASN'T THERE A SPECIAL CUSTOM FOR BRIDEGROOMS OF THE WARRIOR CASTE IN OUR COUNTRY?
YES, BUT YOU'RE DIFFERENT.
YOU'RE JUST TOO WEAK FOR IT.
I DON'T WANT TO BE SOME EXCEPTION! I MARRY PROPERLY, OR I DON'T.
SIDDHARTHA! THE CUSTOM SAYS THAT THE GROOM MUST FIGHT ANY SUITORS THAT COME FORTH IN ORDER TO WIN THE BRIDE.
YES, THAT WAS IT.
I'M SURE PRINCESS YASHODARA HAS HER SHARE OF BOYFRIENDS. LET THEM COME FORTH AND CHALLENGE ME. IF I WIN, SHE WILL BE MINE.

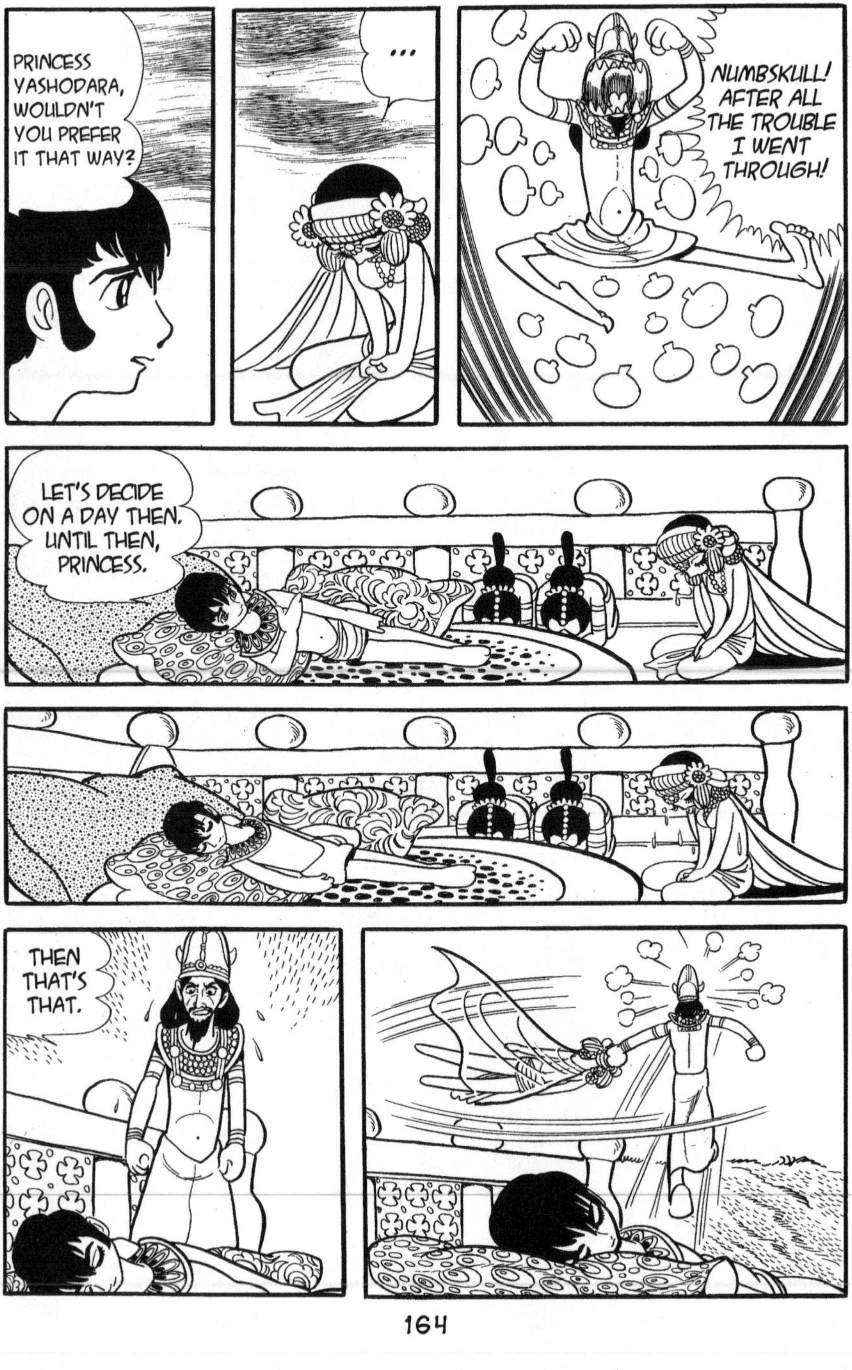
PRINCESS YASHODARA, WOULDN'T YOU PREFER IT THAT WAY?
...
NUMBSKULL! AFTER ALL THE TROUBLE I WENT THROUGH!
LET'S DECIDE ON A DAY THEN. UNTIL THEN, PRINCESS.
THEN THAT'S THAT.

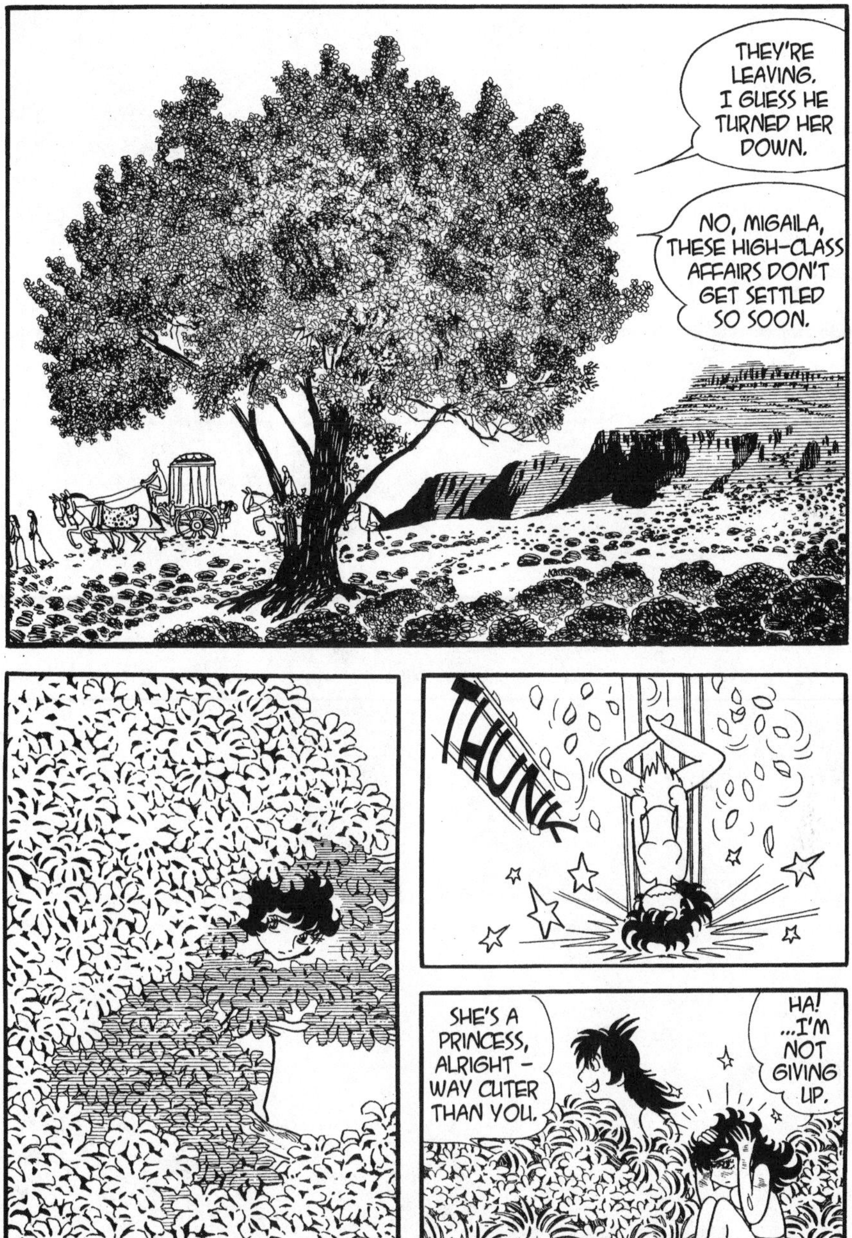
THEY'RE LEAVING. I GUESS HE TURNED HER DOWN.
NO, MIGAILA, THESE HIGH-CLASS AFFAIRS DON'T GET SETTLED SO SOON.
THUNK
SHE'S A PRINCESS, ALRIGHT - WAY CUTER THAN YOU.
HA! ...I'M NOT GIVING UP.

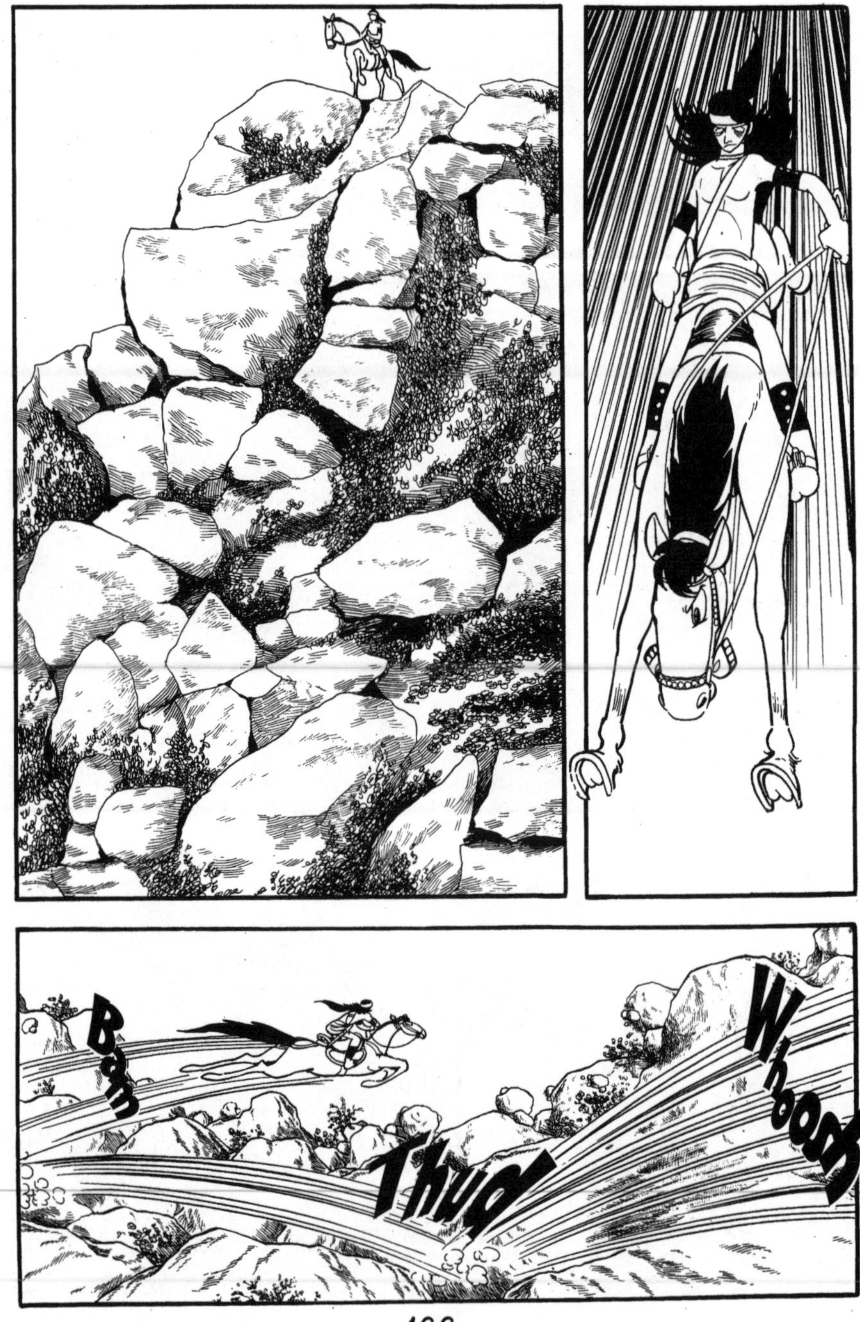
Bam
Thud
Whoosh

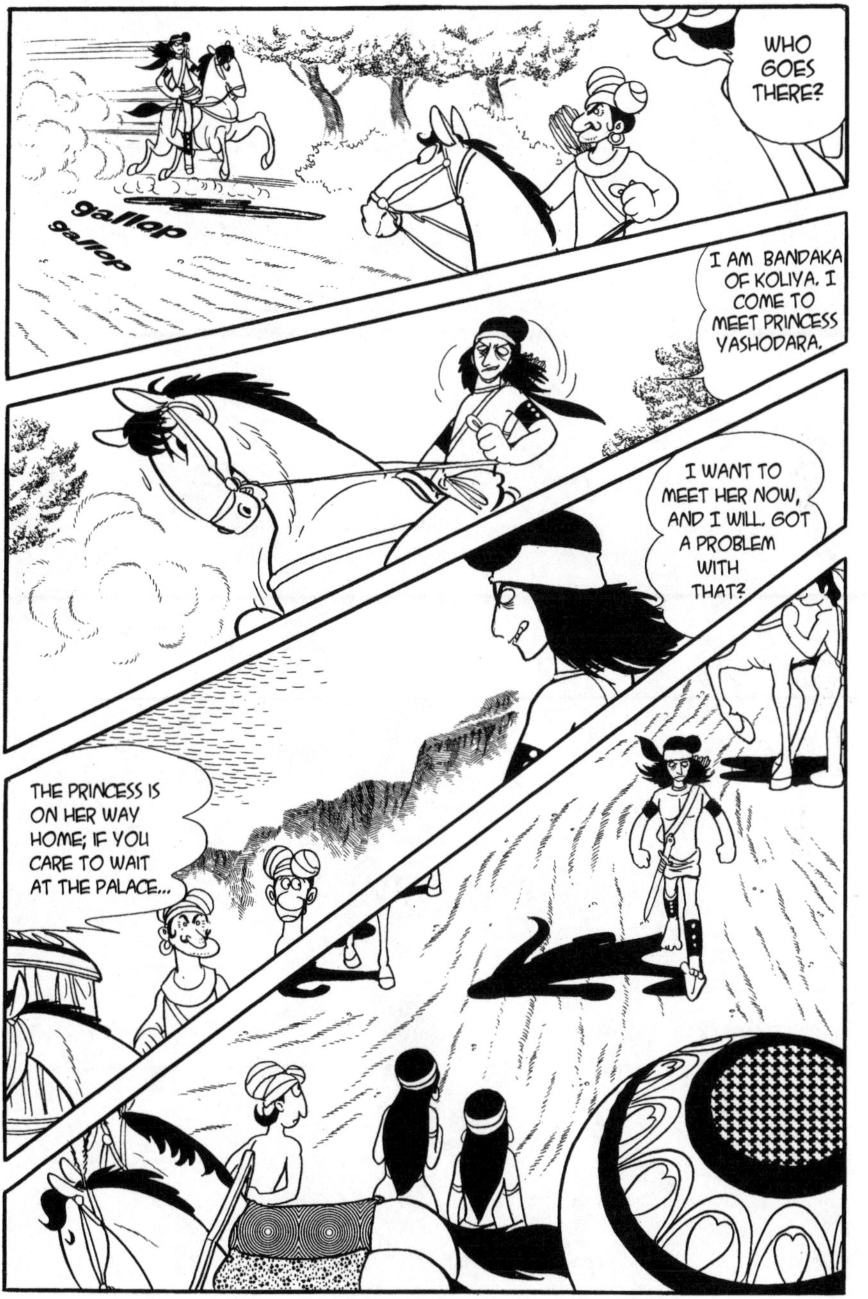

gallop
gallop
WHO GOES THERE?
I AM BANDAKA OF KOLIYA. I COME TO MEET PRINCESS YASHODARA.
I WANT TO MEET HER NOW, AND I WILL. GOT A PROBLEM WITH THAT?
THE PRINCESS IS ON HER WAY HOME; IF YOU CARE TO WAIT AT THE PALACE...

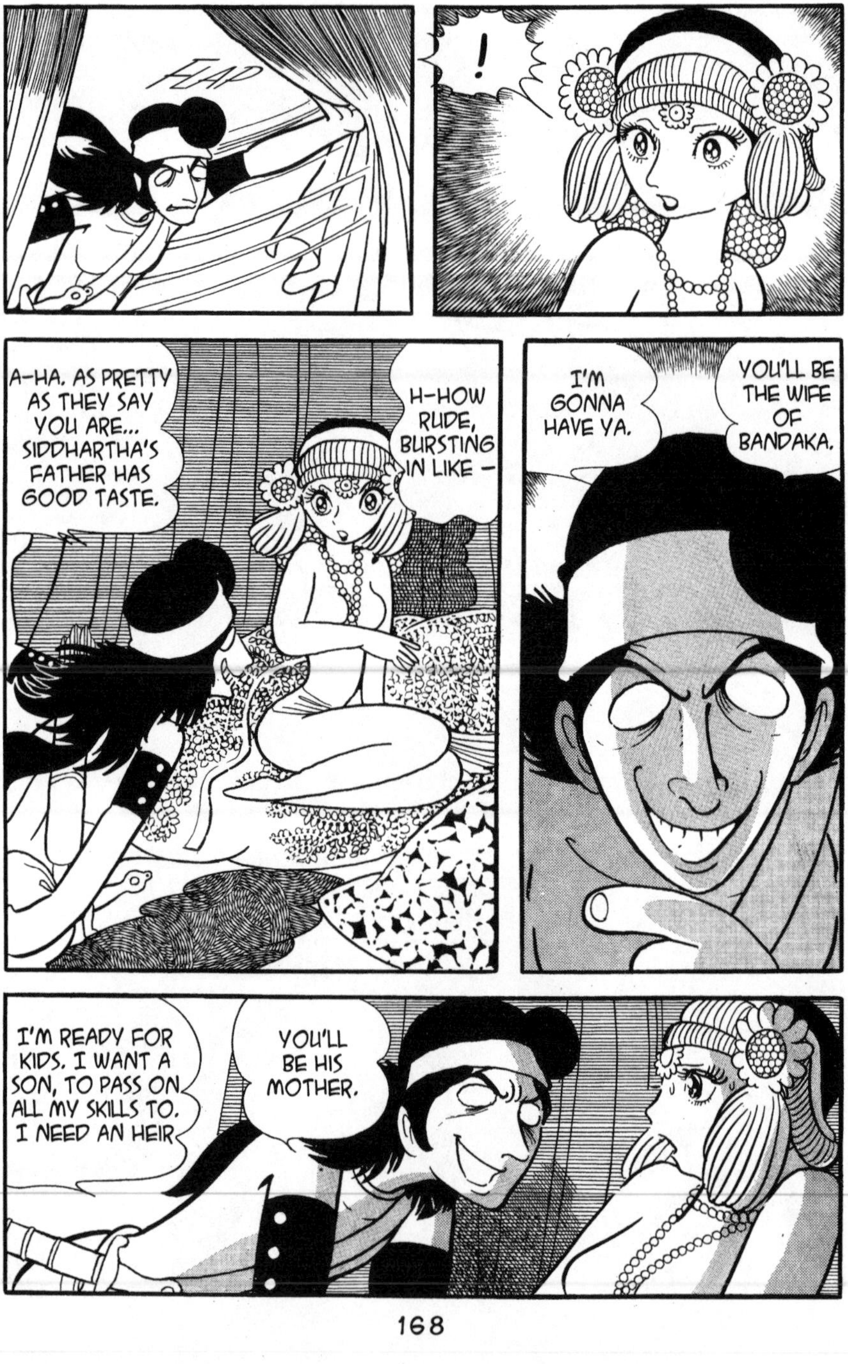
FLAP
!
A-HA. AS PRETTY AS THEY SAY YOU ARE... SIDDHARTHA'S FATHER HAS GOOD TASTE.
H-HOW RUDE, BURSTING IN LIKE —
I'M GONNA HAVE YA.
YOU'LL BE THE WIFE OF BANDAKA.
I'M READY FOR KIDS. I WANT A SON, TO PASS ON ALL MY SKILLS TO. I NEED AN HEIR
YOU'LL BE HIS MOTHER.

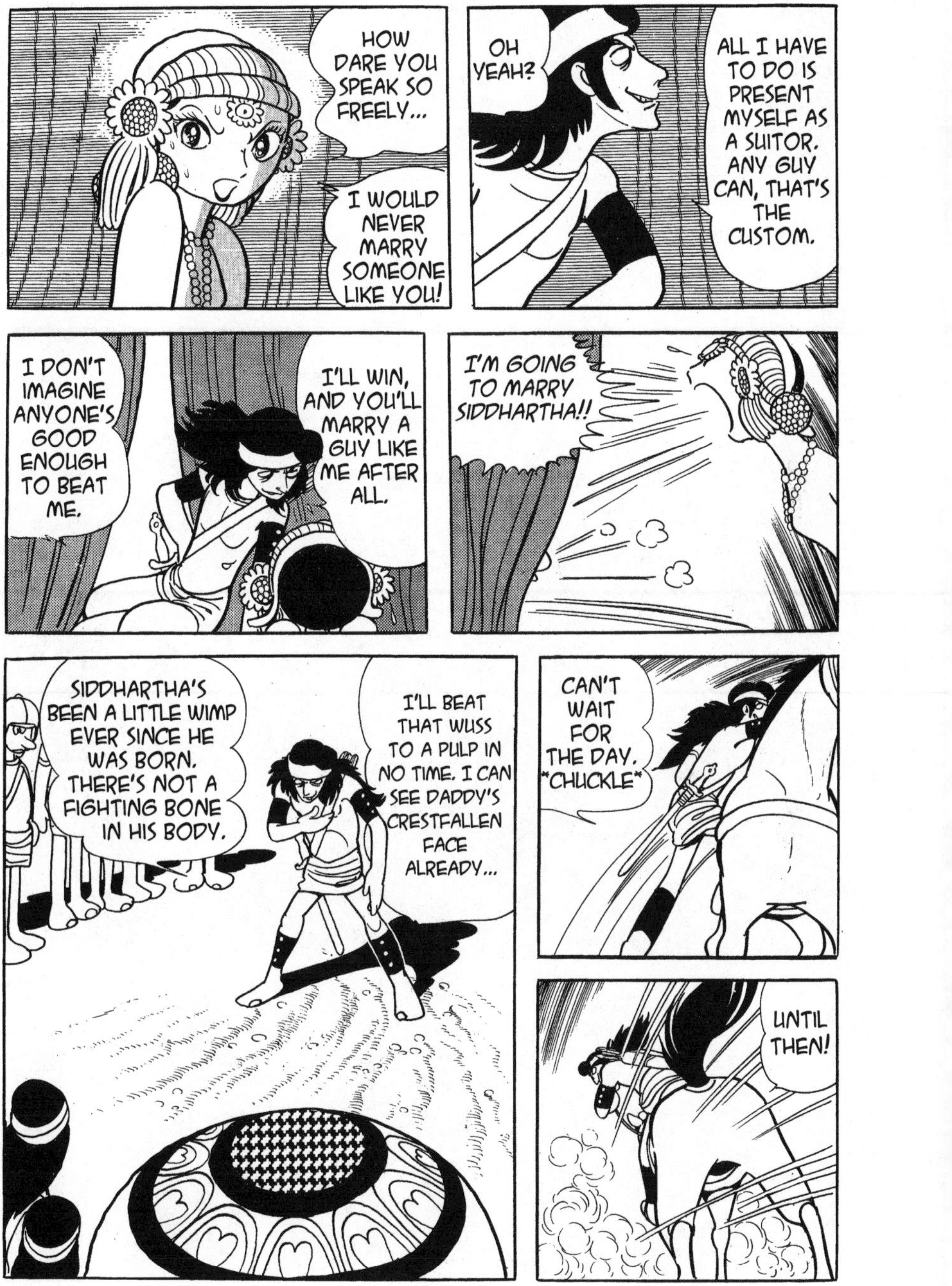
HOW DARE YOU SPEAK SO FREELY...
I WOULD NEVER MARRY SOMEONE LIKE YOU!
OH YEAH?
ALL I HAVE TO DO IS PRESENT MYSELF AS A SUITOR. ANY GUY CAN, THAT'S THE CUSTOM.
I DON'T IMAGINE ANYONE'S GOOD ENOUGH TO BEAT ME.
I'LL WIN, AND YOU'LL MARRY A GUY LIKE ME AFTER ALL.
I'M GOING TO MARRY SIDDHARTHA!!
SIDDHARTHA'S BEEN A LITTLE WIMP EVER SINCE HE WAS BORN. THERE'S NOT A FIGHTING BONE IN HIS BODY.
I'LL BEAT THAT WUSS TO A PULP IN NO TIME. I CAN SEE DADDY'S CRESTFALLEN FACE ALREADY...
CAN'T WAIT FOR THE DAY. *CHUCKLE*
UNTIL THEN!

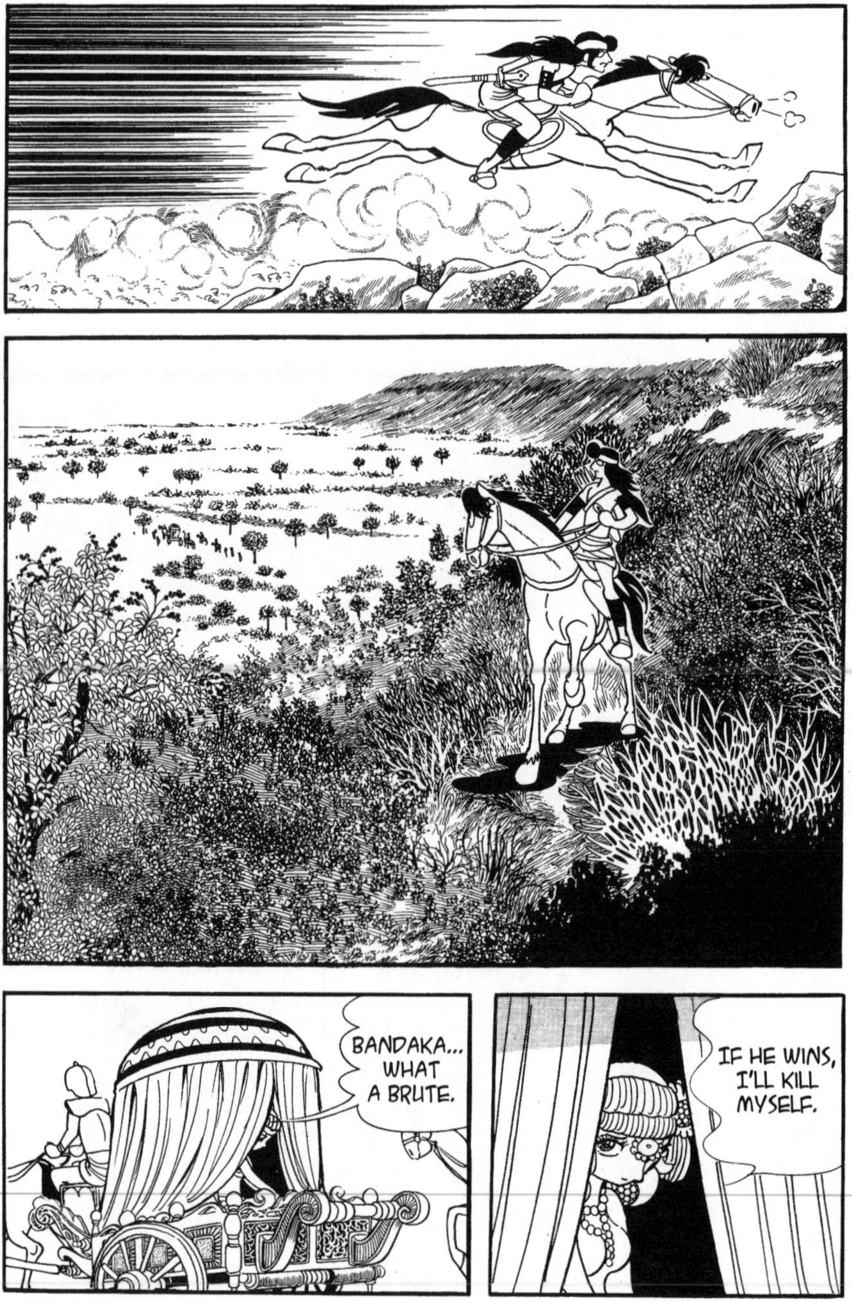
BANDAKA... WHAT A BRUTE.
IF HE WINS, I'LL KILL MYSELF.

CHAPTER FIVE

MIGAILA

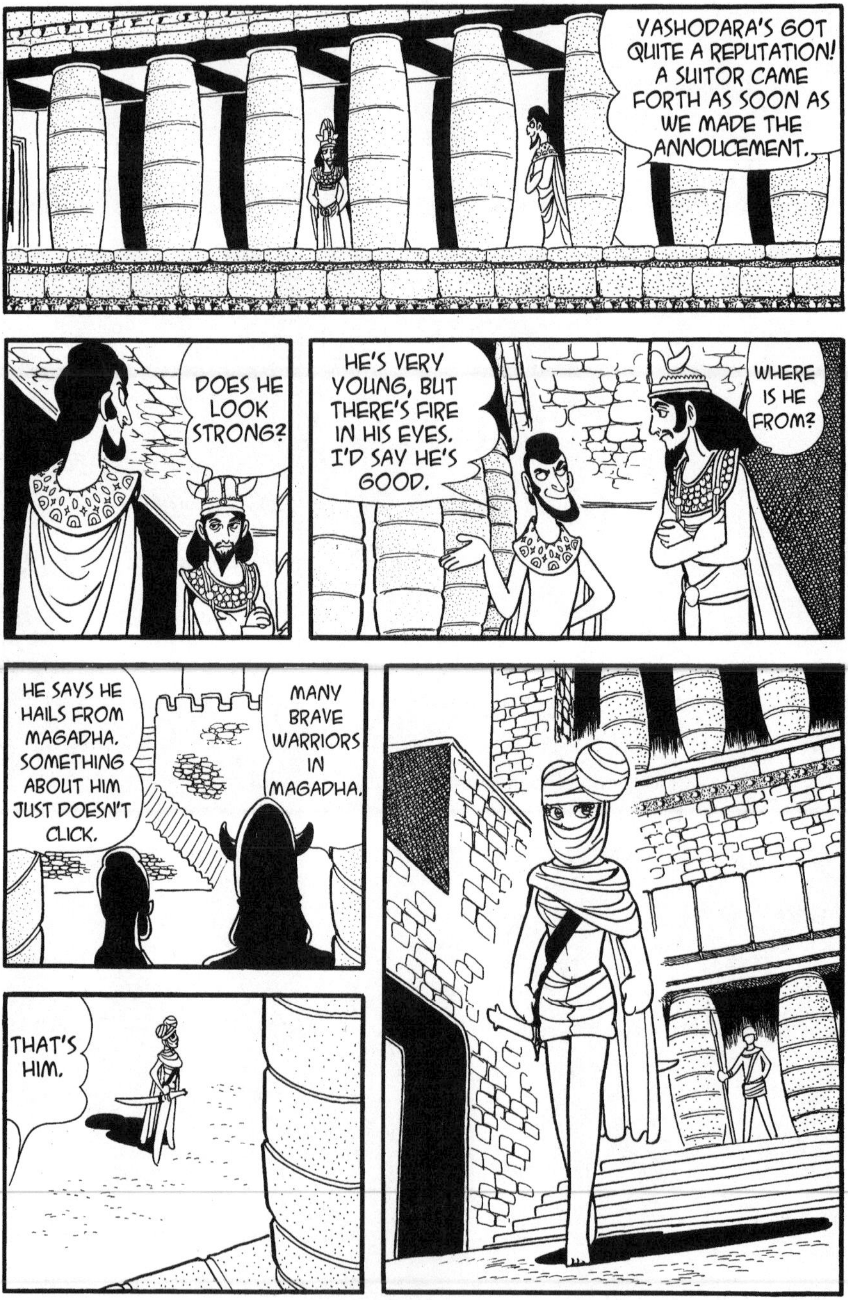

YASHODARA'S GOT QUITE A REPUTATION! A SUITOR CAME FORTH AS SOON AS WE MADE THE ANNOUCEMENT.
DOES HE LOOK STRONG?
HE'S VERY YOUNG, BUT THERE'S FIRE IN HIS EYES. I'D SAY HE'S GOOD.
WHERE IS HE FROM?
HE SAYS HE HAILS FROM MAGADHA. SOMETHING ABOUT HIM JUST DOESN'T CLICK.
MANY BRAVE WARRIORS IN MAGADHA.
THAT'S HIM.

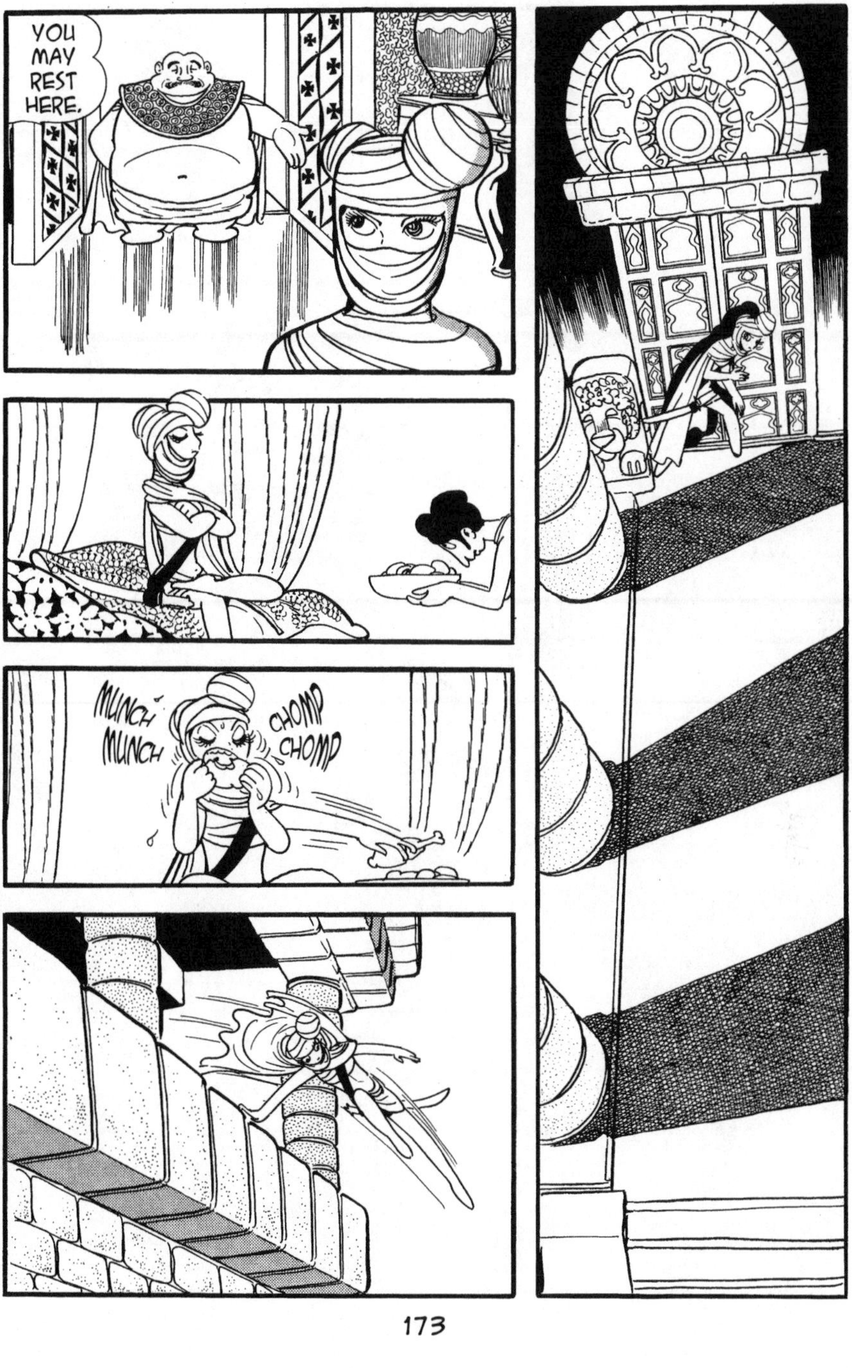
YOU MAY REST HERE.
MUNCH MUNCH
CHOMP CHOMP

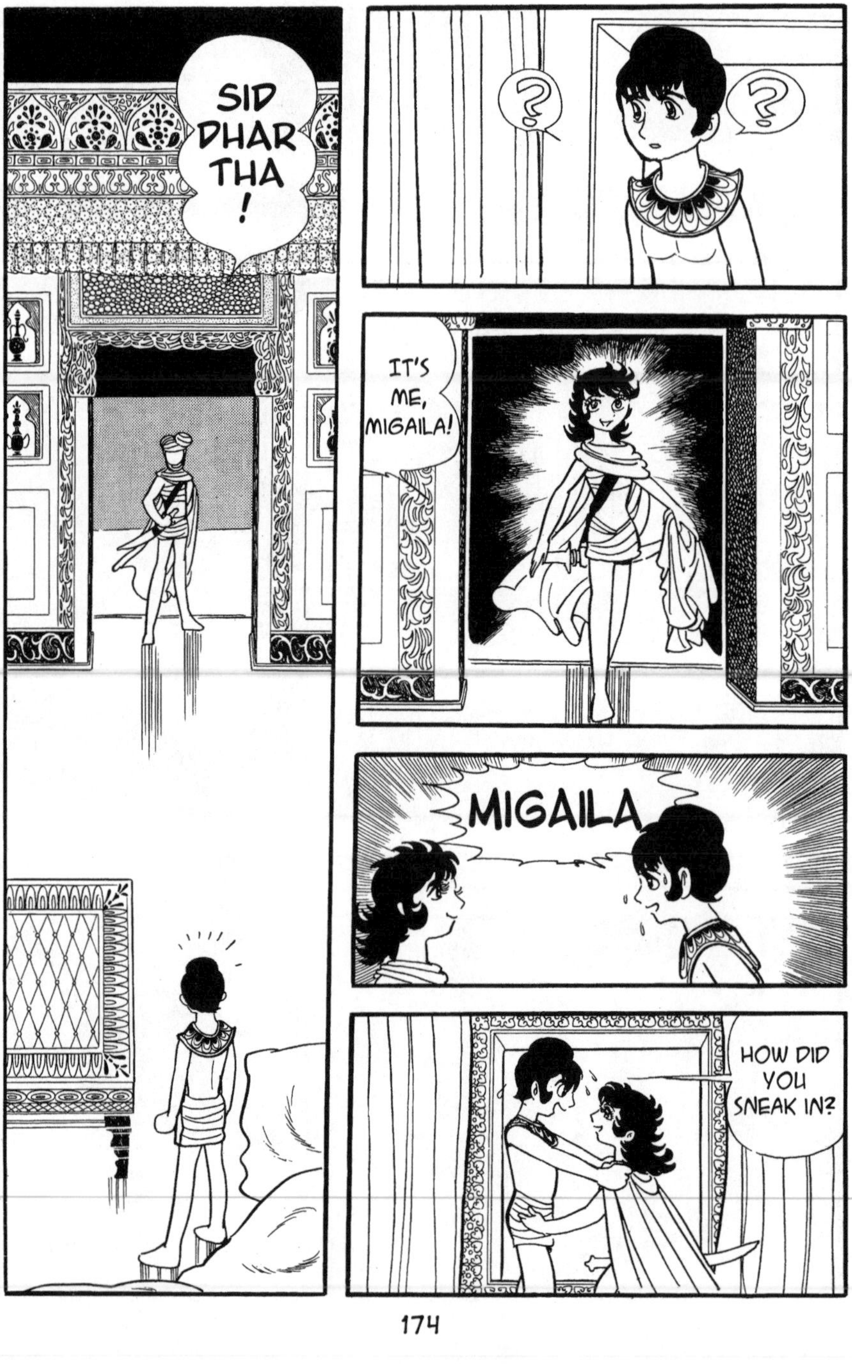
SID DHAR THA!
?
?
IT'S ME, MIGAILA!
MIGAILA
HOW DID YOU SNEAK IN?

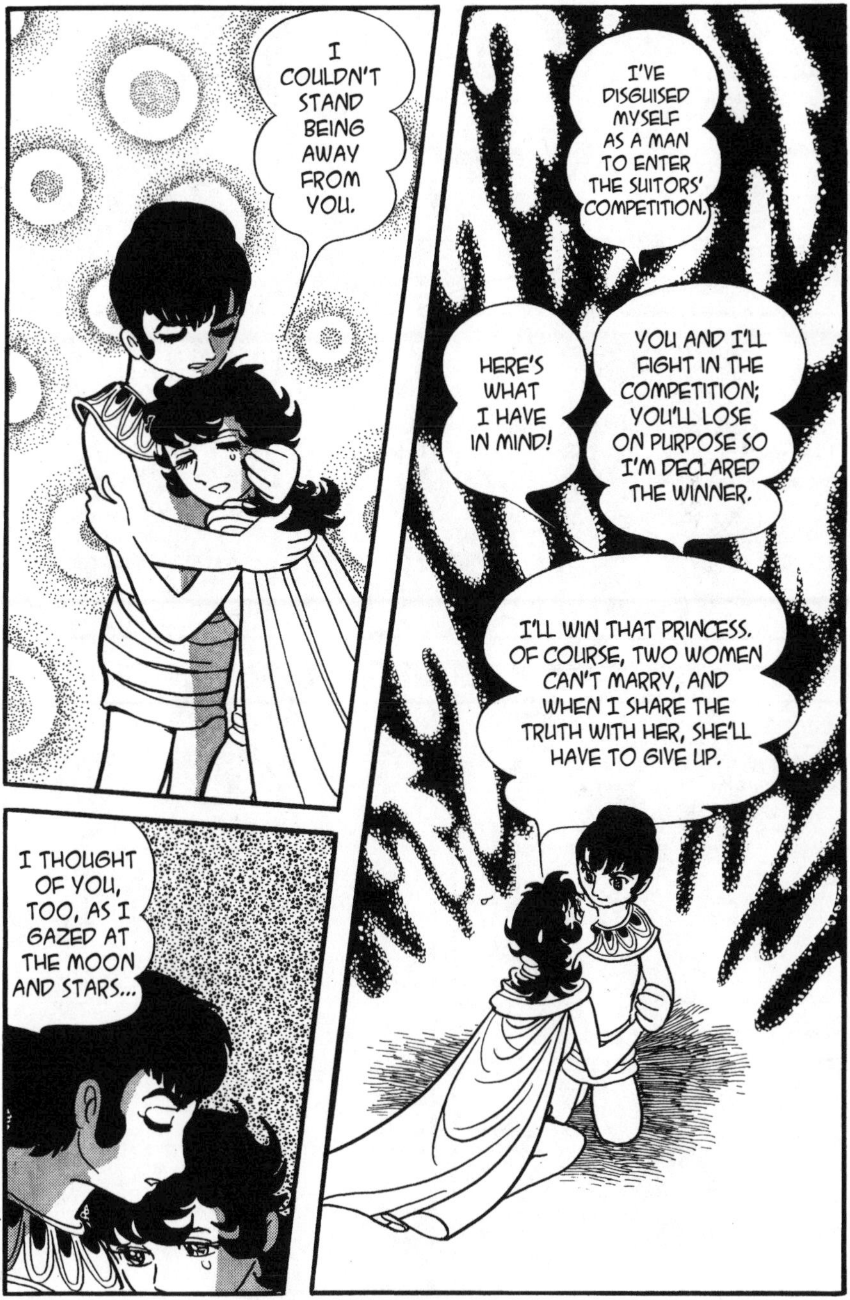
I COULDN'T STAND BEING AWAY FROM YOU.
I THOUGHT OF YOU, TOO, AS I GAZED AT THE MOON AND STARS...
I'VE DISGUISED MYSELF AS A MAN TO ENTER THE SUITORS' COMPETITION.
HERE'S WHAT I HAVE IN MIND!
YOU AND I'LL FIGHT IN THE COMPETITION; YOU'LL LOSE ON PURPOSE SO I'M DECLARED THE WINNER.
I'LL WIN THAT PRINCESS. OF COURSE, TWO WOMEN CAN'T MARRY, AND WHEN I SHARE THE TRUTH WITH HER, SHE'LL HAVE TO GIVE UP.

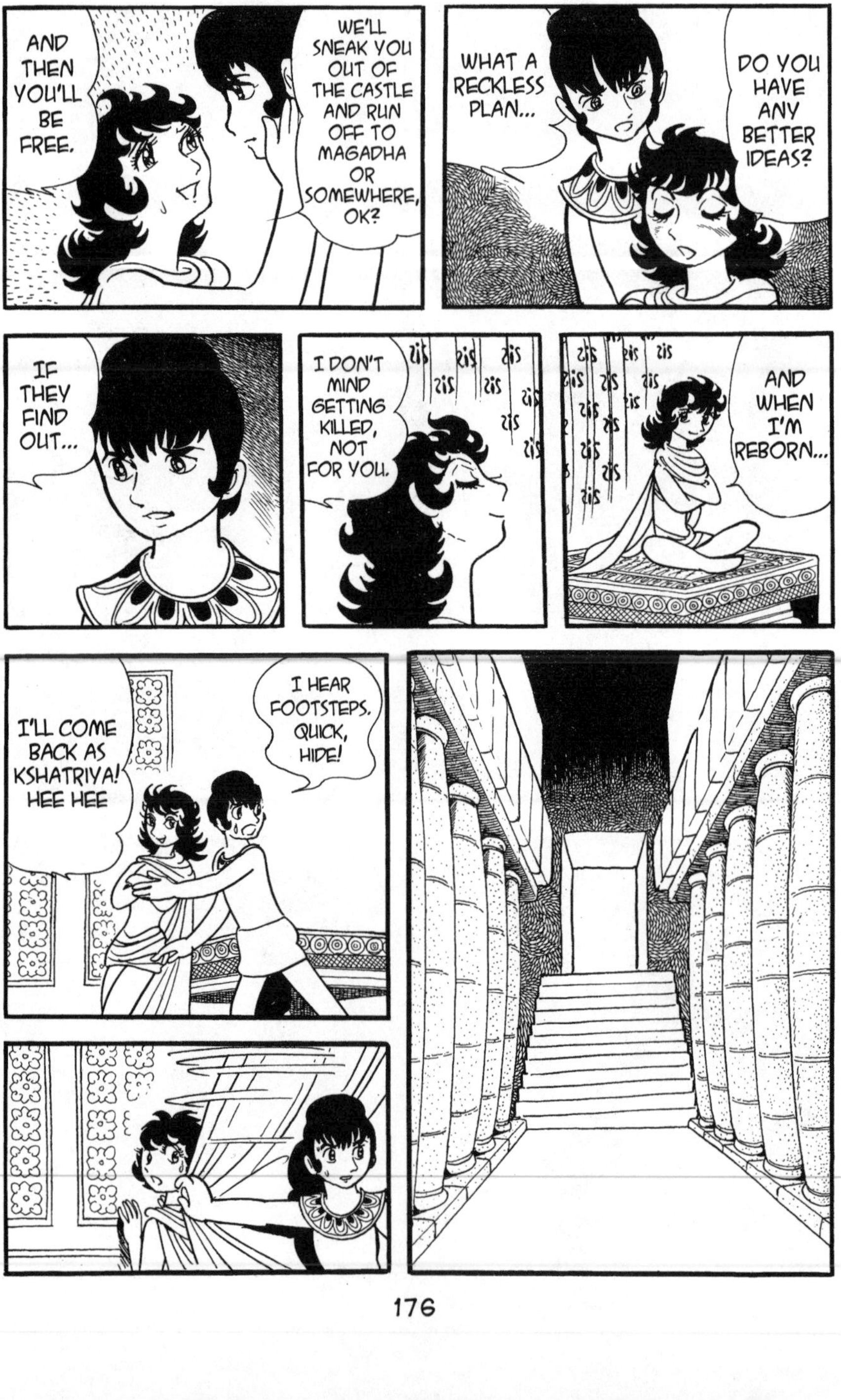

AND THEN YOU'LL BE FREE.
WE'LL SNEAK YOU OUT OF THE CASTLE AND RUN OFF TO MAGADHA OR SOMEWHERE, OK?
WHAT A RECKLESS PLAN...
DO YOU HAVE ANY BETTER IDEAS?
IF THEY FIND OUT...
I DON'T MIND GETTING KILLED, NOT FOR YOU.
AND WHEN I'M REBORN...
I'LL COME BACK AS KSHATRIYA! HEE HEE
I HEAR FOOTSTEPS. QUICK, HIDE!

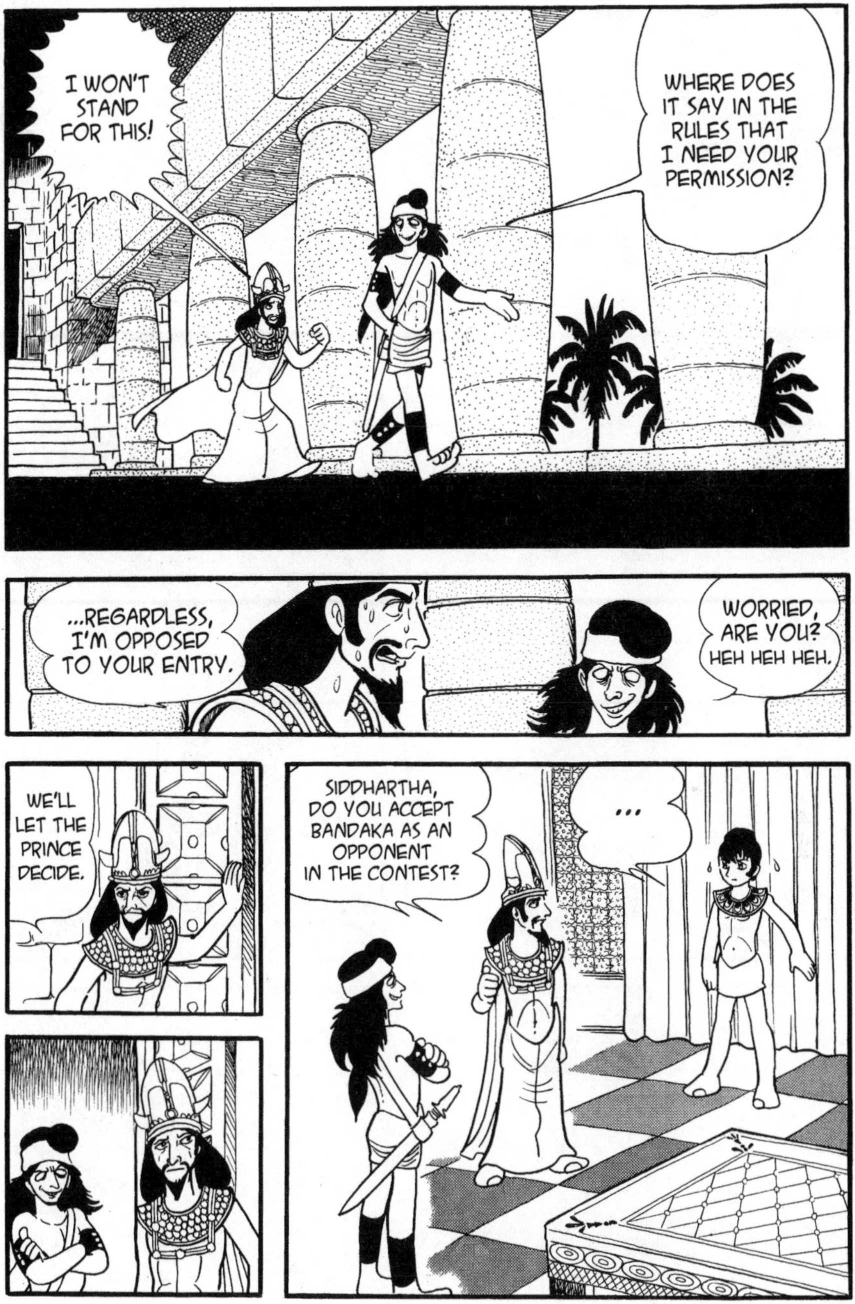
I WON'T STAND FOR THIS!
WHERE DOES IT SAY IN THE RULES THAT I NEED YOUR PERMISSION?
...REGARDLESS, I'M OPPOSED TO YOUR ENTRY.
WORRIED, ARE YOU? HEH HEH HEH.
WE'LL LET THE PRINCE DECIDE.
SIDDHARTHA, DO YOU ACCEPT BANDAKA AS AN OPPONENT IN THE CONTEST?
...

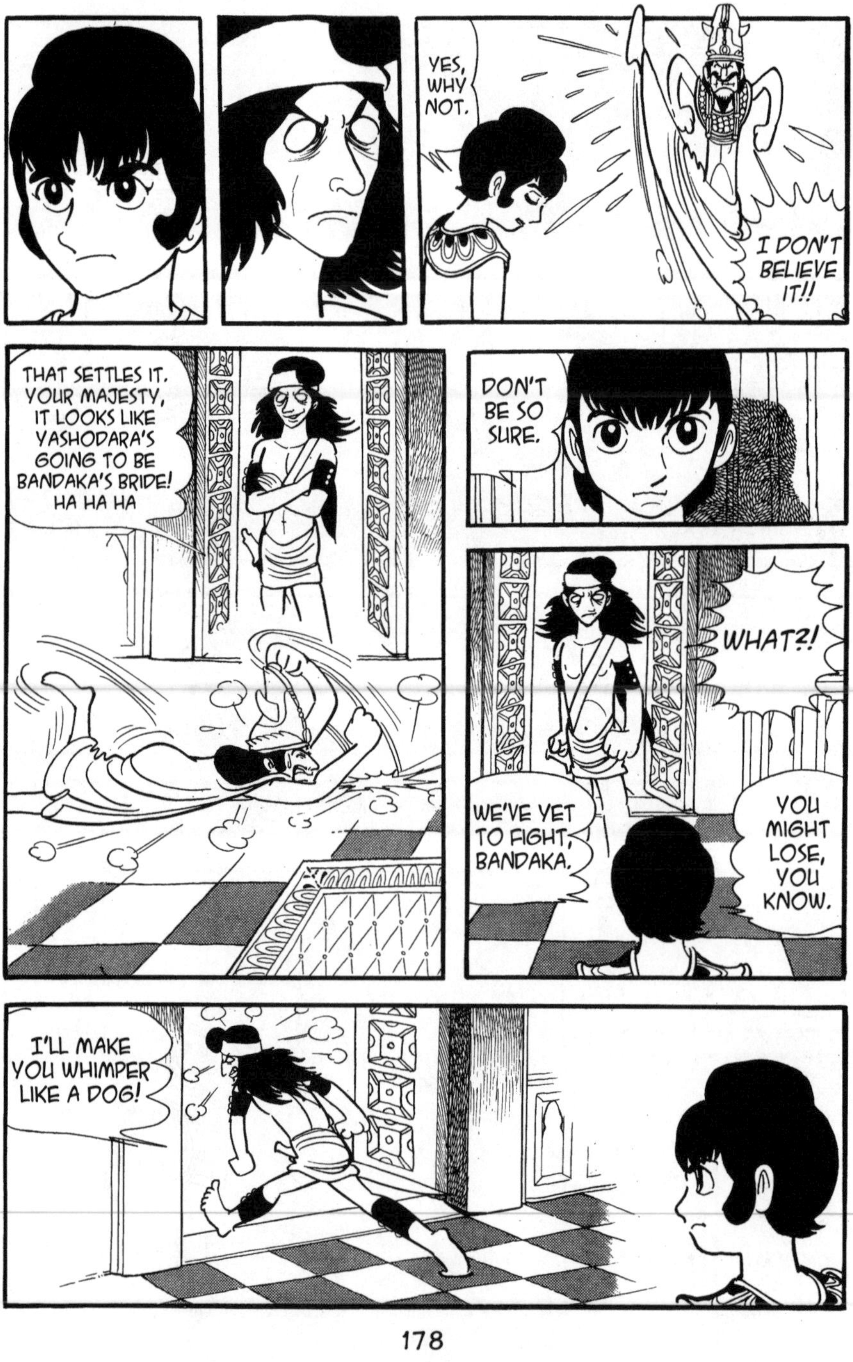
YES, WHY NOT.
I DON'T BELIEVE IT!!
THAT SETTLES IT. YOUR MAJESTY, IT LOOKS LIKE YASHODARA'S GOING TO BE BANDAKA'S BRIDE! HA HA HA
DON'T BE SO SURE.
WHAT?!
WE'VE YET TO FIGHT, BANDAKA.
YOU MIGHT LOSE, YOU KNOW.
I'LL MAKE YOU WHIMPER LIKE A DOG!

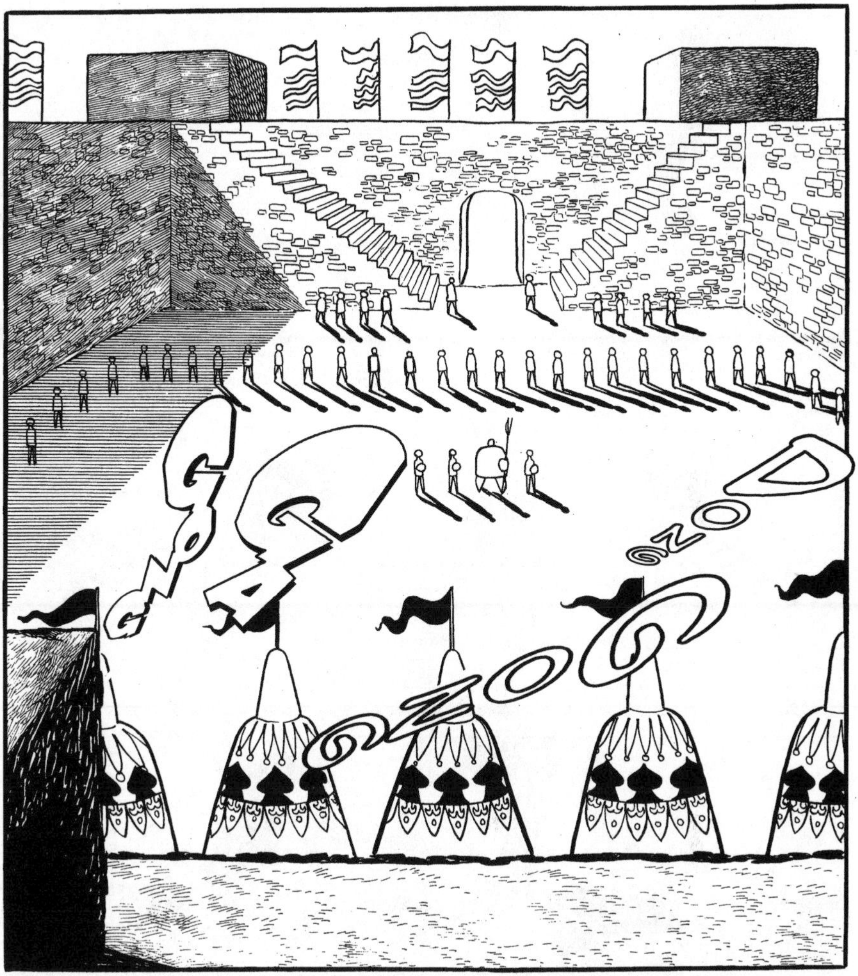
GONG GONG
DONG DONG

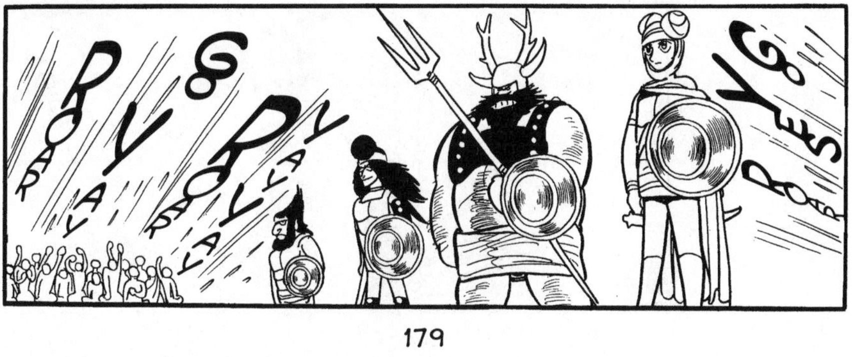
ROAR
ROAR
ROAR

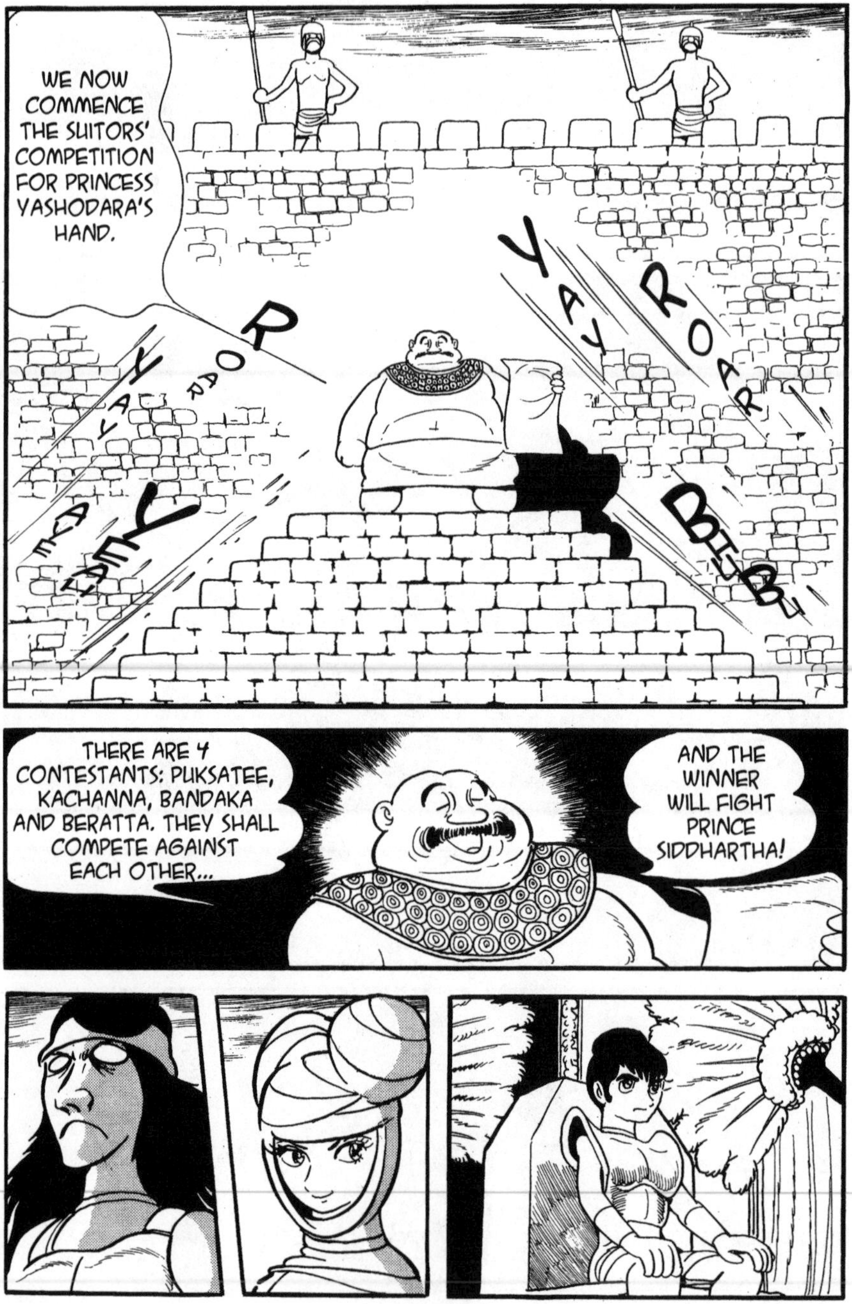
WE NOW COMMENCE THE SUITORS' COMPETITION FOR PRINCESS YASHODARA'S HAND.
YAY
ROAR
ROAR
YAY
YEAH
AYE
BUBU
THERE ARE 4 CONTESTANTS: PUKSATEE, KACHANNA, BANDAKA AND BERATTA. THEY SHALL COMPETE AGAINST EACH OTHER...
AND THE WINNER WILL FIGHT PRINCE SIDDHARTHA!

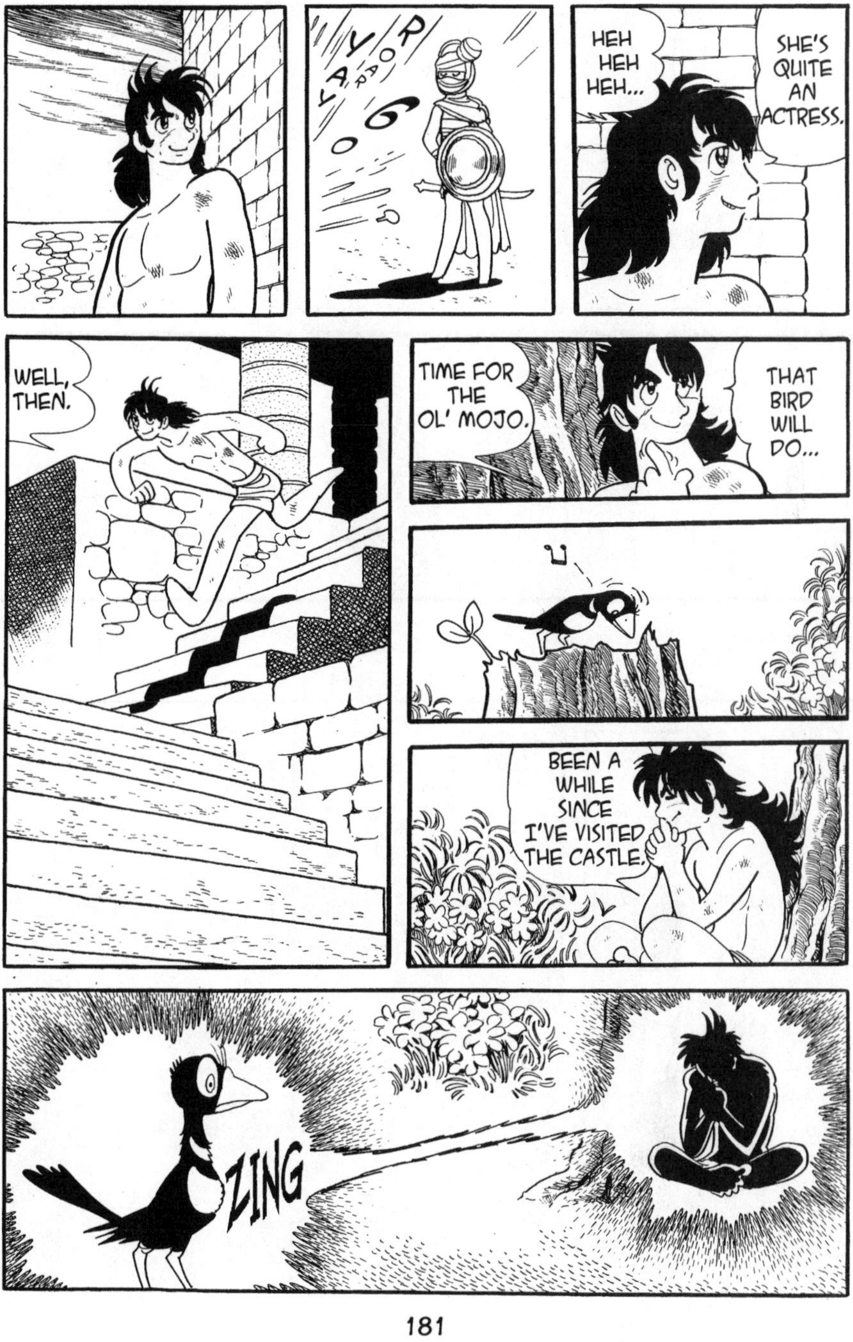
HEH HEH HEH...
SHE'S QUITE AN ACTRESS.
WELL, THEN.
TIME FOR THE OL' MOJO.
THAT BIRD WILL DO...
BEEN A WHILE SINCE I'VE VISITED THE CASTLE.
ZING

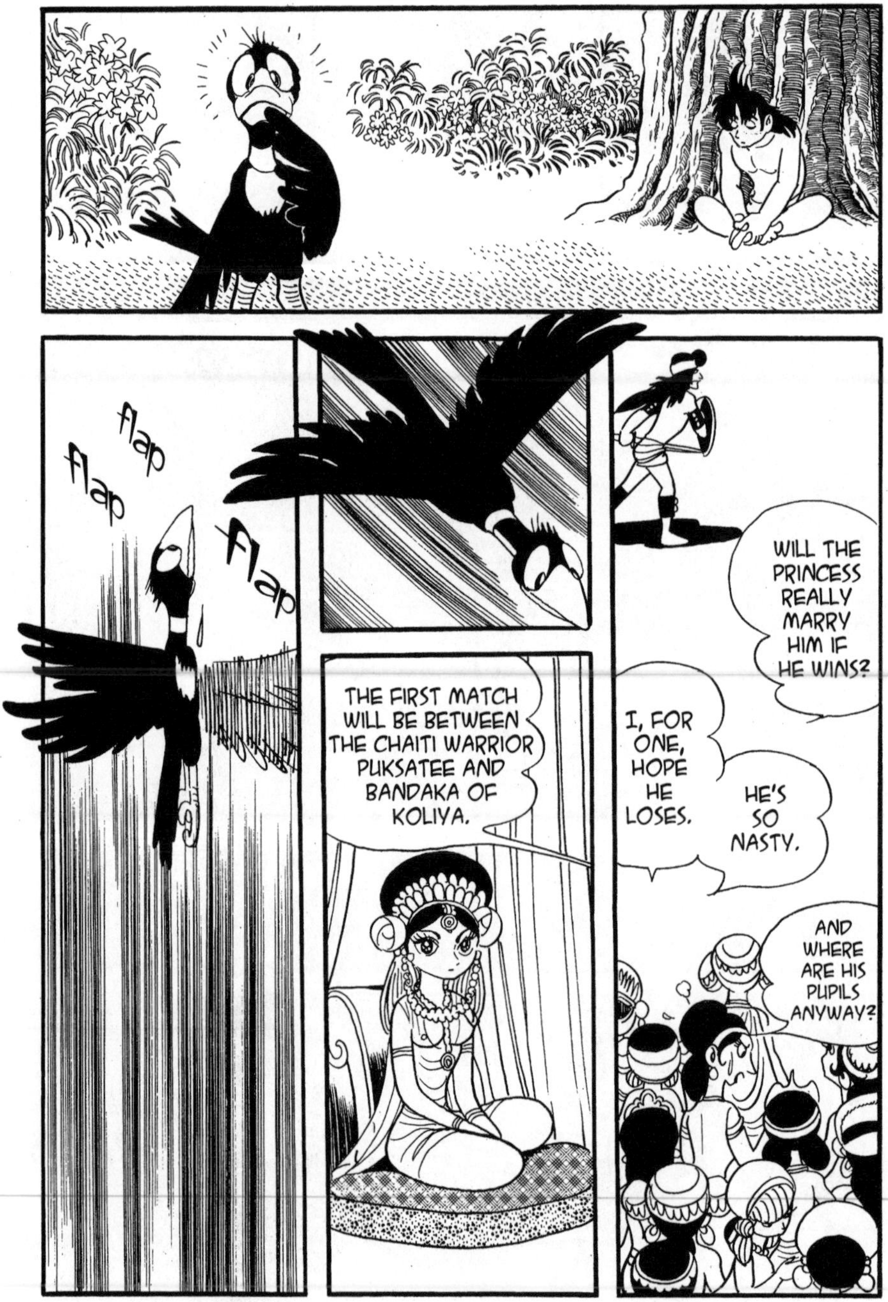
flap
flap
flap
WILL THE PRINCESS REALLY MARRY HIM IF HE WINS?
THE FIRST MATCH WILL BE BETWEEN THE CHAITI WARRIOR PUKSATEE AND BANDAKA OF KOLIYA.
I, FOR ONE, HOPE HE LOSES.
HE'S SO NASTY.
AND WHERE ARE HIS PUPILS ANYWAY?

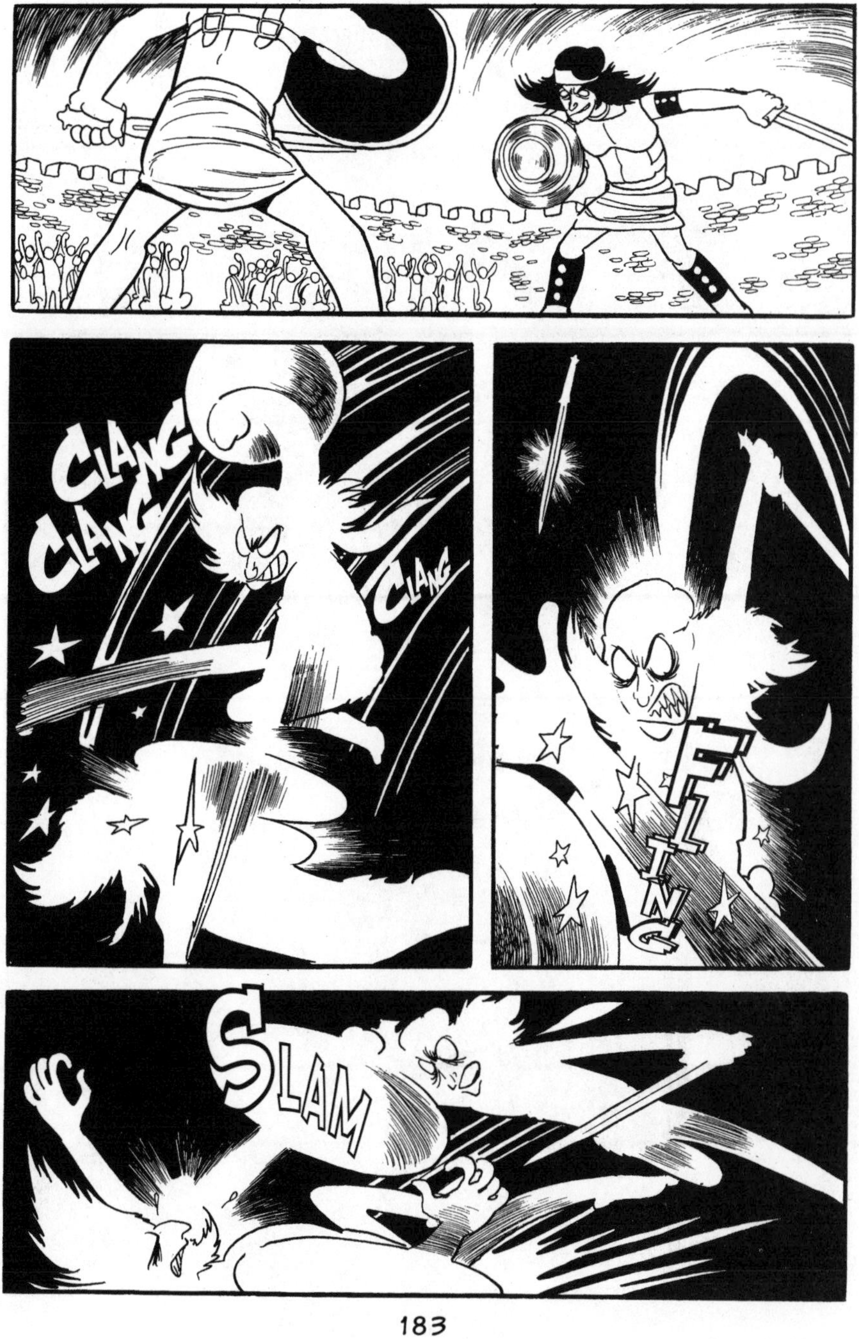
CLANG
CLANG
CLANG
FLING
SLAM

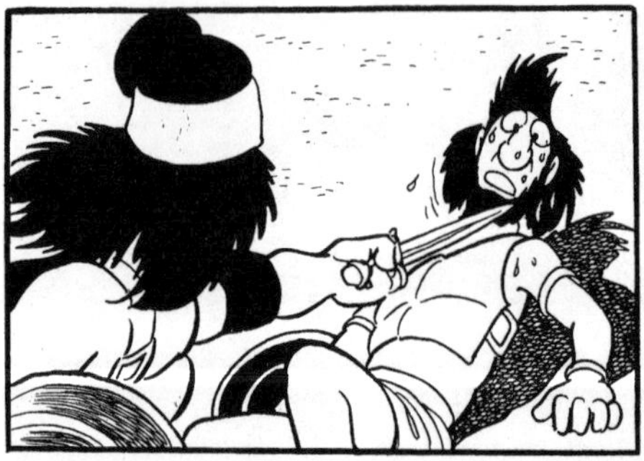

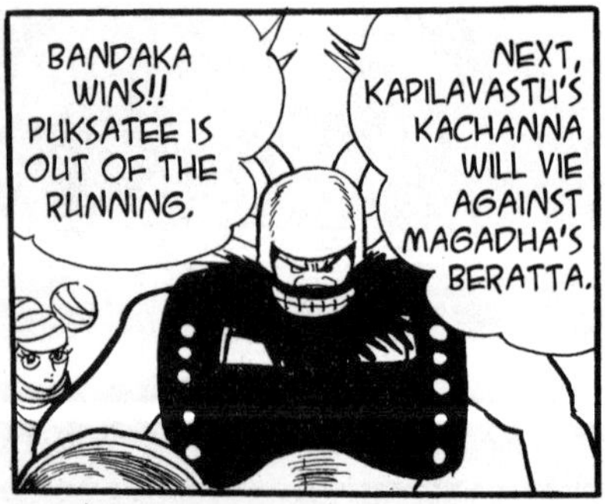
BANDAKA WINS!! PUKSATEE IS OUT OF THE RUNNING.
NEXT, KAPILAVASTU'S KACHANNA WILL VIE AGAINST MAGADHA'S BERATTA.

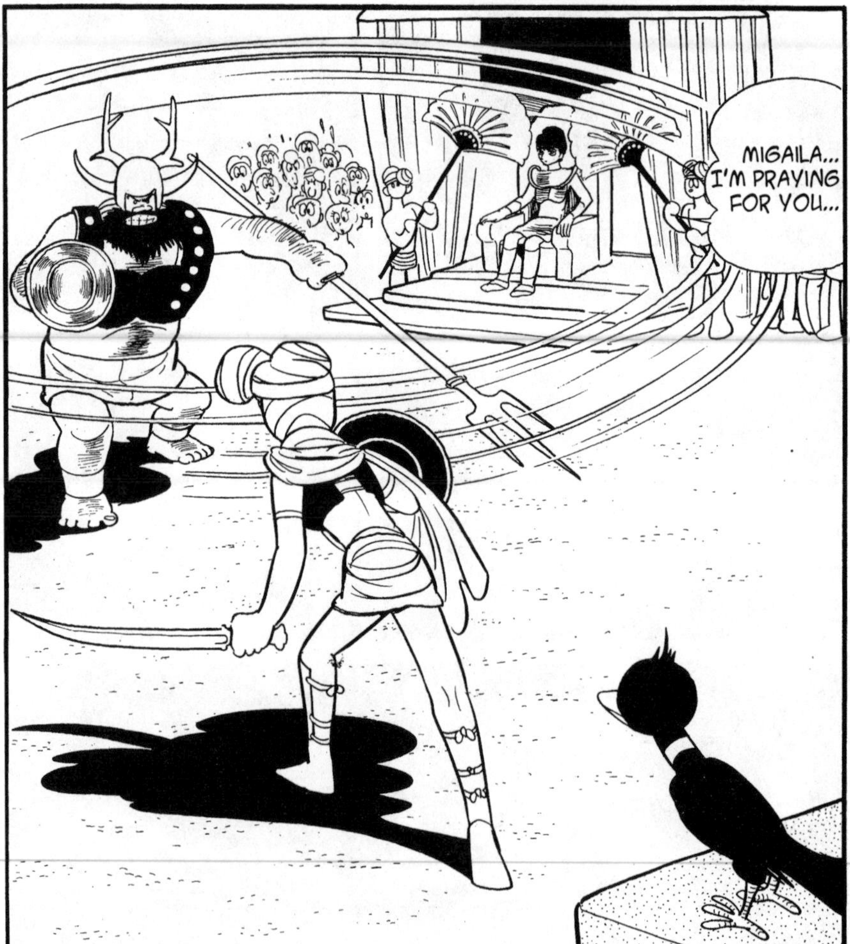
MIGAILA... I'M PRAYING FOR YOU...

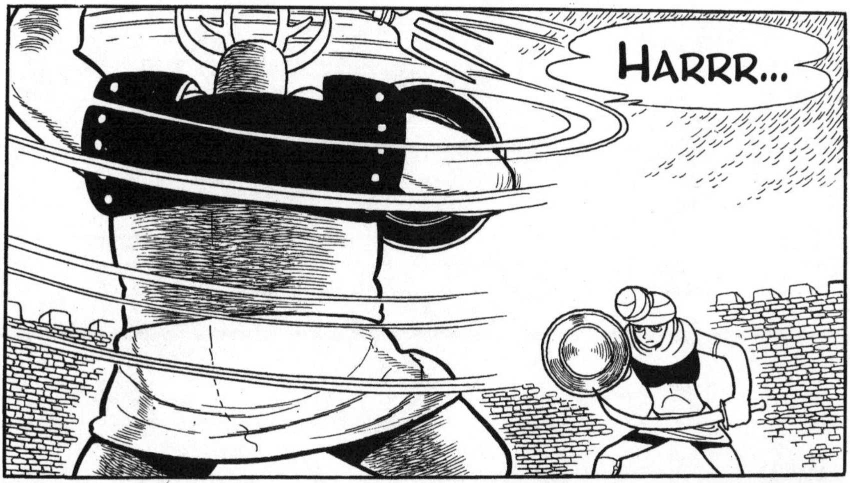
HARRR...

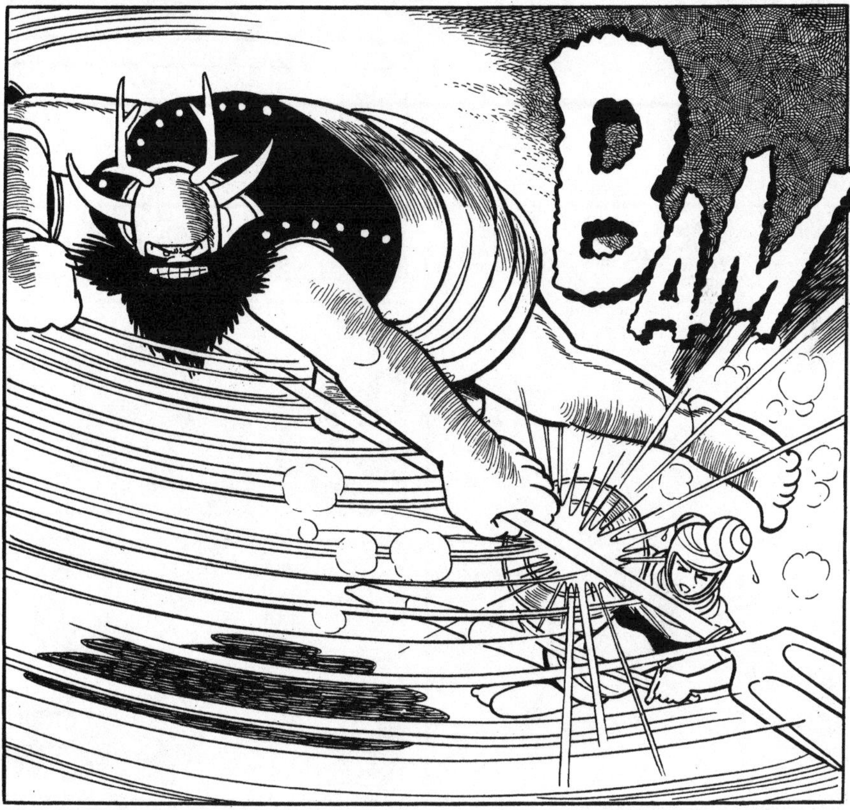
BAM

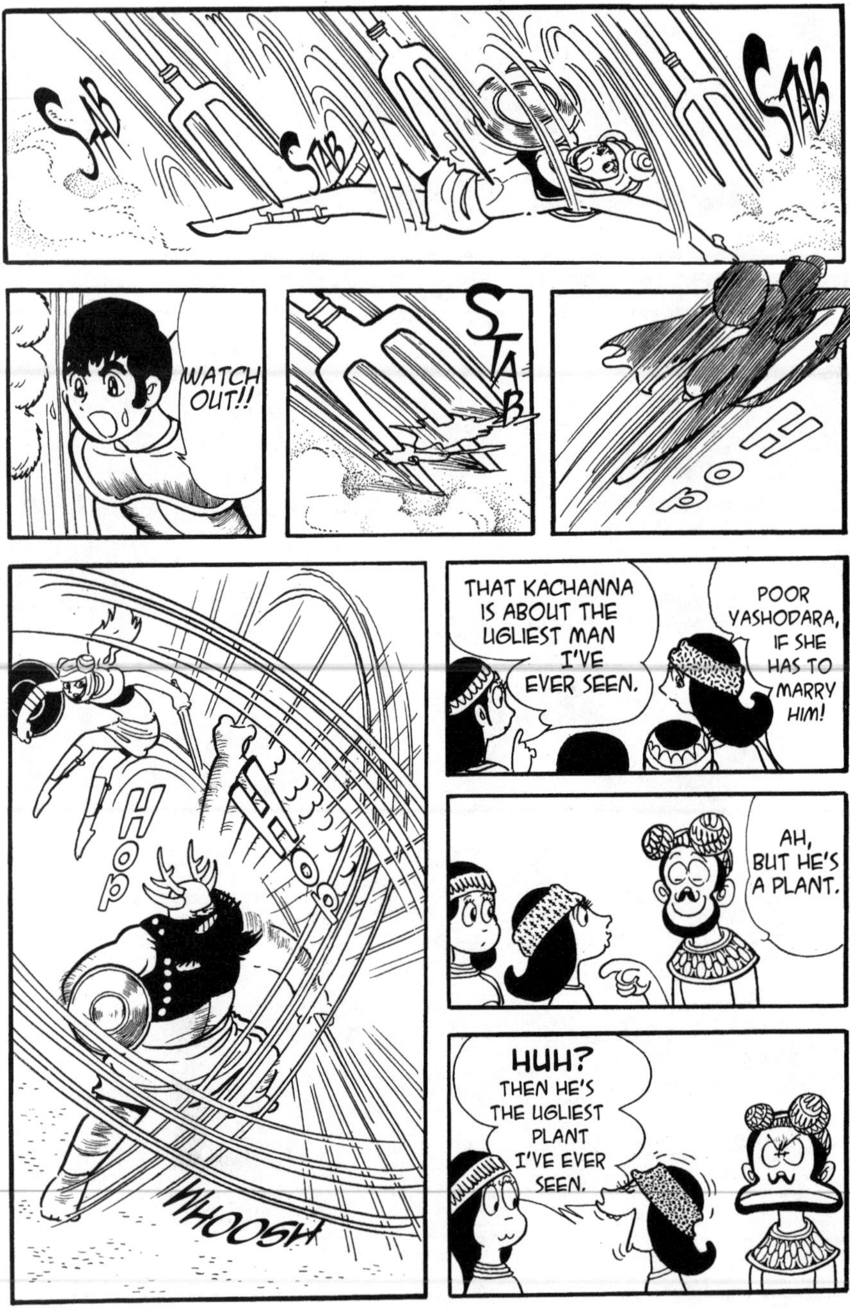
SAB
STAB
STAB
WATCH OUT!!
STAB
Hop
Hop
Hop
WHOOSH
THAT KACHANNA IS ABOUT THE UGLIEST MAN I'VE EVER SEEN.
POOR YASHODARA, IF SHE HAS TO MARRY HIM!
AH, BUT HE'S A PLANT.
HUH? THEN HE'S THE UGLIEST PLANT I'VE EVER SEEN.

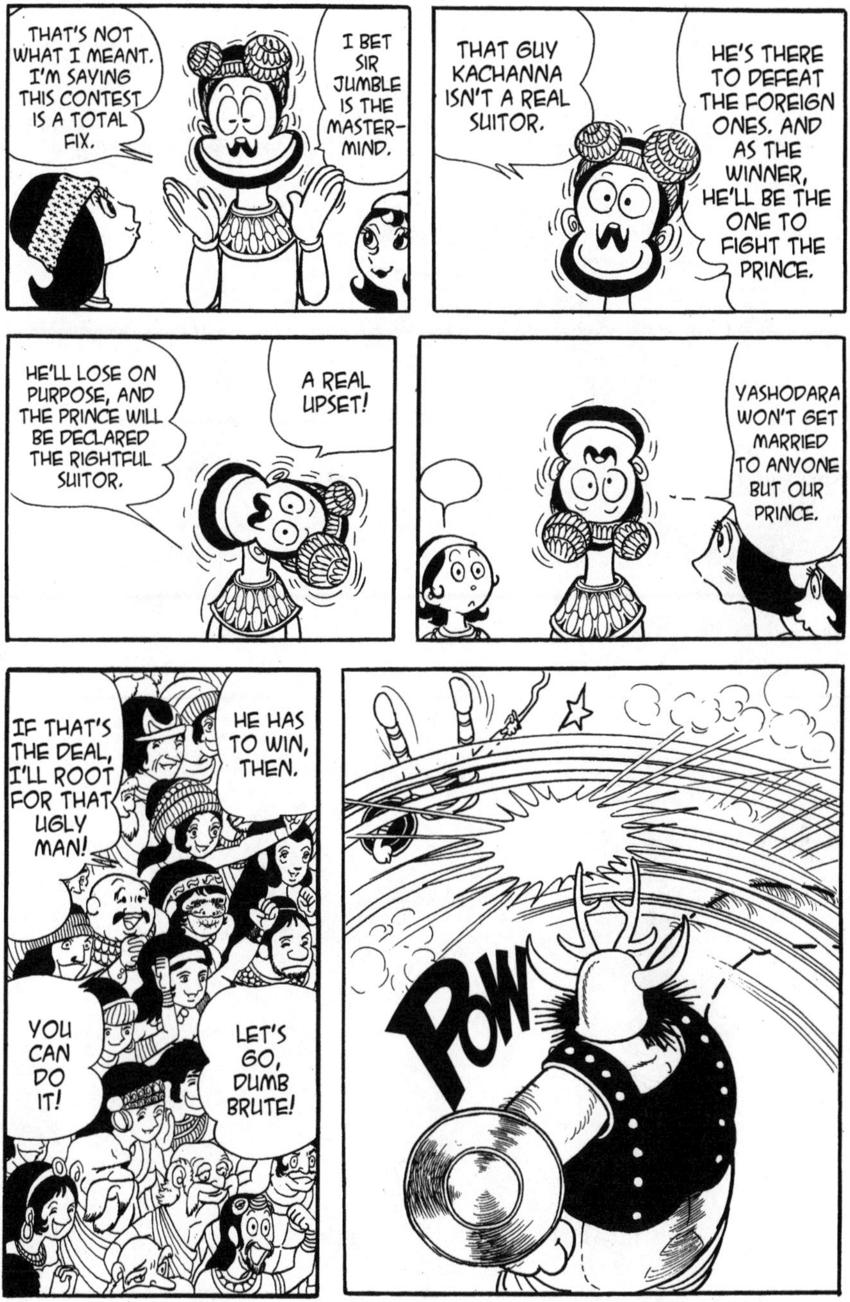
THAT'S NOT WHAT I MEANT. I'M SAYING THIS CONTEST IS A TOTAL FIX.
I BET SIR JUMBLE IS THE MASTER-MIND.
THAT GUY KACHANNA ISN'T A REAL SUITOR.
HE'S THERE TO DEFEAT THE FOREIGN ONES. AND AS THE WINNER, HE'LL BE THE ONE TO FIGHT THE PRINCE.
HE'LL LOSE ON PURPOSE, AND THE PRINCE WILL BE DECLARED THE RIGHTFUL SUITOR.
A REAL UPSET!
YASHODARA WON'T GET MARRIED TO ANYONE BUT OUR PRINCE.
IF THAT'S THE DEAL, I'LL ROOT FOR THAT UGLY MAN!
HE HAS TO WIN, THEN.
YOU CAN DO IT!
LET'S GO, DUMB BRUTE!
POW

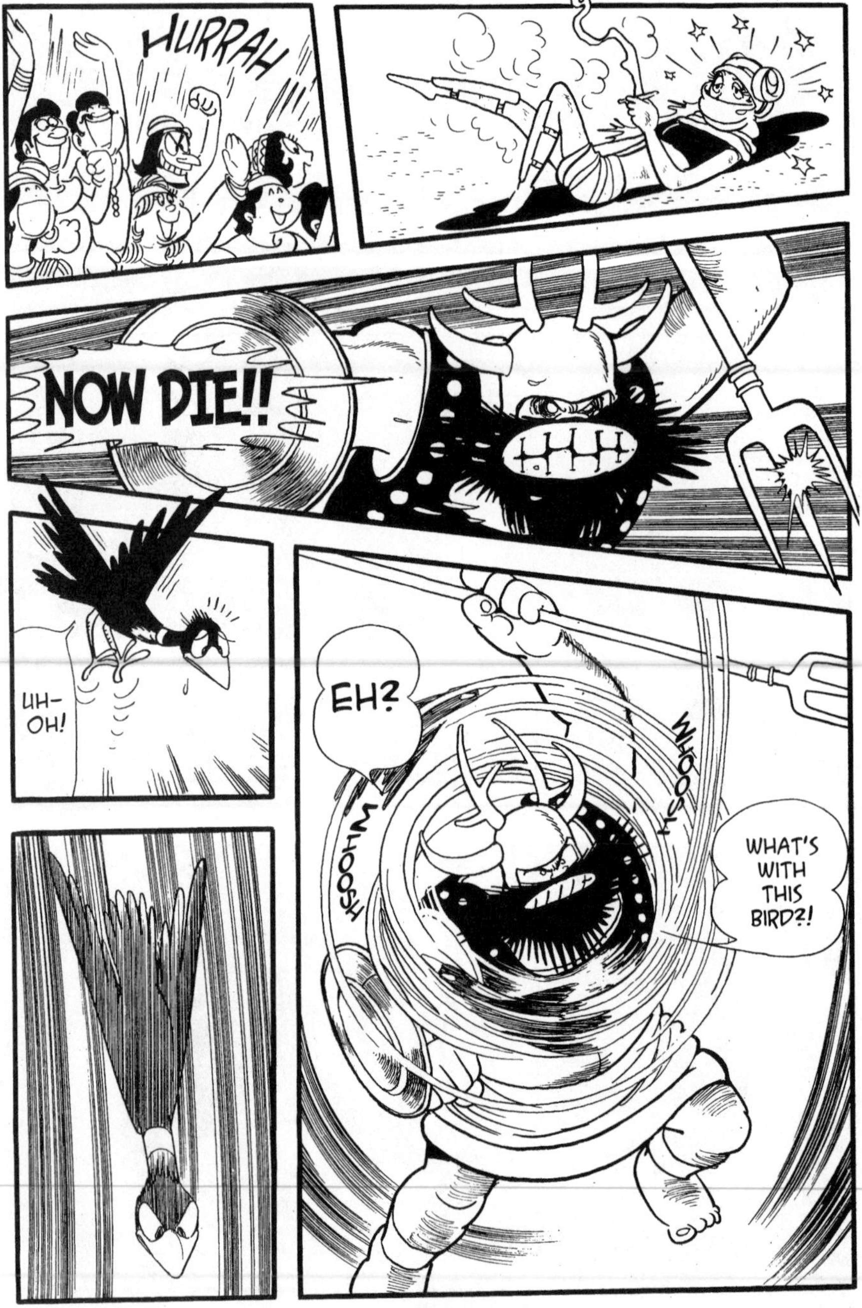
HURRAH
NOW DIE!!
UH-OH!
EH?
WHOOSH
WHOOSH
WHAT'S WITH THIS BIRD?!

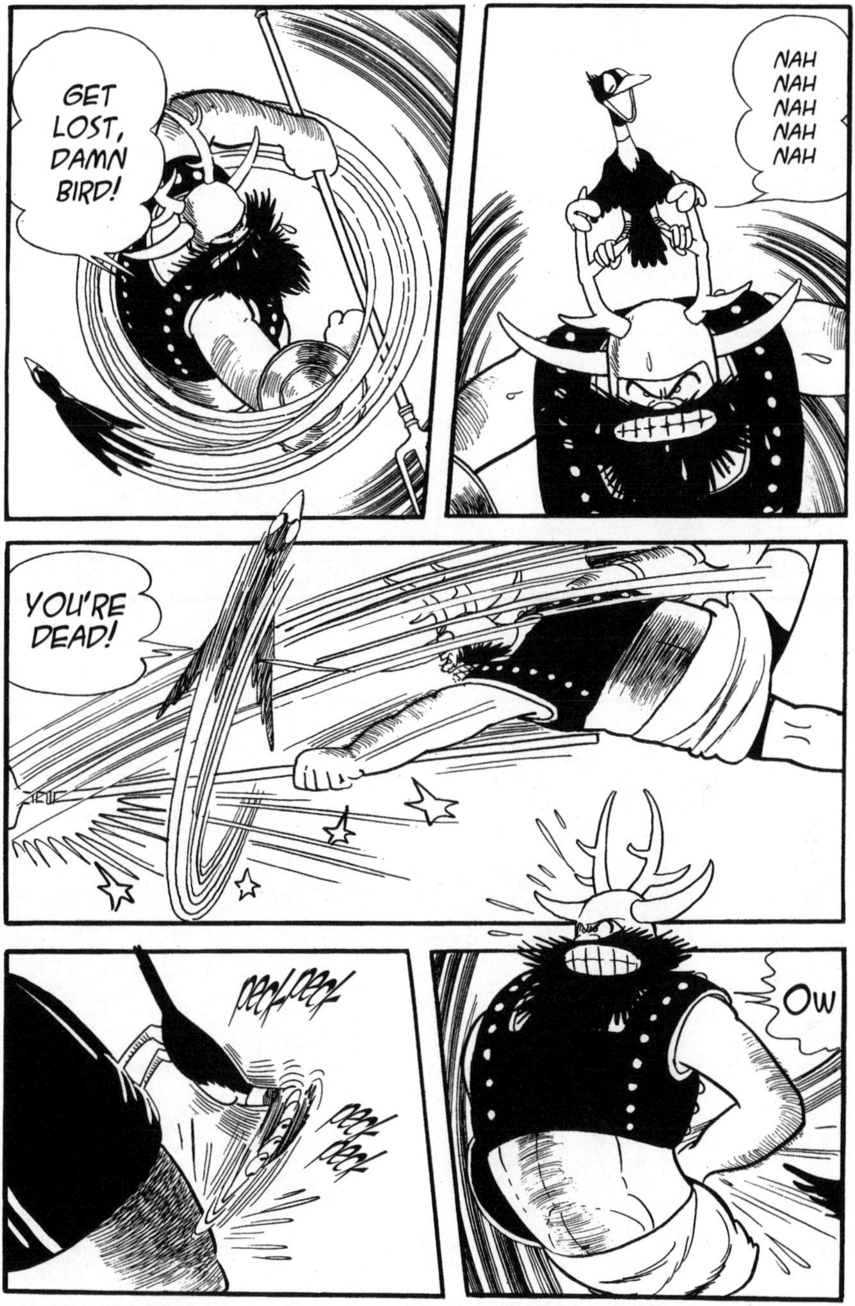
GET LOST, DAMN BIRD!
NAH NAH NAH NAH NAH
YOU'RE DEAD!
peck peck
peck peck
OW

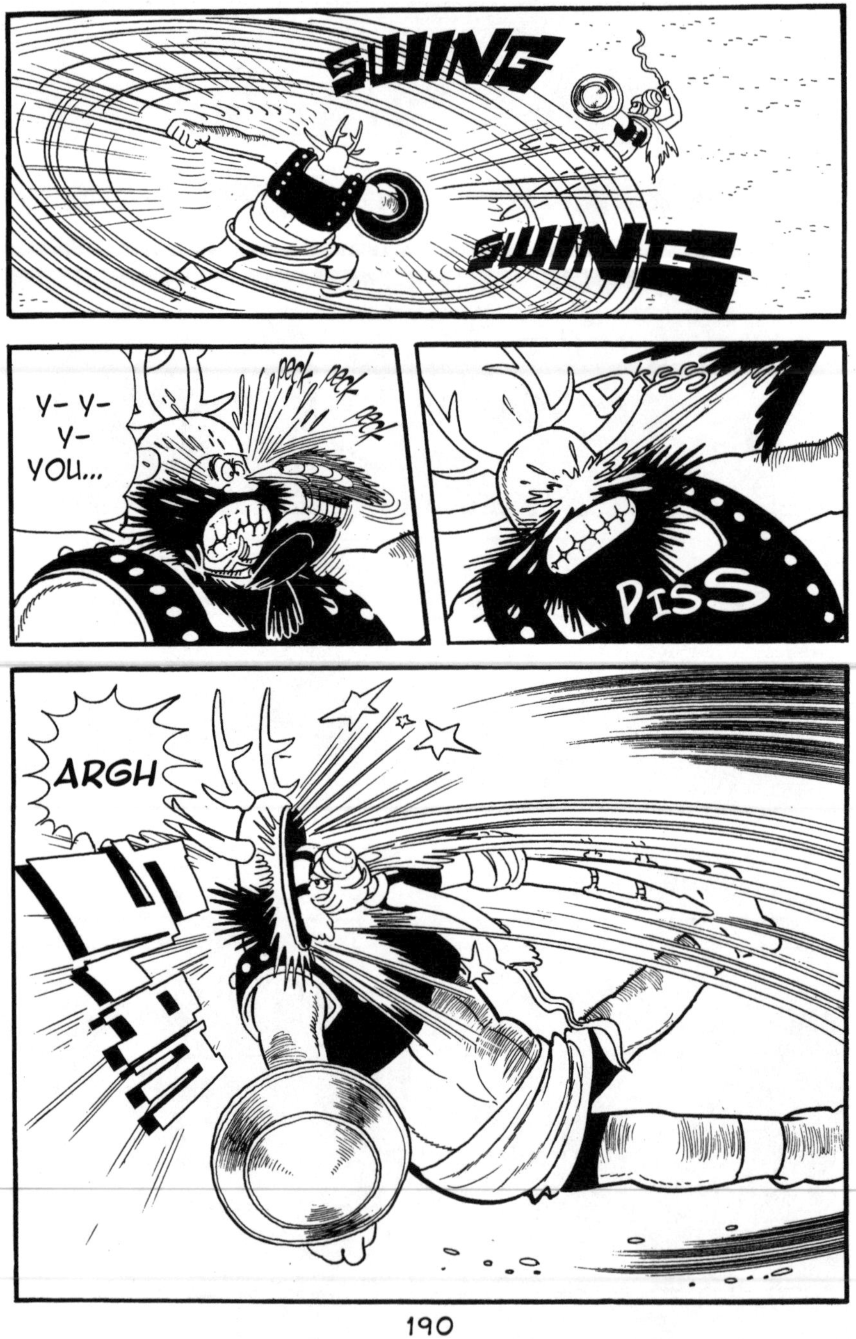
SWING
SWING
Y- Y- Y- YOU...
peck peck peck
PISS
ARGH

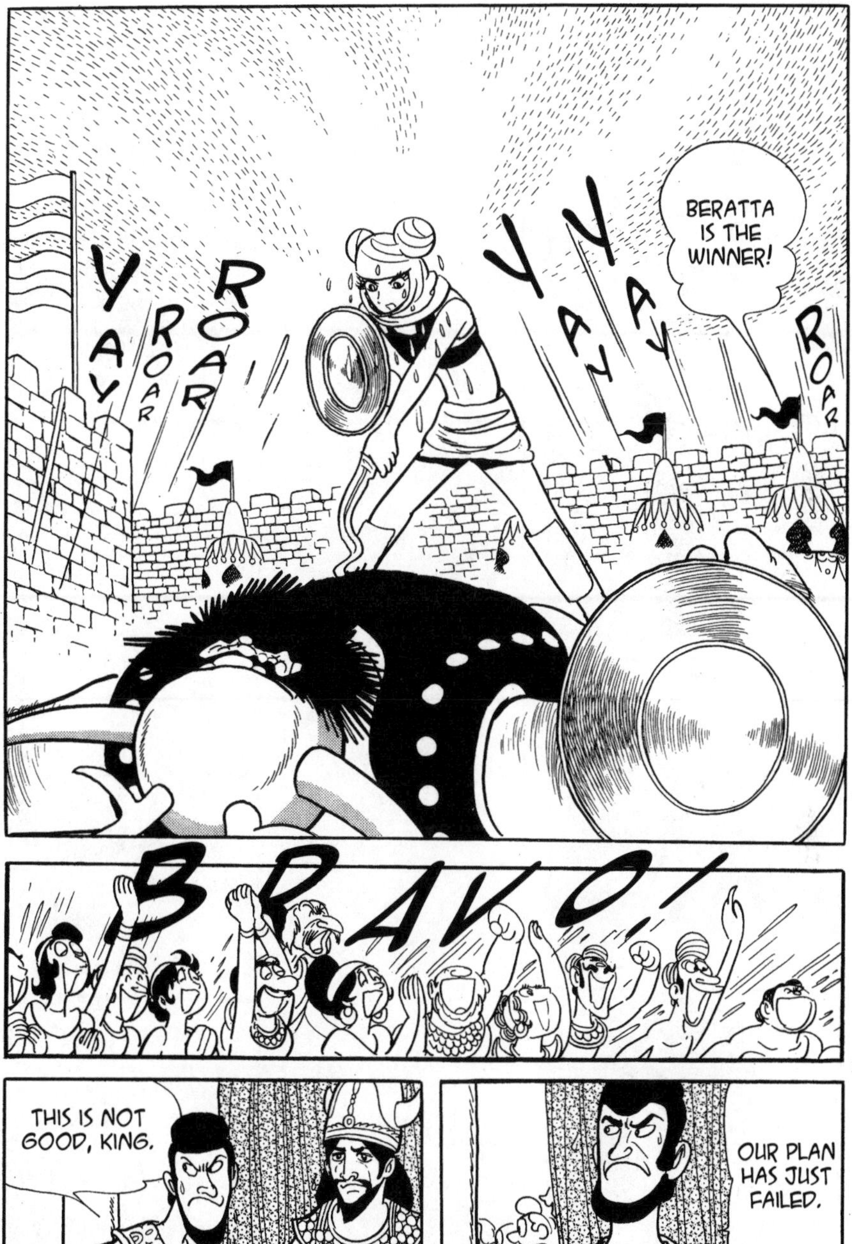
YAY
ROAR
ROAR
YAY
BERATTA IS THE WINNER!
YAY
ROAR
BRAVO!
THIS IS NOT GOOD, KING.
OUR PLAN HAS JUST FAILED.

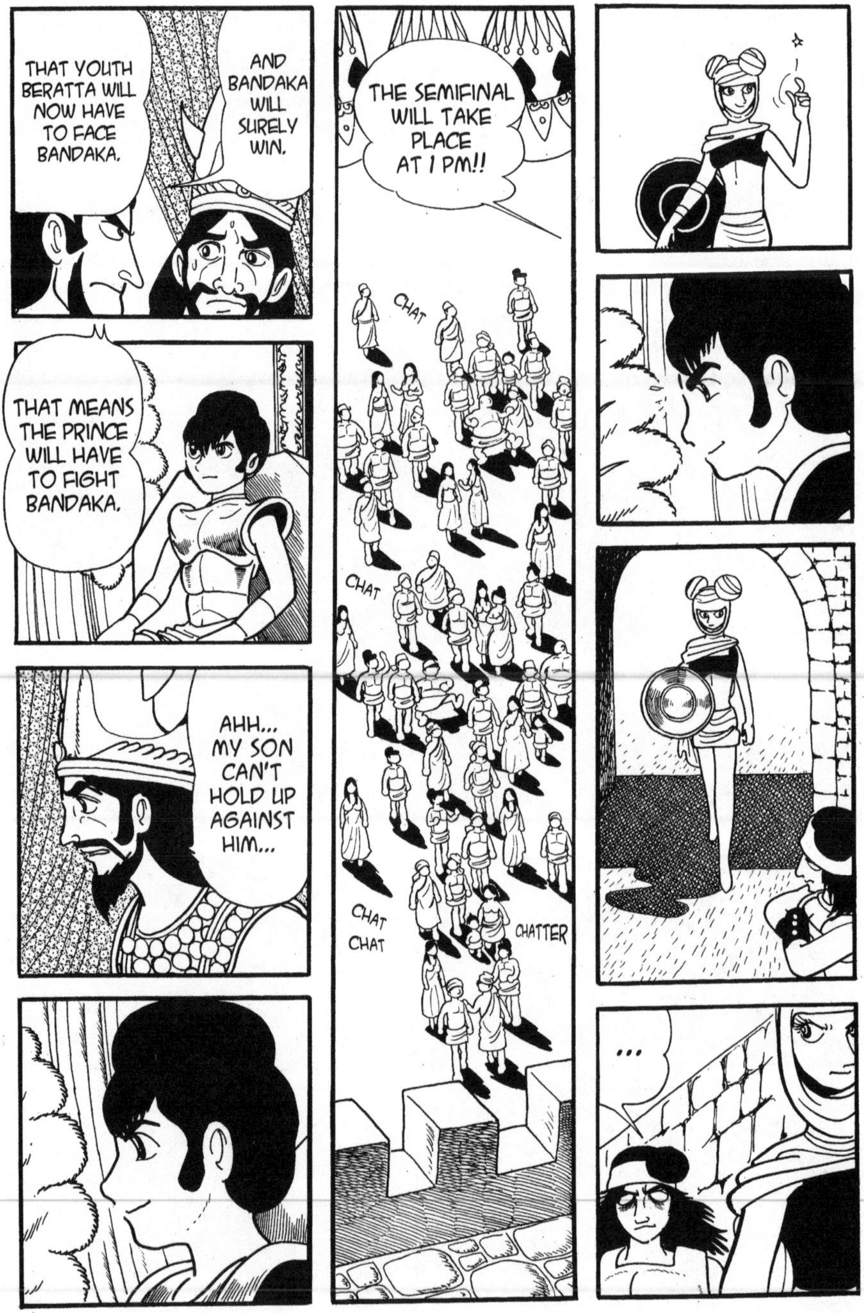
THAT YOUTH BERATTA WILL NOW HAVE TO FACE BANDAKA.
AND BANDAKA WILL SURELY WIN.
THAT MEANS THE PRINCE WILL HAVE TO FIGHT BANDAKA.
AHH... MY SON CAN'T HOLD UP AGAINST HIM...
THE SEMIFINAL WILL TAKE PLACE AT 1 PM!!
CHAT
CHAT
CHAT
CHAT
CHATTER
...

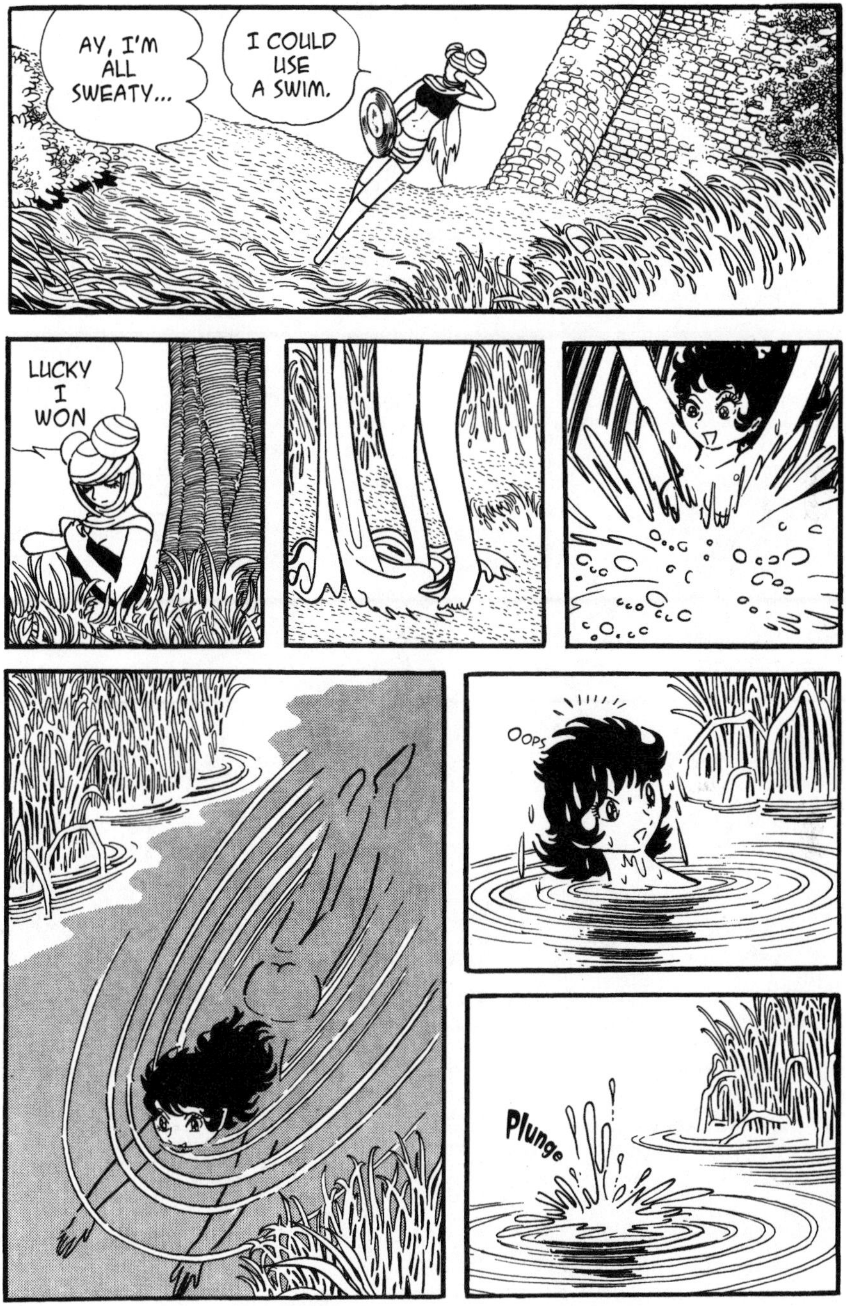
AY, I'M ALL SWEATY...
I COULD USE A SWIM.
LUCKY I WON
OOPS
Plunge

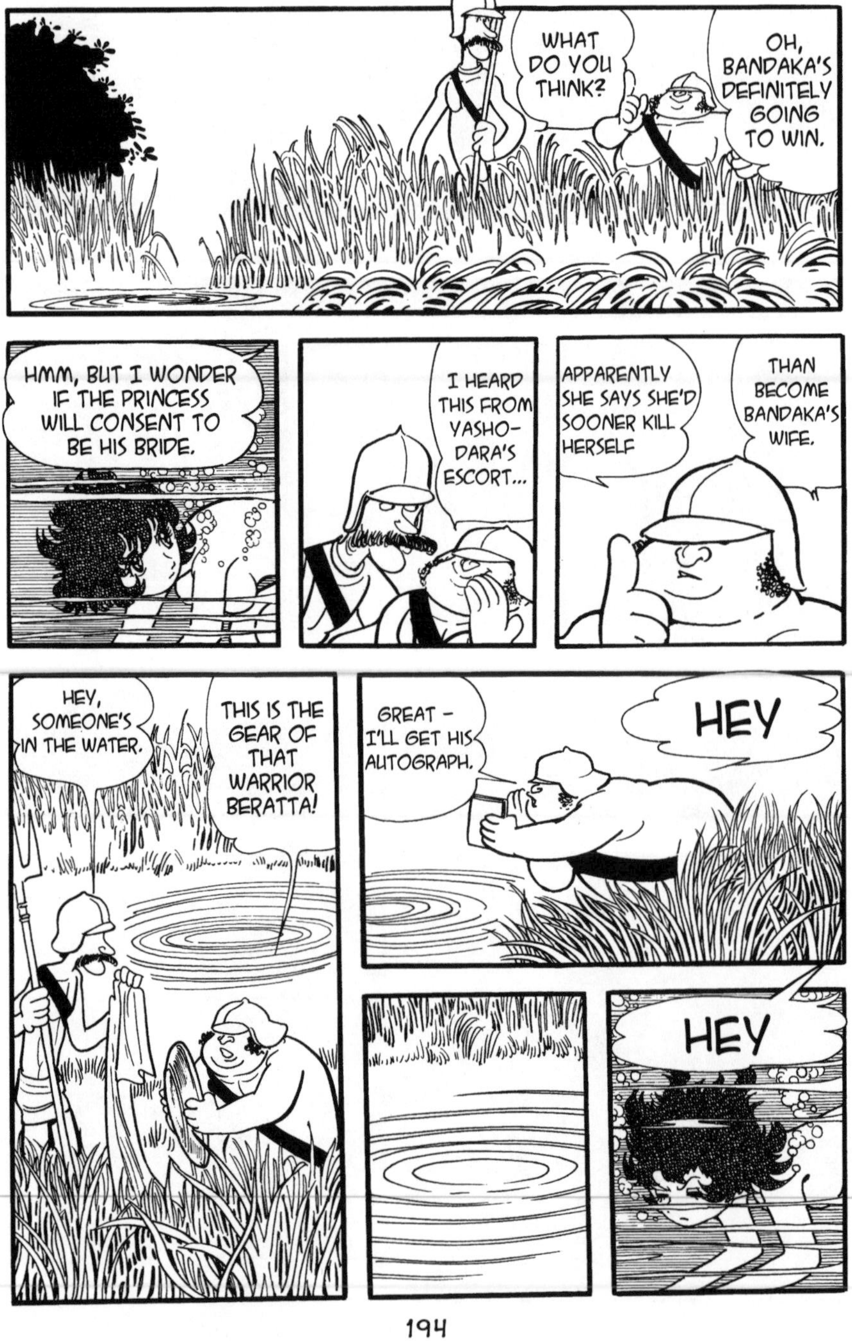
WHAT DO YOU THINK?
OH, BANDAKA'S DEFINITELY GOING TO WIN.
HMM, BUT I WONDER IF THE PRINCESS WILL CONSENT TO BE HIS BRIDE.
I HEARD THIS FROM YASHO-DARA'S ESCORT...
APPARENTLY SHE SAYS SHE'D SOONER KILL HERSELF
THAN BECOME BANDAKA'S WIFE.
HEY, SOMEONE'S IN THE WATER.
THIS IS THE GEAR OF THAT WARRIOR BERATTA!
GREAT - I'LL GET HIS AUTOGRAPH.
HEY
HEY

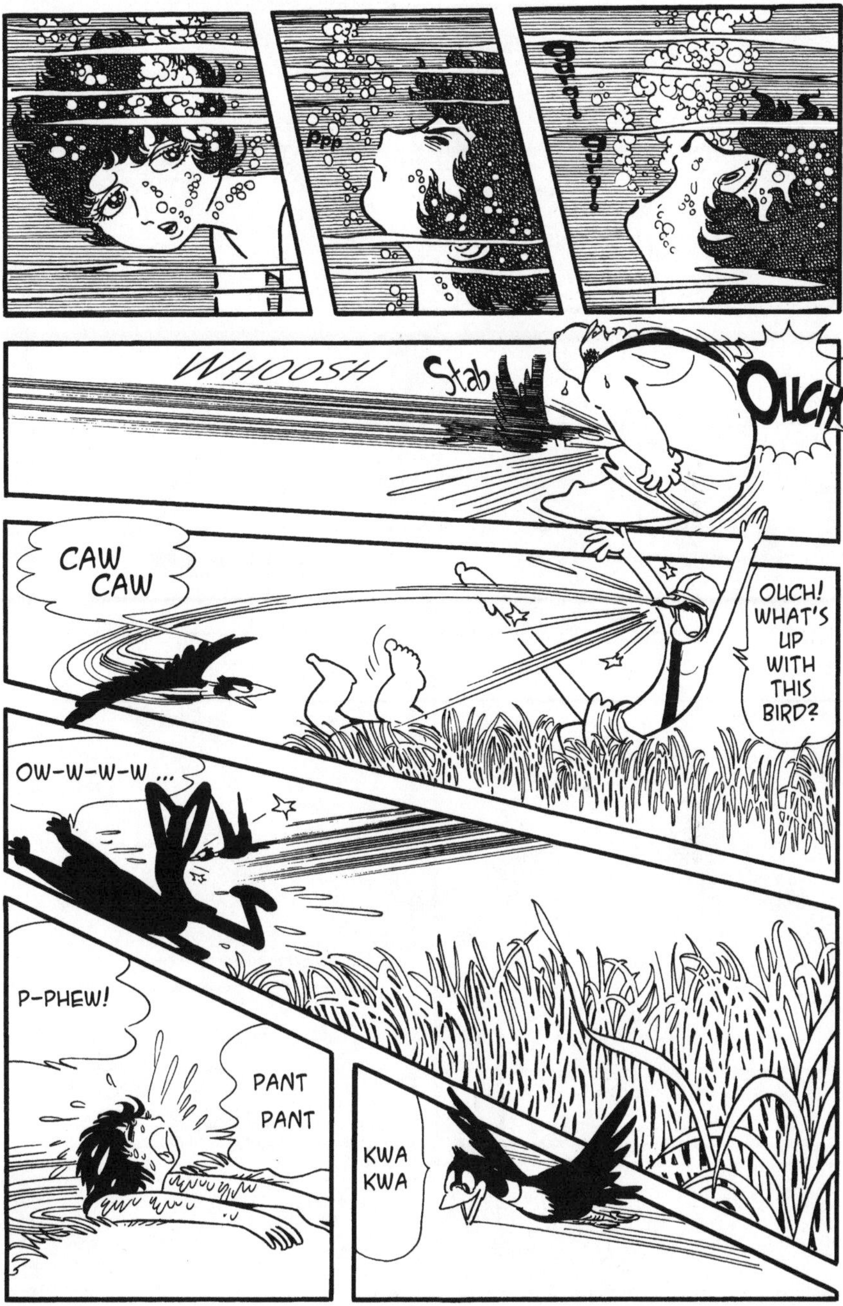
Ppp
gurgl gurgl
WHOOSH
Stab
OUCH
CAW CAW
OUCH! WHAT'S UP WITH THIS BIRD?
OW-W-W-W...
P-PHEW!
PANT PANT
KWA KWA

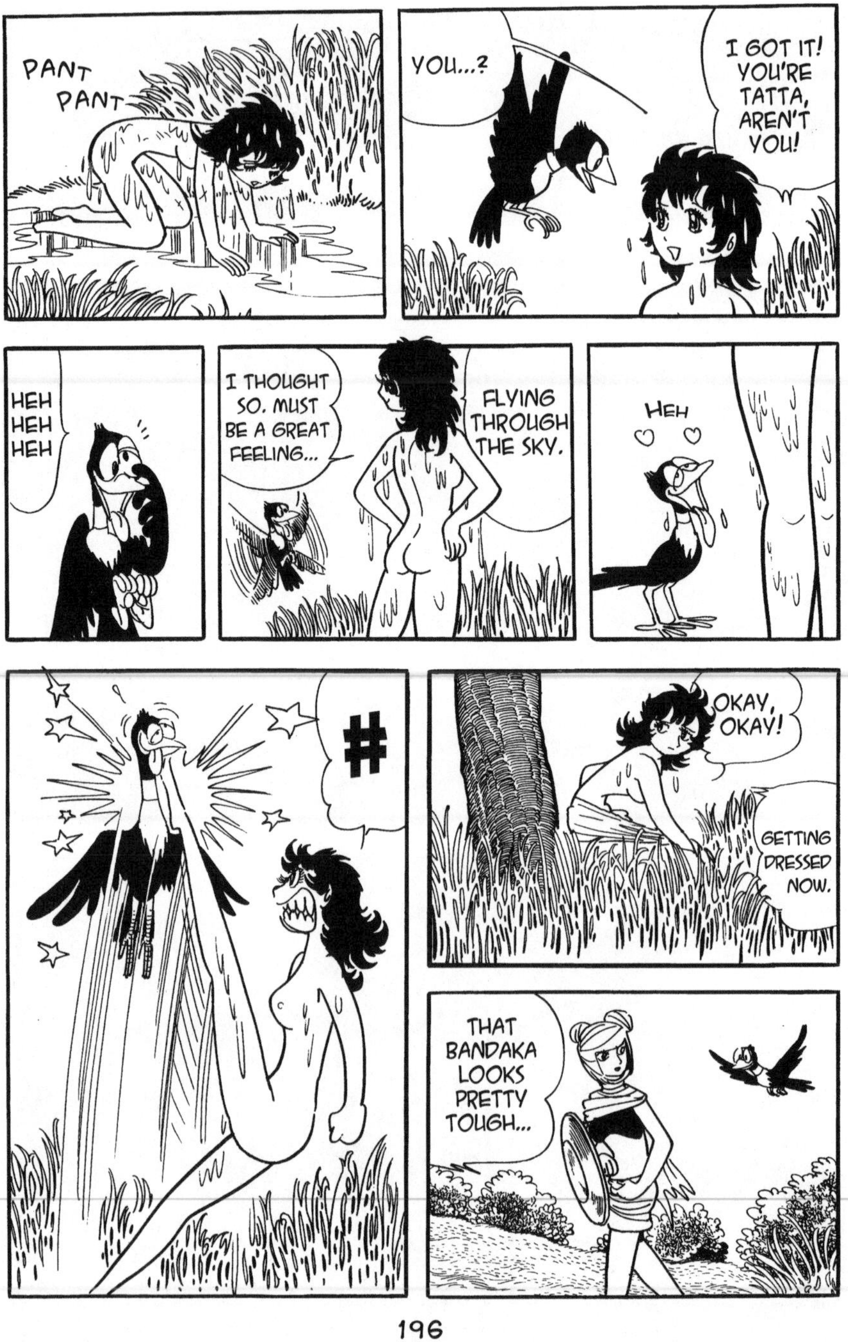
PANT PANT
YOU...?
I GOT IT! YOU'RE TATTA, AREN'T YOU!
HEH HEH HEH
I THOUGHT SO. MUST BE A GREAT FEELING...
FLYING THROUGH THE SKY.
HEH
#
OKAY, OKAY!
GETTING DRESSED NOW.
THAT BANDAKA LOOKS PRETTY TOUGH...

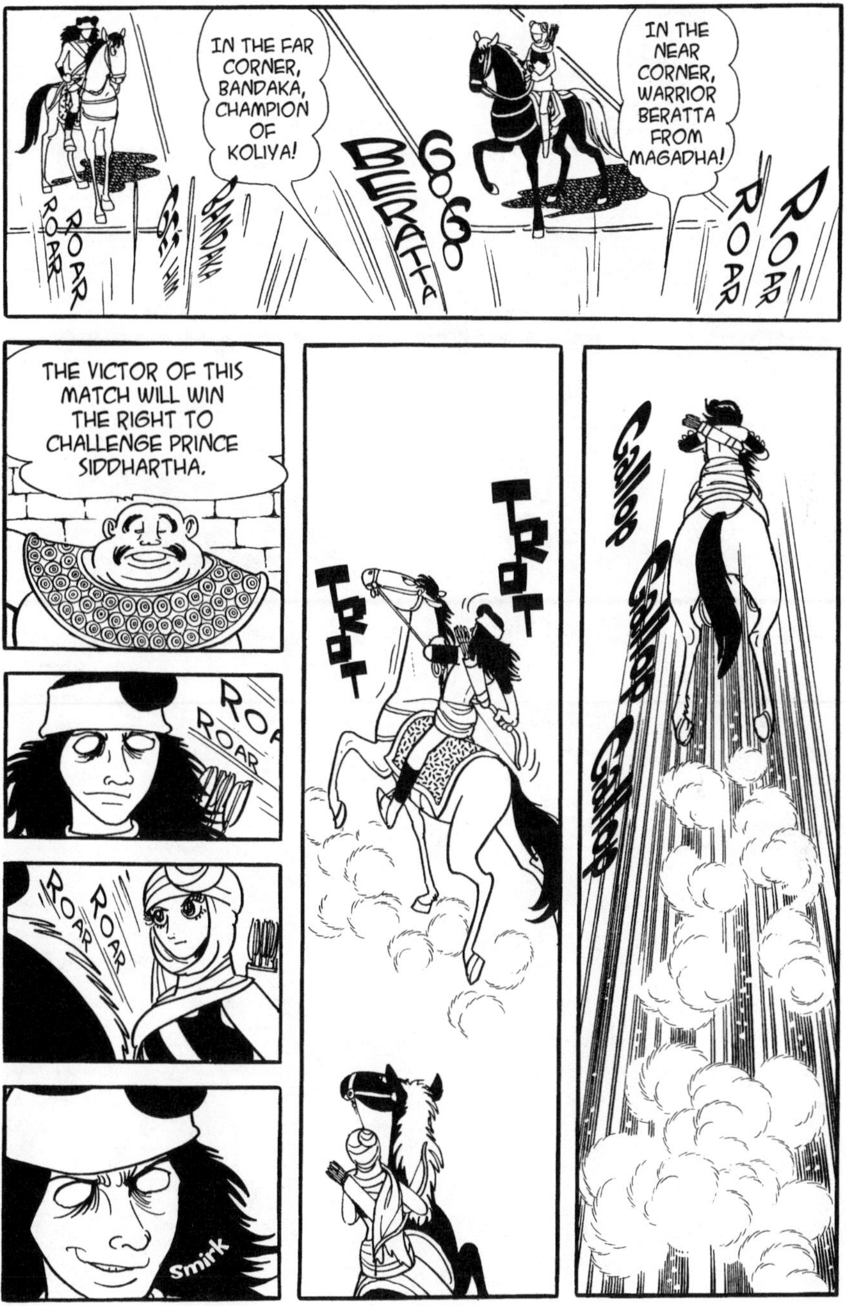
ROAR ROAR
BANDAKA
IN THE FAR CORNER, BANDAKA, CHAMPION OF KOLIYA!
GO GO BERATTA
IN THE NEAR CORNER, WARRIOR BERATTA FROM MAGADHA!
ROAR ROAR
THE VICTOR OF THIS MATCH WILL WIN THE RIGHT TO CHALLENGE PRINCE SIDDHARTHA.
TROT TROT
Gallop Gallop Gallop
ROAR ROAR
ROAR ROAR
Smirk

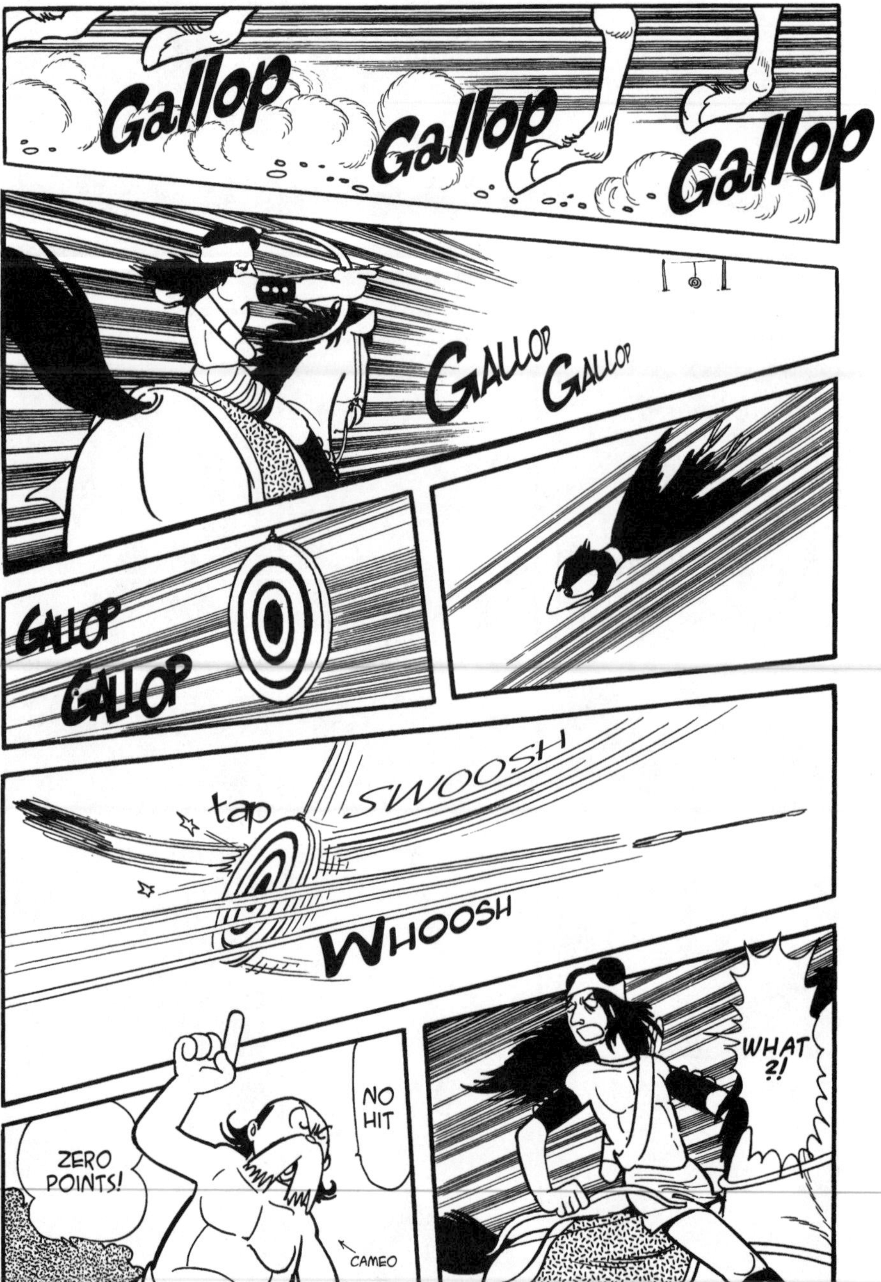

Gallop
Gallop
Gallop
GALLOP
GALLOP
GALLOP
GALLOP
tap
SWOOSH
WHOOSH
ZERO POINTS!
NO HIT
CAMEO
WHAT ?!

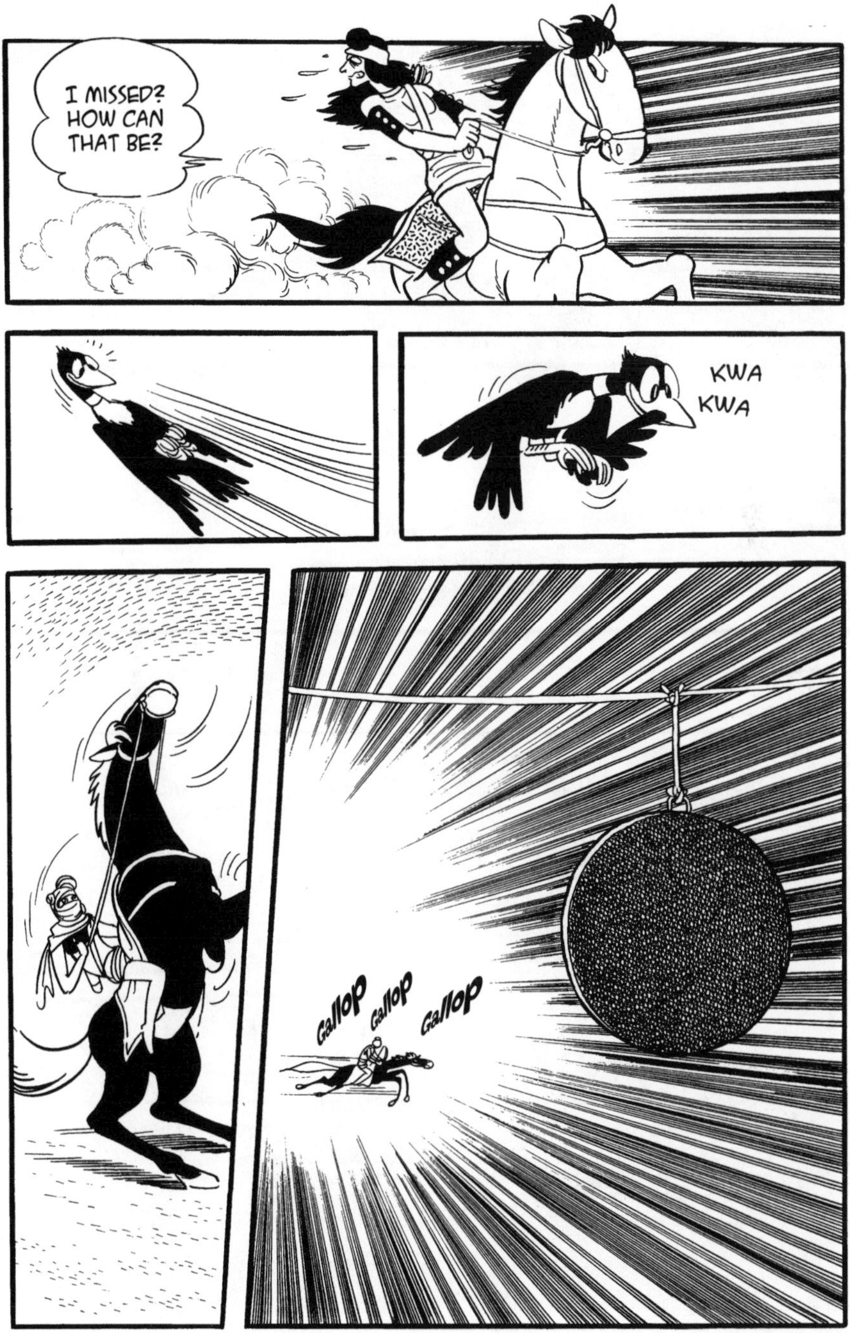
I MISSED? HOW CAN THAT BE?
KWA KWA
Gallop Gallop Gallop

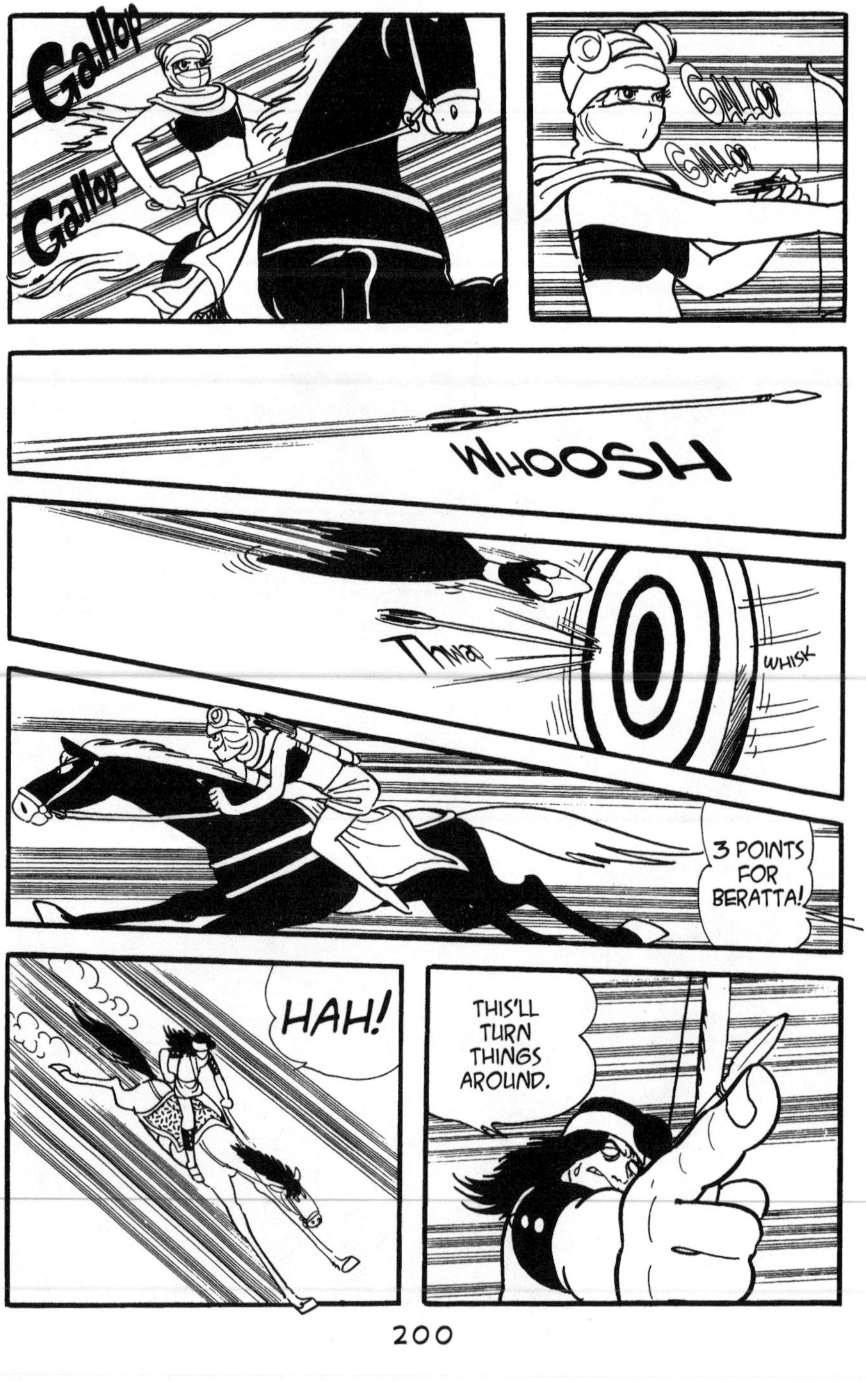
Gallop
Gallop
GALLOP
GALLOP
WHOOSH
THWAP
WHISK
3 POINTS FOR BERATTA!
HAH!
THIS'LL TURN THINGS AROUND.

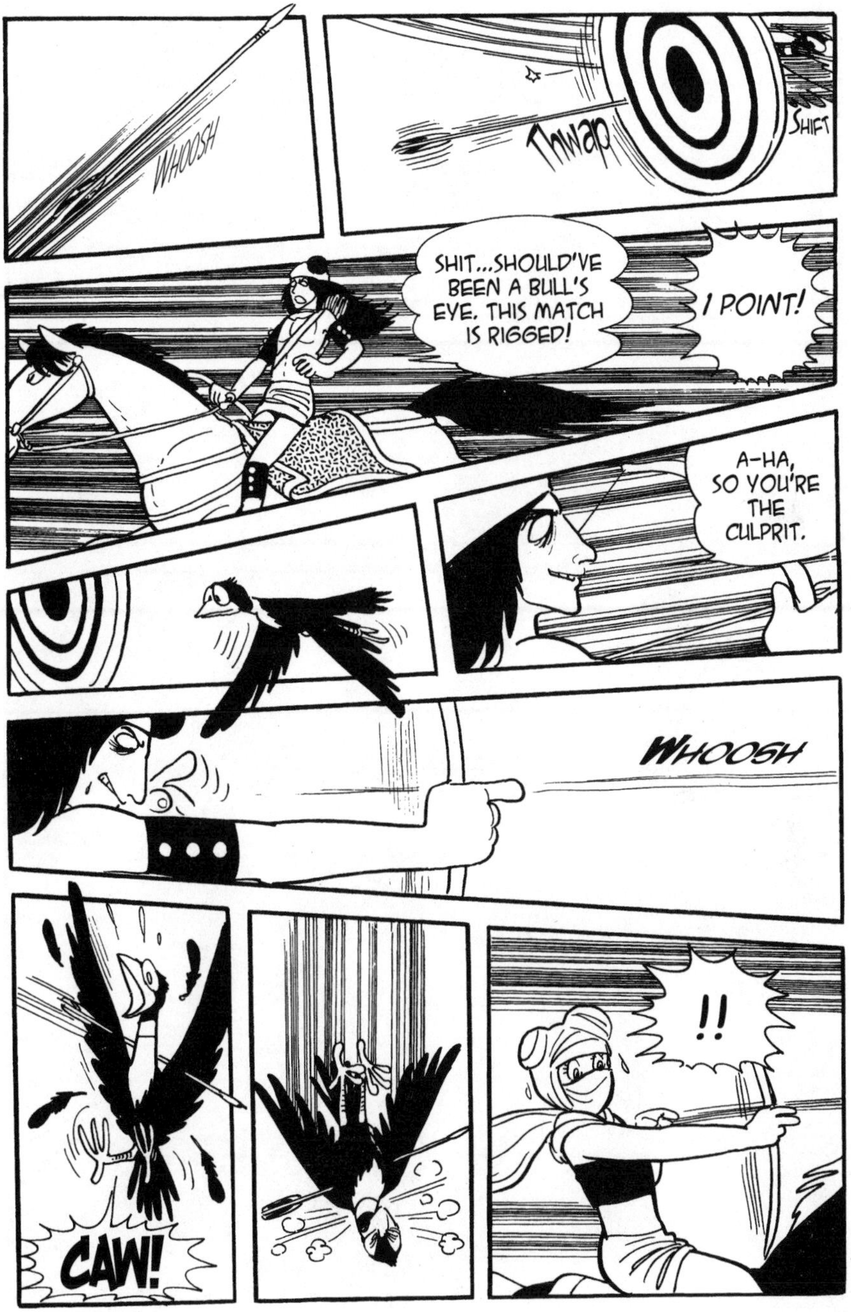
WHOOSH
Thwap
SHIFT
SHIT...SHOULD'VE BEEN A BULL'S EYE. THIS MATCH IS RIGGED!
1 POINT!
A-HA, SO YOU'RE THE CULPRIT.
WHOOSH
CAW!
!!

WHOOSH
BERATTA MISSES!!
CAWK
Neigh

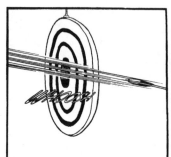

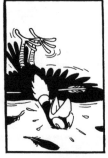

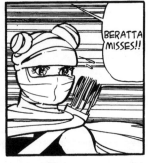

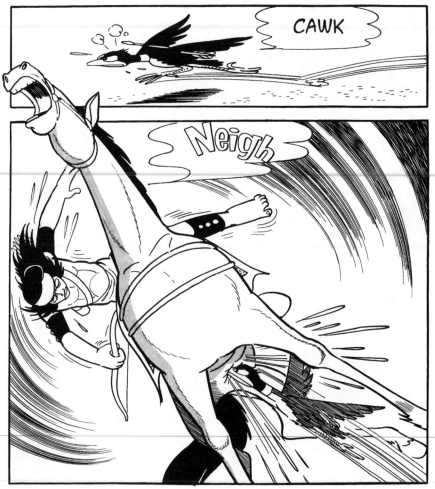

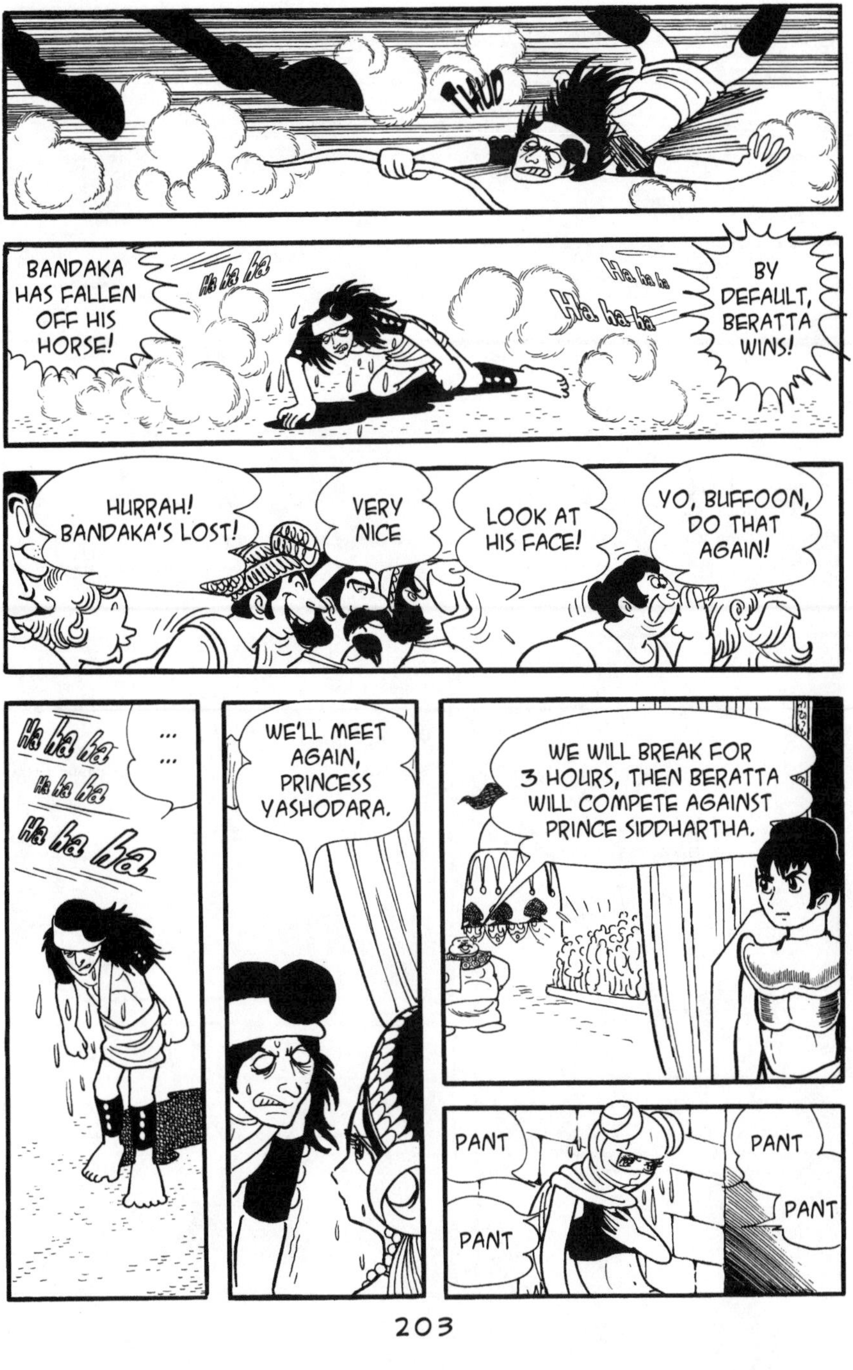
THUD
BANDAKA HAS FALLEN OFF HIS HORSE!
Ha ha ha
Ha ha ha
Ha ha ha
BY DEFAULT, BERATTA WINS!
HURRAH! BANDAKA'S LOST!
VERY NICE
LOOK AT HIS FACE!
YO, BUFFOON, DO THAT AGAIN!
Ha ha ha
Ha ha ha
Ha ha ha
... ...
WE'LL MEET AGAIN, PRINCESS YASHODARA.
WE WILL BREAK FOR 3 HOURS, THEN BERATTA WILL COMPETE AGAINST PRINCE SIDDHARTHA.
PANT
PANT
PANT
PANT

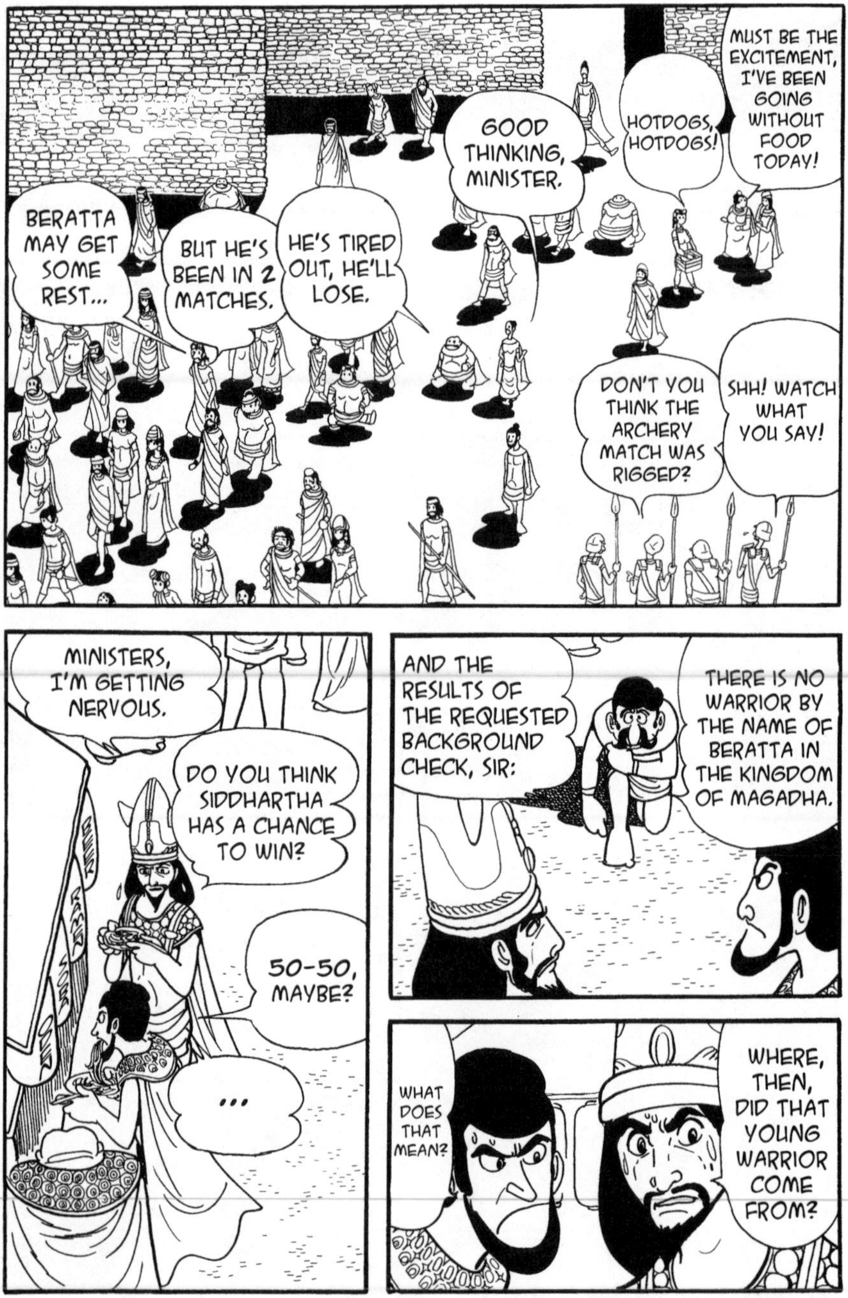
BERATTA MAY GET SOME REST...
BUT HE'S BEEN IN 2 MATCHES.
HE'S TIRED OUT, HE'LL LOSE.
GOOD THINKING, MINISTER.
HOTDOGS, HOTDOGS!
MUST BE THE EXCITEMENT, I'VE BEEN GOING WITHOUT FOOD TODAY!
DON'T YOU THINK THE ARCHERY MATCH WAS RIGGED?
SHH! WATCH WHAT YOU SAY!
MINISTERS, I'M GETTING NERVOUS.
DO YOU THINK SIDDHARTHA HAS A CHANCE TO WIN?
50-50, MAYBE?
...
AND THE RESULTS OF THE REQUESTED BACKGROUND CHECK, SIR:
THERE IS NO WARRIOR BY THE NAME OF BERATTA IN THE KINGDOM OF MAGADHA.
WHAT DOES THAT MEAN?
WHERE, THEN, DID THAT YOUNG WARRIOR COME FROM?

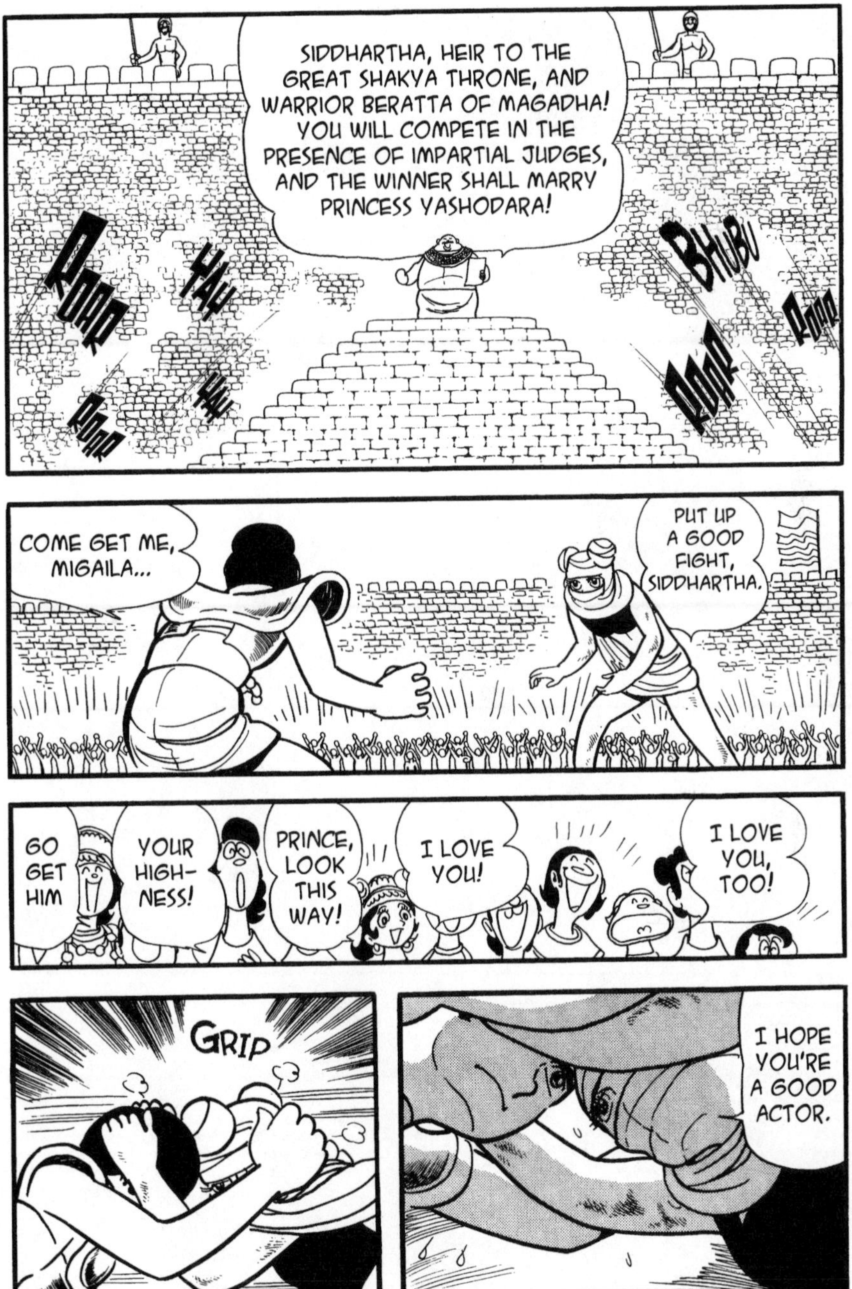
SIDDHARTHA, HEIR TO THE GREAT SHAKYA THRONE, AND WARRIOR BERATTA OF MAGADHA! YOU WILL COMPETE IN THE PRESENCE OF IMPARTIAL JUDGES, AND THE WINNER SHALL MARRY PRINCESS YASHODARA!
ROAR
YAY
YAY
ROAR
BHUBU
ROAR
ROAR
COME GET ME, MIGAILA...
PUT UP A GOOD FIGHT, SIDDHARTHA.
GO GET HIM
YOUR HIGHNESS!
PRINCE, LOOK THIS WAY!
I LOVE YOU!
I LOVE YOU, TOO!
GRIP
I HOPE YOU'RE A GOOD ACTOR.

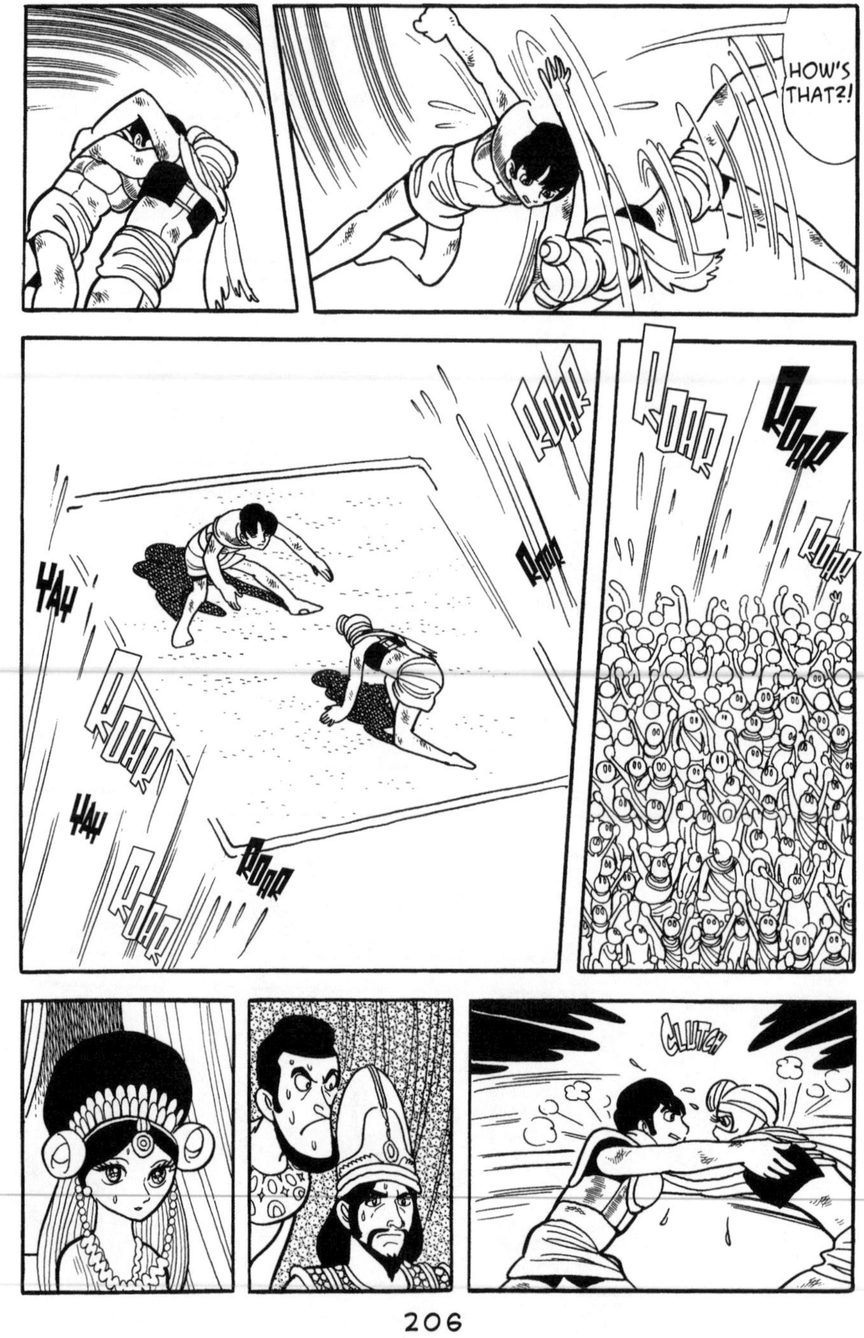
HOW'S THAT?!
ROAR
ROAR
YAH
ROAR
YAH
ROAR
ROAR
ROAR
ROAR
ROAR
CLUTCH

EVEN SUPERMAN DOESN'T HIDE HIS FACE. WHY DOES BERATTA?

NOW THAT YOU MENTION IT, HE HASN'T SHOWN HIS FACE ALL DAY! STRANGE.

WE'LL DO THIS FOR JUST 3 MORE MINUTES, OKAY?

YAA!

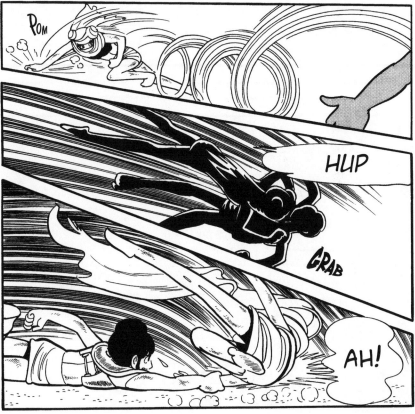

POM

HUP

GRAB

AH!

207

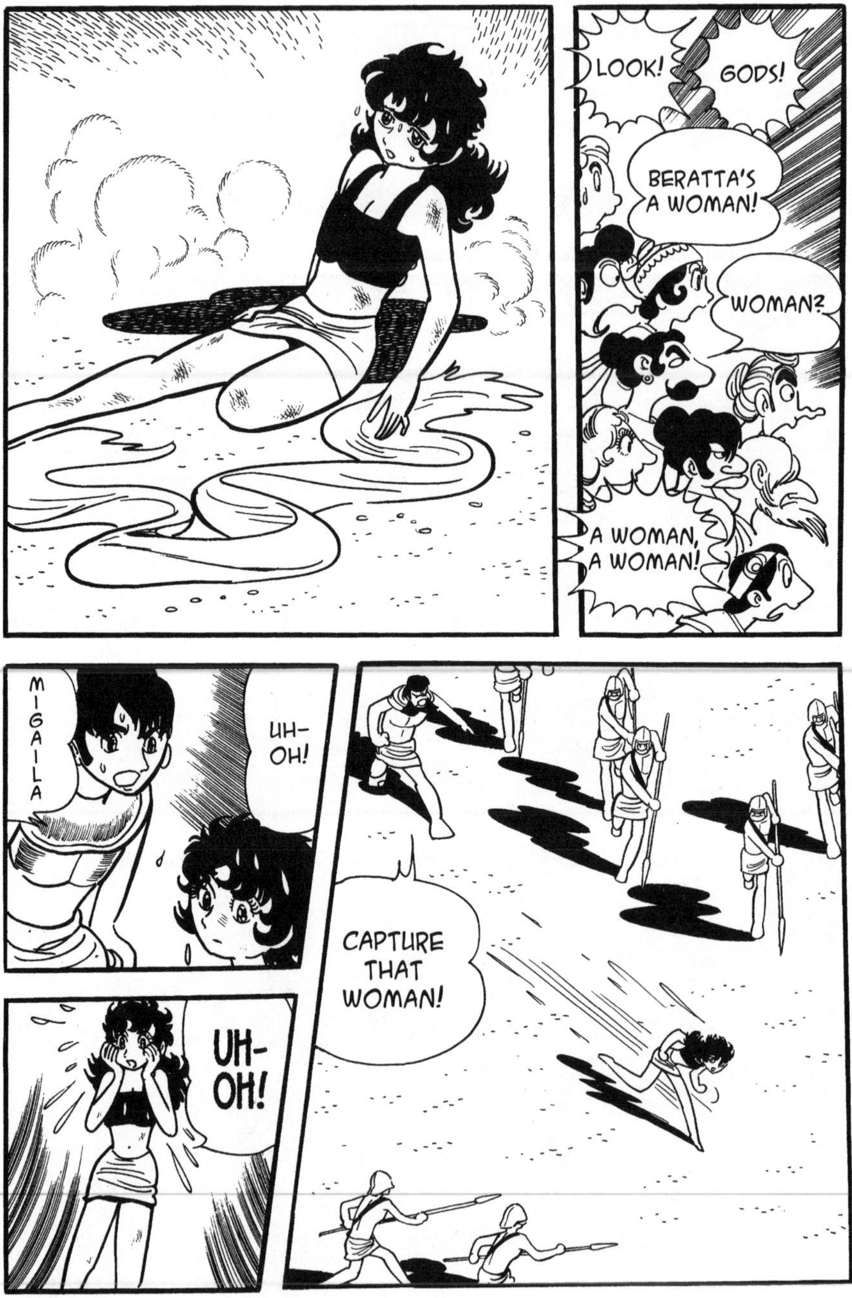
LOOK!
GODS!
BERATTA'S A WOMAN!
WOMAN?
A WOMAN, A WOMAN!
MIGAILA
UH-OH!
UH-OH!
CAPTURE THAT WOMAN!

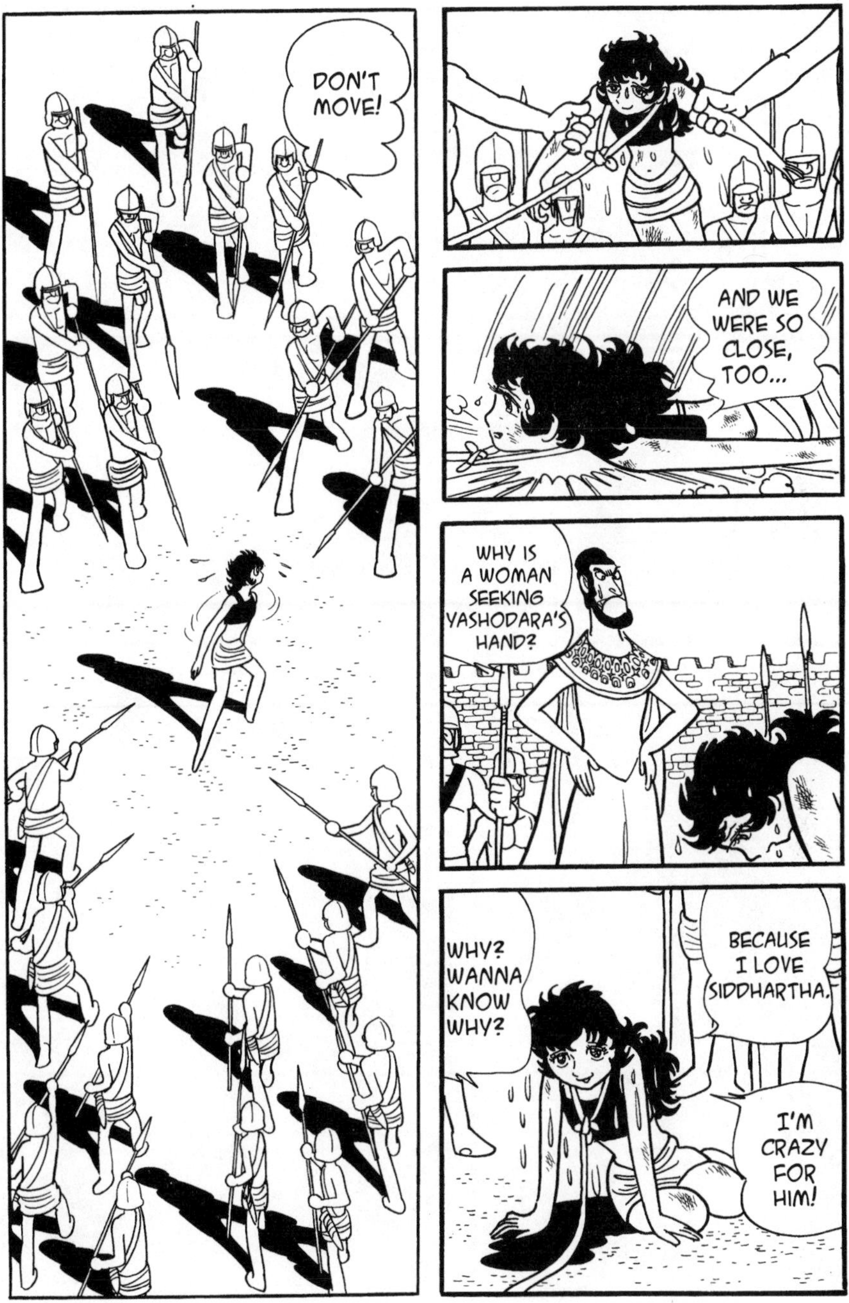
DON'T MOVE!
AND WE WERE SO CLOSE, TOO...
WHY IS A WOMAN SEEKING YASHODARA'S HAND?
WHY? WANNA KNOW WHY?
BECAUSE I LOVE SIDDHARTHA.
I'M CRAZY FOR HIM!

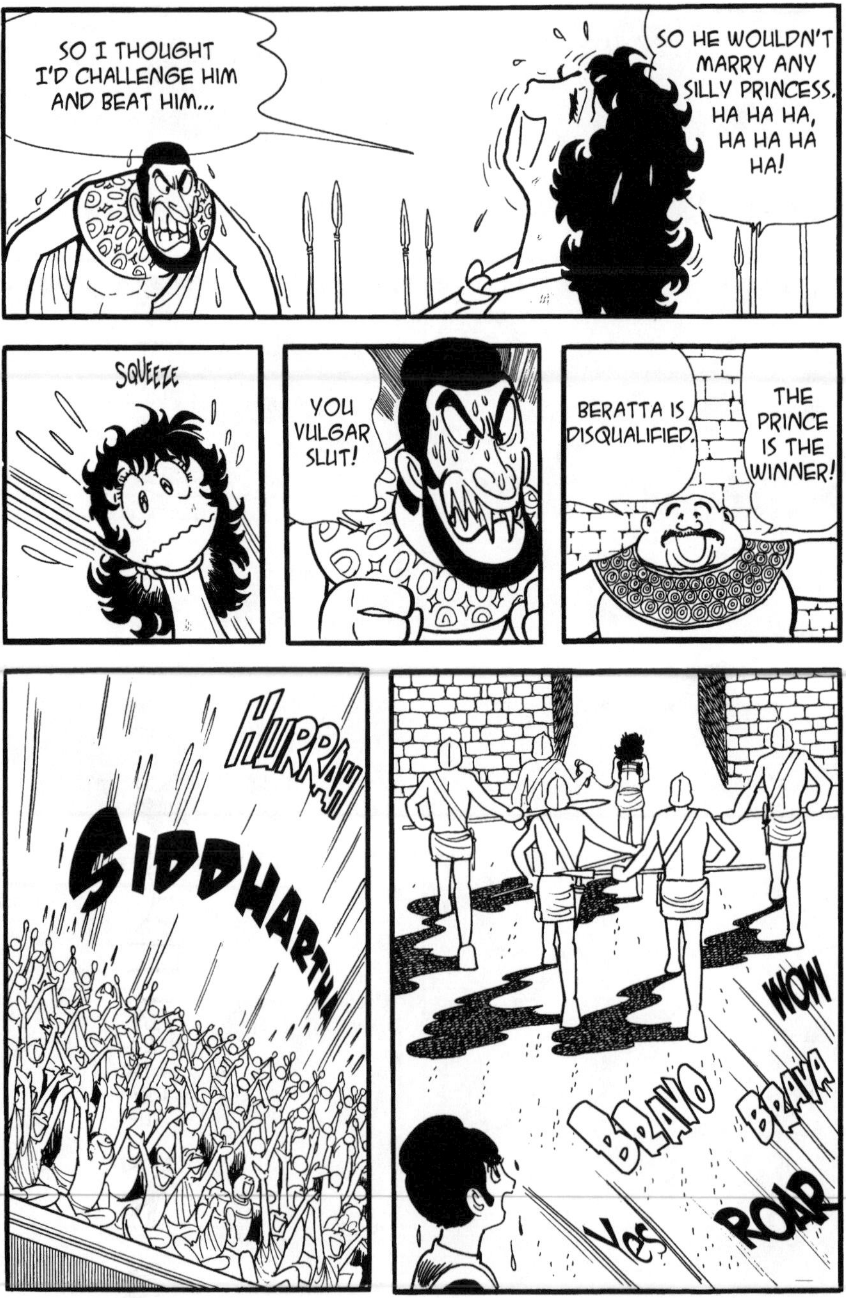
SO I THOUGHT I'D CHALLENGE HIM AND BEAT HIM...
SO HE WOULDN'T MARRY ANY SILLY PRINCESS. HA HA HA, HA HA HA HA!
SQUEEZE
YOU VULGAR SLUT!
BERATTA IS DISQUALIFIED.
THE PRINCE IS THE WINNER!
HURRAH
SIDDHARTHA
WOW
BRAVO
BRAVA
YES
ROAR

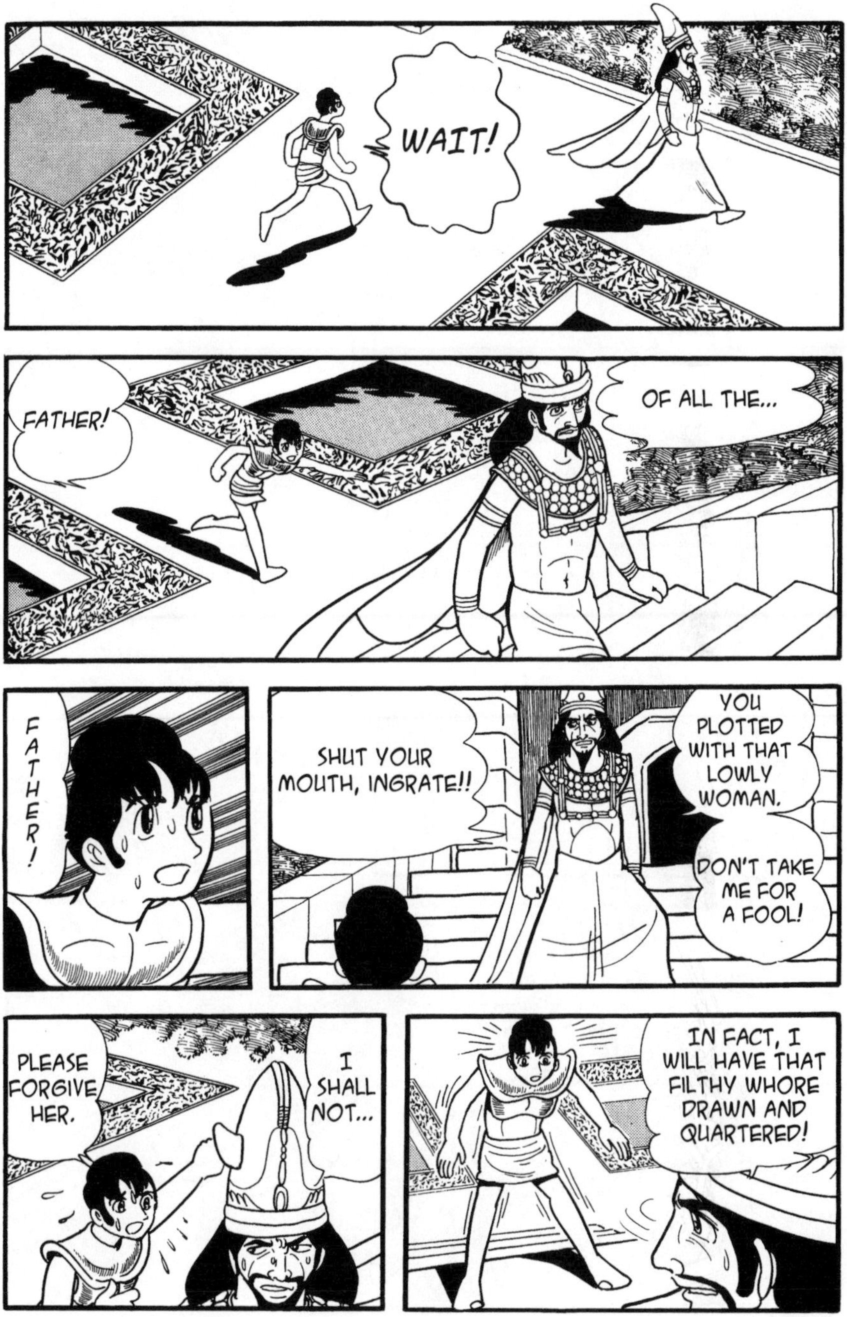
WAIT!
FATHER!
OF ALL THE...
FATHER!
SHUT YOUR MOUTH, INGRATE!!
YOU PLOTTED WITH THAT LOWLY WOMAN.
DON'T TAKE ME FOR A FOOL!
PLEASE FORGIVE HER.
I SHALL NOT...
IN FACT, I WILL HAVE THAT FILTHY WHORE DRAWN AND QUARTERED!

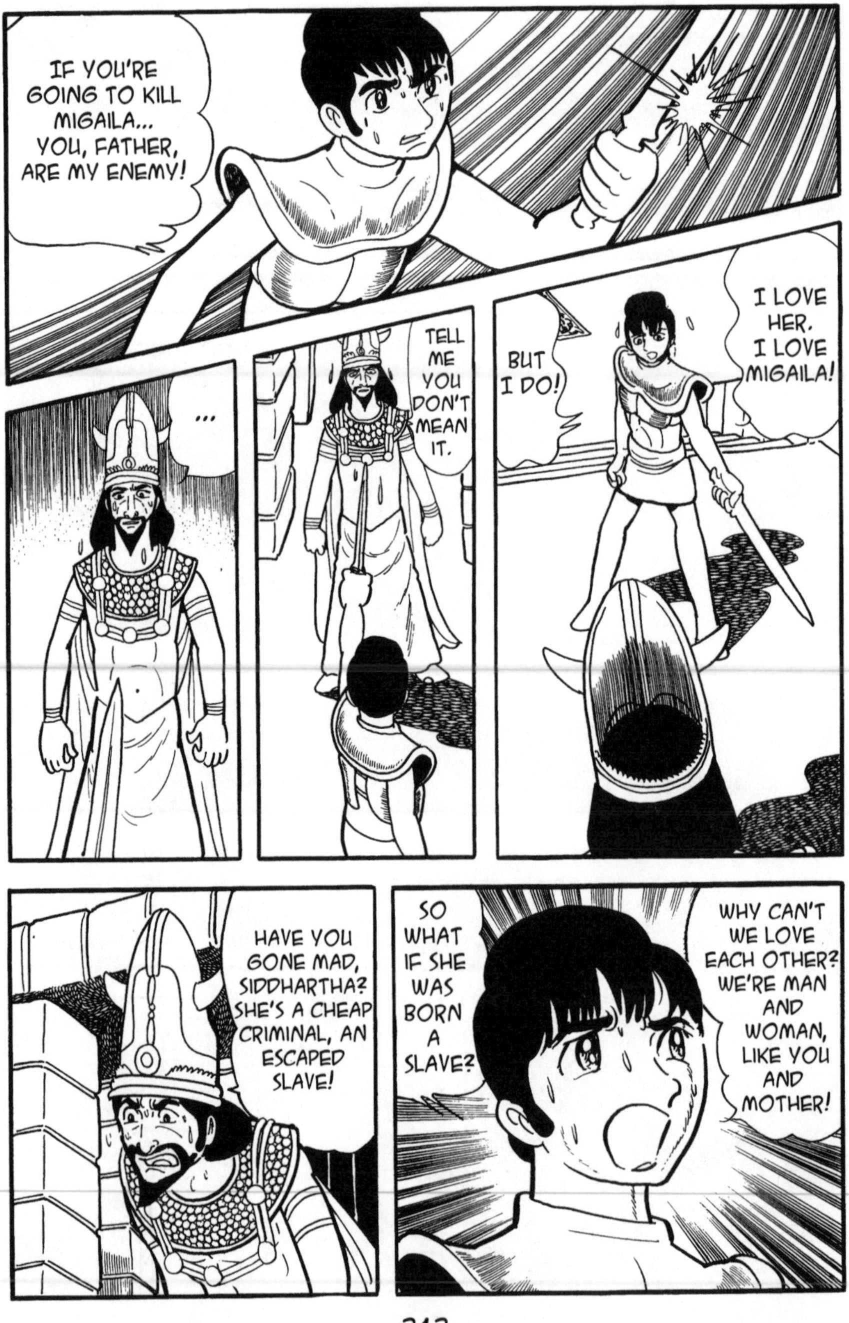
IF YOU'RE GOING TO KILL MIGAILA... YOU, FATHER, ARE MY ENEMY!
...
TELL ME YOU DON'T MEAN IT.
BUT I DO!
I LOVE HER. I LOVE MIGAILA!
HAVE YOU GONE MAD, SIDDHARTHA? SHE'S A CHEAP CRIMINAL, AN ESCAPED SLAVE!
SO WHAT IF SHE WAS BORN A SLAVE?
WHY CAN'T WE LOVE EACH OTHER? WE'RE MAN AND WOMAN, LIKE YOU AND MOTHER!

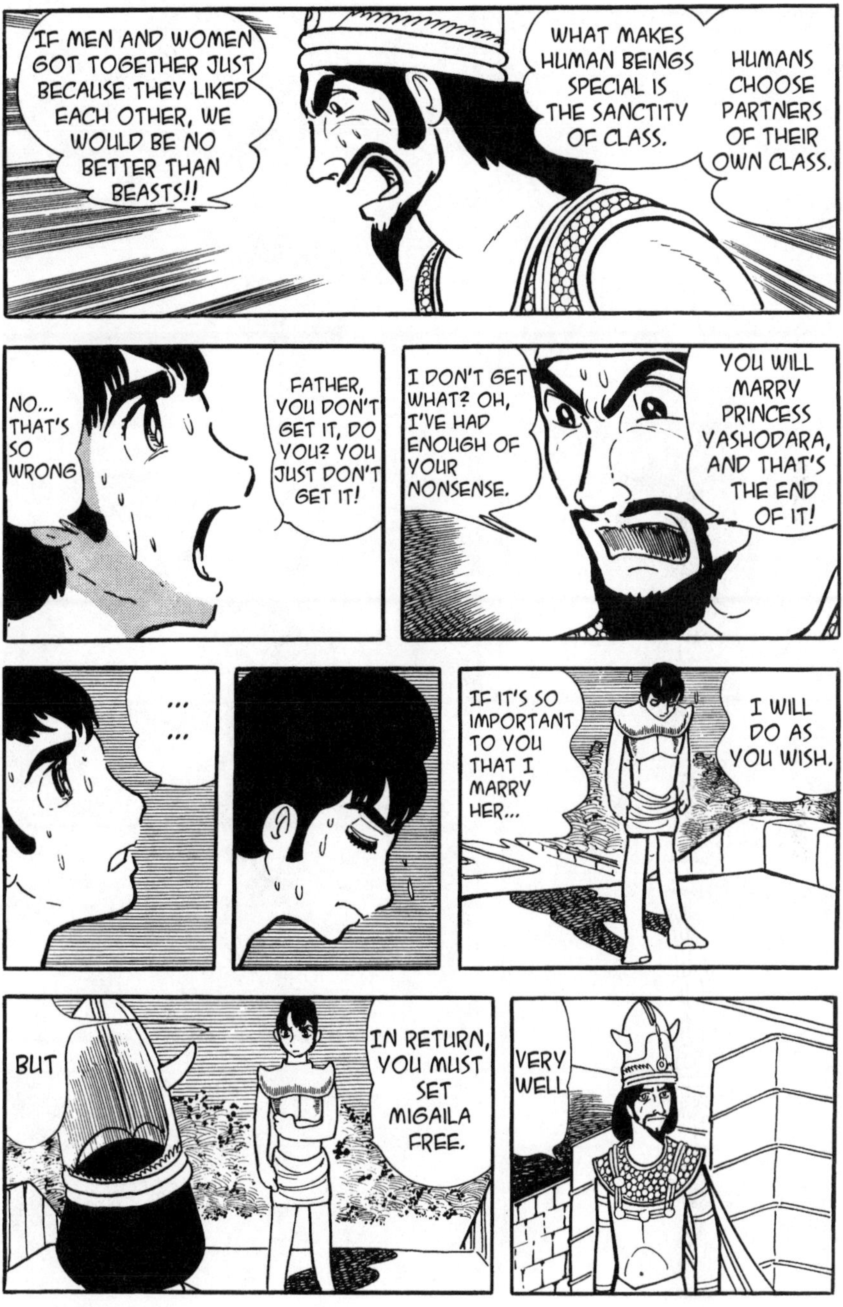
IF MEN AND WOMEN GOT TOGETHER JUST BECAUSE THEY LIKED EACH OTHER, WE WOULD BE NO BETTER THAN BEASTS!!
WHAT MAKES HUMAN BEINGS SPECIAL IS THE SANCTITY OF CLASS.
HUMANS CHOOSE PARTNERS OF THEIR OWN CLASS.
NO... THAT'S SO WRONG
FATHER, YOU DON'T GET IT, DO YOU? YOU JUST DON'T GET IT!
I DON'T GET WHAT? OH, I'VE HAD ENOUGH OF YOUR NONSENSE.
YOU WILL MARRY PRINCESS YASHODARA, AND THAT'S THE END OF IT!
...
...
IF IT'S SO IMPORTANT TO YOU THAT I MARRY HER...
I WILL DO AS YOU WISH.
BUT
IN RETURN, YOU MUST SET MIGAILA FREE.
VERY WELL

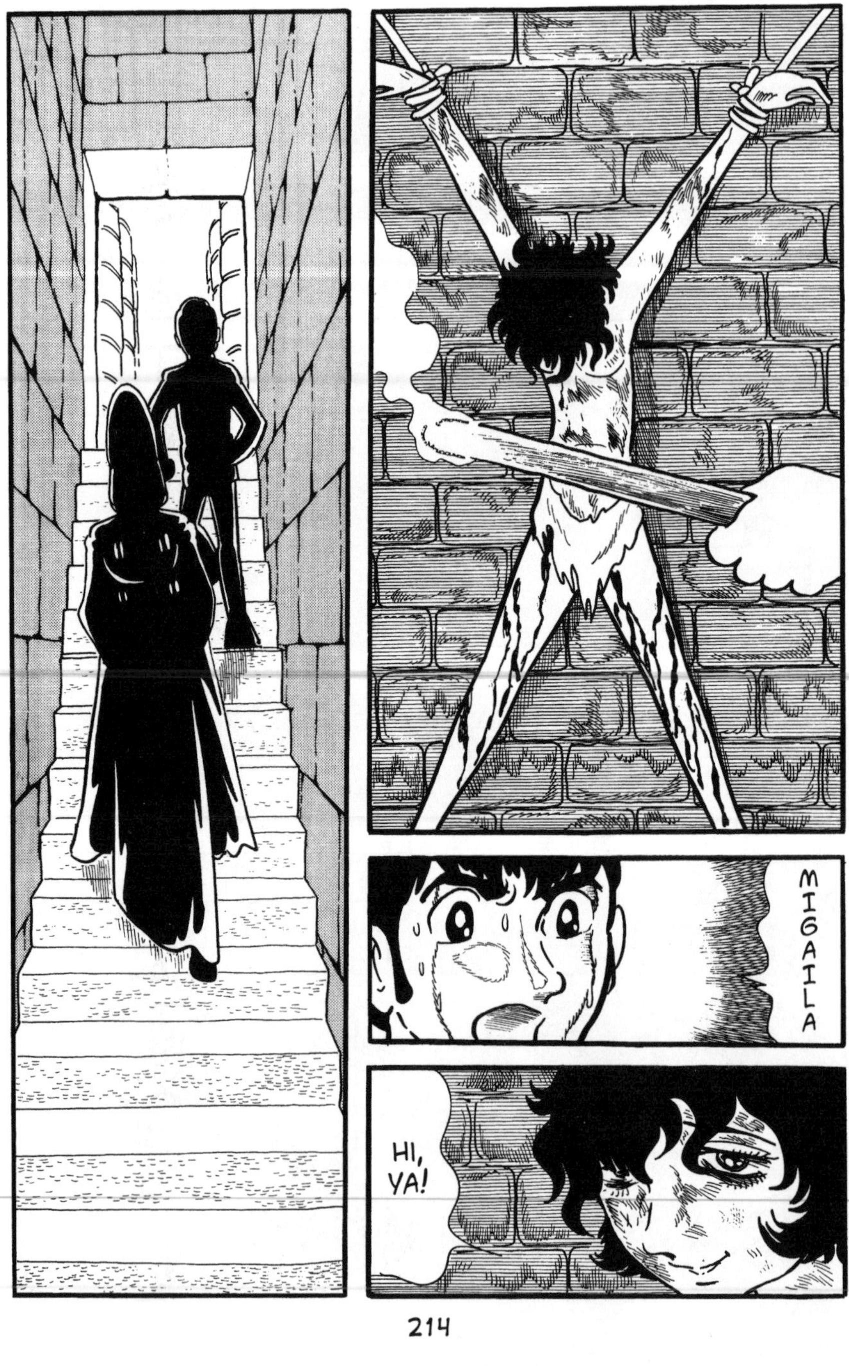
MIGAILA
HI, YA!

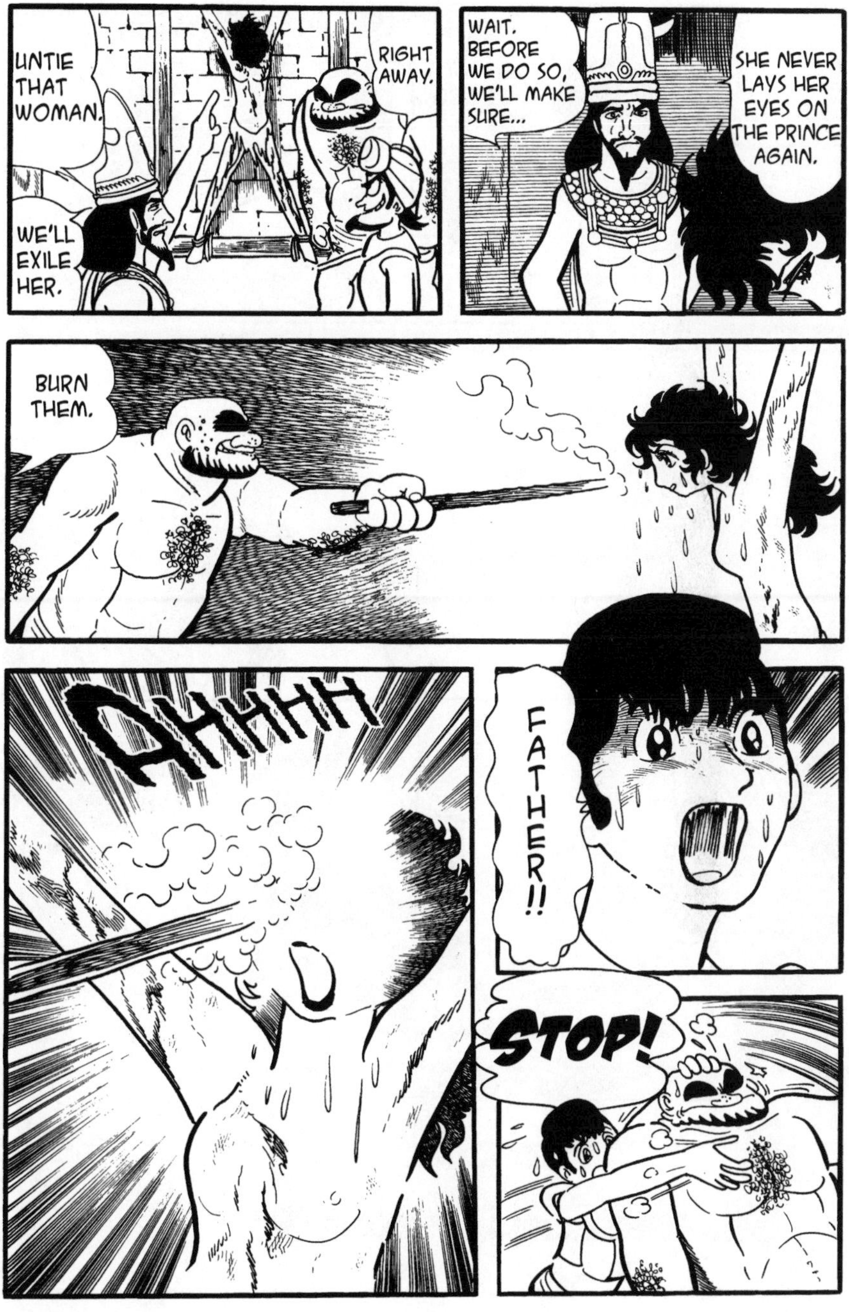
UNTIE THAT WOMAN.
WE'LL EXILE HER.
RIGHT AWAY.
WAIT. BEFORE WE DO SO, WE'LL MAKE SURE...
SHE NEVER LAYS HER EYES ON THE PRINCE AGAIN.
BURN THEM.
AHHHH
FATHER!!
STOP!

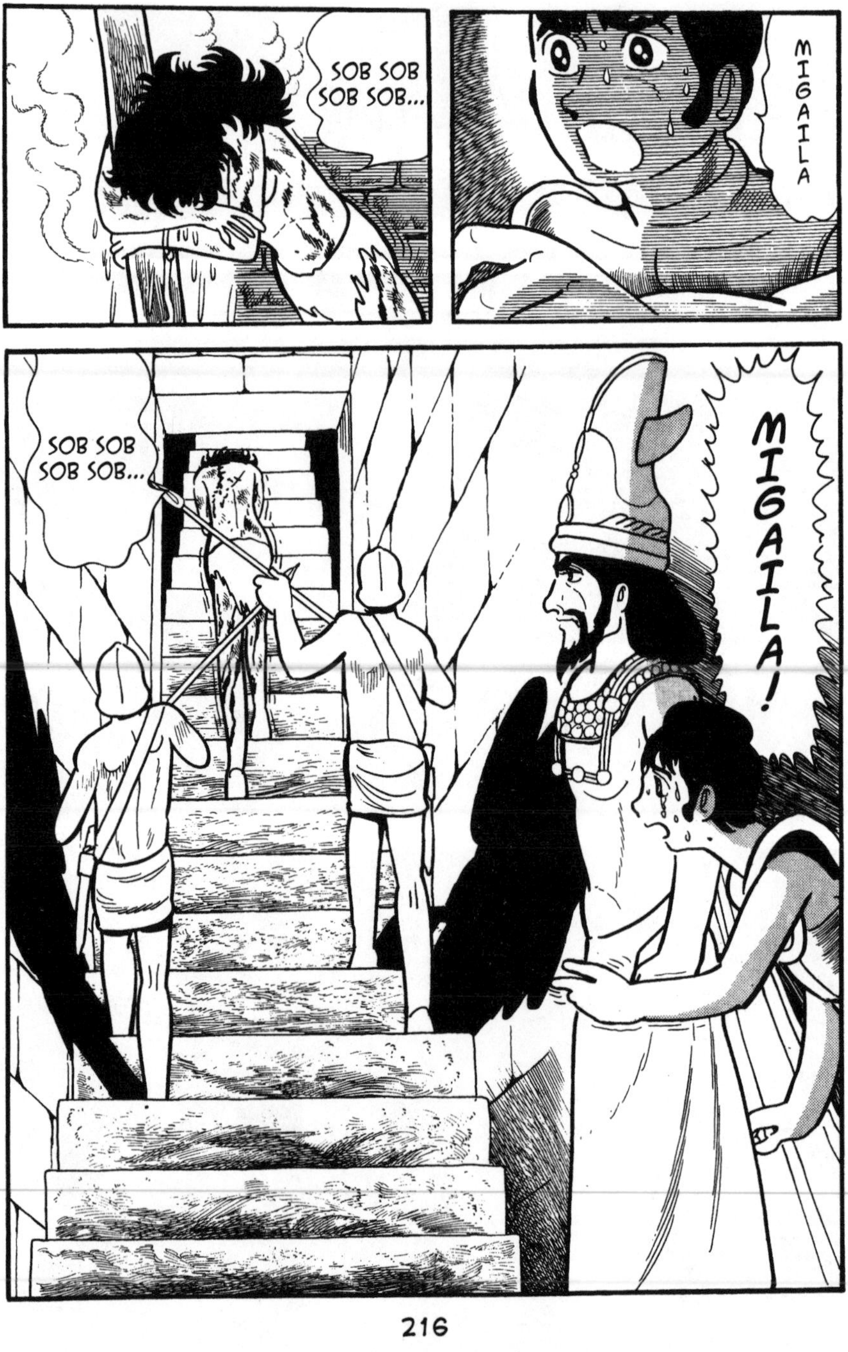
SOB SOB
SOB SOB...
MIGAILA
SOB SOB
SOB SOB...
MIGAILA!

CHAPTER SIX

THE FOUR ENCOUNTERS

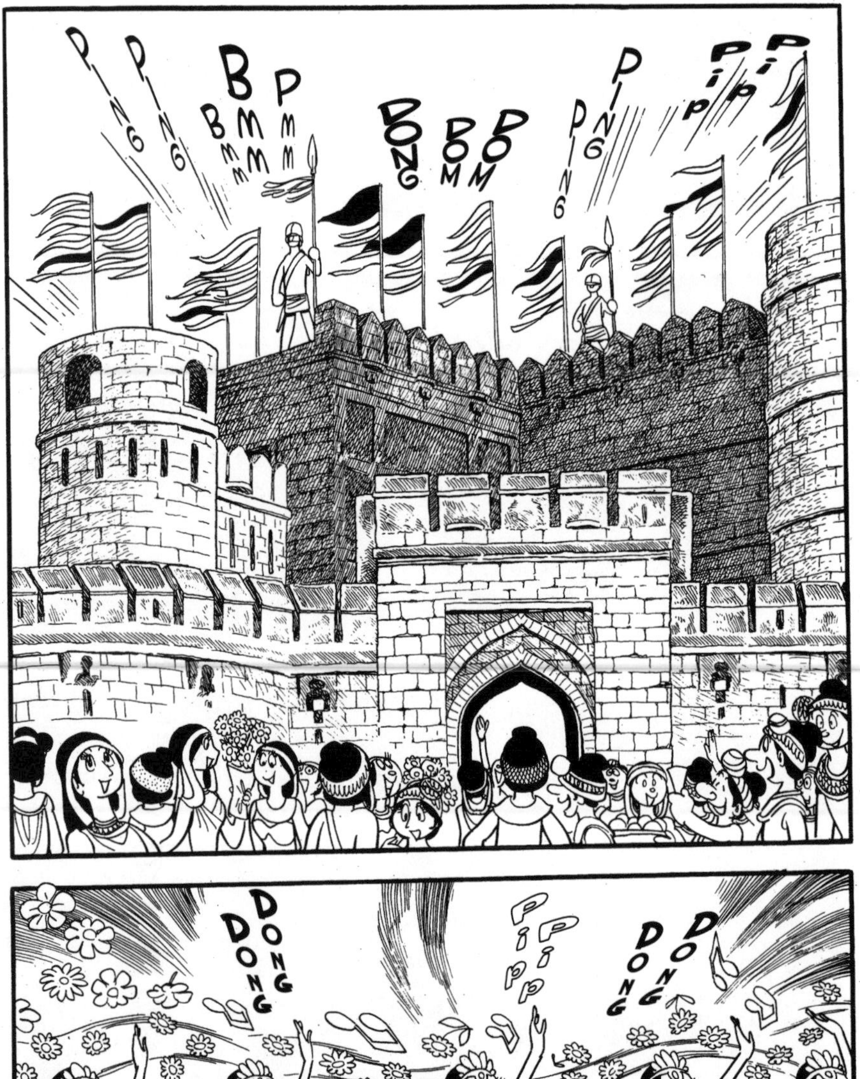
PING
PING
BMMM
BMMM
PMMM
DONG
DOM
DOM
PING
PING
PIP
PIP
PI

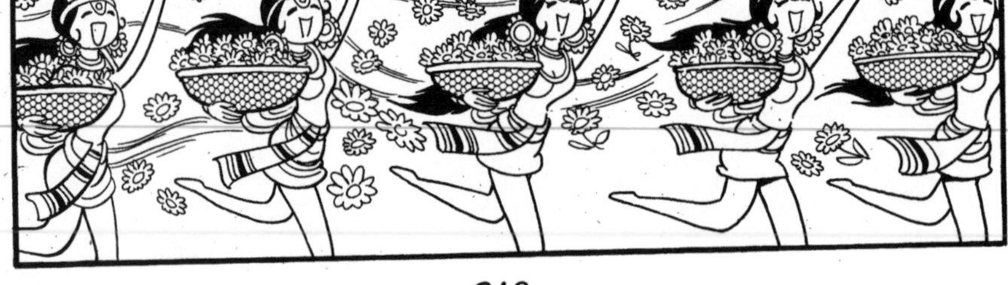
DONG
DONG
PIP
PIP
DONG
DONG

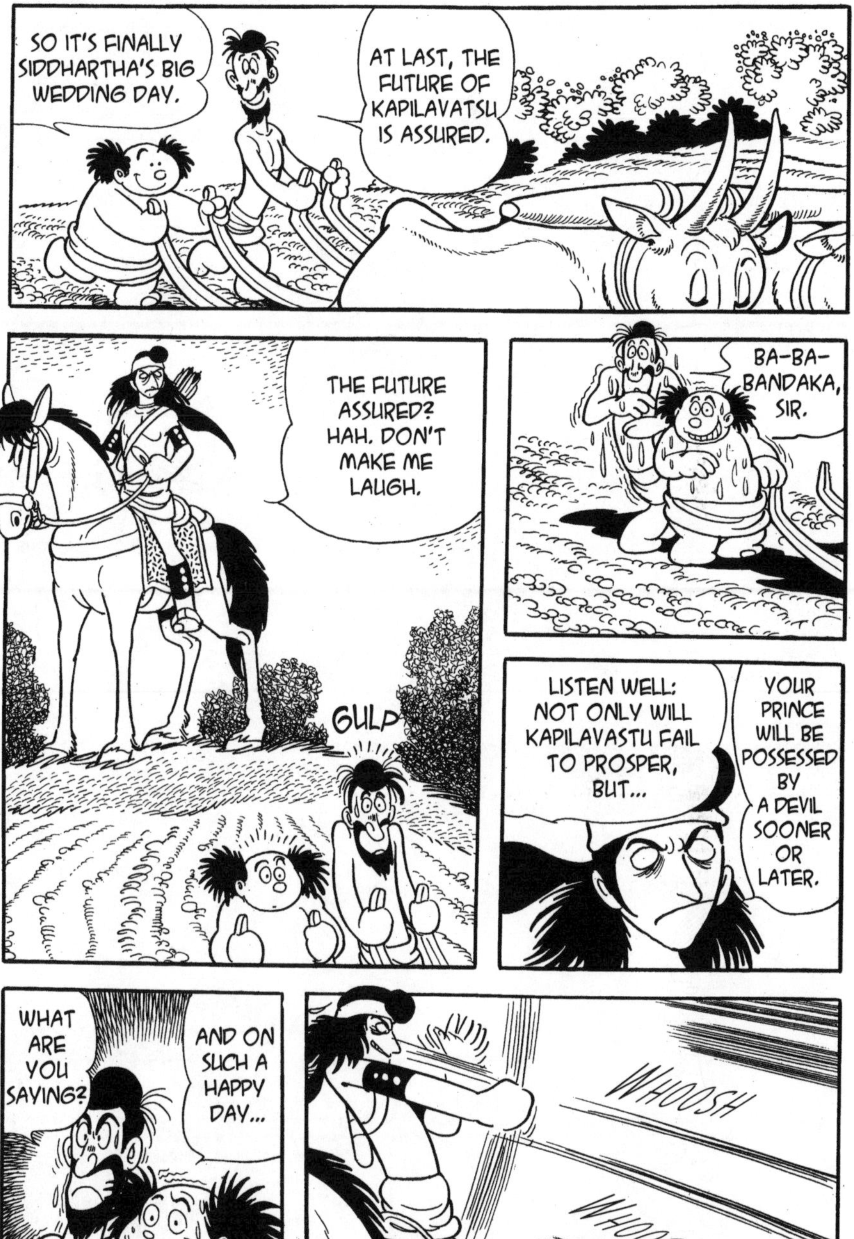
SO IT'S FINALLY SIDDHARTHA'S BIG WEDDING DAY.
AT LAST, THE FUTURE OF KAPILAVATSU IS ASSURED.
THE FUTURE ASSURED? HAH. DON'T MAKE ME LAUGH.
GULP
BA-BA-BANDAKA, SIR.
LISTEN WELL: NOT ONLY WILL KAPILAVASTU FAIL TO PROSPER, BUT...
YOUR PRINCE WILL BE POSSESSED BY A DEVIL SOONER OR LATER.
WHAT ARE YOU SAYING?
AND ON SUCH A HAPPY DAY...
WHOOSH
WHOOSH

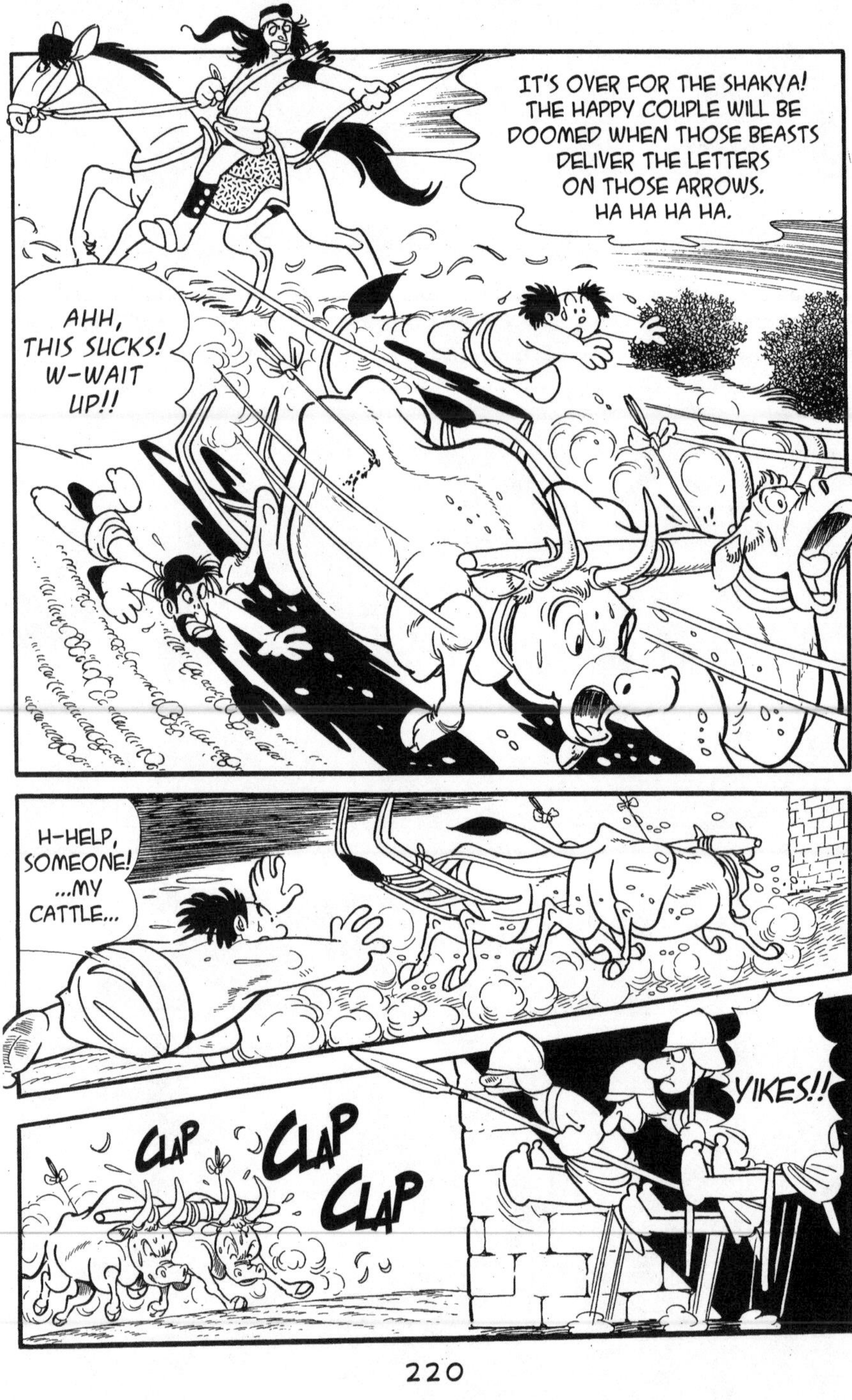
IT'S OVER FOR THE SHAKYA! THE HAPPY COUPLE WILL BE DOOMED WHEN THOSE BEASTS DELIVER THE LETTERS ON THOSE ARROWS. HA HA HA HA.
AHH, THIS SUCKS! W-WAIT UP!!
H-HELP, SOMEONE! ...MY CATTLE...
CLAP CLAP CLAP
YIKES!!

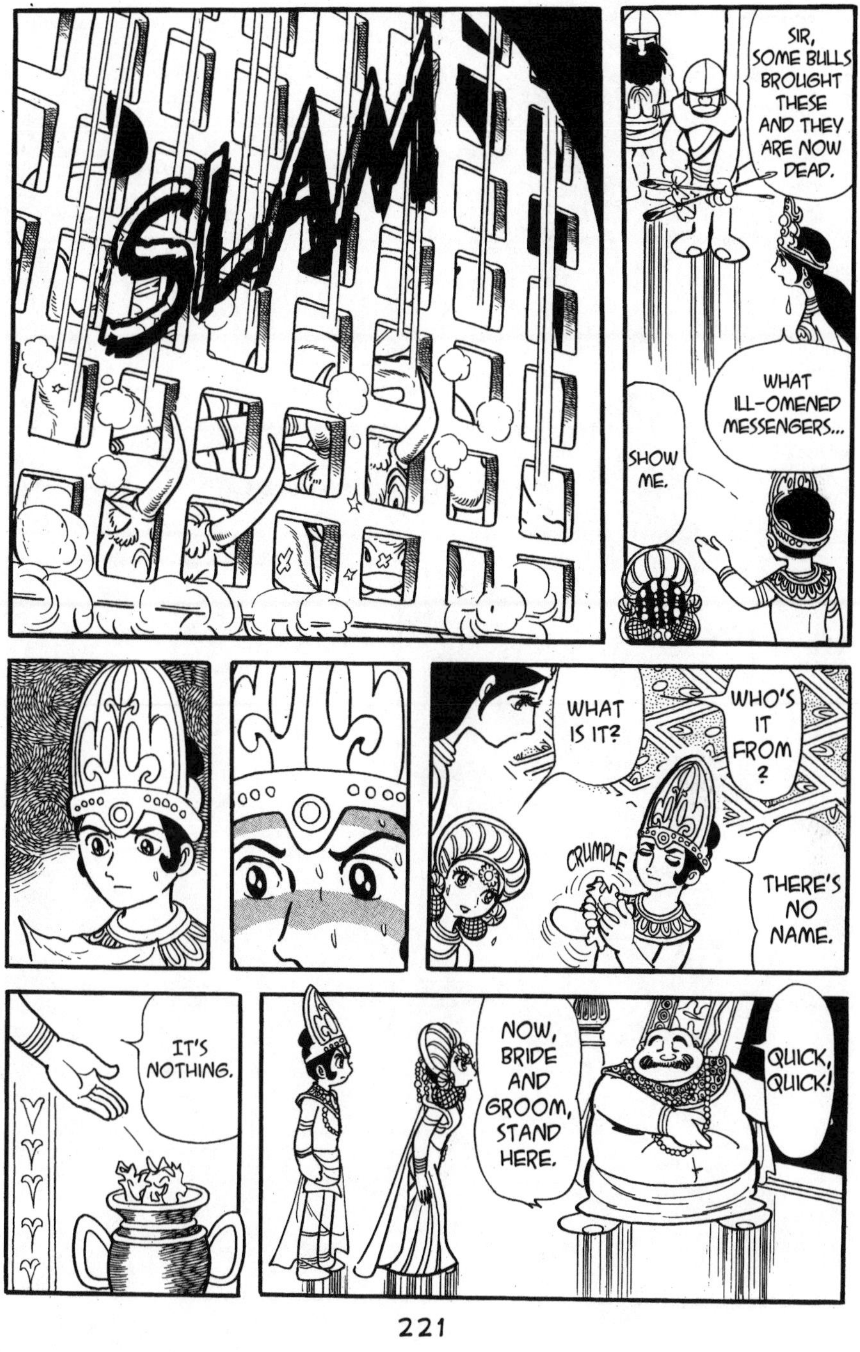
SLAM
SIR, SOME BULLS BROUGHT THESE AND THEY ARE NOW DEAD.
WHAT ILL-OMENED MESSENGERS...
SHOW ME.
WHAT IS IT?
WHO'S IT FROM?
CRUMPLE
THERE'S NO NAME.
IT'S NOTHING.
NOW, BRIDE AND GROOM, STAND HERE.
QUICK, QUICK!

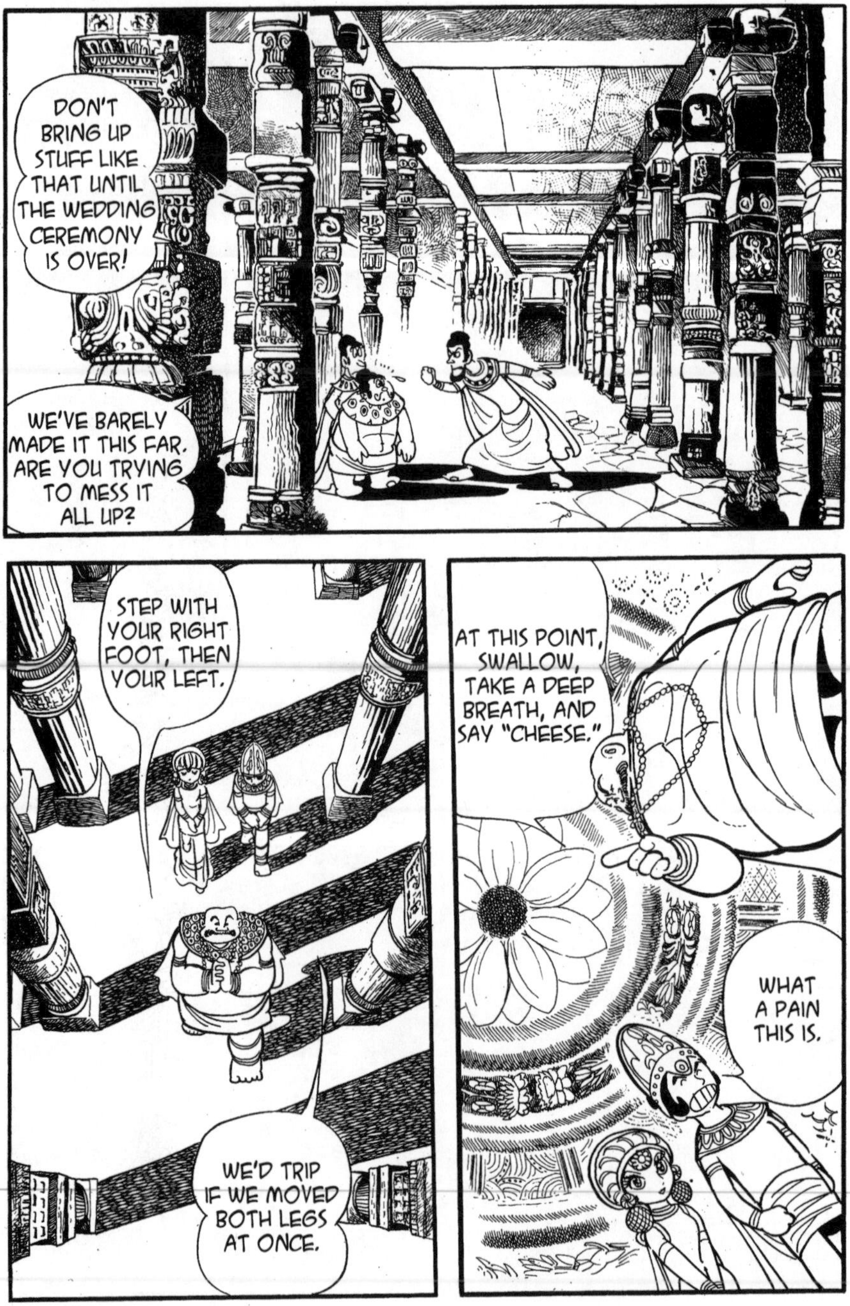
DON'T BRING UP STUFF LIKE THAT UNTIL THE WEDDING CEREMONY IS OVER!
WE'VE BARELY MADE IT THIS FAR. ARE YOU TRYING TO MESS IT ALL UP?
STEP WITH YOUR RIGHT FOOT, THEN YOUR LEFT.
WE'D TRIP IF WE MOVED BOTH LEGS AT ONCE.
AT THIS POINT, SWALLOW, TAKE A DEEP BREATH, AND SAY "CHEESE."
WHAT A PAIN THIS IS.

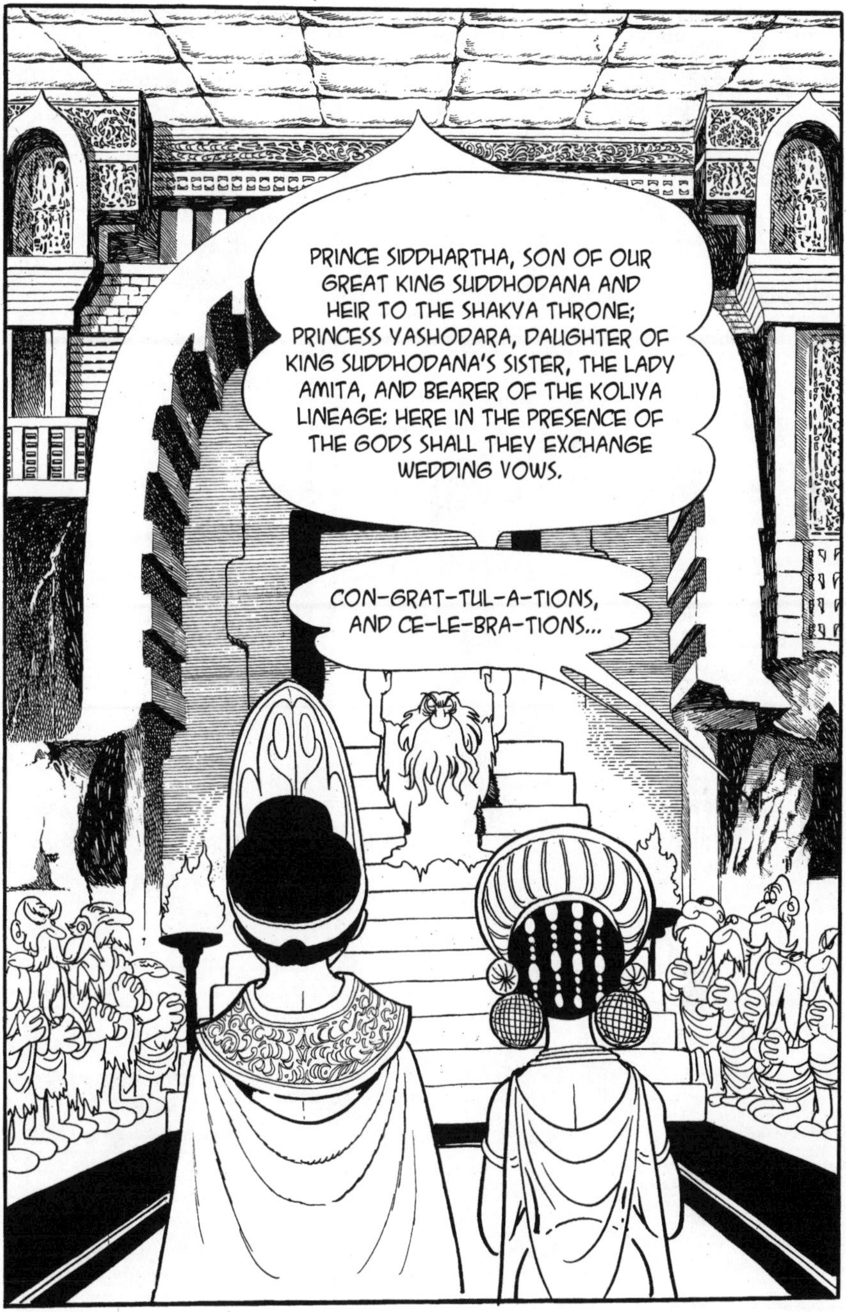
PRINCE SIDDHARTHA, SON OF OUR GREAT KING SUDDHODANA AND HEIR TO THE SHAKYA THRONE; PRINCESS YASHODARA, DAUGHTER OF KING SUDDHODANA'S SISTER, THE LADY AMITA, AND BEARER OF THE KOLIYA LINEAGE: HERE IN THE PRESENCE OF THE GODS SHALL THEY EXCHANGE WEDDING VOWS.
CON-GRAT-TUL-A-TIONS, AND CE-LE-BRA-TIONS...

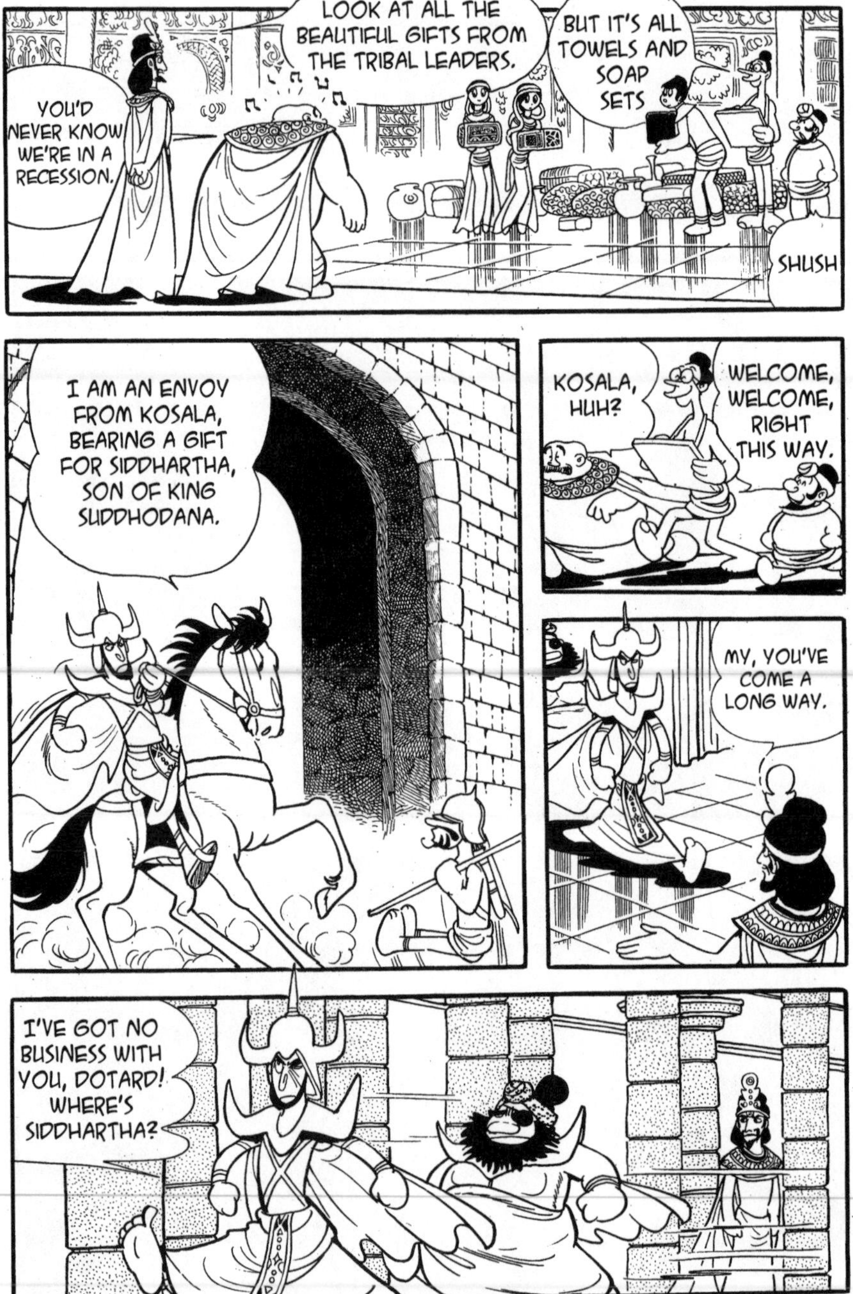
LOOK AT ALL THE BEAUTIFUL GIFTS FROM THE TRIBAL LEADERS.
YOU'D NEVER KNOW WE'RE IN A RECESSION.
BUT IT'S ALL TOWELS AND SOAP SETS
SHUSH
I AM AN ENVOY FROM KOSALA, BEARING A GIFT FOR SIDDHARTHA, SON OF KING SUDDHODANA.
KOSALA, HUH?
WELCOME, WELCOME, RIGHT THIS WAY.
MY, YOU'VE COME A LONG WAY.
I'VE GOT NO BUSINESS WITH YOU, DOTARD! WHERE'S SIDDHARTHA?

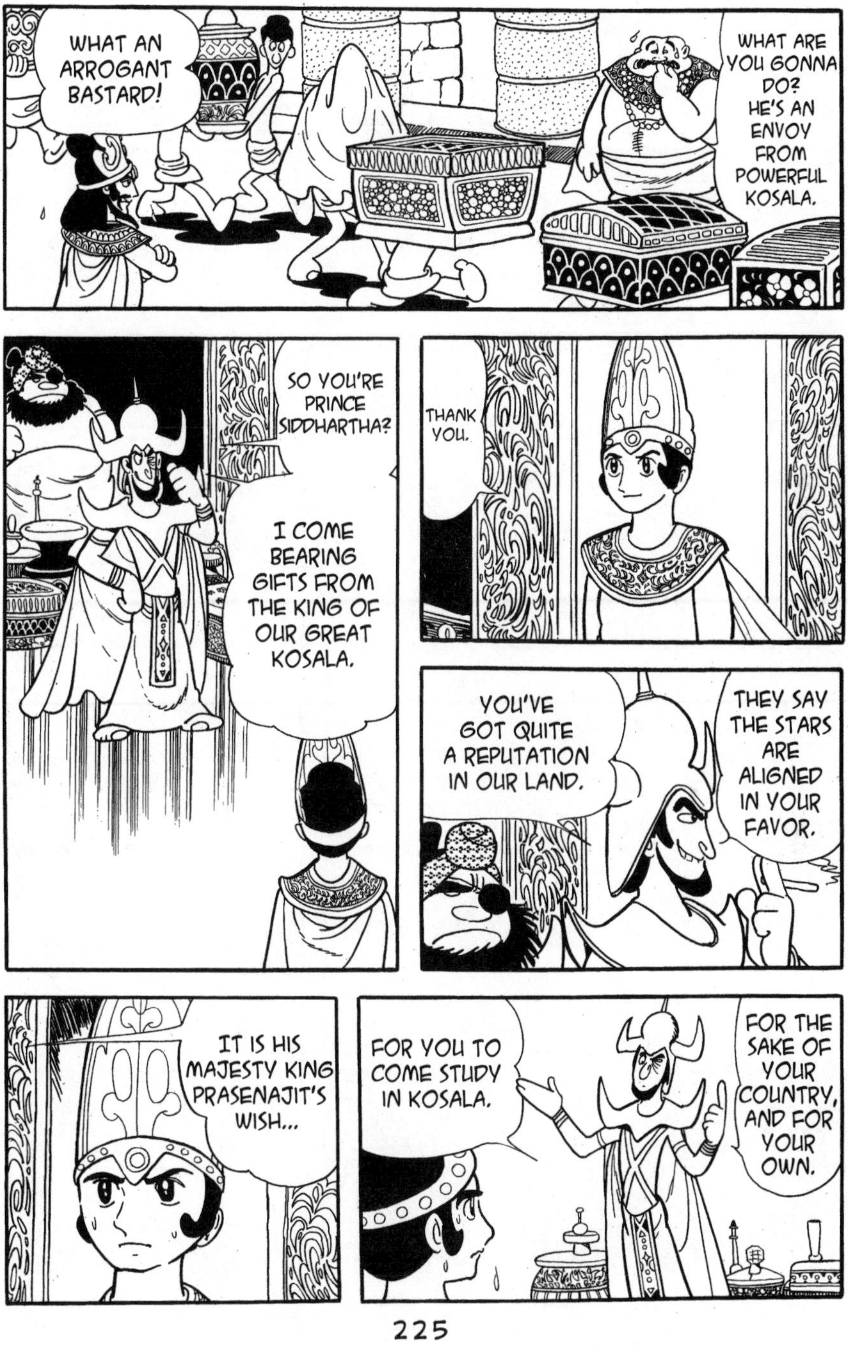
WHAT AN ARROGANT BASTARD!
WHAT ARE YOU GONNA DO? HE'S AN ENVOY FROM POWERFUL KOSALA.
SO YOU'RE PRINCE SIDDHARTHA?
I COME BEARING GIFTS FROM THE KING OF OUR GREAT KOSALA.
THANK YOU.
YOU'VE GOT QUITE A REPUTATION IN OUR LAND.
THEY SAY THE STARS ARE ALIGNED IN YOUR FAVOR.
IT IS HIS MAJESTY KING PRASENAJIT'S WISH...
FOR YOU TO COME STUDY IN KOSALA.
FOR THE SAKE OF YOUR COUNTRY, AND FOR YOUR OWN.

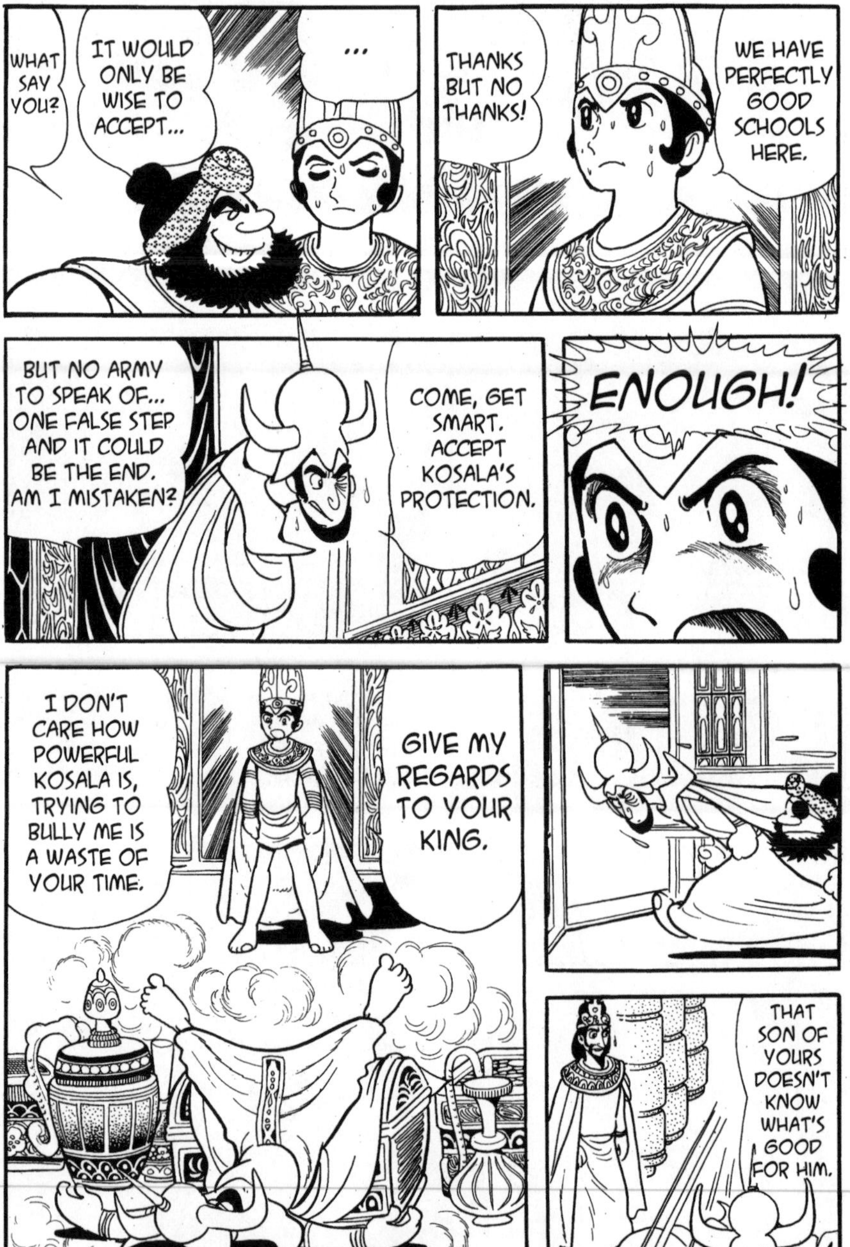
WHAT SAY YOU?
IT WOULD ONLY BE WISE TO ACCEPT...
...
THANKS BUT NO THANKS!
WE HAVE PERFECTLY GOOD SCHOOLS HERE.
BUT NO ARMY TO SPEAK OF... ONE FALSE STEP AND IT COULD BE THE END. AM I MISTAKEN?
COME, GET SMART. ACCEPT KOSALA'S PROTECTION.
ENOUGH!
I DON'T CARE HOW POWERFUL KOSALA IS, TRYING TO BULLY ME IS A WASTE OF YOUR TIME.
GIVE MY REGARDS TO YOUR KING.
THAT SON OF YOURS DOESN'T KNOW WHAT'S GOOD FOR HIM.

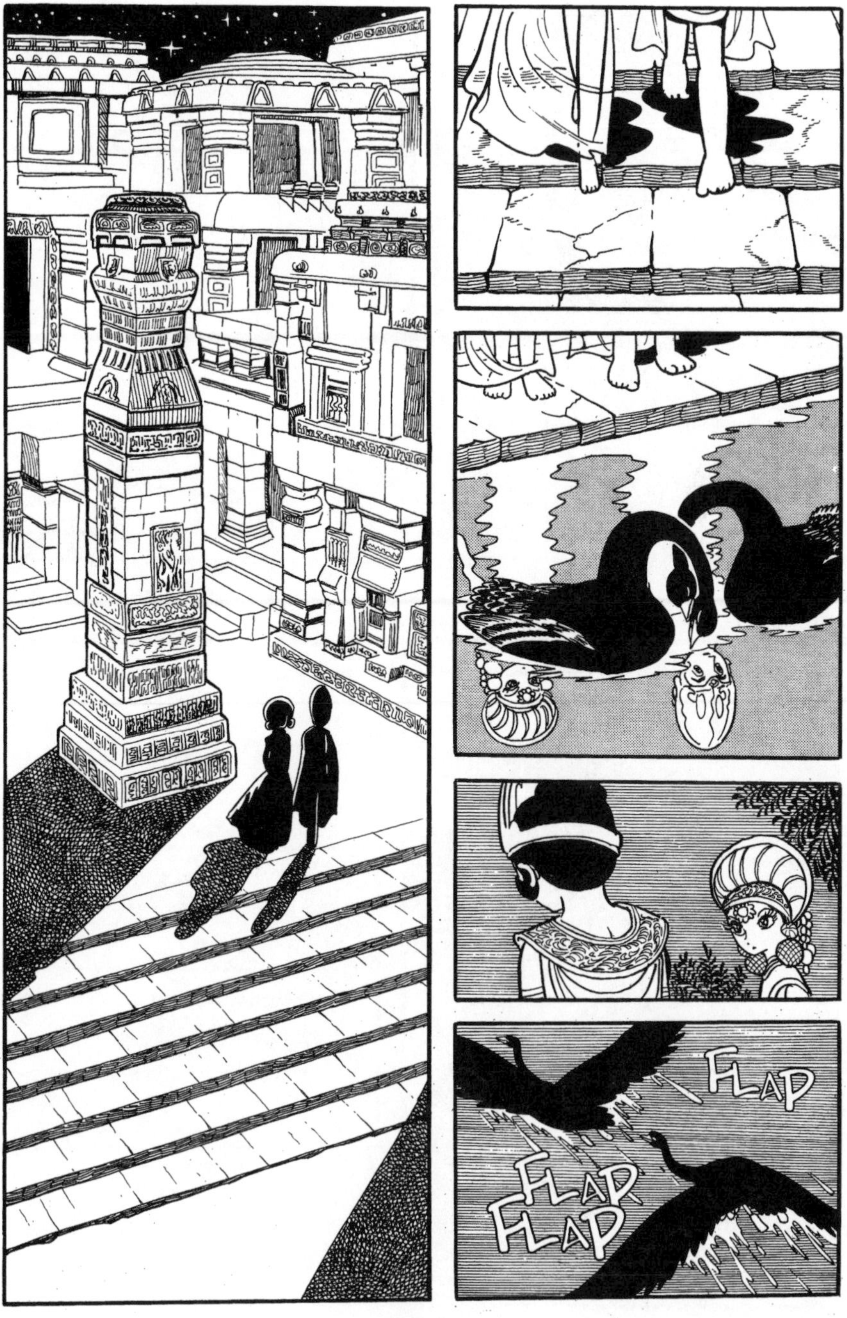
FLAP
FLAP
FLAP

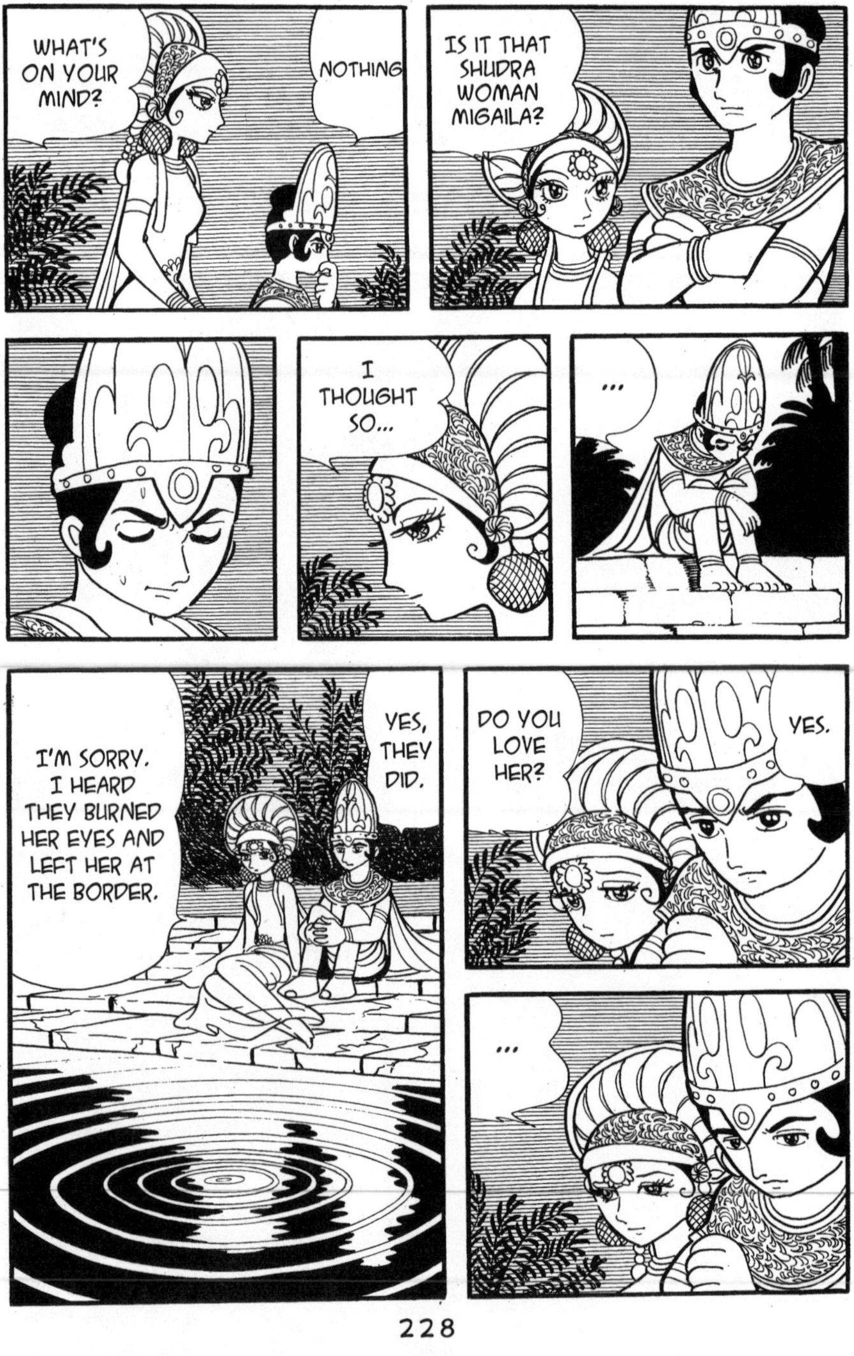
WHAT'S ON YOUR MIND?
NOTHING
IS IT THAT SHUDRA WOMAN MIGAILA?
I THOUGHT SO...
...
I'M SORRY. I HEARD THEY BURNED HER EYES AND LEFT HER AT THE BORDER.
YES, THEY DID.
DO YOU LOVE HER?
YES.
...

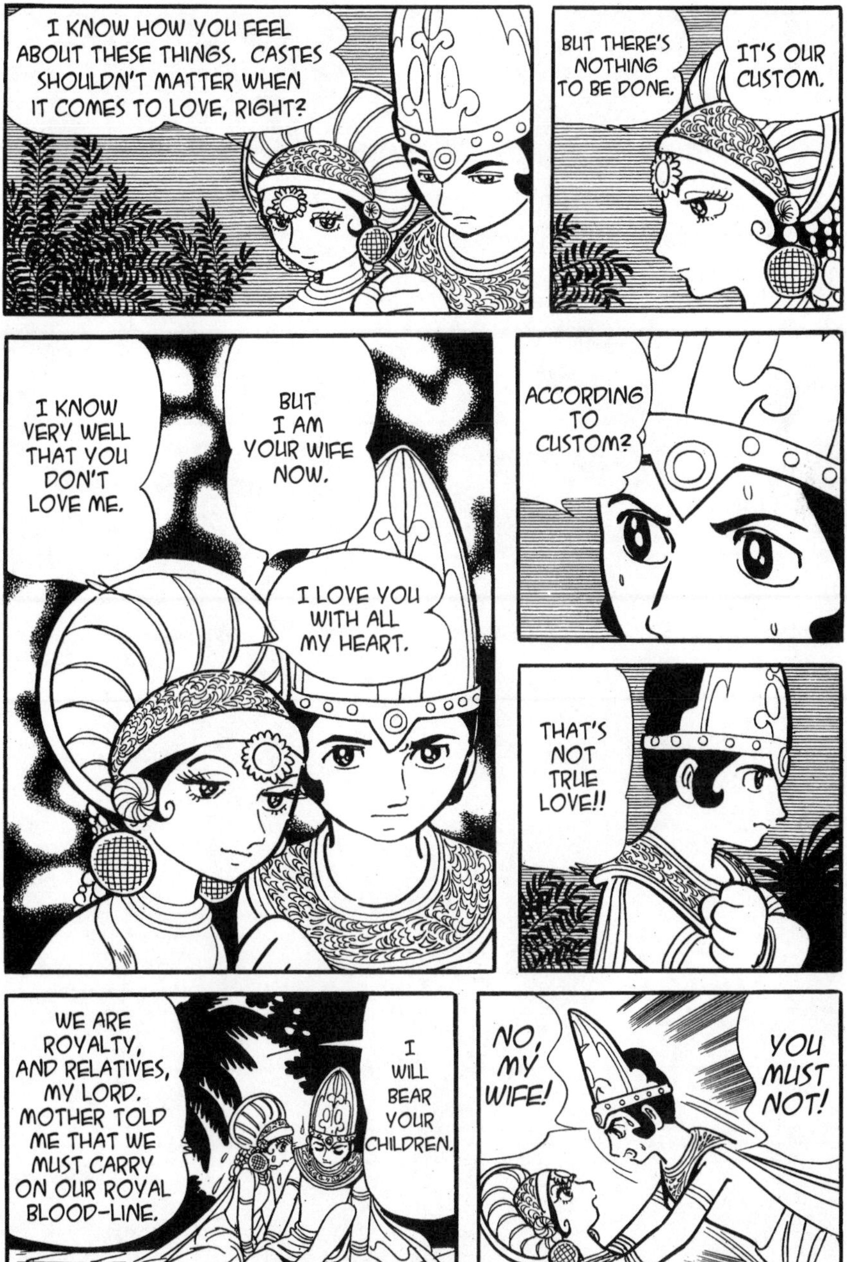
I KNOW HOW YOU FEEL ABOUT THESE THINGS. CASTES SHOULDN'T MATTER WHEN IT COMES TO LOVE, RIGHT?
BUT THERE'S NOTHING TO BE DONE.
IT'S OUR CUSTOM.
I KNOW VERY WELL THAT YOU DON'T LOVE ME.
BUT I AM YOUR WIFE NOW.
I LOVE YOU WITH ALL MY HEART.
ACCORDING TO CUSTOM?
THAT'S NOT TRUE LOVE!!
WE ARE ROYALTY, AND RELATIVES, MY LORD. MOTHER TOLD ME THAT WE MUST CARRY ON OUR ROYAL BLOOD-LINE.
I WILL BEAR YOUR CHILDREN.
NO, MY WIFE!
YOU MUST NOT!

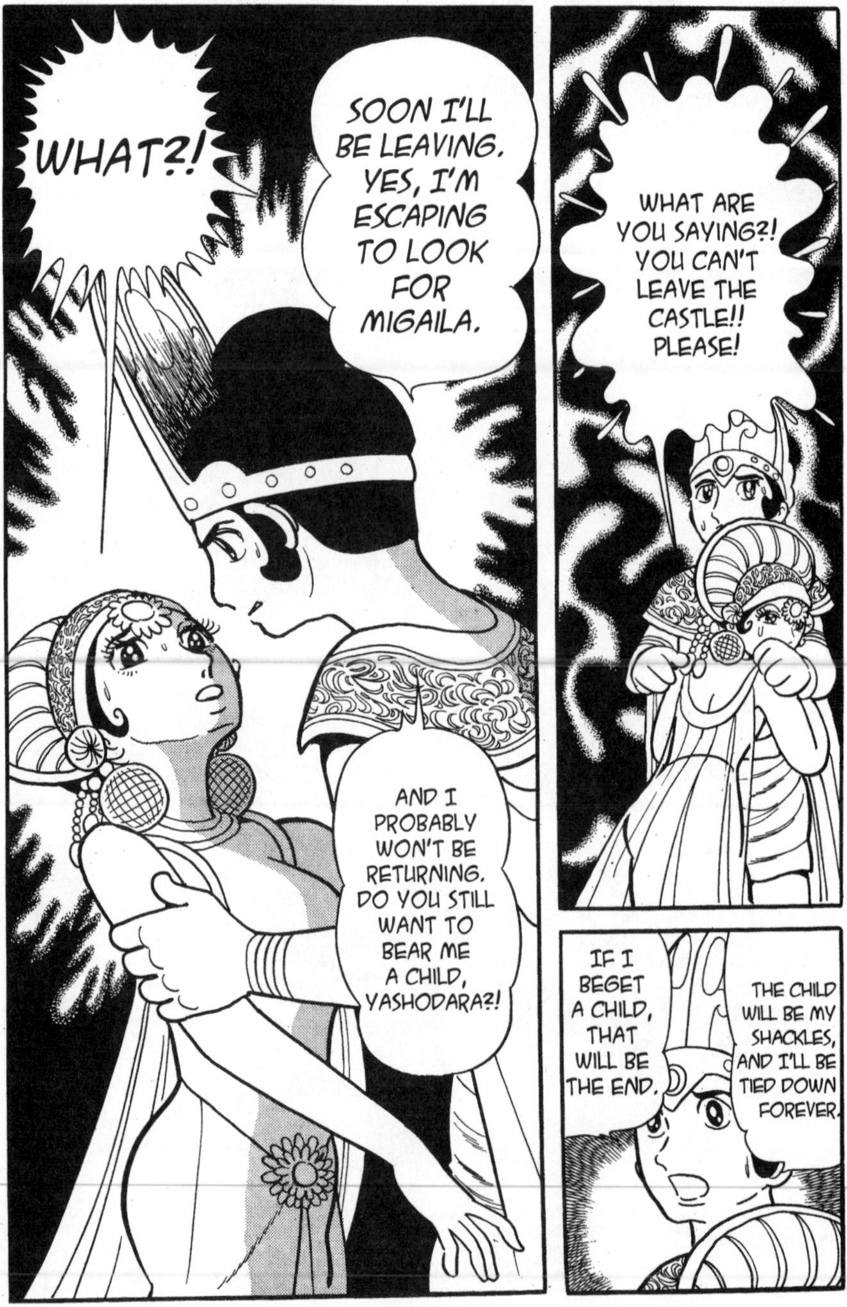
WHAT?!
SOON I'LL BE LEAVING. YES, I'M ESCAPING TO LOOK FOR MIGAILA.
AND I PROBABLY WON'T BE RETURNING. DO YOU STILL WANT TO BEAR ME A CHILD, YASHODARA?!
WHAT ARE YOU SAYING?! YOU CAN'T LEAVE THE CASTLE!! PLEASE!
IF I BEGET A CHILD, THAT WILL BE THE END.
THE CHILD WILL BE MY SHACKLES, AND I'LL BE TIED DOWN FOREVER.

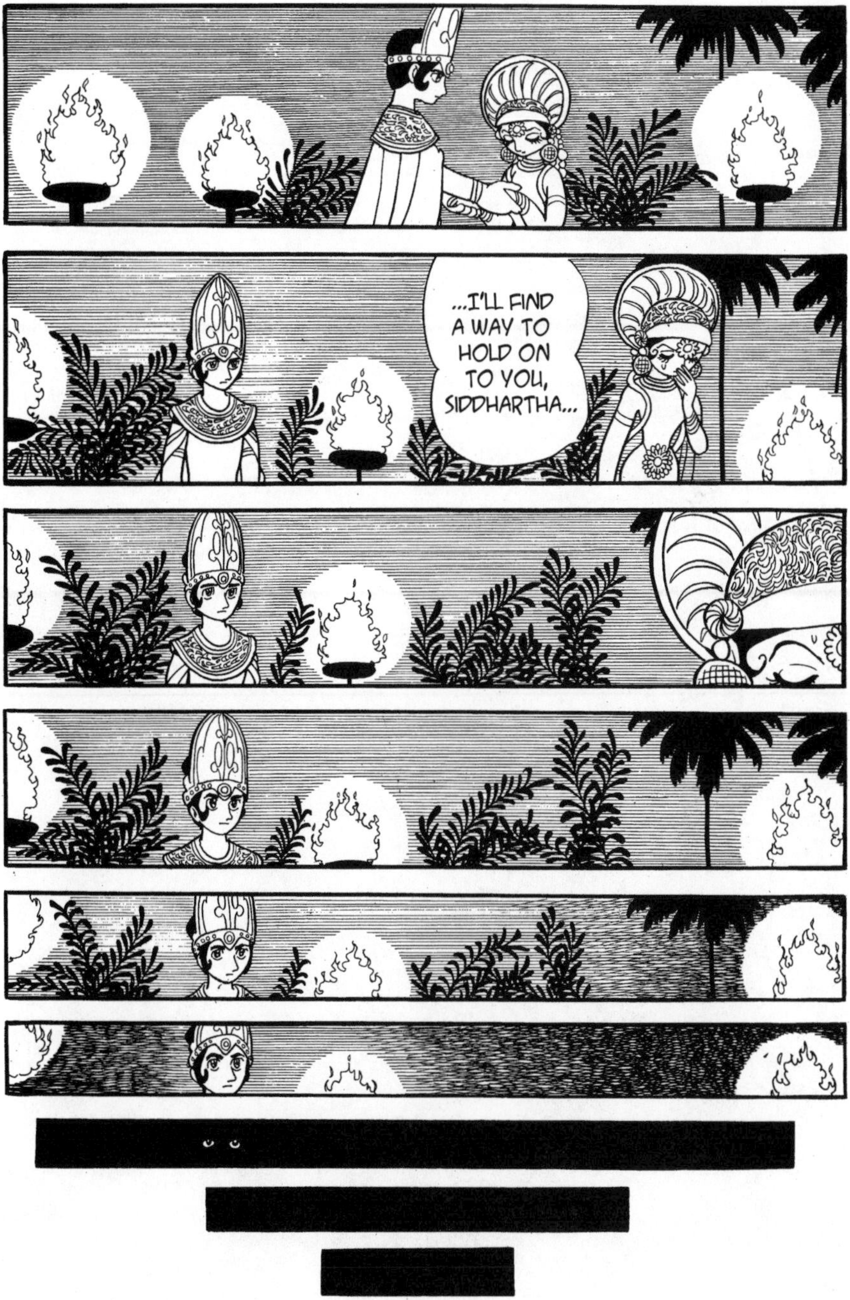
...I'LL FIND A WAY TO HOLD ON TO YOU, SIDDHARTHA...

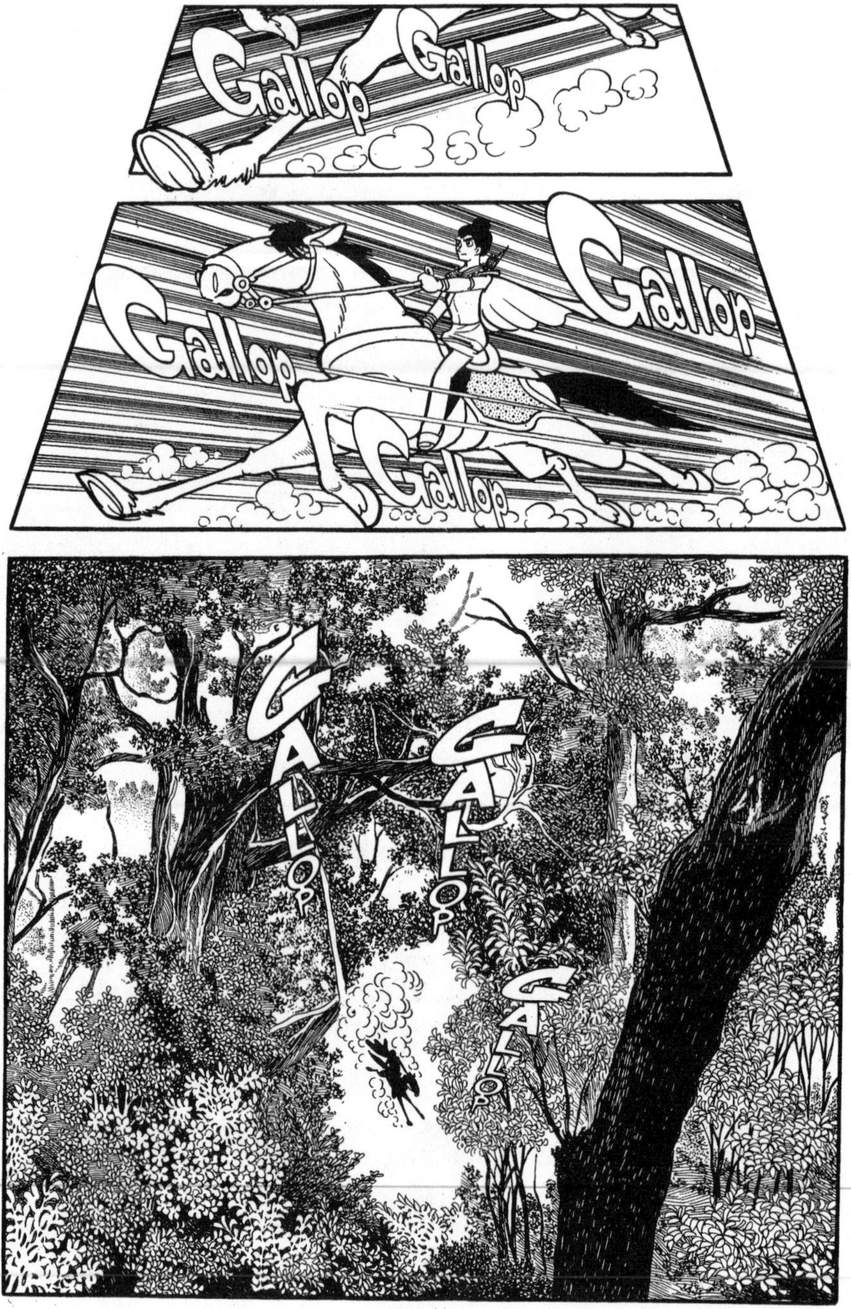
Gallop
Gallop
Gallop
Gallop
Gallop
GALLOP
GALLOP
GALLOP

233

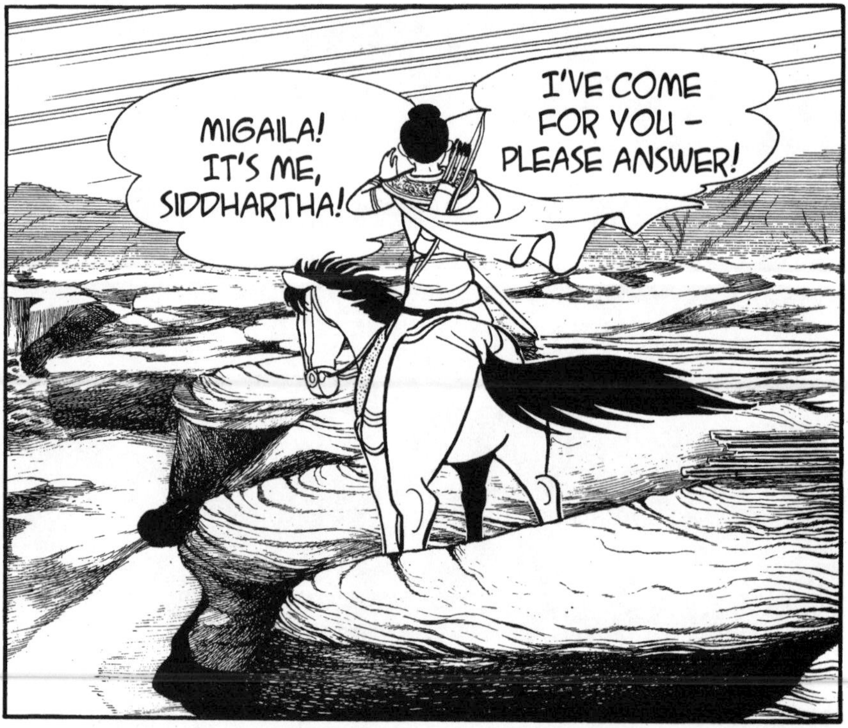
MIGAILA! IT'S ME, SIDDHARTHA!
I'VE COME FOR YOU - PLEASE ANSWER!

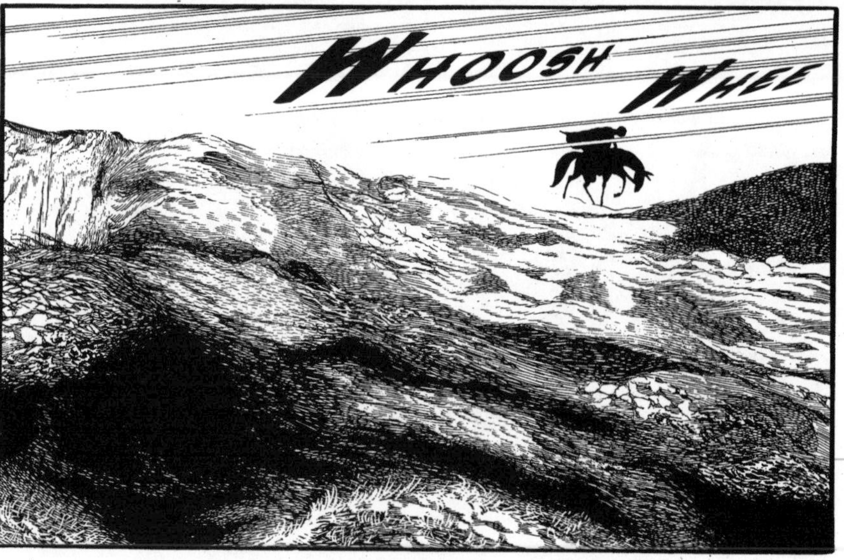
WHOOSH
WHEE

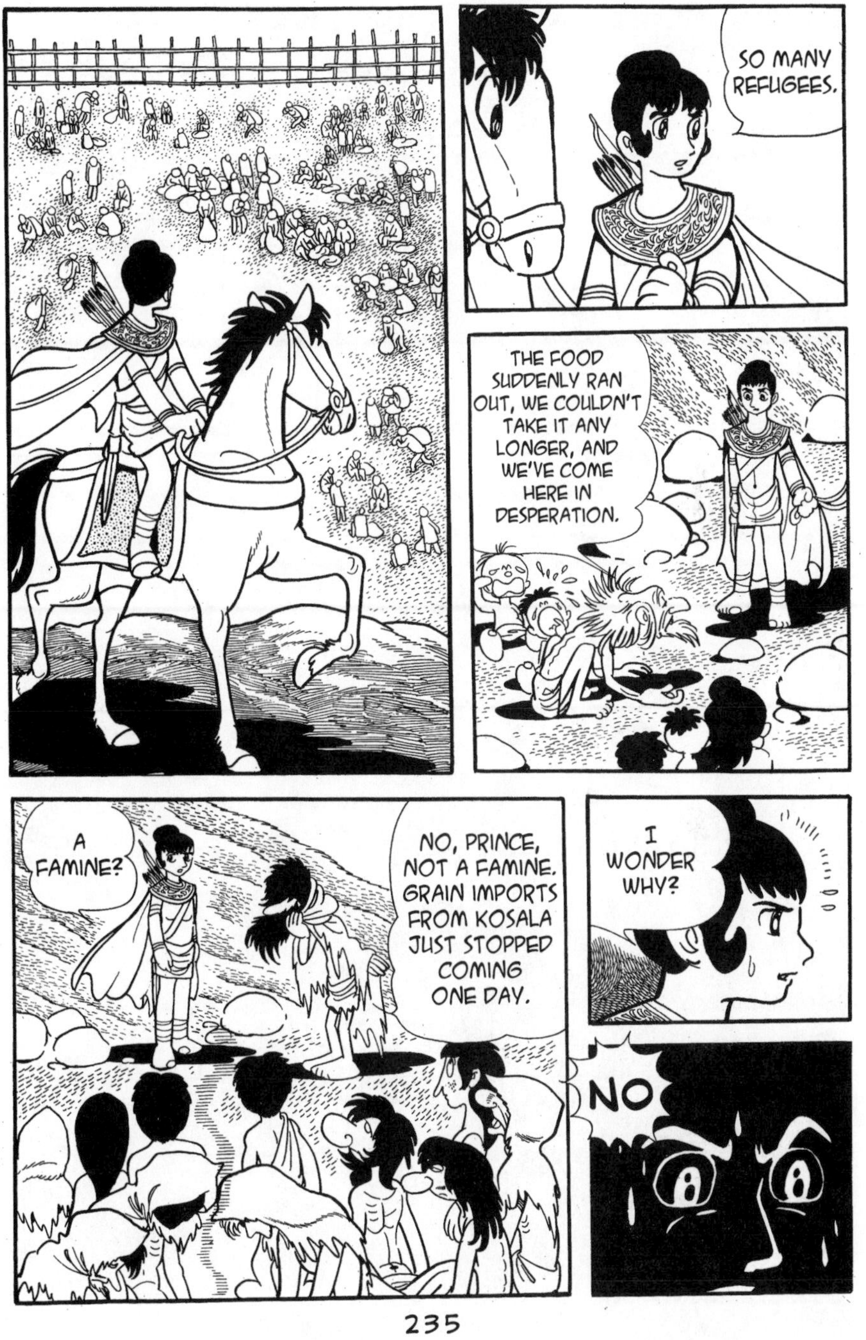
SO MANY REFUGEES.
THE FOOD SUDDENLY RAN OUT, WE COULDN'T TAKE IT ANY LONGER, AND WE'VE COME HERE IN DESPERATION.
A FAMINE?
NO, PRINCE, NOT A FAMINE. GRAIN IMPORTS FROM KOSALA JUST STOPPED COMING ONE DAY.
I WONDER WHY?
NO

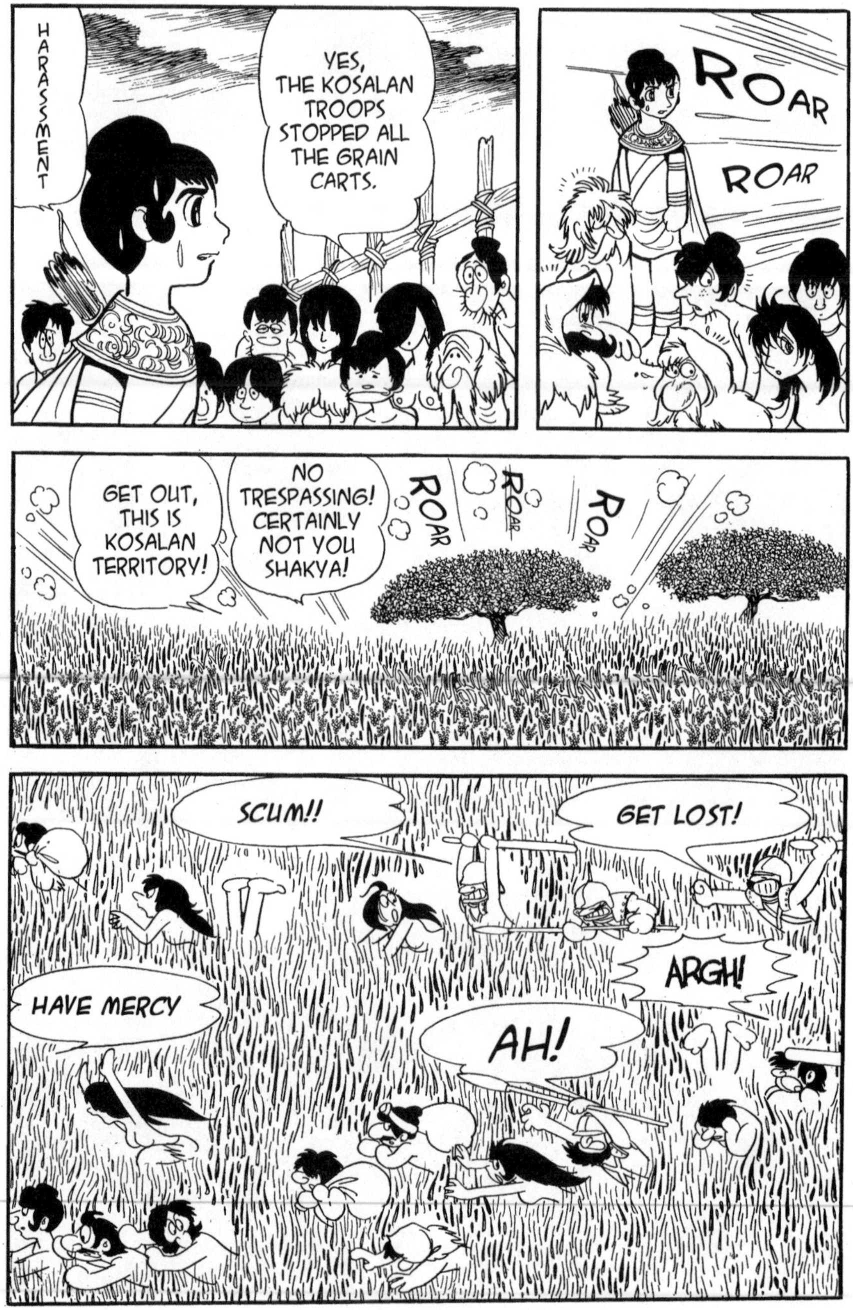
HARASSMENT
YES, THE KOSALAN TROOPS STOPPED ALL THE GRAIN CARTS.
ROAR
ROAR
GET OUT, THIS IS KOSALAN TERRITORY!
NO TRESPASSING! CERTAINLY NOT YOU SHAKYA!
ROAR
ROAR
ROAR
SCUM!!
GET LOST!
ARGH!
HAVE MERCY
AH!

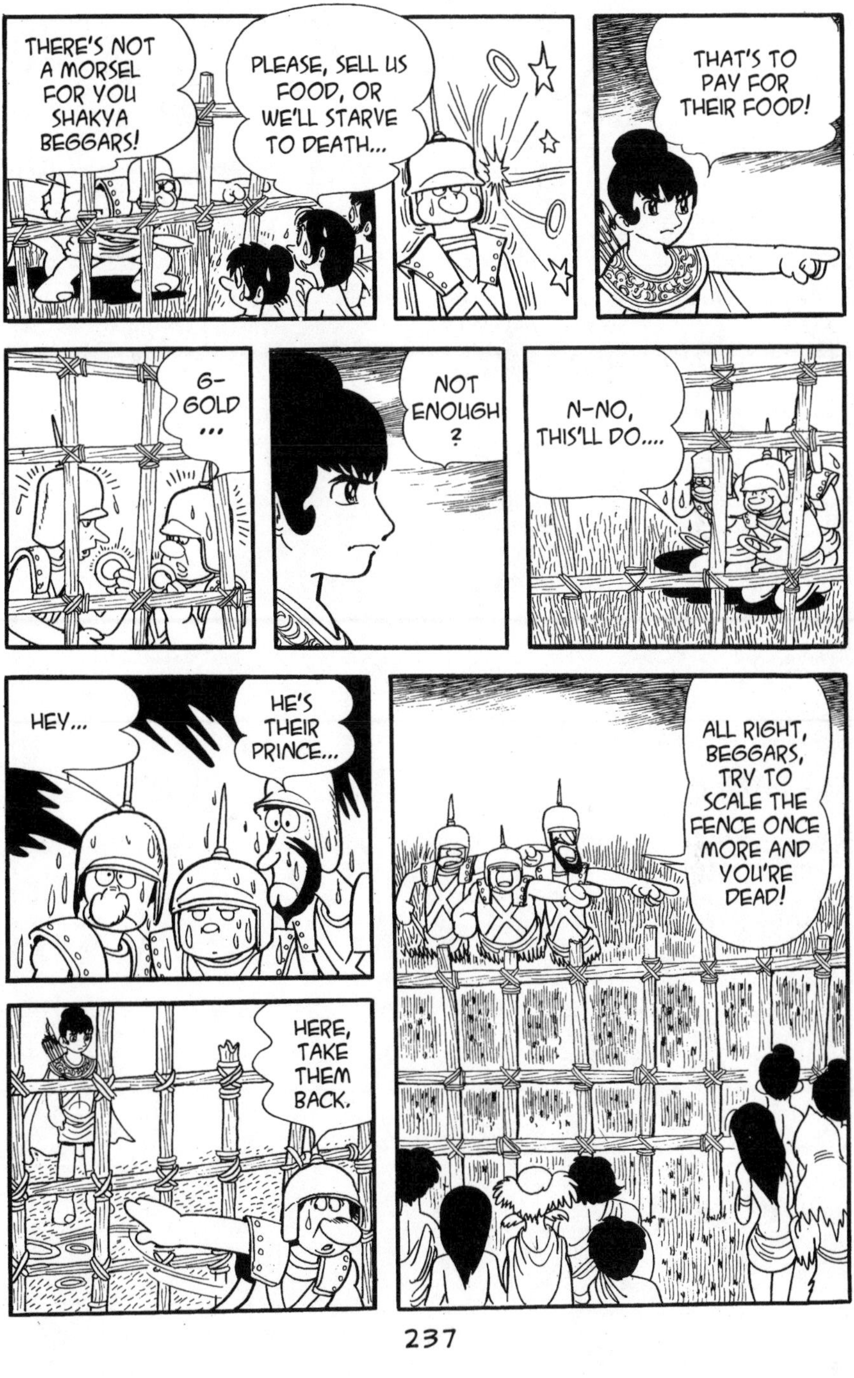
THERE'S NOT A MORSEL FOR YOU SHAKYA BEGGARS!
PLEASE, SELL US FOOD, OR WE'LL STARVE TO DEATH...
THAT'S TO PAY FOR THEIR FOOD!
G-GOLD ...
NOT ENOUGH ?
N-NO, THIS'LL DO....
HEY...
HE'S THEIR PRINCE...
HERE, TAKE THEM BACK.
ALL RIGHT, BEGGARS, TRY TO SCALE THE FENCE ONCE MORE AND YOU'RE DEAD!

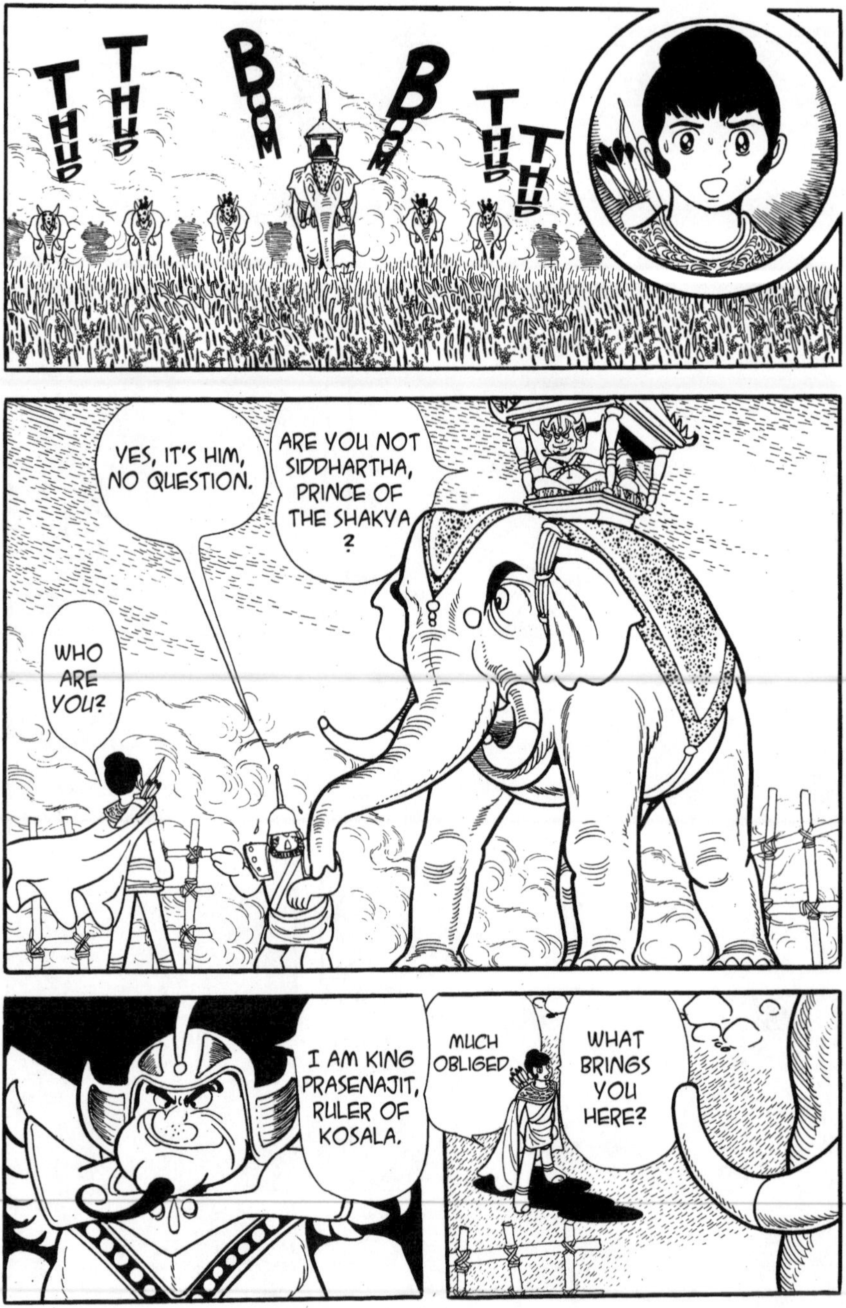
THUD
THUD
BOOM
BOOM
THUD
THUD
YES, IT'S HIM, NO QUESTION.
ARE YOU NOT SIDDHARTHA, PRINCE OF THE SHAKYA?
WHO ARE YOU?
I AM KING PRASENAJIT, RULER OF KOSALA.
MUCH OBLIGED.
WHAT BRINGS YOU HERE?

HM, YOUR EVERY WORD AND DEED...

SEEMS TO RUB ME THE WRONG WAY.

MY ENVOY TELLS ME YOU'VE REJECTED MY OFFER – MY VERY *GENEROUS* OFFER.

THAT IS SO.

WELL, YOU ACTED RASHLY. DON'T FORGET YOU'RE A BIG FISH IN A SMALL POND.

RUMOR HAS IT THAT, ACCORDING TO A BRAHMIN'S PROPHECY, YOU'RE TO BE KING OF THE WORLD.

YOU SEE, I CAN'T ALLOW THAT.

LOOK! THE 500 ELEPHANTS BEHIND ME ARE ITCHING TO STAMPEDE ACROSS THE BORDER!

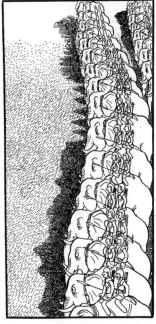

239

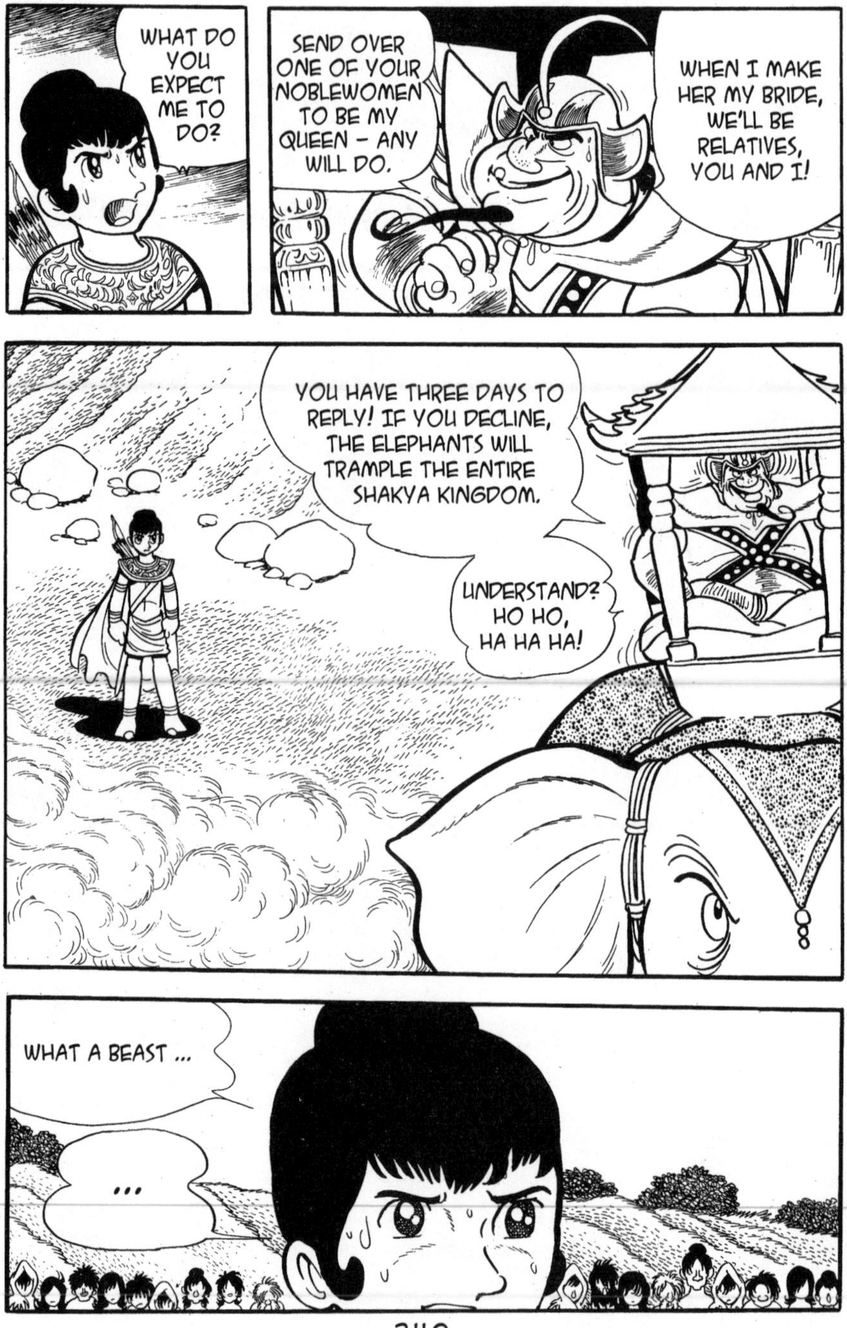
WHAT DO YOU EXPECT ME TO DO?
SEND OVER ONE OF YOUR NOBLEWOMEN TO BE MY QUEEN – ANY WILL DO.
WHEN I MAKE HER MY BRIDE, WE'LL BE RELATIVES, YOU AND I!
YOU HAVE THREE DAYS TO REPLY! IF YOU DECLINE, THE ELEPHANTS WILL TRAMPLE THE ENTIRE SHAKYA KINGDOM.
UNDERSTAND? HO HO, HA HA HA!
WHAT A BEAST ...
...

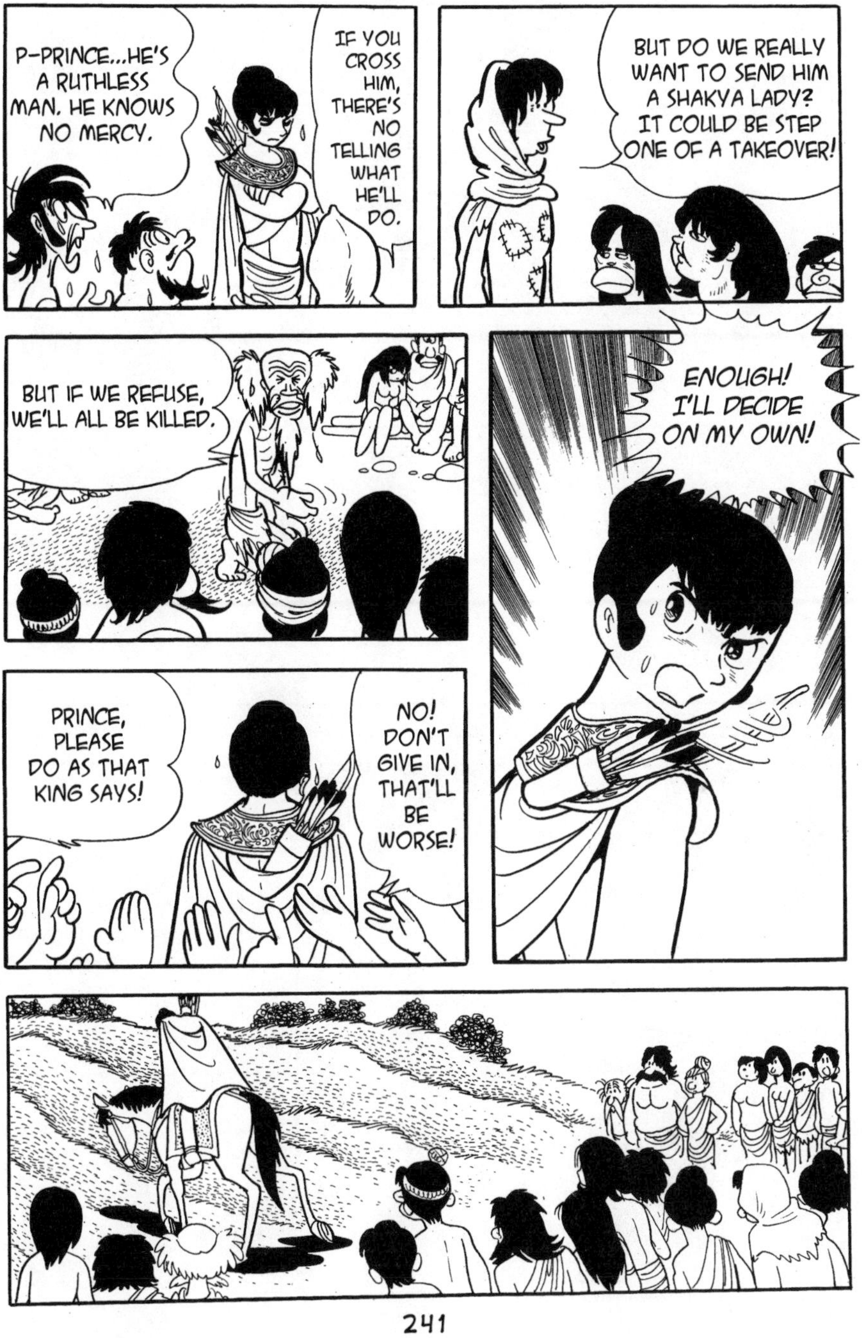
P-PRINCE...HE'S A RUTHLESS MAN. HE KNOWS NO MERCY.
IF YOU CROSS HIM, THERE'S NO TELLING WHAT HE'LL DO.
BUT DO WE REALLY WANT TO SEND HIM A SHAKYA LADY? IT COULD BE STEP ONE OF A TAKEOVER!
BUT IF WE REFUSE, WE'LL ALL BE KILLED.
PRINCE, PLEASE DO AS THAT KING SAYS!
NO! DON'T GIVE IN, THAT'LL BE WORSE!
ENOUGH! I'LL DECIDE ON MY OWN!

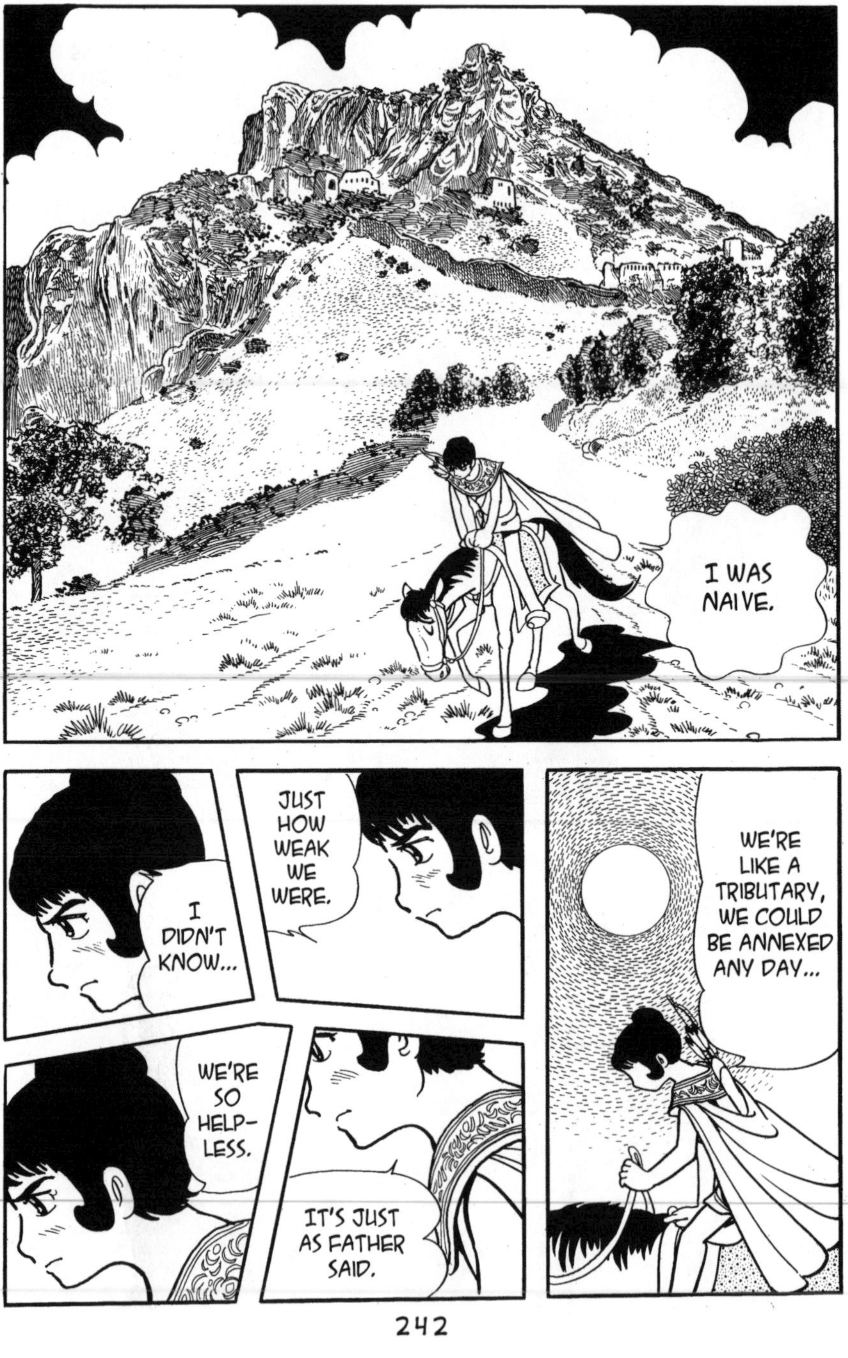
I WAS NAIVE.
I DIDN'T KNOW...
JUST HOW WEAK WE WERE.
WE'RE LIKE A TRIBUTARY, WE COULD BE ANNEXED ANY DAY...
WE'RE SO HELP-LESS.
IT'S JUST AS FATHER SAID.

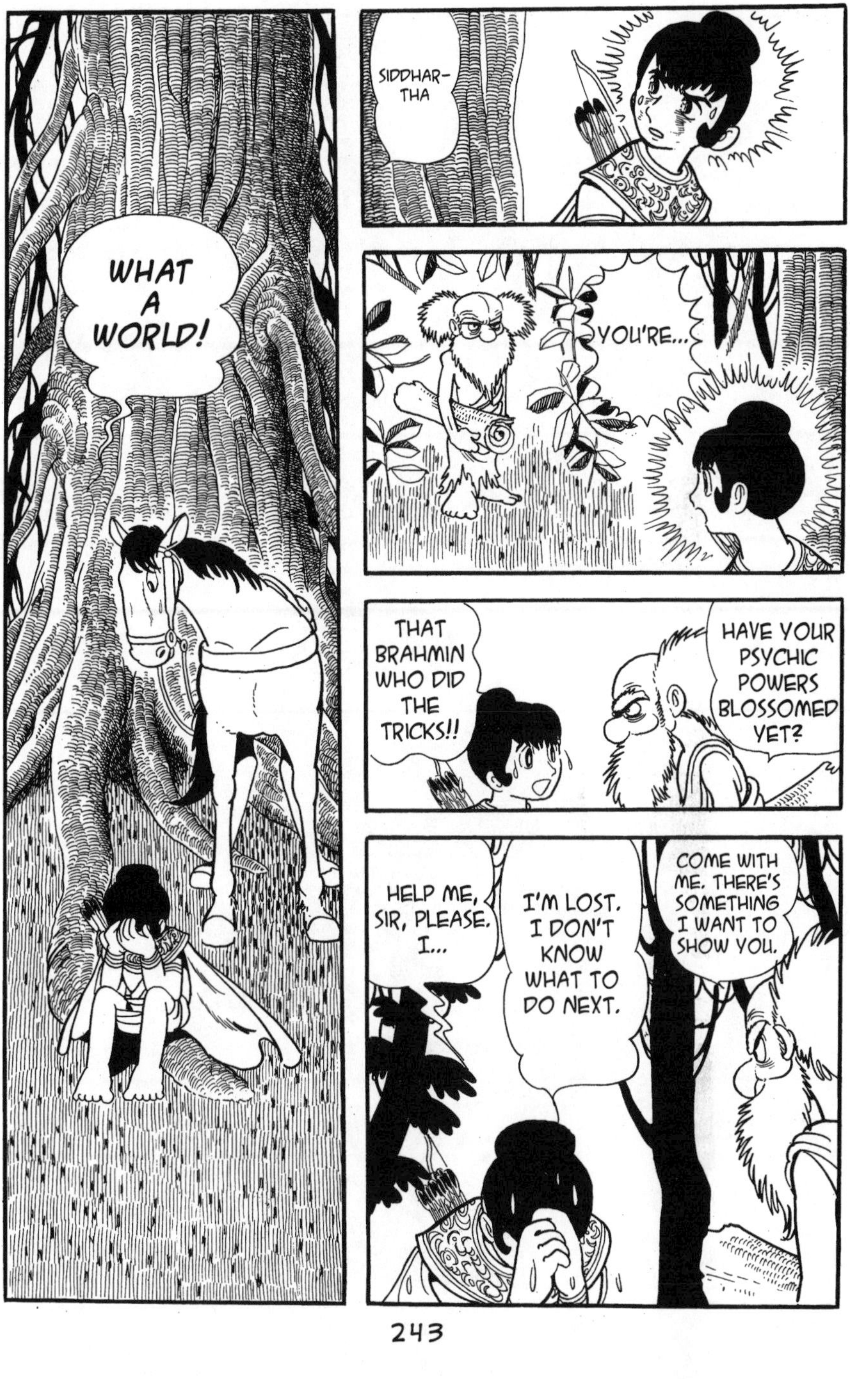

WHAT A WORLD!
SIDDHAR-THA
YOU'RE...
THAT BRAHMIN WHO DID THE TRICKS!!
HAVE YOUR PSYCHIC POWERS BLOSSOMED YET?
HELP ME, SIR, PLEASE. I...
I'M LOST. I DON'T KNOW WHAT TO DO NEXT.
COME WITH ME. THERE'S SOMETHING I WANT TO SHOW YOU.

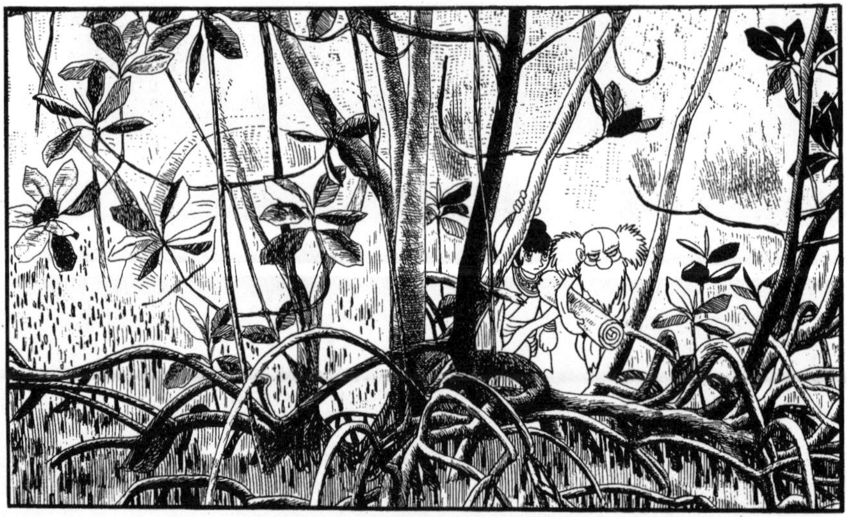

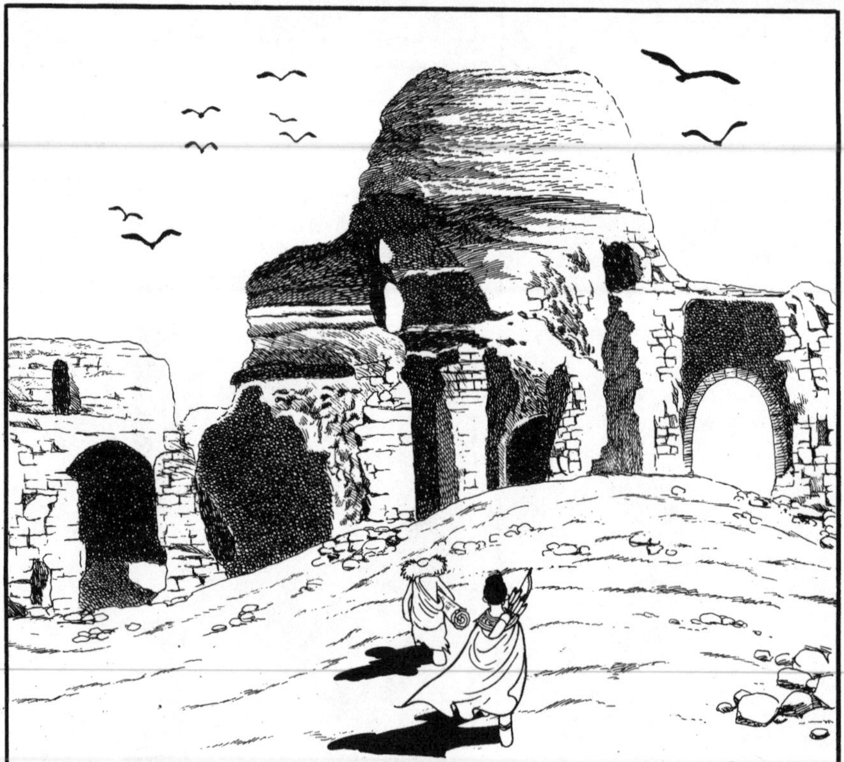

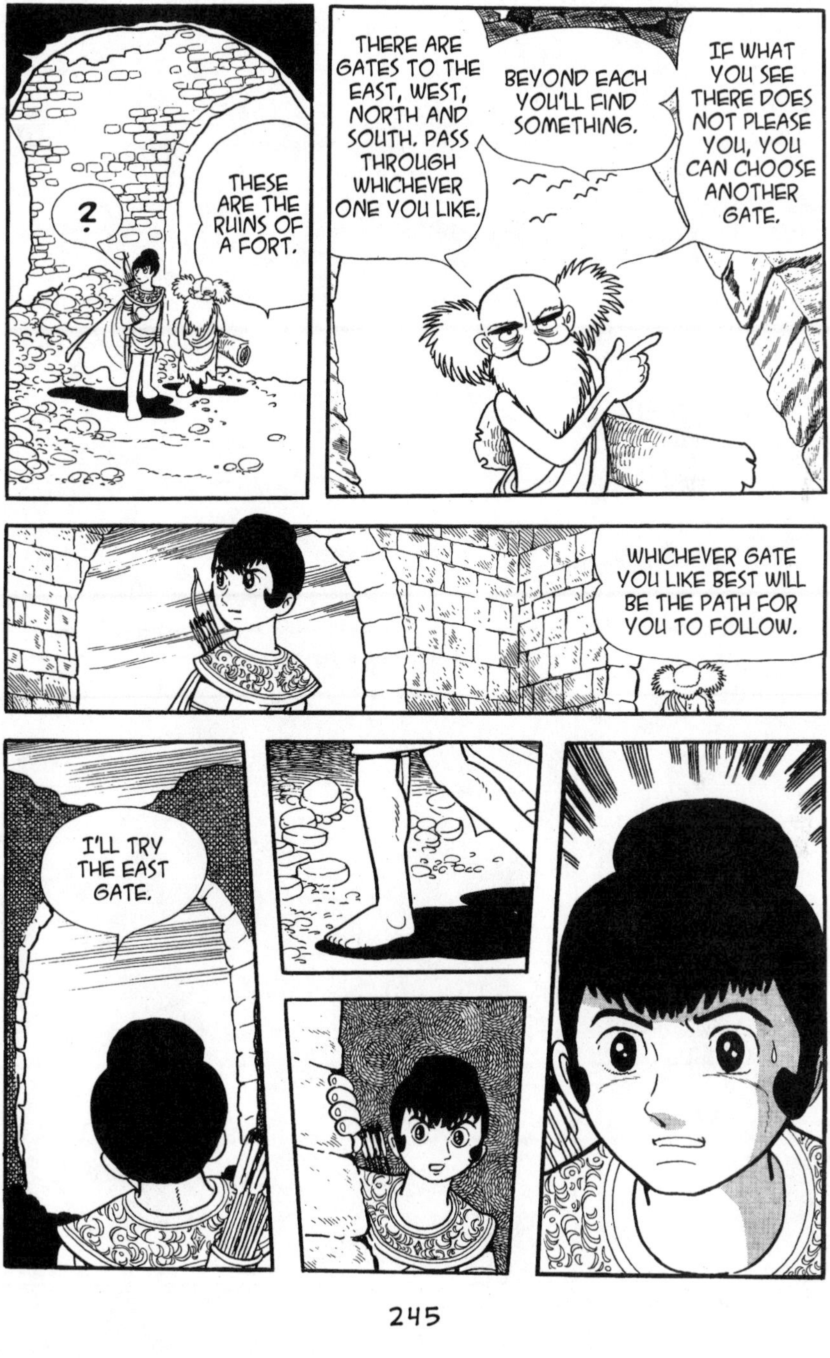
?
THESE ARE THE RUINS OF A FORT.
THERE ARE GATES TO THE EAST, WEST, NORTH AND SOUTH. PASS THROUGH WHICHEVER ONE YOU LIKE.
BEYOND EACH YOU'LL FIND SOMETHING.
IF WHAT YOU SEE THERE DOES NOT PLEASE YOU, YOU CAN CHOOSE ANOTHER GATE.
WHICHEVER GATE YOU LIKE BEST WILL BE THE PATH FOR YOU TO FOLLOW.
I'LL TRY THE EAST GATE.

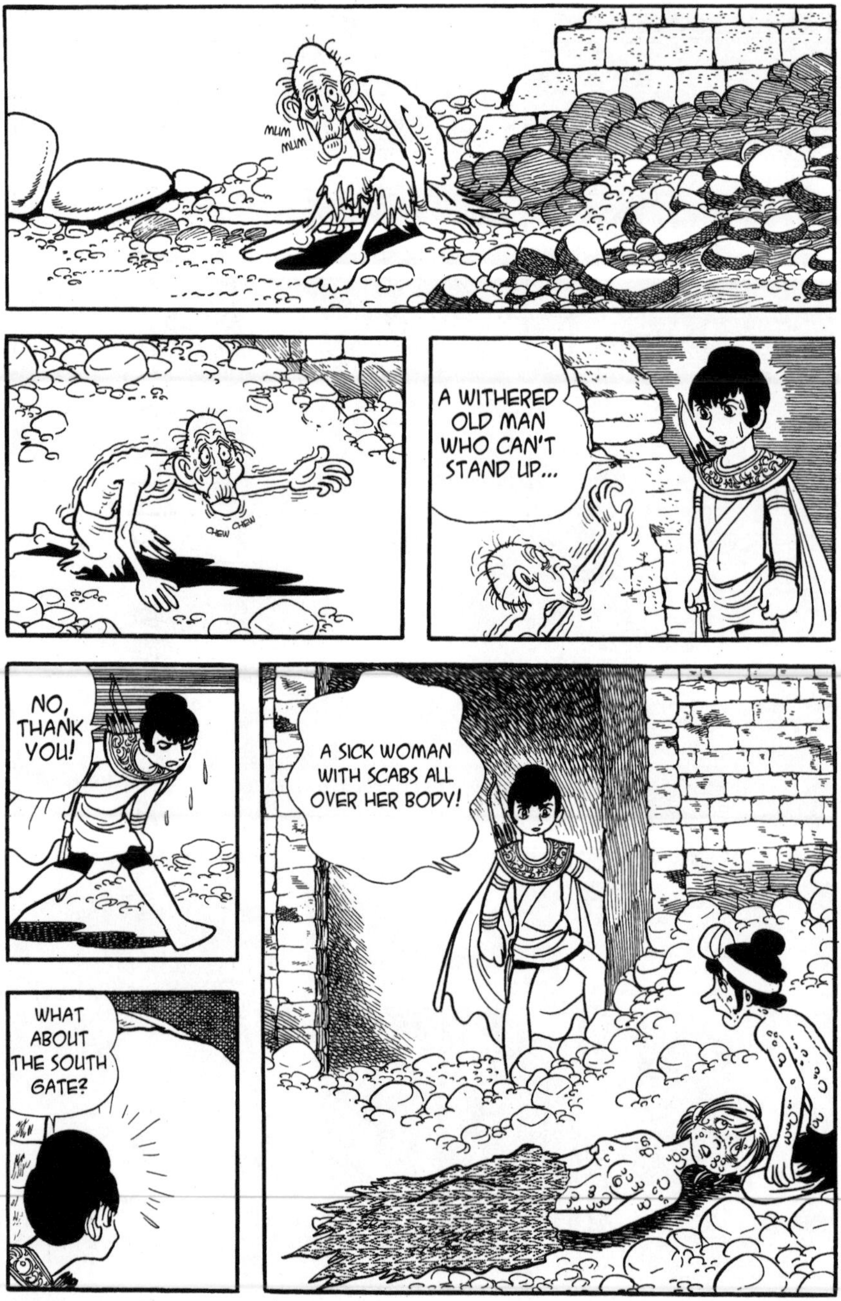
MUM MUM
CHEW CHEW
A WITHERED OLD MAN WHO CAN'T STAND UP...
NO, THANK YOU!
WHAT ABOUT THE SOUTH GATE?
A SICK WOMAN WITH SCABS ALL OVER HER BODY!

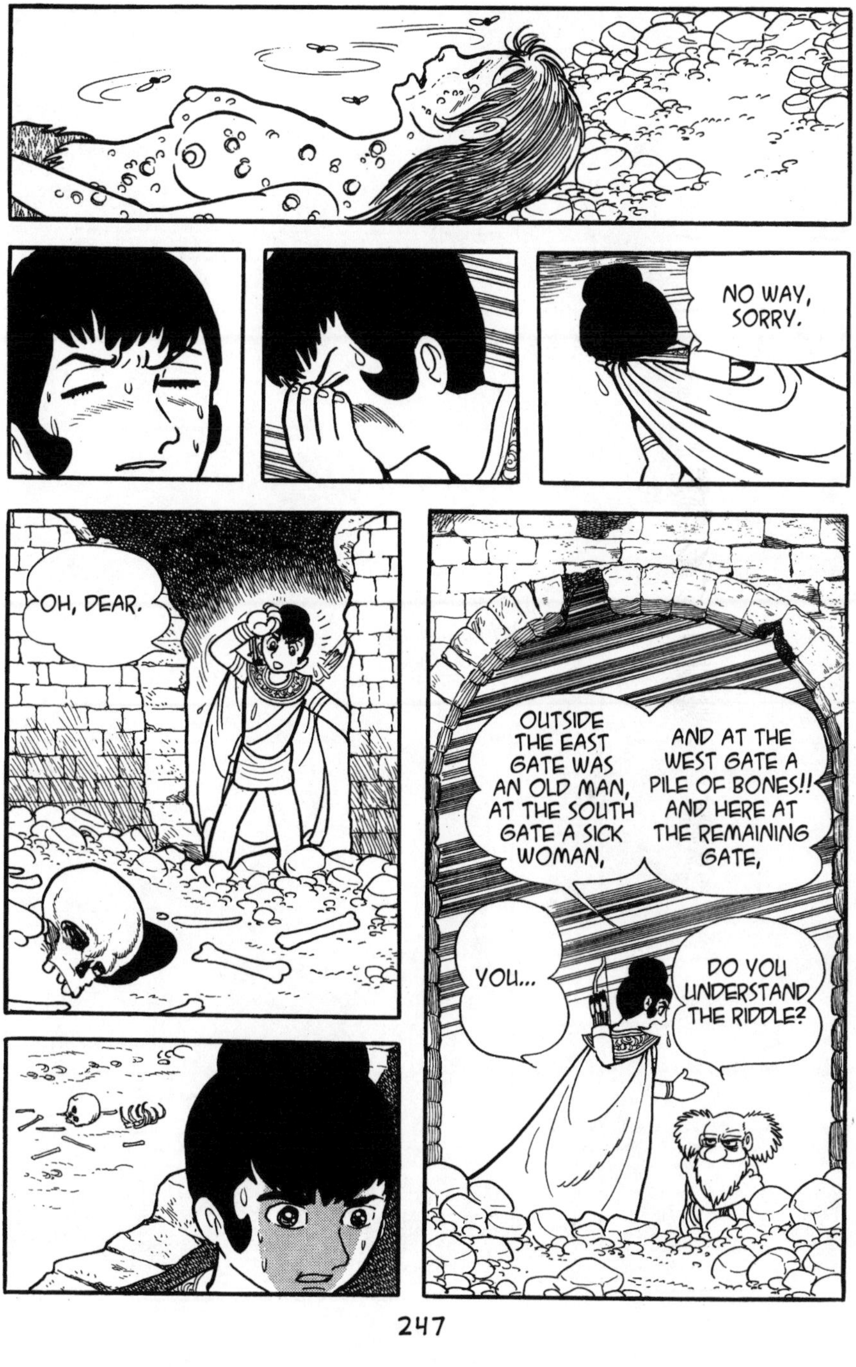
NO WAY, SORRY.
OH, DEAR.
OUTSIDE THE EAST GATE WAS AN OLD MAN, AT THE SOUTH GATE A SICK WOMAN,
AND AT THE WEST GATE A PILE OF BONES!! AND HERE AT THE REMAINING GATE,
YOU...
DO YOU UNDERSTAND THE RIDDLE?

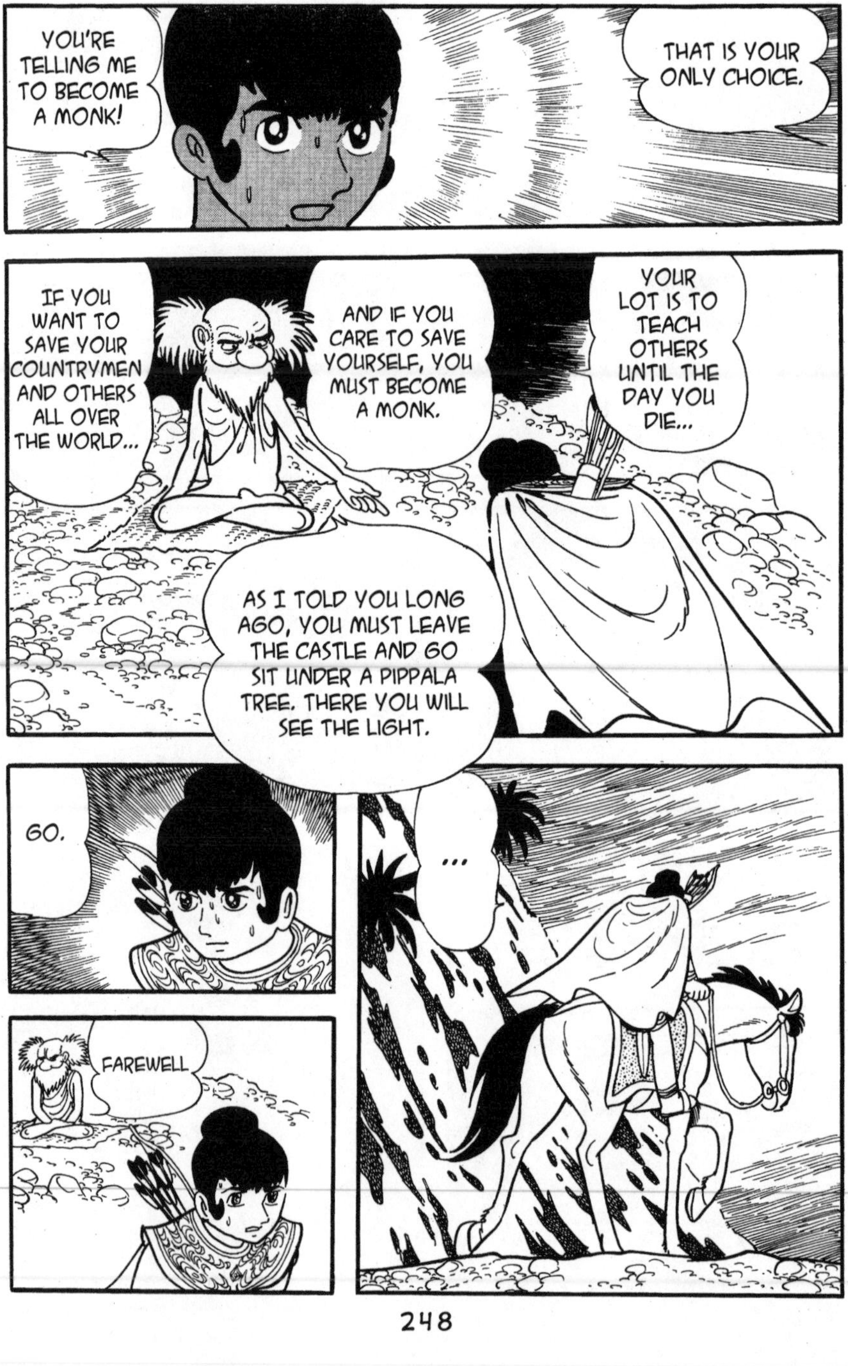
YOU'RE TELLING ME TO BECOME A MONK!
THAT IS YOUR ONLY CHOICE.
IF YOU WANT TO SAVE YOUR COUNTRYMEN AND OTHERS ALL OVER THE WORLD...
AND IF YOU CARE TO SAVE YOURSELF, YOU MUST BECOME A MONK.
YOUR LOT IS TO TEACH OTHERS UNTIL THE DAY YOU DIE...
AS I TOLD YOU LONG AGO, YOU MUST LEAVE THE CASTLE AND GO SIT UNDER A PIPPALA TREE. THERE YOU WILL SEE THE LIGHT.
GO.
FAREWELL
...

KING PRASENAJIT HELD MUCH POWER IN KOSALA, BUT BEHIND HIS BACK PEOPLE SAID HE WAS REALLY A NOBODY.

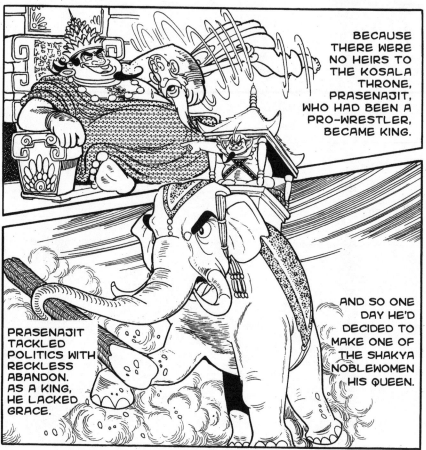

BECAUSE THERE WERE NO HEIRS TO THE KOSALA THRONE, PRASENAJIT, WHO HAD BEEN A PRO-WRESTLER, BECAME KING.

PRASENAJIT TACKLED POLITICS WITH RECKLESS ABANDON. AS A KING, HE LACKED GRACE.

AND SO ONE DAY HE'D DECIDED TO MAKE ONE OF THE SHAKYA NOBLEWOMEN HIS QUEEN.

249

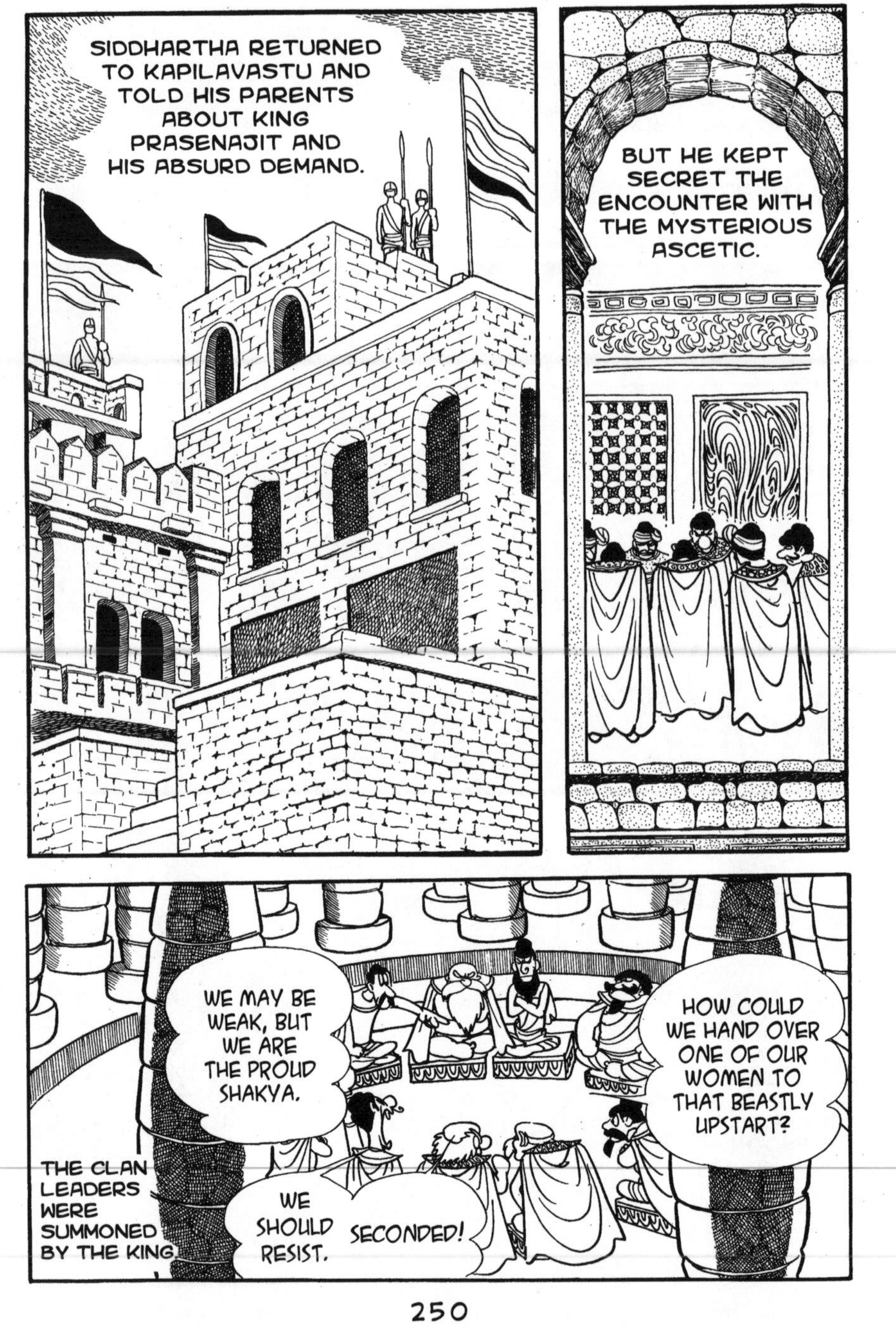
SIDDHARTHA RETURNED TO KAPILAVASTU AND TOLD HIS PARENTS ABOUT KING PRASENAJIT AND HIS ABSURD DEMAND.
BUT HE KEPT SECRET THE ENCOUNTER WITH THE MYSTERIOUS ASCETIC.
WE MAY BE WEAK, BUT WE ARE THE PROUD SHAKYA.
HOW COULD WE HAND OVER ONE OF OUR WOMEN TO THAT BEASTLY UPSTART?
THE CLAN LEADERS WERE SUMMONED BY THE KING.
WE SHOULD RESIST.
SECONDED!

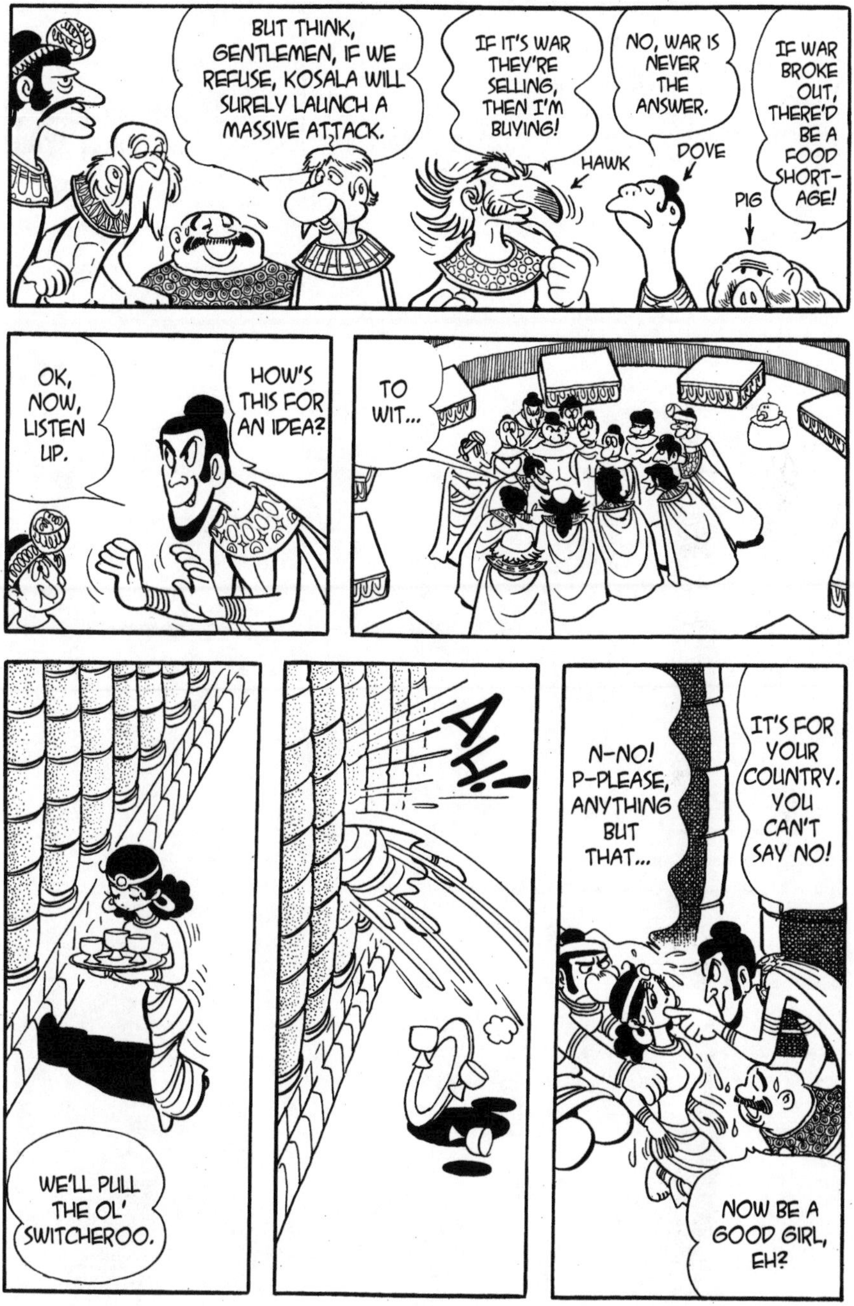
BUT THINK, GENTLEMEN, IF WE REFUSE, KOSALA WILL SURELY LAUNCH A MASSIVE ATTACK.
IF IT'S WAR THEY'RE SELLING, THEN I'M BUYING!
HAWK
NO, WAR IS NEVER THE ANSWER.
DOVE
IF WAR BROKE OUT, THERE'D BE A FOOD SHORTAGE!
PIG
OK, NOW, LISTEN UP.
HOW'S THIS FOR AN IDEA?
TO WIT...
WE'LL PULL THE OL' SWITCHEROO.
AH!!
N-NO! P-PLEASE, ANYTHING BUT THAT...
IT'S FOR YOUR COUNTRY. YOU CAN'T SAY NO!
NOW BE A GOOD GIRL, EH?

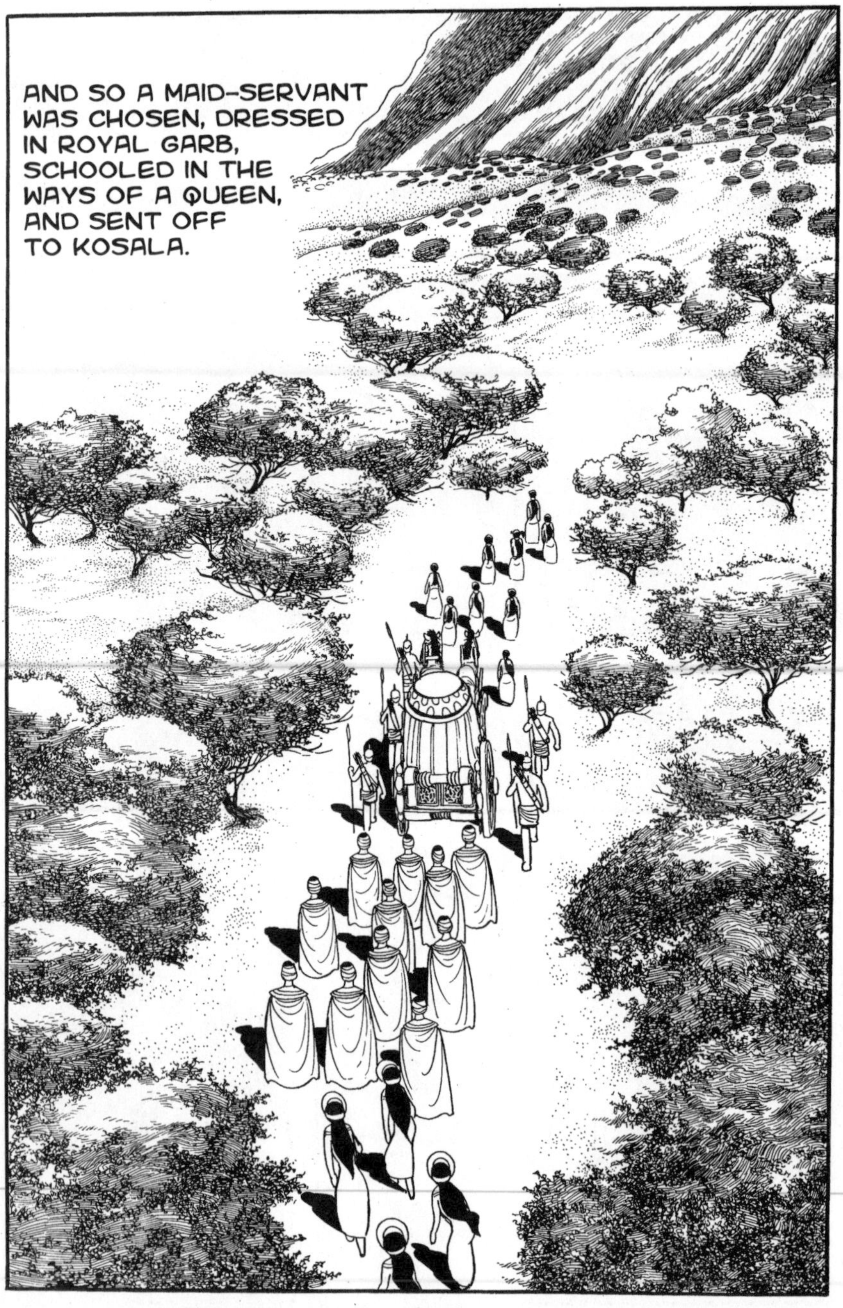
AND SO A MAID-SERVANT WAS CHOSEN, DRESSED IN ROYAL GARB, SCHOOLED IN THE WAYS OF A QUEEN, AND SENT OFF TO KOSALA.

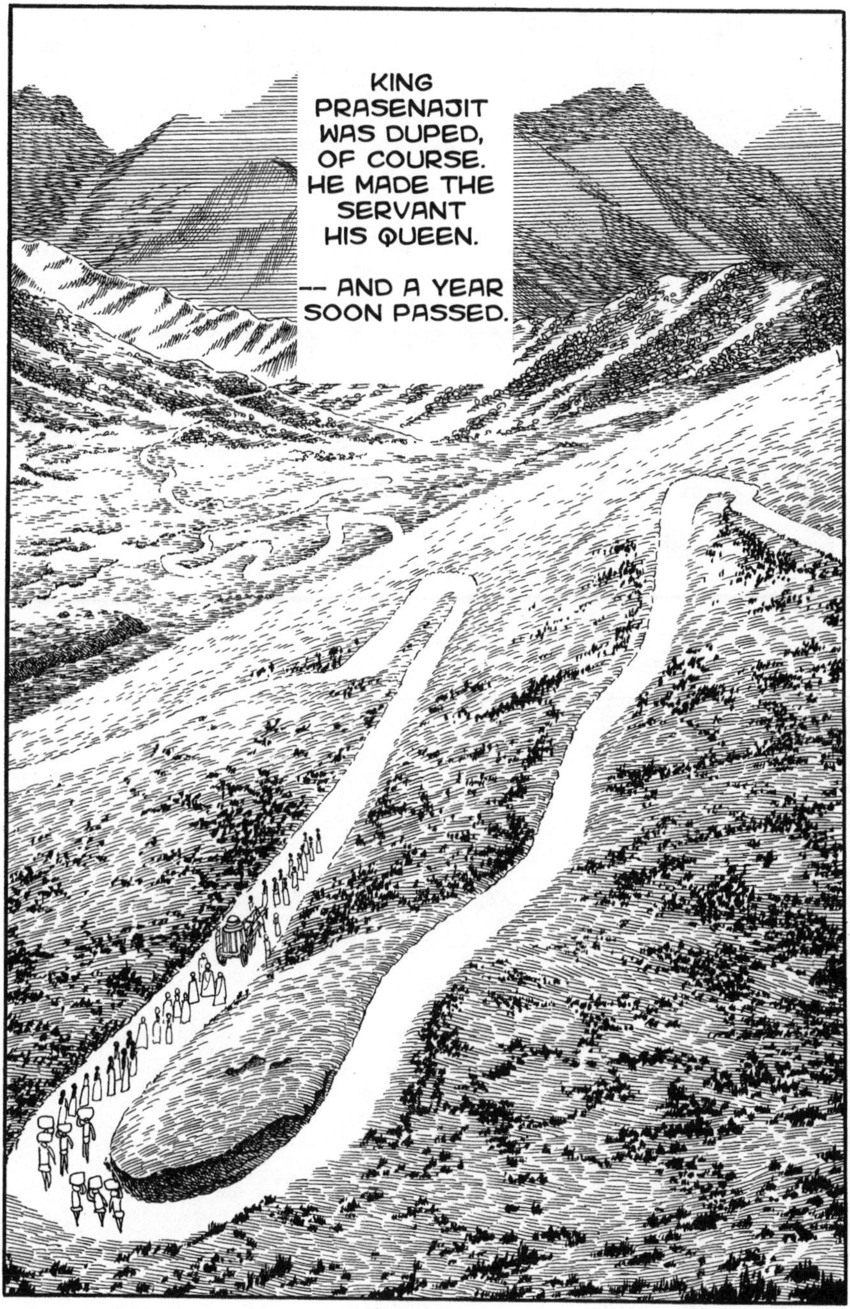
KING PRASENAJIT WAS DUPED, OF COURSE. HE MADE THE SERVANT HIS QUEEN.
-- AND A YEAR SOON PASSED.

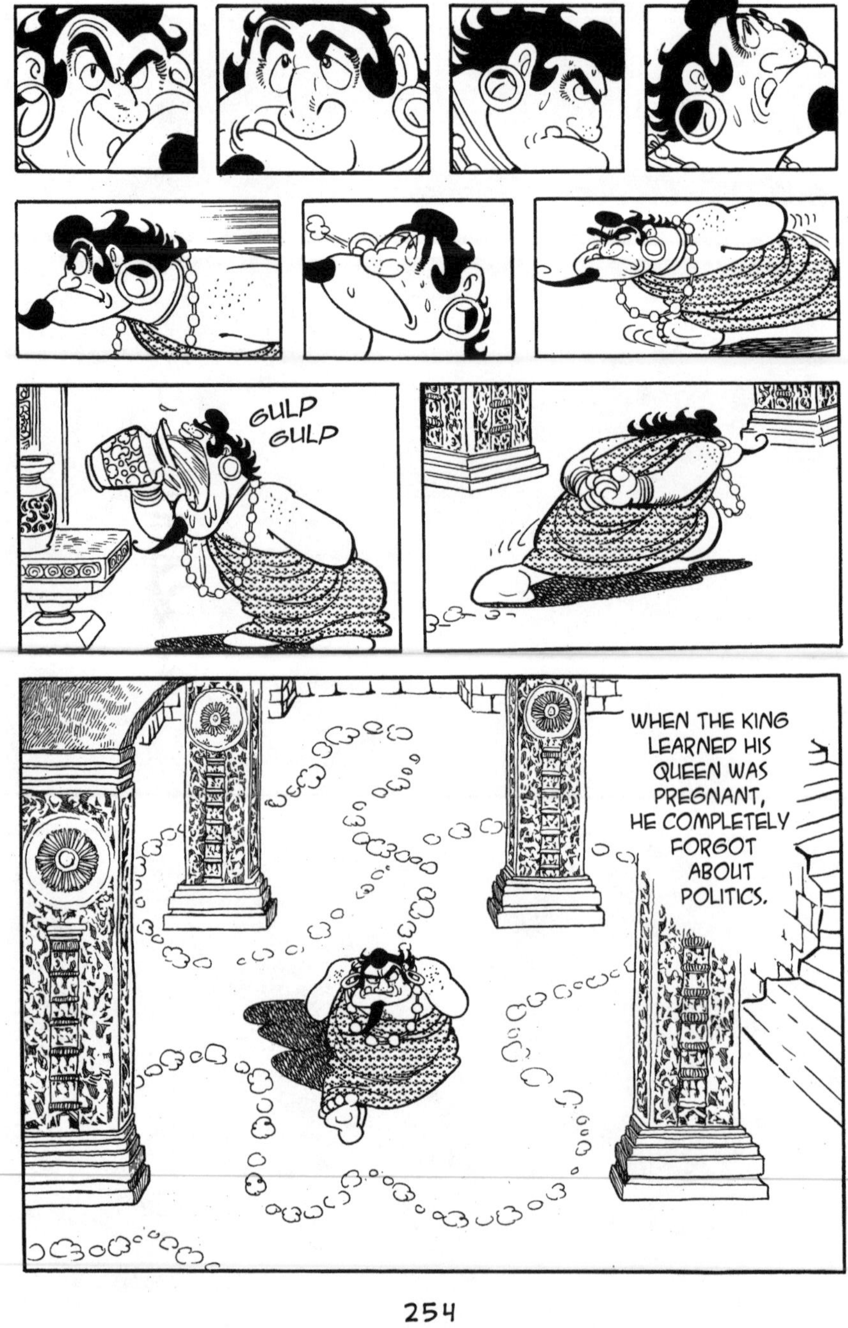
GULP GULP
WHEN THE KING LEARNED HIS QUEEN WAS PREGNANT, HE COMPLETELY FORGOT ABOUT POLITICS.

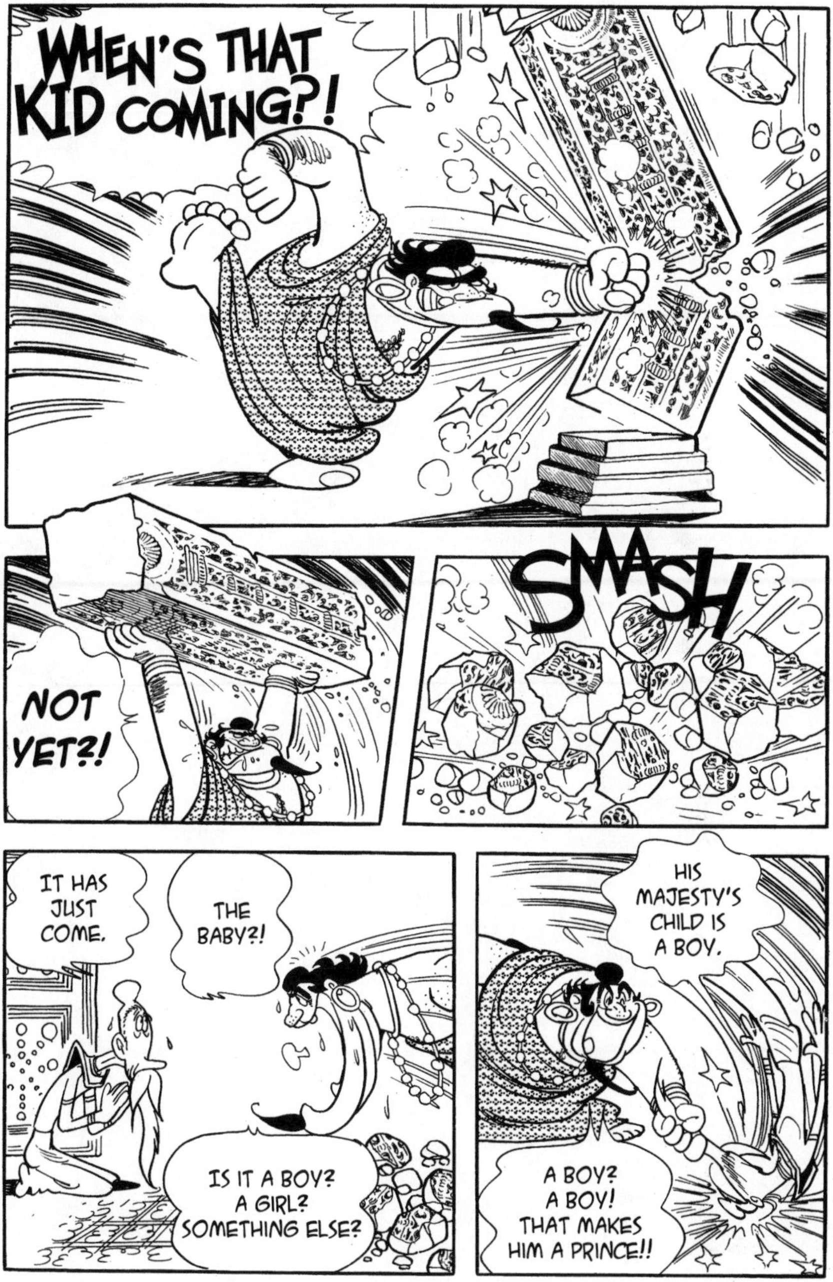
WHEN'S THAT KID COMING?!
NOT YET?!
SMASH
IT HAS JUST COME.
THE BABY?!
IS IT A BOY? A GIRL? SOMETHING ELSE?
HIS MAJESTY'S CHILD IS A BOY.
A BOY? A BOY! THAT MAKES HIM A PRINCE!!

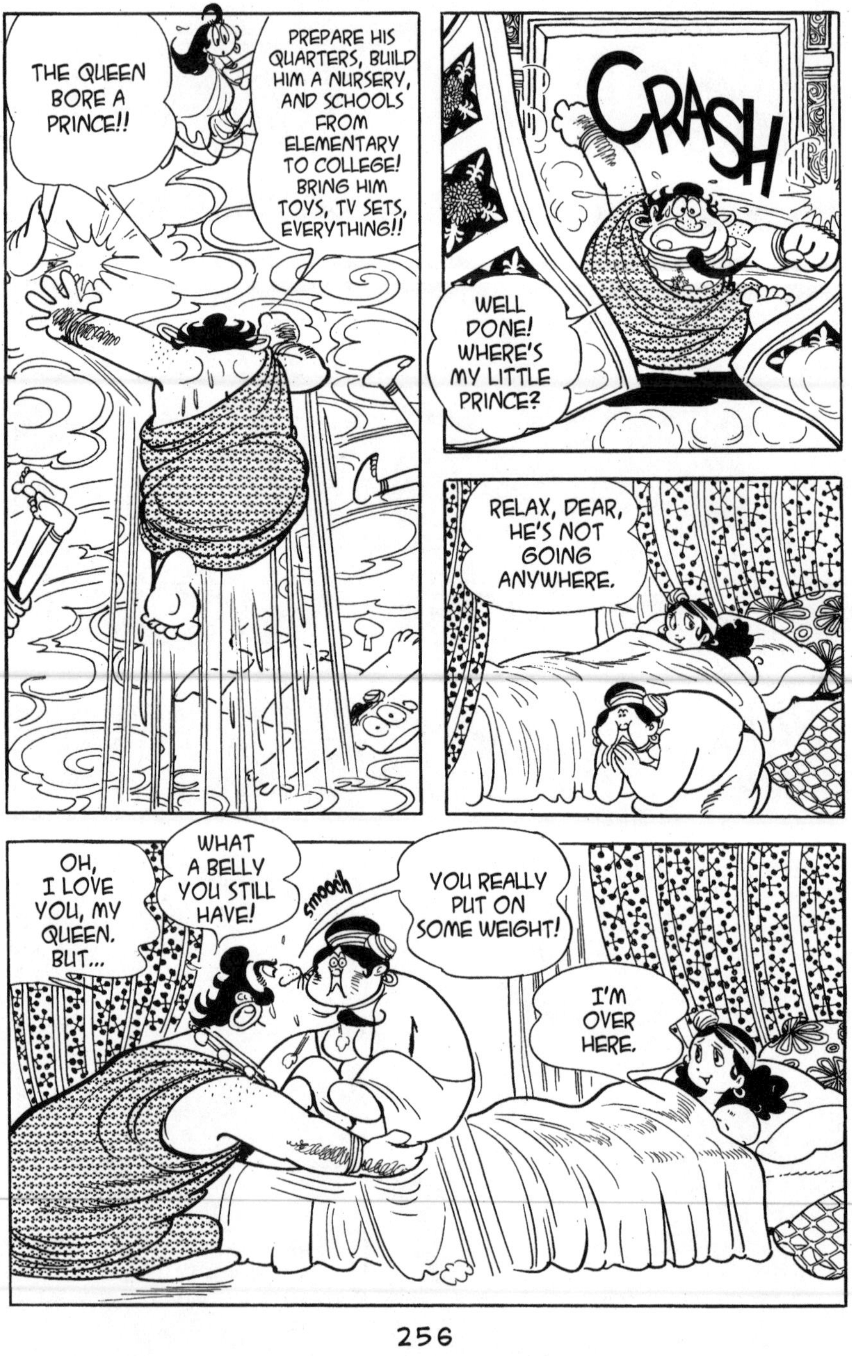
THE QUEEN BORE A PRINCE!!
PREPARE HIS QUARTERS, BUILD HIM A NURSERY, AND SCHOOLS FROM ELEMENTARY TO COLLEGE! BRING HIM TOYS, TV SETS, EVERYTHING!!
CRASH
WELL DONE! WHERE'S MY LITTLE PRINCE?
RELAX, DEAR, HE'S NOT GOING ANYWHERE.
OH, I LOVE YOU, MY QUEEN. BUT...
WHAT A BELLY YOU STILL HAVE!
SMOOCH
YOU REALLY PUT ON SOME WEIGHT!
I'M OVER HERE.

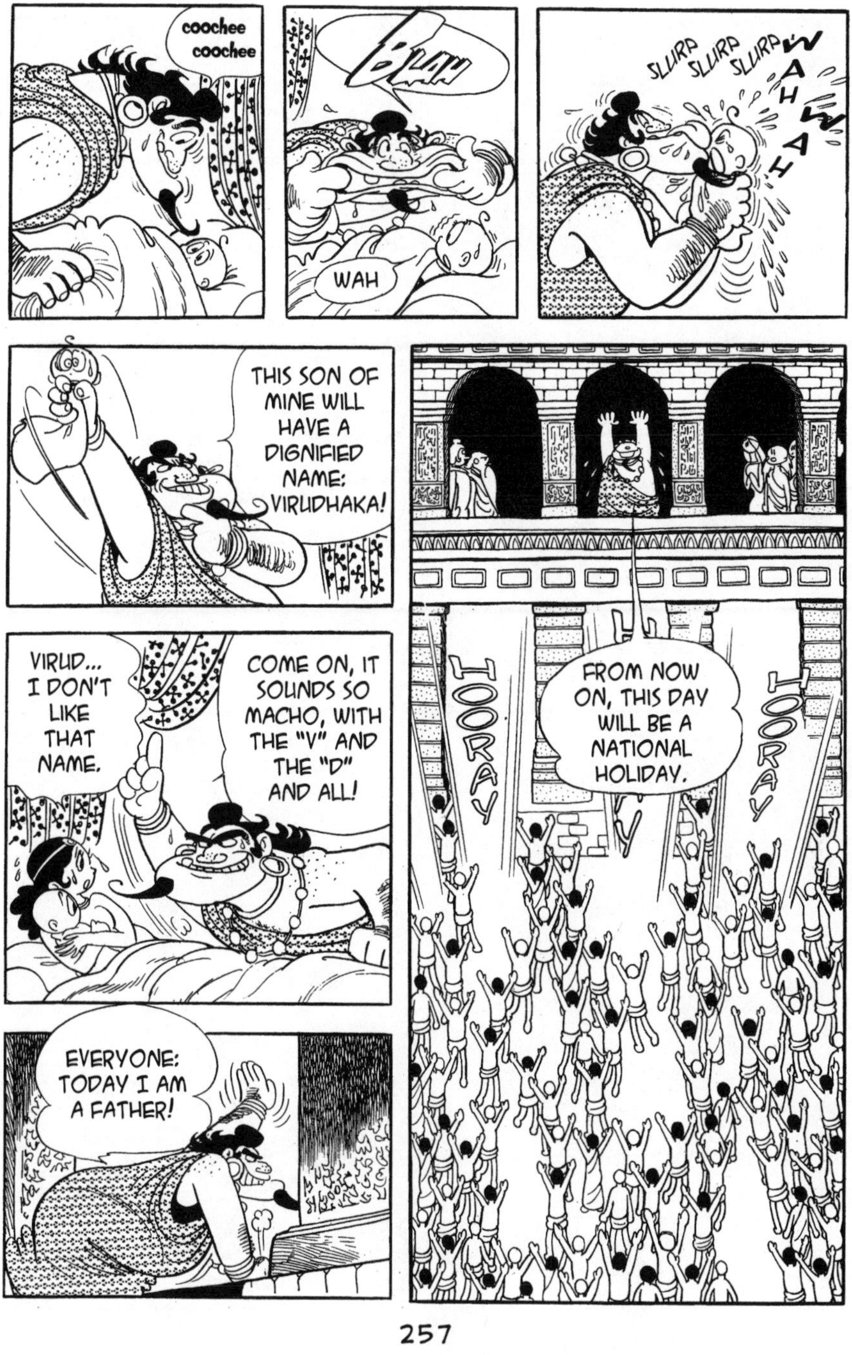
coochee coochee
WAH
SLURP SLURP SLURP
WAHWAH
THIS SON OF MINE WILL HAVE A DIGNIFIED NAME: VIRUDHAKA!
VIRUD... I DON'T LIKE THAT NAME.
COME ON, IT SOUNDS SO MACHO, WITH THE "V" AND THE "D" AND ALL!
EVERYONE: TODAY I AM A FATHER!
HOORAY
FROM NOW ON, THIS DAY WILL BE A NATIONAL HOLIDAY.
HOORAY

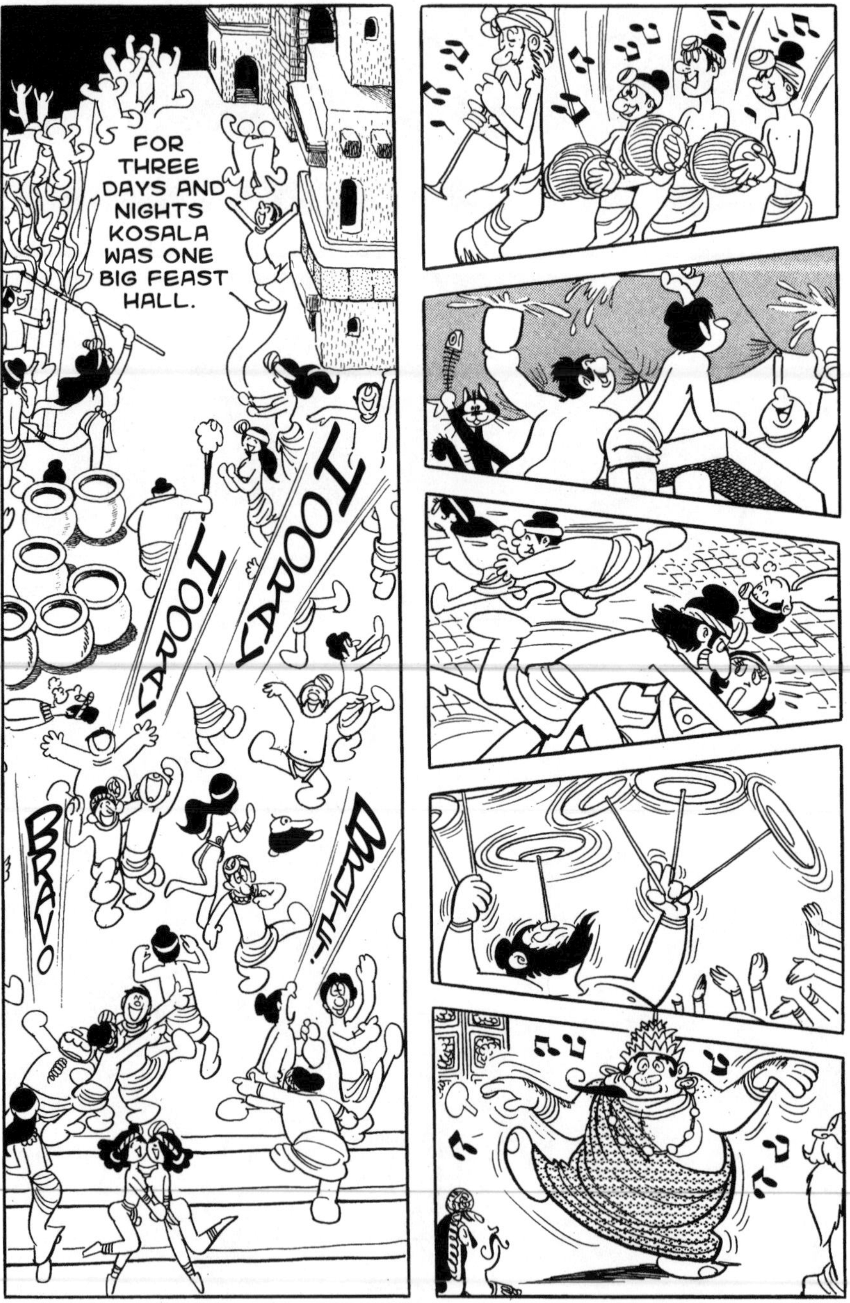
FOR THREE DAYS AND NIGHTS KOSALA WAS ONE BIG FEAST HALL.
BRAVO

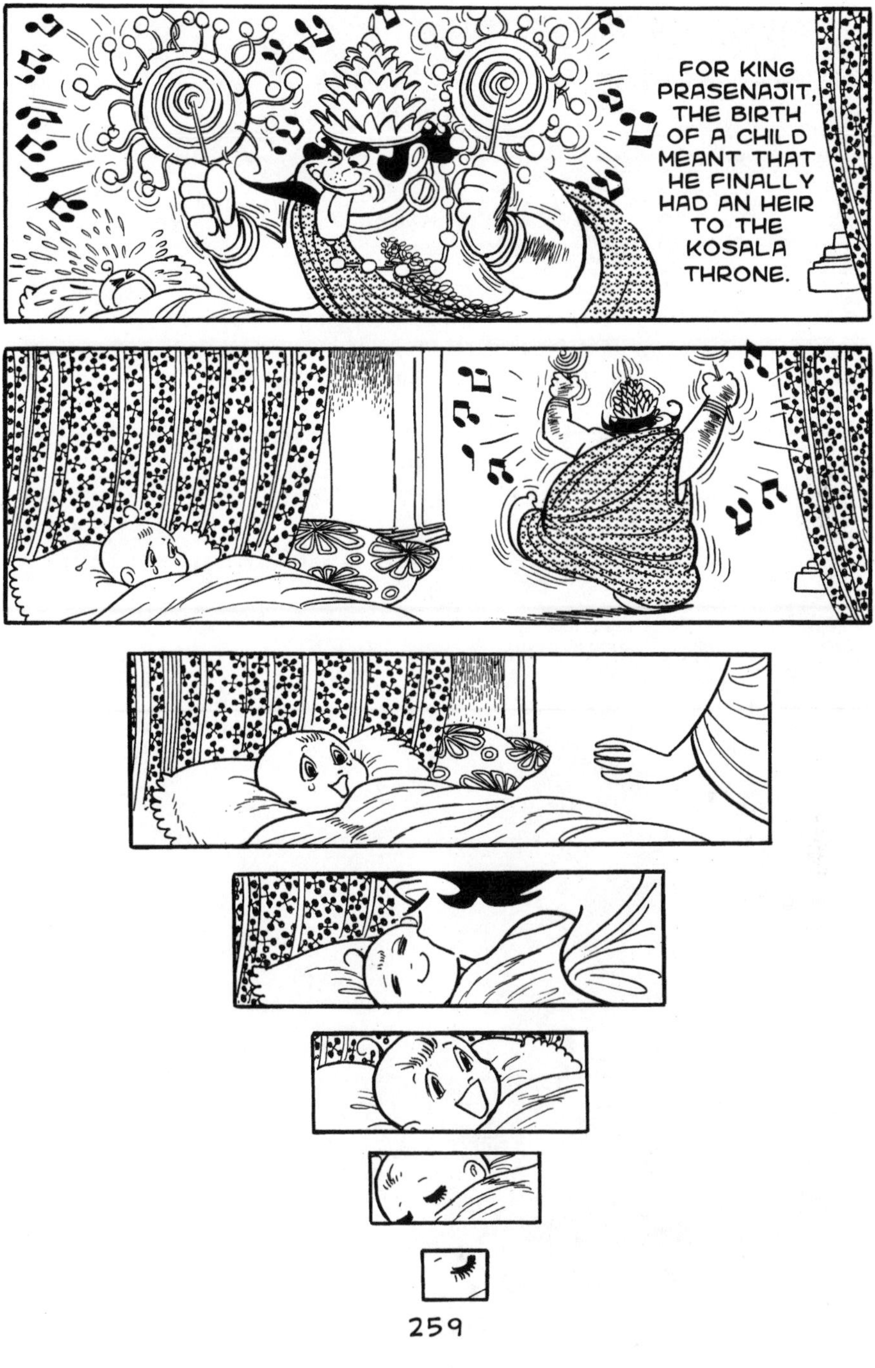
FOR KING PRASENAJIT, THE BIRTH OF A CHILD MEANT THAT HE FINALLY HAD AN HEIR TO THE KOSALA THRONE.

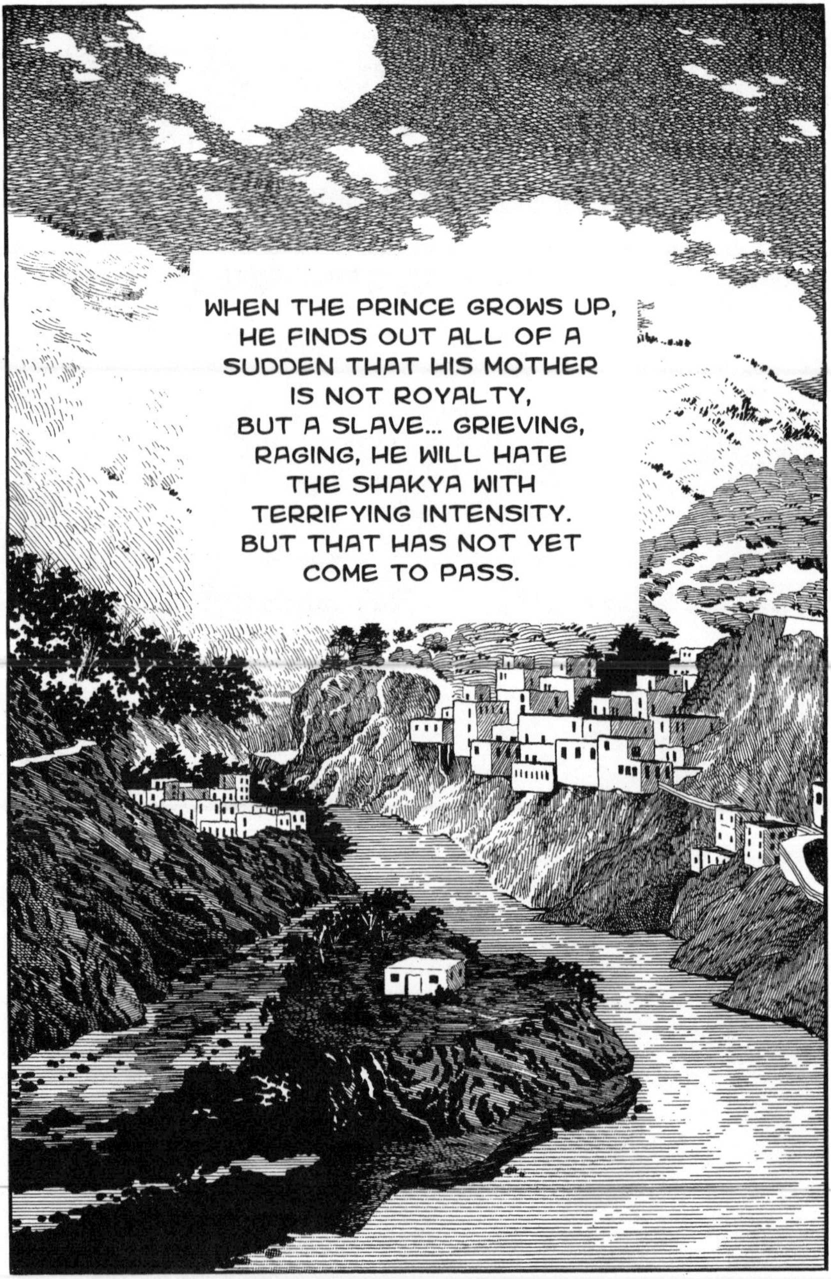
WHEN THE PRINCE GROWS UP, HE FINDS OUT ALL OF A SUDDEN THAT HIS MOTHER IS NOT ROYALTY, BUT A SLAVE... GRIEVING, RAGING, HE WILL HATE THE SHAKYA WITH TERRIFYING INTENSITY. BUT THAT HAS NOT YET COME TO PASS.

CHAPTER SEVEN

RAHULA

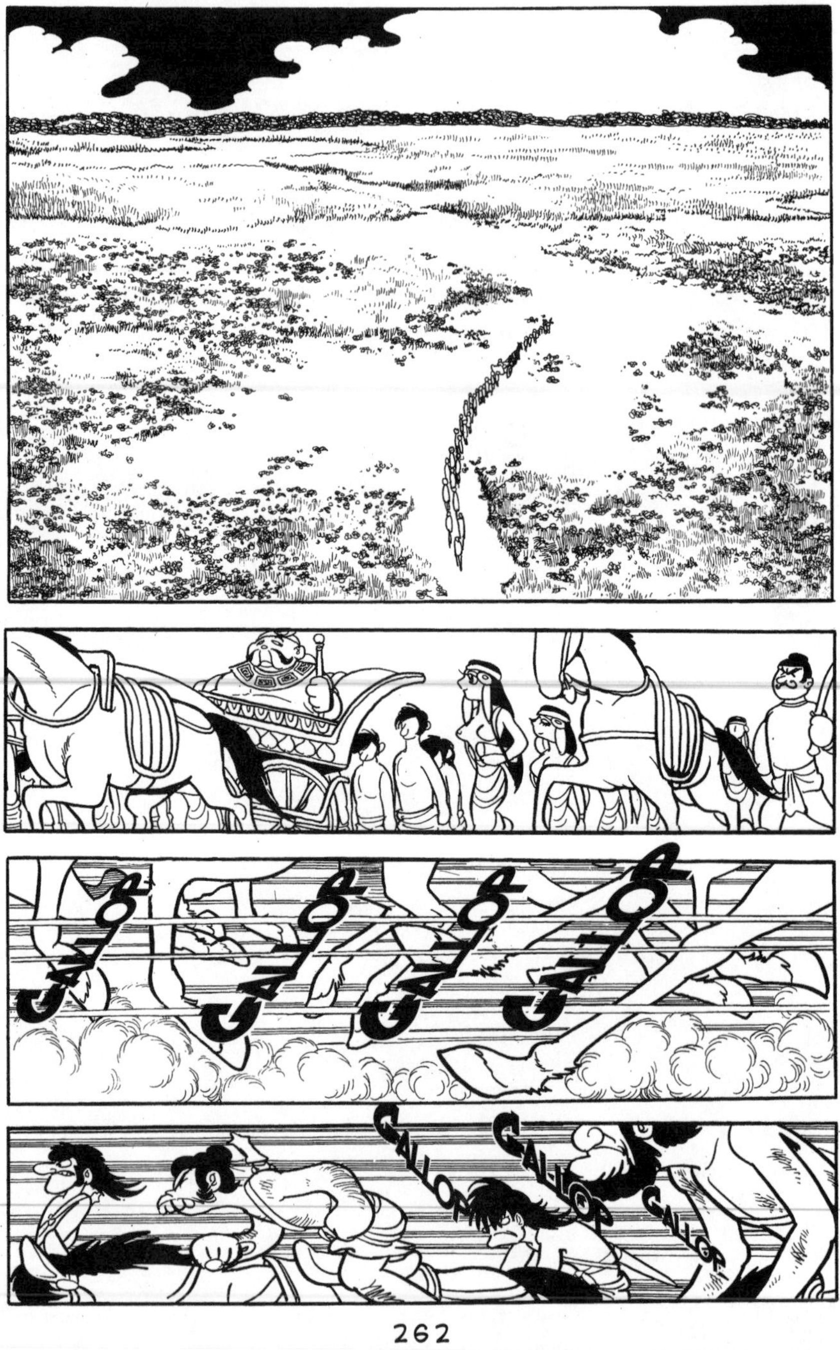
GALLOP
GALLOP
GALLOP
GALLOP
GALLOP
GALLOP
GALLOP

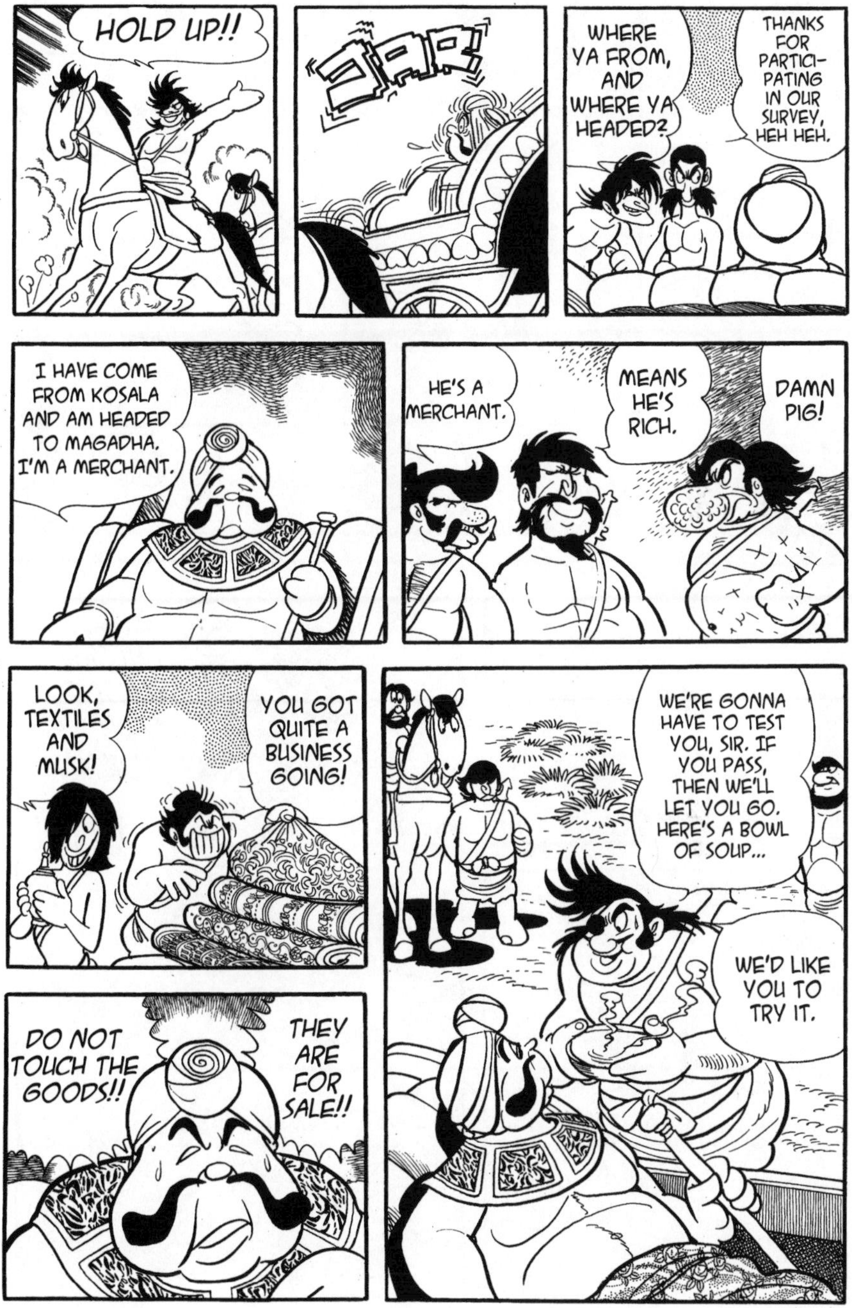
HOLD UP!!
JAR
WHERE YA FROM, AND WHERE YA HEADED?
THANKS FOR PARTICIPATING IN OUR SURVEY, HEH HEH.
I HAVE COME FROM KOSALA AND AM HEADED TO MAGADHA. I'M A MERCHANT.
HE'S A MERCHANT.
MEANS HE'S RICH.
DAMN PIG!
LOOK, TEXTILES AND MUSK!
YOU GOT QUITE A BUSINESS GOING!
DO NOT TOUCH THE GOODS!!
THEY ARE FOR SALE!!
WE'RE GONNA HAVE TO TEST YOU, SIR. IF YOU PASS, THEN WE'LL LET YOU GO. HERE'S A BOWL OF SOUP...
WE'D LIKE YOU TO TRY IT.

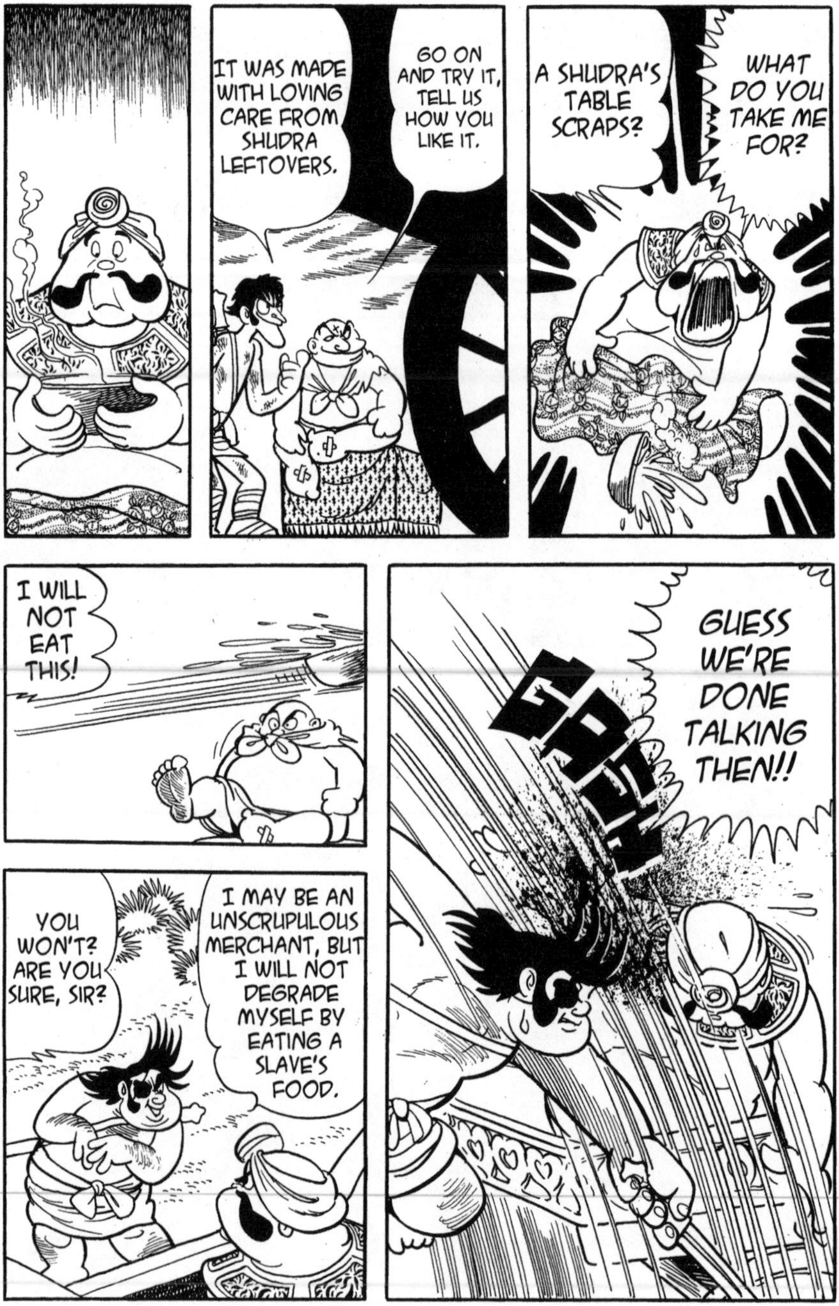
IT WAS MADE WITH LOVING CARE FROM SHUDRA LEFTOVERS.
GO ON AND TRY IT, TELL US HOW YOU LIKE IT.
A SHUDRA'S TABLE SCRAPS?
WHAT DO YOU TAKE ME FOR?
I WILL NOT EAT THIS!
YOU WON'T? ARE YOU SURE, SIR?
I MAY BE AN UNSCRUPULOUS MERCHANT, BUT I WILL NOT DEGRADE MYSELF BY EATING A SLAVE'S FOOD.
GUESS WE'RE DONE TALKING THEN!!

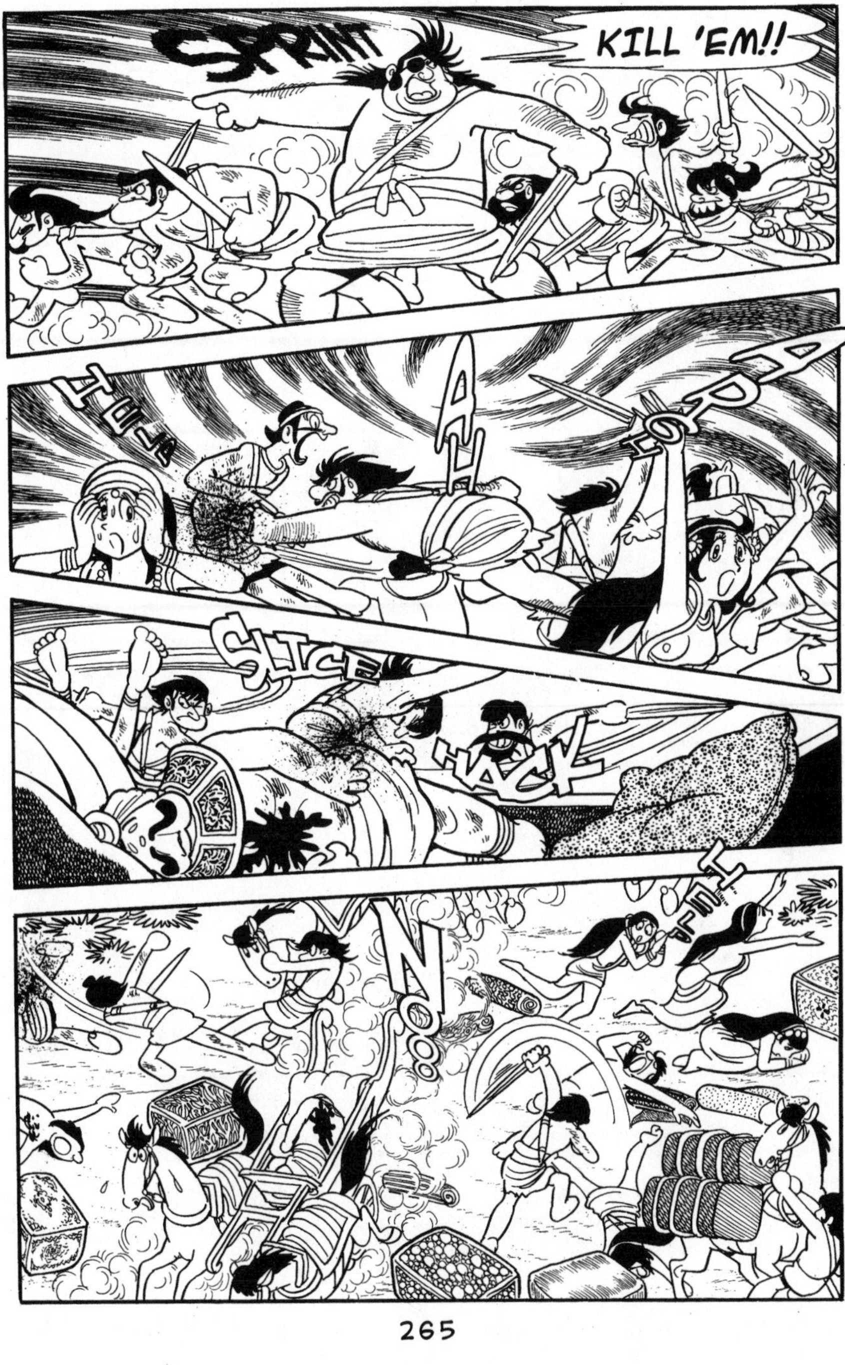
SPRINT
KILL 'EM!!
AH
SLICE
HACK
NOOOO
HELP

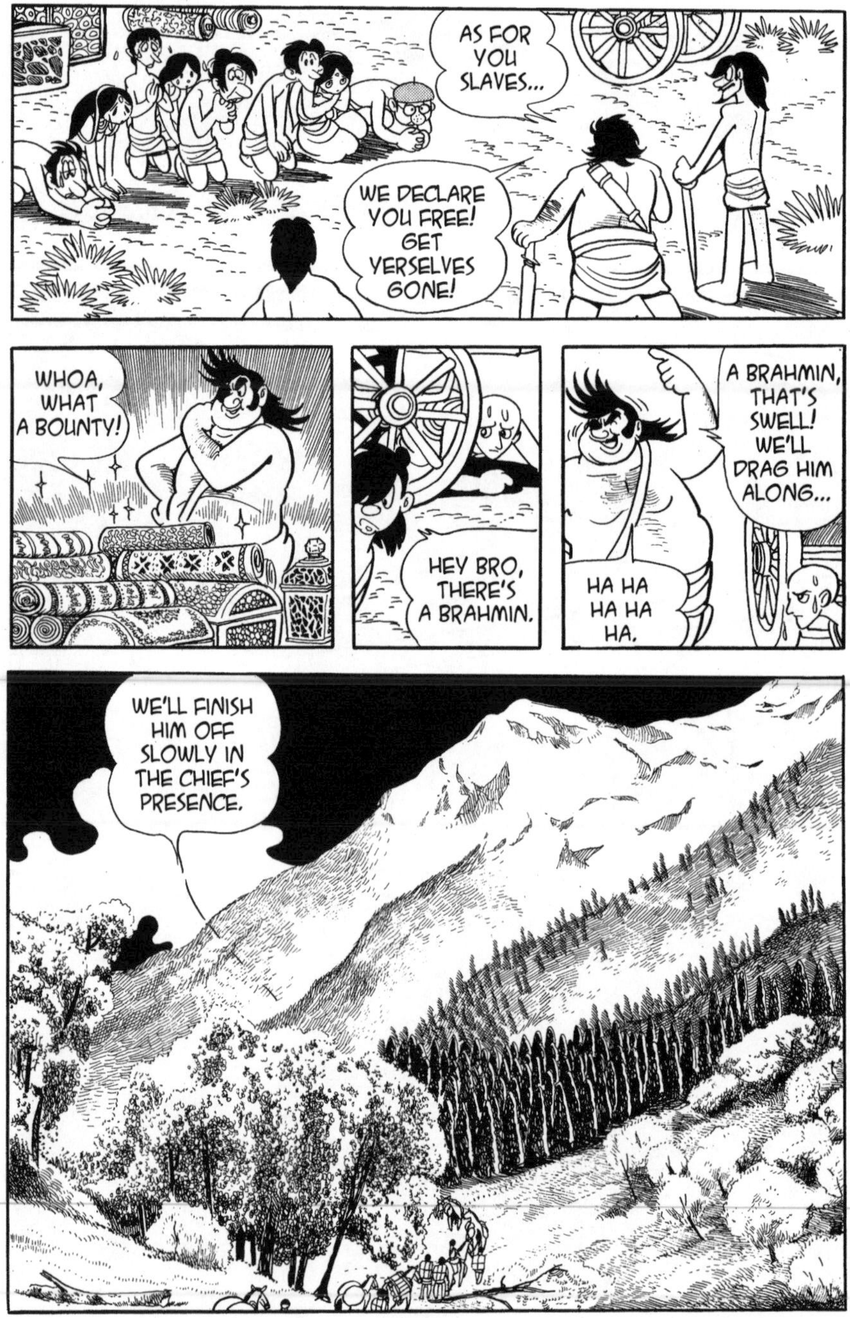
AS FOR YOU SLAVES...
WE DECLARE YOU FREE! GET YERSELVES GONE!
WHOA, WHAT A BOUNTY!
HEY BRO, THERE'S A BRAHMIN.
A BRAHMIN, THAT'S SWELL! WE'LL DRAG HIM ALONG...
HA HA HA HA HA.
WE'LL FINISH HIM OFF SLOWLY IN THE CHIEF'S PRESENCE.

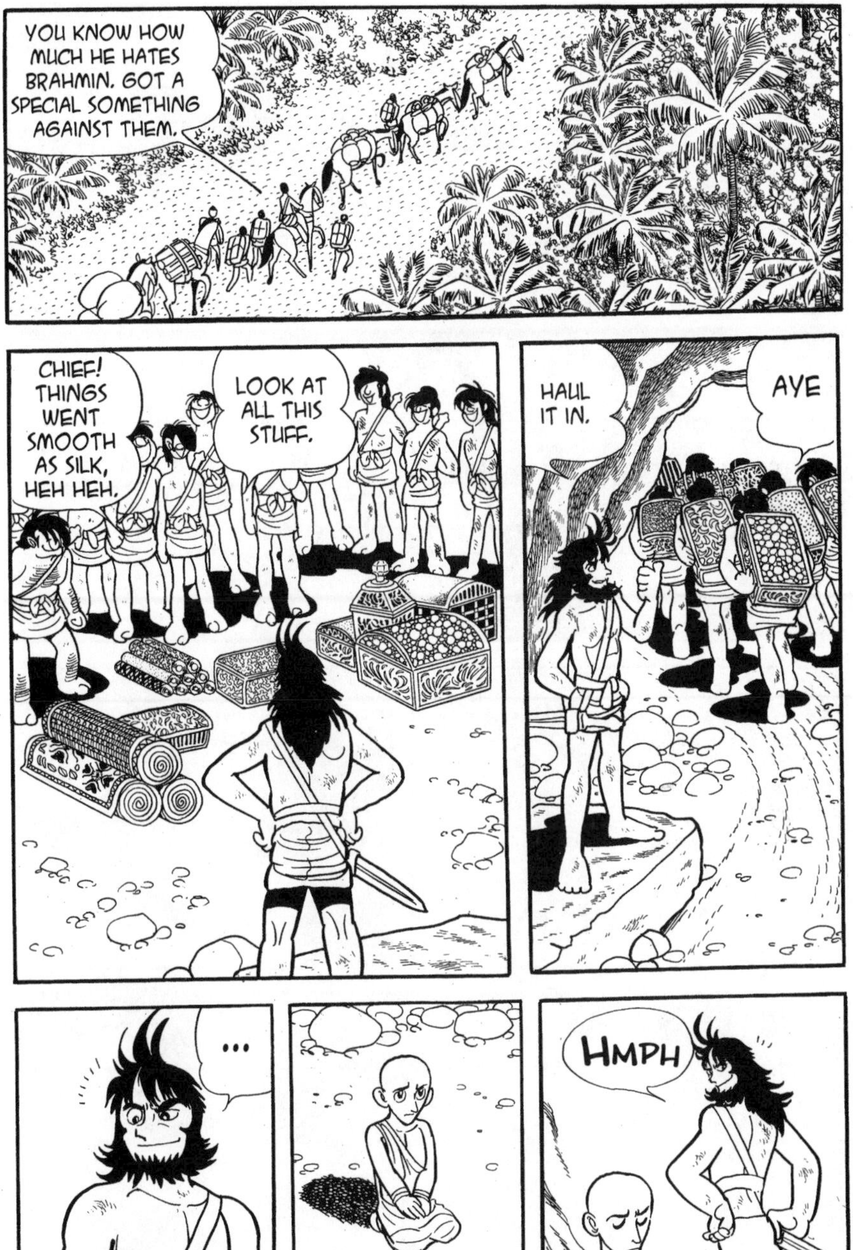
YOU KNOW HOW MUCH HE HATES BRAHMIN. GOT A SPECIAL SOMETHING AGAINST THEM.
CHIEF! THINGS WENT SMOOTH AS SILK, HEH HEH.
LOOK AT ALL THIS STUFF.
HAUL IT IN.
AYE
...
HMPH

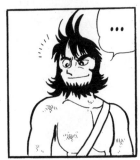

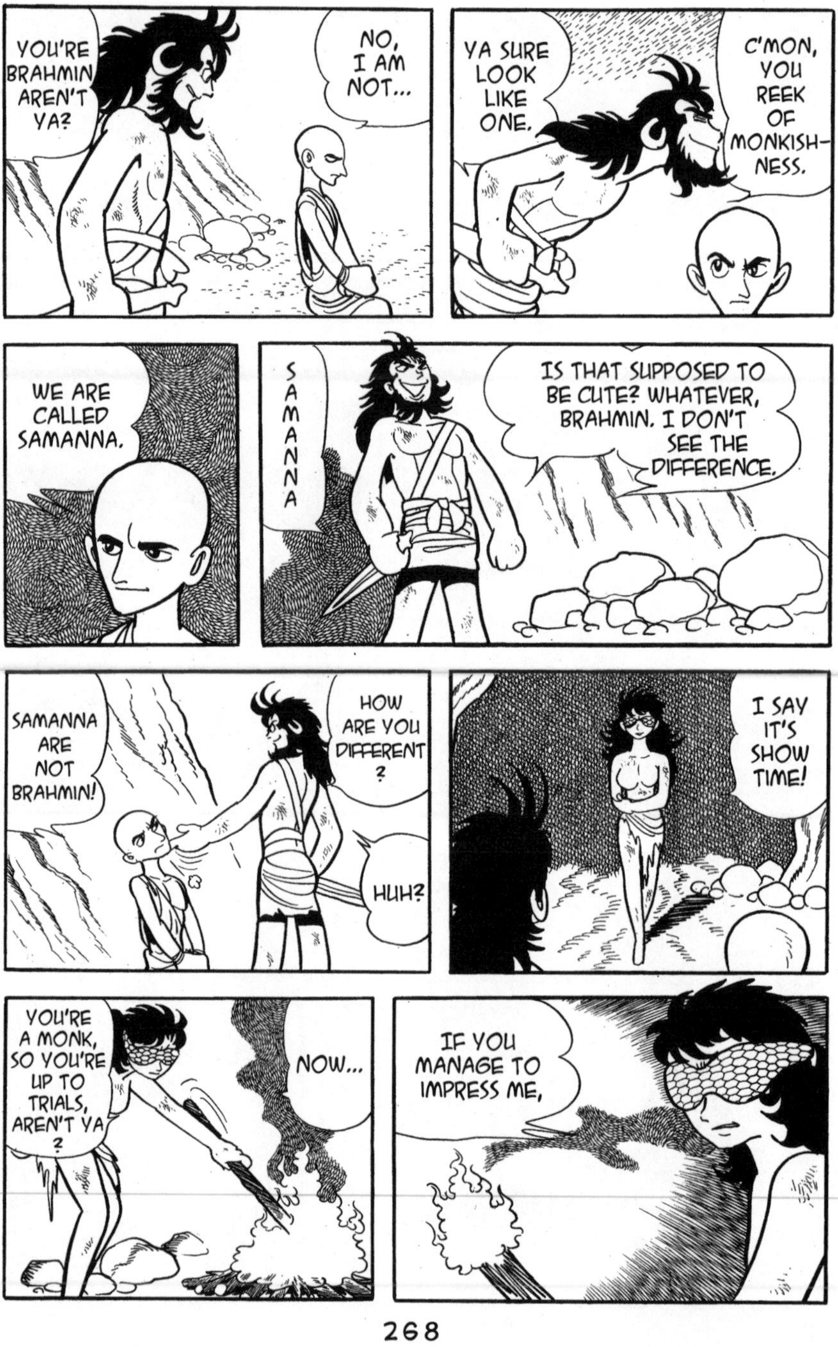
YOU'RE BRAHMIN AREN'T YA?
NO, I AM NOT...
YA SURE LOOK LIKE ONE.
C'MON, YOU REEK OF MONKISHNESS.
WE ARE CALLED SAMANNA.
SAMANNA
IS THAT SUPPOSED TO BE CUTE? WHATEVER, BRAHMIN. I DON'T SEE THE DIFFERENCE.
SAMANNA ARE NOT BRAHMIN!
HOW ARE YOU DIFFERENT?
HUH?
I SAY IT'S SHOW TIME!
YOU'RE A MONK, SO YOU'RE UP TO TRIALS, AREN'T YA?
NOW...
IF YOU MANAGE TO IMPRESS ME,

WE'LL LET YOU GO.

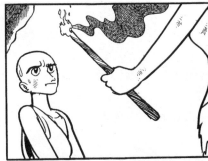

POKE THAT BURNING STICK IN YOUR EYE.

GO AHEAD, LET'S SEE YOU PUT OUT YOUR OWN EYE. IF YOU CAN DO IT, YOU'RE FREE.

BRAHMIN COWARD CAN'T DO IT!

MAYBE HE CAN BECAUSE...

HE ISN'T A DAMN BRAHMIN?

269

SIZZLE
OH, AH, UGH UGH
SIZZLE
HE REALLY DID IT!! HOW'S THAT FOR A SURPRISE.
MAYBE "SAMANNA" MEANS "IDIOT"?
IF YOU STILL WISH TO TRY ME...
CUT OFF MY HANDS!
WHY, YOU...
DON'T!!
NO POINT IN KILLING HIM...

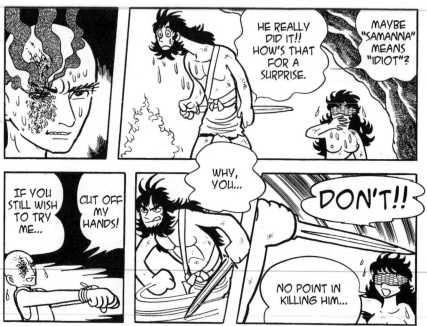

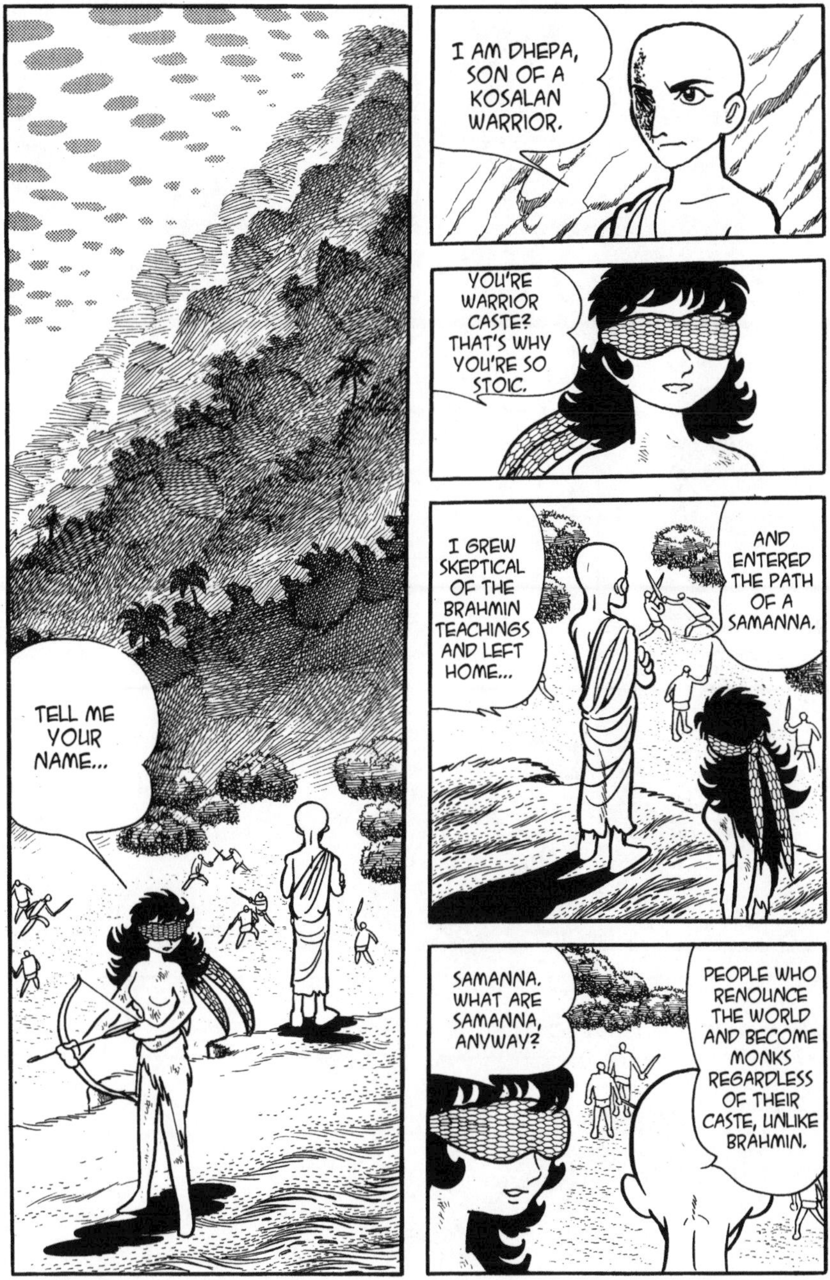
TELL ME YOUR NAME...
I AM DHEPA, SON OF A KOSALAN WARRIOR.
YOU'RE WARRIOR CASTE? THAT'S WHY YOU'RE SO STOIC.
I GREW SKEPTICAL OF THE BRAHMIN TEACHINGS AND LEFT HOME...
AND ENTERED THE PATH OF A SAMANNA.
SAMANNA. WHAT ARE SAMANNA, ANYWAY?
PEOPLE WHO RENOUNCE THE WORLD AND BECOME MONKS REGARDLESS OF THEIR CASTE, UNLIKE BRAHMIN.

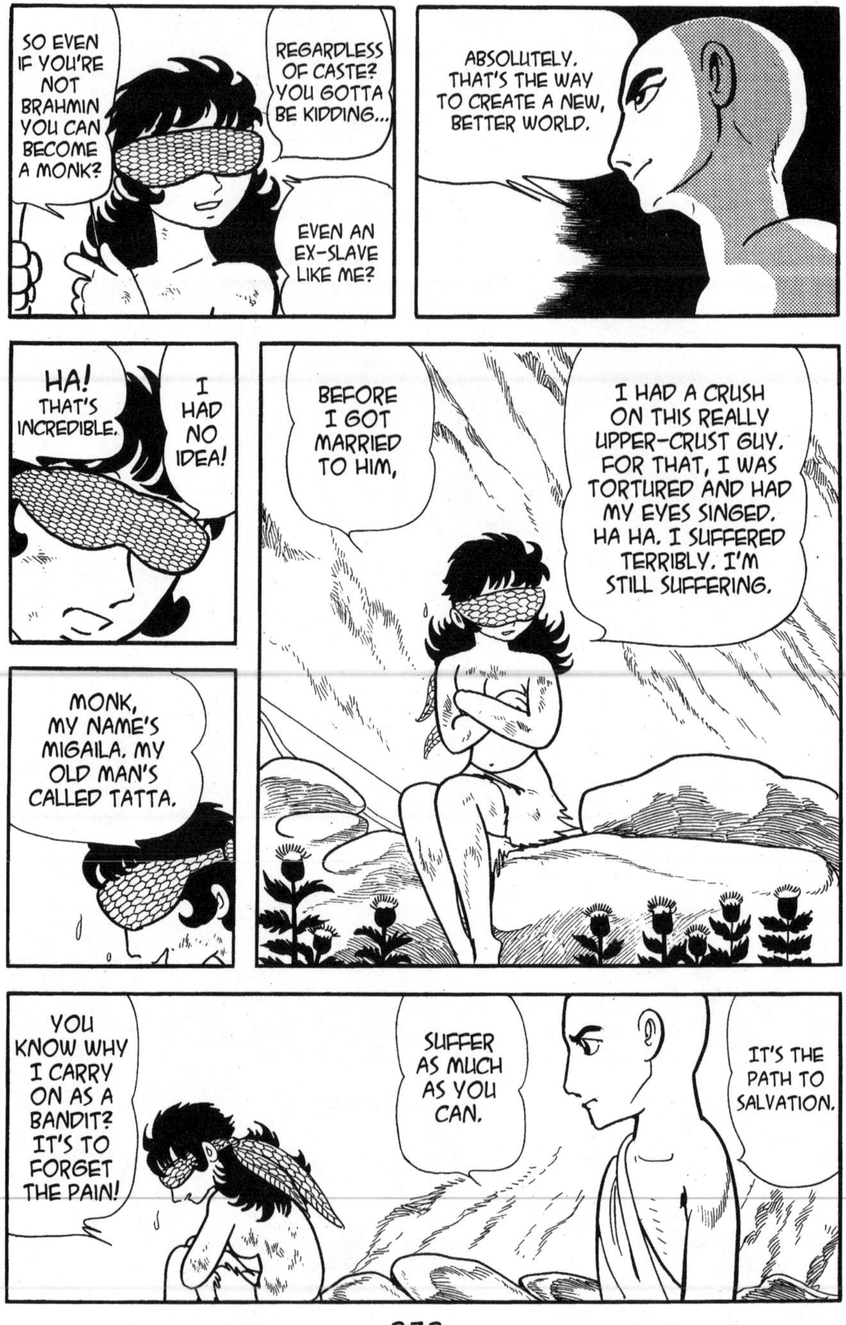
SO EVEN IF YOU'RE NOT BRAHMIN YOU CAN BECOME A MONK?
REGARDLESS OF CASTE? YOU GOTTA BE KIDDING...
EVEN AN EX-SLAVE LIKE ME?
ABSOLUTELY. THAT'S THE WAY TO CREATE A NEW, BETTER WORLD.
HA! THAT'S INCREDIBLE.
I HAD NO IDEA!
MONK, MY NAME'S MIGAILA. MY OLD MAN'S CALLED TATTA.
BEFORE I GOT MARRIED TO HIM,
I HAD A CRUSH ON THIS REALLY UPPER-CRUST GUY. FOR THAT, I WAS TORTURED AND HAD MY EYES SINGED. HA HA. I SUFFERED TERRIBLY. I'M STILL SUFFERING.
YOU KNOW WHY I CARRY ON AS A BANDIT? IT'S TO FORGET THE PAIN!
SUFFER AS MUCH AS YOU CAN.
IT'S THE PATH TO SALVATION.

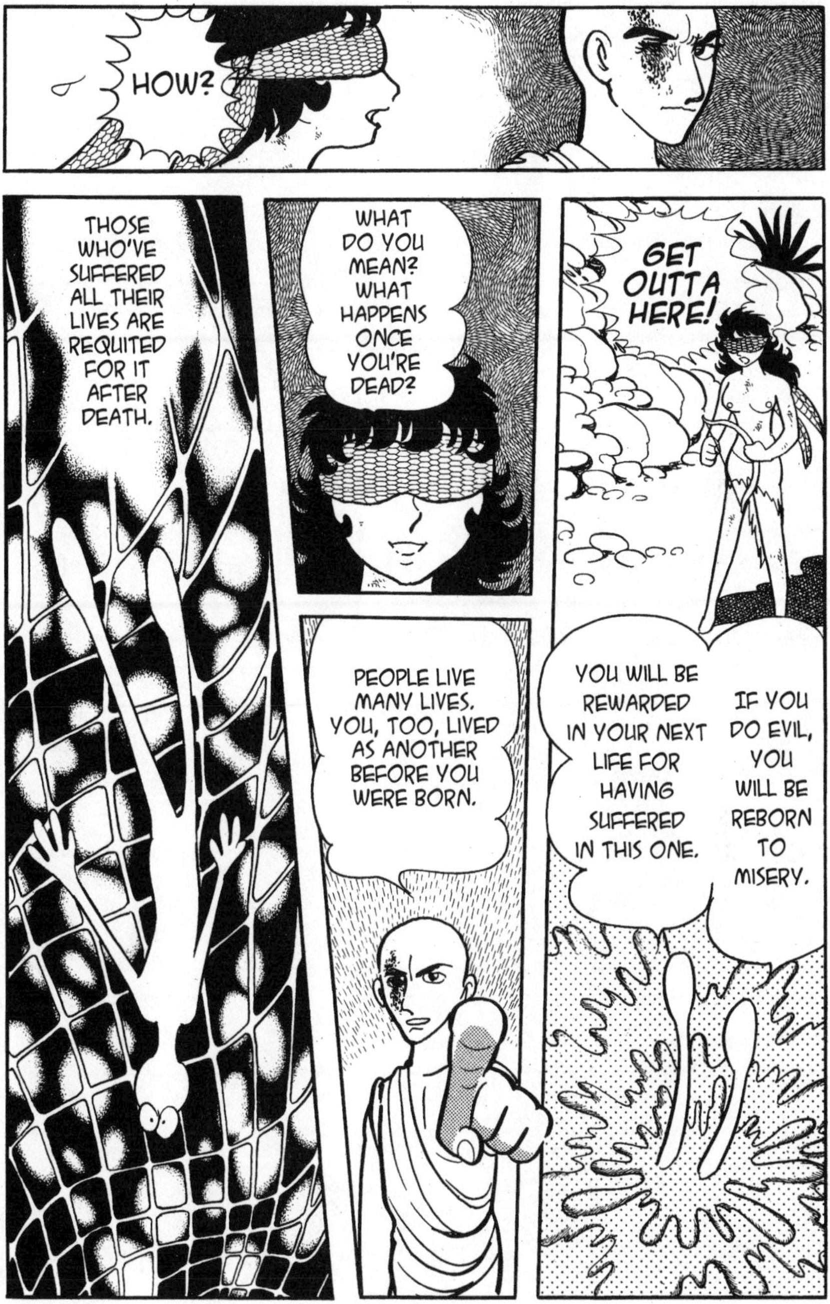
HOW?
THOSE WHO'VE SUFFERED ALL THEIR LIVES ARE REQUITED FOR IT AFTER DEATH.
WHAT DO YOU MEAN? WHAT HAPPENS ONCE YOU'RE DEAD?
GET OUTTA HERE!
PEOPLE LIVE MANY LIVES. YOU, TOO, LIVED AS ANOTHER BEFORE YOU WERE BORN.
YOU WILL BE REWARDED IN YOUR NEXT LIFE FOR HAVING SUFFERED IN THIS ONE.
IF YOU DO EVIL, YOU WILL BE REBORN TO MISERY.

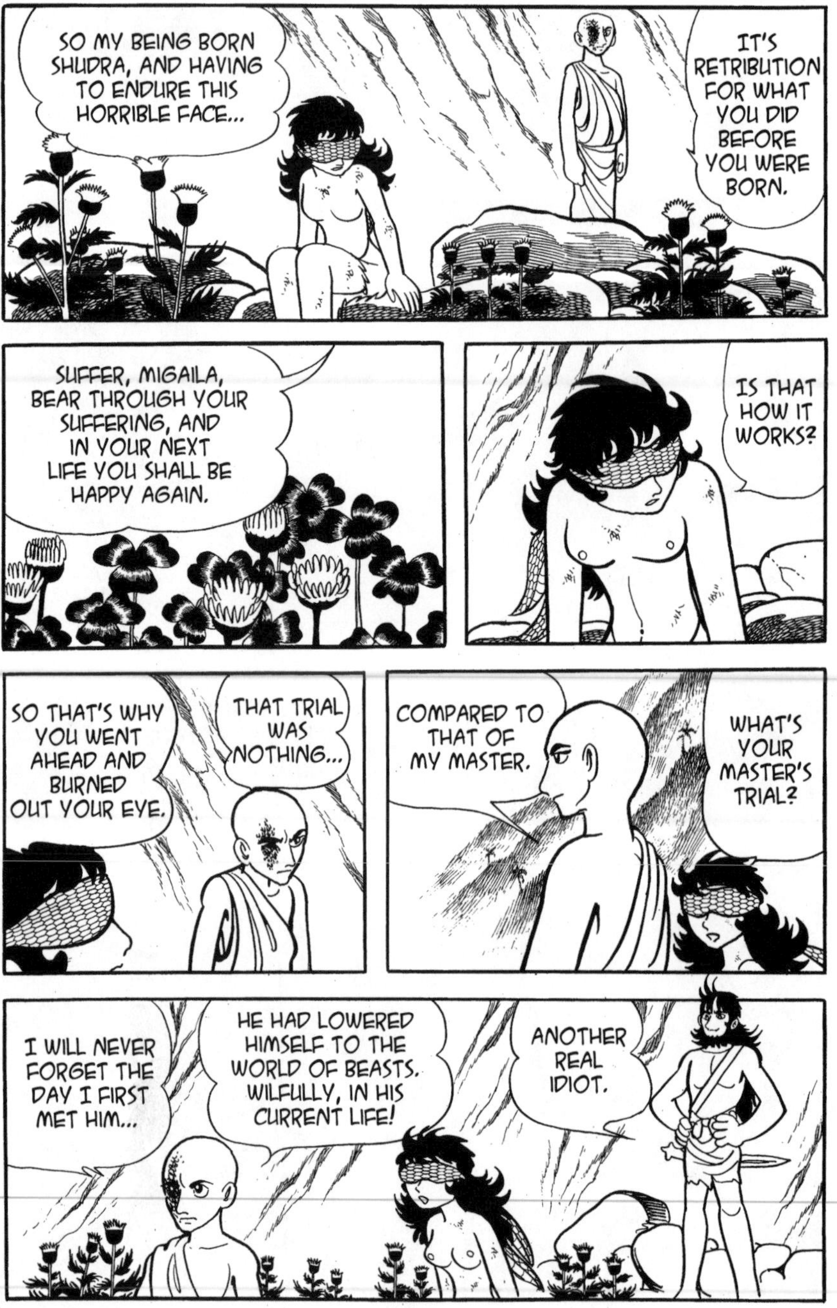
SO MY BEING BORN SHUDRA, AND HAVING TO ENDURE THIS HORRIBLE FACE...
IT'S RETRIBUTION FOR WHAT YOU DID BEFORE YOU WERE BORN.
SUFFER, MIGAILA, BEAR THROUGH YOUR SUFFERING, AND IN YOUR NEXT LIFE YOU SHALL BE HAPPY AGAIN.
IS THAT HOW IT WORKS?
SO THAT'S WHY YOU WENT AHEAD AND BURNED OUT YOUR EYE.
THAT TRIAL WAS NOTHING...
COMPARED TO THAT OF MY MASTER.
WHAT'S YOUR MASTER'S TRIAL?
I WILL NEVER FORGET THE DAY I FIRST MET HIM...
HE HAD LOWERED HIMSELF TO THE WORLD OF BEASTS. WILFULLY, IN HIS CURRENT LIFE!
ANOTHER REAL IDIOT.

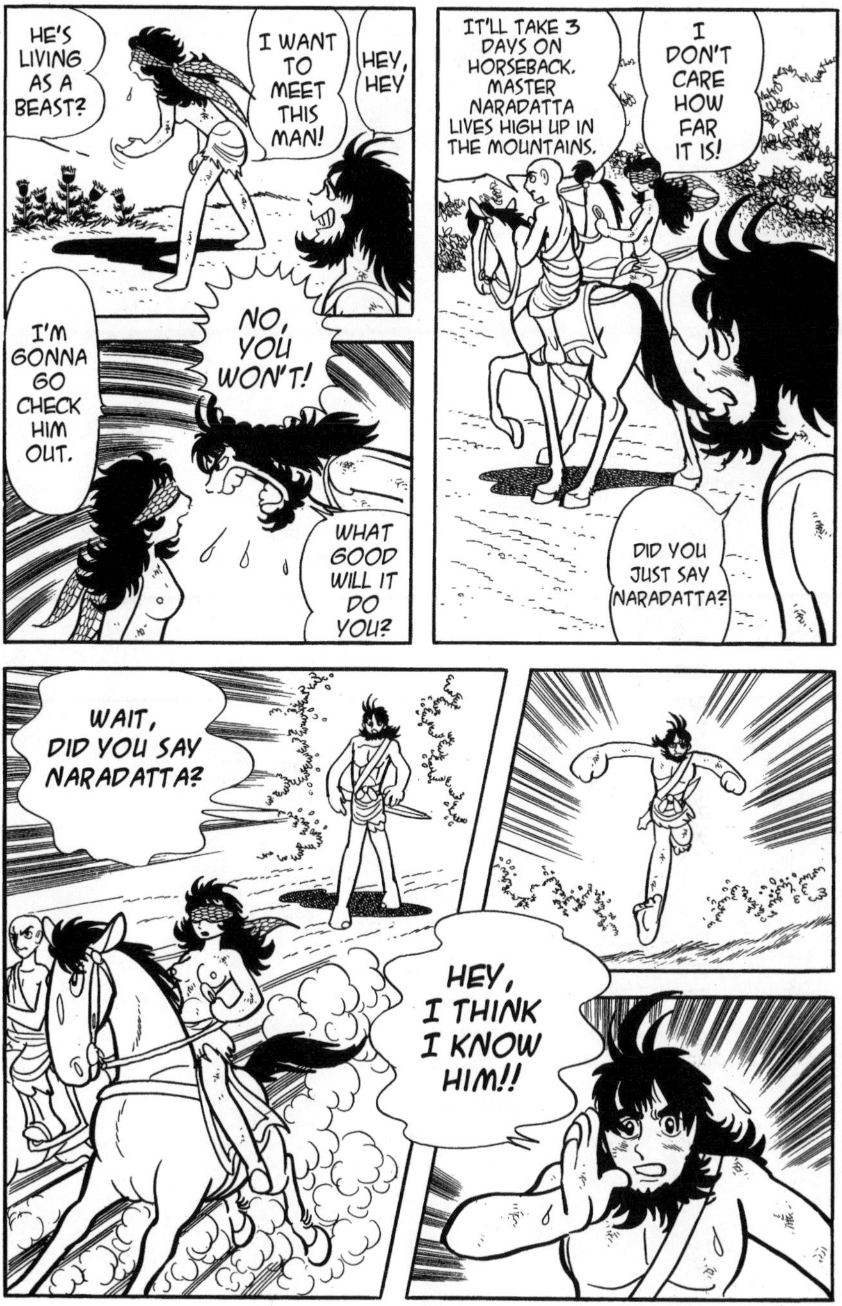
HE'S LIVING AS A BEAST?
I WANT TO MEET THIS MAN!
HEY, HEY
I'M GONNA GO CHECK HIM OUT.
NO, YOU WON'T!
WHAT GOOD WILL IT DO YOU?
IT'LL TAKE 3 DAYS ON HORSEBACK. MASTER NARADATTA LIVES HIGH UP IN THE MOUNTAINS.
I DON'T CARE HOW FAR IT IS!
DID YOU JUST SAY NARADATTA?
WAIT, DID YOU SAY NARADATTA?
HEY, I THINK I KNOW HIM!!

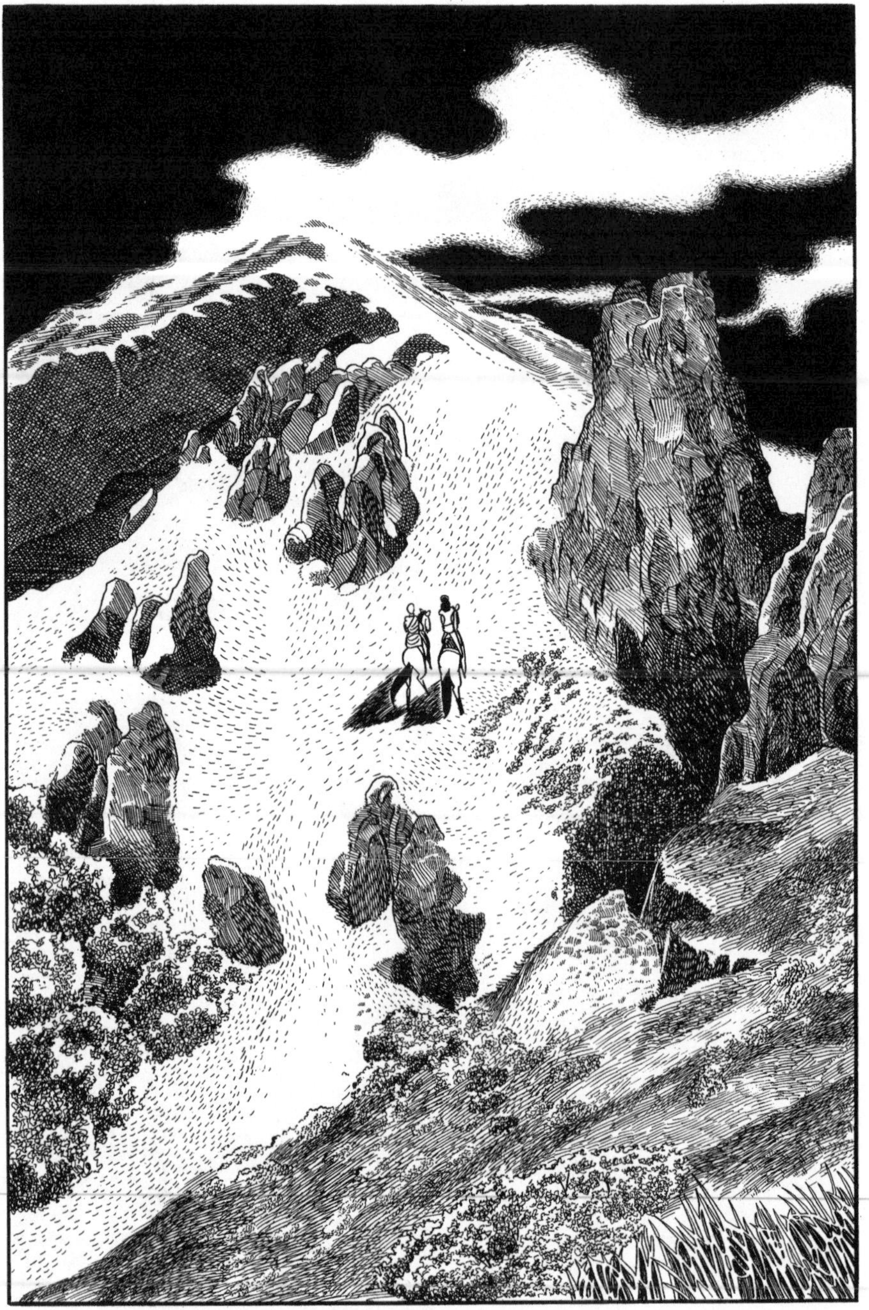

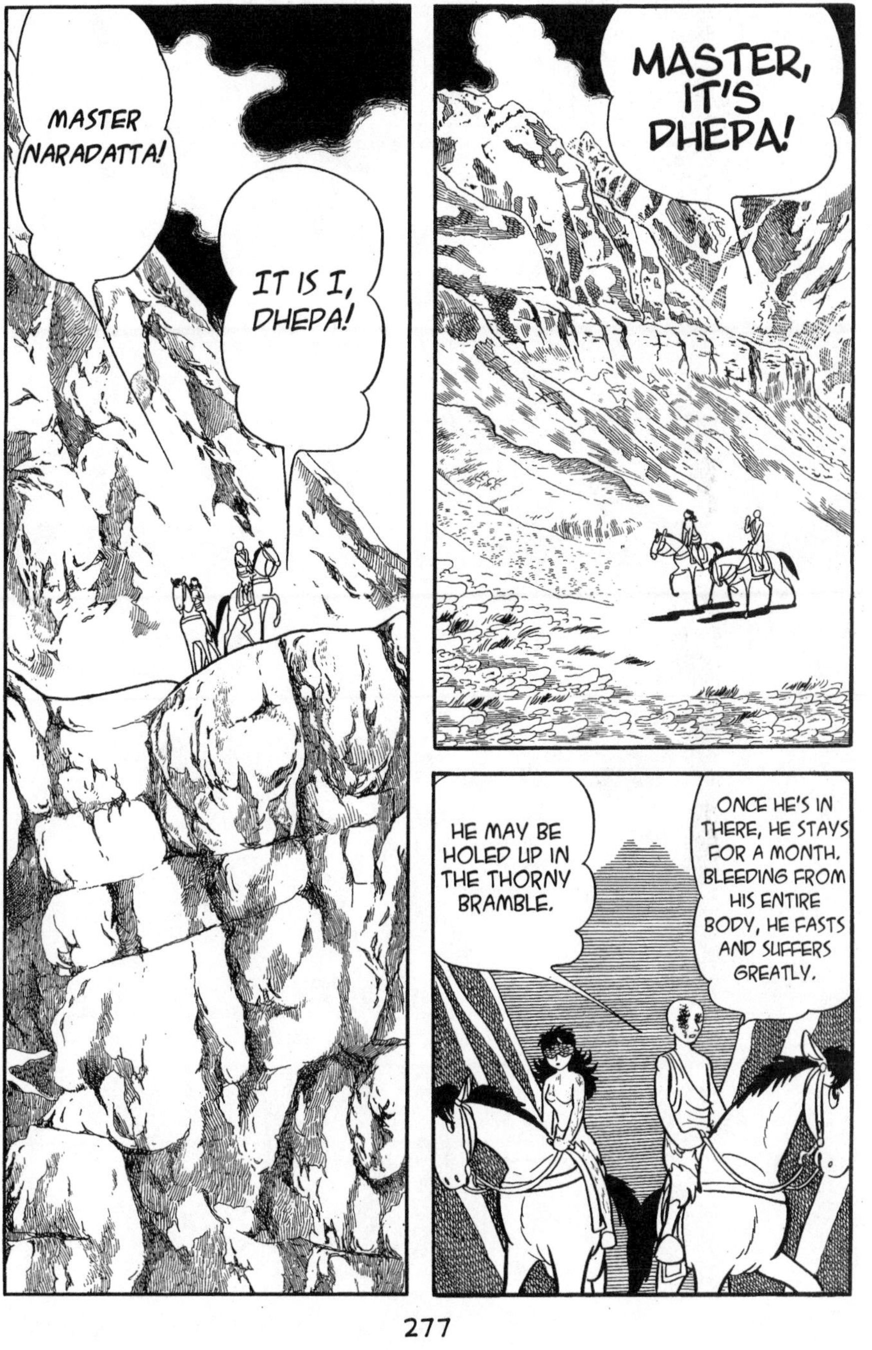
MASTER NARADATTA!
IT IS I, DHEPA!
MASTER, IT'S DHEPA!
HE MAY BE HOLED UP IN THE THORNY BRAMBLE.
ONCE HE'S IN THERE, HE STAYS FOR A MONTH. BLEEDING FROM HIS ENTIRE BODY, HE FASTS AND SUFFERS GREATLY.

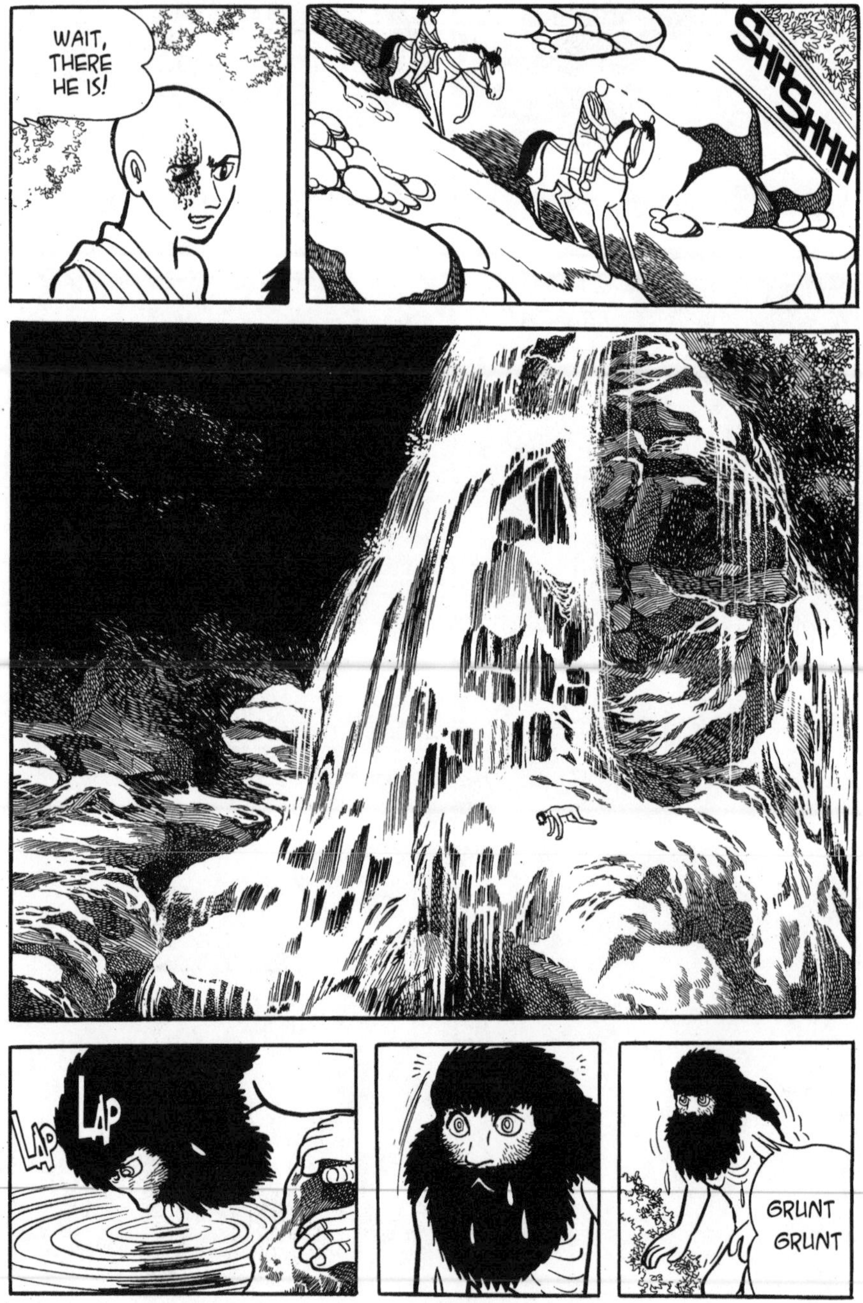
WAIT, THERE HE IS!
SHHSHHH
LAP
LAP
GRUNT GRUNT

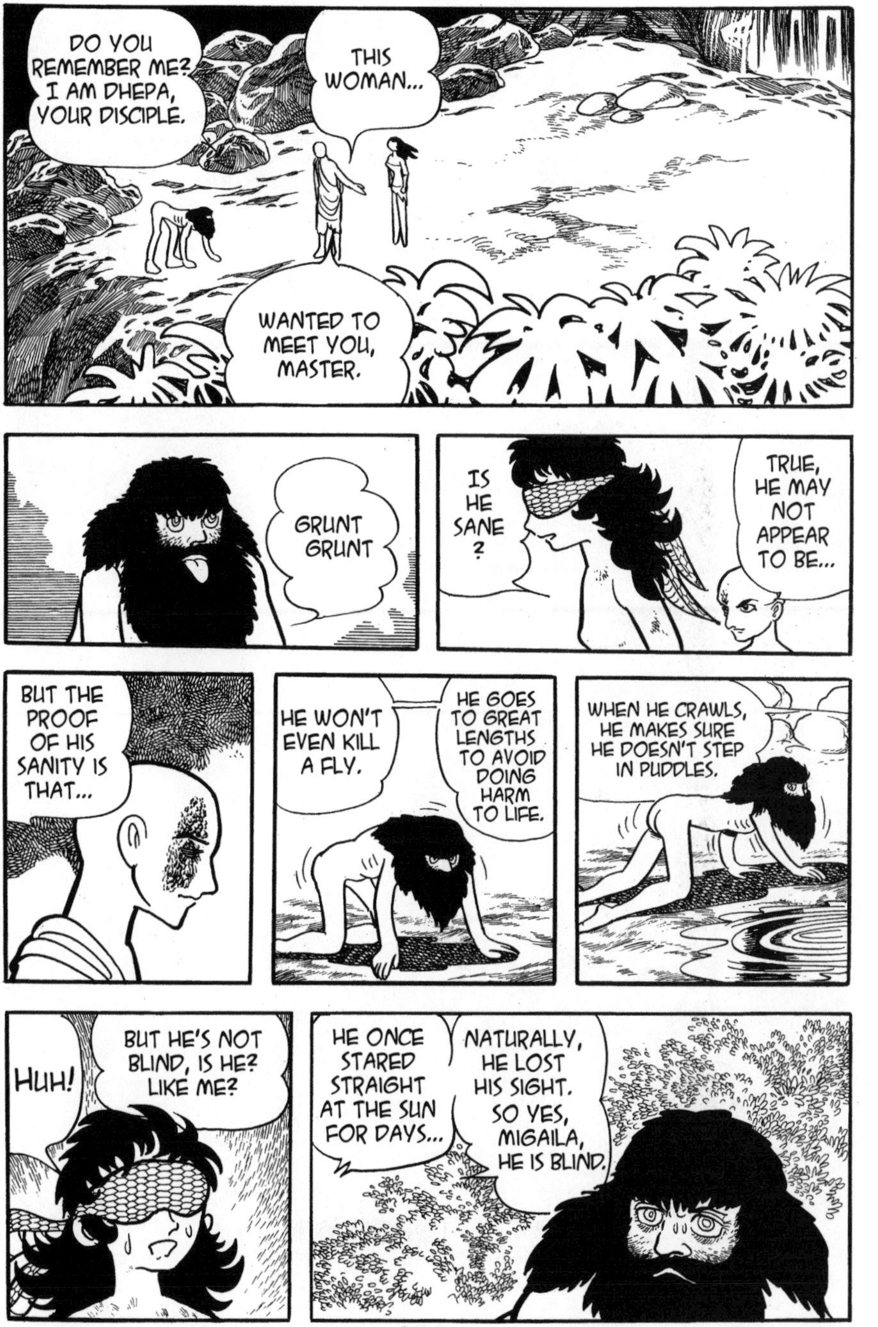
DO YOU REMEMBER ME? I AM DHEPA, YOUR DISCIPLE.
THIS WOMAN...
WANTED TO MEET YOU, MASTER.
GRUNT GRUNT
IS HE SANE?
TRUE, HE MAY NOT APPEAR TO BE...
BUT THE PROOF OF HIS SANITY IS THAT...
HE WON'T EVEN KILL A FLY.
HE GOES TO GREAT LENGTHS TO AVOID DOING HARM TO LIFE.
WHEN HE CRAWLS, HE MAKES SURE HE DOESN'T STEP IN PUDDLES.
HUH!
BUT HE'S NOT BLIND, IS HE? LIKE ME?
HE ONCE STARED STRAIGHT AT THE SUN FOR DAYS...
NATURALLY, HE LOST HIS SIGHT. SO YES, MIGAILA, HE IS BLIND.

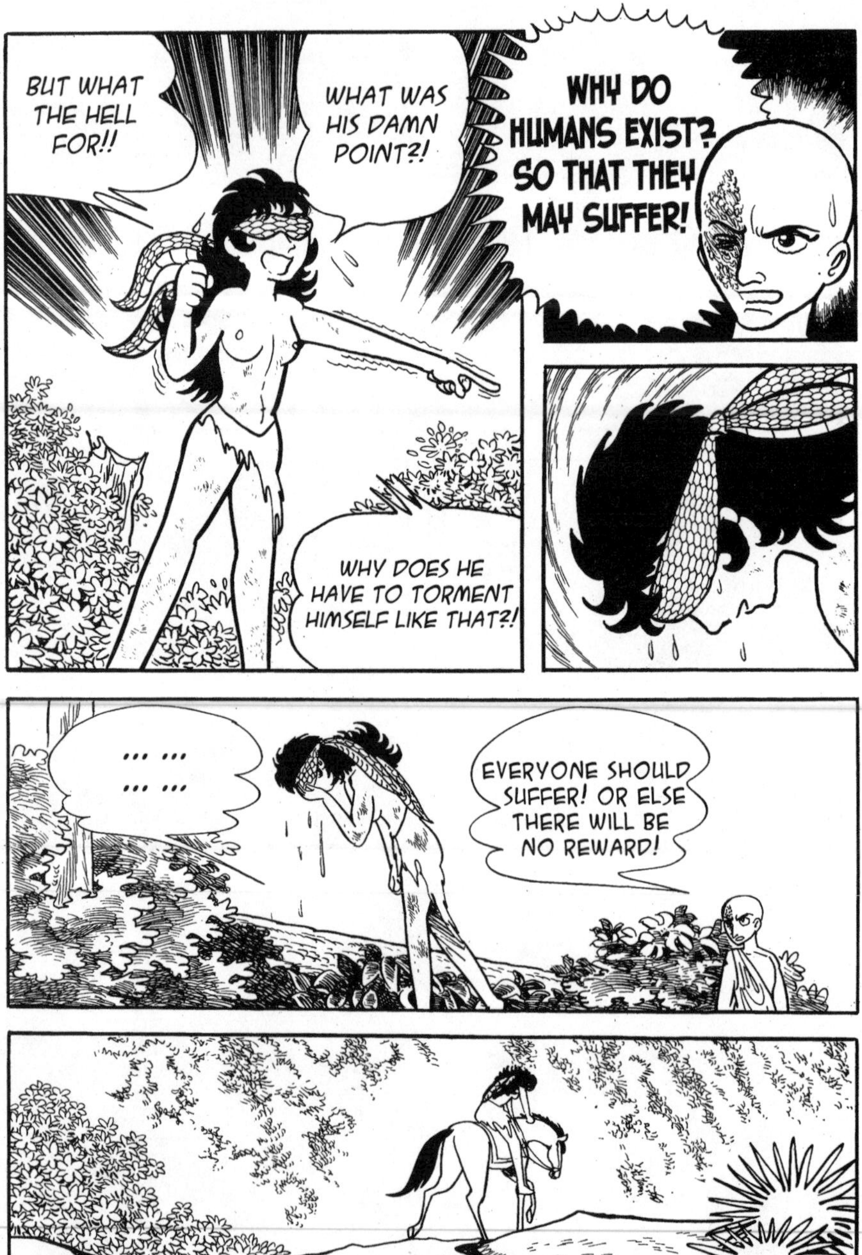
BUT WHAT THE HELL FOR!!
WHAT WAS HIS DAMN POINT?!
WHY DO HUMANS EXIST? SO THAT THEY MAY SUFFER!
WHY DOES HE HAVE TO TORMENT HIMSELF LIKE THAT?!
... ...
EVERYONE SHOULD SUFFER! OR ELSE THERE WILL BE NO REWARD!

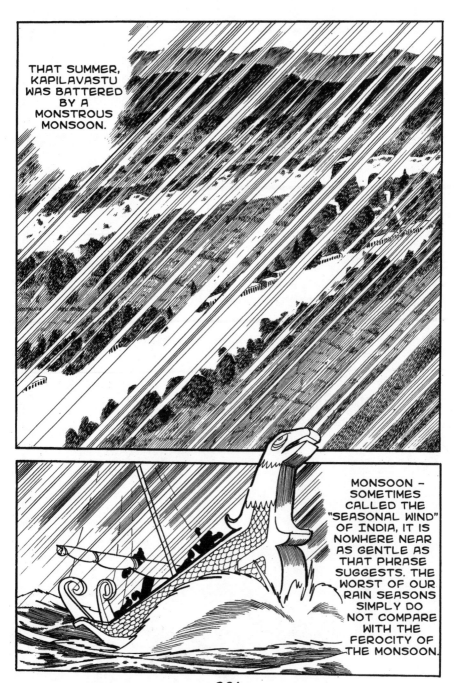

THAT SUMMER, KAPILAVASTU WAS BATTERED BY A MONSTROUS MONSOON.

MONSOON – SOMETIMES CALLED THE "SEASONAL WIND" OF INDIA, IT IS NOWHERE NEAR AS GENTLE AS THAT PHRASE SUGGESTS. THE WORST OF OUR RAIN SEASONS SIMPLY DO NOT COMPARE WITH THE FEROCITY OF THE MONSOON.

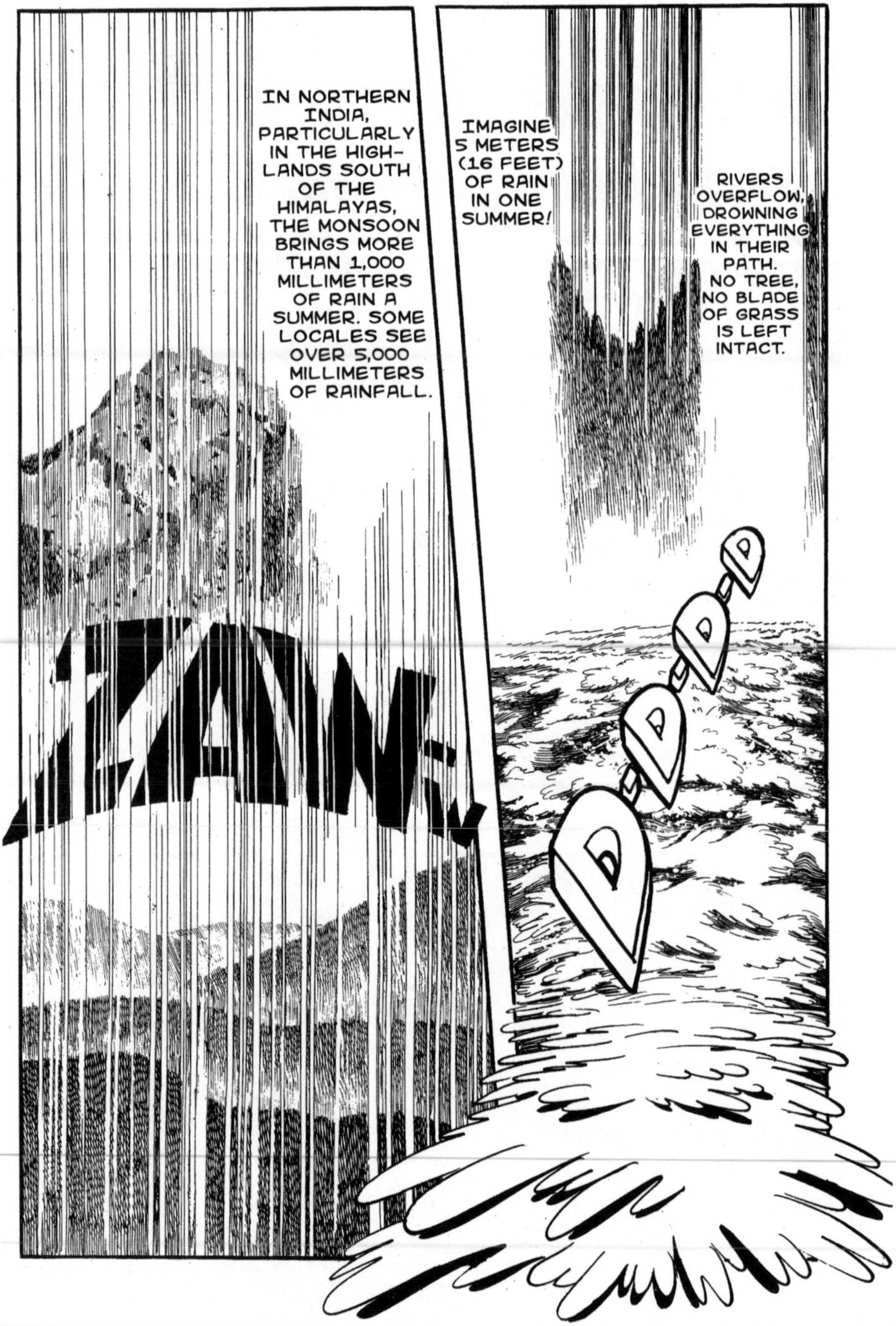
IN NORTHERN INDIA, PARTICULARLY IN THE HIGH-LANDS SOUTH OF THE HIMALAYAS, THE MONSOON BRINGS MORE THAN 1,000 MILLIMETERS OF RAIN A SUMMER. SOME LOCALES SEE OVER 5,000 MILLIMETERS OF RAINFALL.
IMAGINE 5 METERS (16 FEET) OF RAIN IN ONE SUMMER!
RIVERS OVERFLOW, DROWNING EVERYTHING IN THEIR PATH. NO TREE, NO BLADE OF GRASS IS LEFT INTACT.

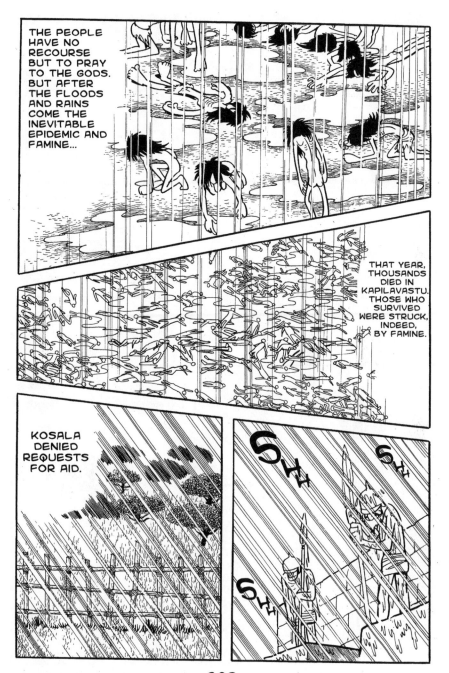

THE PEOPLE HAVE NO RECOURSE BUT TO PRAY TO THE GODS. BUT AFTER THE FLOODS AND RAINS COME THE INEVITABLE EPIDEMIC AND FAMINE...

THAT YEAR, THOUSANDS DIED IN KAPILAVASTU. THOSE WHO SURVIVED WERE STRUCK, INDEED, BY FAMINE.

KOSALA DENIED REQUESTS FOR AID.

SHH

SHH

SHH

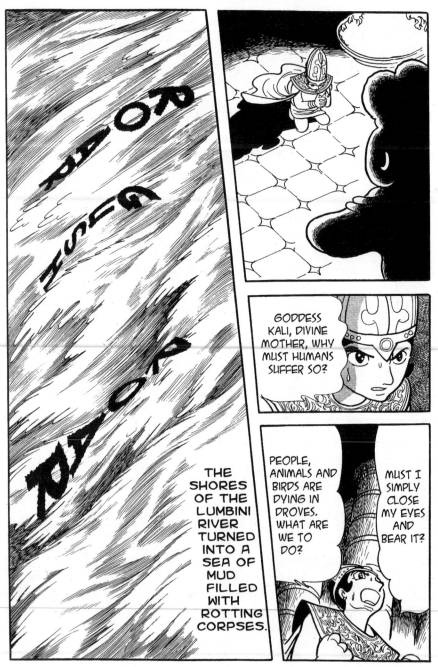

THE SHORES OF THE LUMBINI RIVER TURNED INTO A SEA OF MUD FILLED WITH ROTTING CORPSES.

GODDESS KALI, DIVINE MOTHER, WHY MUST HUMANS SUFFER SO?

PEOPLE, ANIMALS AND BIRDS ARE DYING IN DROVES. WHAT ARE WE TO DO?

MUST I SIMPLY CLOSE MY EYES AND BEAR IT?

ONE DAY WE SHAKYA WILL PERISH EVEN IF THERE IS NO WAR, I SEE NOW...

KALI... GIVE ME COURAGE...

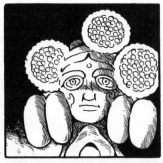

ROUSE YOURSELF, PRINCE! YOUR SOLE PURPOSE FOR THE REST OF YOUR LIFE IS TO TEACH OTHERS!

TEACH? WHAT AM I SUPPOSED TO TEACH?!

HOW TO SAVE HUMANITY. YOU WILL KNOW HOW, ONCE YOU ATTAIN ENLIGHTENMENT.

GO NOW, FORSAKE THE ROYAL LIFE AND DON THE ROBE OF A MONK. GET THEE TO THE PIPPALA TREE.

THERE YOU MUST AWAKEN.

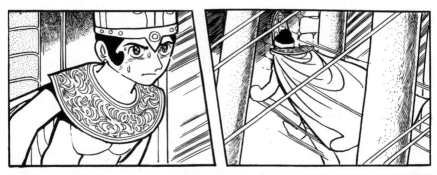

MY LORD, WHERE ARE YOU GOING?

I SHALL LEAVE KAPILAVASTU AFTER ALL. THERE IS NO OTHER WAY FOR ME.

N—NO, YOU MUST NOT!

YOU ARE TO BE KING. IF YOU LEAVE, THIS COUNTRY WILL SURELY GO TO RUIN.

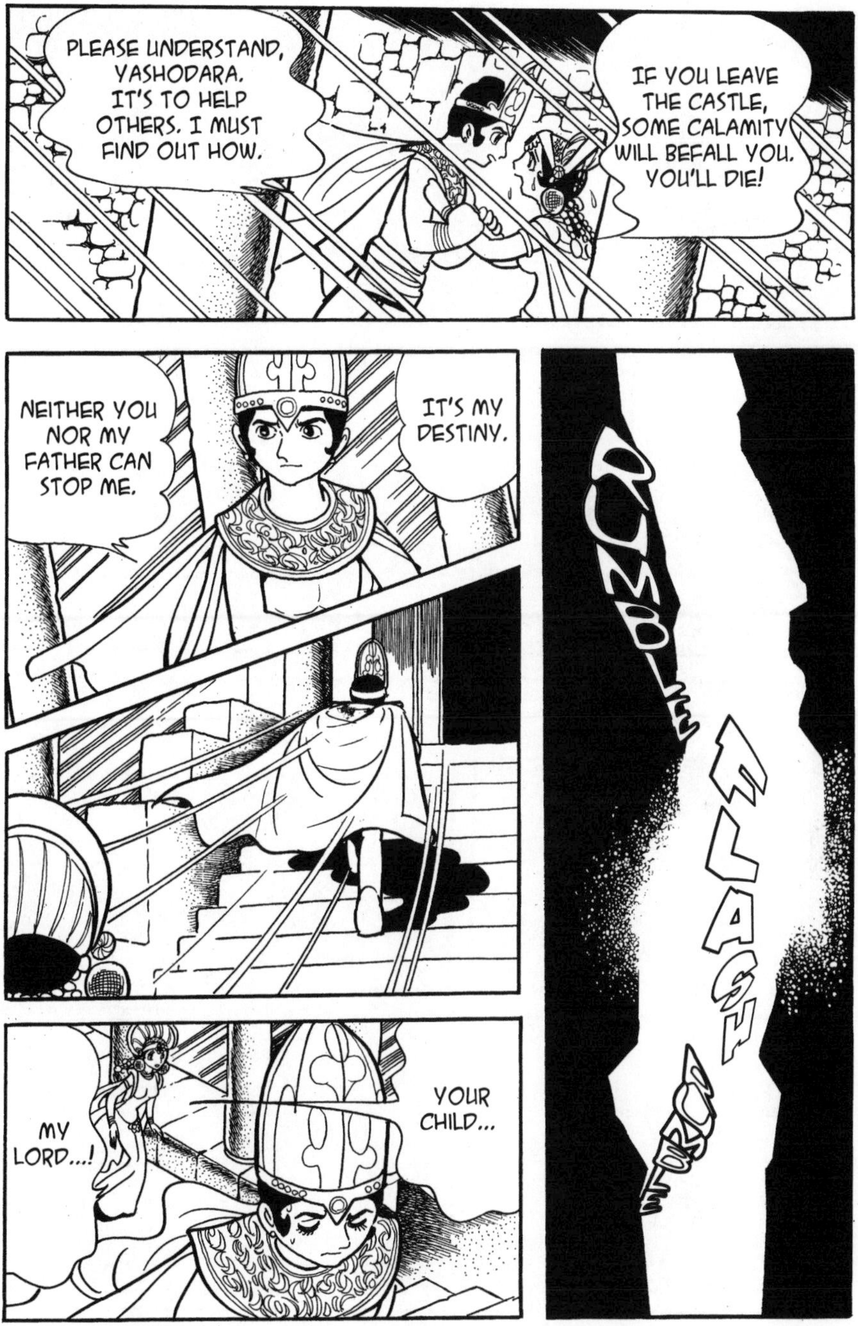
PLEASE UNDERSTAND, YASHODARA. IT'S TO HELP OTHERS. I MUST FIND OUT HOW.
IF YOU LEAVE THE CASTLE, SOME CALAMITY WILL BEFALL YOU. YOU'LL DIE!
NEITHER YOU NOR MY FATHER CAN STOP ME.
IT'S MY DESTINY.
MY LORD...!
YOUR CHILD...
RUMBLE
FLASH

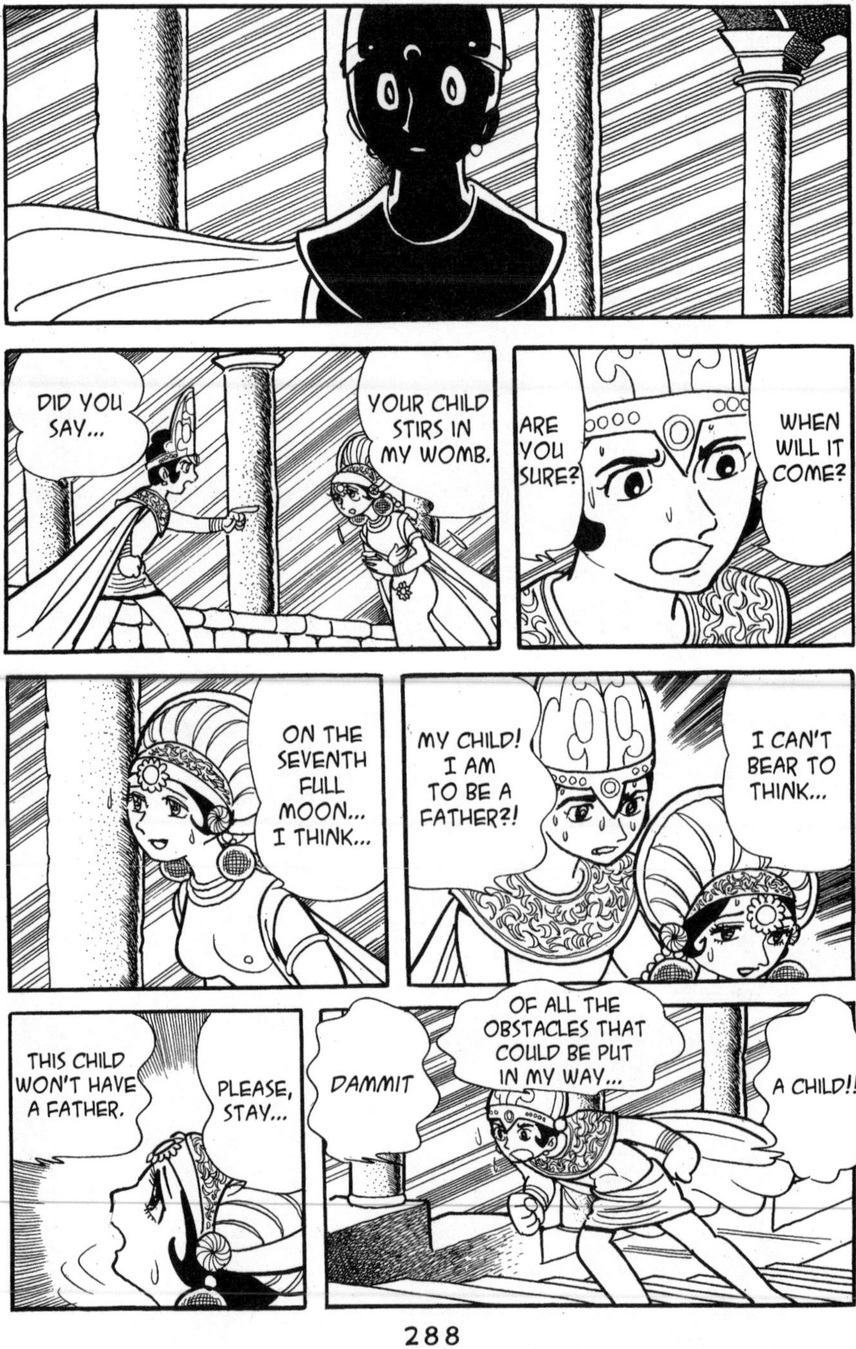
DID YOU SAY...
YOUR CHILD STIRS IN MY WOMB.
ARE YOU SURE?
WHEN WILL IT COME?
ON THE SEVENTH FULL MOON... I THINK...
MY CHILD! I AM TO BE A FATHER?!
I CAN'T BEAR TO THINK...
THIS CHILD WON'T HAVE A FATHER.
PLEASE, STAY...
DAMMIT
OF ALL THE OBSTACLES THAT COULD BE PUT IN MY WAY...
A CHILD!!

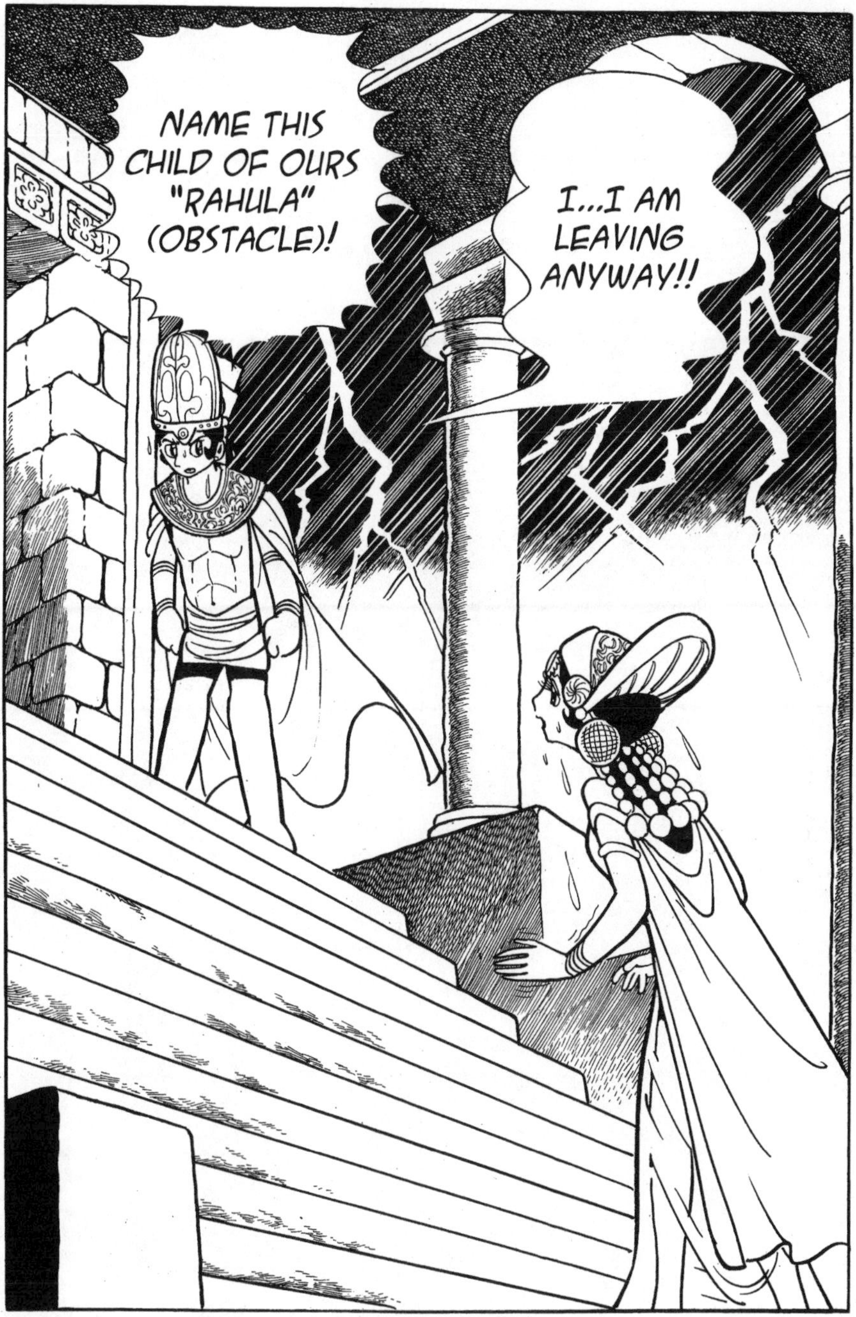
NAME THIS CHILD OF OURS "RAHULA" (OBSTACLE)!
I...I AM LEAVING ANYWAY!!

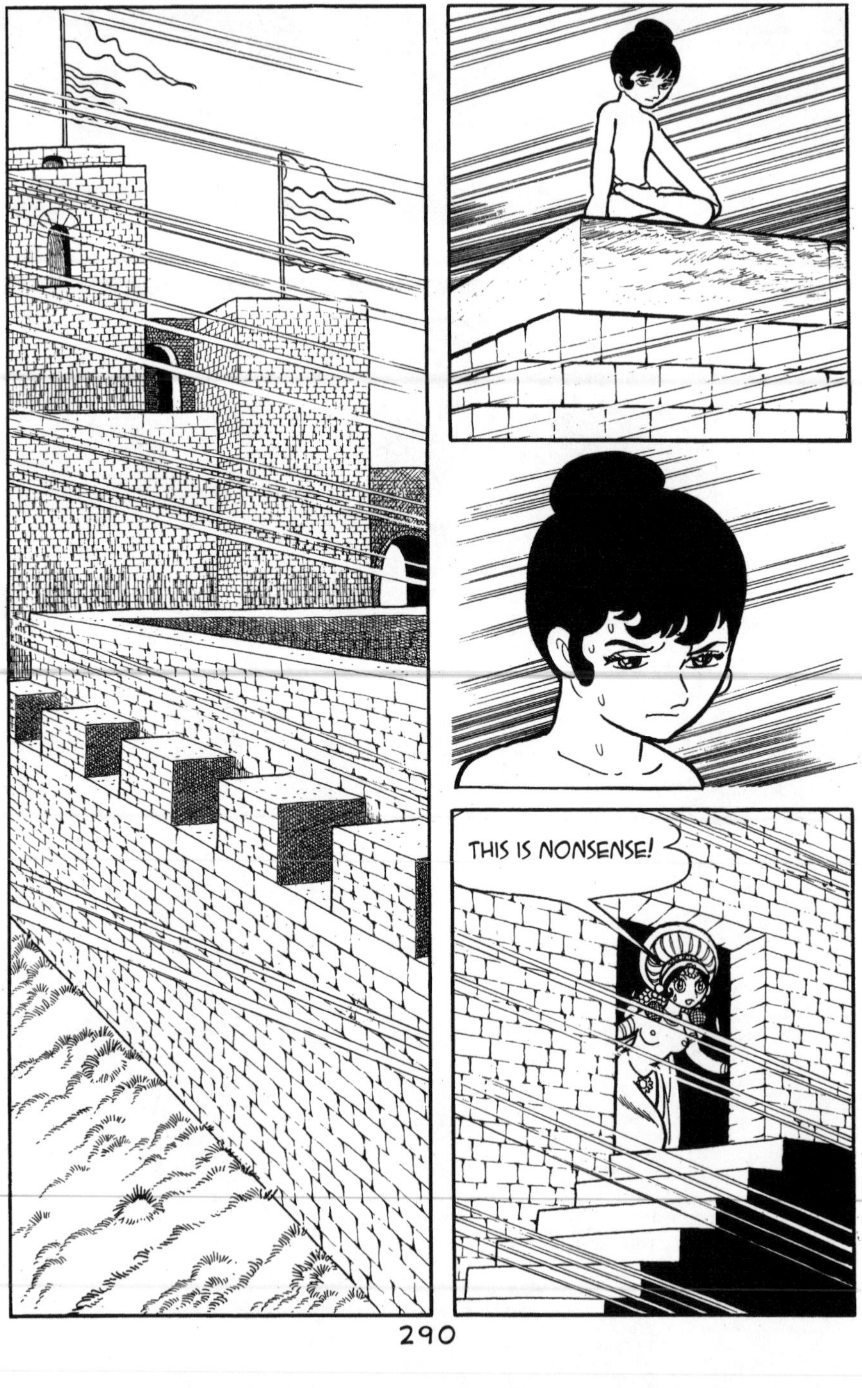
THIS IS NONSENSE!

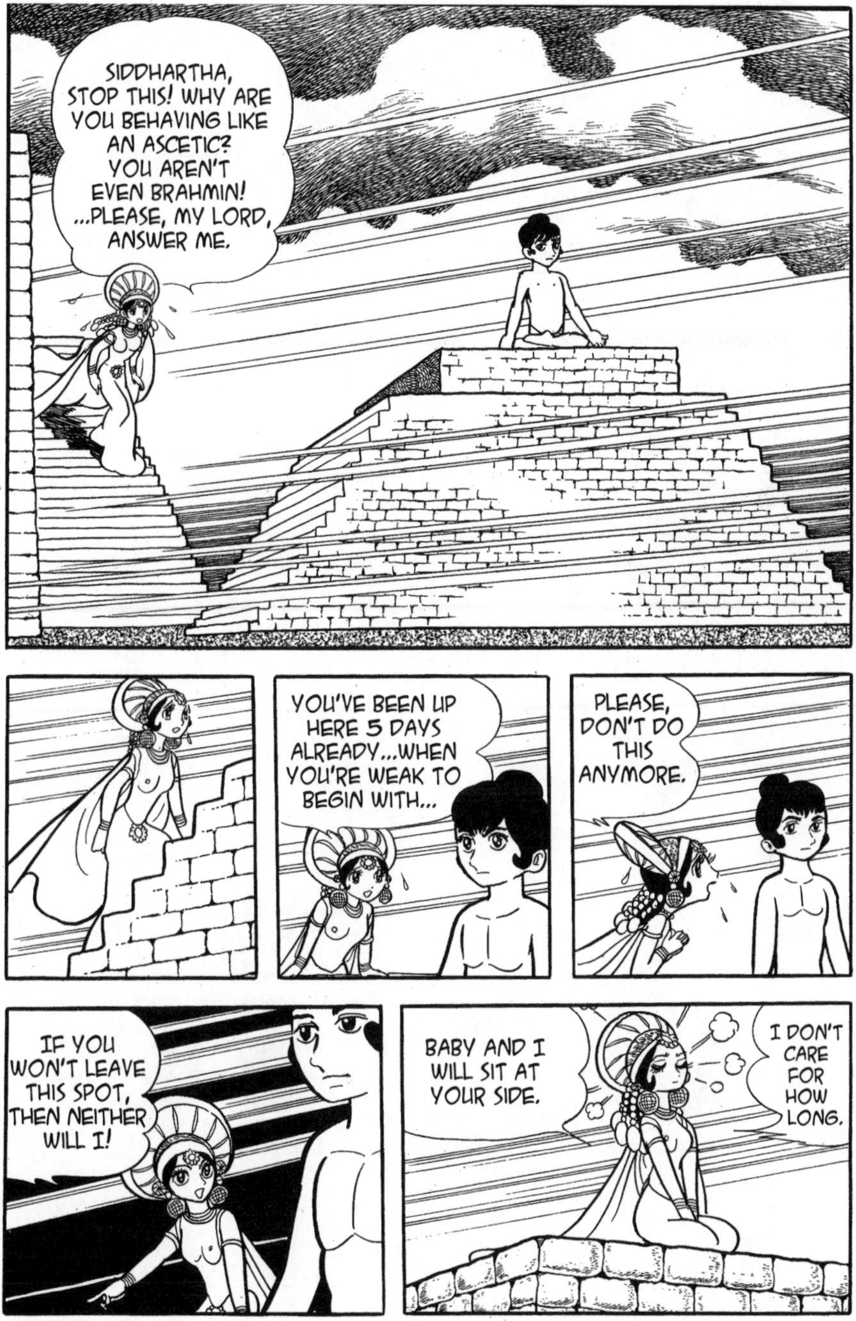
SIDDHARTHA, STOP THIS! WHY ARE YOU BEHAVING LIKE AN ASCETIC? YOU AREN'T EVEN BRAHMIN! ...PLEASE, MY LORD, ANSWER ME.
YOU'VE BEEN UP HERE 5 DAYS ALREADY...WHEN YOU'RE WEAK TO BEGIN WITH...
PLEASE, DON'T DO THIS ANYMORE.
IF YOU WON'T LEAVE THIS SPOT, THEN NEITHER WILL I!
BABY AND I WILL SIT AT YOUR SIDE.
I DON'T CARE FOR HOW LONG.

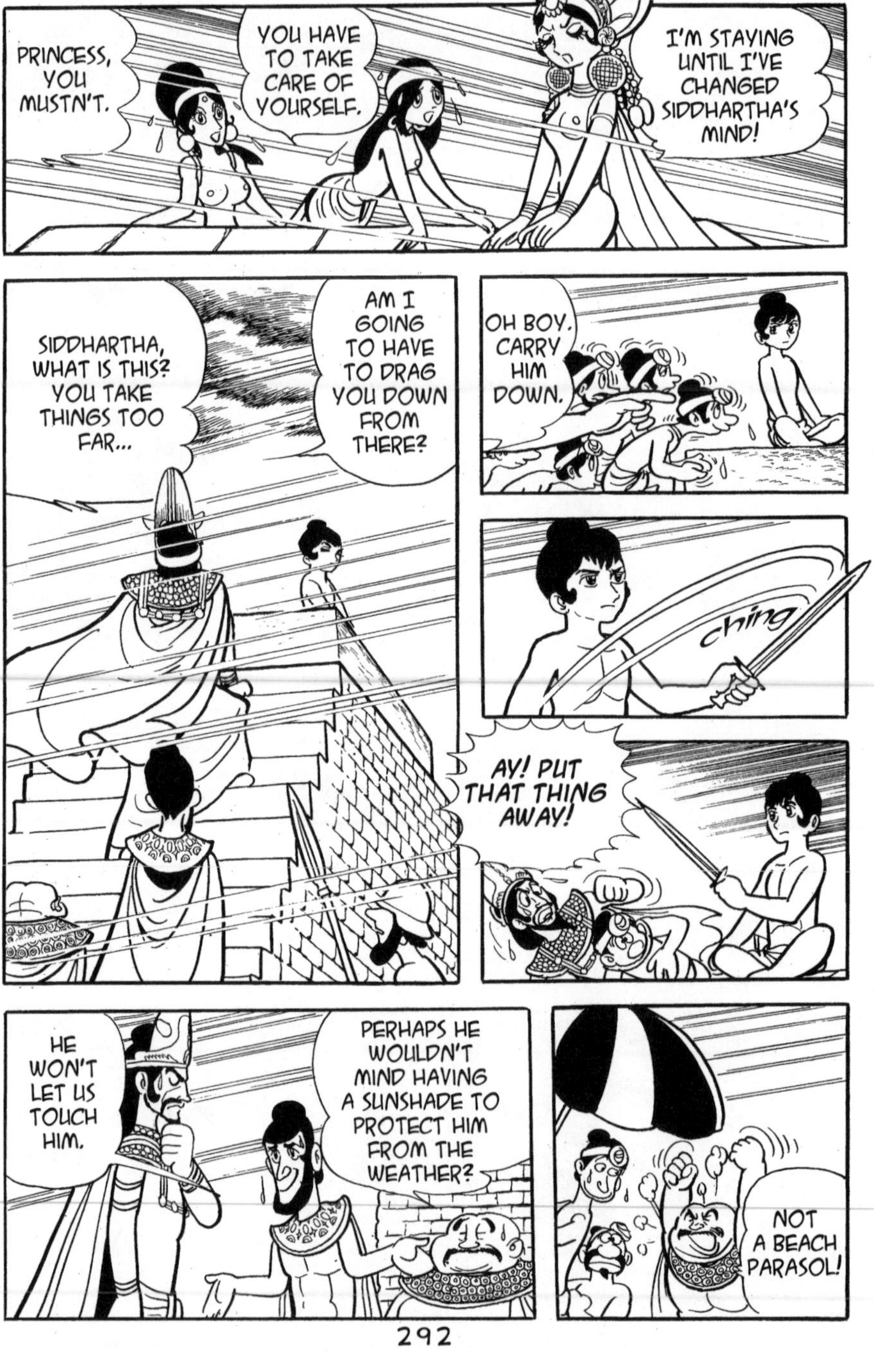
PRINCESS, YOU MUSTN'T.
YOU HAVE TO TAKE CARE OF YOURSELF.
I'M STAYING UNTIL I'VE CHANGED SIDDHARTHA'S MIND!
SIDDHARTHA, WHAT IS THIS? YOU TAKE THINGS TOO FAR...
AM I GOING TO HAVE TO DRAG YOU DOWN FROM THERE?
OH BOY. CARRY HIM DOWN.
ching
AY! PUT THAT THING AWAY!
HE WON'T LET US TOUCH HIM.
PERHAPS HE WOULDN'T MIND HAVING A SUNSHADE TO PROTECT HIM FROM THE WEATHER?
NOT A BEACH PARASOL!

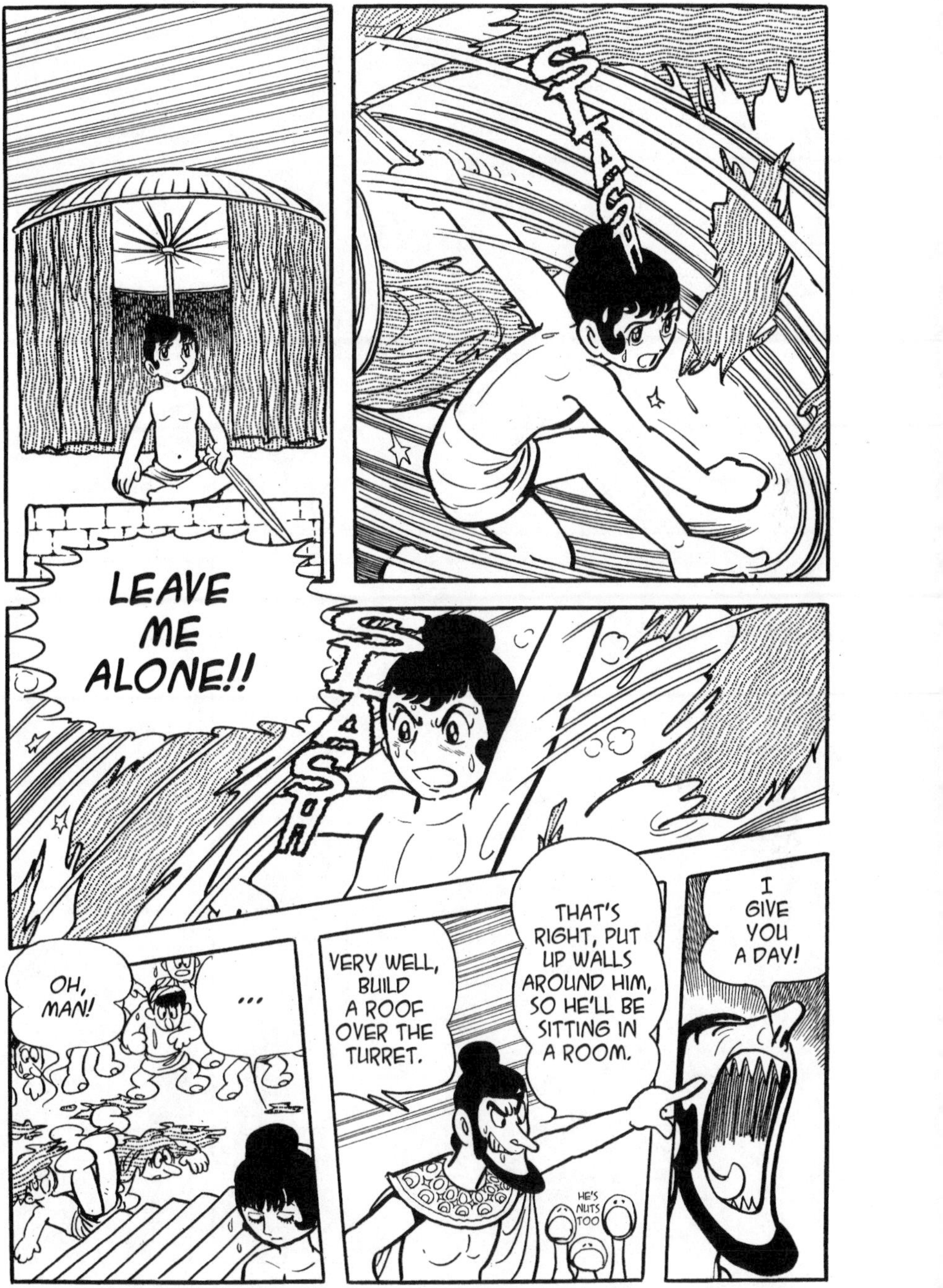
SLASH
LEAVE ME ALONE!!
SLASH
OH, MAN!
...
VERY WELL, BUILD A ROOF OVER THE TURRET.
THAT'S RIGHT, PUT UP WALLS AROUND HIM, SO HE'LL BE SITTING IN A ROOM.
HE'S NUTS TOO
I GIVE YOU A DAY!

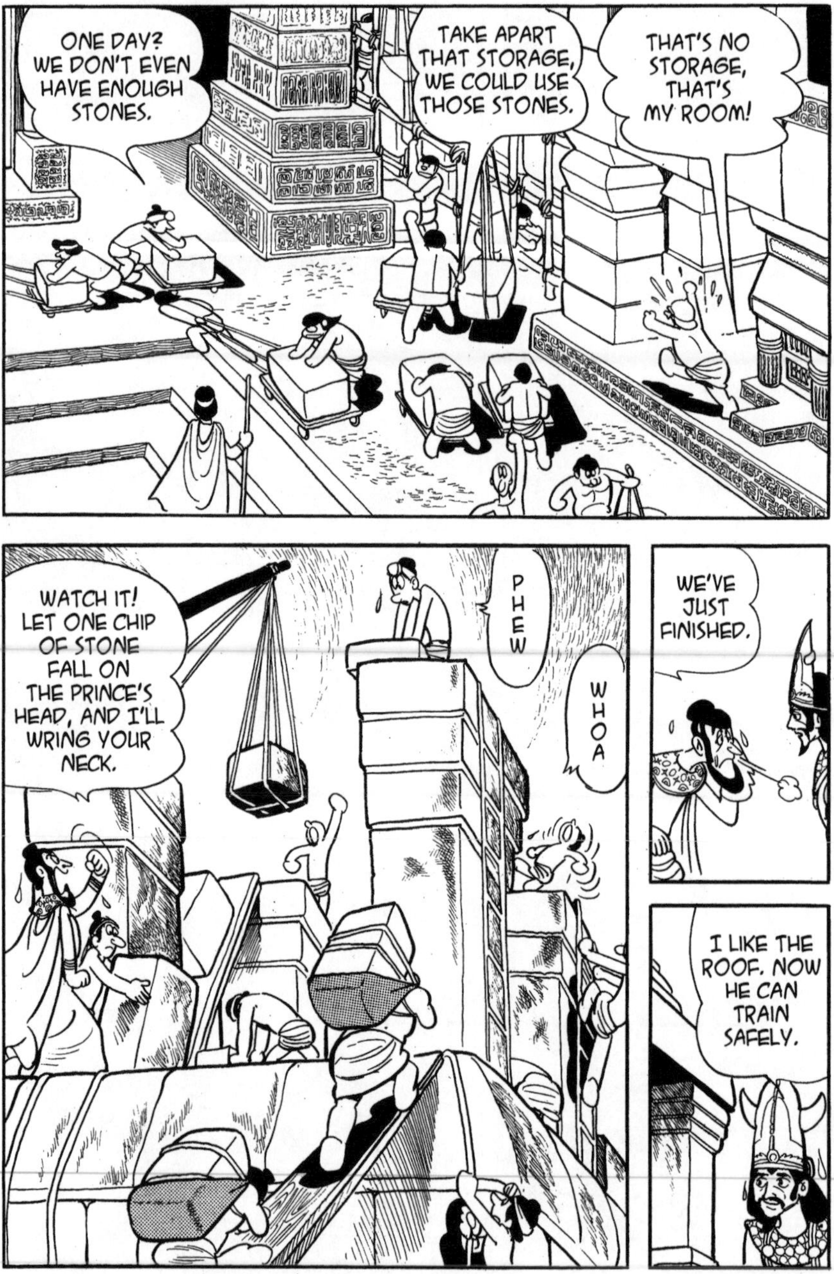
ONE DAY? WE DON'T EVEN HAVE ENOUGH STONES.
TAKE APART THAT STORAGE, WE COULD USE THOSE STONES.
THAT'S NO STORAGE, THAT'S MY ROOM!
WATCH IT! LET ONE CHIP OF STONE FALL ON THE PRINCE'S HEAD, AND I'LL WRING YOUR NECK.
PHEW
WHOA
WE'VE JUST FINISHED.
I LIKE THE ROOF. NOW HE CAN TRAIN SAFELY.

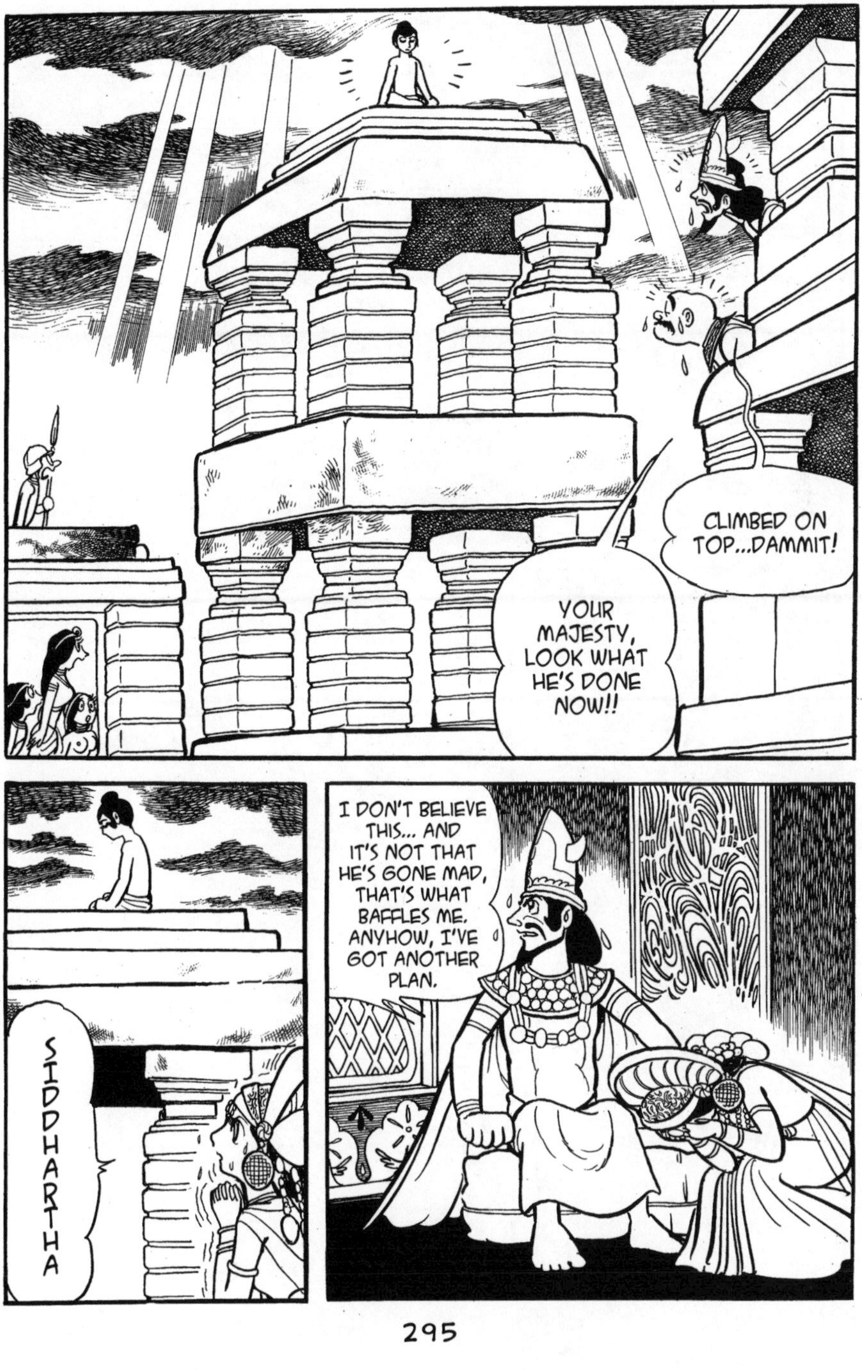
CLIMBED ON TOP...DAMMIT!
YOUR MAJESTY, LOOK WHAT HE'S DONE NOW!!
SIDDHARTHA
I DON'T BELIEVE THIS... AND IT'S NOT THAT HE'S GONE MAD, THAT'S WHAT BAFFLES ME. ANYHOW, I'VE GOT ANOTHER PLAN.

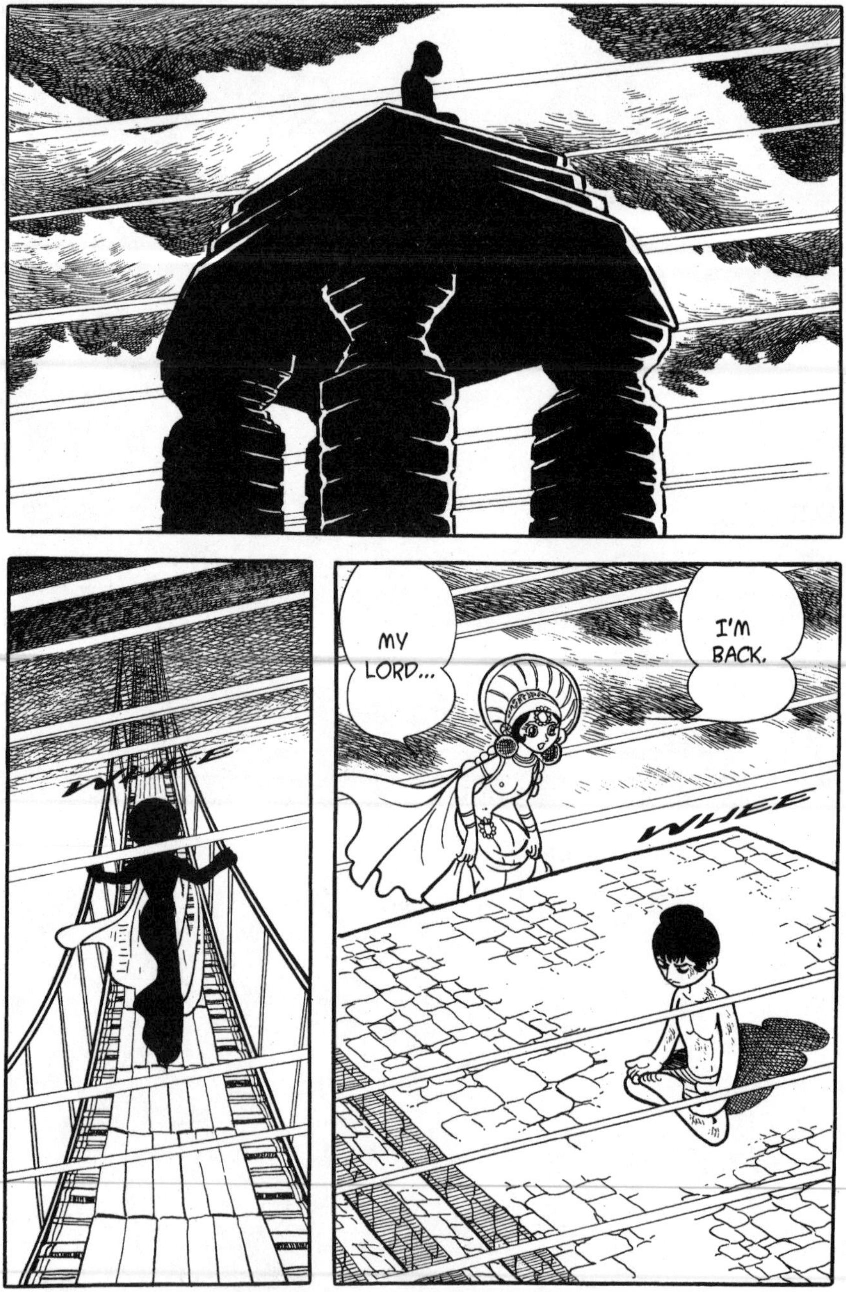
WHEE
MY LORD...
I'M BACK.
WHEE

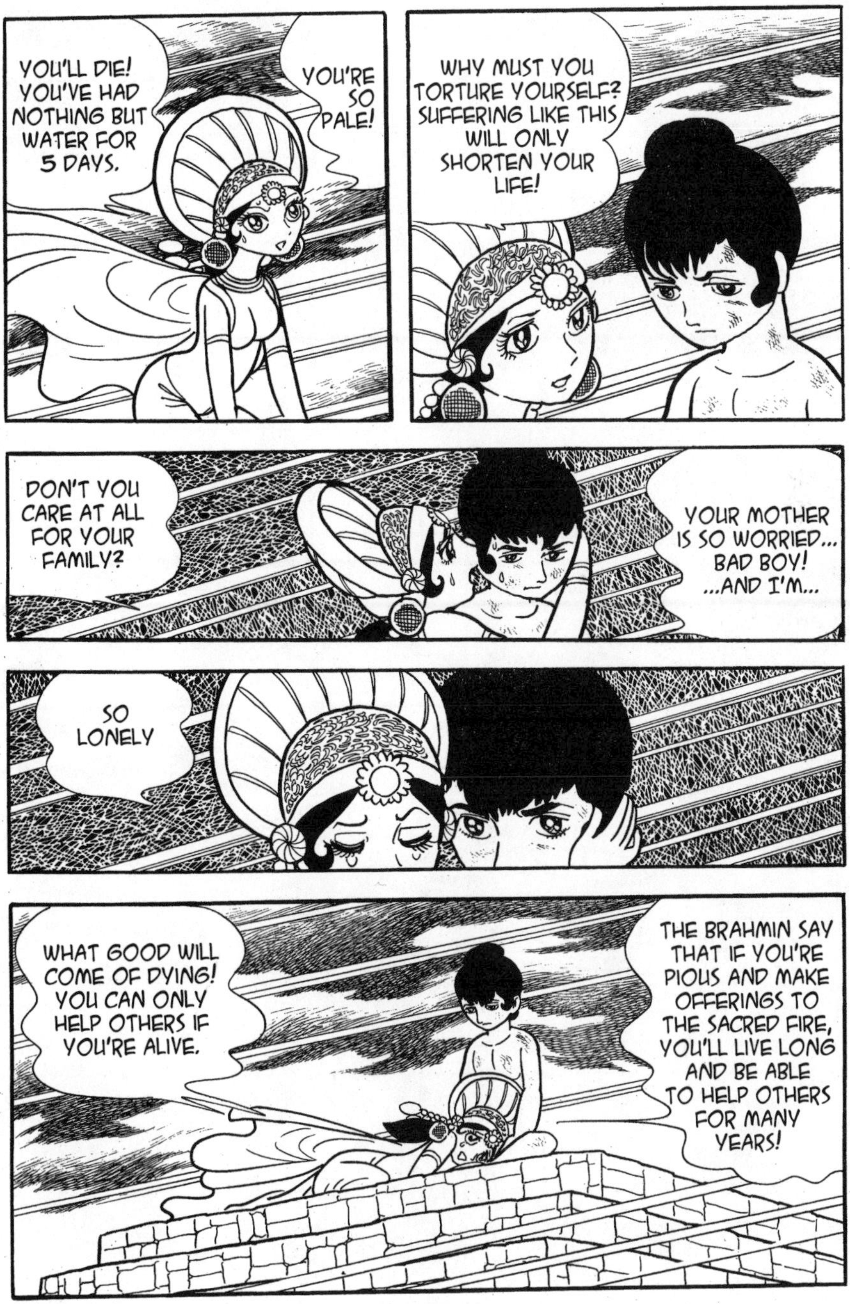

YOU'LL DIE! YOU'VE HAD NOTHING BUT WATER FOR 5 DAYS.
YOU'RE SO PALE!
WHY MUST YOU TORTURE YOURSELF? SUFFERING LIKE THIS WILL ONLY SHORTEN YOUR LIFE!
DON'T YOU CARE AT ALL FOR YOUR FAMILY?
YOUR MOTHER IS SO WORRIED... BAD BOY! ...AND I'M...
SO LONELY
WHAT GOOD WILL COME OF DYING! YOU CAN ONLY HELP OTHERS IF YOU'RE ALIVE.
THE BRAHMIN SAY THAT IF YOU'RE PIOUS AND MAKE OFFERINGS TO THE SACRED FIRE, YOU'LL LIVE LONG AND BE ABLE TO HELP OTHERS FOR MANY YEARS!

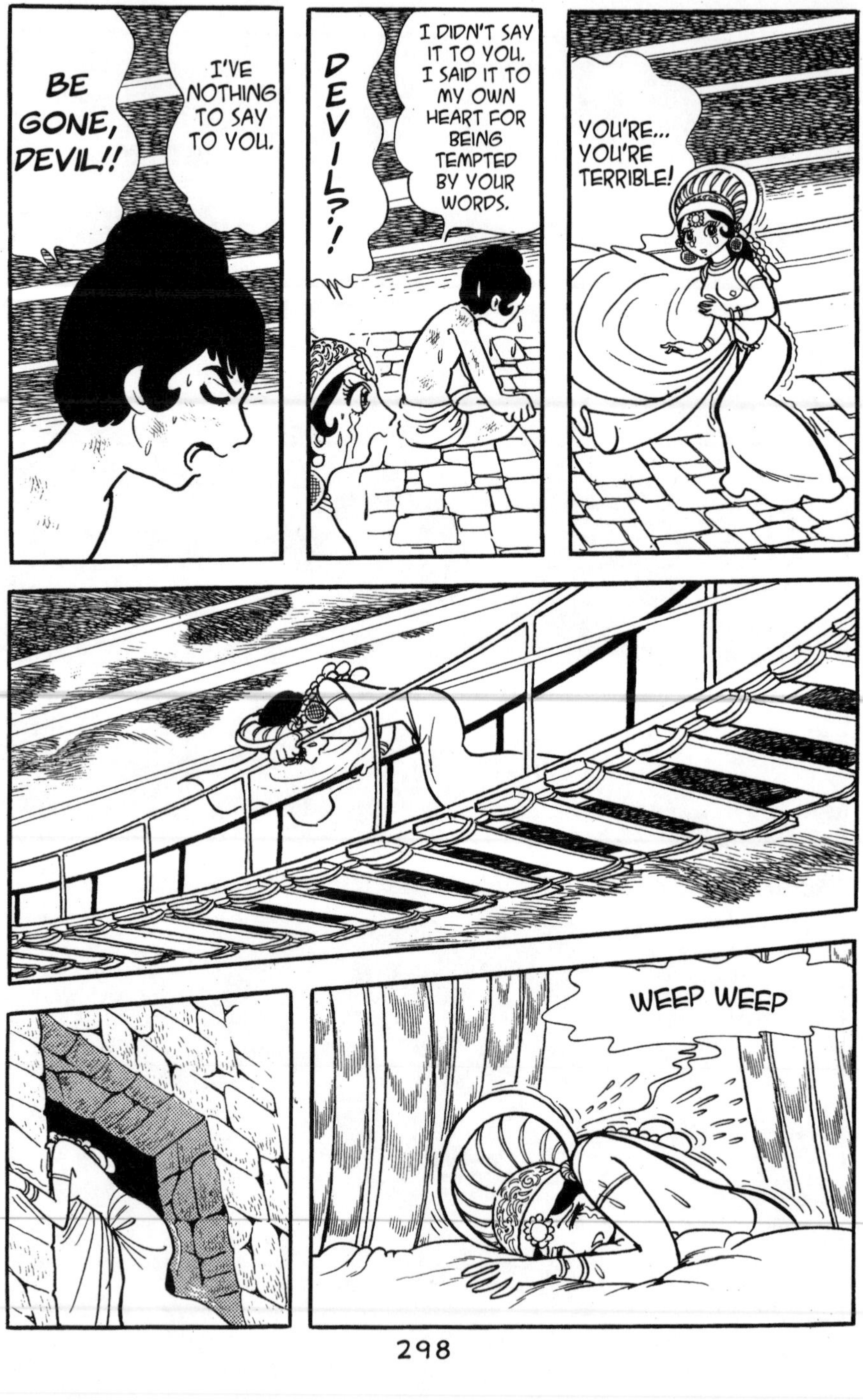
BE GONE, DEVIL!!
I'VE NOTHING TO SAY TO YOU.
DEVIL?!
I DIDN'T SAY IT TO YOU. I SAID IT TO MY OWN HEART FOR BEING TEMPTED BY YOUR WORDS.
YOU'RE... YOU'RE TERRIBLE!
WEEP WEEP

CHAPTER EIGHT

THE FIVE ASCETICS

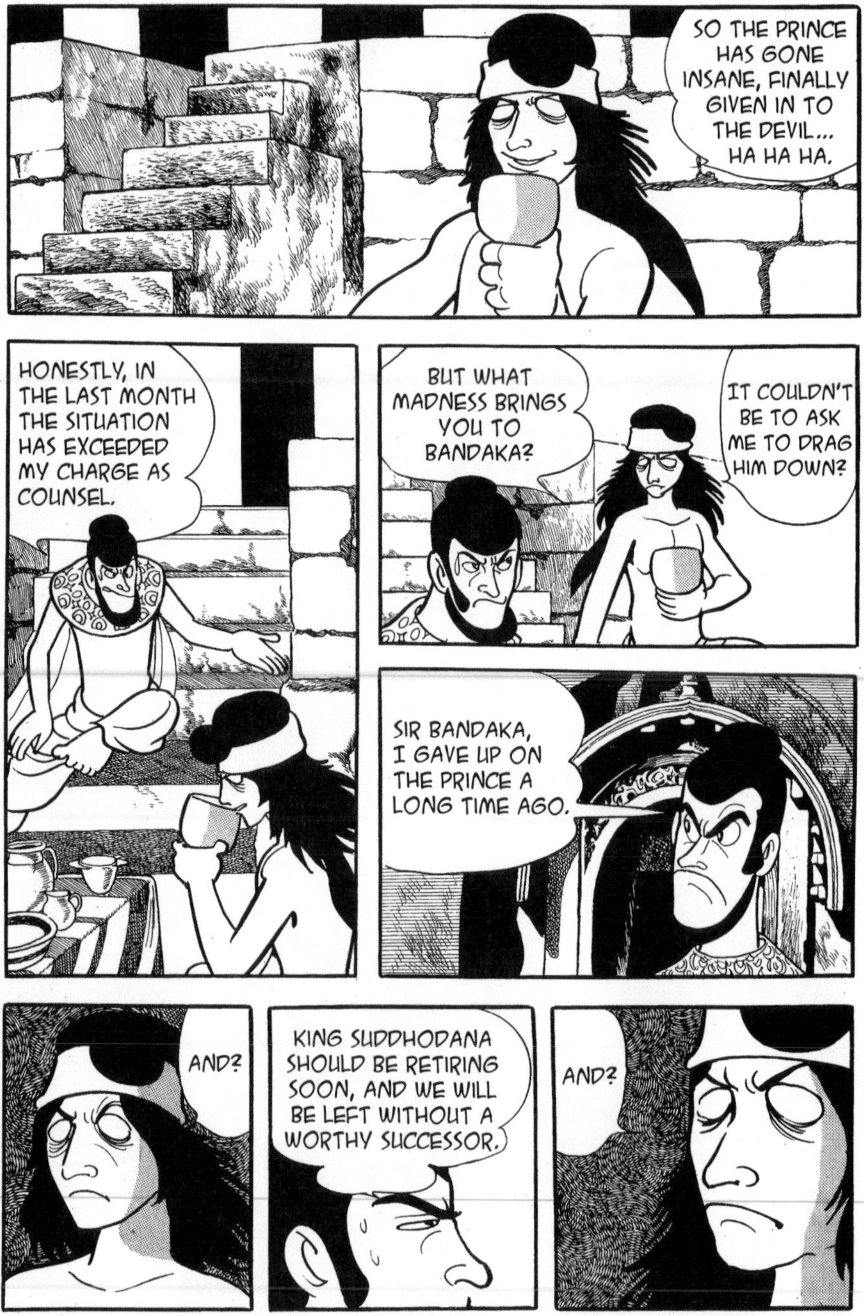
SO THE PRINCE HAS GONE INSANE, FINALLY GIVEN IN TO THE DEVIL... HA HA HA.
HONESTLY, IN THE LAST MONTH THE SITUATION HAS EXCEEDED MY CHARGE AS COUNSEL.
BUT WHAT MADNESS BRINGS YOU TO BANDAKA?
IT COULDN'T BE TO ASK ME TO DRAG HIM DOWN?
SIR BANDAKA, I GAVE UP ON THE PRINCE A LONG TIME AGO.
AND?
KING SUDDHODANA SHOULD BE RETIRING SOON, AND WE WILL BE LEFT WITHOUT A WORTHY SUCCESSOR.
AND?

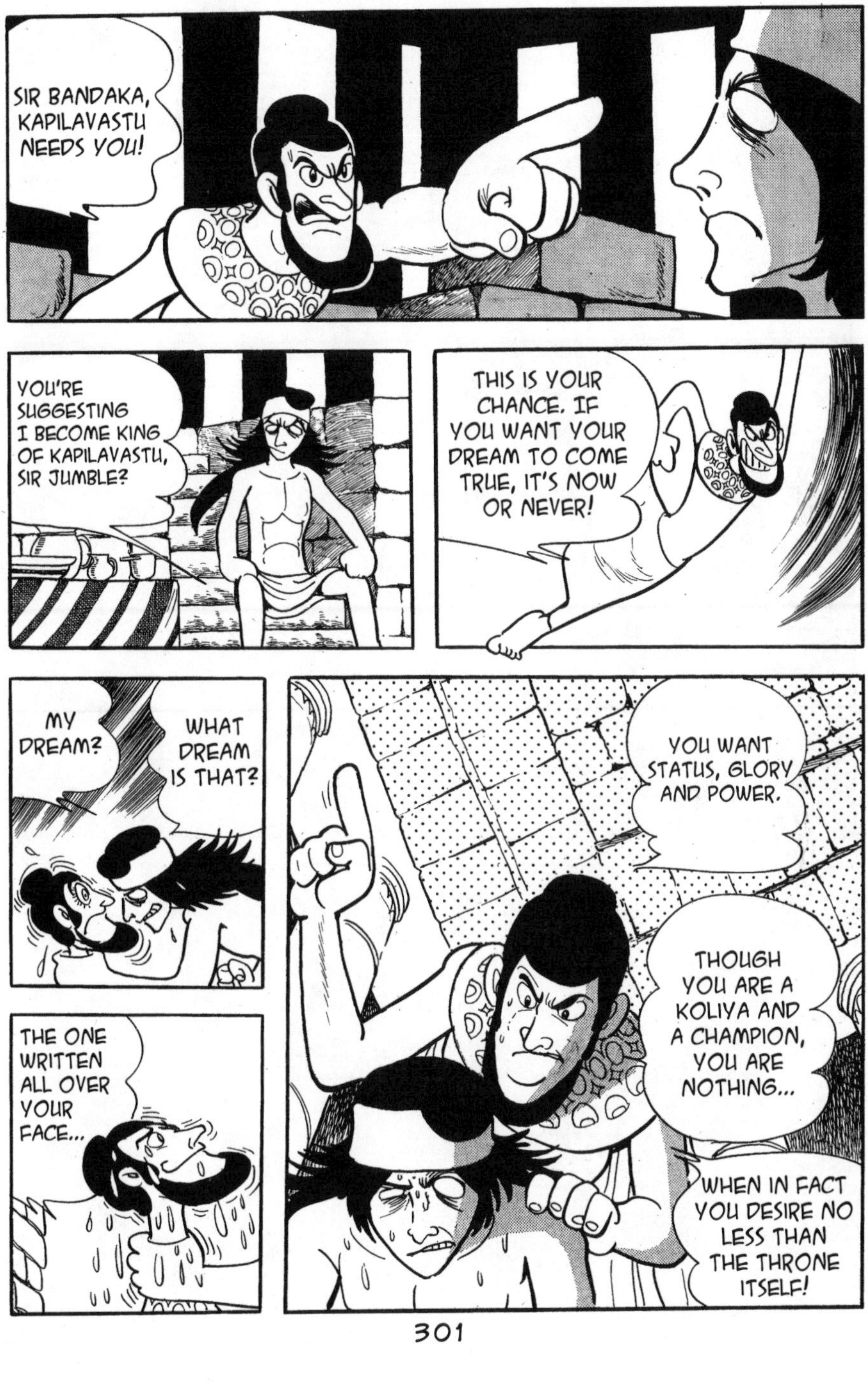
SIR BANDAKA, KAPILAVASTU NEEDS YOU!
YOU'RE SUGGESTING I BECOME KING OF KAPILAVASTU, SIR JUMBLE?
THIS IS YOUR CHANCE. IF YOU WANT YOUR DREAM TO COME TRUE, IT'S NOW OR NEVER!
MY DREAM?
WHAT DREAM IS THAT?
THE ONE WRITTEN ALL OVER YOUR FACE...
YOU WANT STATUS, GLORY AND POWER.
THOUGH YOU ARE A KOLIYA AND A CHAMPION, YOU ARE NOTHING...
WHEN IN FACT YOU DESIRE NO LESS THAN THE THRONE ITSELF!

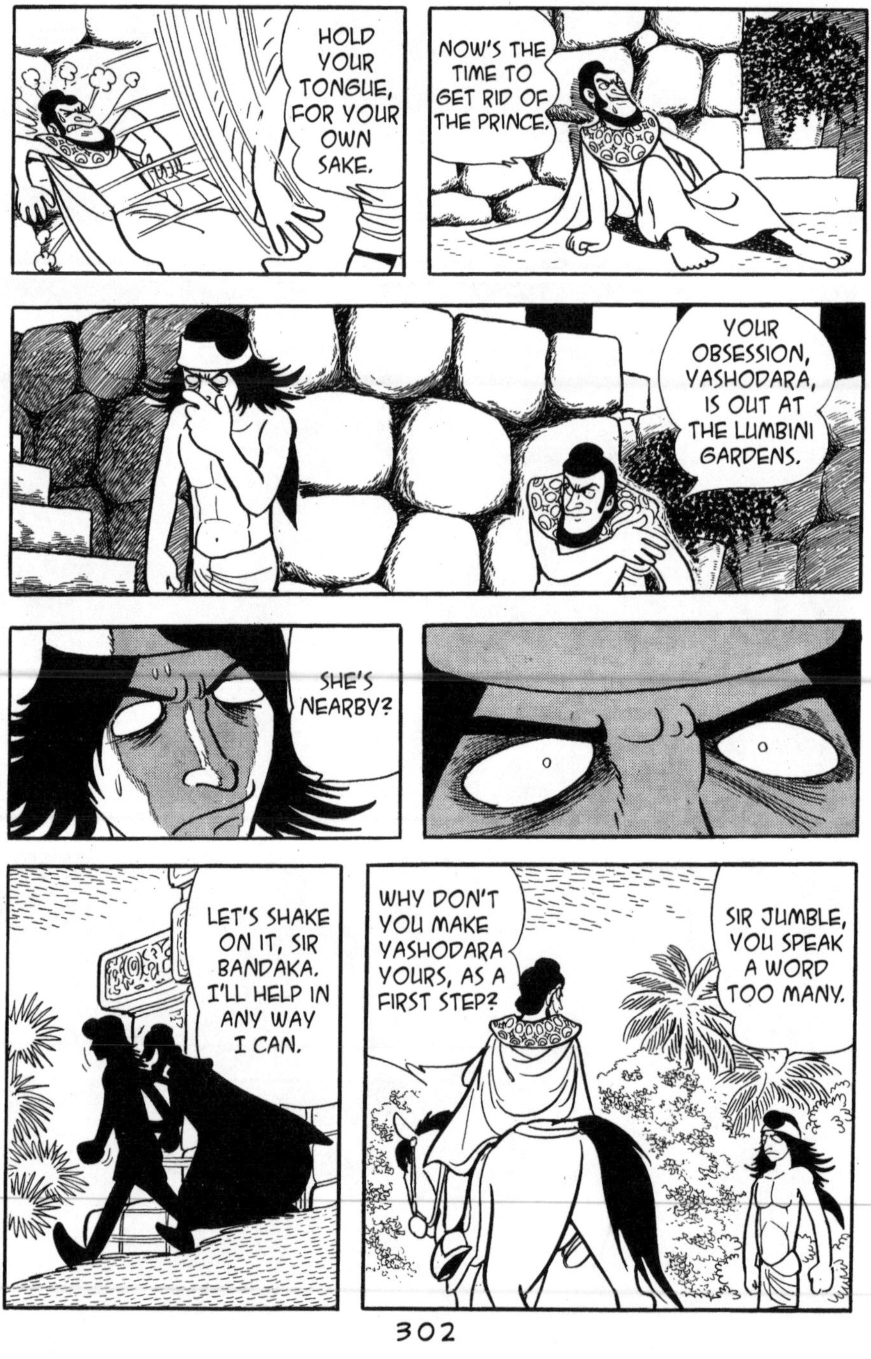
HOLD YOUR TONGUE, FOR YOUR OWN SAKE.
NOW'S THE TIME TO GET RID OF THE PRINCE.
YOUR OBSESSION, YASHODARA, IS OUT AT THE LUMBINI GARDENS.
SHE'S NEARBY?
LET'S SHAKE ON IT, SIR BANDAKA. I'LL HELP IN ANY WAY I CAN.
WHY DON'T YOU MAKE YASHODARA YOURS, AS A FIRST STEP?
SIR JUMBLE, YOU SPEAK A WORD TOO MANY.

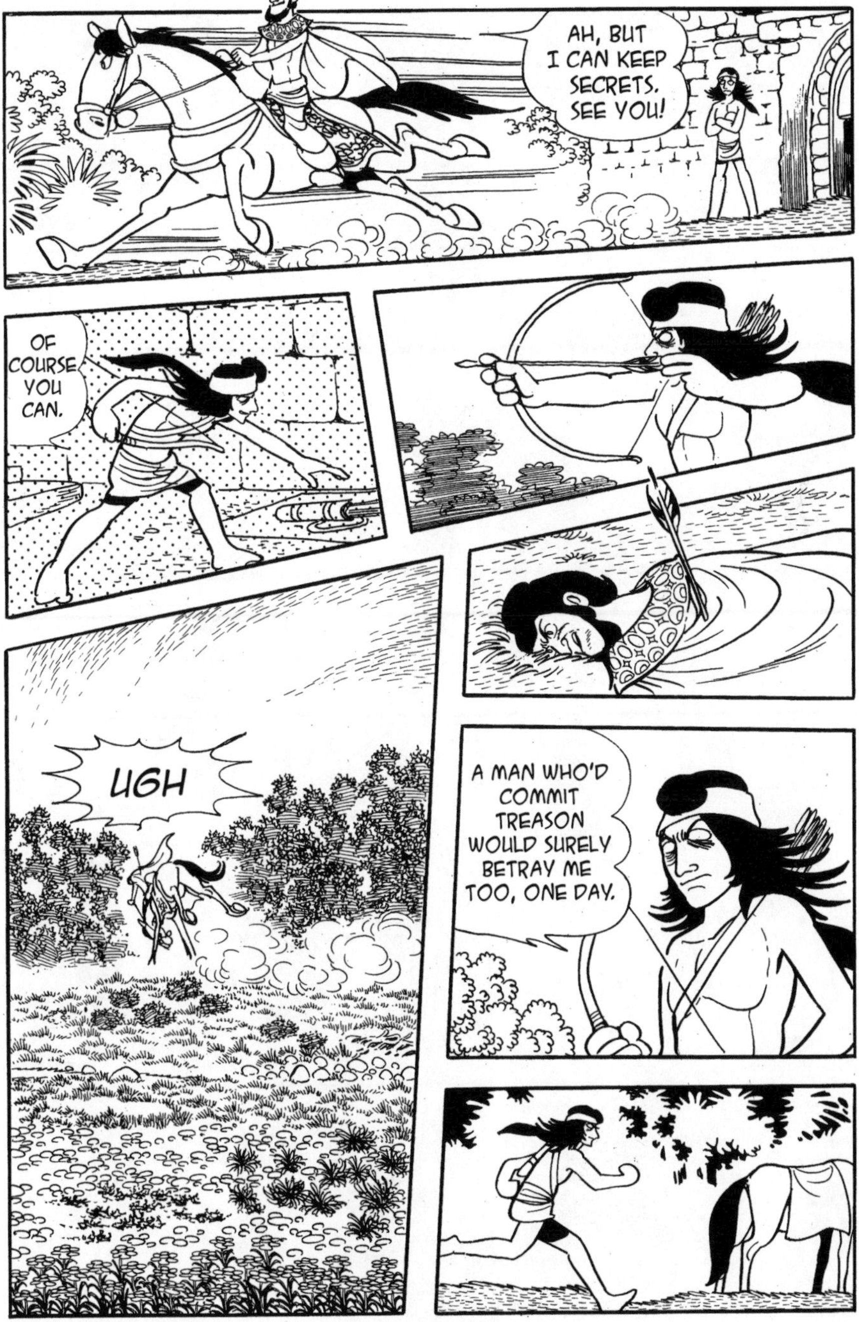
AH, BUT I CAN KEEP SECRETS. SEE YOU!
OF COURSE YOU CAN.
UGH
A MAN WHO'D COMMIT TREASON WOULD SURELY BETRAY ME TOO, ONE DAY.

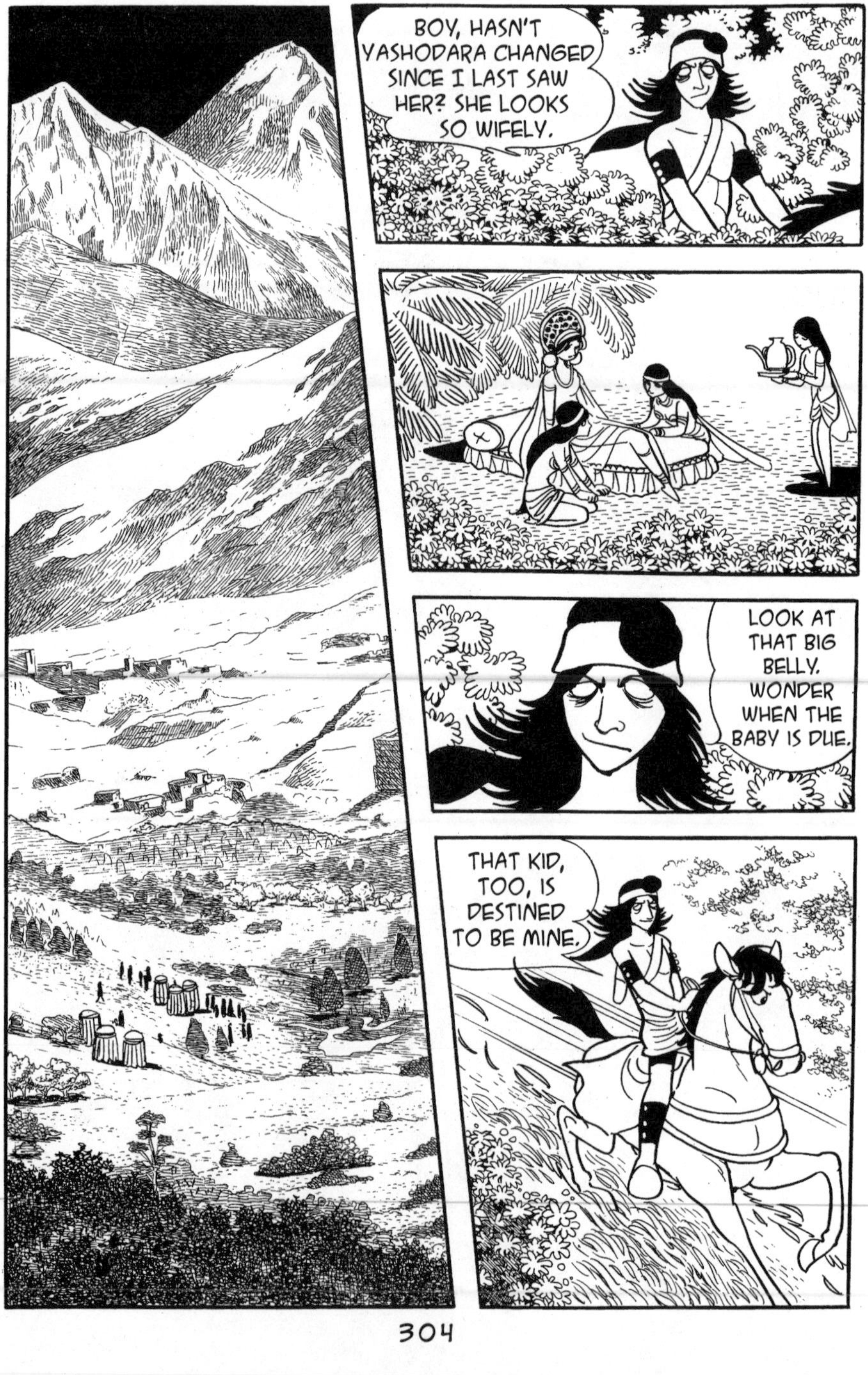
BOY, HASN'T YASHODARA CHANGED SINCE I LAST SAW HER? SHE LOOKS SO WIFELY.
LOOK AT THAT BIG BELLY. WONDER WHEN THE BABY IS DUE.
THAT KID, TOO, IS DESTINED TO BE MINE.

OH DEAR, IT'S SIR BANDAKA.

I'M SCARED...

SIR BANDAKA IS HERE...

REALLY?

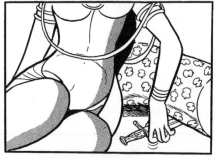

YASHODARA!

I HEARD ABOUT SIDDHARTHA. AH, I CAN SEE YOU'RE IN PAIN. IT'S NOT GOOD FOR THE BABY.

I HAVE NOTHING TO SAY TO YOU, IT'S NONE OF YOUR BUSINESS.

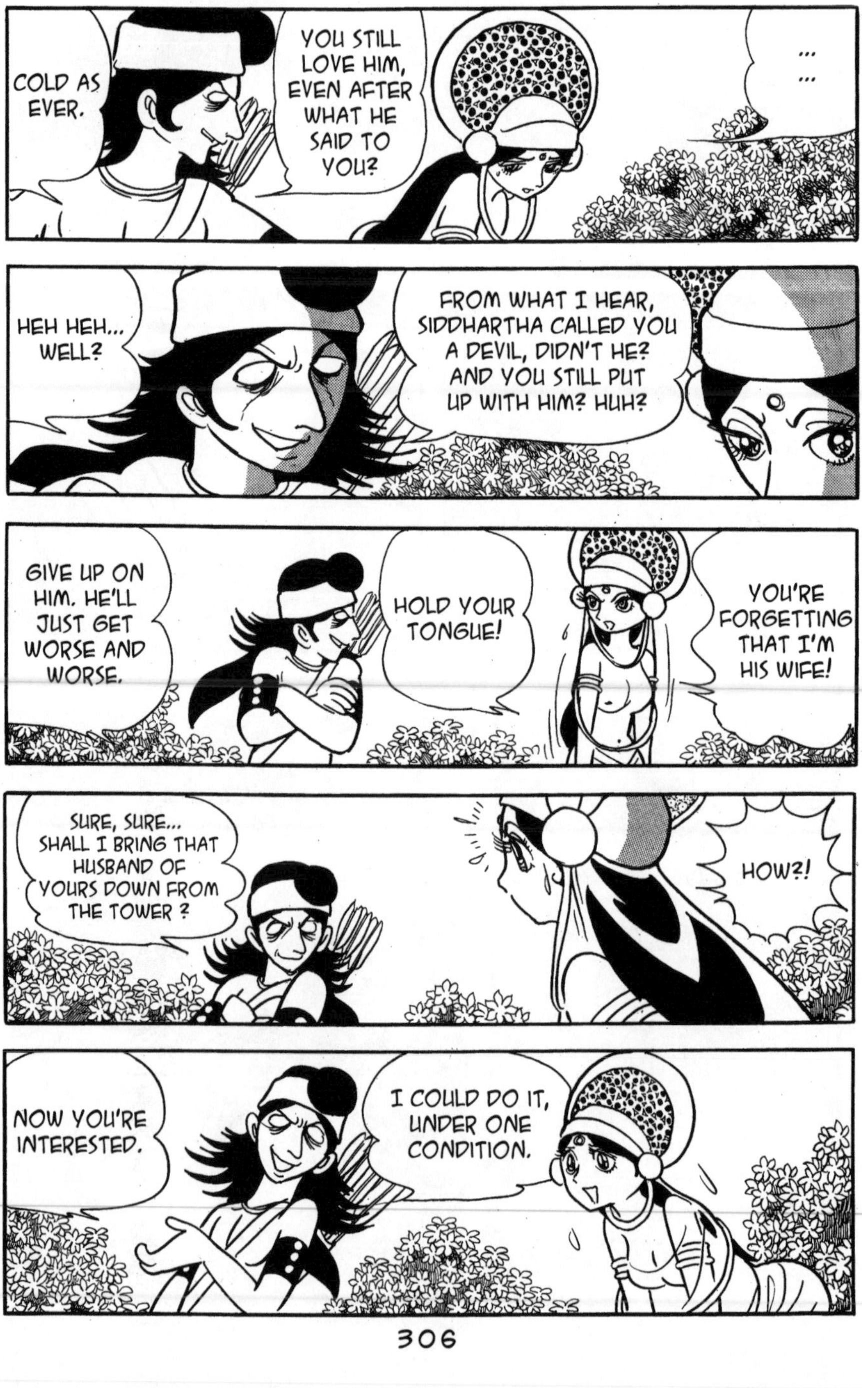
COLD AS EVER.
YOU STILL LOVE HIM, EVEN AFTER WHAT HE SAID TO YOU?
... ...
HEH HEH... WELL?
FROM WHAT I HEAR, SIDDHARTHA CALLED YOU A DEVIL, DIDN'T HE? AND YOU STILL PUT UP WITH HIM? HUH?
GIVE UP ON HIM. HE'LL JUST GET WORSE AND WORSE.
HOLD YOUR TONGUE!
YOU'RE FORGETTING THAT I'M HIS WIFE!
SURE, SURE... SHALL I BRING THAT HUSBAND OF YOURS DOWN FROM THE TOWER?
HOW?!
NOW YOU'RE INTERESTED.
I COULD DO IT, UNDER ONE CONDITION.

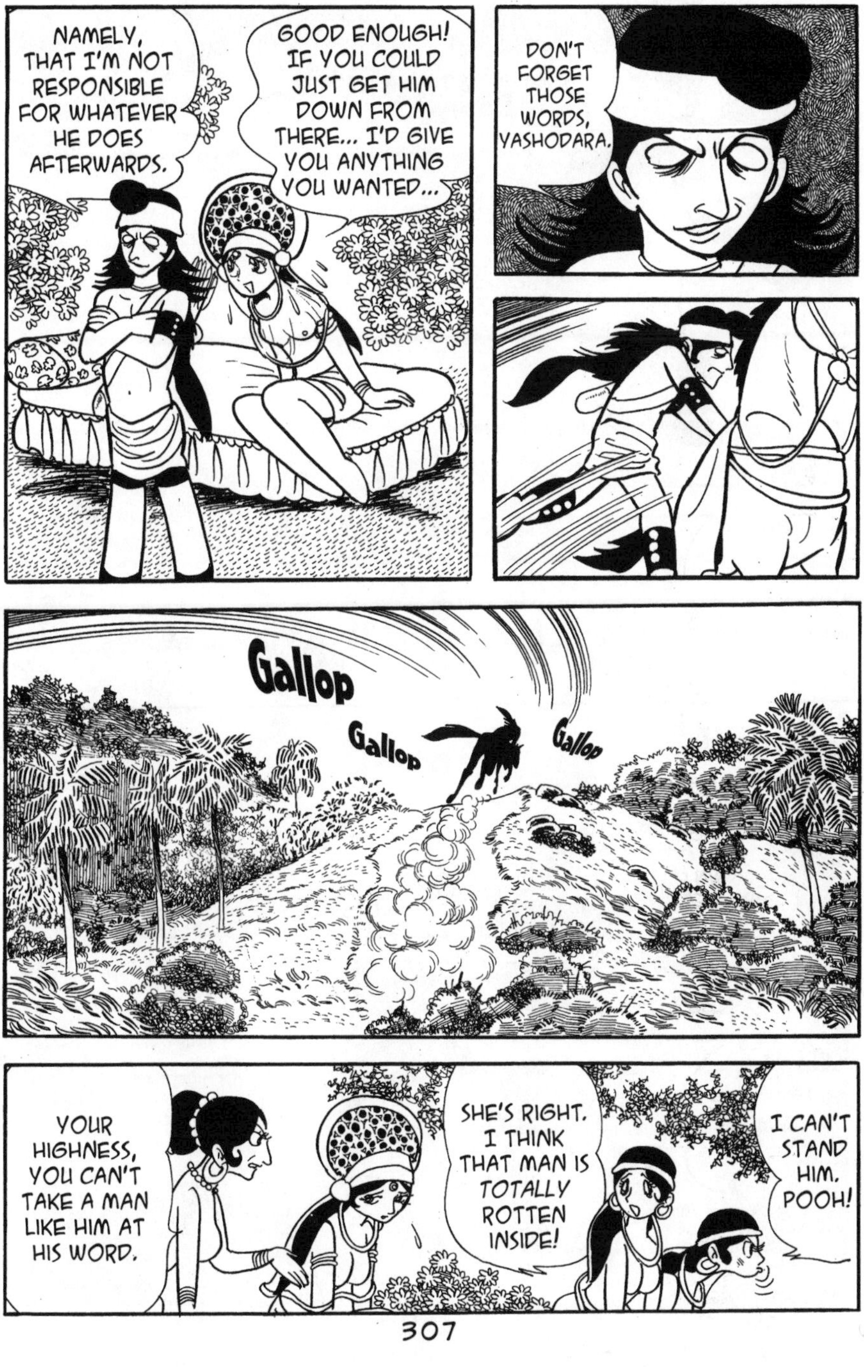
NAMELY, THAT I'M NOT RESPONSIBLE FOR WHATEVER HE DOES AFTERWARDS.
GOOD ENOUGH! IF YOU COULD JUST GET HIM DOWN FROM THERE... I'D GIVE YOU ANYTHING YOU WANTED...
DON'T FORGET THOSE WORDS, YASHODARA.
Gallop
Gallop
Gallop
YOUR HIGHNESS, YOU CAN'T TAKE A MAN LIKE HIM AT HIS WORD.
SHE'S RIGHT. I THINK THAT MAN IS TOTALLY ROTTEN INSIDE!
I CAN'T STAND HIM. POOH!

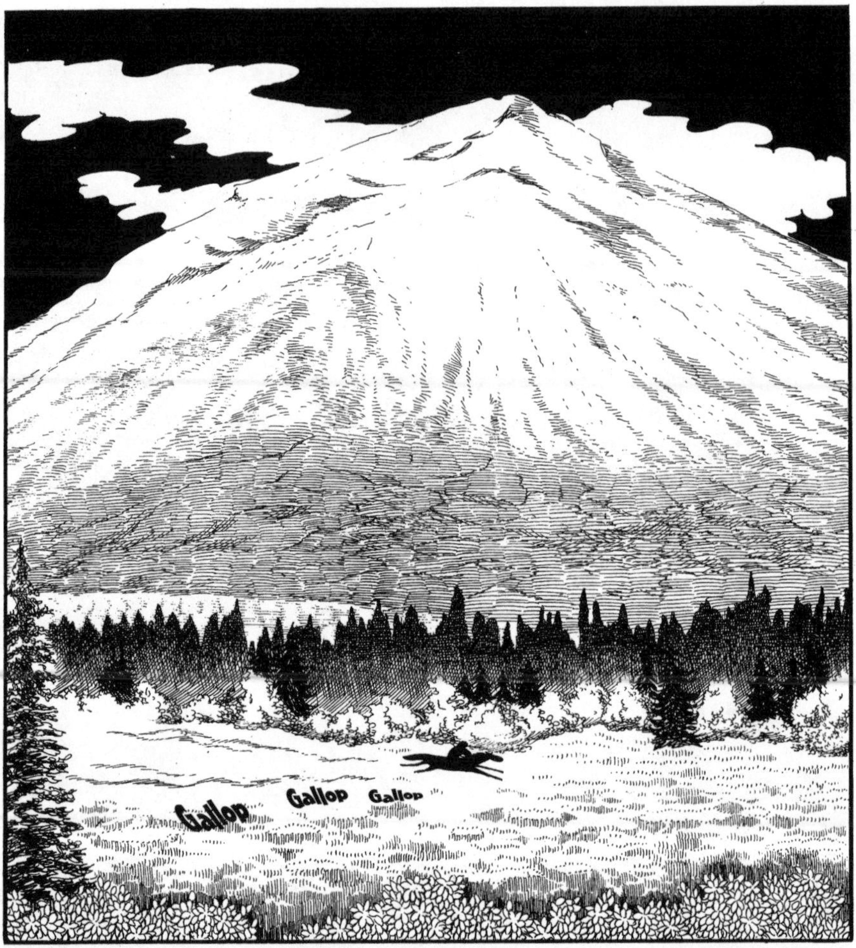
Gallop
Gallop
Gallop
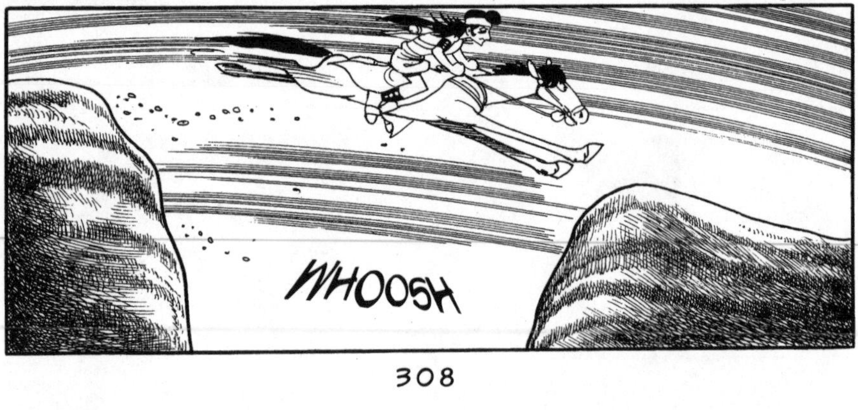
WHOOSH

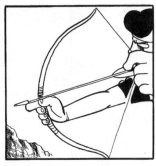

TWMACK

TWMACK

I BETTER BRING SOME GIFTS TO THOSE GUYS, HEH HEH...

Gallop Gallop Gallop

HELLO?

WHO IS IT?

IT'S ME, BANDAKA, WARRIOR OF KOLIYA!!

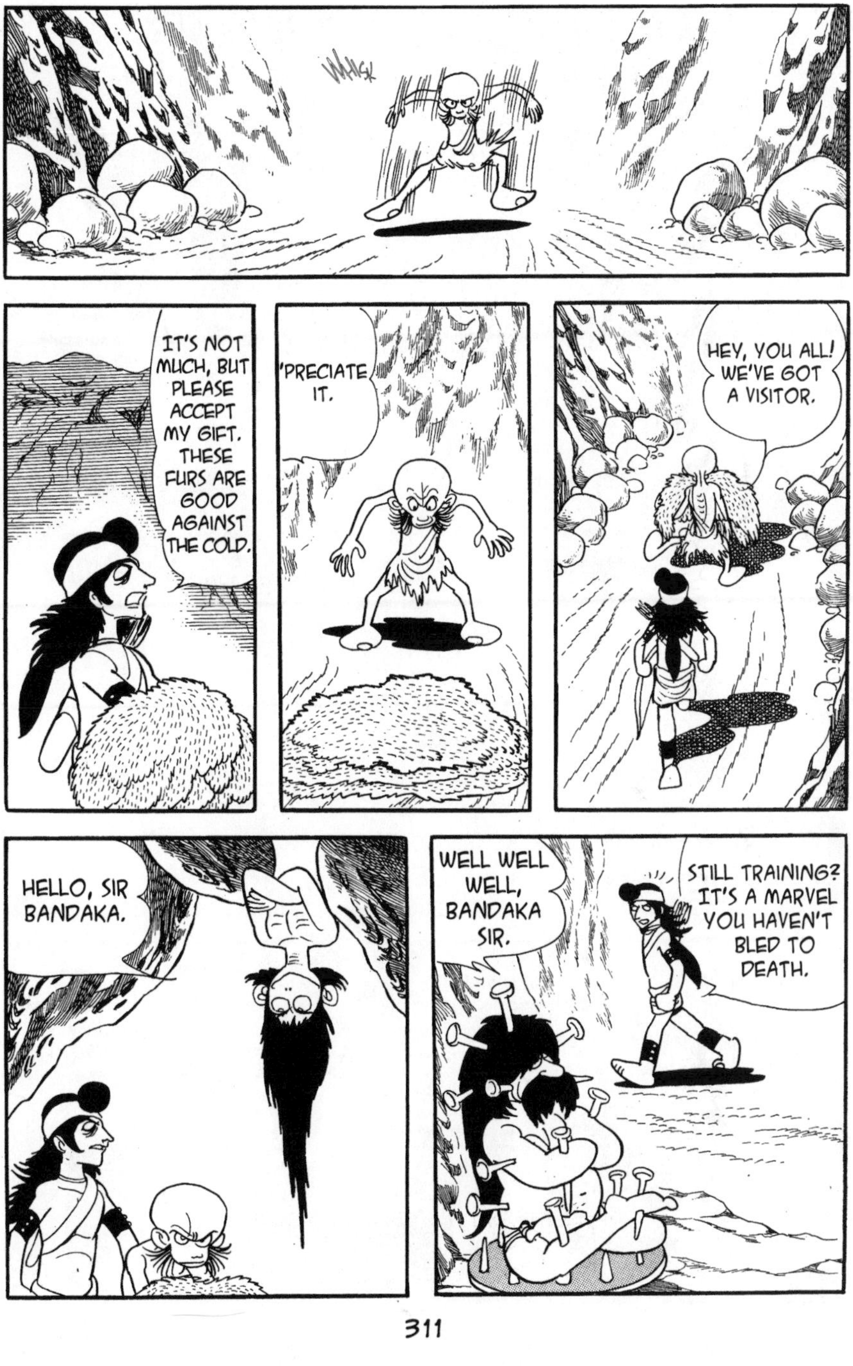
WHISK
IT'S NOT MUCH, BUT PLEASE ACCEPT MY GIFT. THESE FURS ARE GOOD AGAINST THE COLD.
'PRECIATE IT.
HEY, YOU ALL! WE'VE GOT A VISITOR.
HELLO, SIR BANDAKA.
WELL WELL WELL, BANDAKA SIR.
STILL TRAINING? IT'S A MARVEL YOU HAVEN'T BLED TO DEATH.

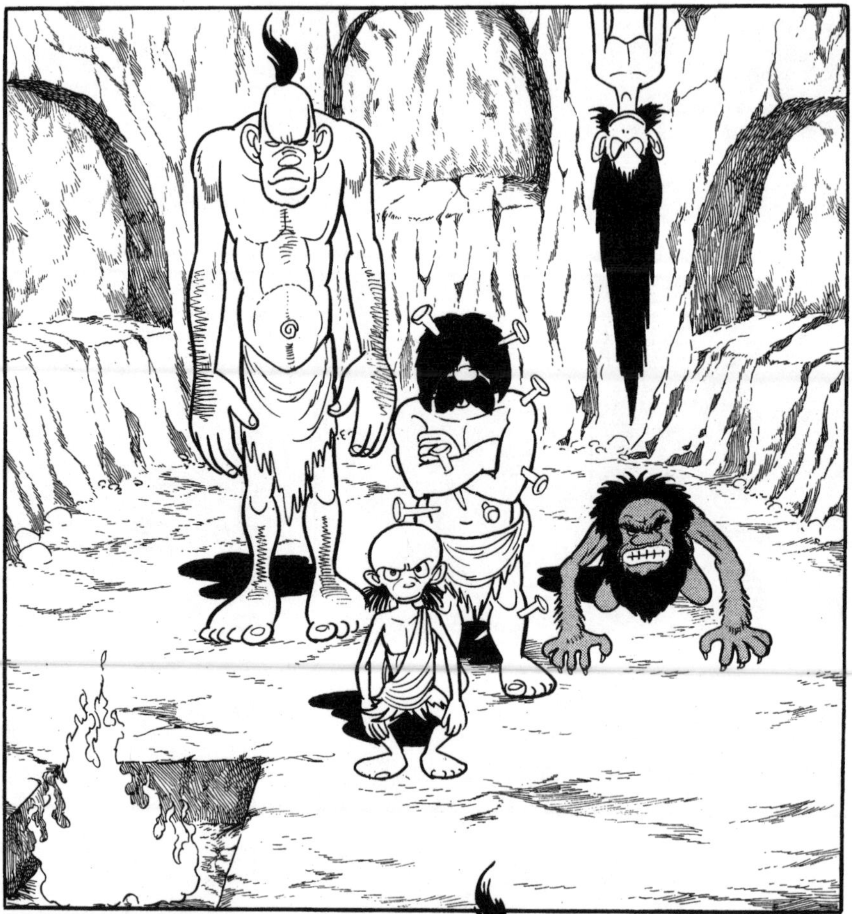

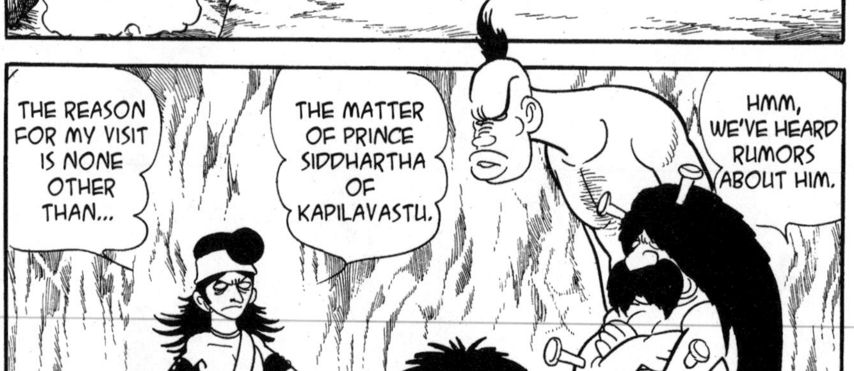
THE REASON FOR MY VISIT IS NONE OTHER THAN...
THE MATTER OF PRINCE SIDDHARTHA OF KAPILAVASTU.
HMM, WE'VE HEARD RUMORS ABOUT HIM.

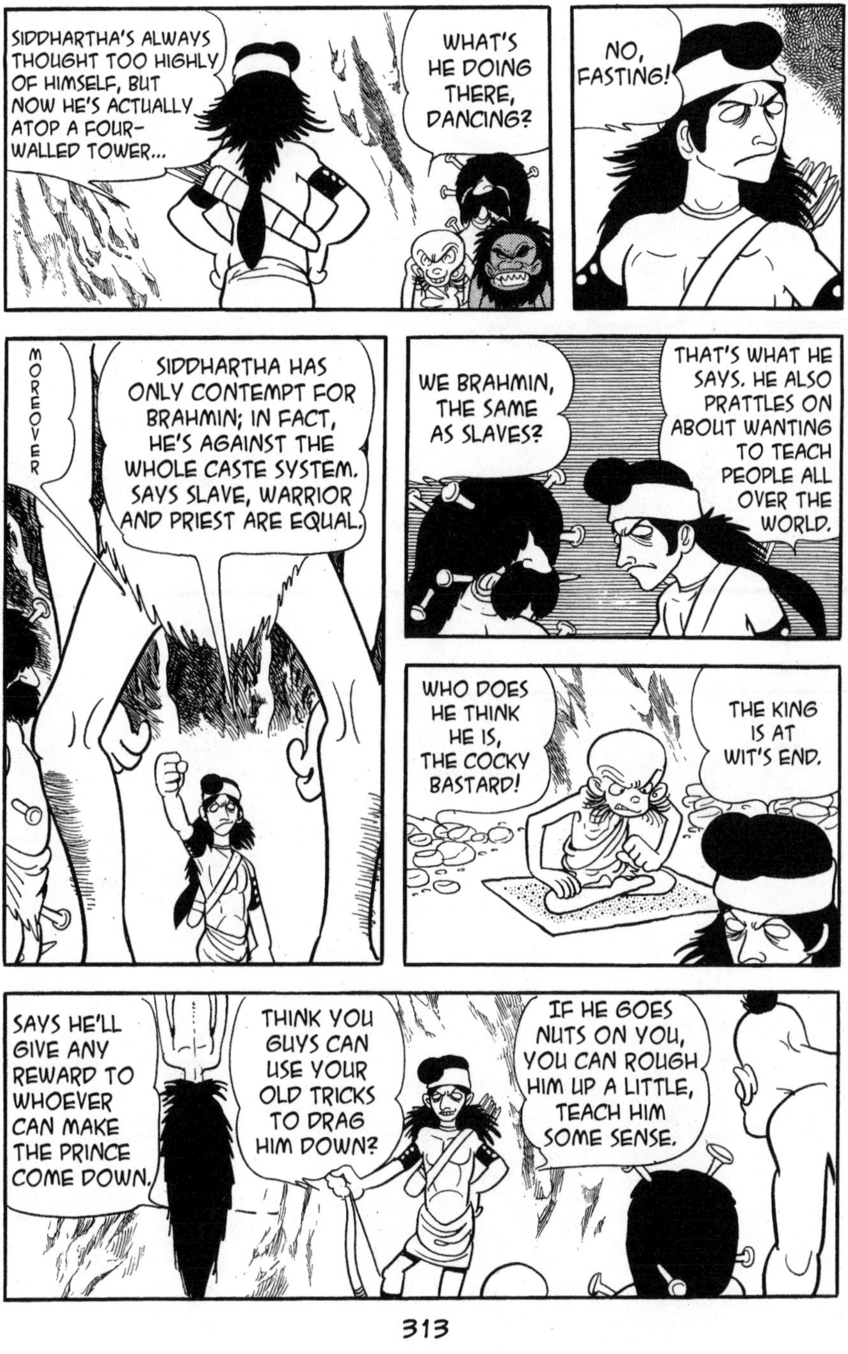
SIDDHARTHA'S ALWAYS THOUGHT TOO HIGHLY OF HIMSELF, BUT NOW HE'S ACTUALLY ATOP A FOUR-WALLED TOWER...
WHAT'S HE DOING THERE, DANCING?
NO, FASTING!
MOREOVER
SIDDHARTHA HAS ONLY CONTEMPT FOR BRAHMIN; IN FACT, HE'S AGAINST THE WHOLE CASTE SYSTEM. SAYS SLAVE, WARRIOR AND PRIEST ARE EQUAL.
WE BRAHMIN, THE SAME AS SLAVES?
THAT'S WHAT HE SAYS. HE ALSO PRATTLES ON ABOUT WANTING TO TEACH PEOPLE ALL OVER THE WORLD.
WHO DOES HE THINK HE IS, THE COCKY BASTARD!
THE KING IS AT WIT'S END.
SAYS HE'LL GIVE ANY REWARD TO WHOEVER CAN MAKE THE PRINCE COME DOWN.
THINK YOU GUYS CAN USE YOUR OLD TRICKS TO DRAG HIM DOWN?
IF HE GOES NUTS ON YOU, YOU CAN ROUGH HIM UP A LITTLE, TEACH HIM SOME SENSE.

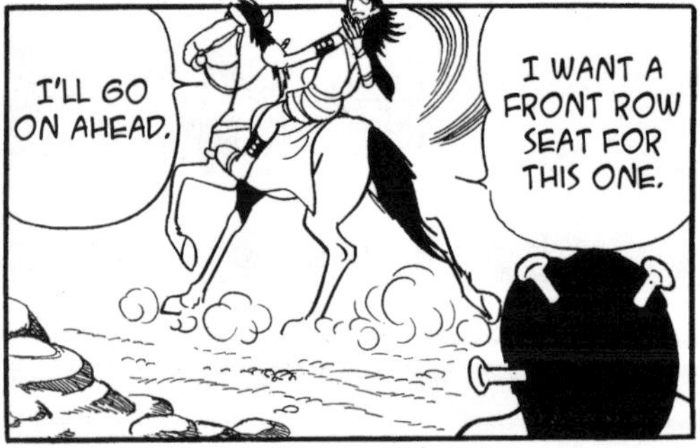
I'LL GO ON AHEAD.
I WANT A FRONT ROW SEAT FOR THIS ONE.

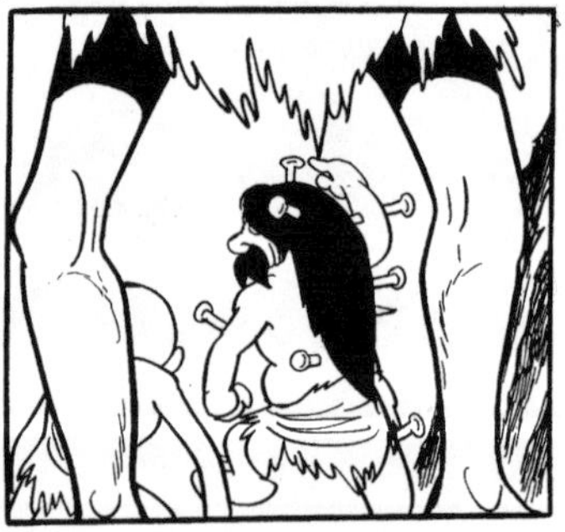

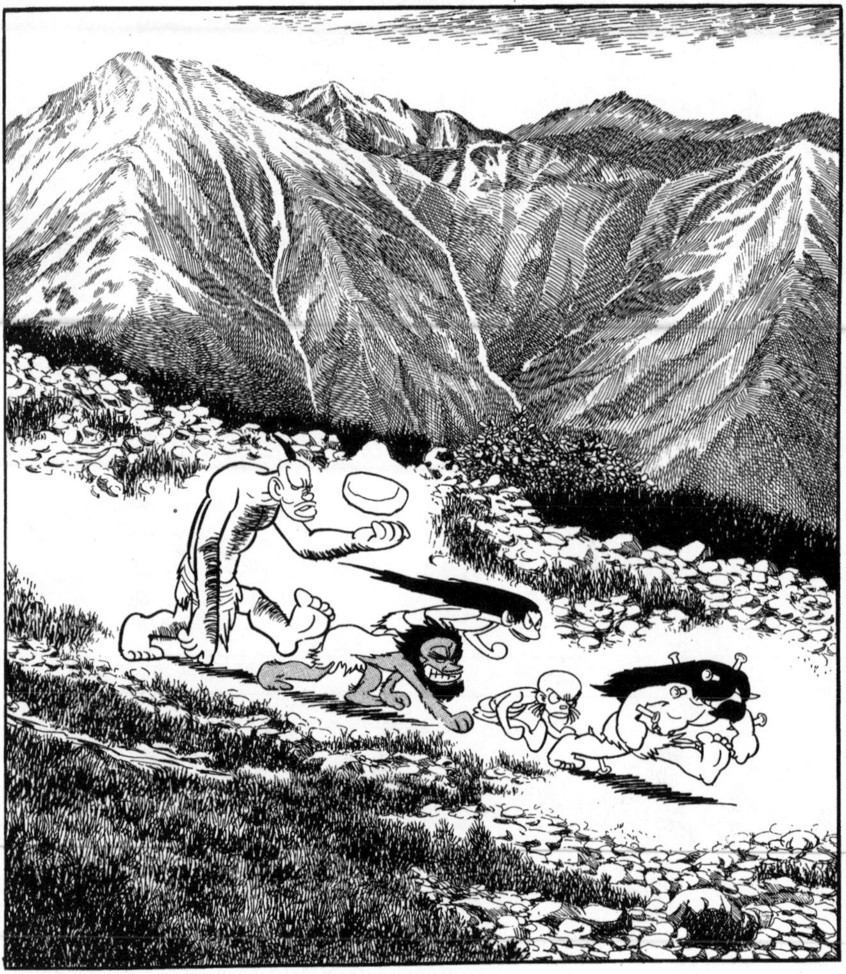

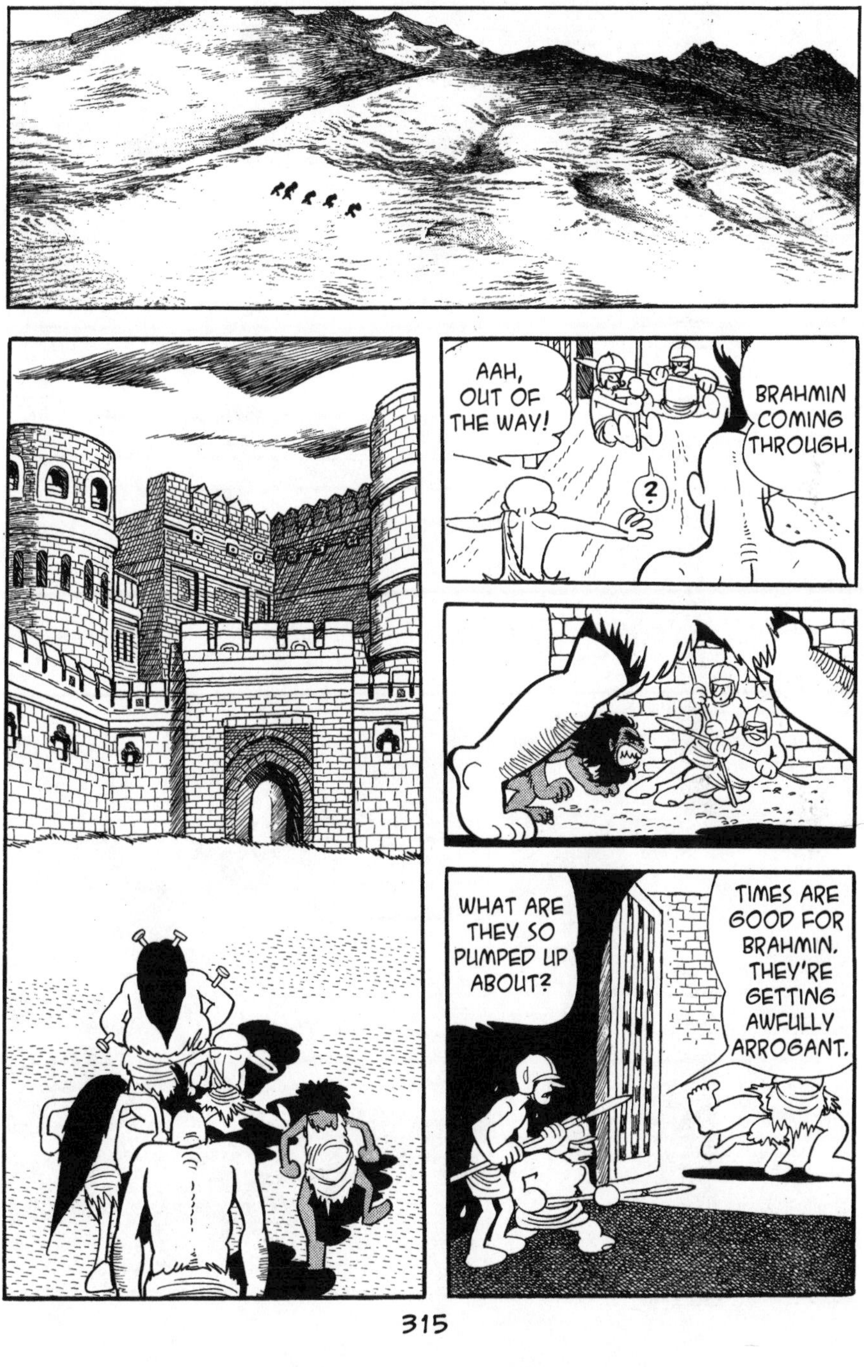
AAH, OUT OF THE WAY!
BRAHMIN COMING THROUGH.
?
WHAT ARE THEY SO PUMPED UP ABOUT?
TIMES ARE GOOD FOR BRAHMIN. THEY'RE GETTING AWFULLY ARROGANT.

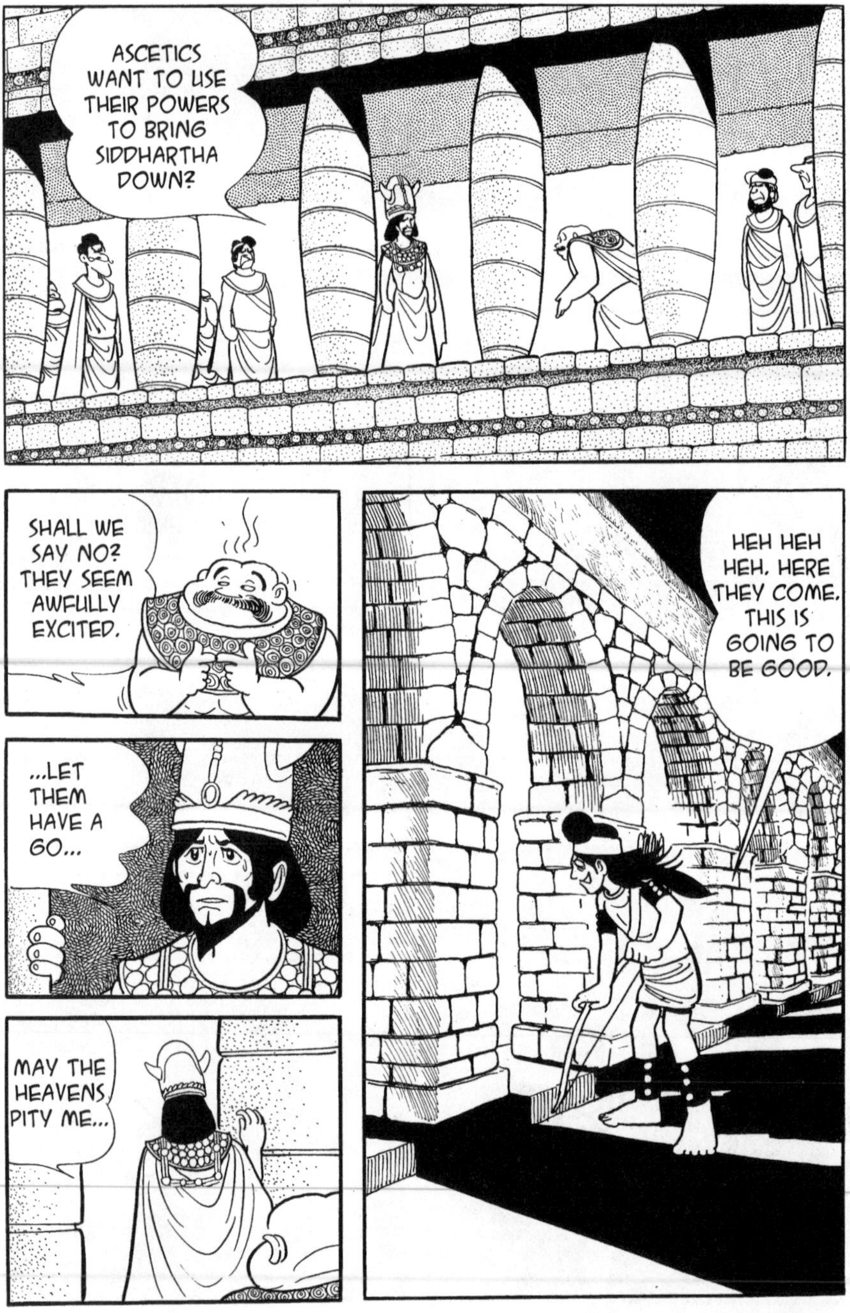
ASCETICS WANT TO USE THEIR POWERS TO BRING SIDDHARTHA DOWN?
SHALL WE SAY NO? THEY SEEM AWFULLY EXCITED.
...LET THEM HAVE A GO...
MAY THE HEAVENS PITY ME...
HEH HEH HEH. HERE THEY COME. THIS IS GOING TO BE GOOD.

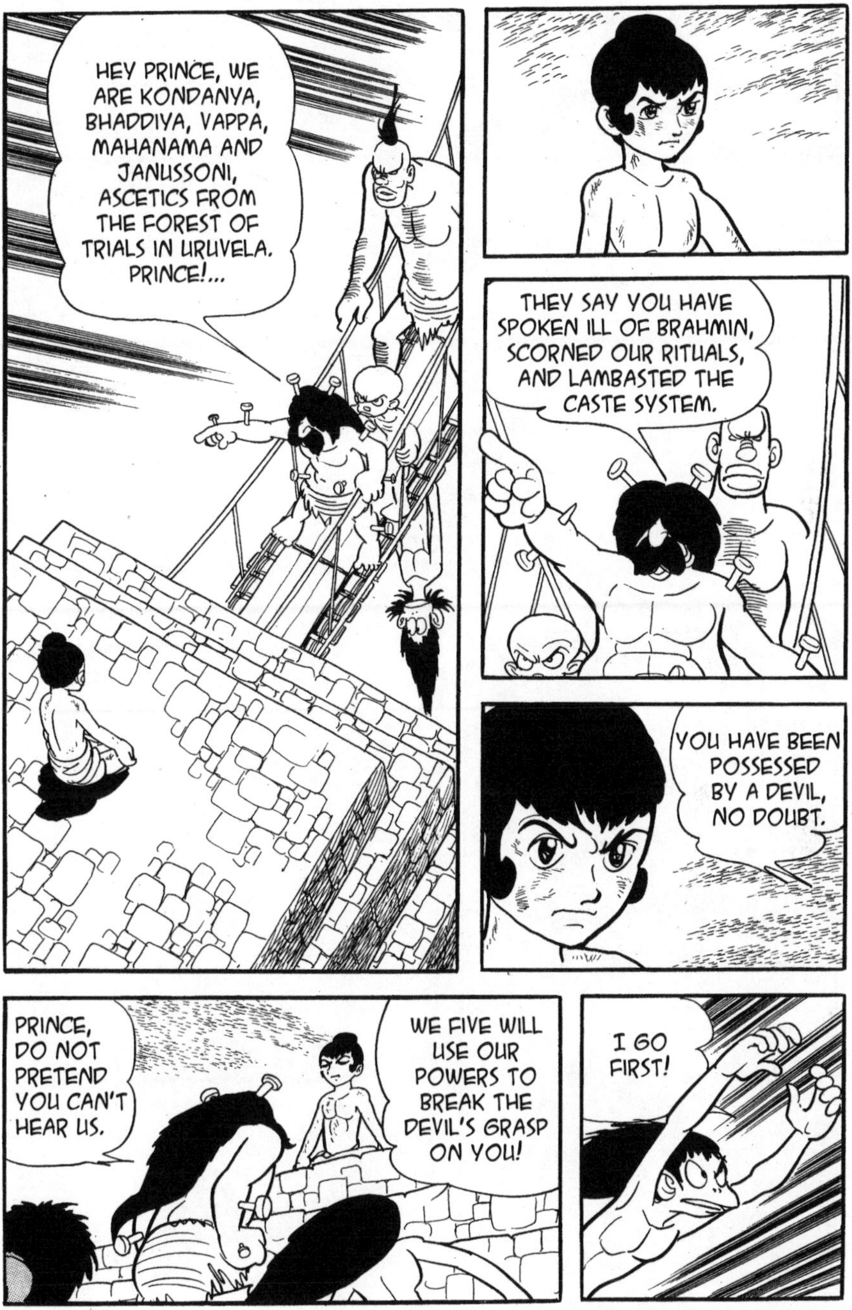
HEY PRINCE, WE ARE KONDANYA, BHADDIYA, VAPPA, MAHANAMA AND JANUSSONI, ASCETICS FROM THE FOREST OF TRIALS IN URUVELA. PRINCE!...
THEY SAY YOU HAVE SPOKEN ILL OF BRAHMIN, SCORNED OUR RITUALS, AND LAMBASTED THE CASTE SYSTEM.
YOU HAVE BEEN POSSESSED BY A DEVIL, NO DOUBT.
PRINCE, DO NOT PRETEND YOU CAN'T HEAR US.
WE FIVE WILL USE OUR POWERS TO BREAK THE DEVIL'S GRASP ON YOU!
I GO FIRST!

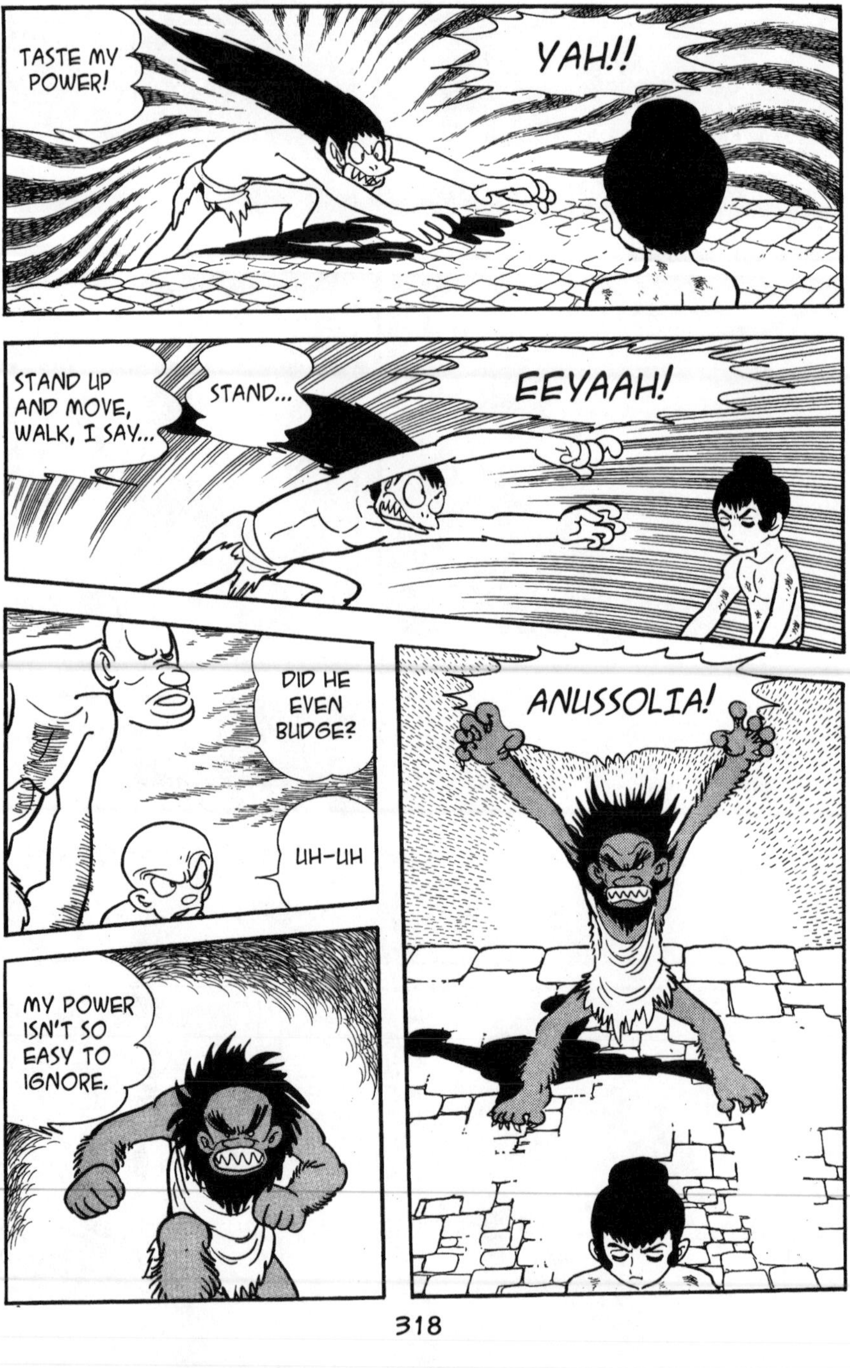
TASTE MY POWER!
YAH!!
STAND UP AND MOVE, WALK, I SAY...
STAND...
EEYAAH!
DID HE EVEN BUDGE?
UH-UH
ANUSSOLIA!
MY POWER ISN'T SO EASY TO IGNORE.

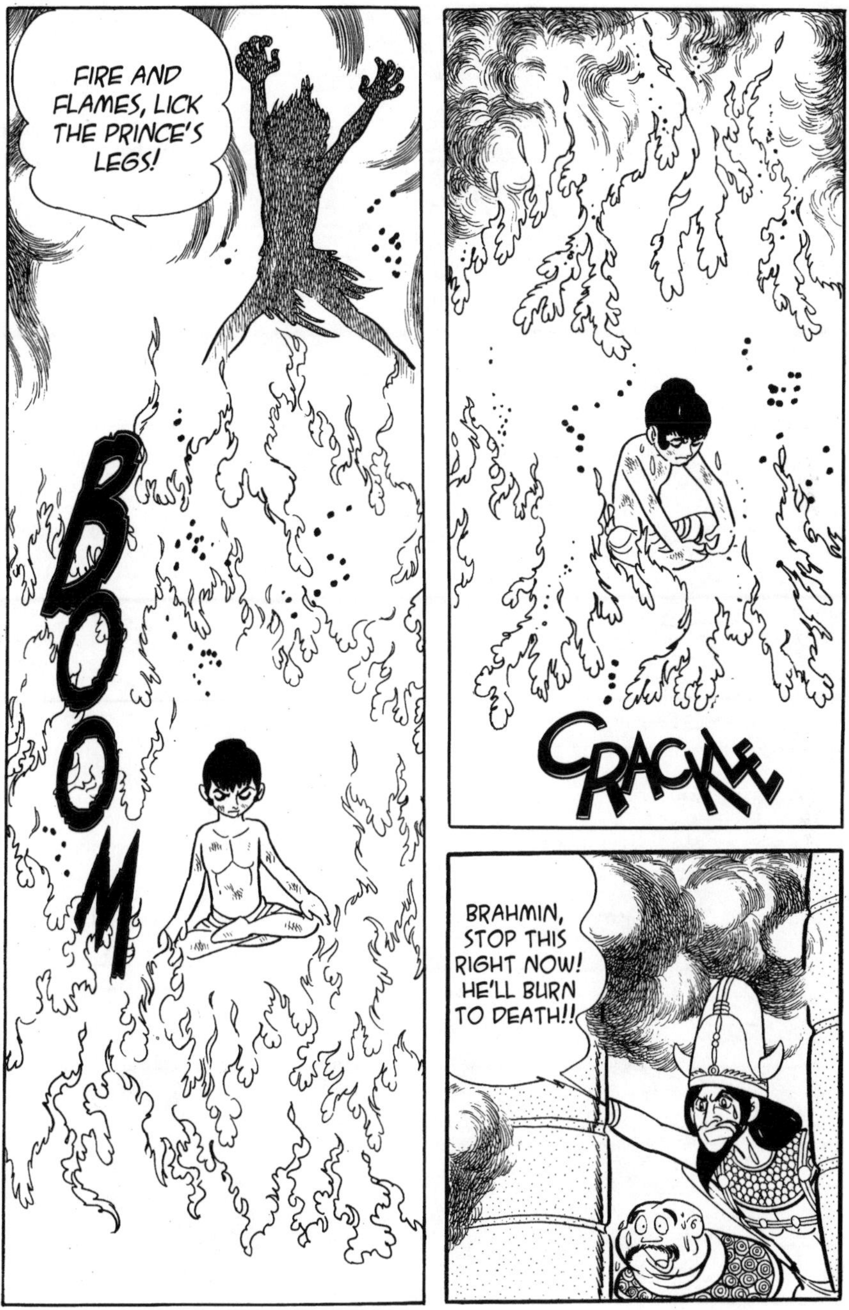
FIRE AND FLAMES, LICK THE PRINCE'S LEGS!
BOOM
CRACKLE
BRAHMIN, STOP THIS RIGHT NOW! HE'LL BURN TO DEATH!!

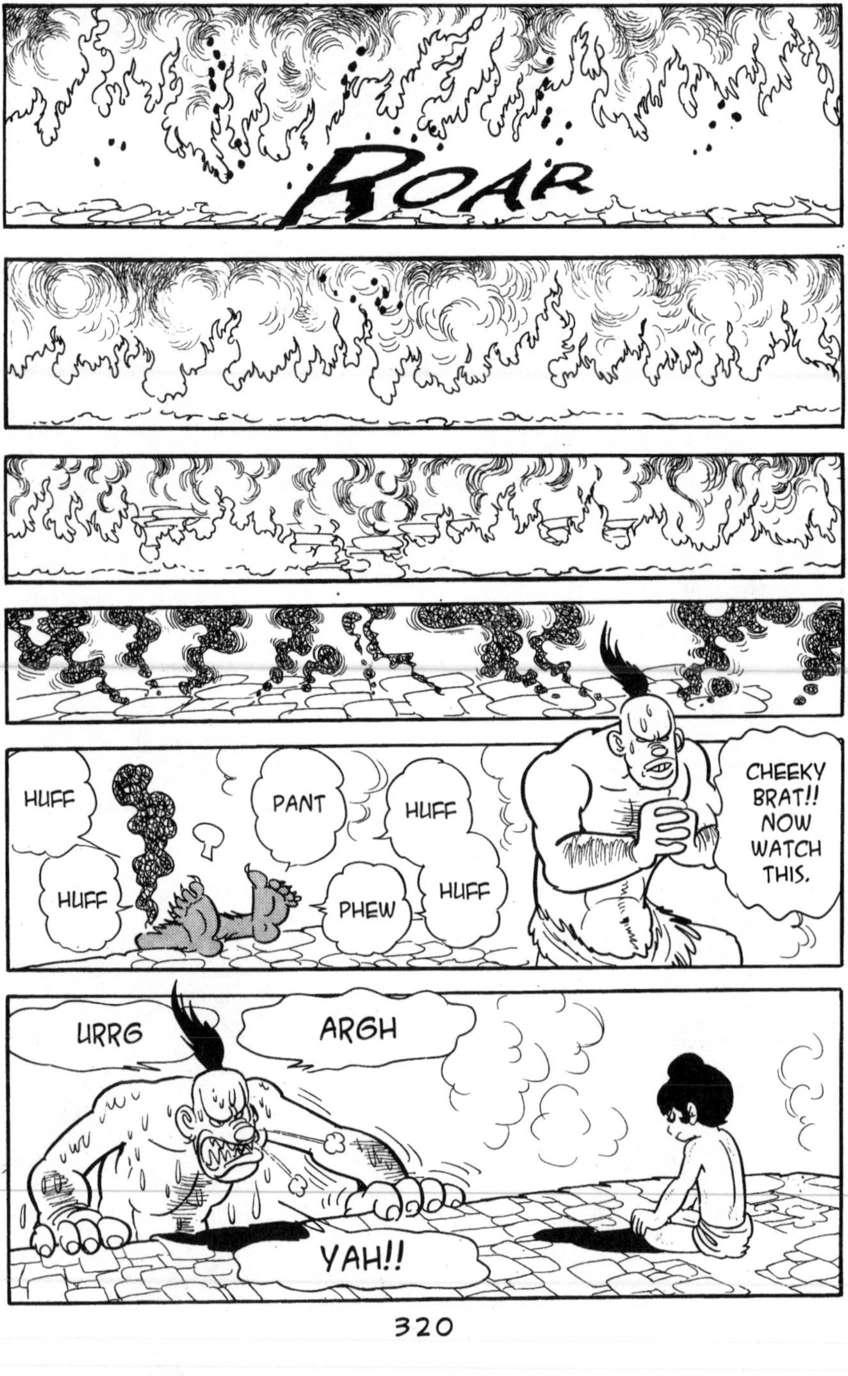
ROAR
HUFF
HUFF
PANT
PHEW
HUFF
HUFF
CHEEKY BRAT!! NOW WATCH THIS.
URRG
ARGH
YAH!!

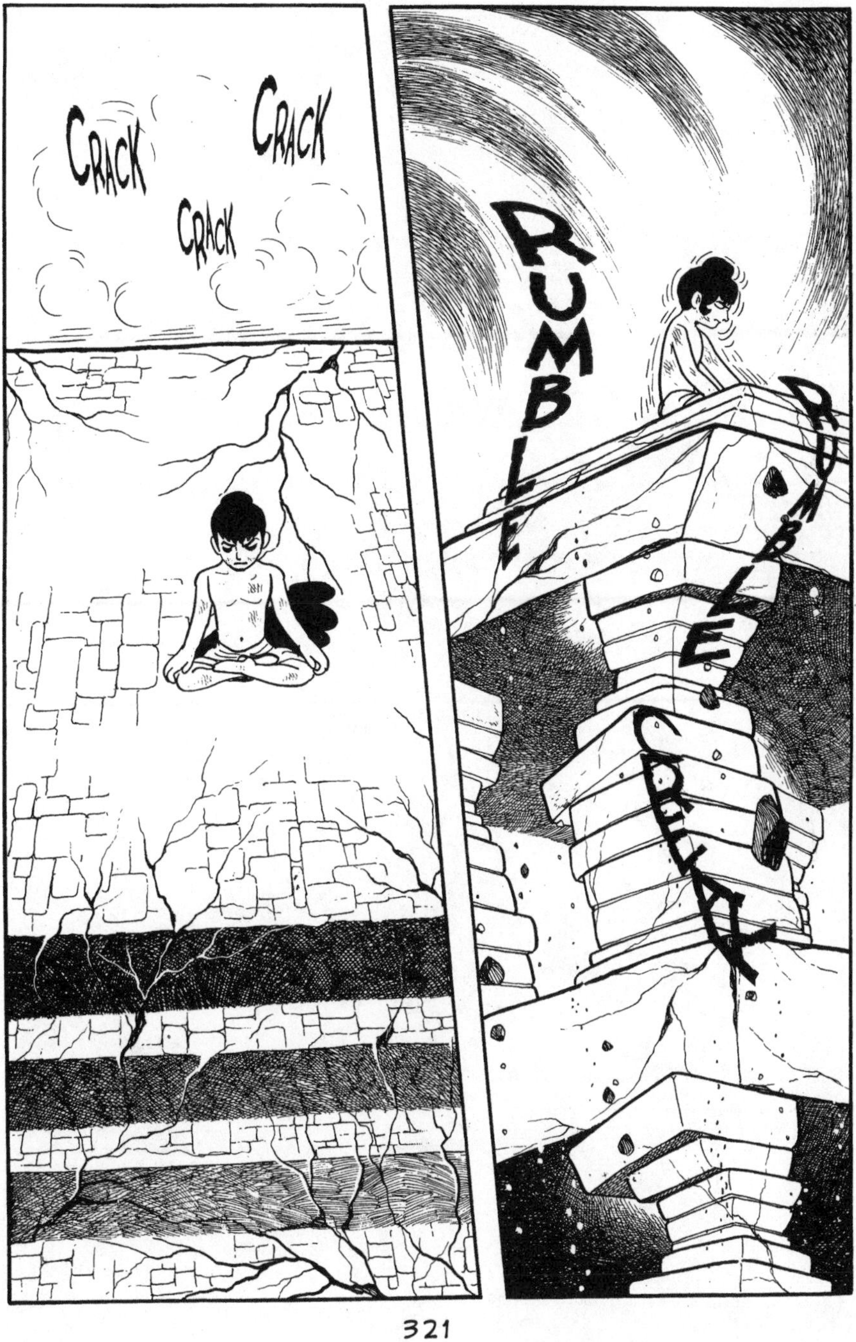
CRACK
CRACK
CRACK
RUMBLE
RUMBLE
CREAK

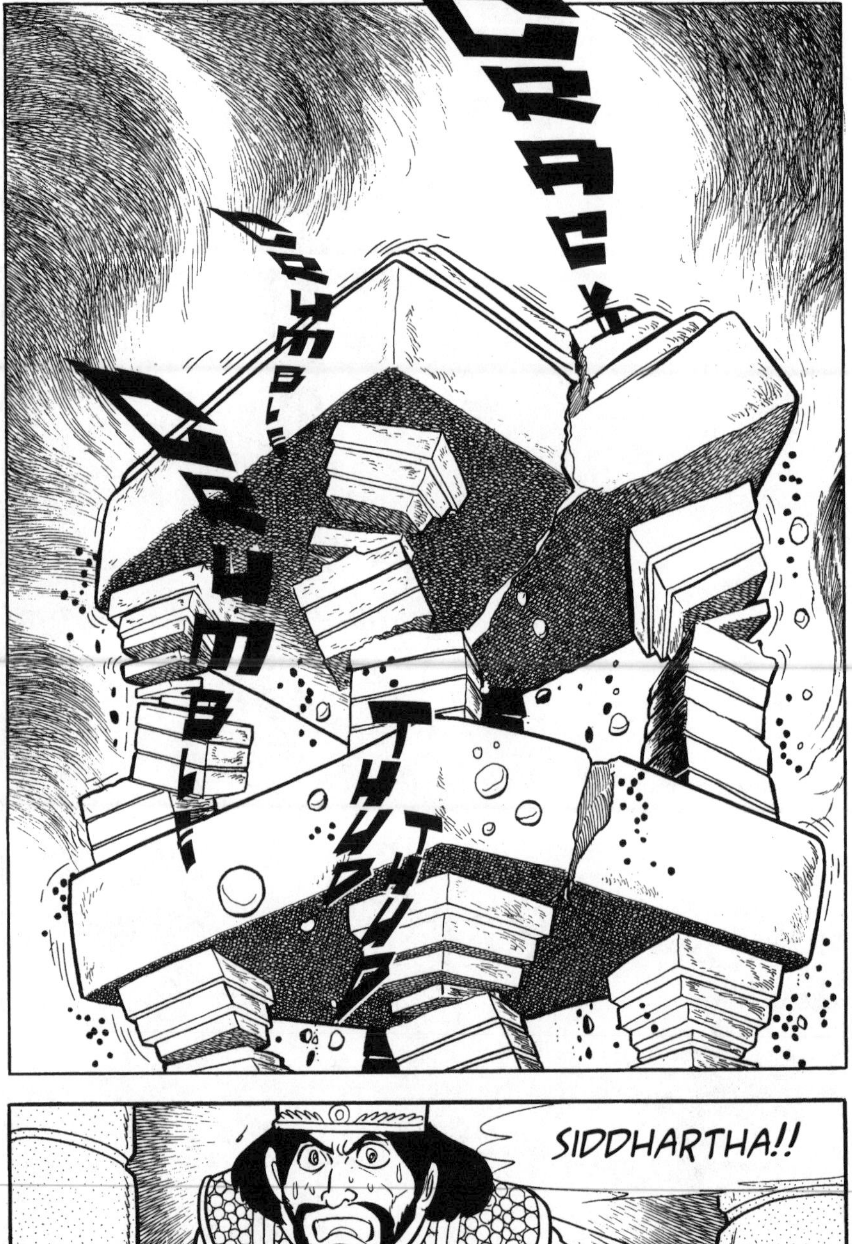
CRACK
CRUMBLE
CRUMBLE
THUD
THUD
SIDDHARTHA!!

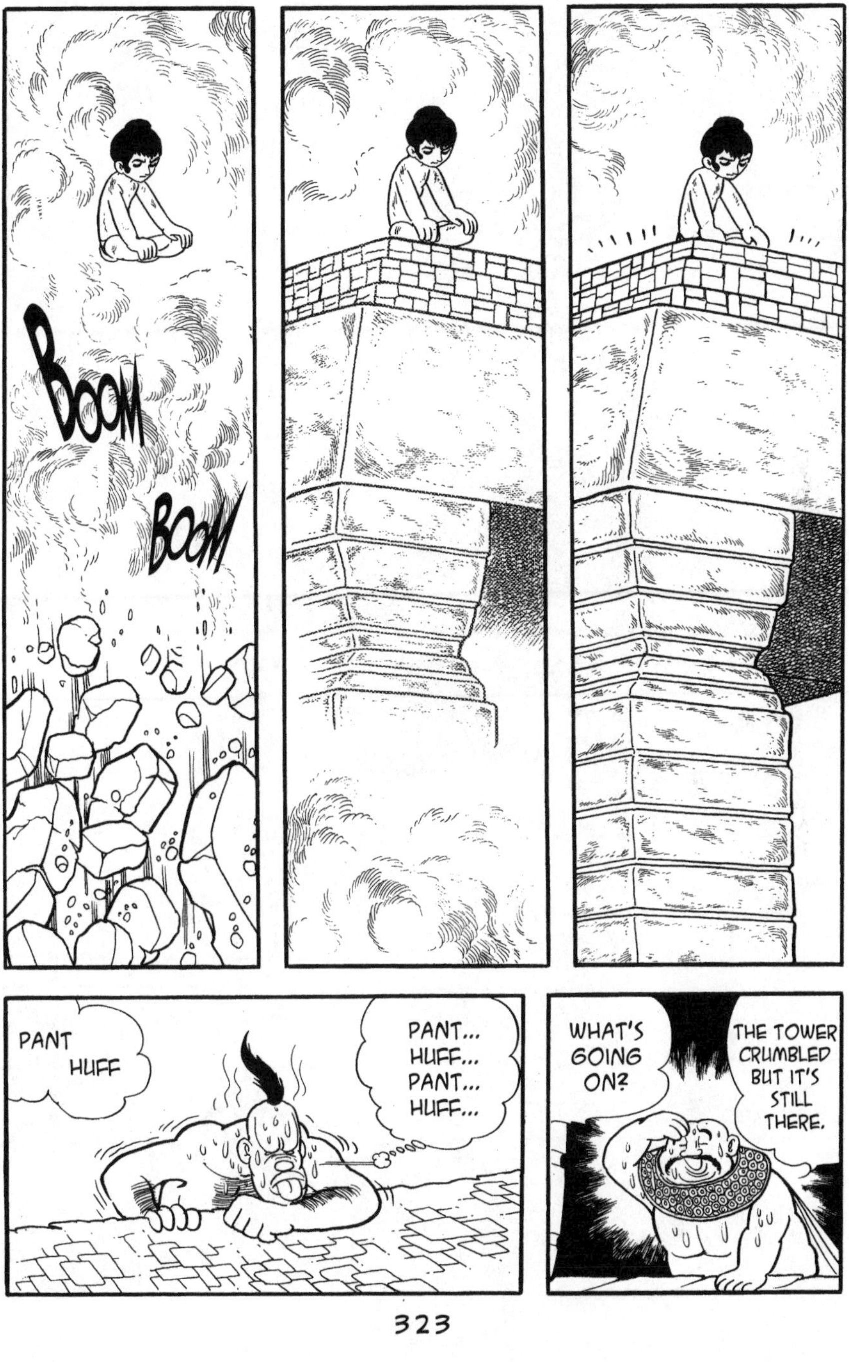
BOOM
BOOM
PANT
HUFF
PANT... HUFF... PANT... HUFF...
WHAT'S GOING ON?
THE TOWER CRUMBLED BUT IT'S STILL THERE.

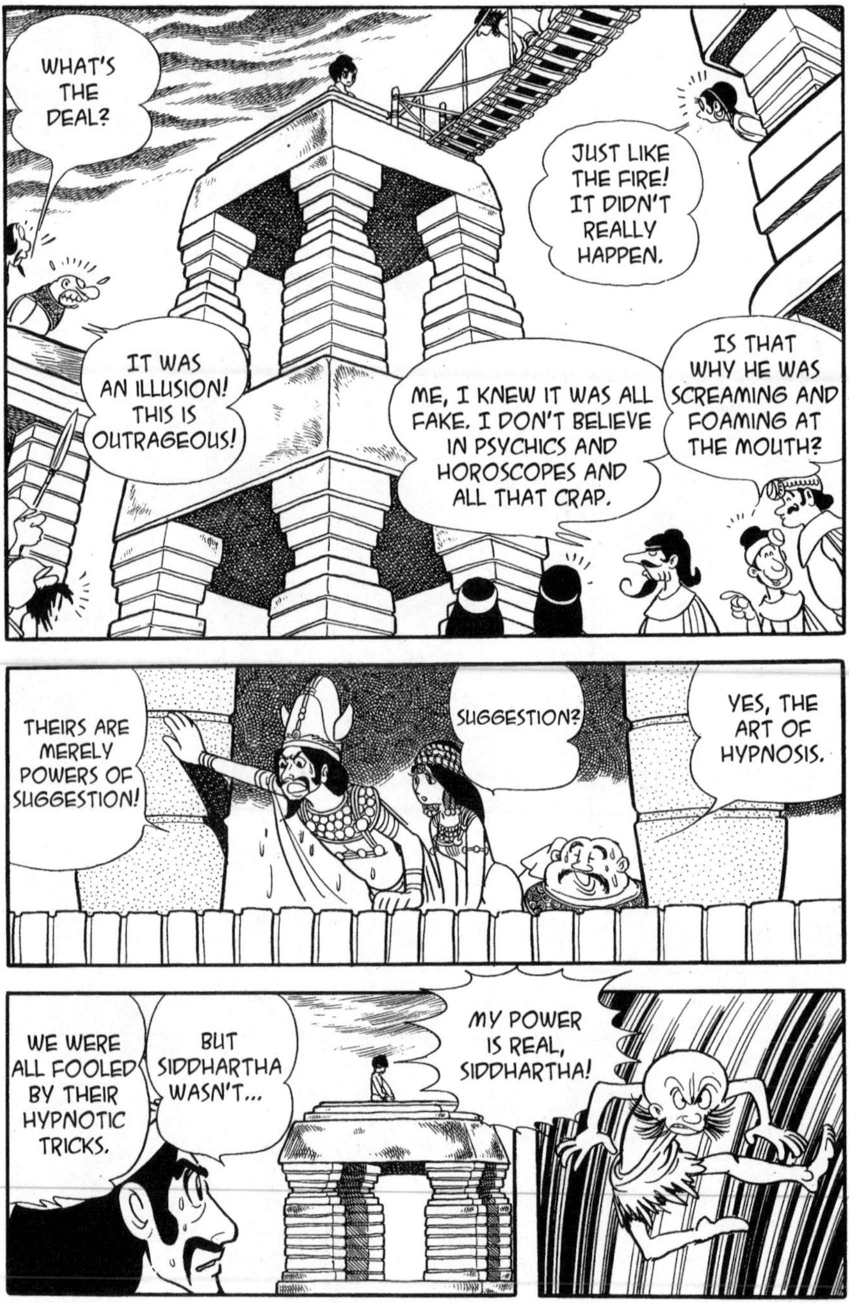
WHAT'S THE DEAL?
JUST LIKE THE FIRE! IT DIDN'T REALLY HAPPEN.
IT WAS AN ILLUSION! THIS IS OUTRAGEOUS!
ME, I KNEW IT WAS ALL FAKE. I DON'T BELIEVE IN PSYCHICS AND HOROSCOPES AND ALL THAT CRAP.
IS THAT WHY HE WAS SCREAMING AND FOAMING AT THE MOUTH?
THEIRS ARE MERELY POWERS OF SUGGESTION!
SUGGESTION?
YES, THE ART OF HYPNOSIS.
WE WERE ALL FOOLED BY THEIR HYPNOTIC TRICKS.
BUT SIDDHARTHA WASN'T...
MY POWER IS REAL, SIDDHARTHA!

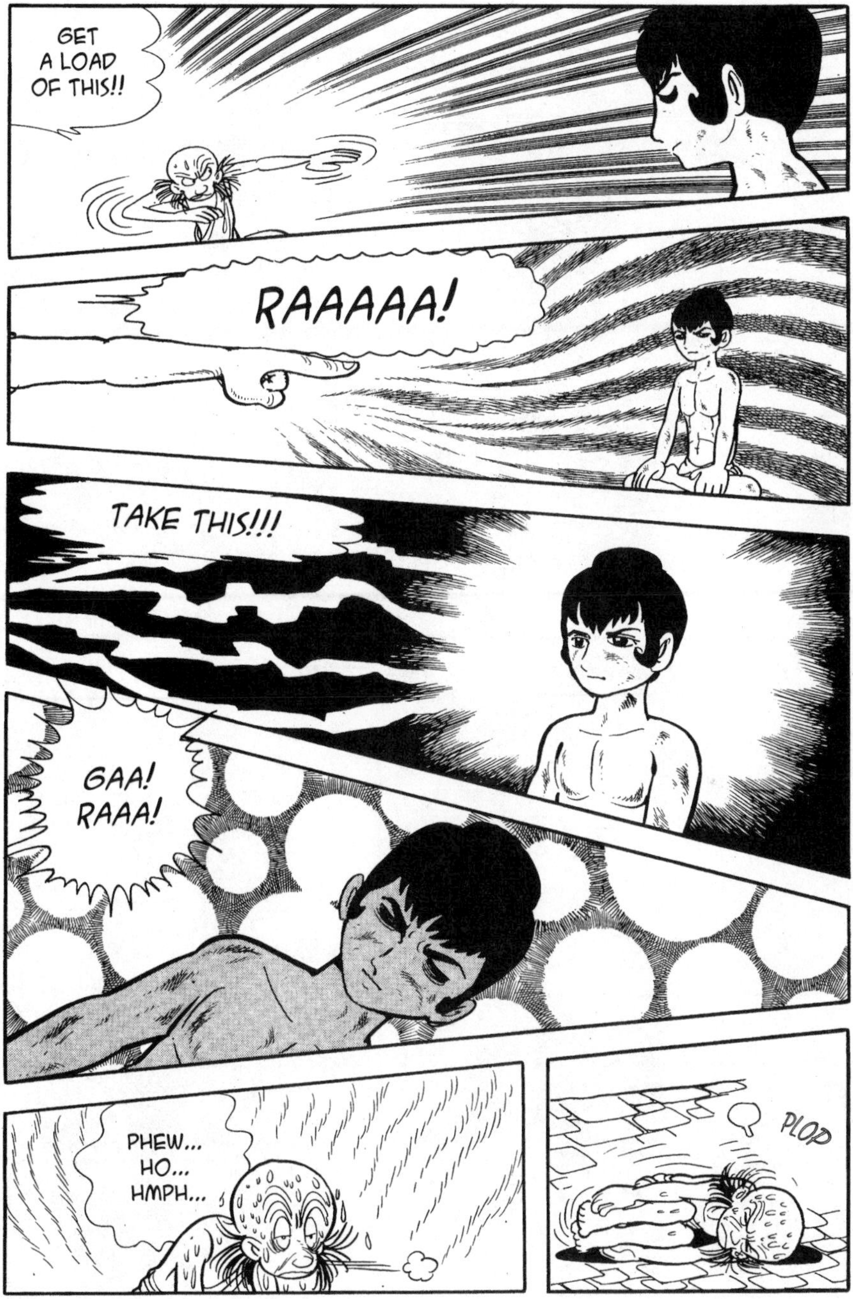
GET A LOAD OF THIS!!
RAAAAA!
TAKE THIS!!!
GAA! RAAA!
PHEW... HO... HMPH...
PLOP

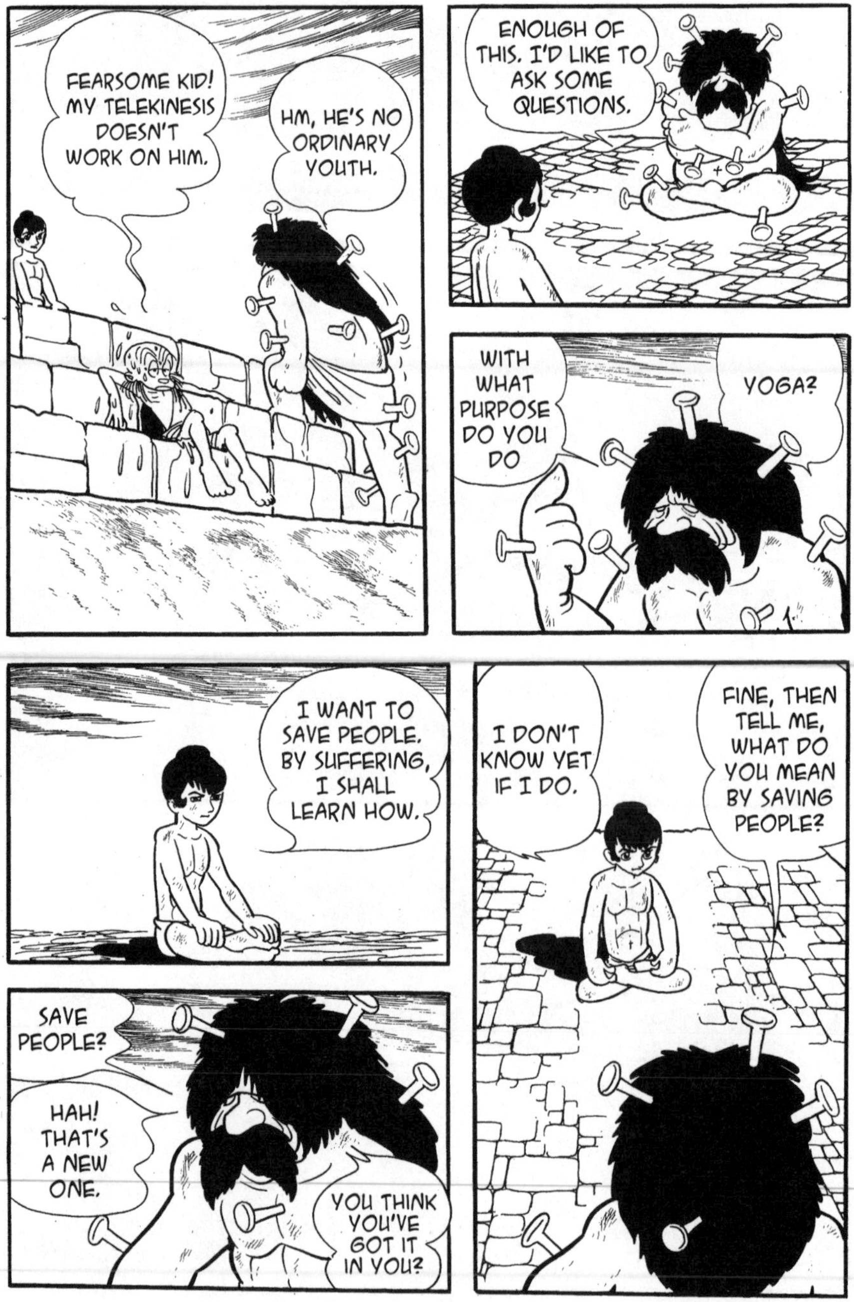
FEARSOME KID! MY TELEKINESIS DOESN'T WORK ON HIM.
HM, HE'S NO ORDINARY YOUTH.
ENOUGH OF THIS. I'D LIKE TO ASK SOME QUESTIONS.
WITH WHAT PURPOSE DO YOU DO
YOGA?
I WANT TO SAVE PEOPLE. BY SUFFERING, I SHALL LEARN HOW.
SAVE PEOPLE?
HAH! THAT'S A NEW ONE.
YOU THINK YOU'VE GOT IT IN YOU?
FINE, THEN TELL ME, WHAT DO YOU MEAN BY SAVING PEOPLE?
I DON'T KNOW YET IF I DO.

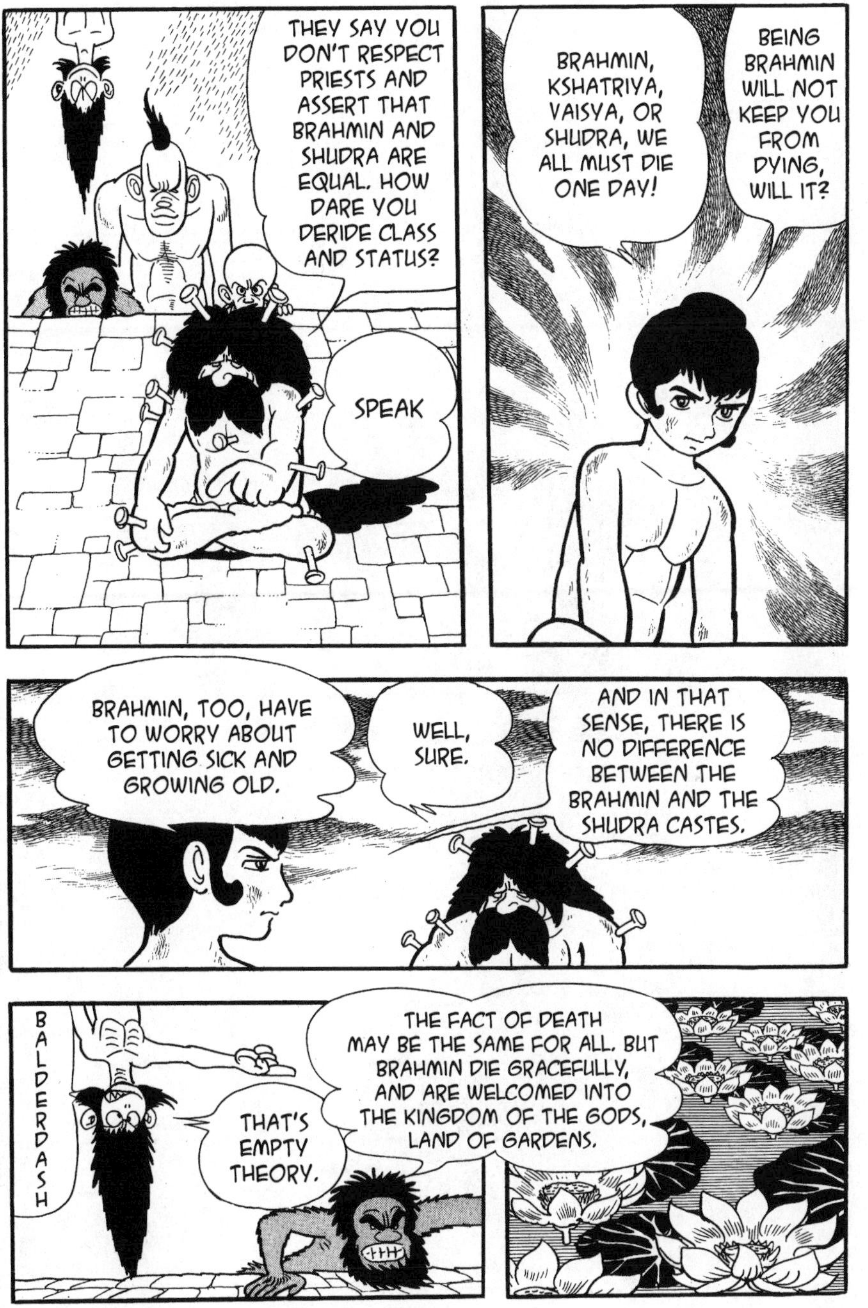
THEY SAY YOU DON'T RESPECT PRIESTS AND ASSERT THAT BRAHMIN AND SHUDRA ARE EQUAL. HOW DARE YOU DERIDE CLASS AND STATUS?
SPEAK
BRAHMIN, KSHATRIYA, VAISYA, OR SHUDRA, WE ALL MUST DIE ONE DAY!
BEING BRAHMIN WILL NOT KEEP YOU FROM DYING, WILL IT?
BRAHMIN, TOO, HAVE TO WORRY ABOUT GETTING SICK AND GROWING OLD.
WELL, SURE.
AND IN THAT SENSE, THERE IS NO DIFFERENCE BETWEEN THE BRAHMIN AND THE SHUDRA CASTES.
BALDERDASH
THAT'S EMPTY THEORY.
THE FACT OF DEATH MAY BE THE SAME FOR ALL. BUT BRAHMIN DIE GRACEFULLY, AND ARE WELCOMED INTO THE KINGDOM OF THE GODS, LAND OF GARDENS.

LOWLY SHUDRA, ON THE OTHER HAND, DIE LIKE DOGS AND GET THE FLESH RIPPED OFF THEIR BONES BY WOLVES, IN SOME DARK PIT.

HOW'S THAT FOR DYING ALL THE SAME?

I ONCE SAW HUNDREDS DIE FROM AN EPIDEMIC. DOES DISEASE DISTINGUISH BETWEEN SHUDRA AND BRAHMIN?

EHH... DISEASE IS SPECIAL. WE DO GET SICK, WHATEVER OUR CASTES.

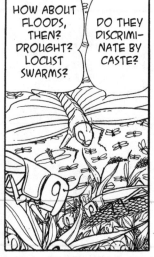

HOW ABOUT FLOODS, THEN? DROUGHT? LOCUST SWARMS?

DO THEY DISCRIMI-NATE BY CASTE?

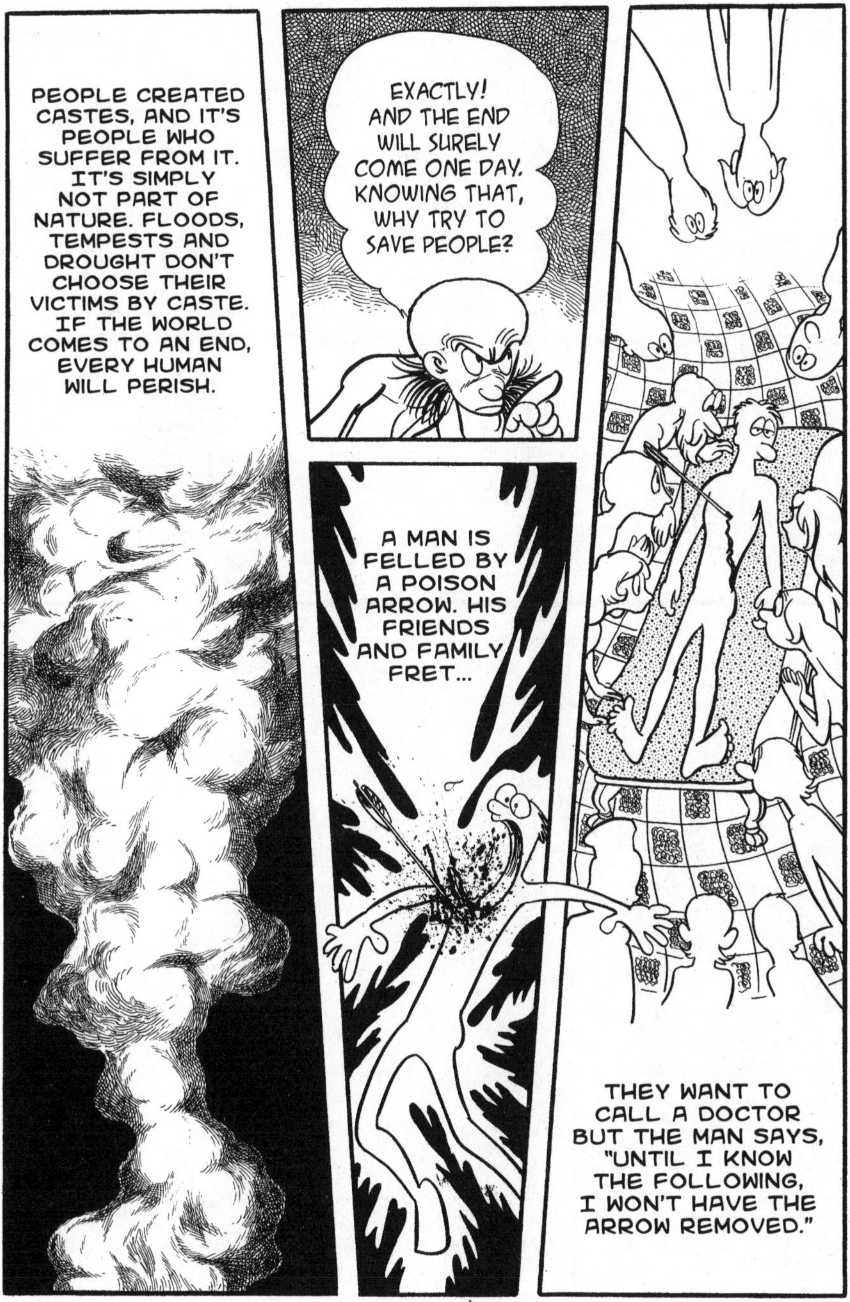
PEOPLE CREATED CASTES, AND IT'S PEOPLE WHO SUFFER FROM IT. IT'S SIMPLY NOT PART OF NATURE. FLOODS, TEMPESTS AND DROUGHT DON'T CHOOSE THEIR VICTIMS BY CASTE. IF THE WORLD COMES TO AN END, EVERY HUMAN WILL PERISH.
EXACTLY! AND THE END WILL SURELY COME ONE DAY. KNOWING THAT, WHY TRY TO SAVE PEOPLE?
A MAN IS FELLED BY A POISON ARROW. HIS FRIENDS AND FAMILY FRET...
THEY WANT TO CALL A DOCTOR BUT THE MAN SAYS, "UNTIL I KNOW THE FOLLOWING, I WON'T HAVE THE ARROW REMOVED."

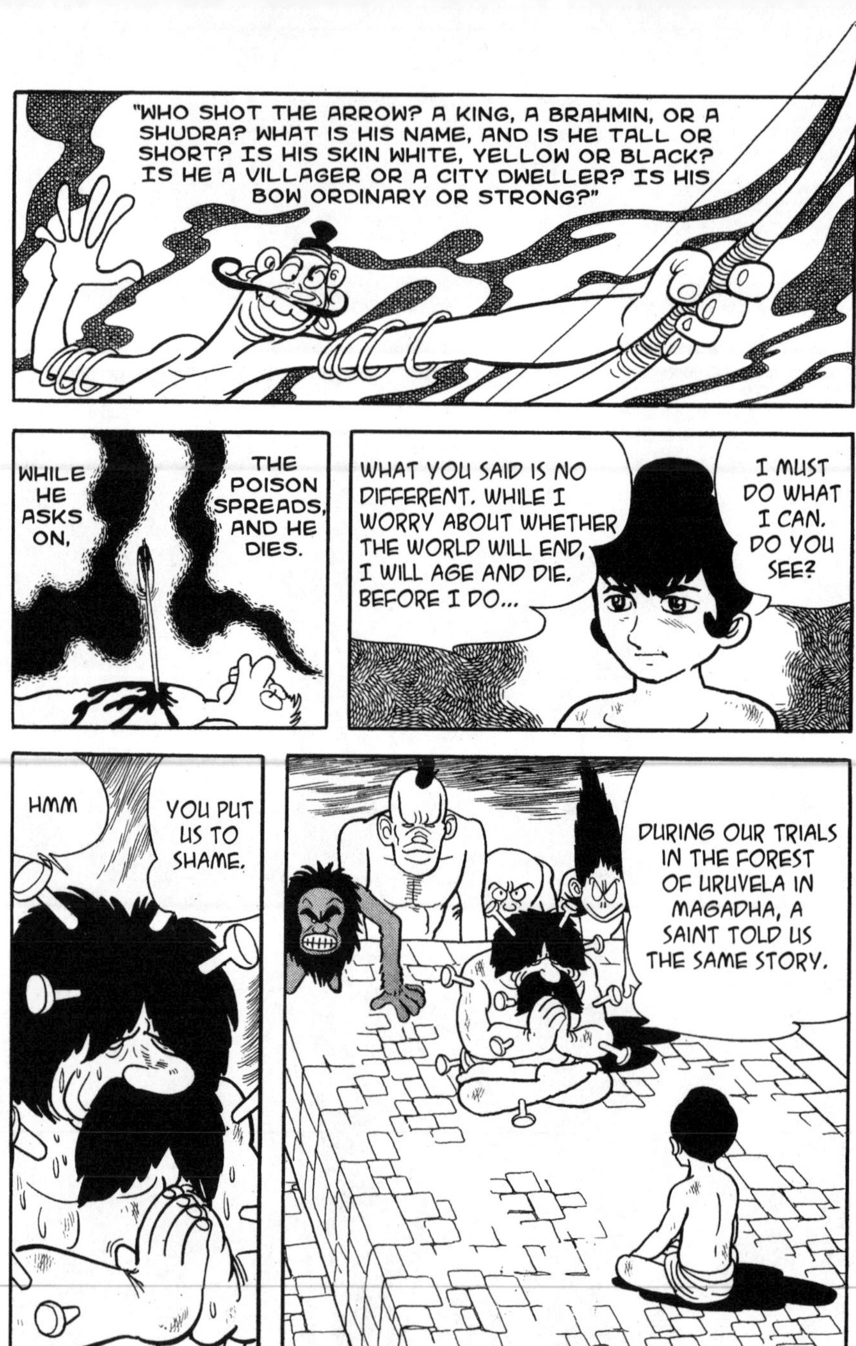
"WHO SHOT THE ARROW? A KING, A BRAHMIN, OR A SHUDRA? WHAT IS HIS NAME, AND IS HE TALL OR SHORT? IS HIS SKIN WHITE, YELLOW OR BLACK? IS HE A VILLAGER OR A CITY DWELLER? IS HIS BOW ORDINARY OR STRONG?"
WHILE HE ASKS ON,
THE POISON SPREADS, AND HE DIES.
WHAT YOU SAID IS NO DIFFERENT. WHILE I WORRY ABOUT WHETHER THE WORLD WILL END, I WILL AGE AND DIE. BEFORE I DO...
I MUST DO WHAT I CAN. DO YOU SEE?
HMM
YOU PUT US TO SHAME.
DURING OUR TRIALS IN THE FOREST OF URUVELA IN MAGADHA, A SAINT TOLD US THE SAME STORY.

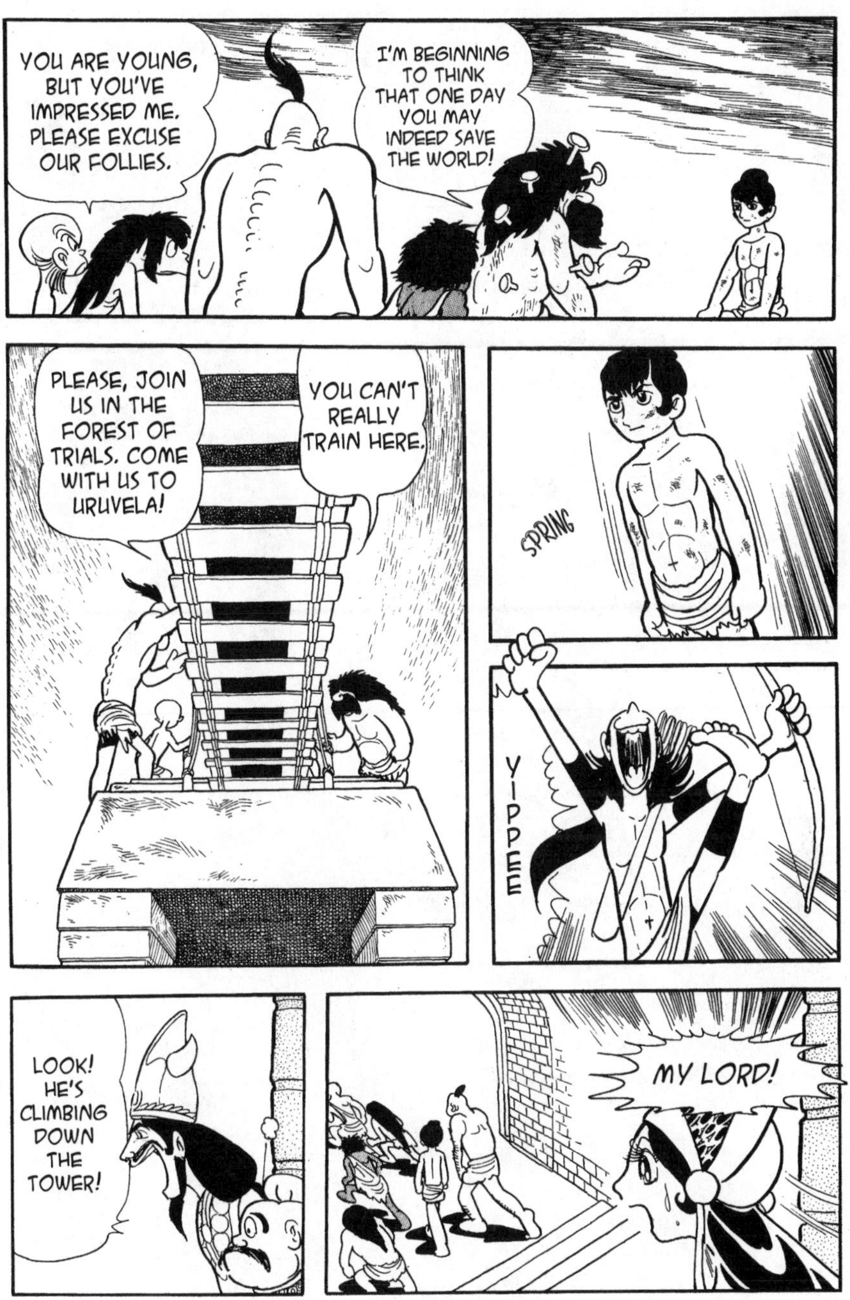
YOU ARE YOUNG, BUT YOU'VE IMPRESSED ME. PLEASE EXCUSE OUR FOLLIES.
I'M BEGINNING TO THINK THAT ONE DAY YOU MAY INDEED SAVE THE WORLD!
PLEASE, JOIN US IN THE FOREST OF TRIALS. COME WITH US TO URUVELA!
YOU CAN'T REALLY TRAIN HERE.
SPRING
YIPPEE
LOOK! HE'S CLIMBING DOWN THE TOWER!
MY LORD!

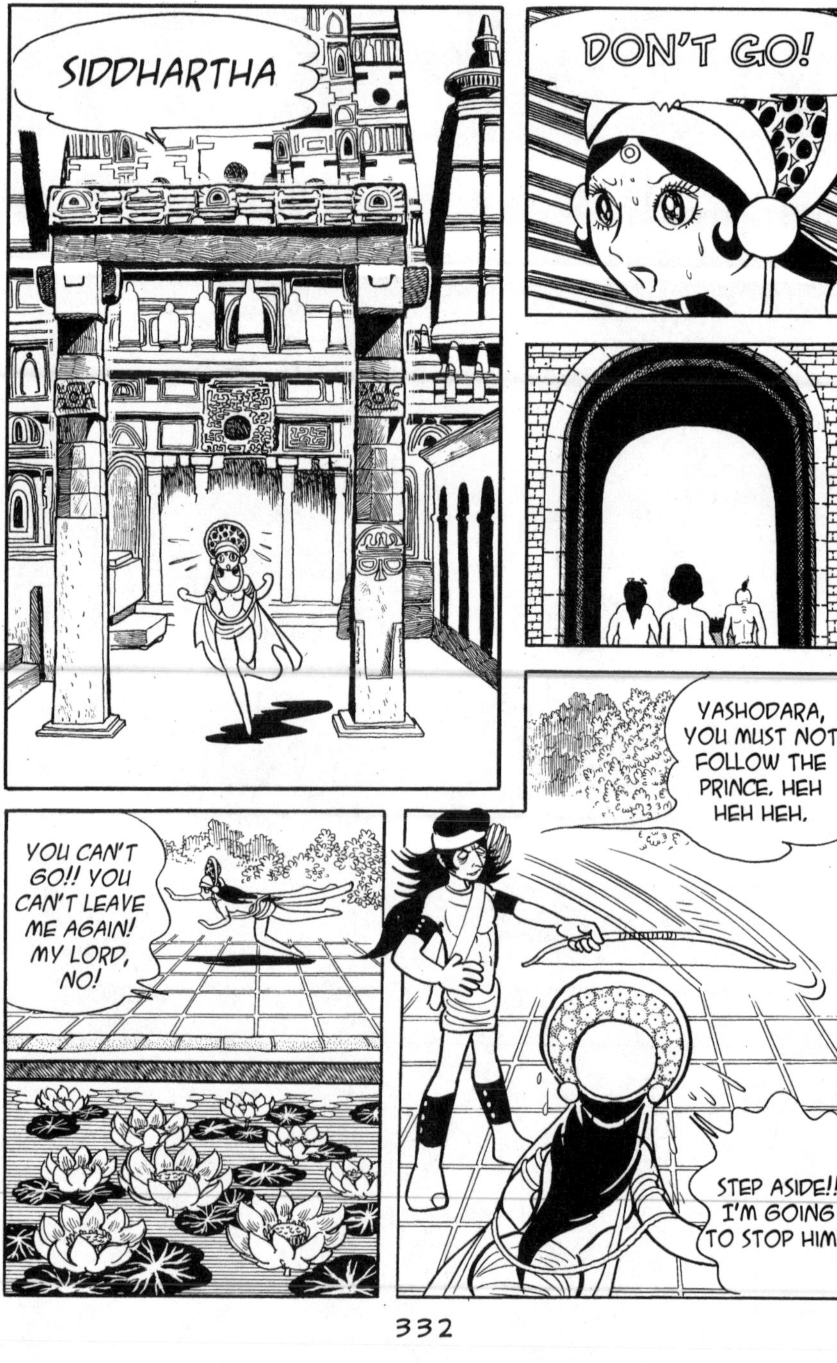
SIDDHARTHA
DON'T GO!
YASHODARA, YOU MUST NOT FOLLOW THE PRINCE. HEH HEH HEH.
YOU CAN'T GO!! YOU CAN'T LEAVE ME AGAIN! MY LORD, NO!
STEP ASIDE!! I'M GOING TO STOP HIM!

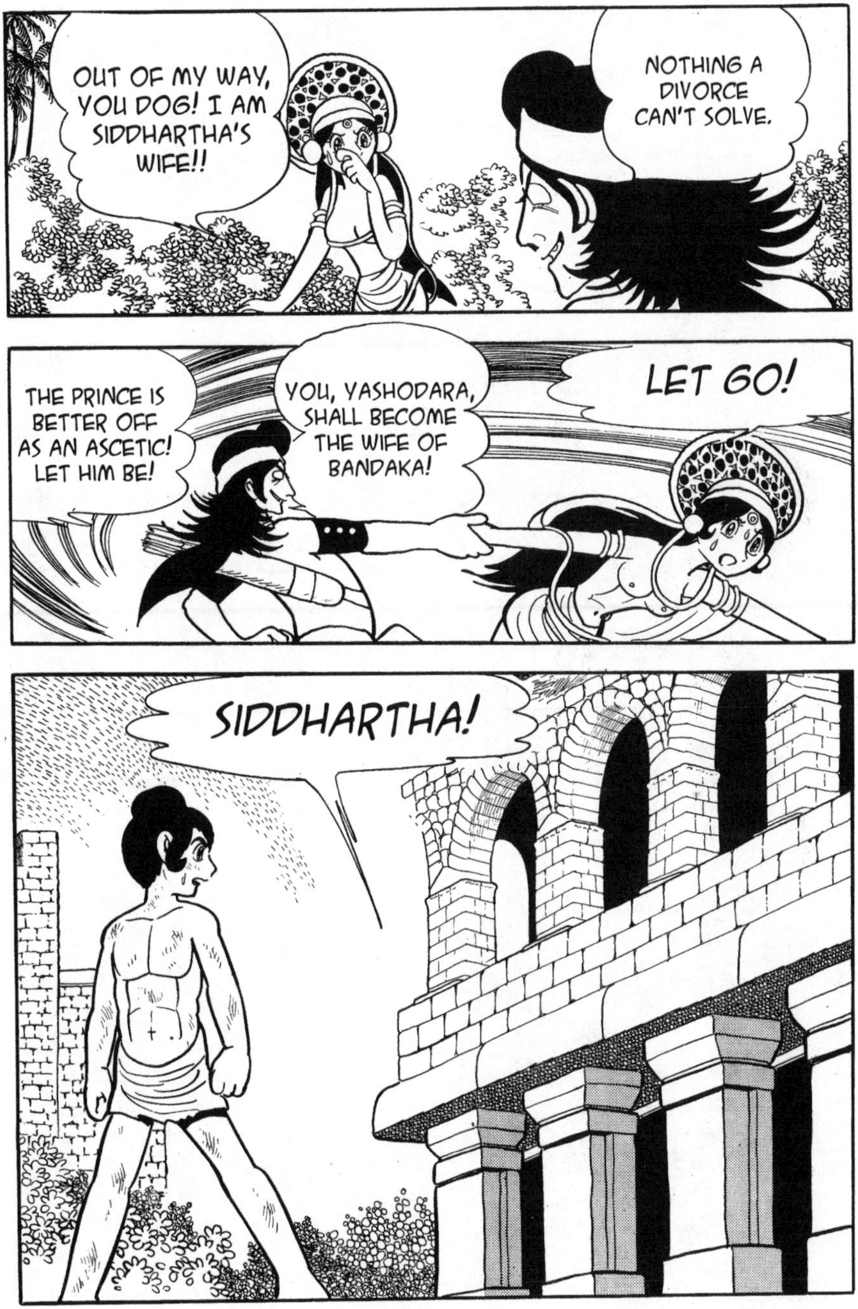
OUT OF MY WAY, YOU DOG! I AM SIDDHARTHA'S WIFE!!
NOTHING A DIVORCE CAN'T SOLVE.
THE PRINCE IS BETTER OFF AS AN ASCETIC! LET HIM BE!
YOU, YASHODARA, SHALL BECOME THE WIFE OF BANDAKA!
LET GO!
SIDDHARTHA!

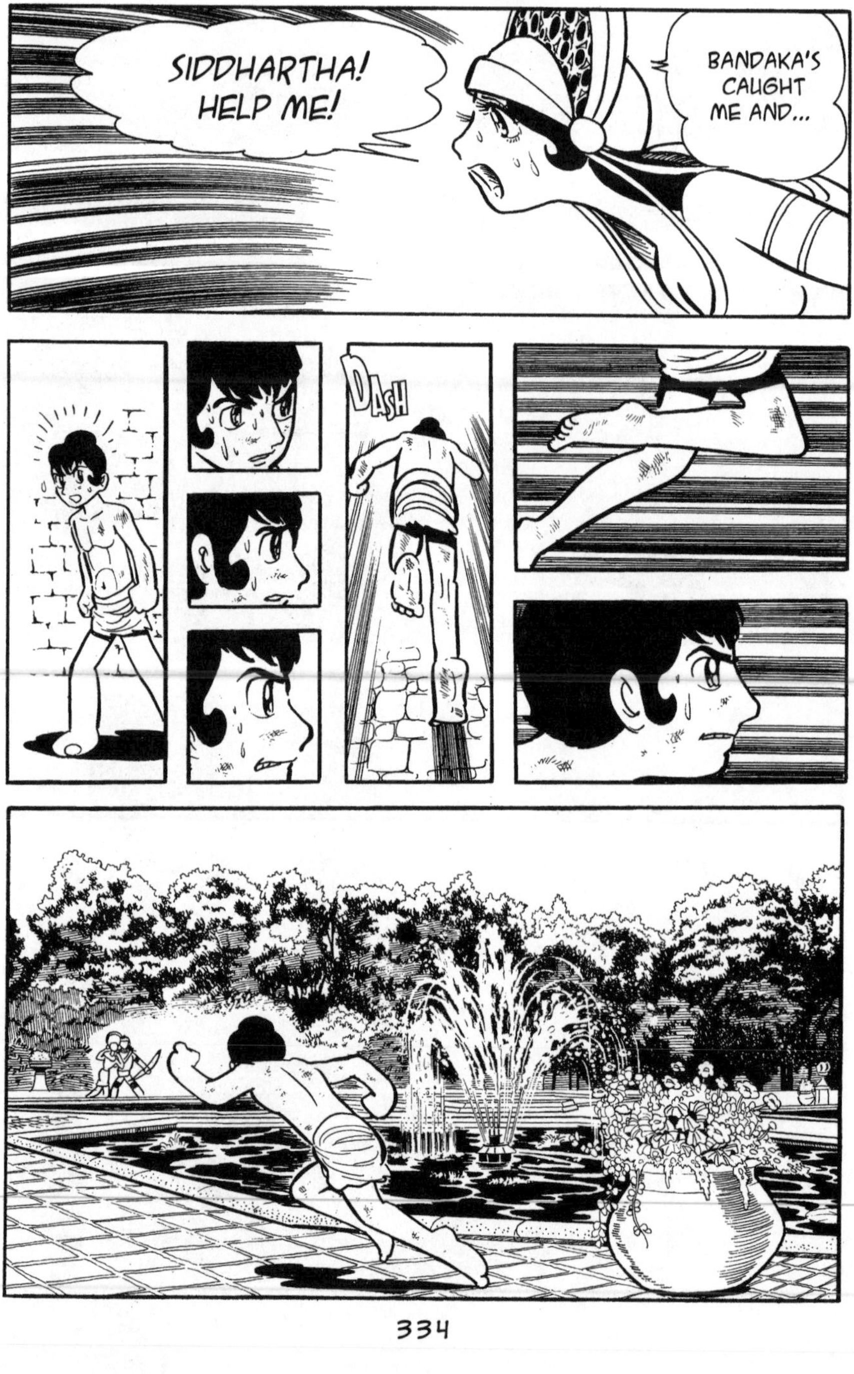
SIDDHARTHA! HELP ME!
BANDAKA'S CAUGHT ME AND...
DASH

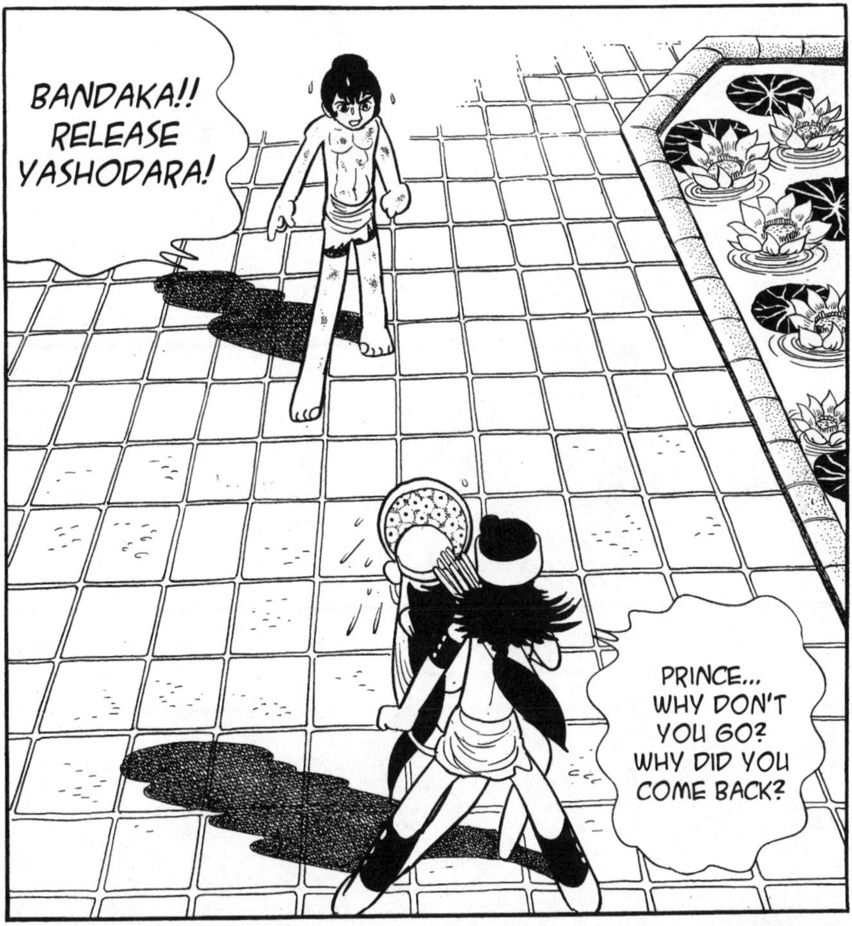
BANDAKA!! RELEASE YASHODARA!
PRINCE... WHY DON'T YOU GO? WHY DID YOU COME BACK?

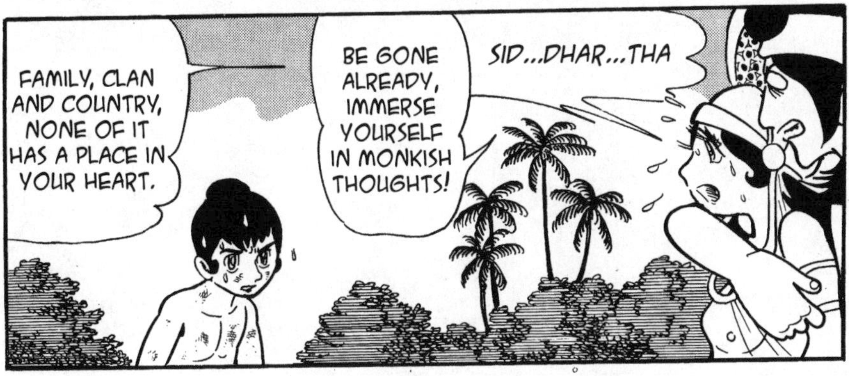
FAMILY, CLAN AND COUNTRY, NONE OF IT HAS A PLACE IN YOUR HEART.
BE GONE ALREADY, IMMERSE YOURSELF IN MONKISH THOUGHTS!
SID...DHAR...THA

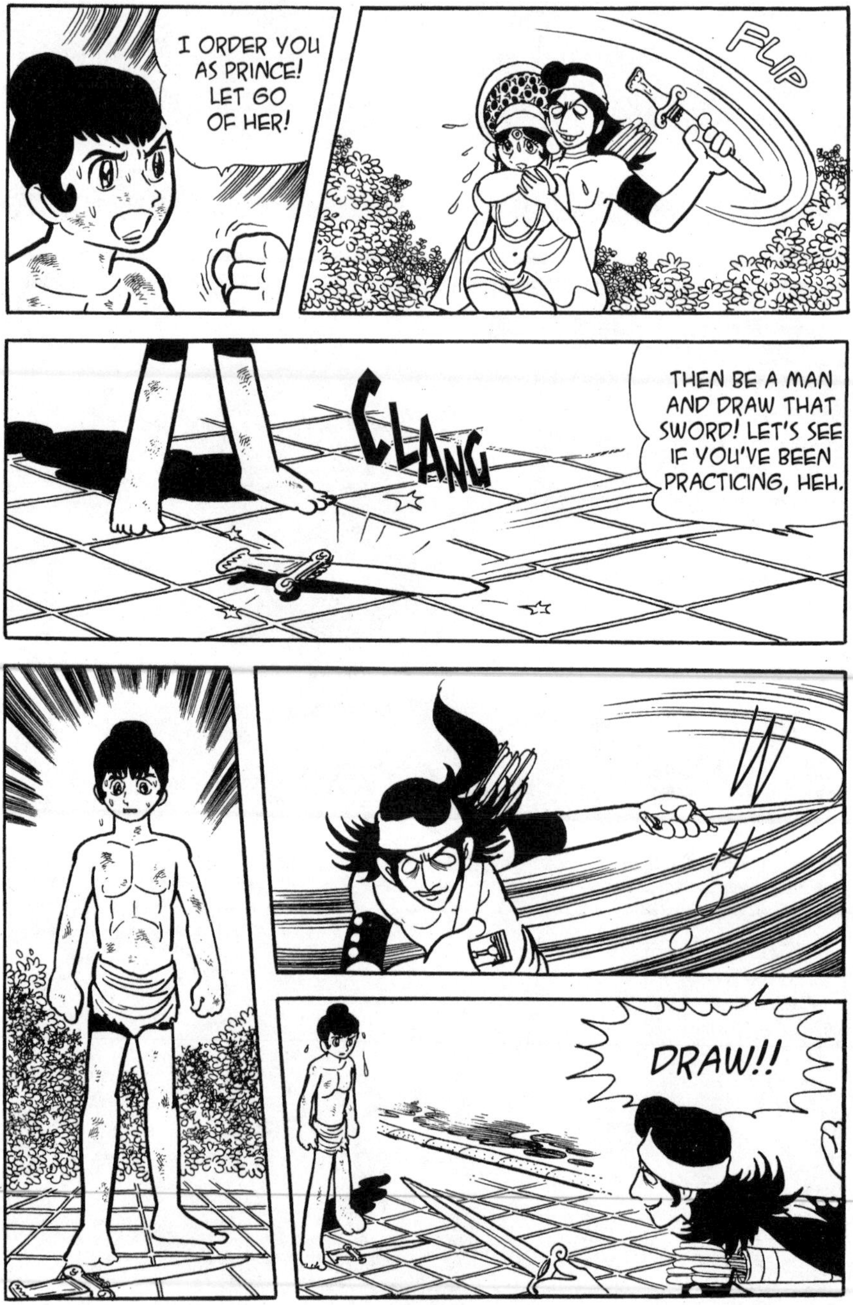
I ORDER YOU AS PRINCE! LET GO OF HER!
FLIP
CLANG
THEN BE A MAN AND DRAW THAT SWORD! LET'S SEE IF YOU'VE BEEN PRACTICING, HEH.
DRAW!!

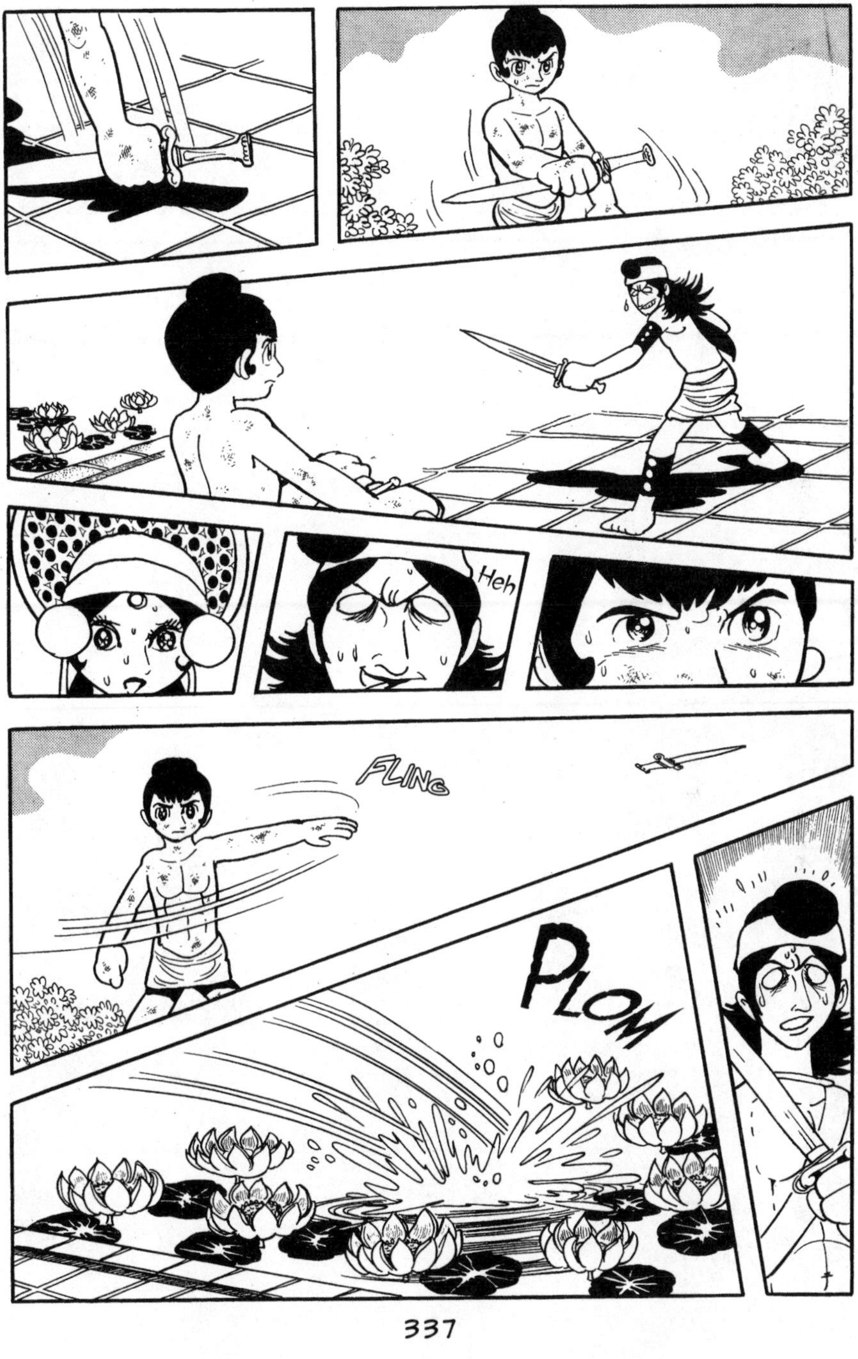
Heh
FLING
PLOM

SQUEEZE

AH

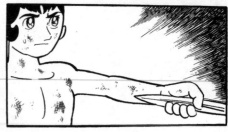

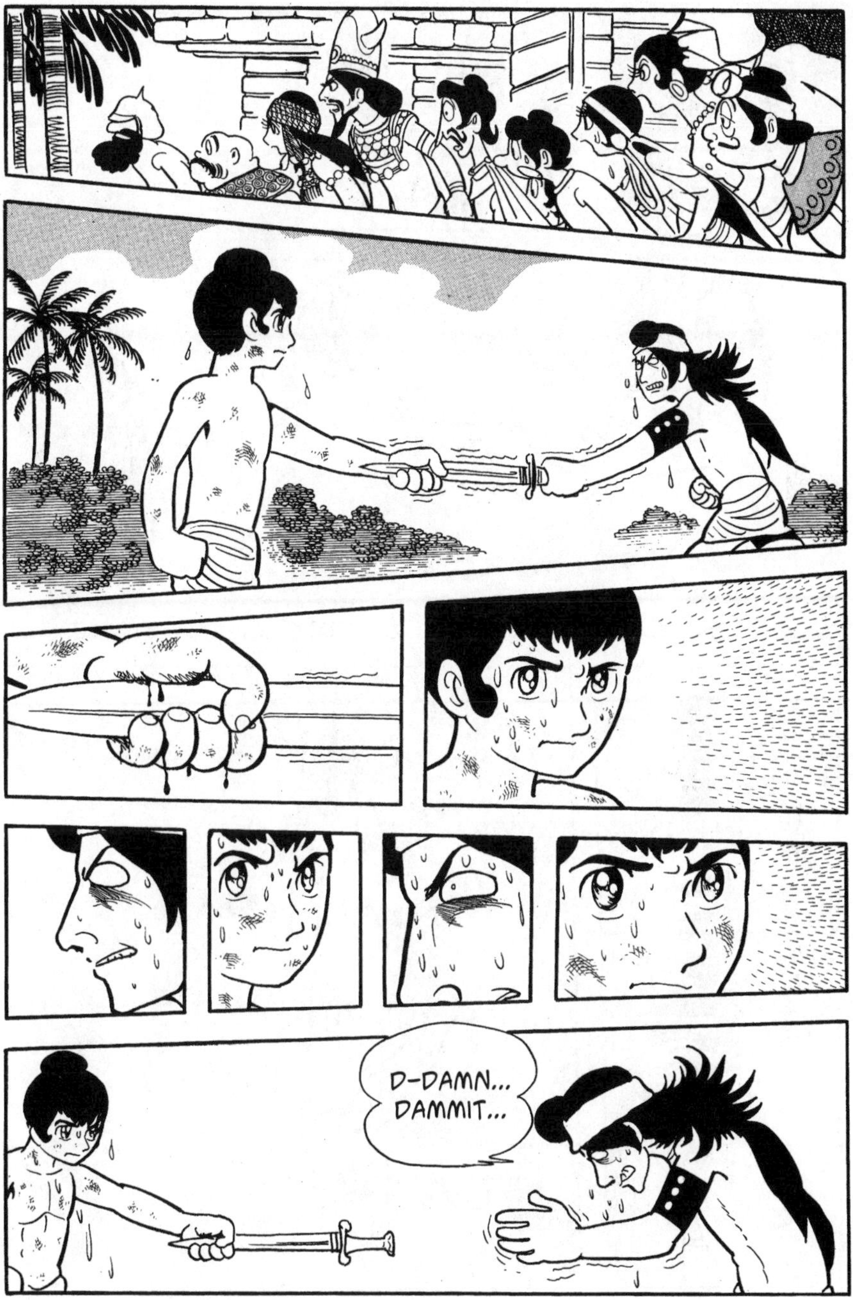
D-DAMN... DAMMIT...

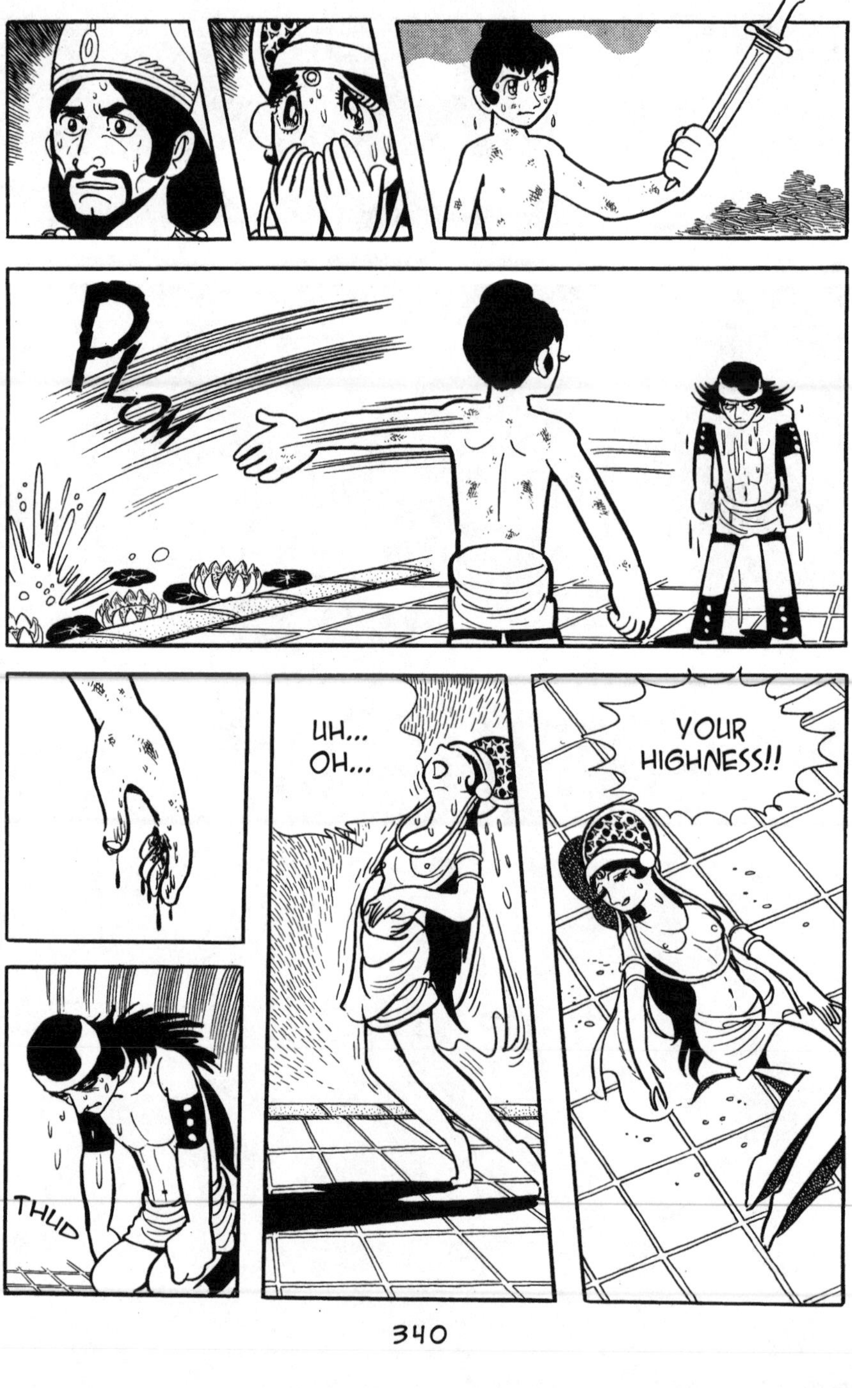
PLOM
UH... OH...
YOUR HIGHNESS!!
THUD

CHAPTER NINE

DAWN OF THE JOURNEY

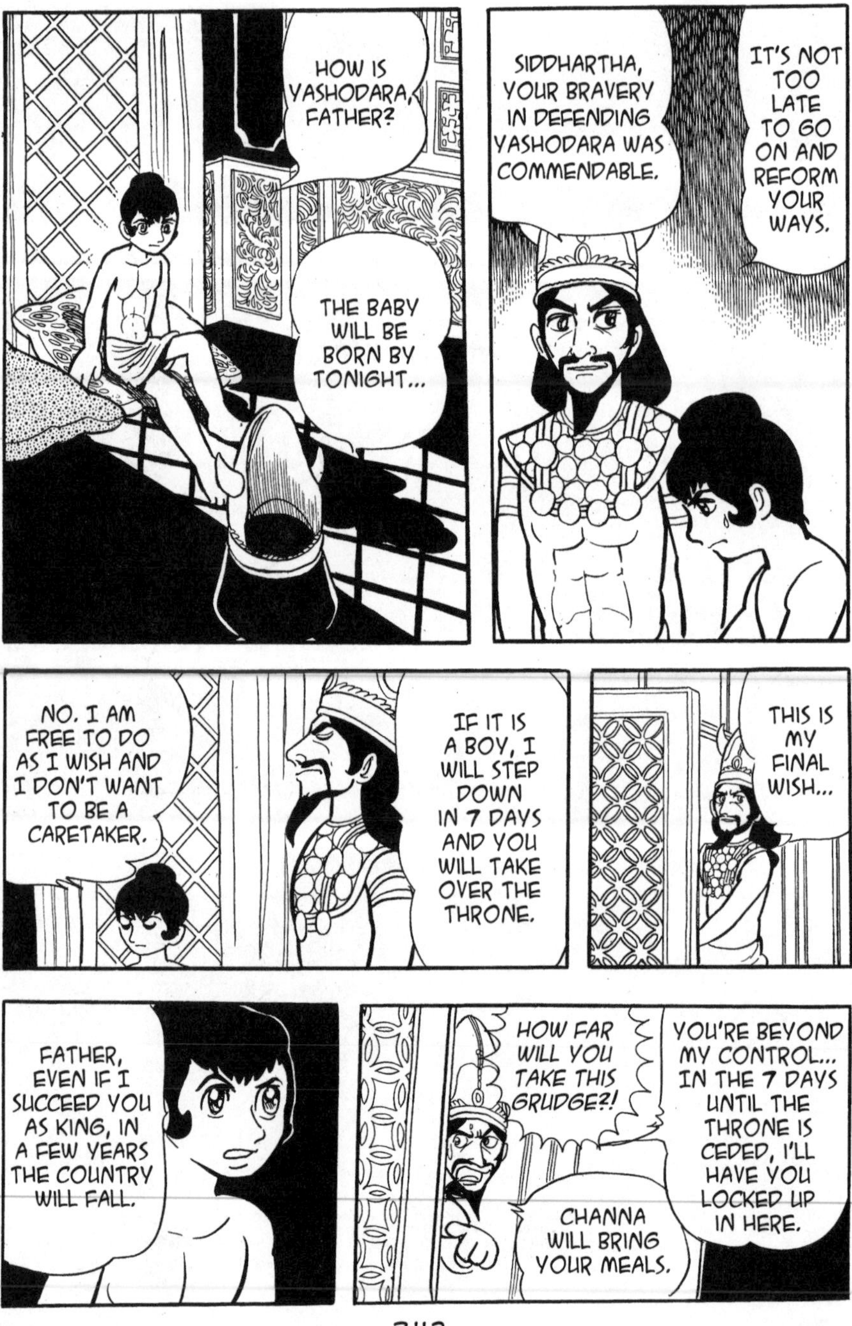
HOW IS YASHODARA, FATHER?
THE BABY WILL BE BORN BY TONIGHT...
SIDDHARTHA, YOUR BRAVERY IN DEFENDING YASHODARA WAS COMMENDABLE.
IT'S NOT TOO LATE TO GO ON AND REFORM YOUR WAYS.
NO. I AM FREE TO DO AS I WISH AND I DON'T WANT TO BE A CARETAKER.
IF IT IS A BOY, I WILL STEP DOWN IN 7 DAYS AND YOU WILL TAKE OVER THE THRONE.
THIS IS MY FINAL WISH...
FATHER, EVEN IF I SUCCEED YOU AS KING, IN A FEW YEARS THE COUNTRY WILL FALL.
HOW FAR WILL YOU TAKE THIS GRUDGE?!
YOU'RE BEYOND MY CONTROL... IN THE 7 DAYS UNTIL THE THRONE IS CEDED, I'LL HAVE YOU LOCKED UP IN HERE.
CHANNA WILL BRING YOUR MEALS.

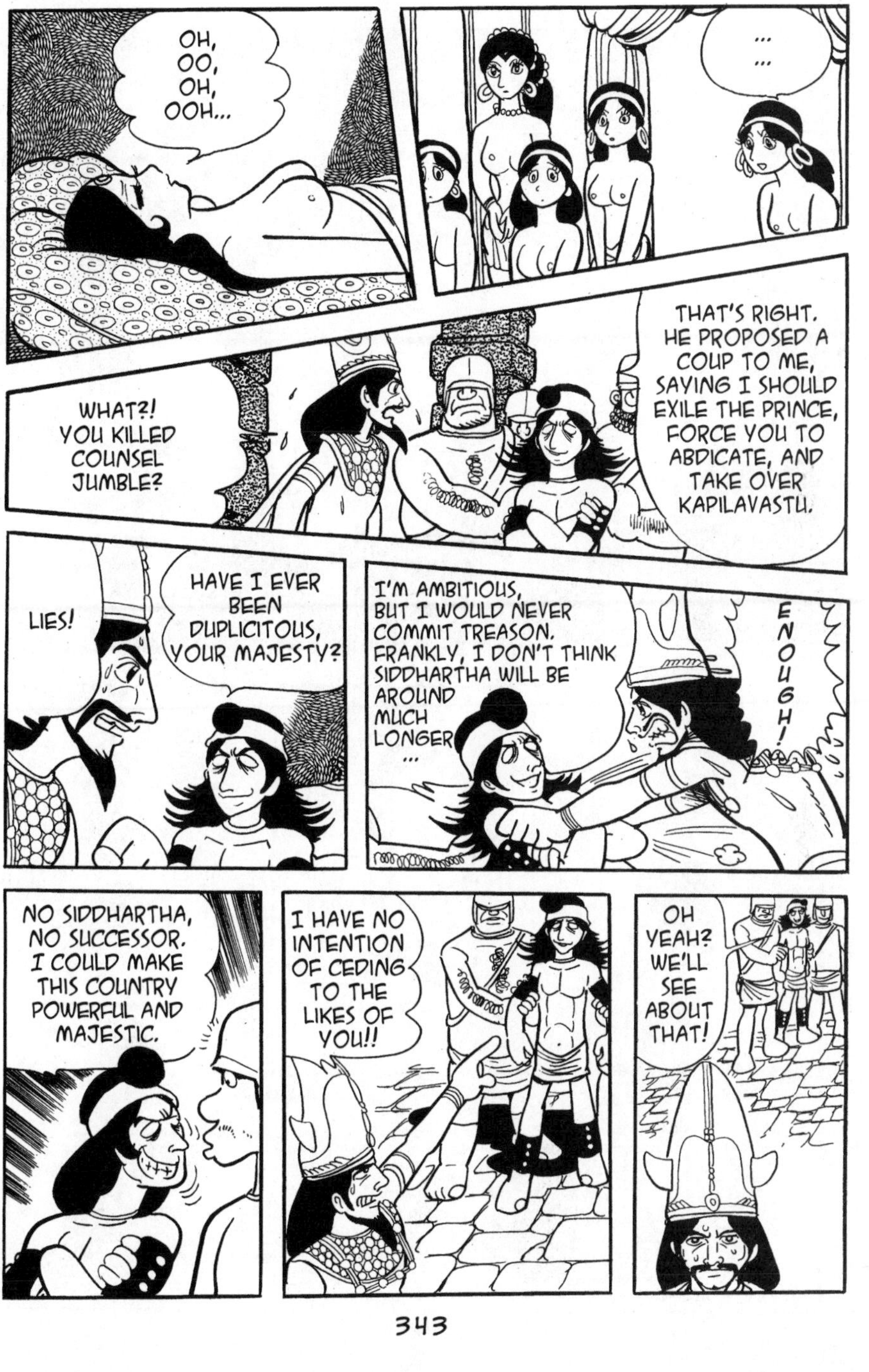
OH, OO, OH, OOH...
...
...
WHAT?! YOU KILLED COUNSEL JUMBLE?
THAT'S RIGHT. HE PROPOSED A COUP TO ME, SAYING I SHOULD EXILE THE PRINCE, FORCE YOU TO ABDICATE, AND TAKE OVER KAPILAVASTU.
LIES!
HAVE I EVER BEEN DUPLICITOUS, YOUR MAJESTY?
I'M AMBITIOUS, BUT I WOULD NEVER COMMIT TREASON. FRANKLY, I DON'T THINK SIDDHARTHA WILL BE AROUND MUCH LONGER ...
ENOUGH!
NO SIDDHARTHA, NO SUCCESSOR. I COULD MAKE THIS COUNTRY POWERFUL AND MAJESTIC.
I HAVE NO INTENTION OF CEDING TO THE LIKES OF YOU!!
OH YEAH? WE'LL SEE ABOUT THAT!

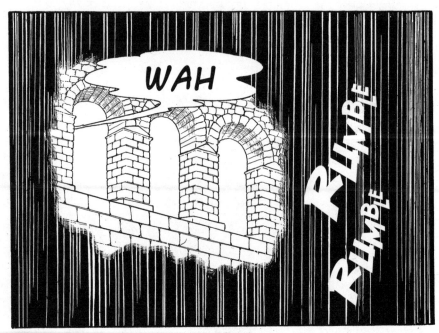

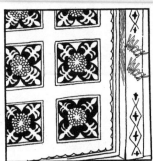

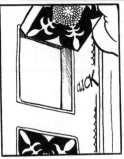

WAH
RUMBLE
RUMBLE
KNOCK
KNOCK
CLICK
PRINCE, IT IS I, CHANNA.
THE HEIR IS BORN.
AH.... A BOY OR A GIRL?
A PRINCE!
A PRINCE LIKE A JEWEL

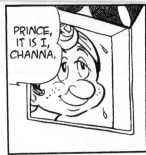

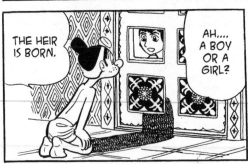

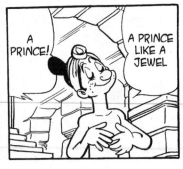

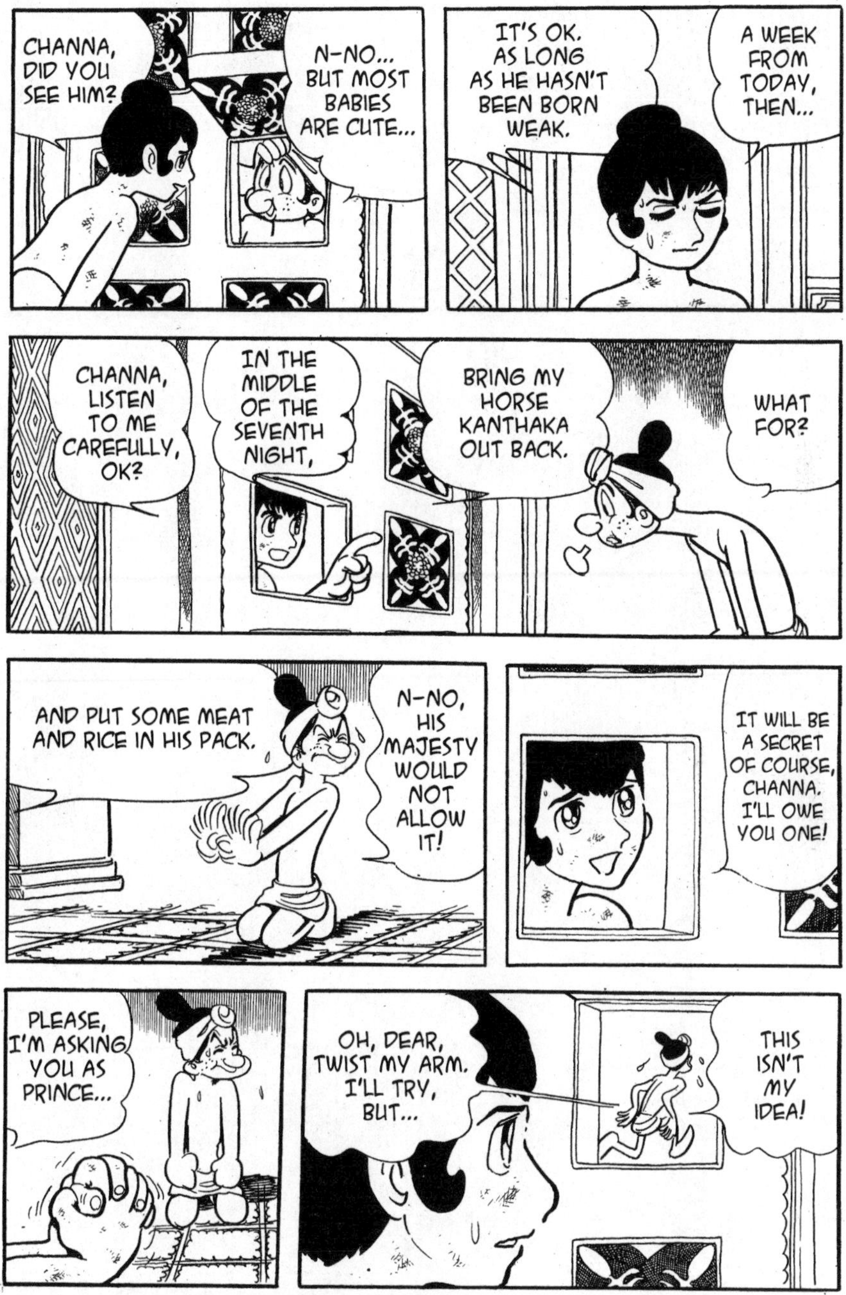
CHANNA, DID YOU SEE HIM?
N-NO... BUT MOST BABIES ARE CUTE...
IT'S OK. AS LONG AS HE HASN'T BEEN BORN WEAK.
A WEEK FROM TODAY, THEN...
CHANNA, LISTEN TO ME CAREFULLY, OK?
IN THE MIDDLE OF THE SEVENTH NIGHT,
BRING MY HORSE KANTHAKA OUT BACK.
WHAT FOR?
AND PUT SOME MEAT AND RICE IN HIS PACK.
N-NO, HIS MAJESTY WOULD NOT ALLOW IT!
IT WILL BE A SECRET OF COURSE, CHANNA. I'LL OWE YOU ONE!
PLEASE, I'M ASKING YOU AS PRINCE...
OH, DEAR, TWIST MY ARM. I'LL TRY, BUT...
THIS ISN'T MY IDEA!

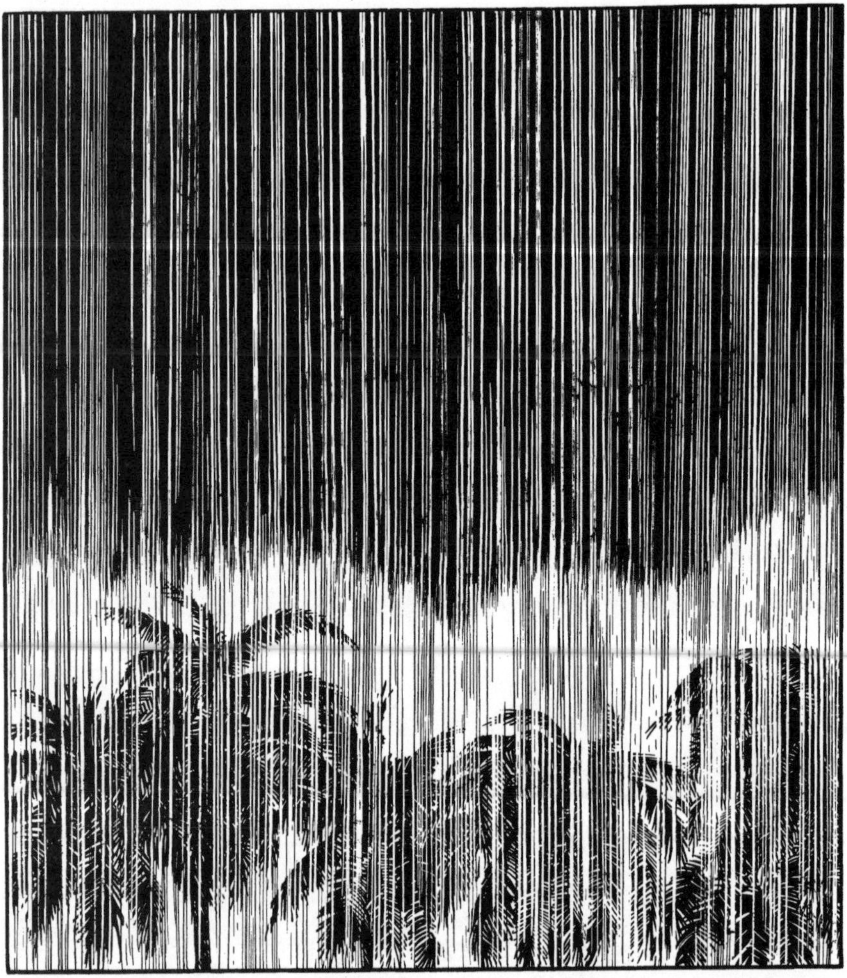

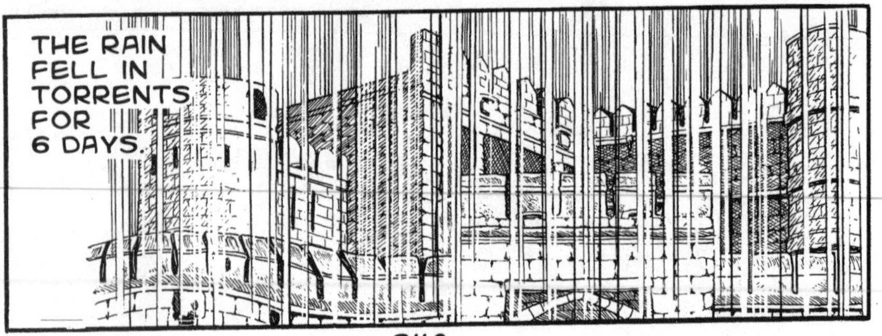
THE RAIN FELL IN TORRENTS FOR 6 DAYS.

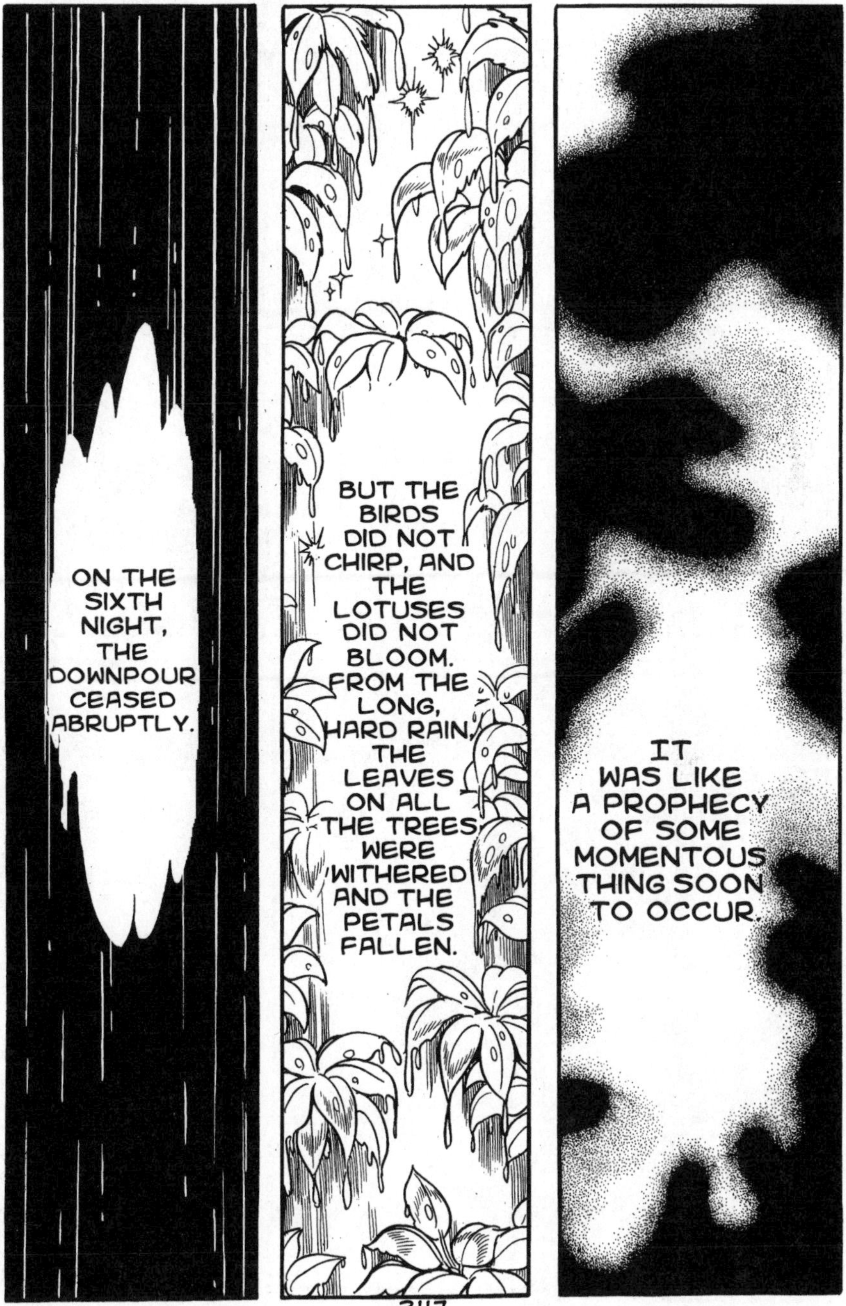
ON THE SIXTH NIGHT, THE DOWNPOUR CEASED ABRUPTLY.
BUT THE BIRDS DID NOT CHIRP, AND THE LOTUSES DID NOT BLOOM. FROM THE LONG, HARD RAIN, THE LEAVES ON ALL THE TREES WERE WITHERED AND THE PETALS FALLEN.
IT WAS LIKE A PROPHECY OF SOME MOMENTOUS THING SOON TO OCCUR.

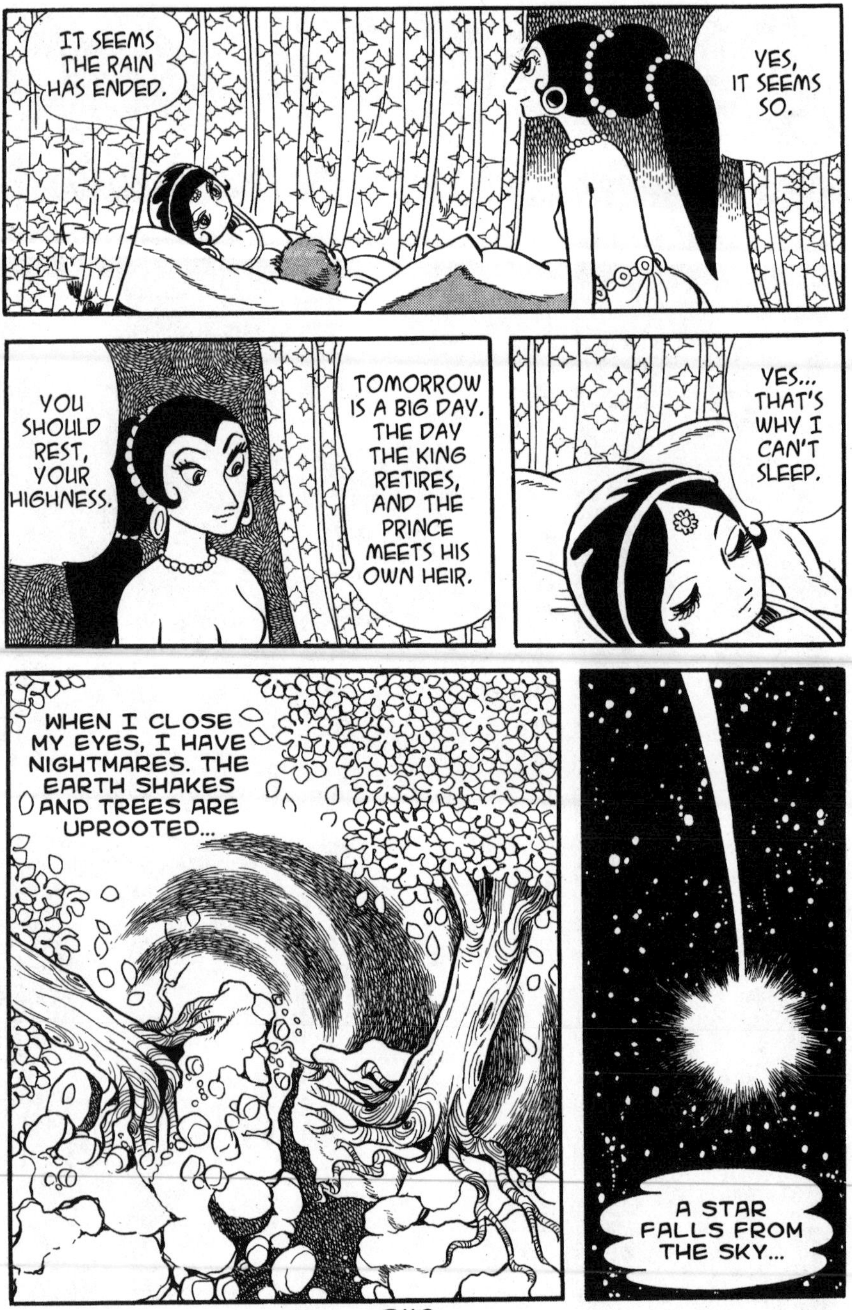
IT SEEMS THE RAIN HAS ENDED.
YES, IT SEEMS SO.
YOU SHOULD REST, YOUR HIGHNESS.
TOMORROW IS A BIG DAY. THE DAY THE KING RETIRES, AND THE PRINCE MEETS HIS OWN HEIR.
YES... THAT'S WHY I CAN'T SLEEP.
WHEN I CLOSE MY EYES, I HAVE NIGHTMARES. THE EARTH SHAKES AND TREES ARE UPROOTED...
A STAR FALLS FROM THE SKY...

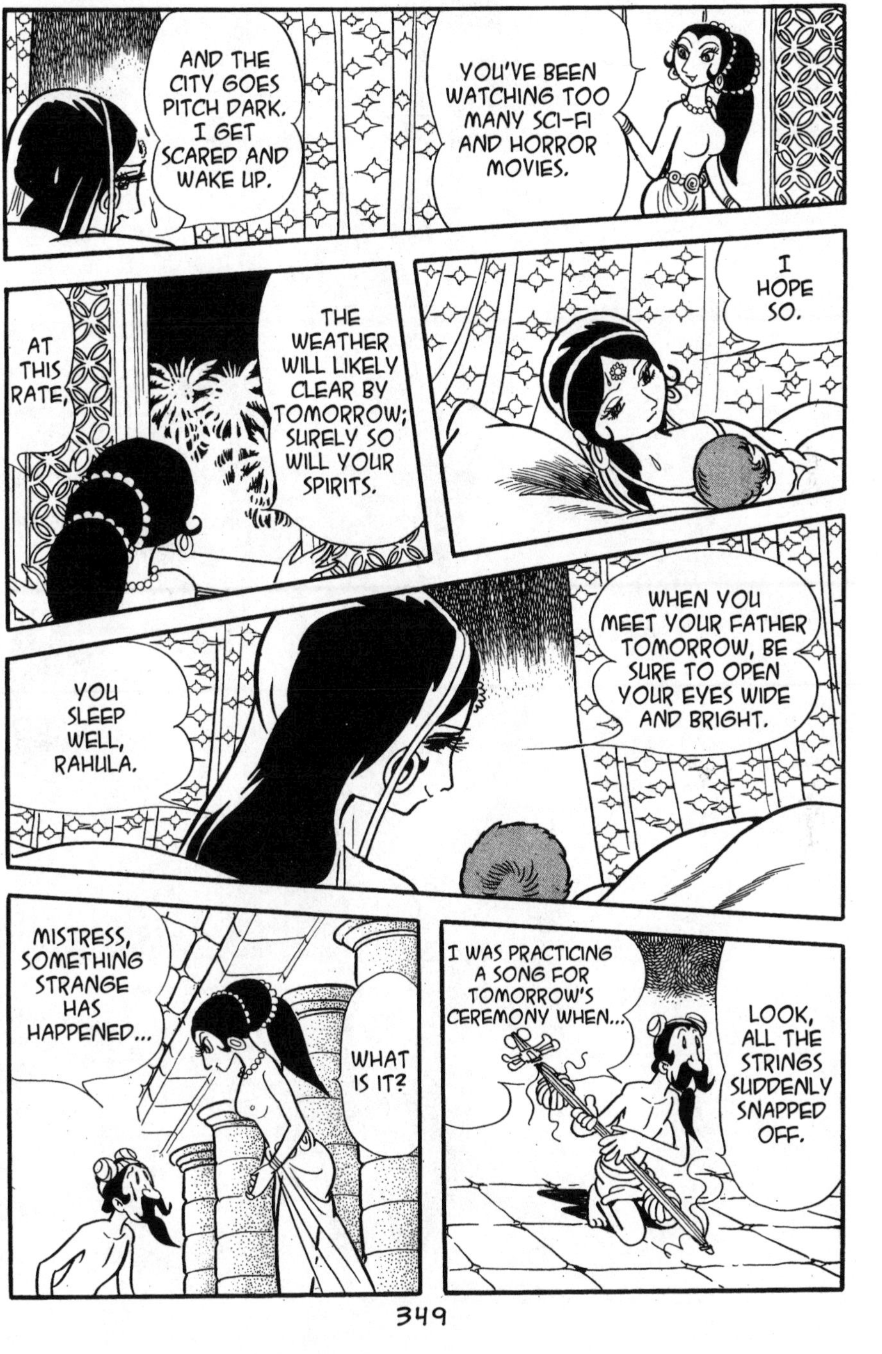
AND THE CITY GOES PITCH DARK. I GET SCARED AND WAKE UP.
YOU'VE BEEN WATCHING TOO MANY SCI-FI AND HORROR MOVIES.
AT THIS RATE,
THE WEATHER WILL LIKELY CLEAR BY TOMORROW; SURELY SO WILL YOUR SPIRITS.
I HOPE SO.
YOU SLEEP WELL, RAHULA.
WHEN YOU MEET YOUR FATHER TOMORROW, BE SURE TO OPEN YOUR EYES WIDE AND BRIGHT.
MISTRESS, SOMETHING STRANGE HAS HAPPENED...
WHAT IS IT?
I WAS PRACTICING A SONG FOR TOMORROW'S CEREMONY WHEN...
LOOK, ALL THE STRINGS SUDDENLY SNAPPED OFF.

IT'S NOT A VERY GOOD OMEN.

TELL NO ONE ABOUT THIS, LEAST OF ALL THE QUEEN.

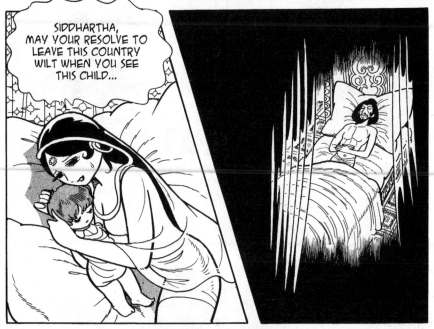

SIDDHARTHA, MAY YOUR RESOLVE TO LEAVE THIS COUNTRY WILT WHEN YOU SEE THIS CHILD...

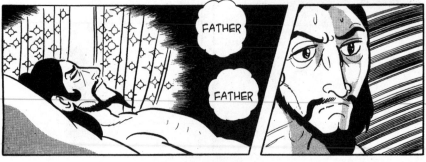

FATHER

FATHER

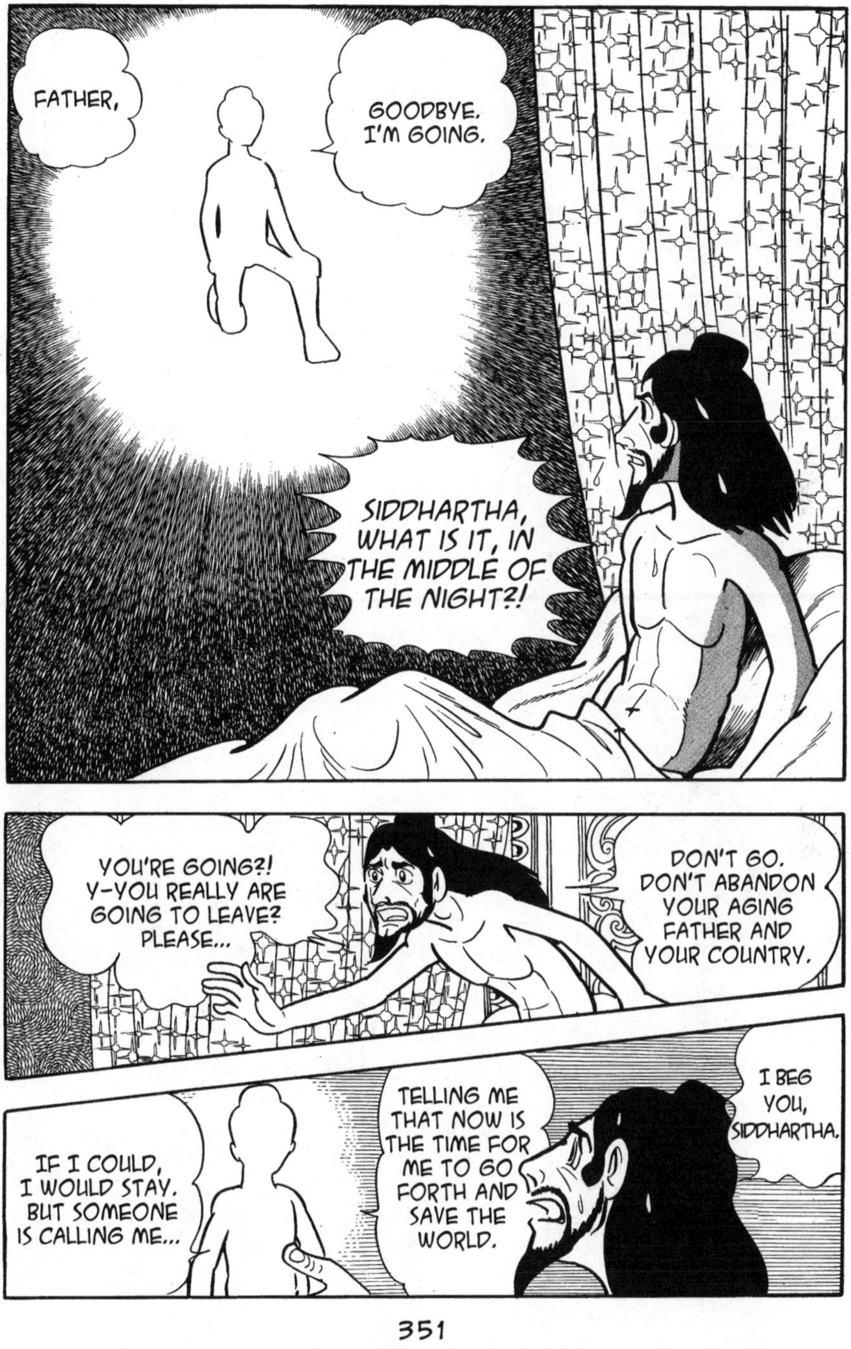
FATHER,
GOODBYE. I'M GOING.
SIDDHARTHA, WHAT IS IT, IN THE MIDDLE OF THE NIGHT?!
YOU'RE GOING?! Y-YOU REALLY ARE GOING TO LEAVE? PLEASE...
DON'T GO. DON'T ABANDON YOUR AGING FATHER AND YOUR COUNTRY.
IF I COULD, I WOULD STAY. BUT SOMEONE IS CALLING ME...
TELLING ME THAT NOW IS THE TIME FOR ME TO GO FORTH AND SAVE THE WORLD.
I BEG YOU, SIDDHARTHA.

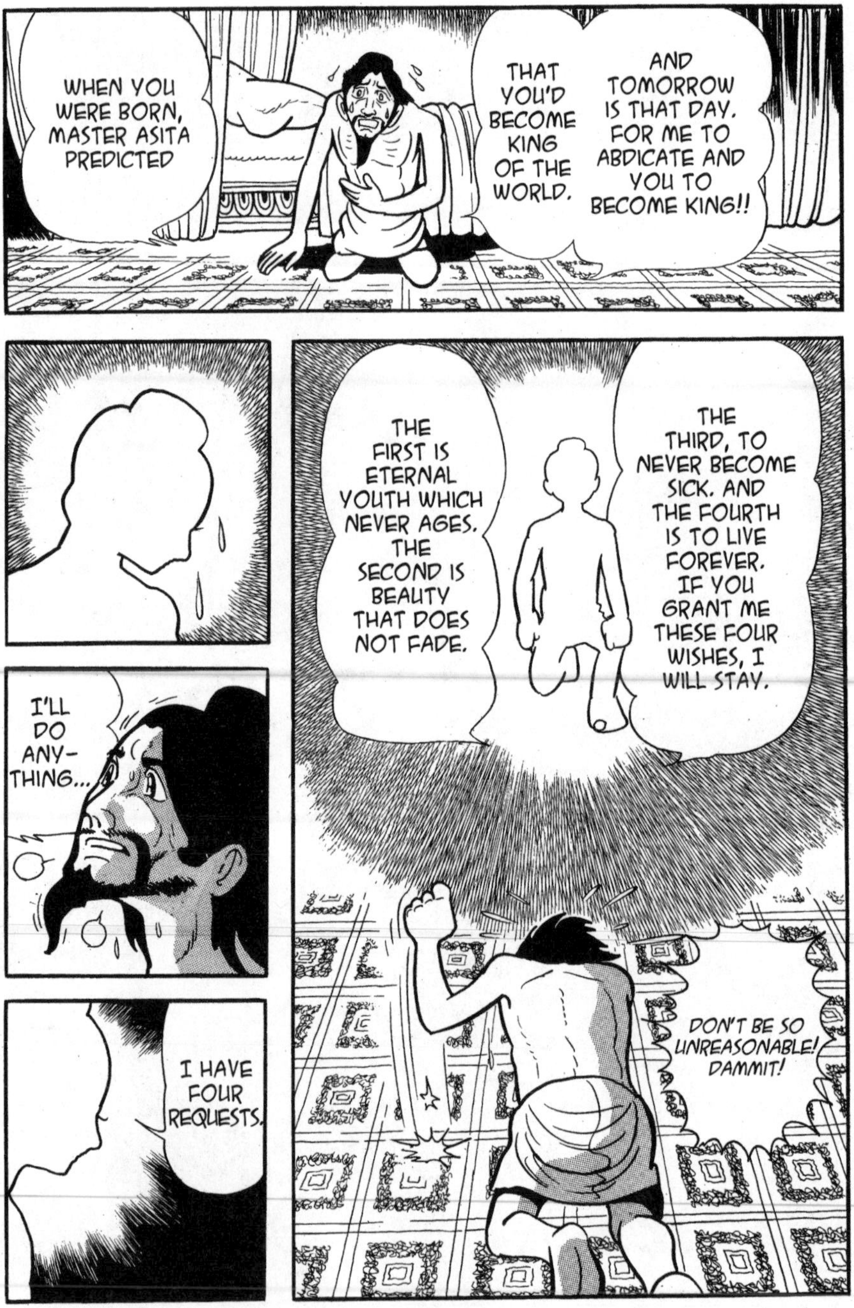
WHEN YOU WERE BORN, MASTER ASITA PREDICTED
THAT YOU'D BECOME KING OF THE WORLD.
AND TOMORROW IS THAT DAY. FOR ME TO ABDICATE AND YOU TO BECOME KING!!
I'LL DO ANY-THING...
I HAVE FOUR REQUESTS.
THE FIRST IS ETERNAL YOUTH WHICH NEVER AGES. THE SECOND IS BEAUTY THAT DOES NOT FADE.
THE THIRD, TO NEVER BECOME SICK. AND THE FOURTH IS TO LIVE FOREVER. IF YOU GRANT ME THESE FOUR WISHES, I WILL STAY.
DON'T BE SO UNREASONABLE! DAMMIT!

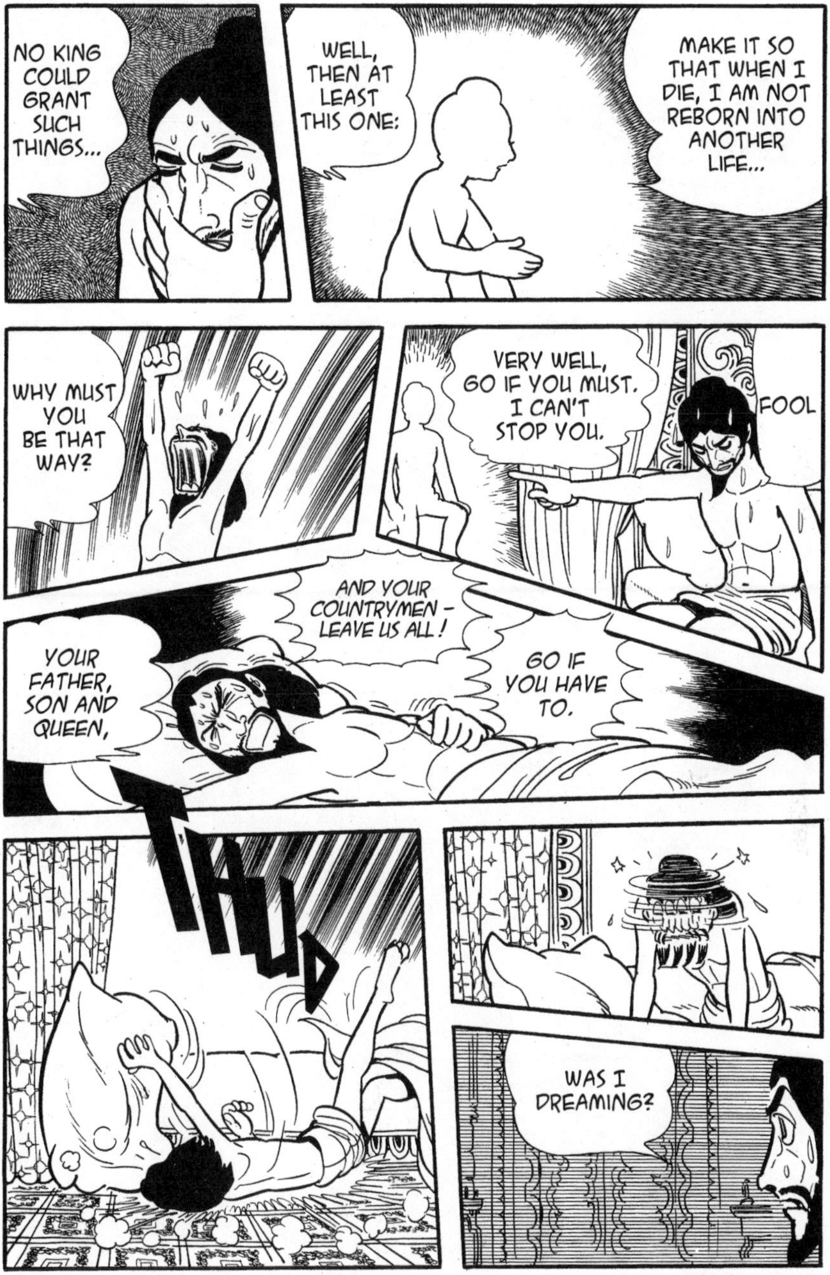
NO KING COULD GRANT SUCH THINGS...
WELL, THEN AT LEAST THIS ONE:
MAKE IT SO THAT WHEN I DIE, I AM NOT REBORN INTO ANOTHER LIFE...
WHY MUST YOU BE THAT WAY?
VERY WELL, GO IF YOU MUST. I CAN'T STOP YOU.
FOOL
YOUR FATHER, SON AND QUEEN,
AND YOUR COUNTRYMEN - LEAVE US ALL!
GO IF YOU HAVE TO.
THUD
WAS I DREAMING?

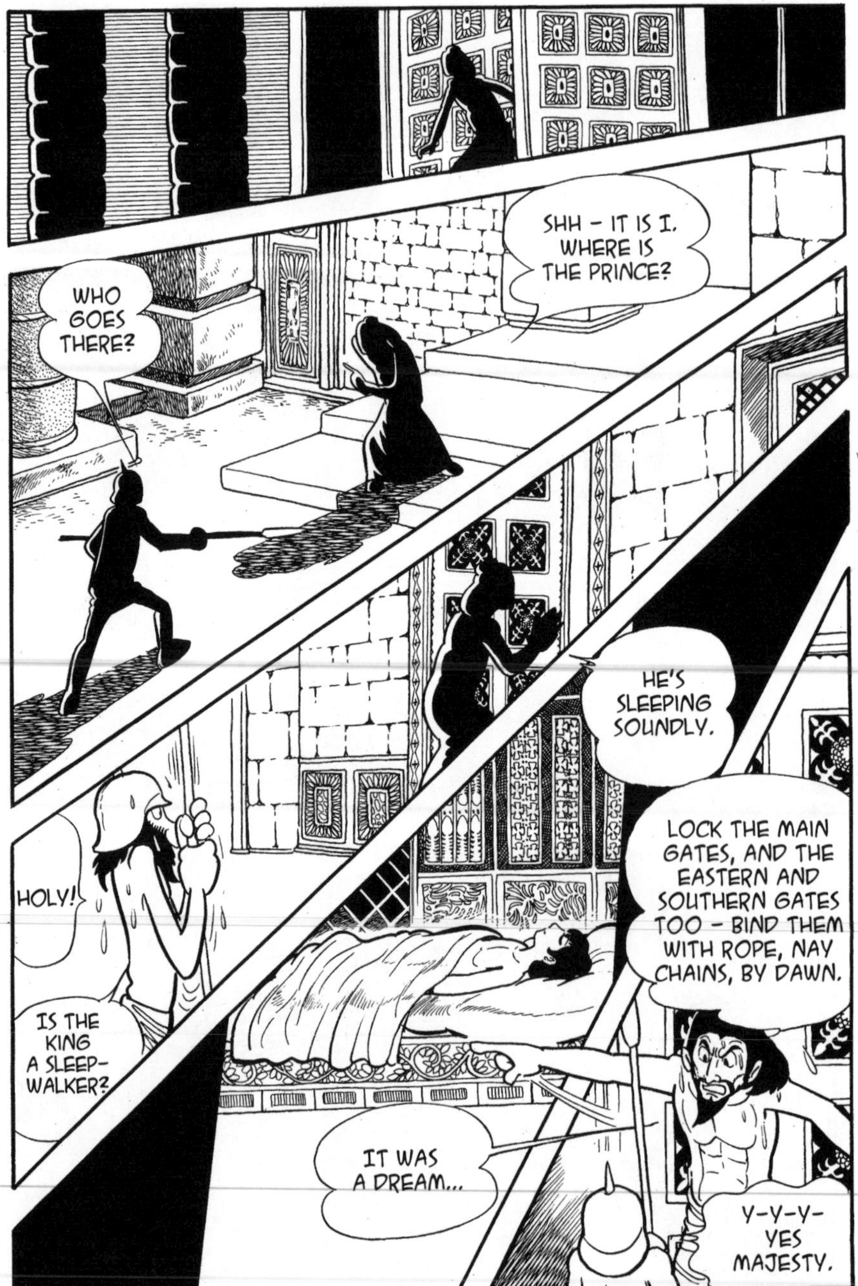
WHO GOES THERE?
SHH - IT IS I. WHERE IS THE PRINCE?
HE'S SLEEPING SOUNDLY.
HOLY!
IS THE KING A SLEEP-WALKER?
IT WAS A DREAM...
LOCK THE MAIN GATES, AND THE EASTERN AND SOUTHERN GATES TOO - BIND THEM WITH ROPE, NAY CHAINS, BY DAWN.
Y-Y-Y-YES MAJESTY.

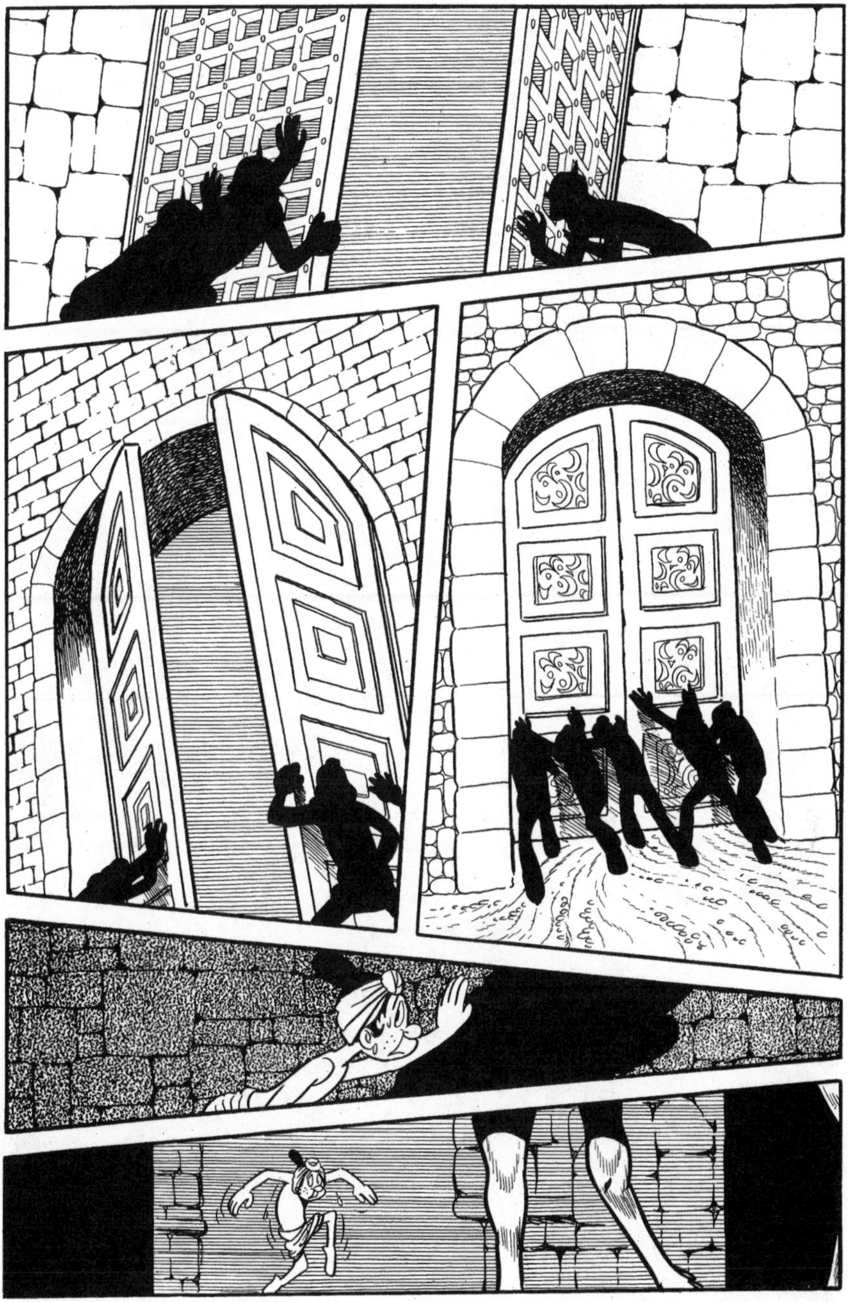

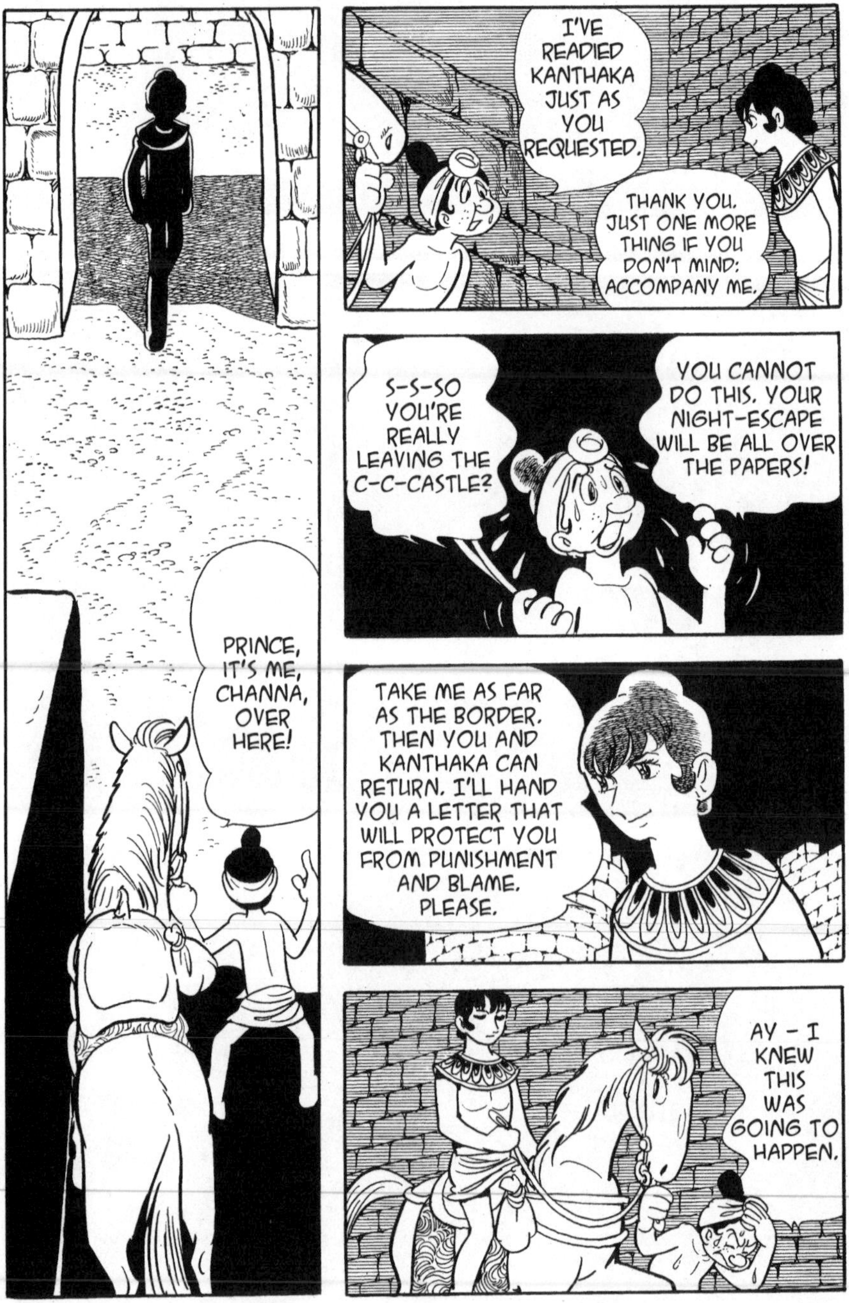
PRINCE, IT'S ME, CHANNA, OVER HERE!
I'VE READIED KANTHAKA JUST AS YOU REQUESTED.
THANK YOU. JUST ONE MORE THING IF YOU DON'T MIND: ACCOMPANY ME.
S-S-SO YOU'RE REALLY LEAVING THE C-C-CASTLE?
YOU CANNOT DO THIS. YOUR NIGHT-ESCAPE WILL BE ALL OVER THE PAPERS!
TAKE ME AS FAR AS THE BORDER. THEN YOU AND KANTHAKA CAN RETURN. I'LL HAND YOU A LETTER THAT WILL PROTECT YOU FROM PUNISHMENT AND BLAME. PLEASE.
AY - I KNEW THIS WAS GOING TO HAPPEN.

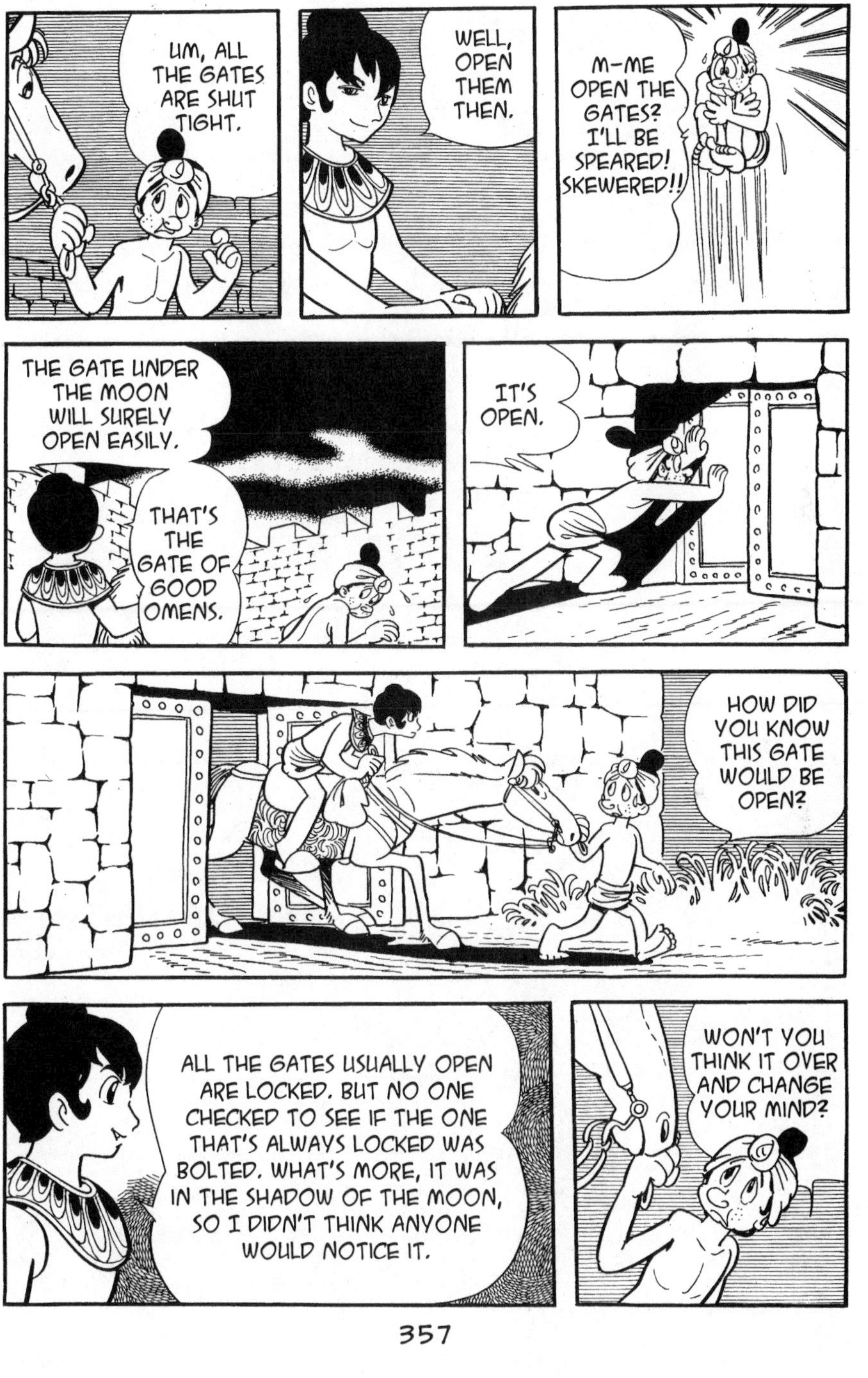
UM, ALL THE GATES ARE SHUT TIGHT.
WELL, OPEN THEM THEN.
M-ME OPEN THE GATES? I'LL BE SPEARED! SKEWERED!!
THE GATE UNDER THE MOON WILL SURELY OPEN EASILY.
THAT'S THE GATE OF GOOD OMENS.
IT'S OPEN.
HOW DID YOU KNOW THIS GATE WOULD BE OPEN?
ALL THE GATES USUALLY OPEN ARE LOCKED. BUT NO ONE CHECKED TO SEE IF THE ONE THAT'S ALWAYS LOCKED WAS BOLTED. WHAT'S MORE, IT WAS IN THE SHADOW OF THE MOON, SO I DIDN'T THINK ANYONE WOULD NOTICE IT.
WON'T YOU THINK IT OVER AND CHANGE YOUR MIND?

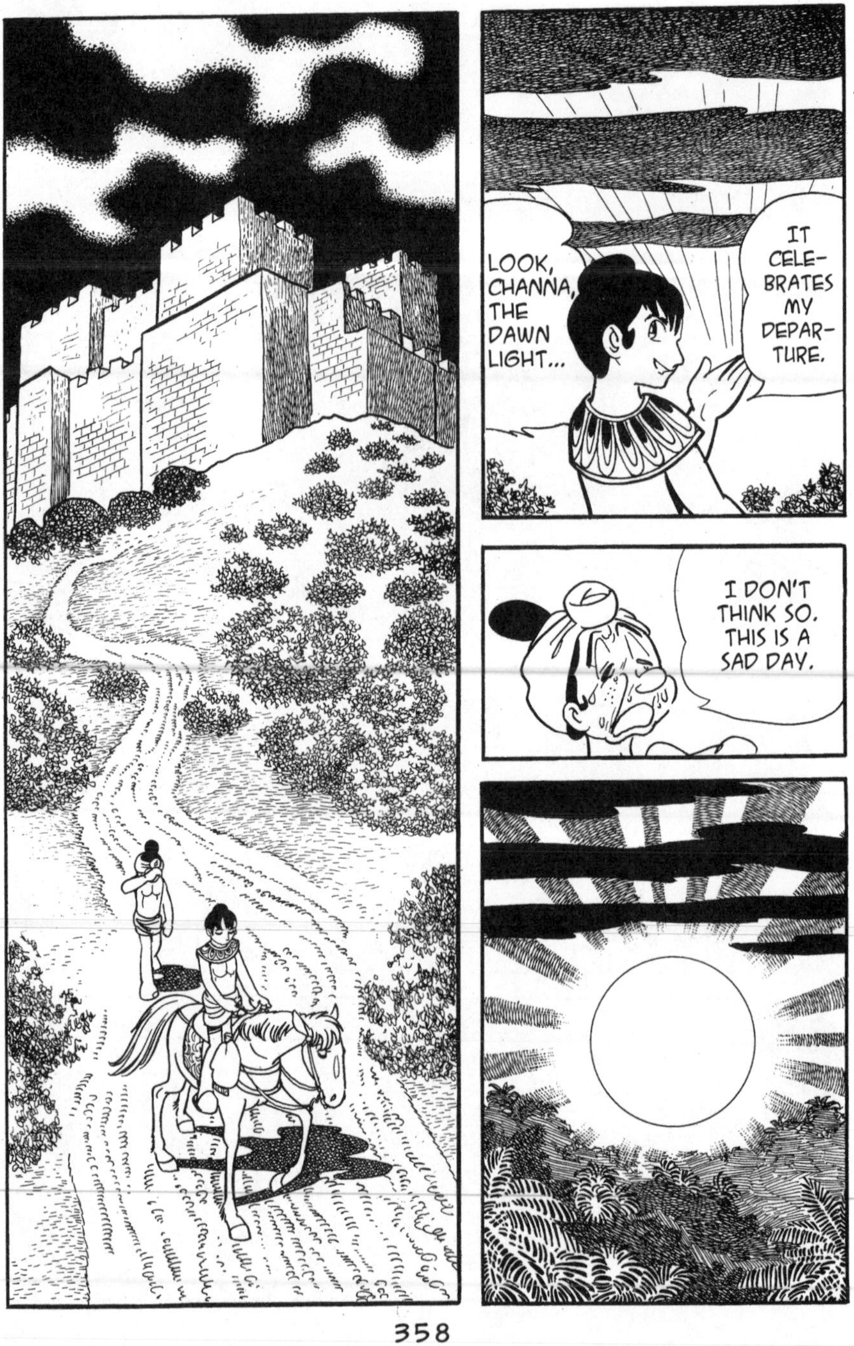
LOOK, CHANNA, THE DAWN LIGHT...
IT CELEBRATES MY DEPARTURE.
I DON'T THINK SO. THIS IS A SAD DAY.

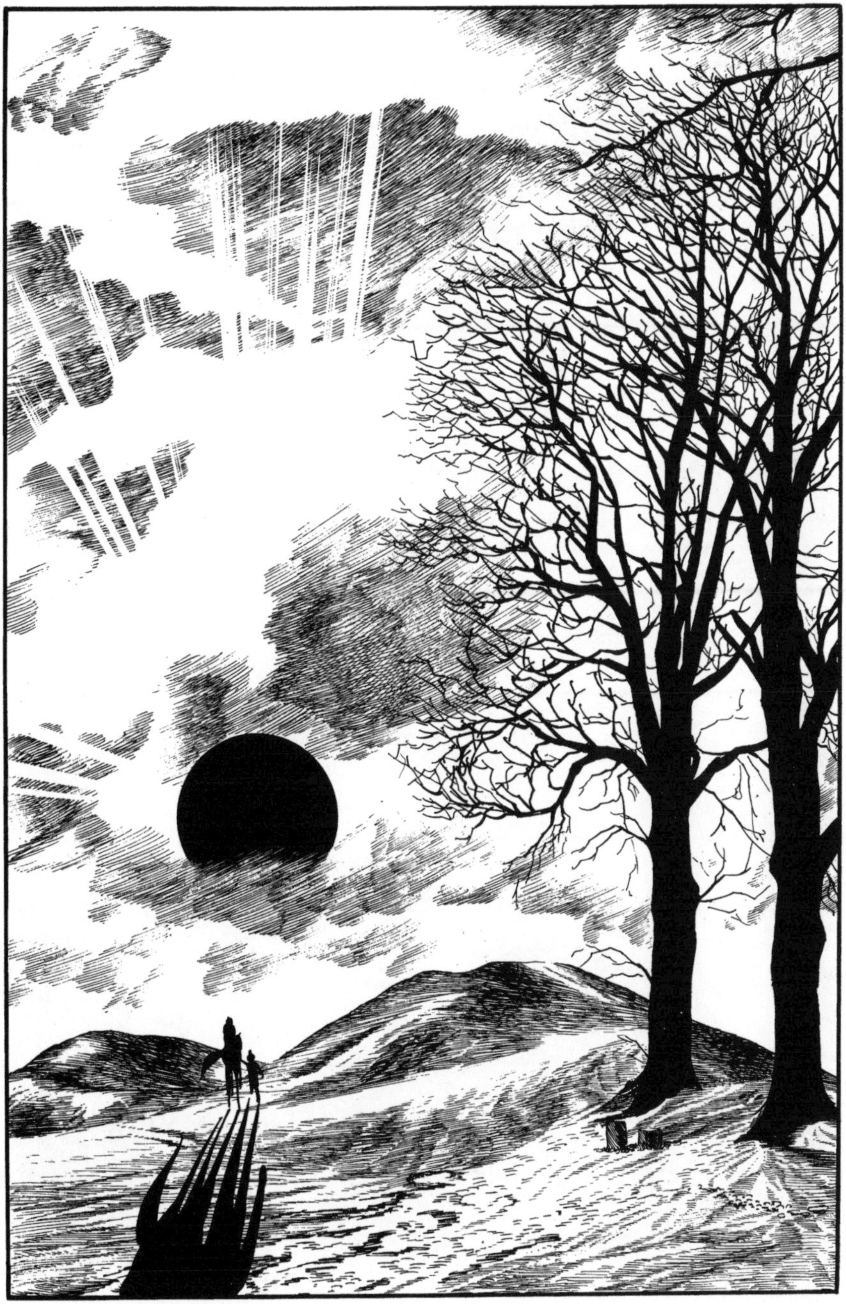

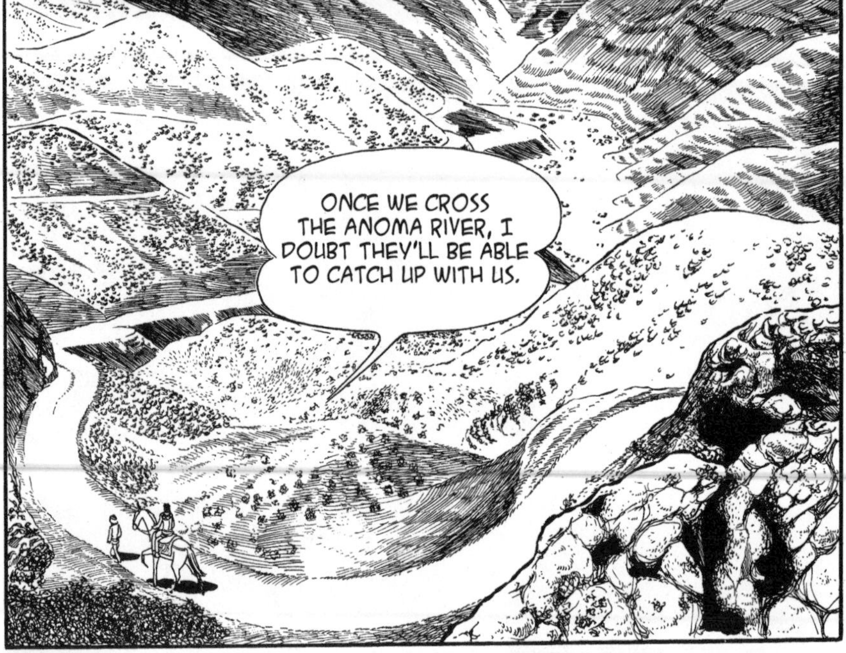
ONCE WE CROSS THE ANOMA RIVER, I DOUBT THEY'LL BE ABLE TO CATCH UP WITH US.

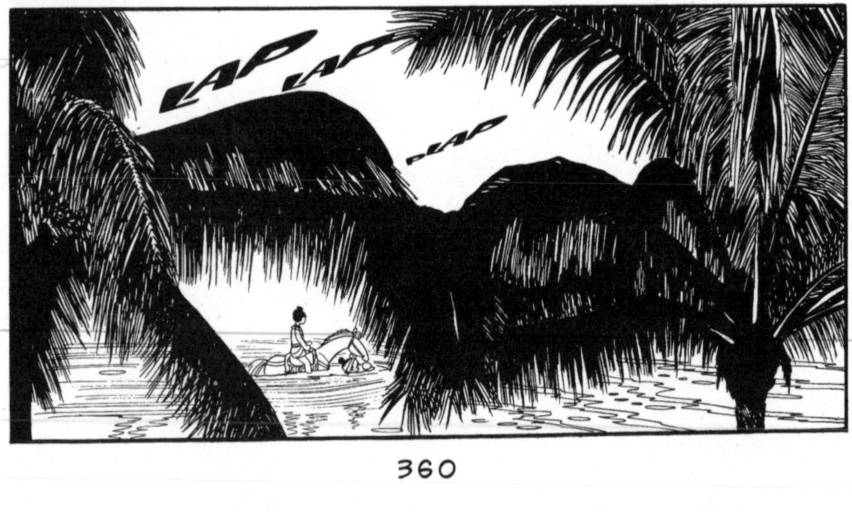
LAP
LAP
PLAP

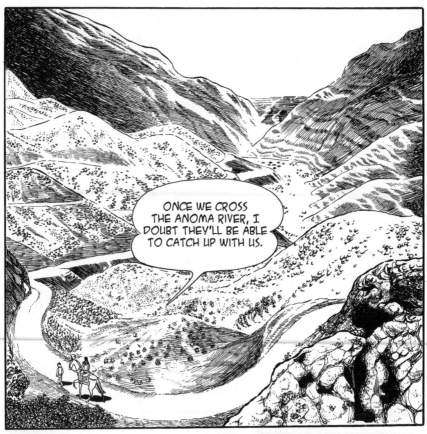

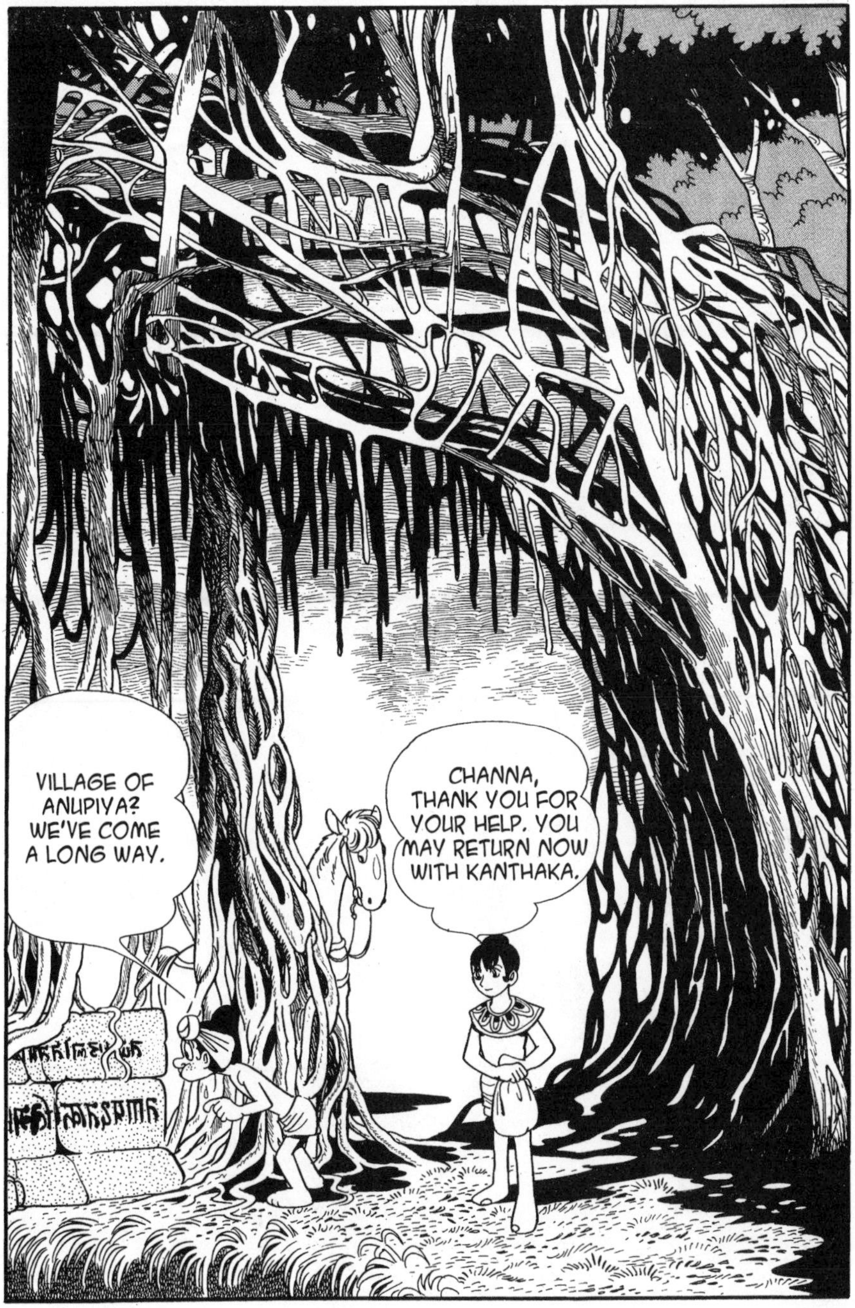
VILLAGE OF ANUPIYA? WE'VE COME A LONG WAY.
CHANNA, THANK YOU FOR YOUR HELP. YOU MAY RETURN NOW WITH KANTHAKA.

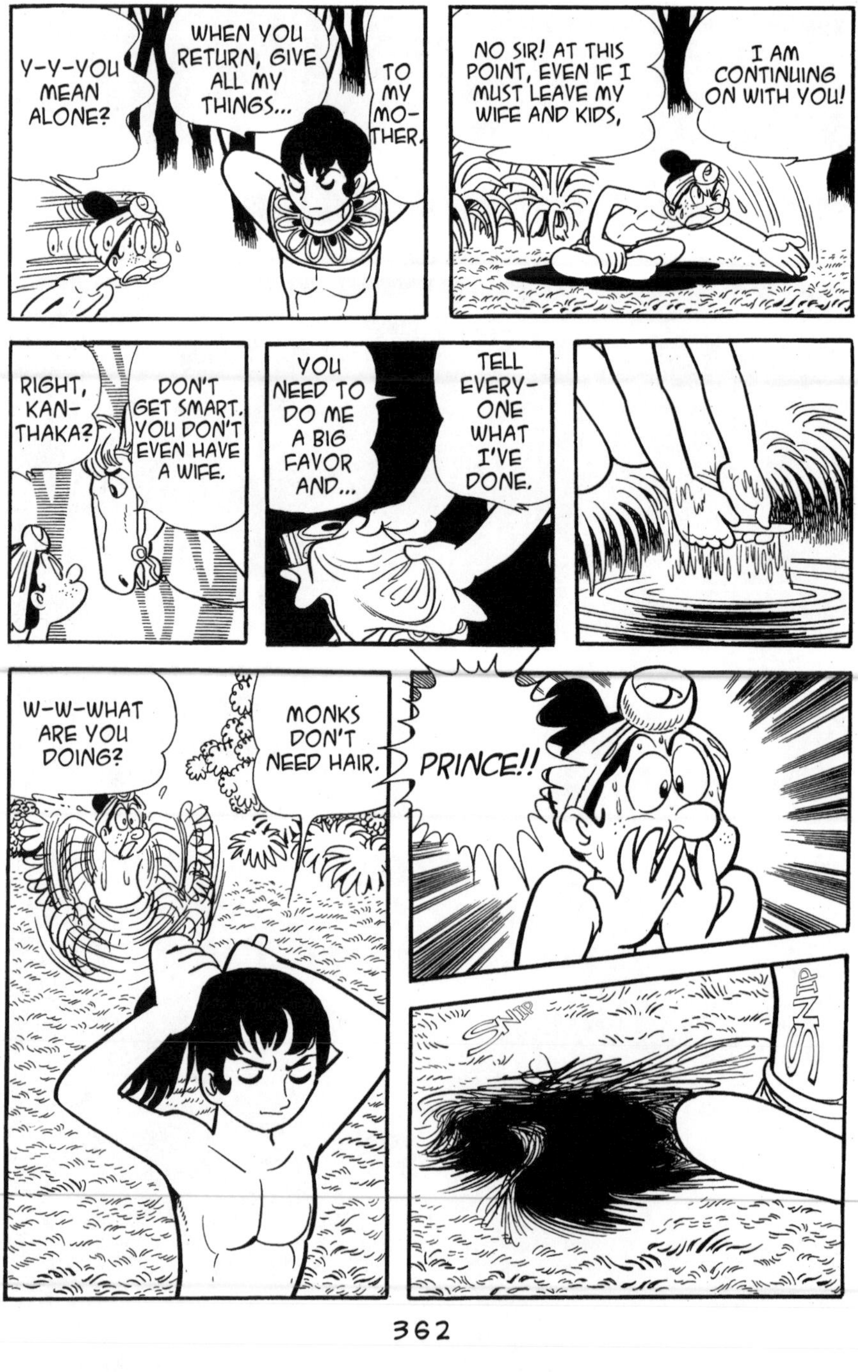

Y-Y-YOU MEAN ALONE?
WHEN YOU RETURN, GIVE ALL MY THINGS...
TO MY MOTHER.
NO SIR! AT THIS POINT, EVEN IF I MUST LEAVE MY WIFE AND KIDS,
I AM CONTINUING ON WITH YOU!
RIGHT, KANTHAKA?
DON'T GET SMART. YOU DON'T EVEN HAVE A WIFE.
YOU NEED TO DO ME A BIG FAVOR AND...
TELL EVERYONE WHAT I'VE DONE.
W-W-WHAT ARE YOU DOING?
MONKS DON'T NEED HAIR.
PRINCE!!
SNIP
SNIP

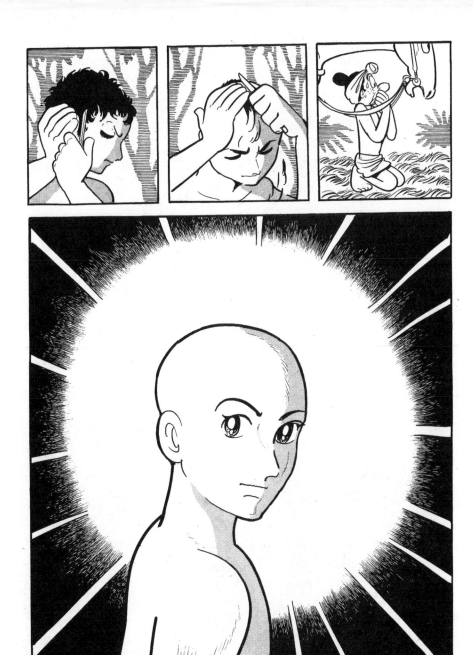

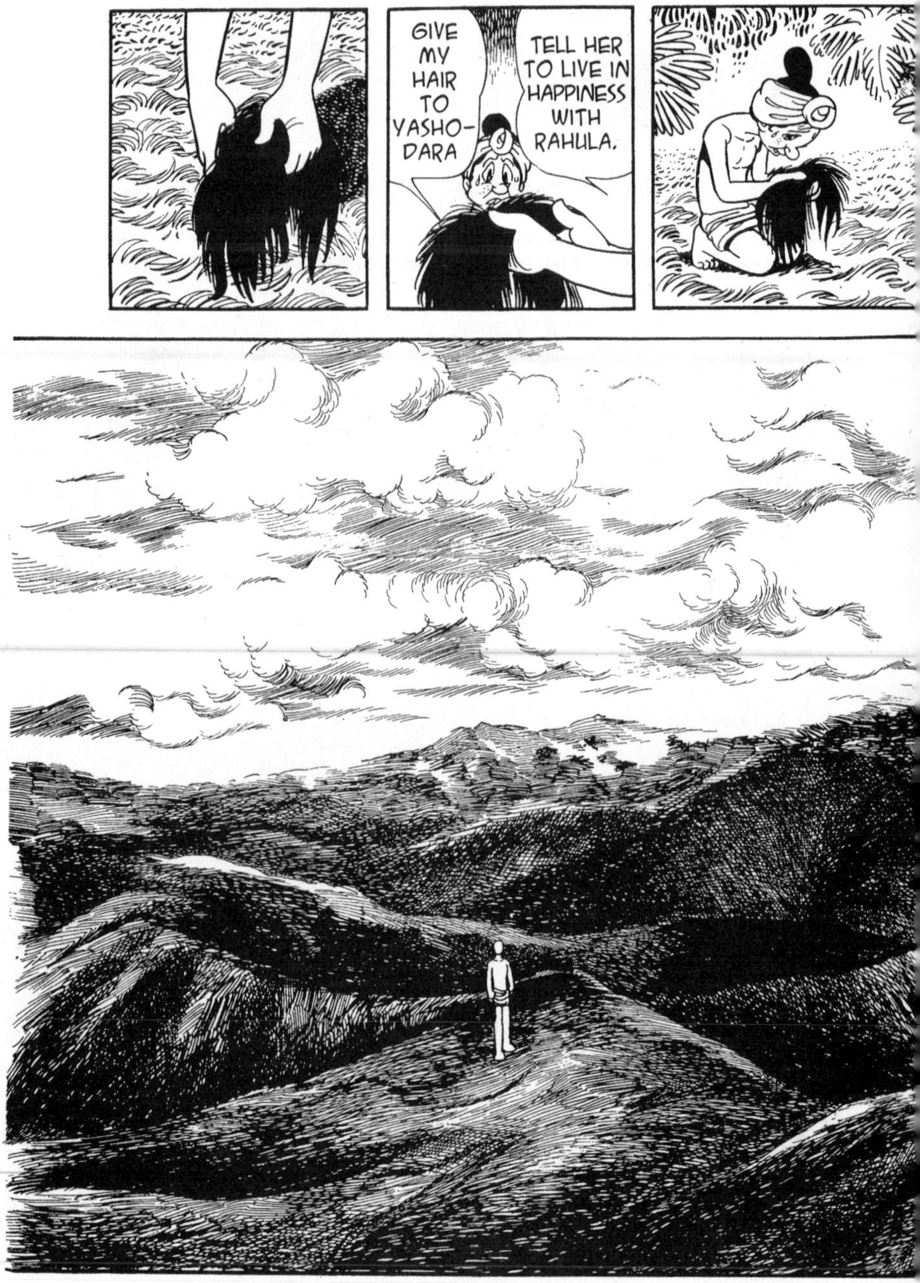
GIVE MY HAIR TO YASHO-DARA
TELL HER TO LIVE IN HAPPINESS WITH RAHULA.

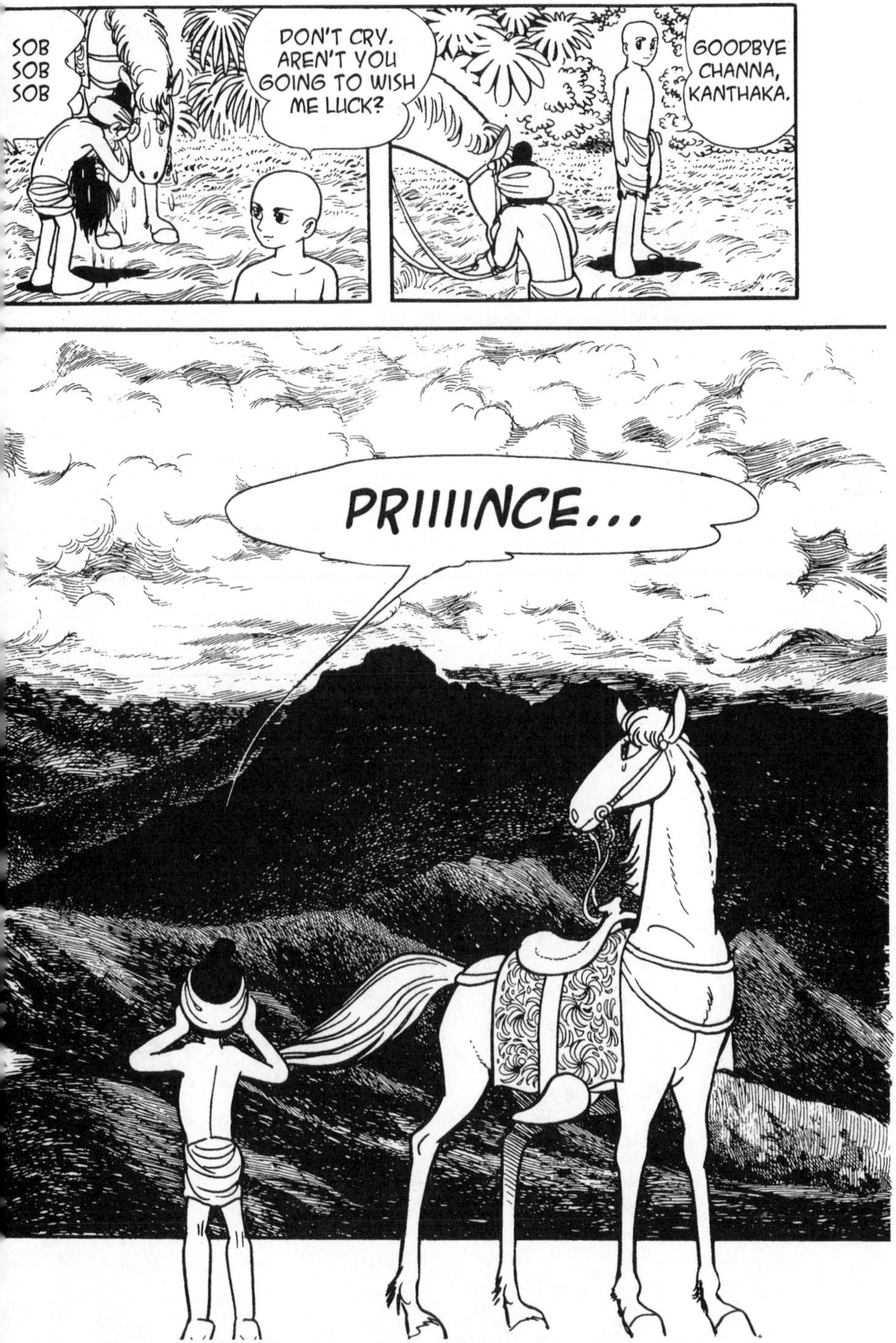
SOB SOB SOB
DON'T CRY. AREN'T YOU GOING TO WISH ME LUCK?
GOODBYE CHANNA, KANTHAKA.
PRIIIINCE...

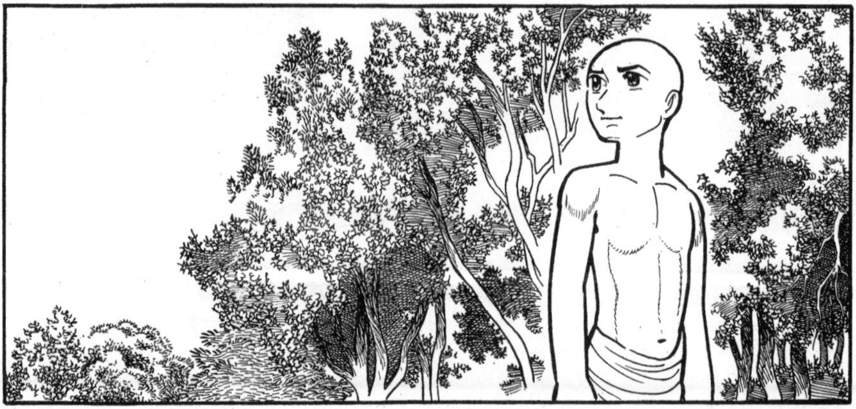
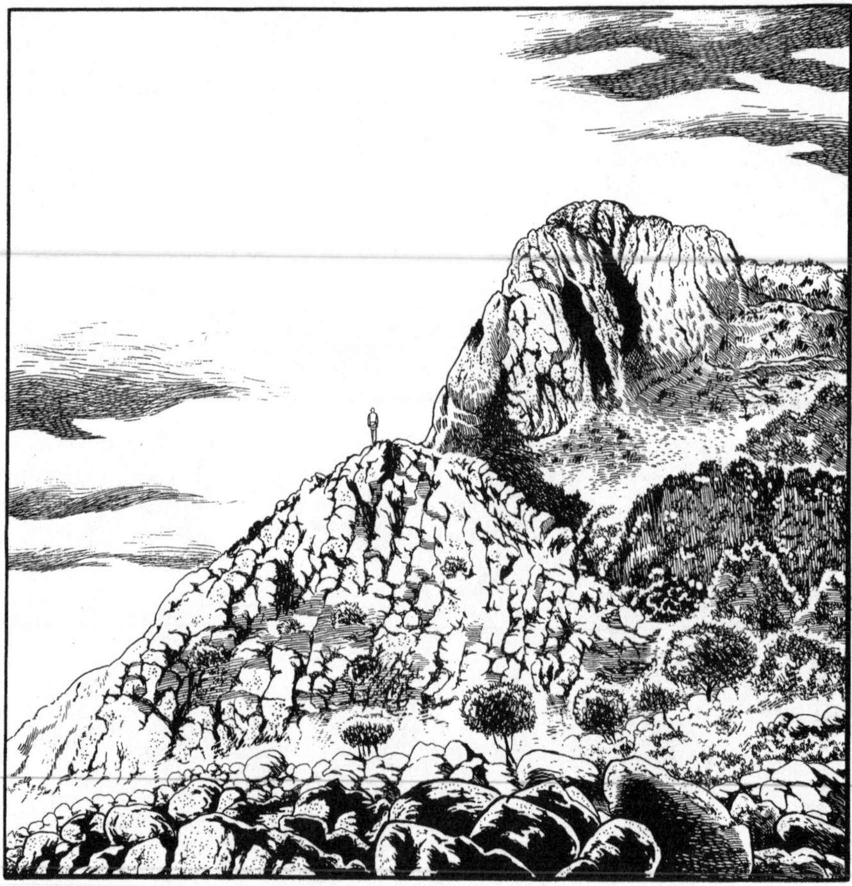

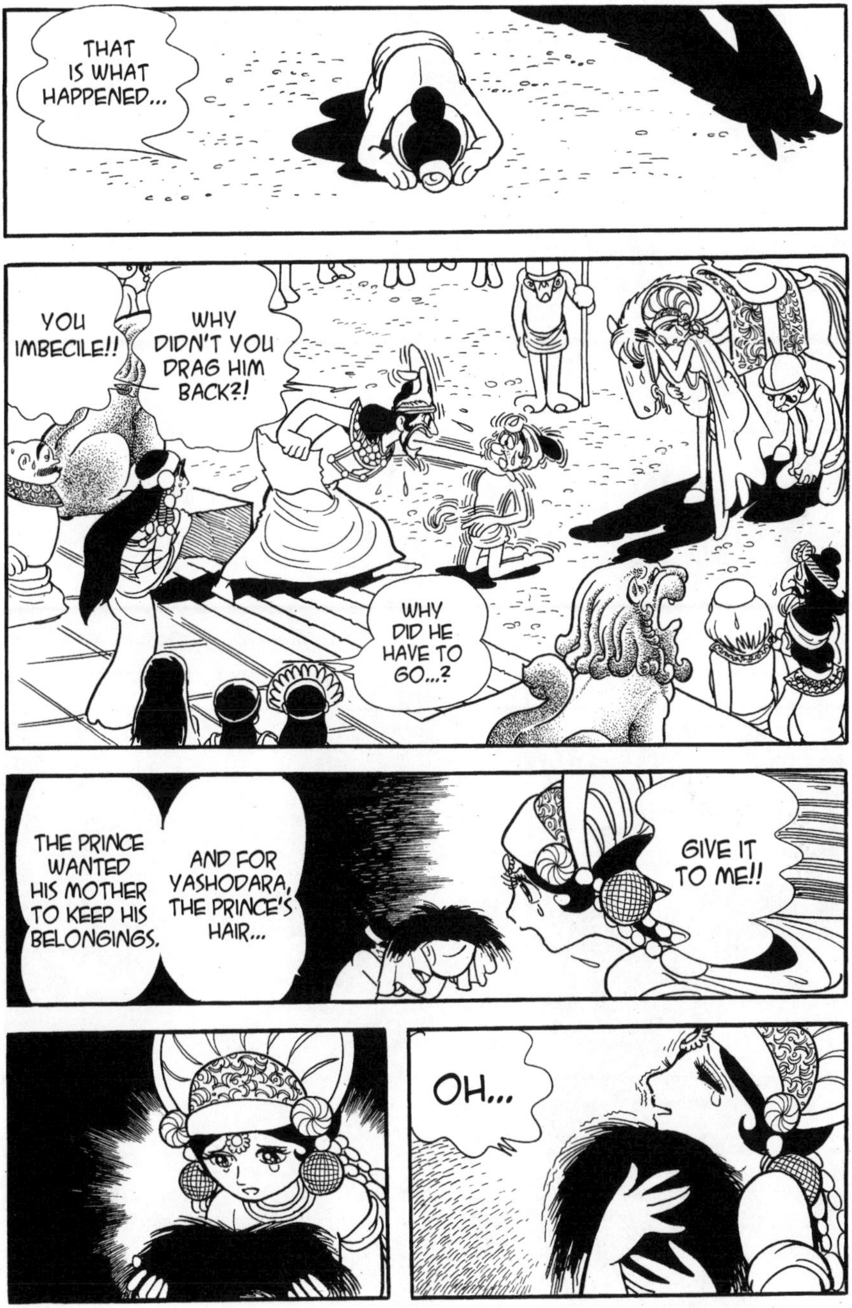
THAT IS WHAT HAPPENED...
YOU IMBECILE!!
WHY DIDN'T YOU DRAG HIM BACK?!
WHY DID HE HAVE TO GO...?
THE PRINCE WANTED HIS MOTHER TO KEEP HIS BELONGINGS.
AND FOR YASHODARA, THE PRINCE'S HAIR...
GIVE IT TO ME!!
OH...

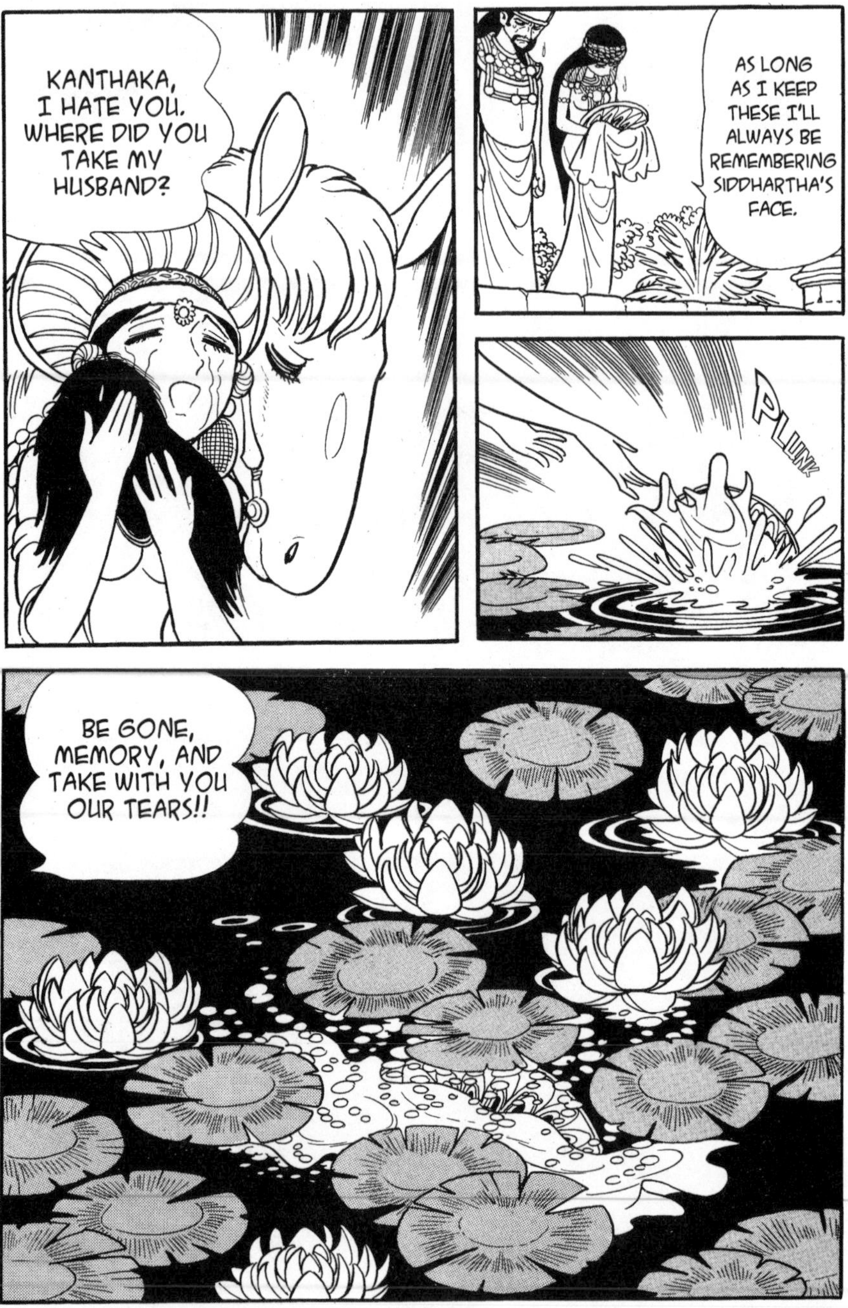

KANTHAKA, I HATE YOU. WHERE DID YOU TAKE MY HUSBAND?
AS LONG AS I KEEP THESE I'LL ALWAYS BE REMEMBERING SIDDHARTHA'S FACE.
PLUNK
BE GONE, MEMORY, AND TAKE WITH YOU OUR TEARS!!

CHAPTER TEN

THE DEATH OF BANDAKA

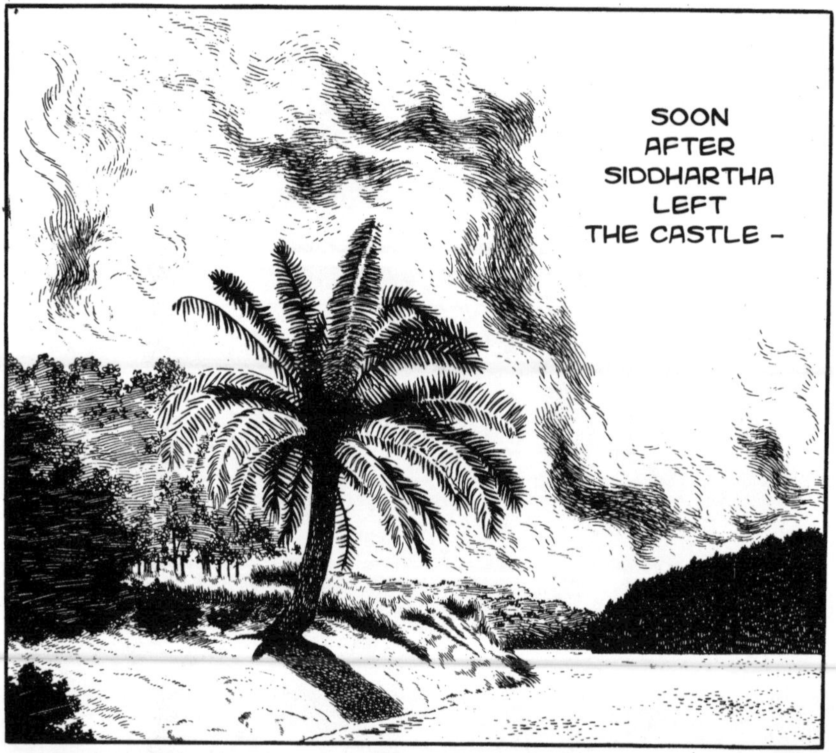
SOON AFTER SIDDHARTHA LEFT THE CASTLE -
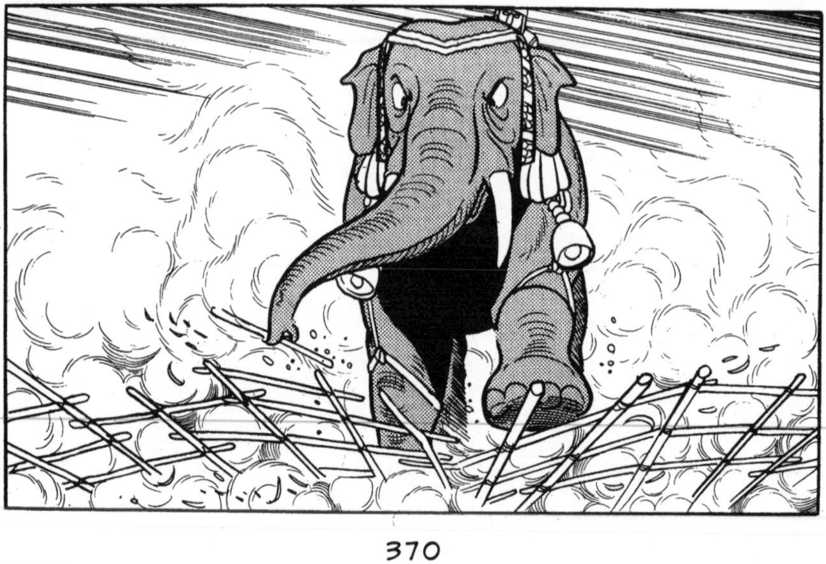

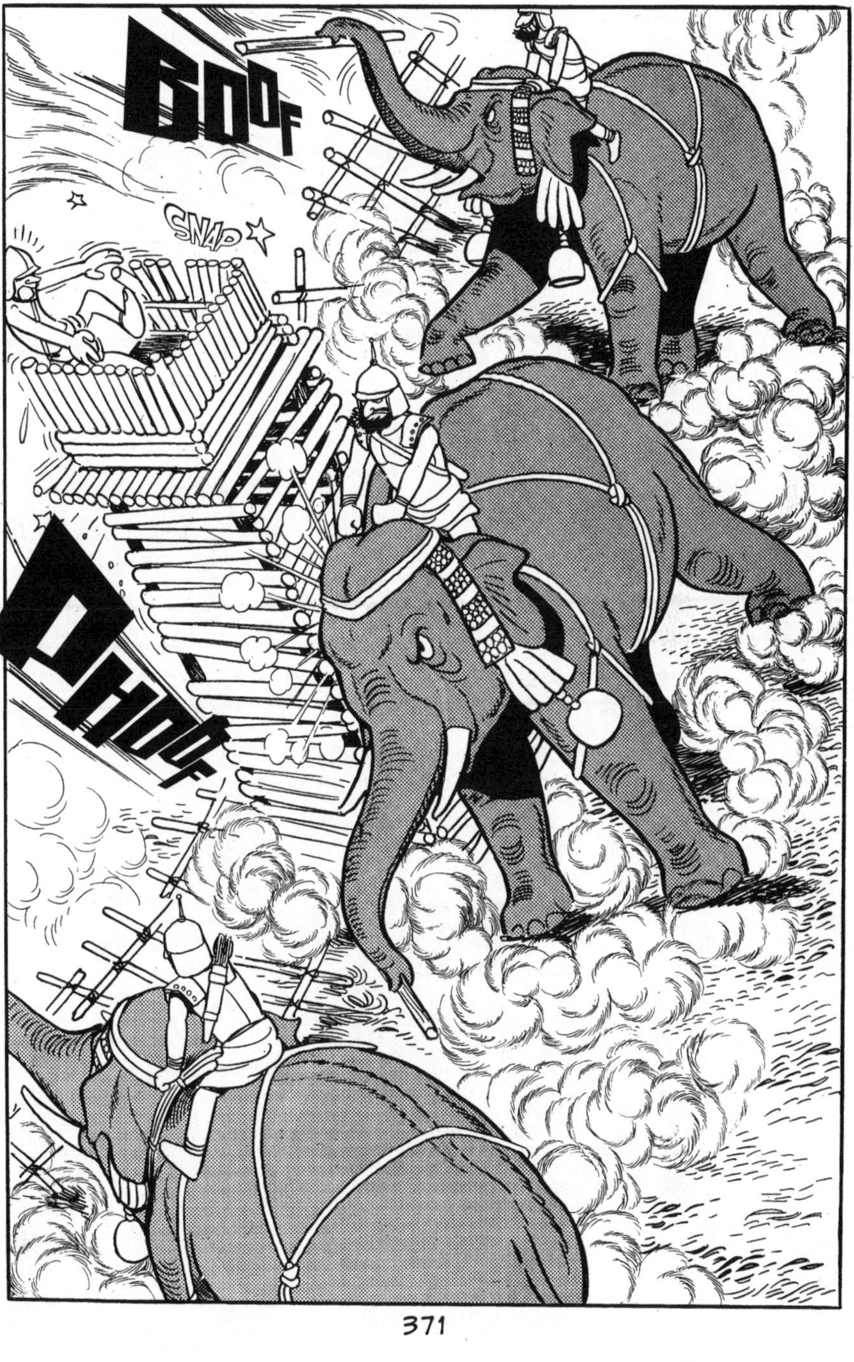
BOOF
SNAP
PROOF

KOSALA IS AT US AGAIN?
ELEPHANTS, A WHOLE ARMY OF THEM ...
THIS TIME THEY'VE GONE TOO FAR. TEARING DOWN THE BORDER WALL AND CRUSHING THE GUARD POSTS.
THEY'RE MAKING COMPLETE FOOLS OF US.
COMPARED TO MIGHTY KOSALA, WE ARE LIKE A HELPLESS FAWN.
BUT, YOUR MAJESTY,
A FAWN GROWS STRONG ANTLERS IN DUE TIME, AND FACES HIS ENEMY EVENTUALLY.
IF WE SHAKYA ONLY HAD A GREAT KING, WE WOULD NOT SUFFER THIS SHAME.
AND WHERE IS THIS GREAT KING?!
WITH MY SON GONE, WHO IS GOING TO DEFEND THIS COUNTRY?

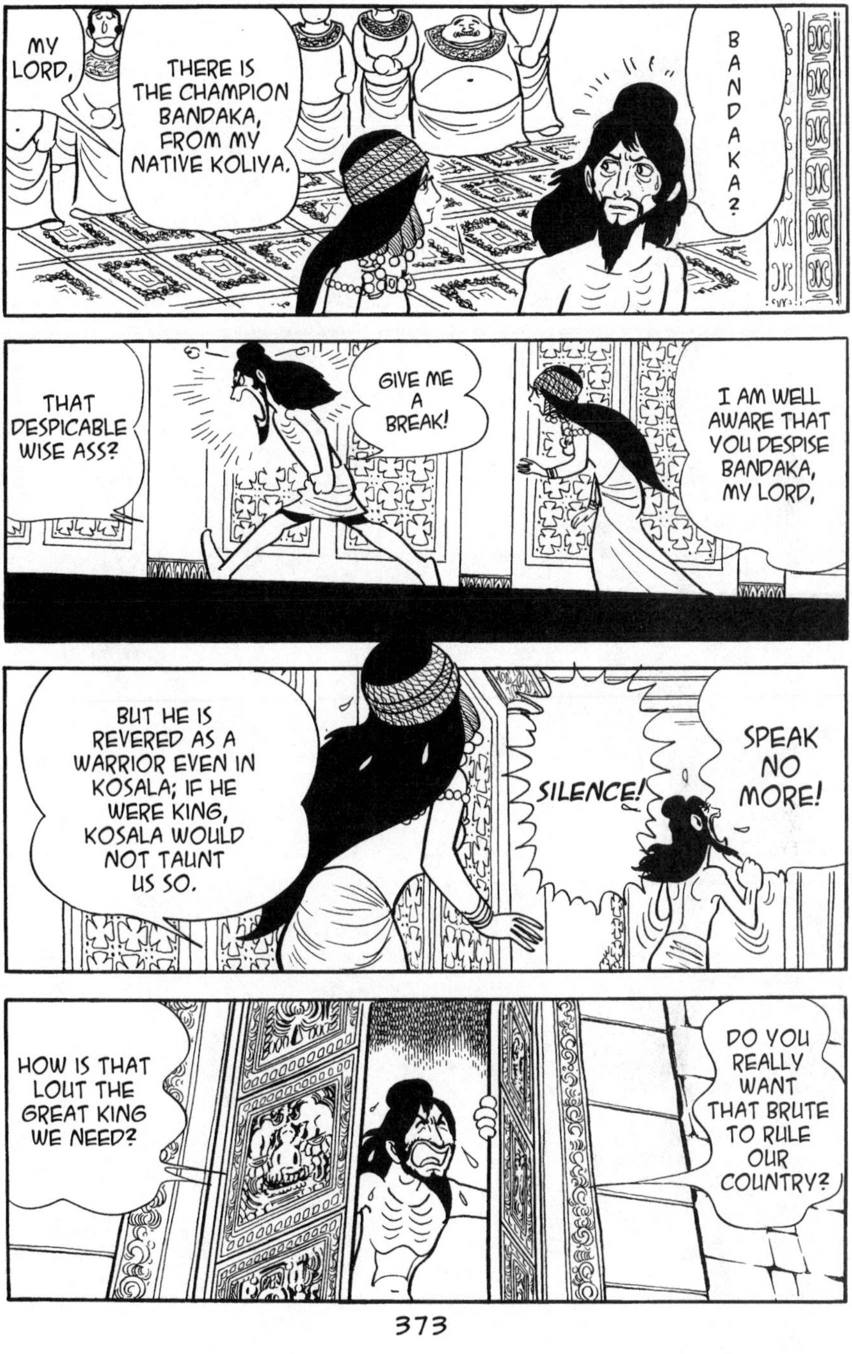
MY LORD,
THERE IS THE CHAMPION BANDAKA, FROM MY NATIVE KOLIYA.
BANDAKA?
THAT DESPICABLE WISE ASS?
GIVE ME A BREAK!
I AM WELL AWARE THAT YOU DESPISE BANDAKA, MY LORD,
BUT HE IS REVERED AS A WARRIOR EVEN IN KOSALA; IF HE WERE KING, KOSALA WOULD NOT TAUNT US SO.
SILENCE!
SPEAK NO MORE!
HOW IS THAT LOUT THE GREAT KING WE NEED?
DO YOU REALLY WANT THAT BRUTE TO RULE OUR COUNTRY?

YOUR MAJESTY, THIS IS A CRISIS...

IF NOT KING, AT LEAST HE COULD BE YOUR COMMANDER IN CHIEF.

LETTING HIM LEAD THE ARMY WOULD BE LETTING HIM RUN THE COUNTRY!

FEEBLE I MAY BE, BUT I AM STILL KING. I WILL NOT TRUST THE COUNTRY TO HIM.

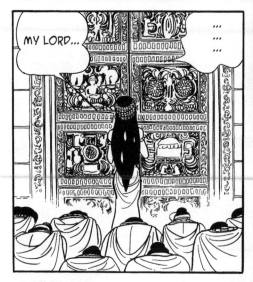

MY LORD...

...

...

QUEEN, DO NOT TORTURE ME SO...

YOUR MAJESTY, IT IS FOR THE SAKE OF THE KINGDOM. PLEASE, HEED THE QUEEN'S WORDS.

...ALL RIGHT THEN...

CALL BANDAKA OVER.

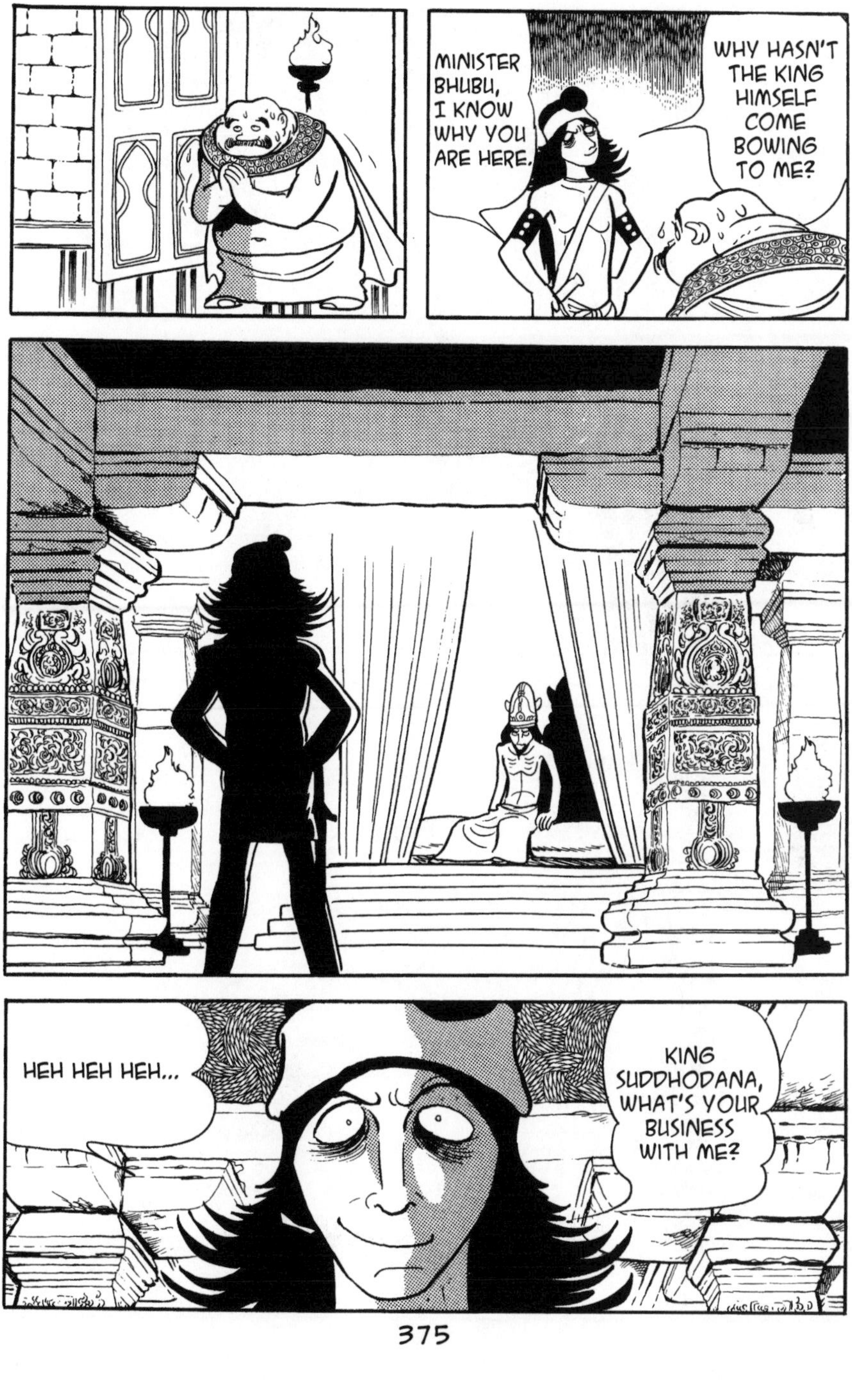
MINISTER BHUBU, I KNOW WHY YOU ARE HERE.
WHY HASN'T THE KING HIMSELF COME BOWING TO ME?
HEH HEH HEH...
KING SUDDHODANA, WHAT'S YOUR BUSINESS WITH ME?

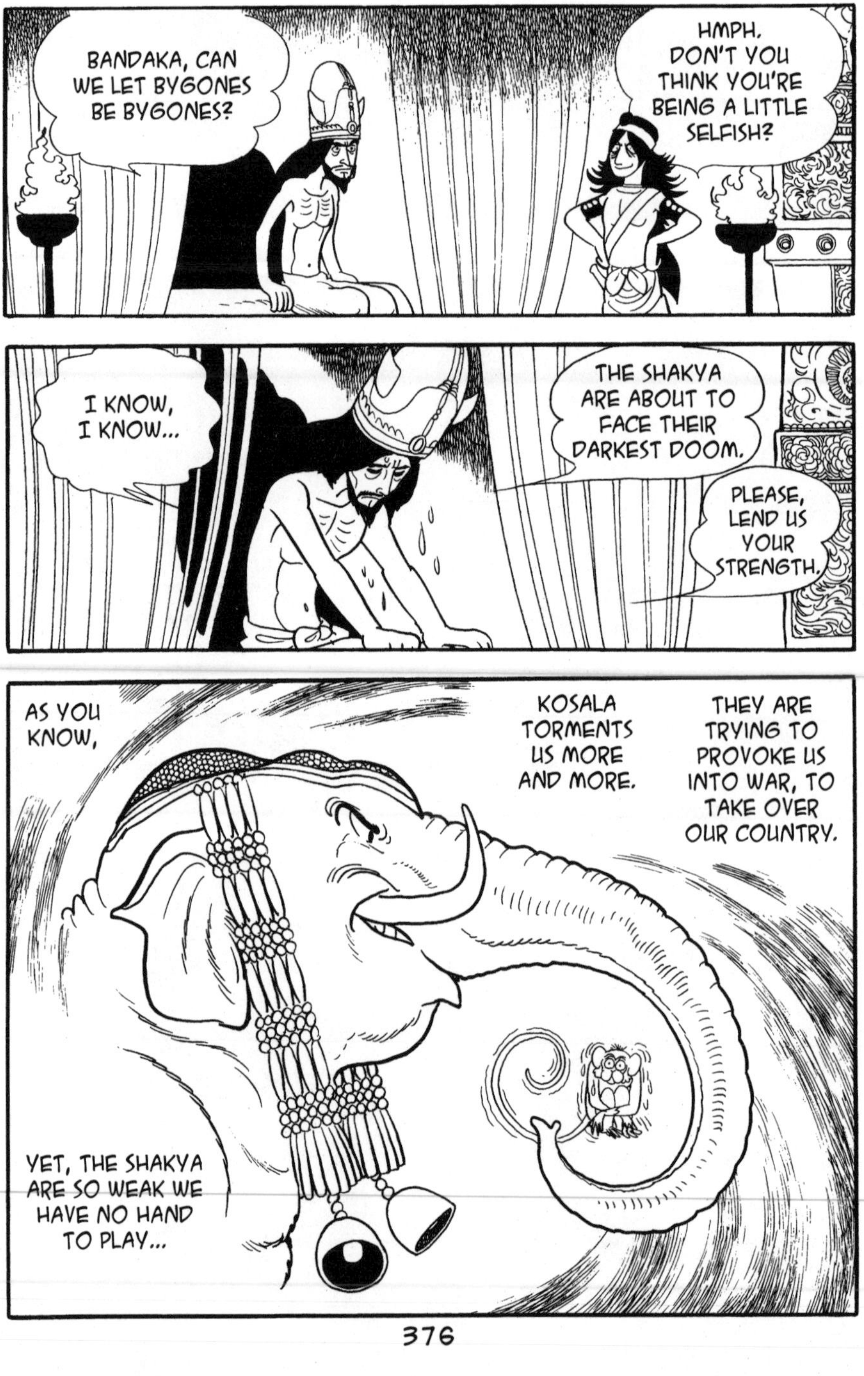
BANDAKA, CAN WE LET BYGONES BE BYGONES?
HMPH. DON'T YOU THINK YOU'RE BEING A LITTLE SELFISH?
I KNOW, I KNOW...
THE SHAKYA ARE ABOUT TO FACE THEIR DARKEST DOOM.
PLEASE, LEND US YOUR STRENGTH.
AS YOU KNOW,
KOSALA TORMENTS US MORE AND MORE.
THEY ARE TRYING TO PROVOKE US INTO WAR, TO TAKE OVER OUR COUNTRY.
YET, THE SHAKYA ARE SO WEAK WE HAVE NO HAND TO PLAY...

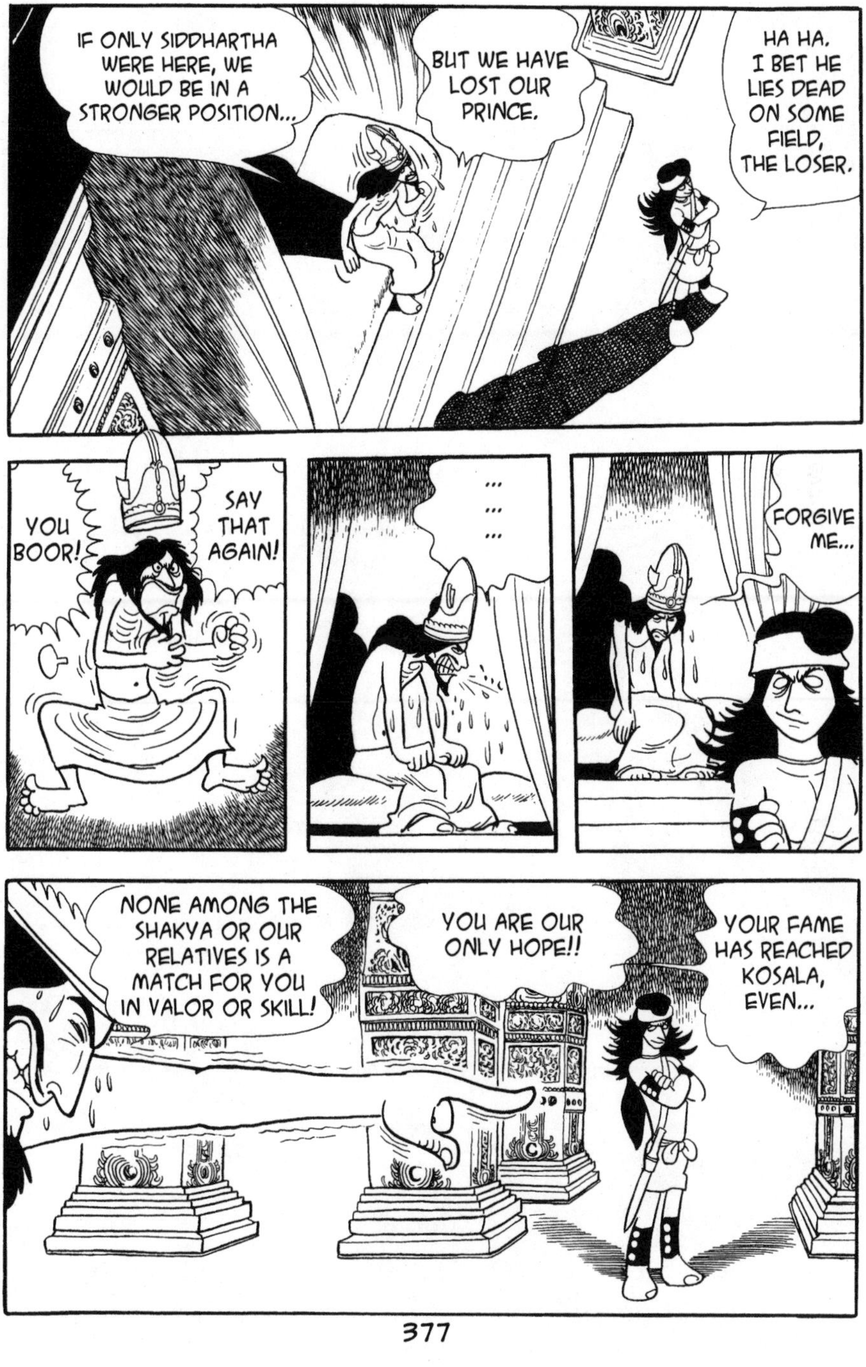
IF ONLY SIDDHARTHA WERE HERE, WE WOULD BE IN A STRONGER POSITION...
BUT WE HAVE LOST OUR PRINCE.
HA HA, I BET HE LIES DEAD ON SOME FIELD, THE LOSER.
YOU BOOR!
SAY THAT AGAIN!
...
...
...
FORGIVE ME...
NONE AMONG THE SHAKYA OR OUR RELATIVES IS A MATCH FOR YOU IN VALOR OR SKILL!
YOU ARE OUR ONLY HOPE!!
YOUR FAME HAS REACHED KOSALA, EVEN...

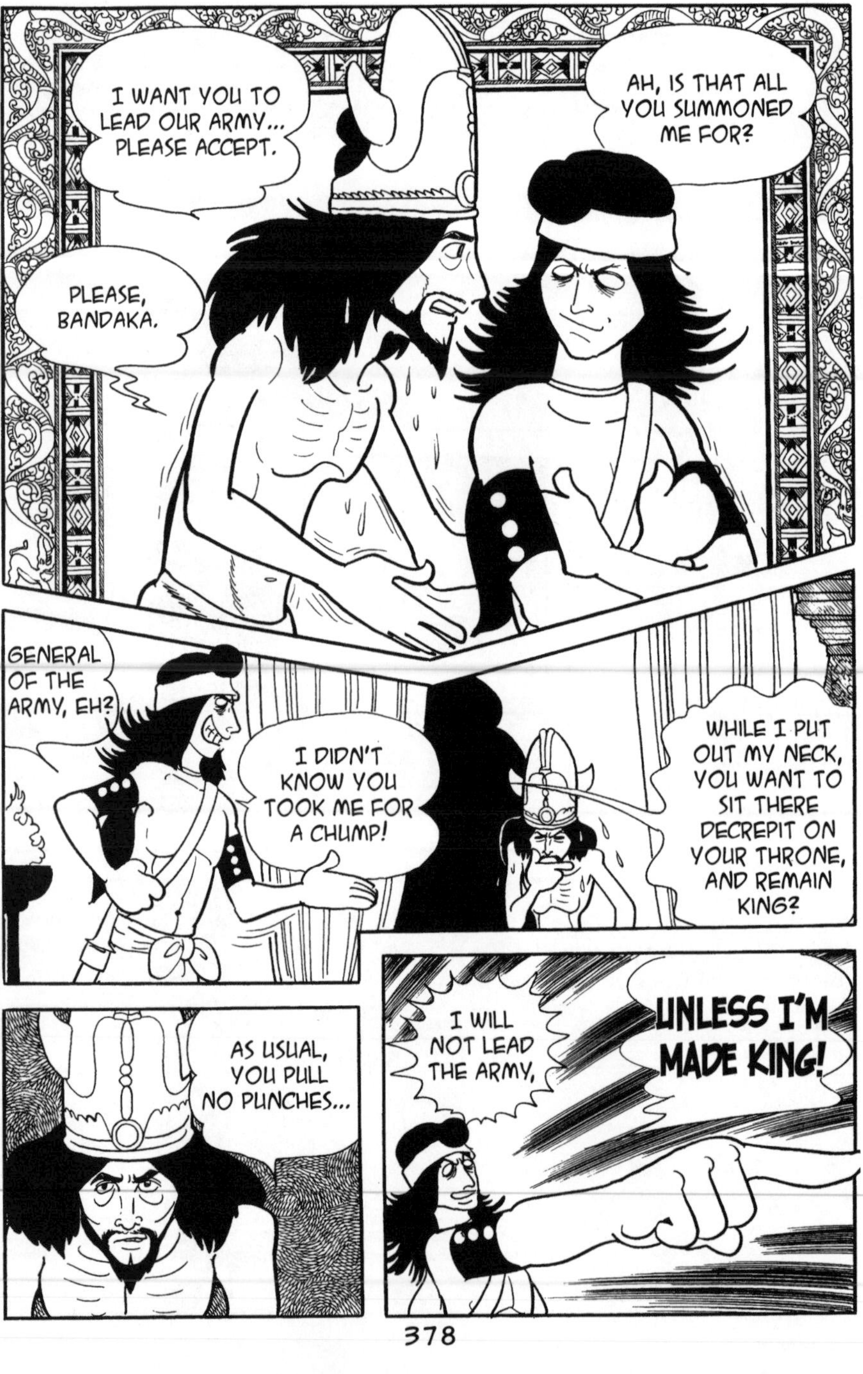
I WANT YOU TO LEAD OUR ARMY... PLEASE ACCEPT.
AH, IS THAT ALL YOU SUMMONED ME FOR?
PLEASE, BANDAKA.
GENERAL OF THE ARMY, EH?
I DIDN'T KNOW YOU TOOK ME FOR A CHUMP!
WHILE I PUT OUT MY NECK, YOU WANT TO SIT THERE DECREPIT ON YOUR THRONE, AND REMAIN KING?
AS USUAL, YOU PULL NO PUNCHES...
I WILL NOT LEAD THE ARMY,
UNLESS I'M MADE KING!

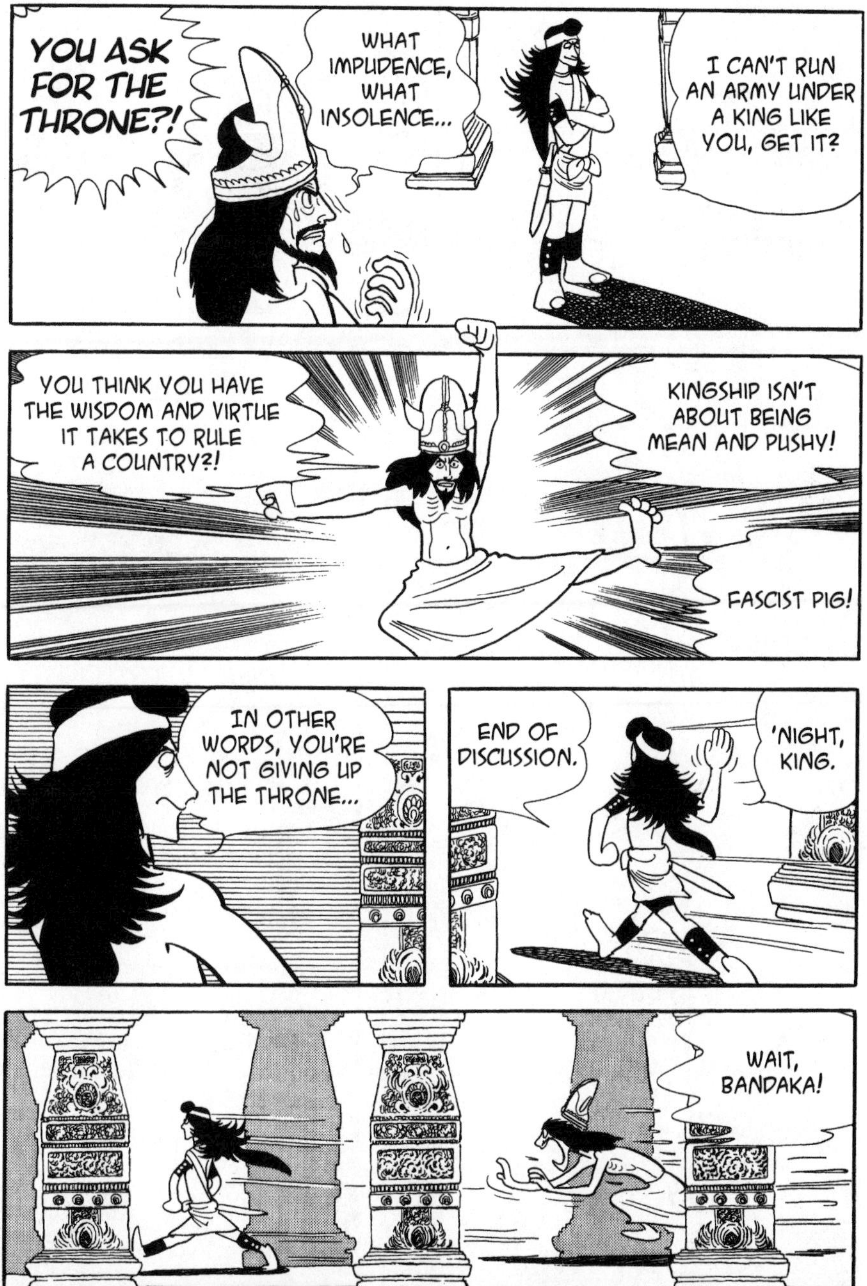
YOU ASK FOR THE THRONE?!
WHAT IMPUDENCE, WHAT INSOLENCE...
I CAN'T RUN AN ARMY UNDER A KING LIKE YOU, GET IT?
YOU THINK YOU HAVE THE WISDOM AND VIRTUE IT TAKES TO RULE A COUNTRY?!
KINGSHIP ISN'T ABOUT BEING MEAN AND PUSHY!
FASCIST PIG!
IN OTHER WORDS, YOU'RE NOT GIVING UP THE THRONE...
END OF DISCUSSION.
'NIGHT, KING.
WAIT, BANDAKA!

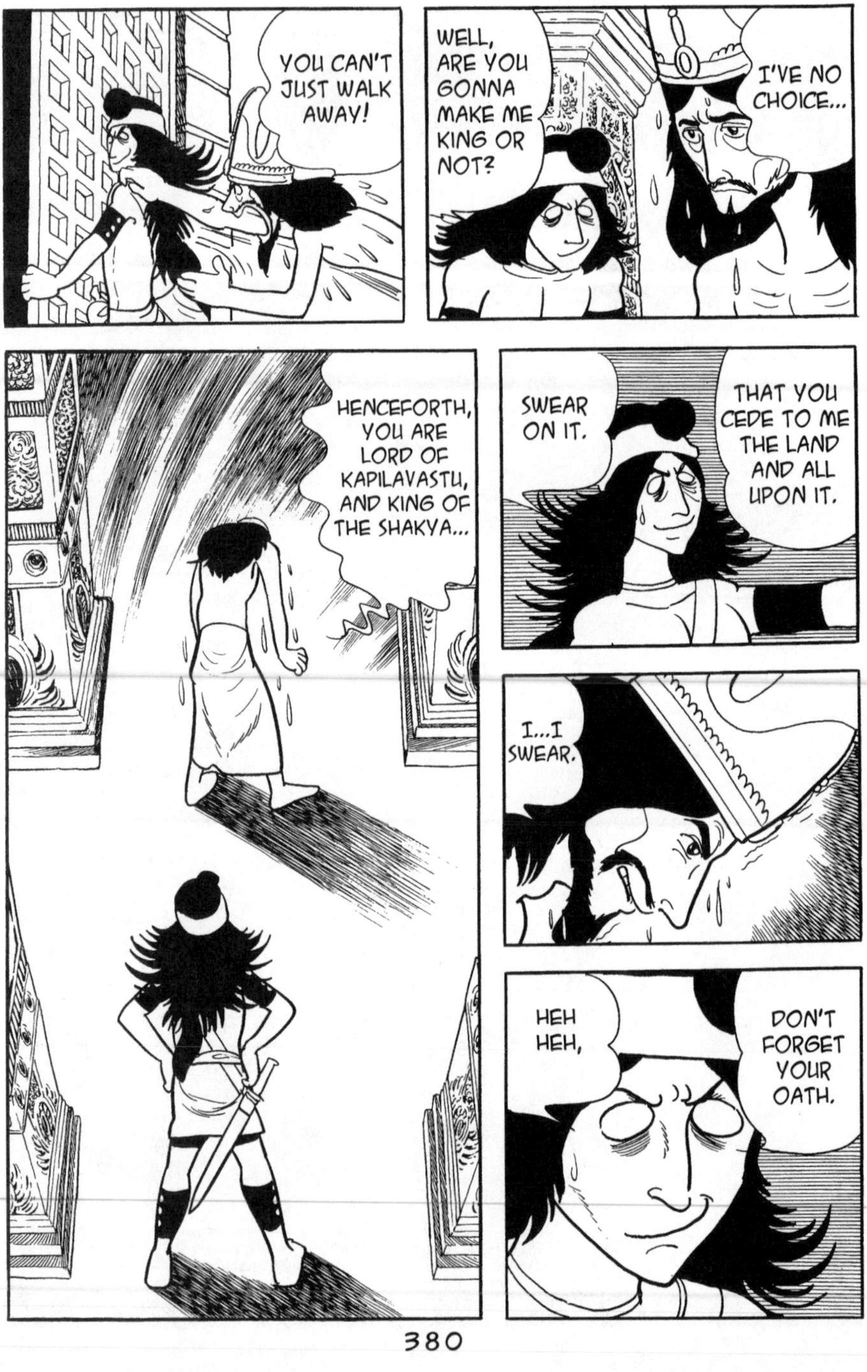
YOU CAN'T JUST WALK AWAY!
WELL, ARE YOU GONNA MAKE ME KING OR NOT?
I'VE NO CHOICE...
HENCEFORTH, YOU ARE LORD OF KAPILAVASTU, AND KING OF THE SHAKYA...
SWEAR ON IT.
THAT YOU CEDE TO ME THE LAND AND ALL UPON IT.
I...I SWEAR.
HEH HEH,
DON'T FORGET YOUR OATH.

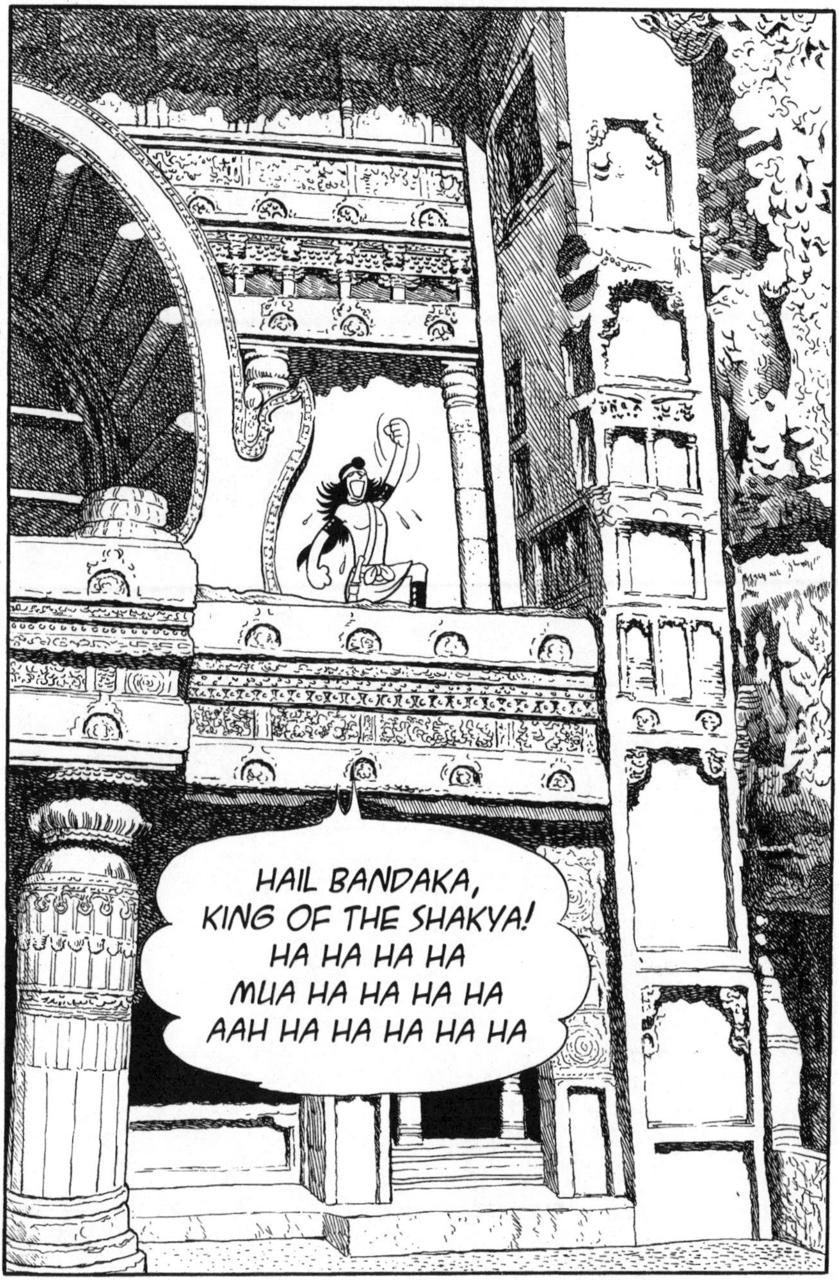
HAIL BANDAKA, KING OF THE SHAKYA! HA HA HA HA MUA HA HA HA HA AAH HA HA HA HA HA

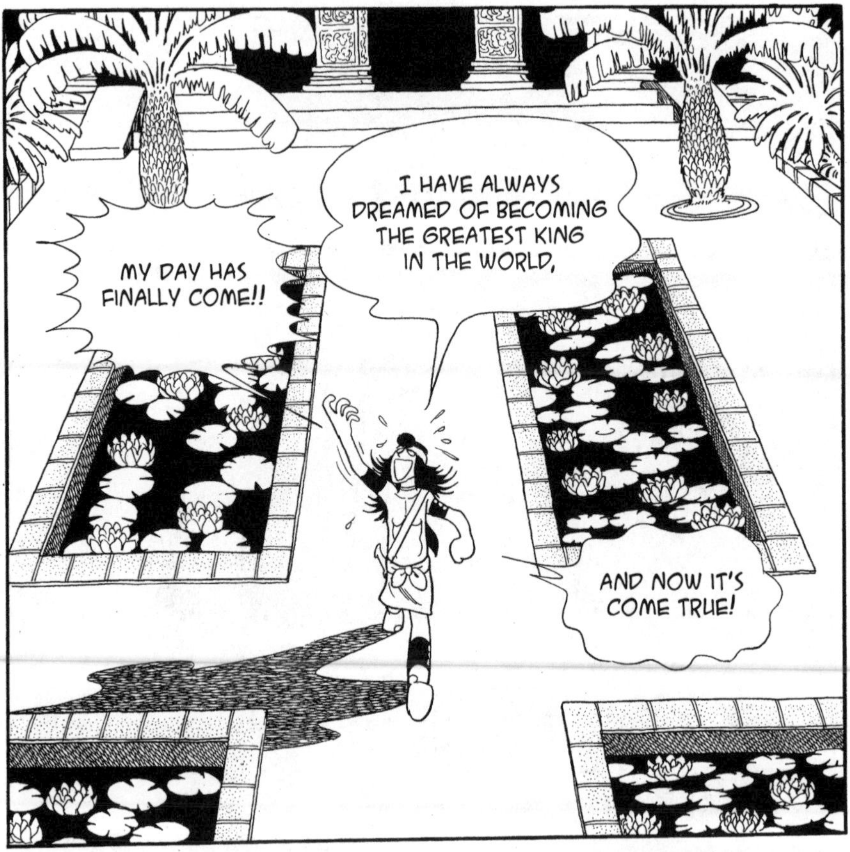
MY DAY HAS FINALLY COME!!
I HAVE ALWAYS DREAMED OF BECOMING THE GREATEST KING IN THE WORLD,
AND NOW IT'S COME TRUE!

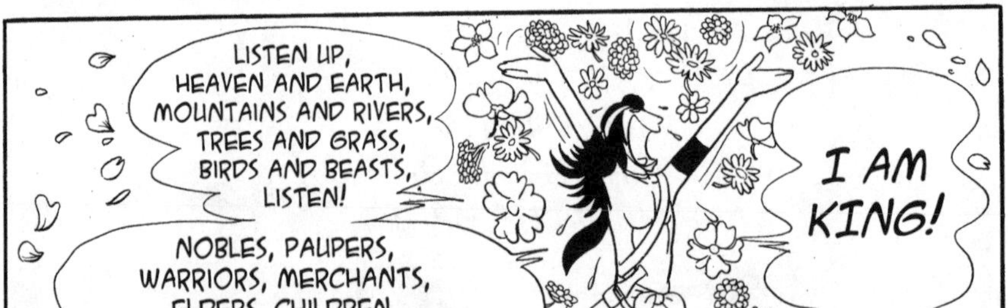
LISTEN UP, HEAVEN AND EARTH, MOUNTAINS AND RIVERS, TREES AND GRASS, BIRDS AND BEASTS, LISTEN!
NOBLES, PAUPERS, WARRIORS, MERCHANTS, ELDERS, CHILDREN, BUSINESSMEN, STUDENTS, REPUBLICANS, DEMOCRATS, MOGULS, CELEBS, FORD, CHAPLIN, ALL OF YOU - LISTEN UP!!
I AM KING!

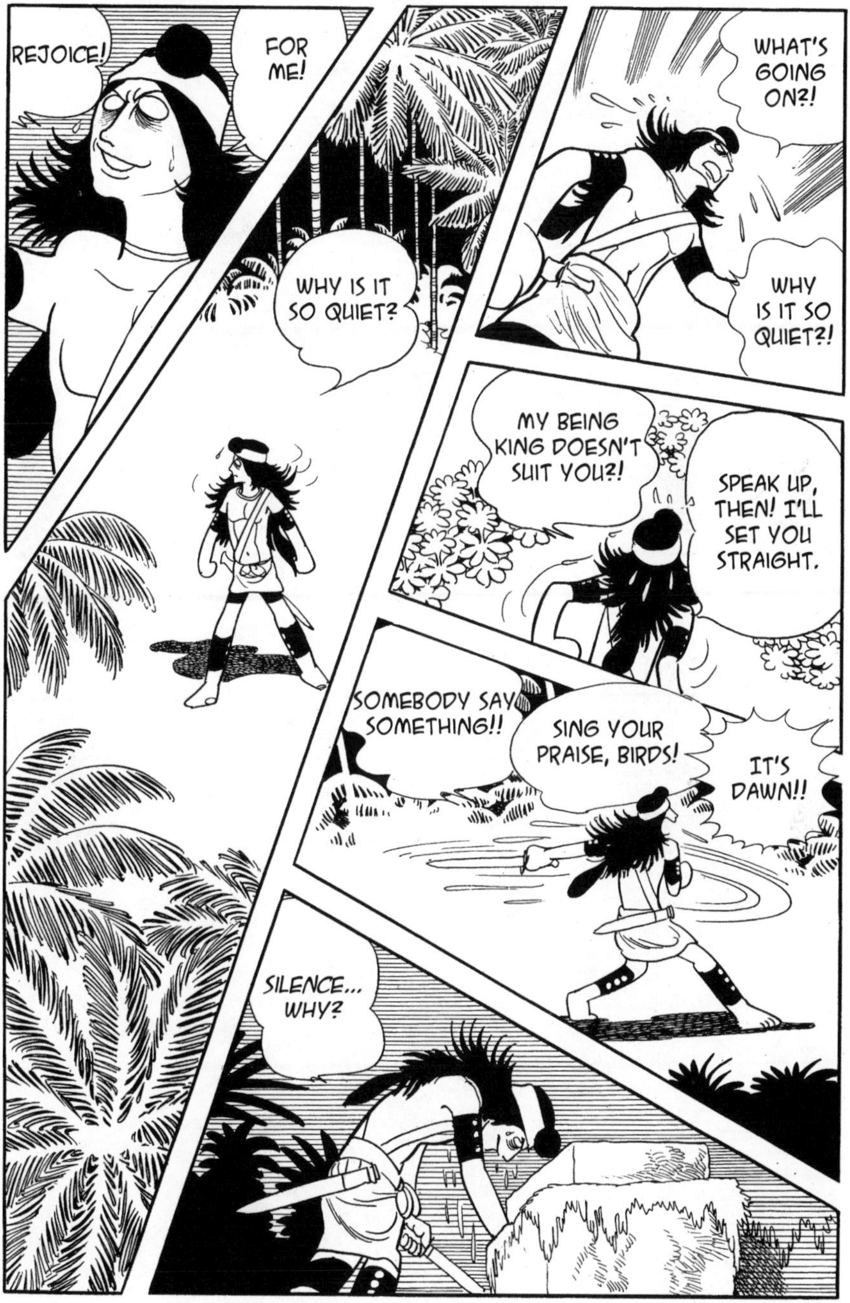
REJOICE!
FOR ME!
WHY IS IT SO QUIET?
WHAT'S GOING ON?!
WHY IS IT SO QUIET?!
MY BEING KING DOESN'T SUIT YOU?!
SPEAK UP, THEN! I'LL SET YOU STRAIGHT.
SOMEBODY SAY SOMETHING!!
SING YOUR PRAISE, BIRDS!
IT'S DAWN!!
SILENCE... WHY?

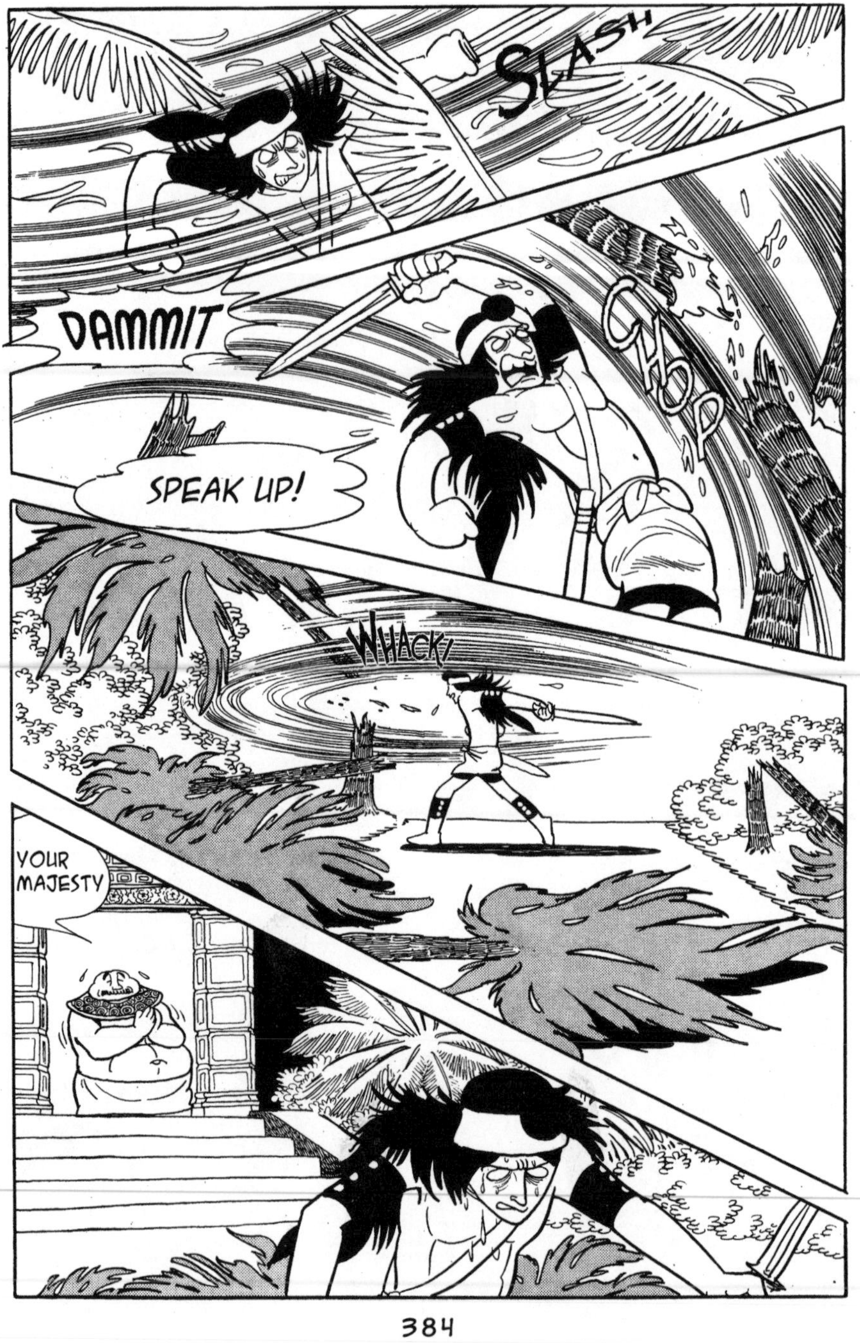
SLASH
DAMMIT
CHOP
SPEAK UP!
WHACK!
YOUR MAJESTY

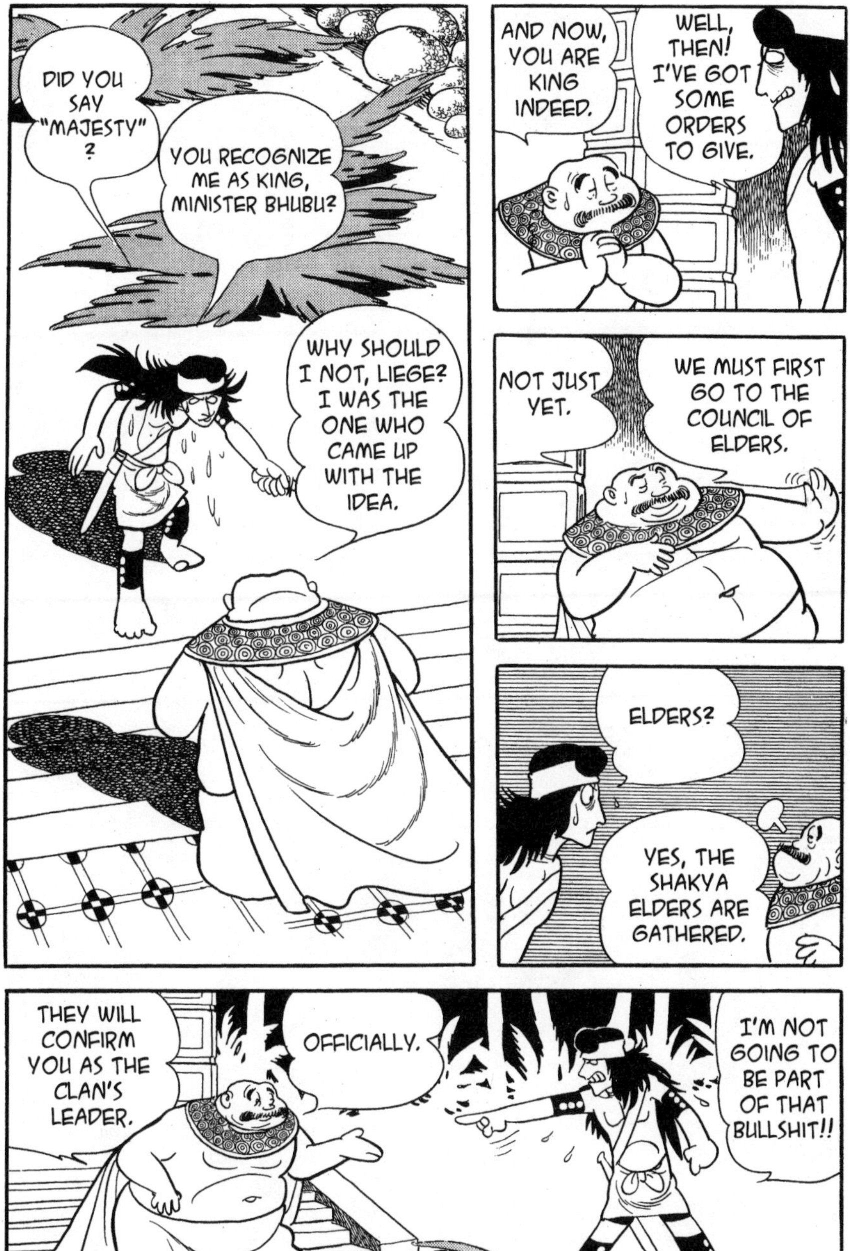
DID YOU SAY "MAJESTY"?
YOU RECOGNIZE ME AS KING, MINISTER BHUBU?
WHY SHOULD I NOT, LIEGE? I WAS THE ONE WHO CAME UP WITH THE IDEA.
AND NOW, YOU ARE KING INDEED.
WELL, THEN! I'VE GOT SOME ORDERS TO GIVE.
NOT JUST YET.
WE MUST FIRST GO TO THE COUNCIL OF ELDERS.
ELDERS?
YES, THE SHAKYA ELDERS ARE GATHERED.
THEY WILL CONFIRM YOU AS THE CLAN'S LEADER.
OFFICIALLY.
I'M NOT GOING TO BE PART OF THAT BULLSHIT!!

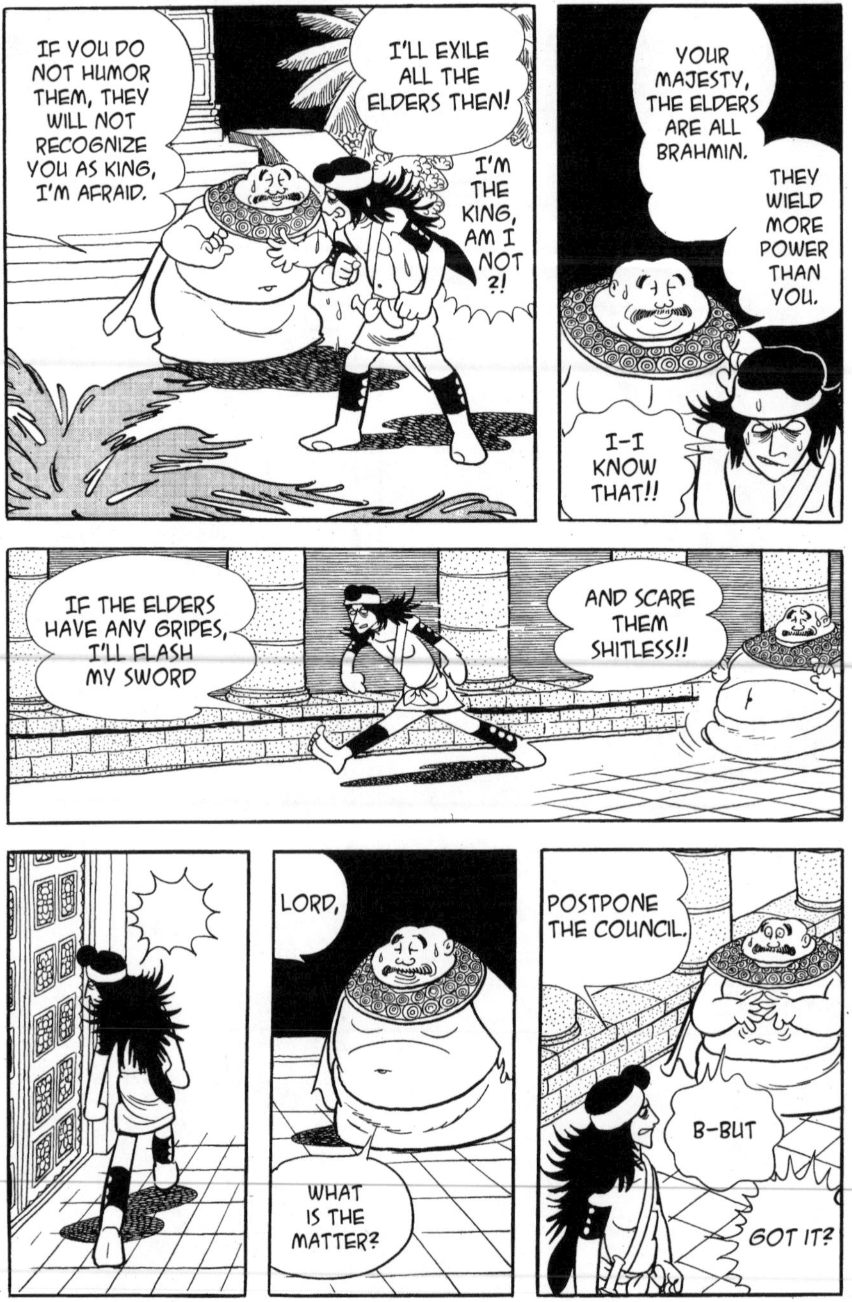
IF YOU DO NOT HUMOR THEM, THEY WILL NOT RECOGNIZE YOU AS KING, I'M AFRAID.
I'LL EXILE ALL THE ELDERS THEN!
I'M THE KING, AM I NOT ?!
YOUR MAJESTY, THE ELDERS ARE ALL BRAHMIN.
THEY WIELD MORE POWER THAN YOU.
I-I KNOW THAT!!
IF THE ELDERS HAVE ANY GRIPES, I'LL FLASH MY SWORD
AND SCARE THEM SHITLESS!!
LORD,
WHAT IS THE MATTER?
POSTPONE THE COUNCIL.
B-BUT
GOT IT?

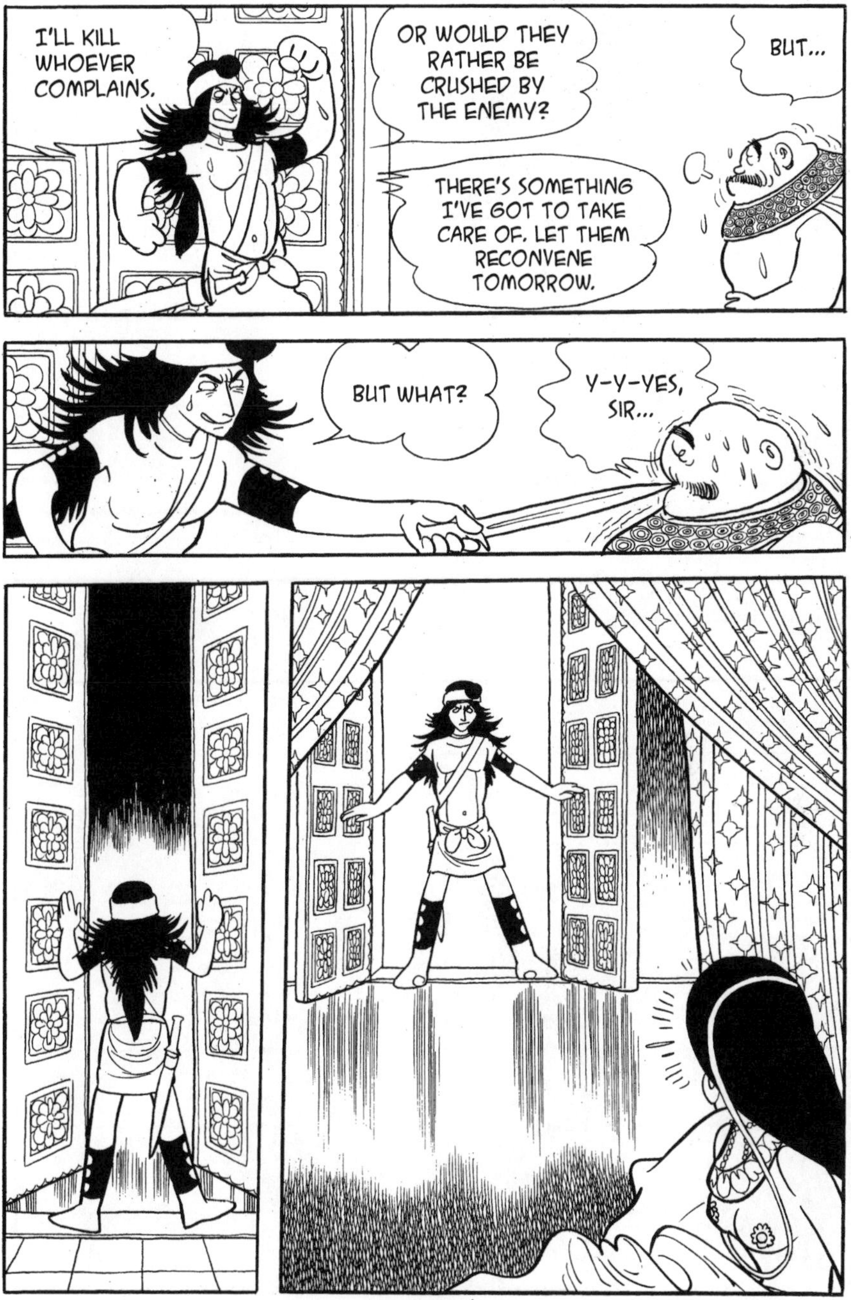
I'LL KILL WHOEVER COMPLAINS.
OR WOULD THEY RATHER BE CRUSHED BY THE ENEMY?
BUT...
THERE'S SOMETHING I'VE GOT TO TAKE CARE OF. LET THEM RECONVENE TOMORROW.
BUT WHAT?
Y-Y-YES, SIR...

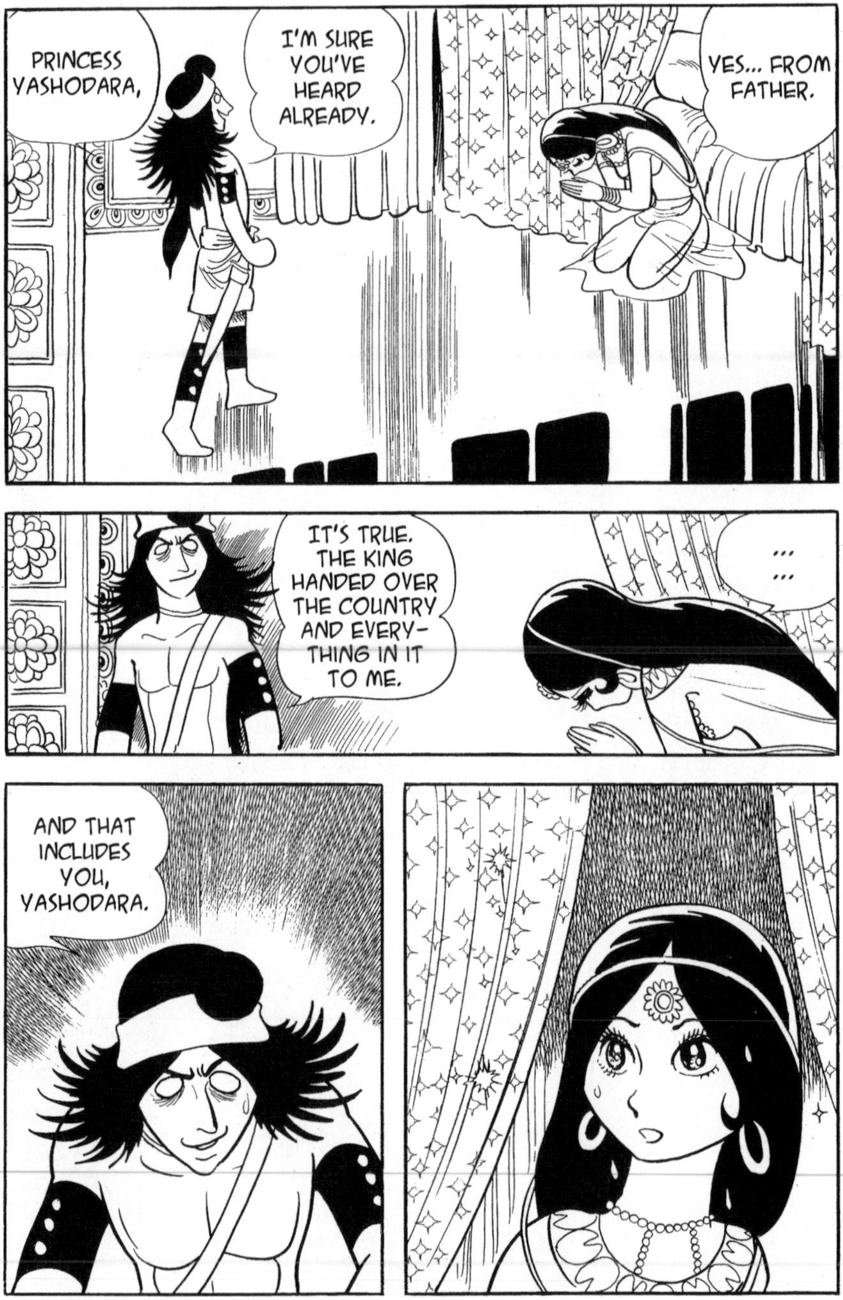
PRINCESS YASHODARA,
I'M SURE YOU'VE HEARD ALREADY.
YES... FROM FATHER.
IT'S TRUE. THE KING HANDED OVER THE COUNTRY AND EVERY-THING IN IT TO ME.
... ...
AND THAT INCLUDES YOU, YASHODARA.

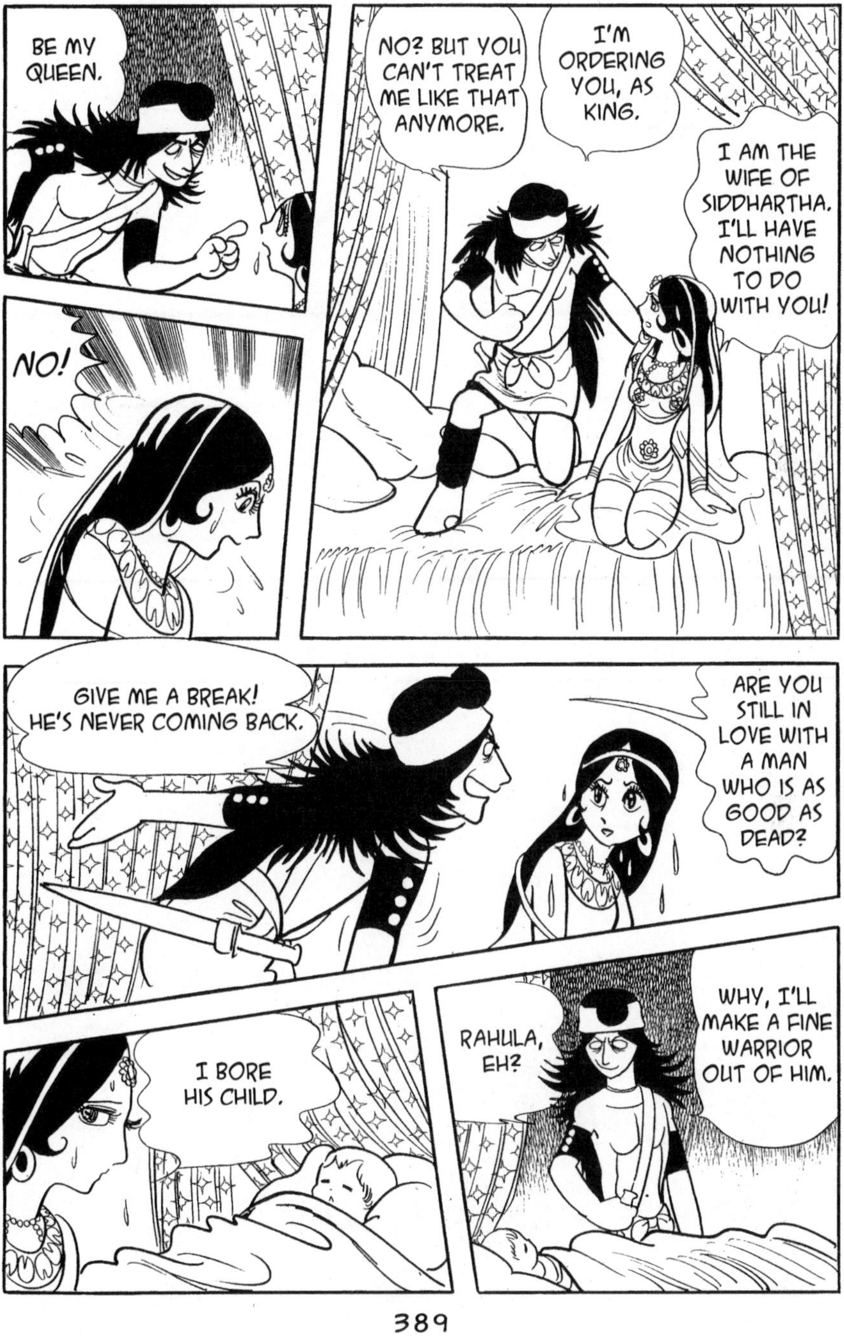
BE MY QUEEN.
NO!
NO? BUT YOU CAN'T TREAT ME LIKE THAT ANYMORE.
I'M ORDERING YOU, AS KING.
I AM THE WIFE OF SIDDHARTHA. I'LL HAVE NOTHING TO DO WITH YOU!
GIVE ME A BREAK! HE'S NEVER COMING BACK.
ARE YOU STILL IN LOVE WITH A MAN WHO IS AS GOOD AS DEAD?
I BORE HIS CHILD.
RAHULA, EH?
WHY, I'LL MAKE A FINE WARRIOR OUT OF HIM.

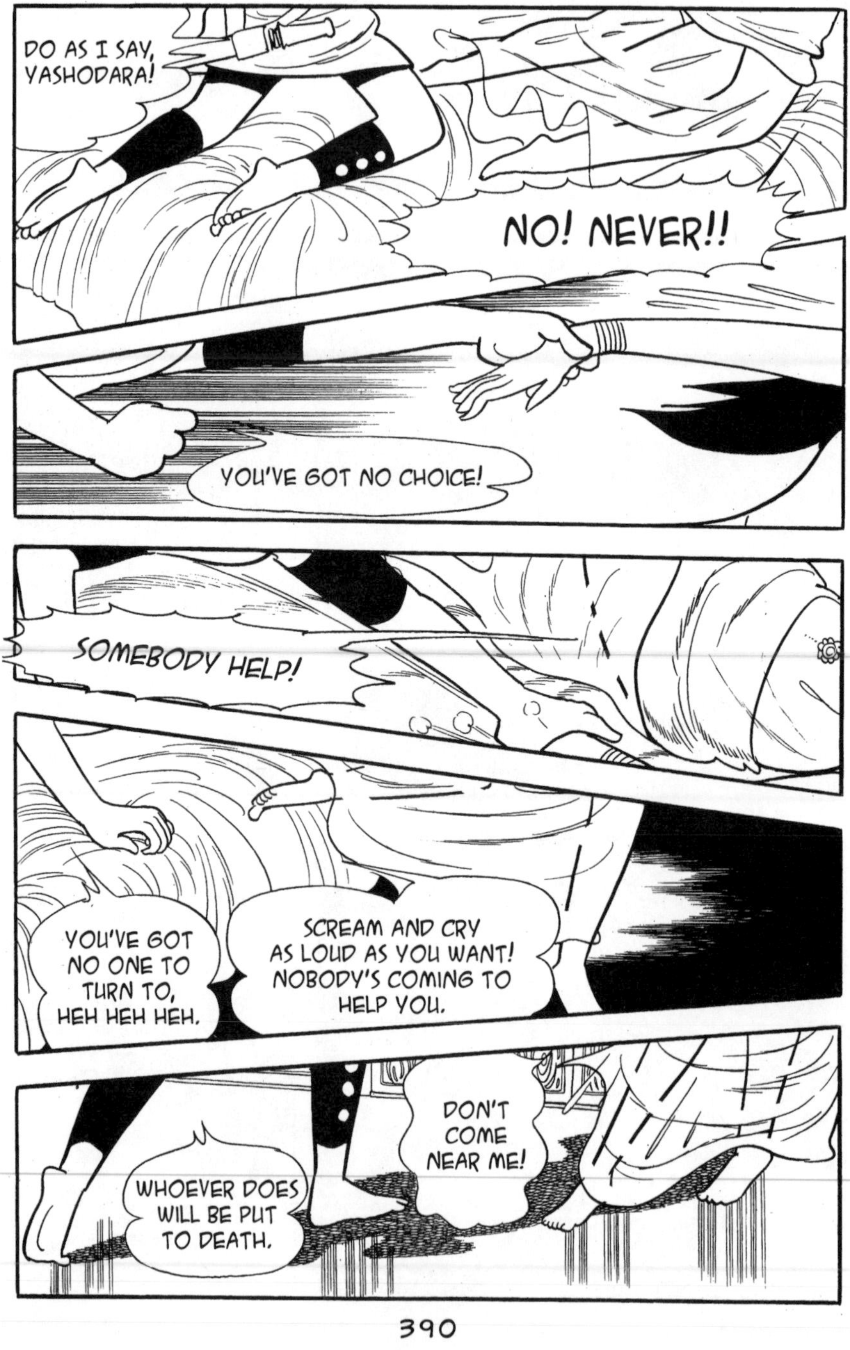
DO AS I SAY, YASHODARA!
NO! NEVER!!
YOU'VE GOT NO CHOICE!
SOMEBODY HELP!
YOU'VE GOT NO ONE TO TURN TO, HEH HEH HEH.
SCREAM AND CRY AS LOUD AS YOU WANT! NOBODY'S COMING TO HELP YOU.
WHOEVER DOES WILL BE PUT TO DEATH.
DON'T COME NEAR ME!

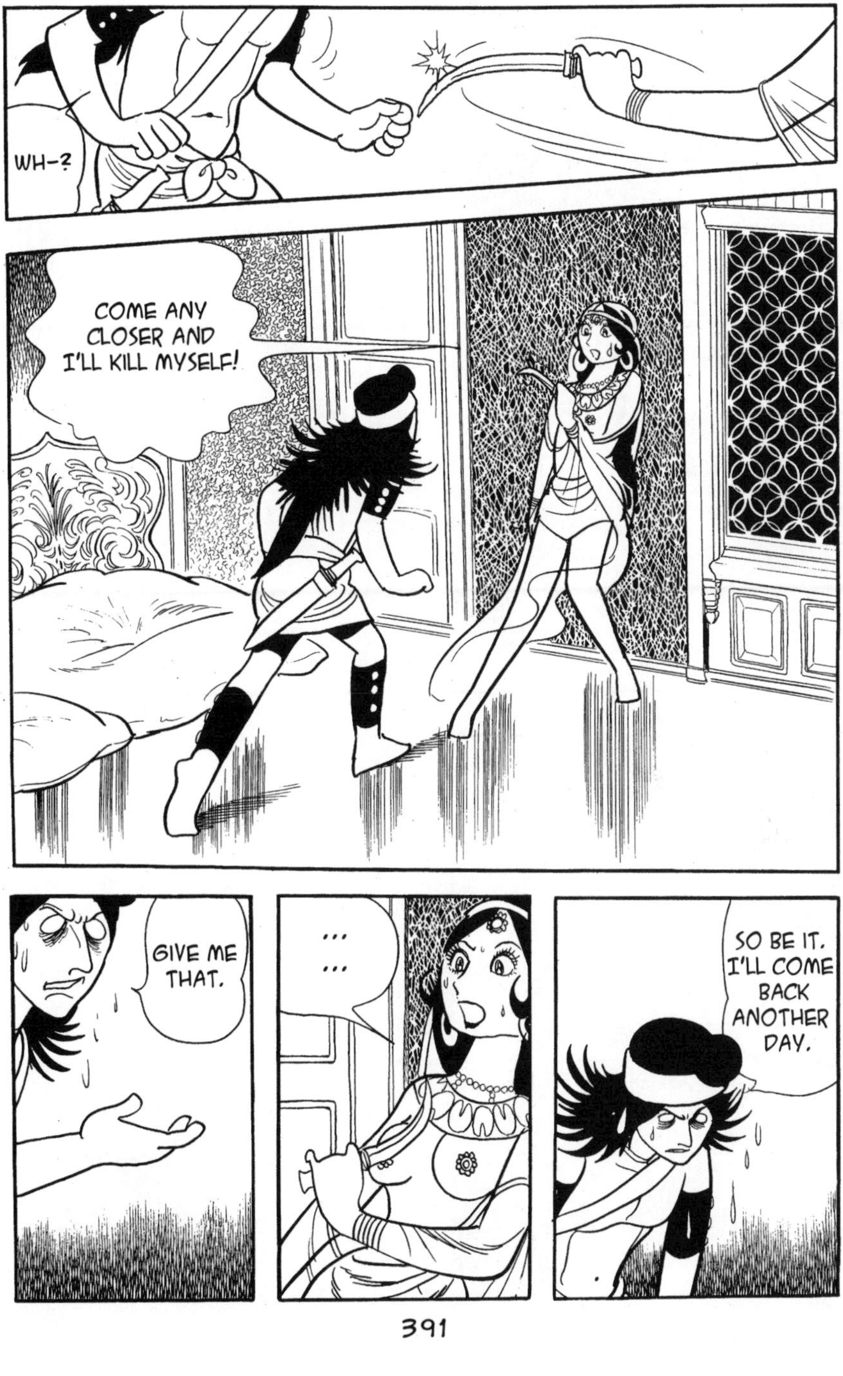
WH-?
COME ANY CLOSER AND I'LL KILL MYSELF!
GIVE ME THAT.
... ...
SO BE IT. I'LL COME BACK ANOTHER DAY.

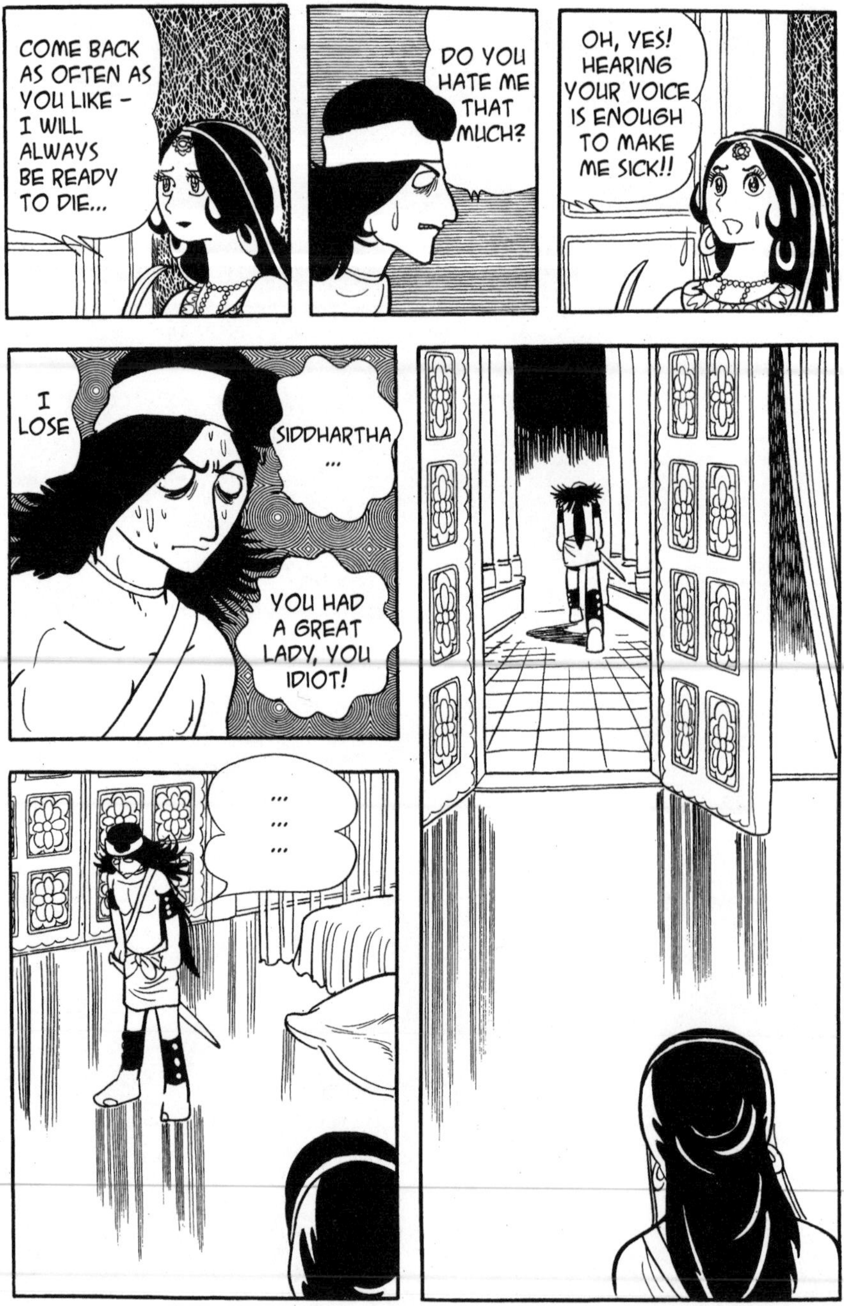
COME BACK AS OFTEN AS YOU LIKE – I WILL ALWAYS BE READY TO DIE...
DO YOU HATE ME THAT MUCH?
OH, YES! HEARING YOUR VOICE IS ENOUGH TO MAKE ME SICK!!
I LOSE
SIDDHARTHA ...
YOU HAD A GREAT LADY, YOU IDIOT!
...
...
...

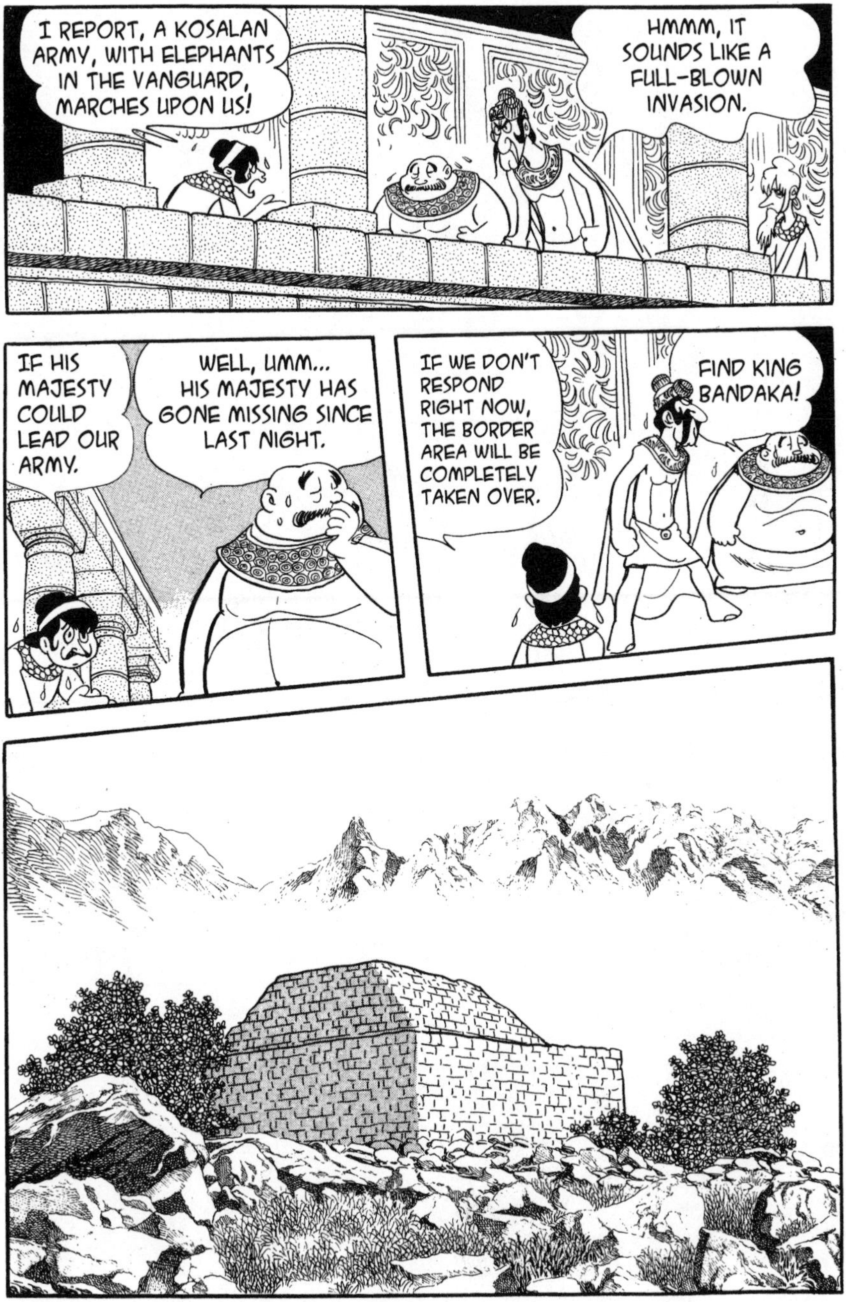
I REPORT, A KOSALAN ARMY, WITH ELEPHANTS IN THE VANGUARD, MARCHES UPON US!
HMMM, IT SOUNDS LIKE A FULL-BLOWN INVASION.
IF HIS MAJESTY COULD LEAD OUR ARMY.
WELL, UMM... HIS MAJESTY HAS GONE MISSING SINCE LAST NIGHT.
IF WE DON'T RESPOND RIGHT NOW, THE BORDER AREA WILL BE COMPLETELY TAKEN OVER.
FIND KING BANDAKA!

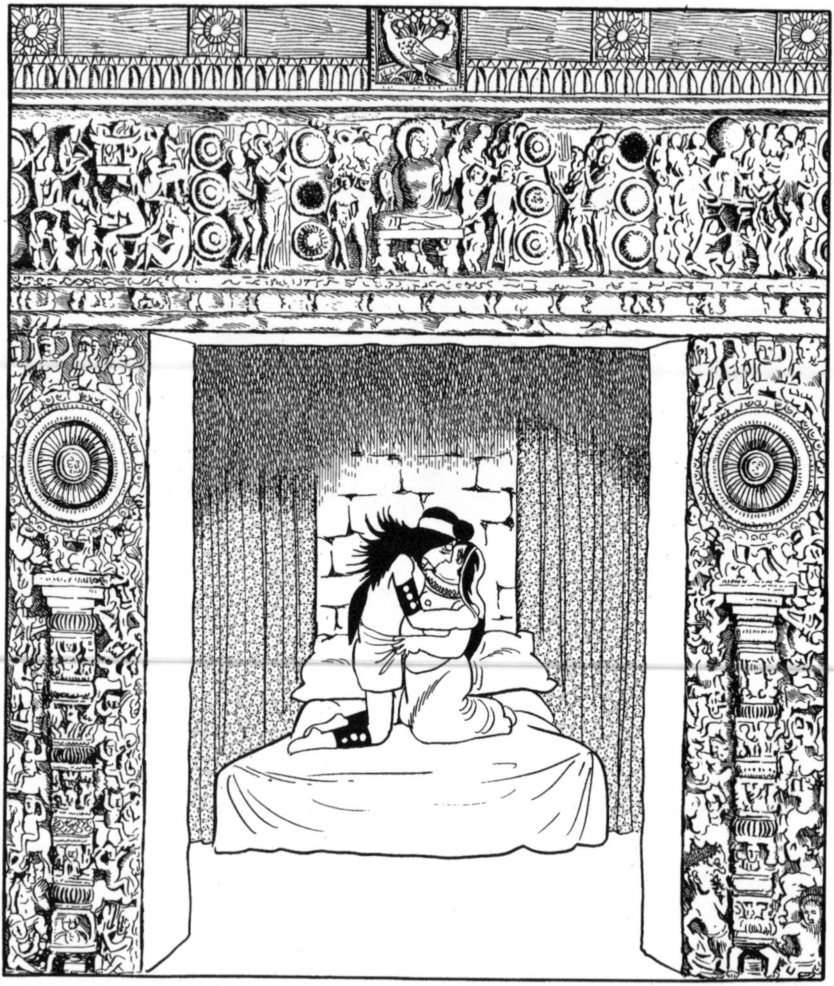

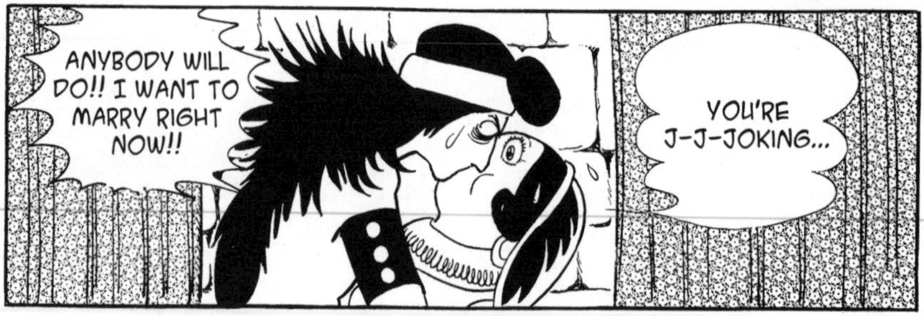
ANYBODY WILL DO!! I WANT TO MARRY RIGHT NOW!!
YOU'RE J-J-JOKING...

HA?

A JOKE, YOU SAY? I'M DEAD SERIOUS.

I'M GONNA MAKE YOU MY QUEEN.

...
...

YOU DON'T WANT THAT?

B-BUT, TO SUDDENLY REQUEST SUCH A THING OF A WOMAN LIKE ME...

CAN'T BELIEVE IT, HUH?

BUT AREN'T YOU AFTER ALL A SHAKYA NOBLE?

YOU'VE GOT A RIGHT TO BE QUEEN, TOO.

WHAT'S MORE, I LOVE CHUBBY GIRLS THAT I CAN BOUNCE AROUND LIKE A BEACH BALL.

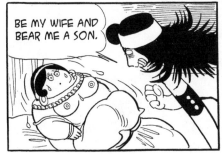

BE MY WIFE AND BEAR ME A SON.

A SON JUST LIKE ME, MANLY, STRONG, AND INTENSE!

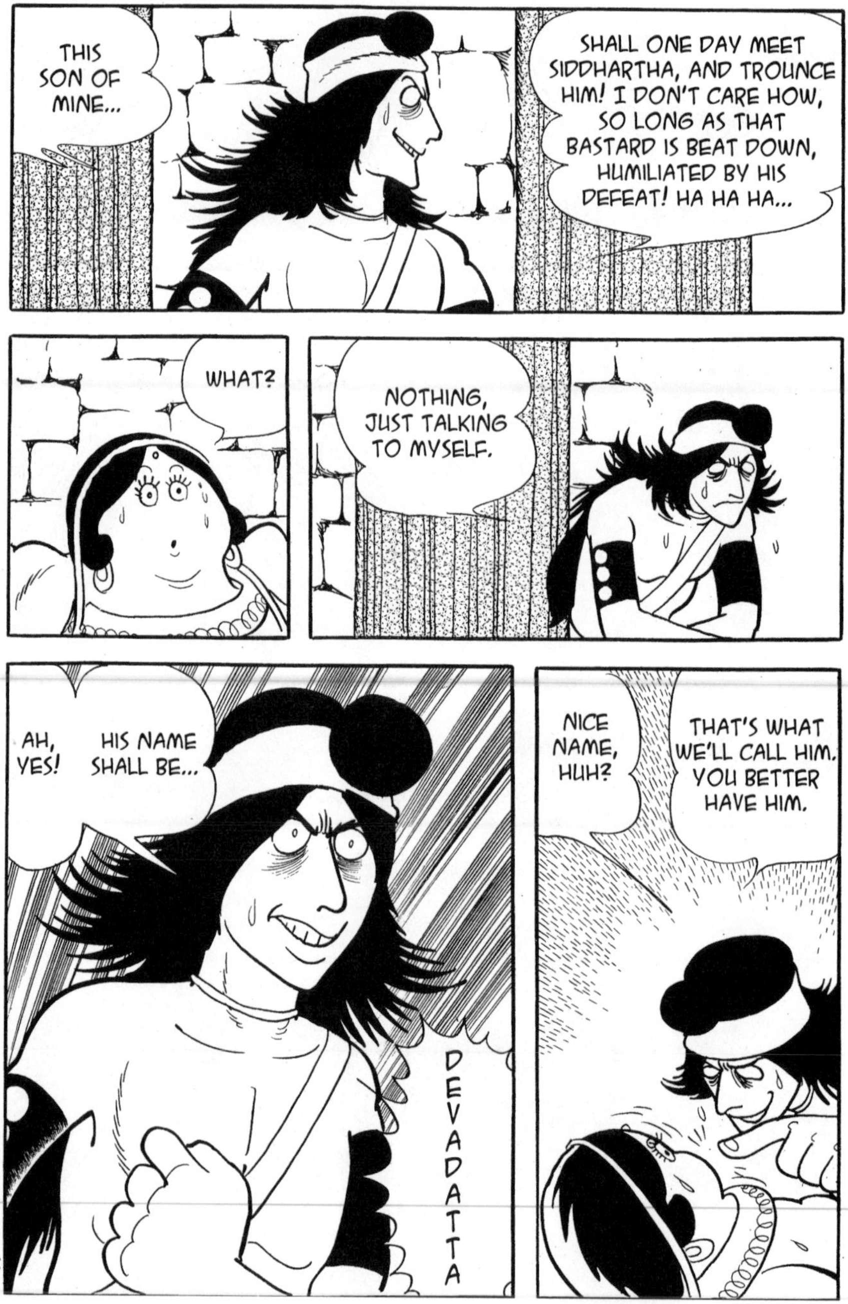
THIS SON OF MINE...
SHALL ONE DAY MEET SIDDHARTHA, AND TROUNCE HIM! I DON'T CARE HOW, SO LONG AS THAT BASTARD IS BEAT DOWN, HUMILIATED BY HIS DEFEAT! HA HA HA...
WHAT?
NOTHING, JUST TALKING TO MYSELF.
AH, YES!
HIS NAME SHALL BE...
DEVADATTA
NICE NAME, HUH?
THAT'S WHAT WE'LL CALL HIM. YOU BETTER HAVE HIM.

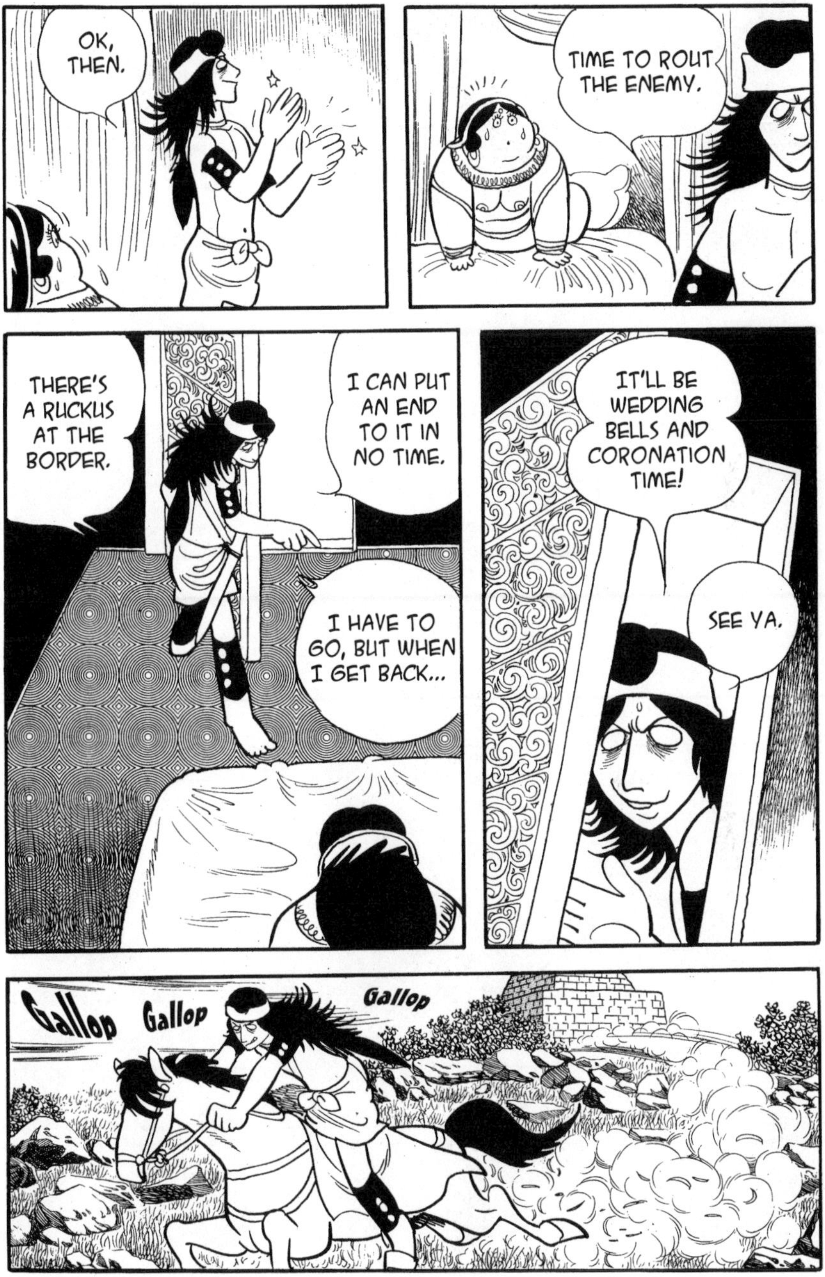
OK, THEN.
TIME TO ROUT THE ENEMY.
THERE'S A RUCKUS AT THE BORDER.
I CAN PUT AN END TO IT IN NO TIME.
I HAVE TO GO, BUT WHEN I GET BACK...
IT'LL BE WEDDING BELLS AND CORONATION TIME!
SEE YA.
Gallop Gallop Gallop

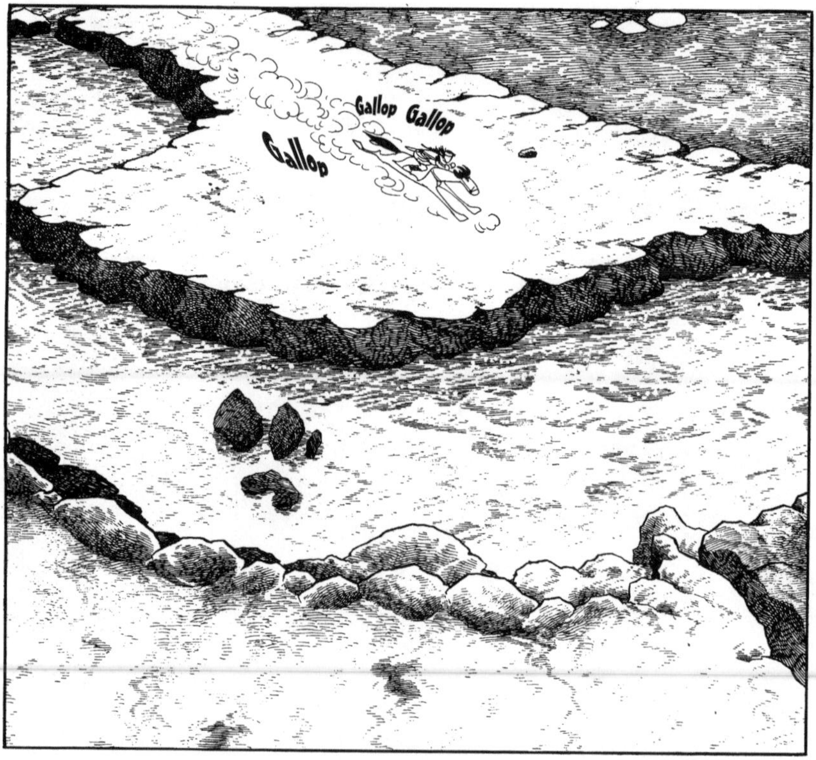
Gallop Gallop
Gallop

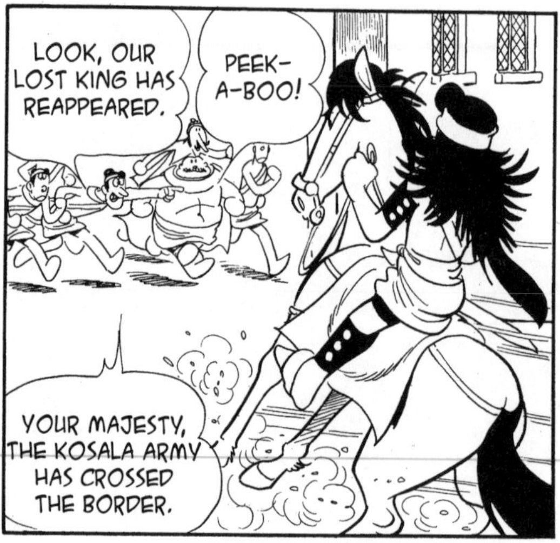
LOOK, OUR LOST KING HAS REAPPEARED.
PEEK-A-BOO!
YOUR MAJESTY, THE KOSALA ARMY HAS CROSSED THE BORDER.

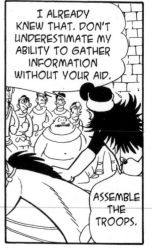

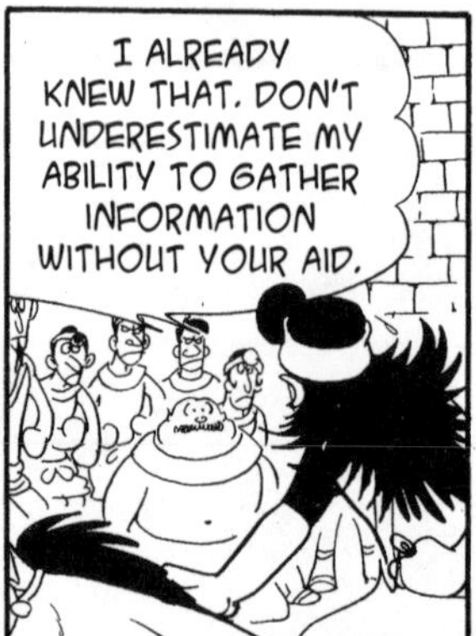
I ALREADY KNEW THAT. DON'T UNDERESTIMATE MY ABILITY TO GATHER INFORMATION WITHOUT YOUR AID.
ASSEMBLE THE TROOPS.

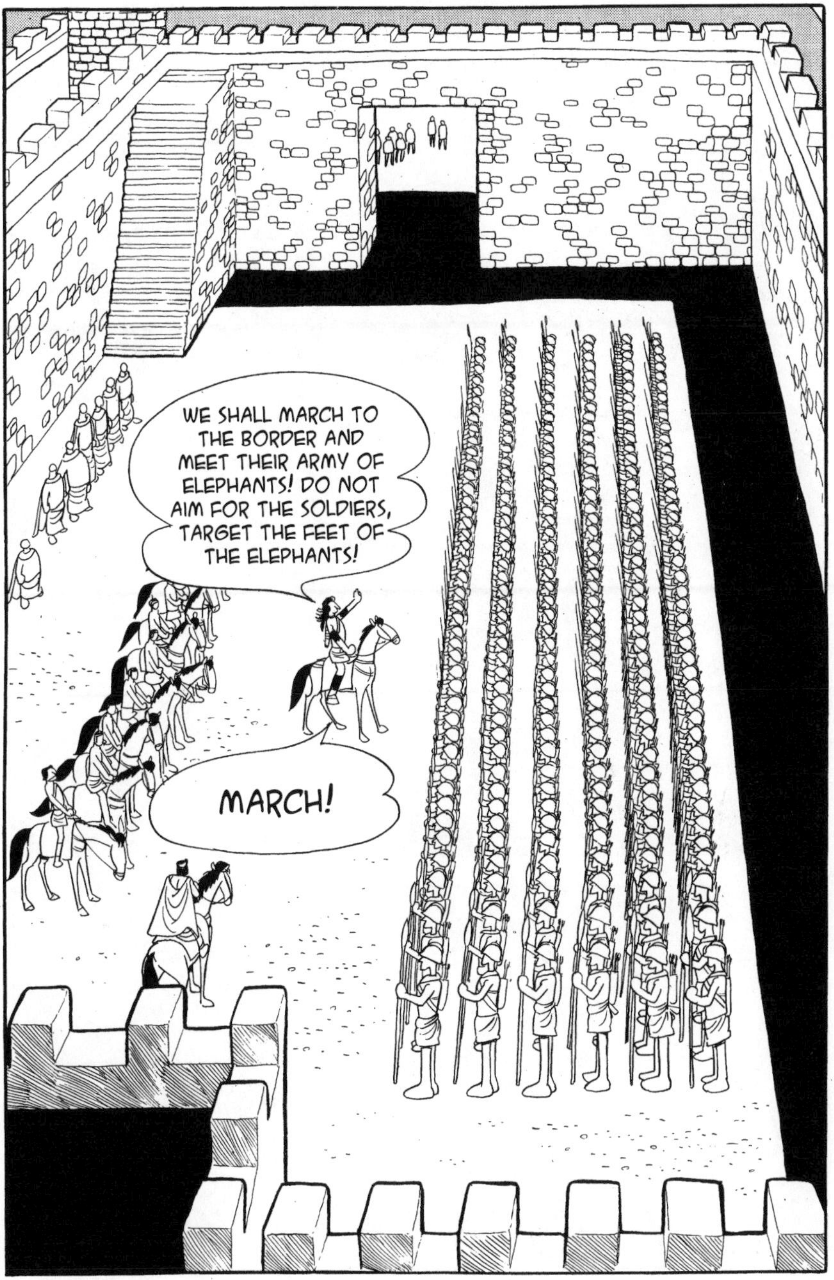
WE SHALL MARCH TO THE BORDER AND MEET THEIR ARMY OF ELEPHANTS! DO NOT AIM FOR THE SOLDIERS, TARGET THE FEET OF THE ELEPHANTS!
MARCH!

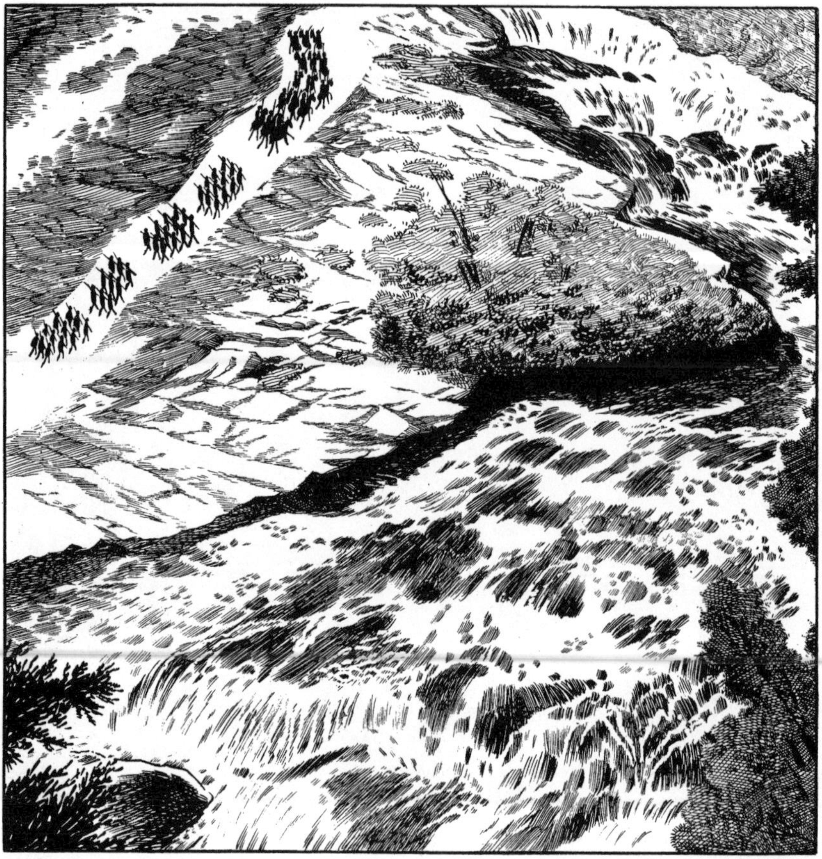

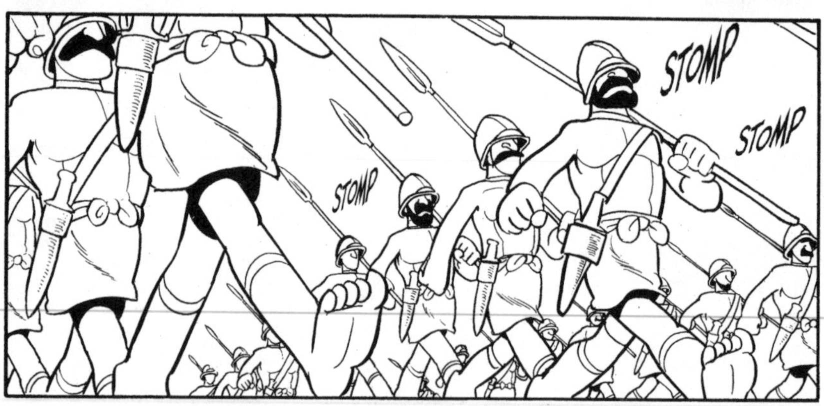
STOMP
STOMP
STOMP

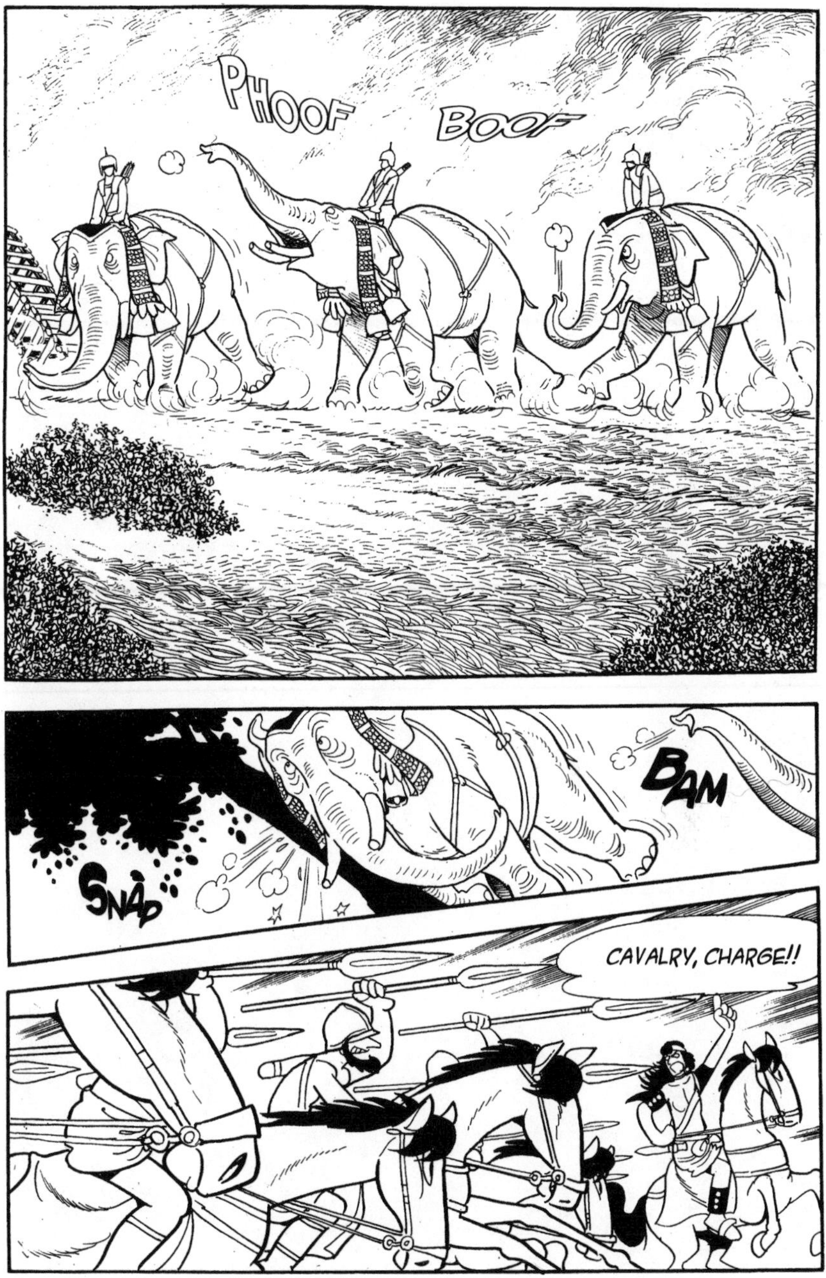
PHOOF
BOOF
BAM
SNAP
CAVALRY, CHARGE!!

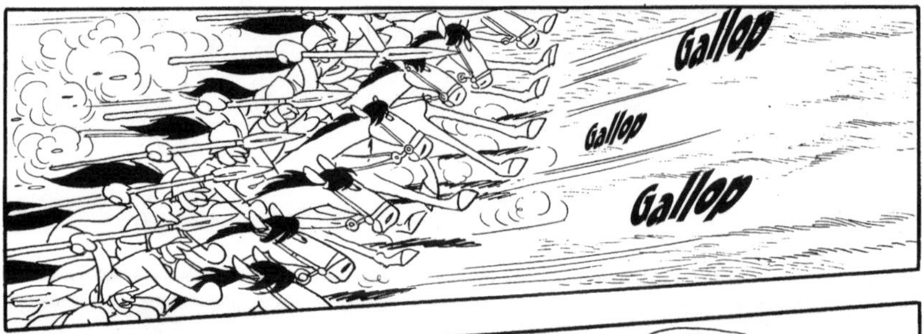
Gallop
Gallop
Gallop
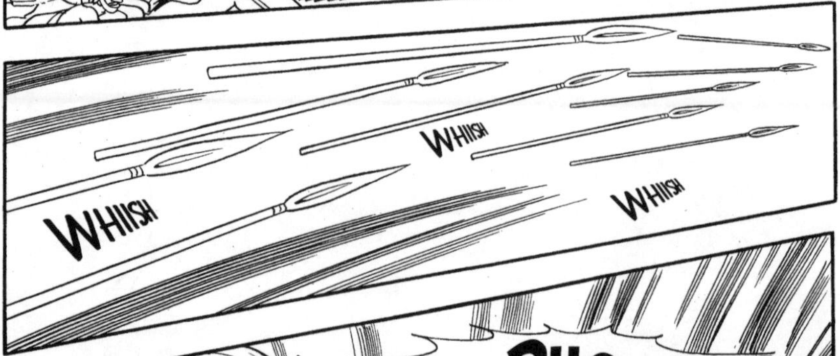
WHIISH
WHIISH
WHIISH
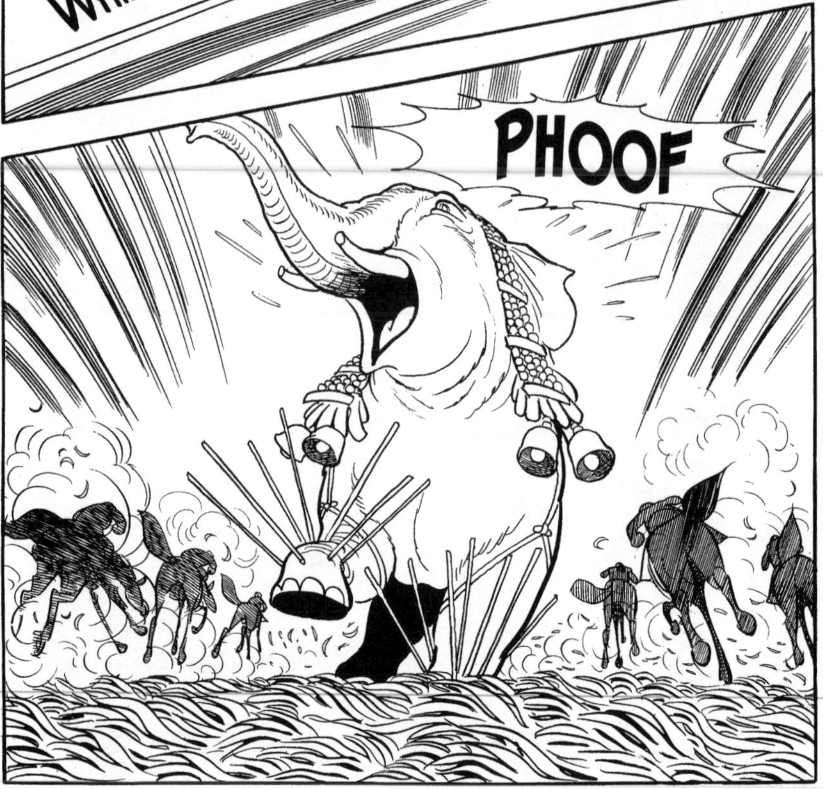
PHOOF

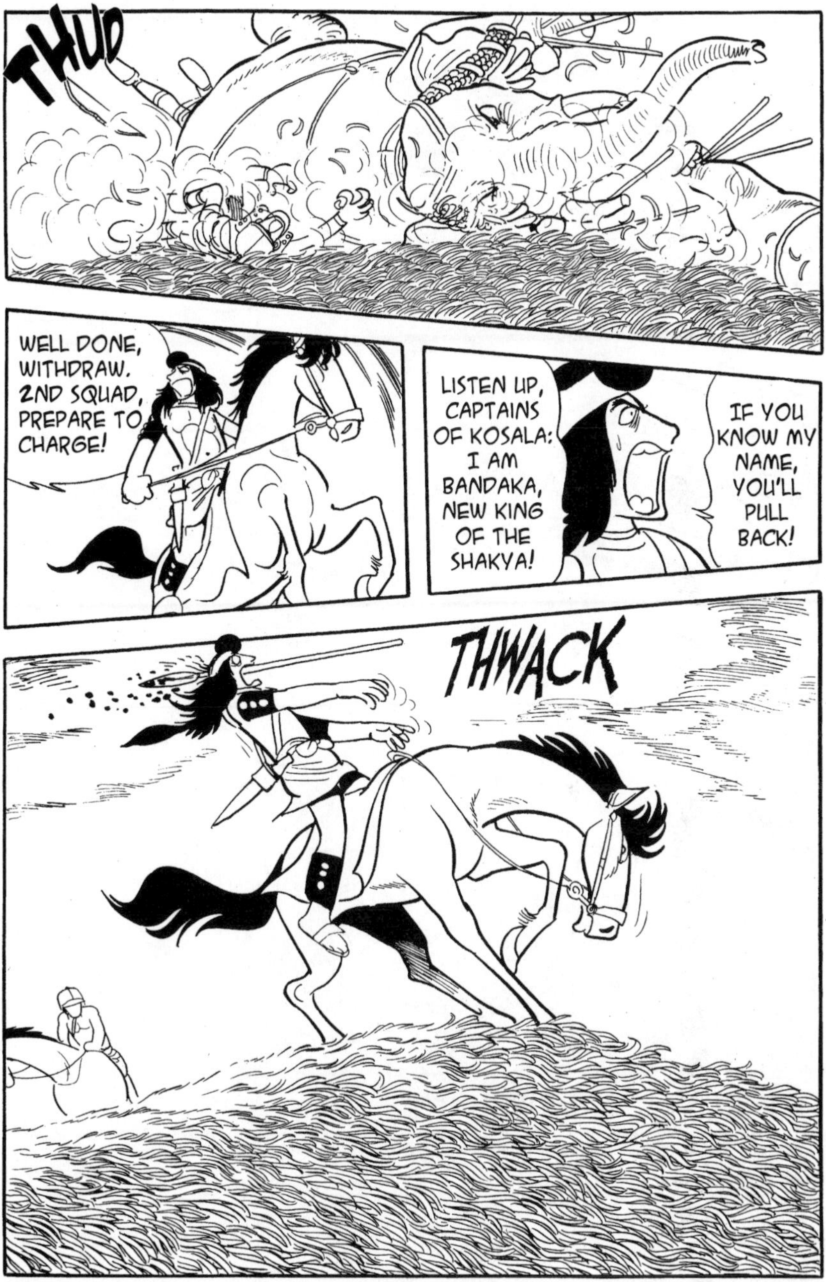
THUD
WELL DONE, WITHDRAW. 2ND SQUAD, PREPARE TO CHARGE!
LISTEN UP, CAPTAINS OF KOSALA: I AM BANDAKA, NEW KING OF THE SHAKYA!
IF YOU KNOW MY NAME, YOU'LL PULL BACK!
THWACK

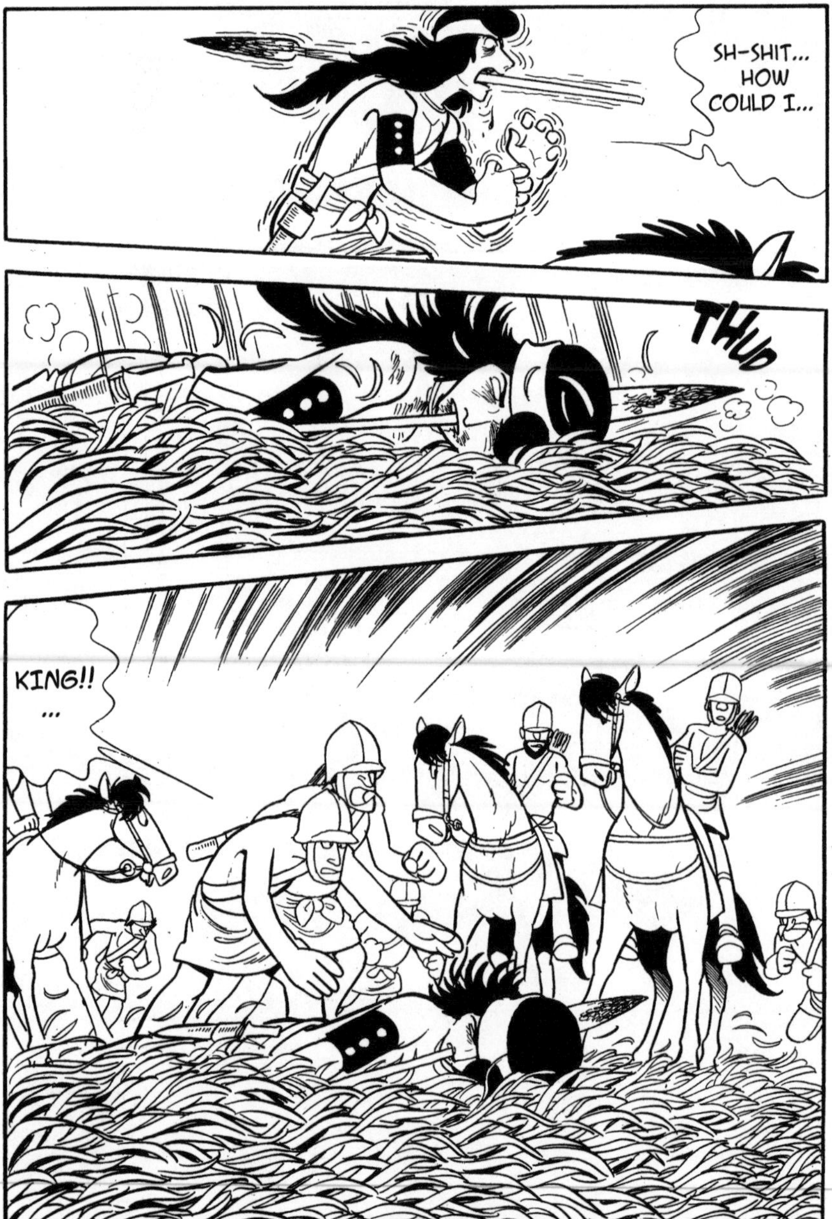
SH-SHIT... HOW COULD I...
THUD
KING!! ...

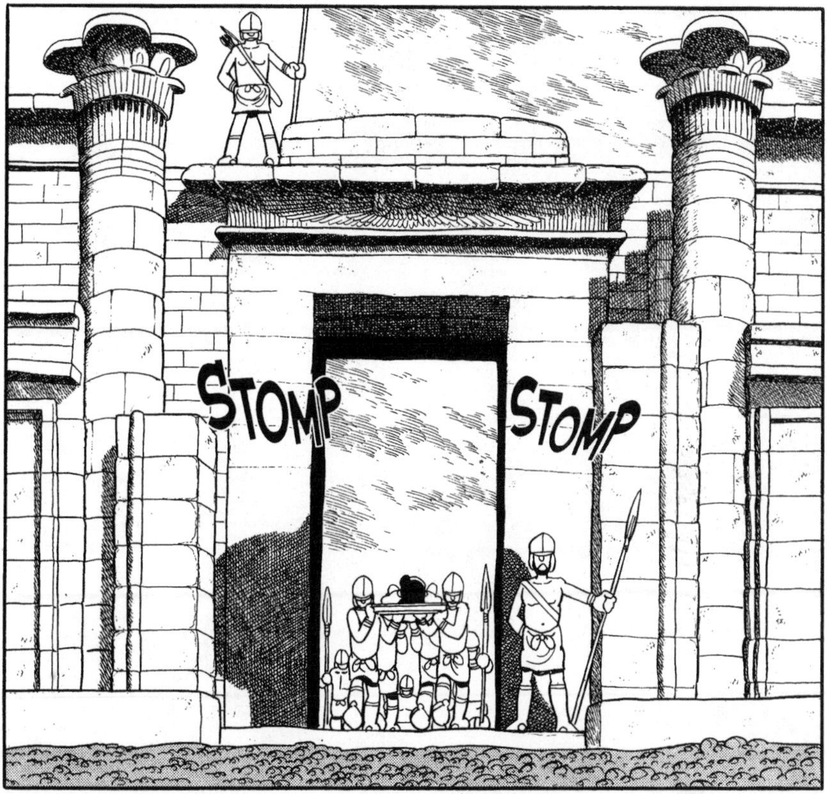
STOMP
STOMP
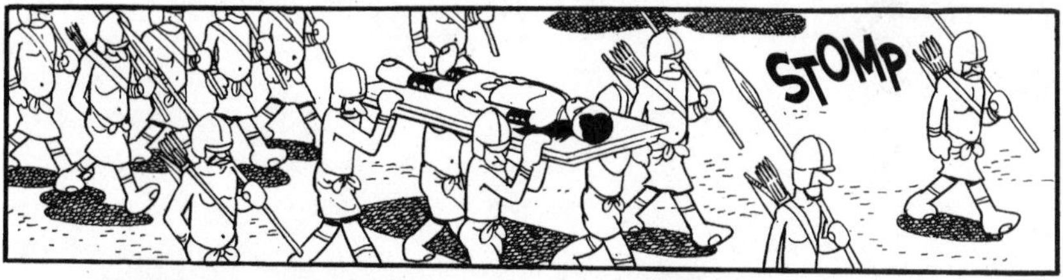
STOMP
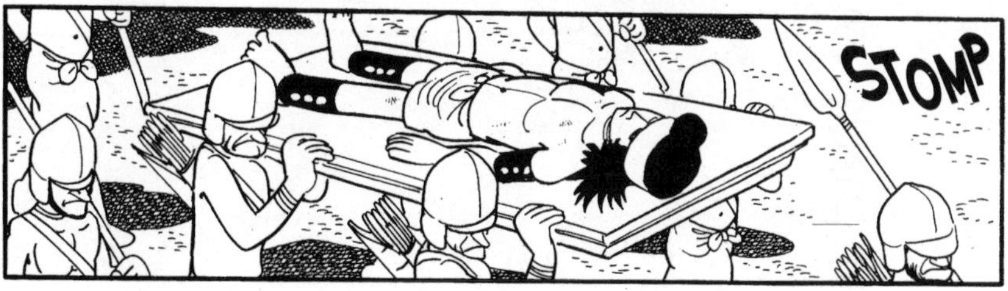
STOMP

WHAT'S WRONG?

WE REPELLED THE KOSALAN INVADERS...

BUT THE KING HAS MET A HEROIC DEATH.

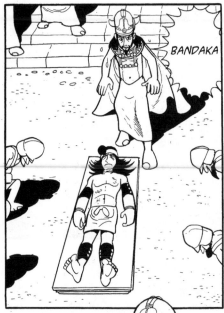

BANDAKA

WHAT AN UNLUCKY MAN YOU ARE.

THE KINGDOM YOU COVETED FINALLY YOURS, YOU HAD TO LEAVE FOR THE KINGDOM OF DEATH...

BUILD A TOMB FIT FOR A KING!

SOUND THE BELLS OF SORROW; LIGHT INCENSE!

THERE SHALL BE A GRAND FUNERAL FOR BANDAKA!!

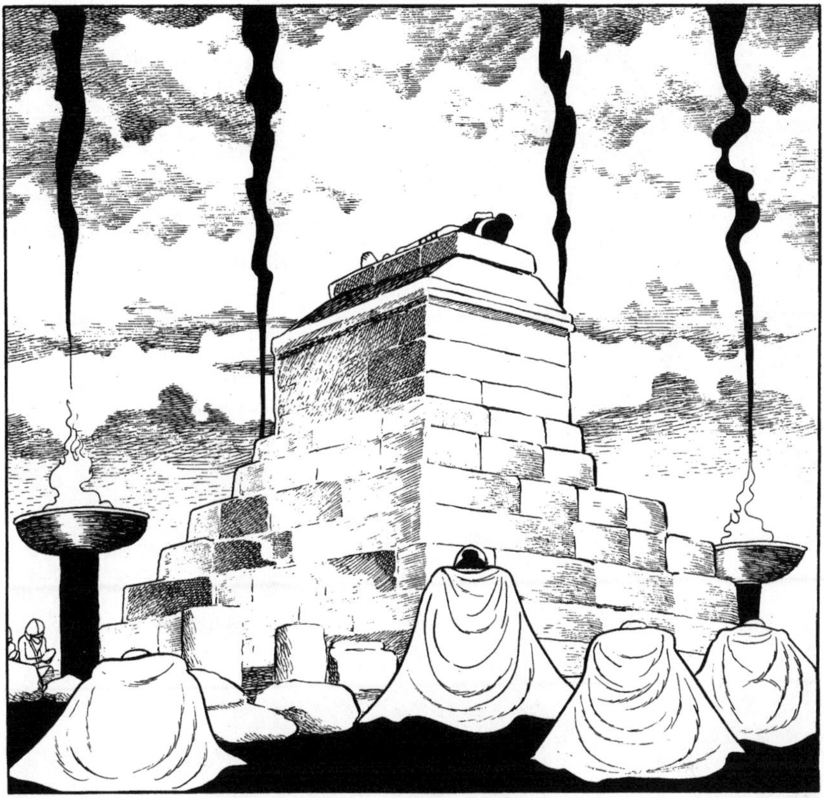

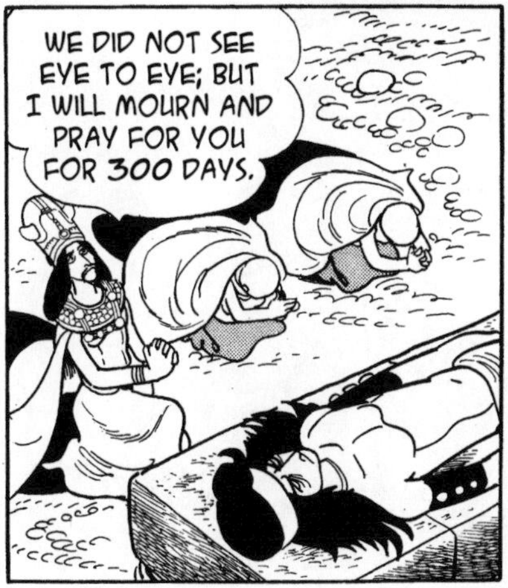
WE DID NOT SEE EYE TO EYE; BUT I WILL MOURN AND PRAY FOR YOU FOR 300 DAYS.

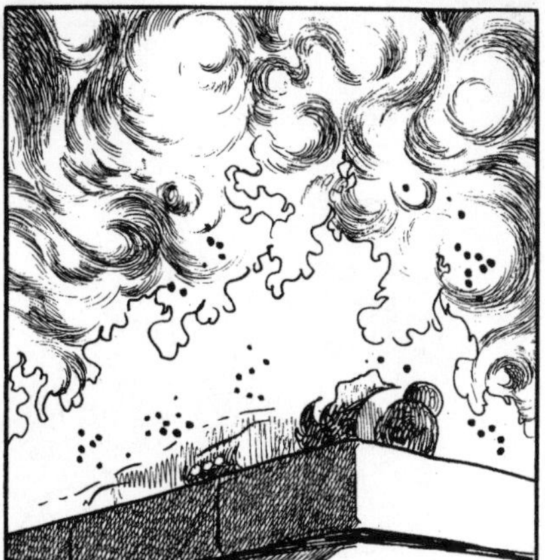

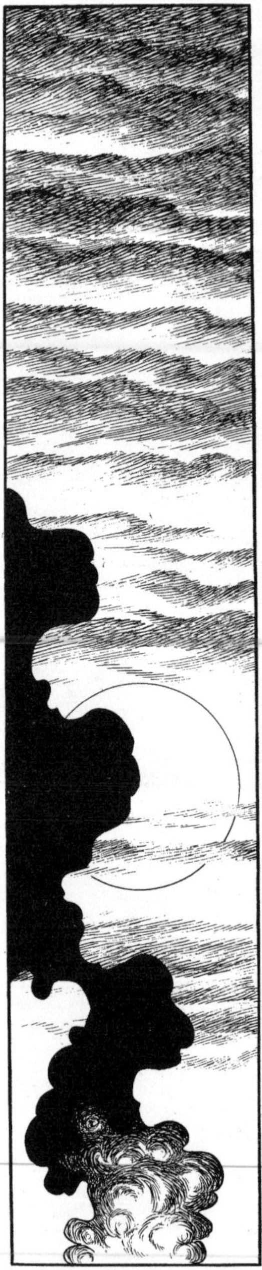
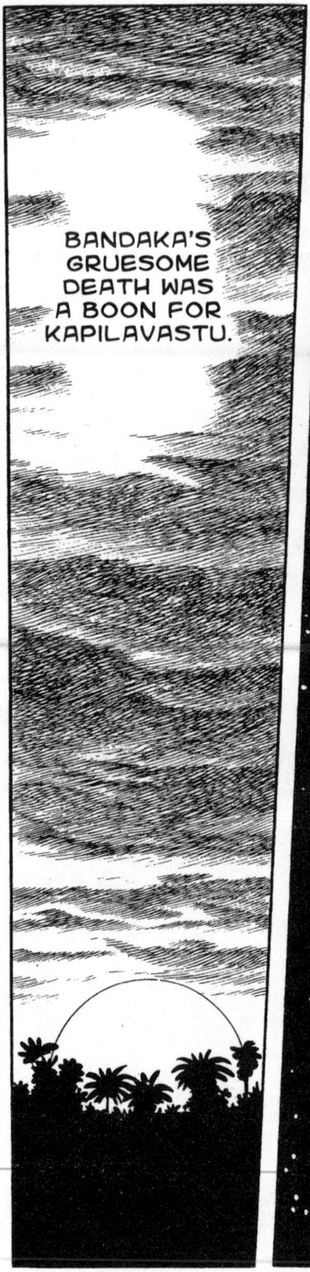
BANDAKA'S GRUESOME DEATH WAS A BOON FOR KAPILAVASTU.
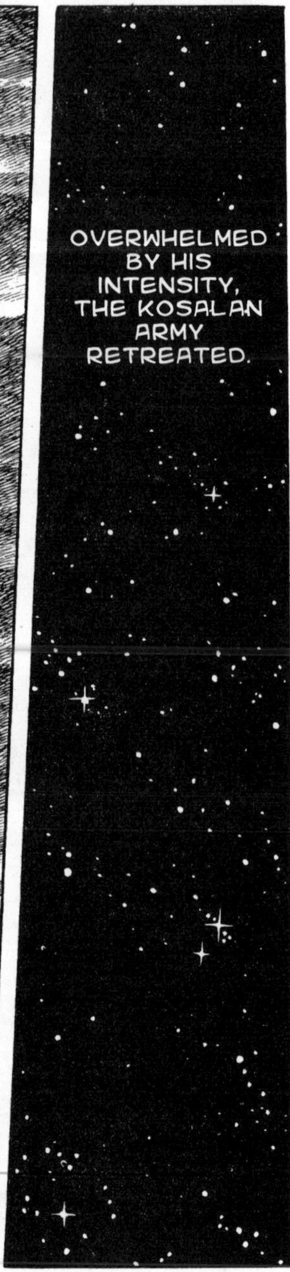
OVERWHELMED BY HIS INTENSITY, THE KOSALAN ARMY RETREATED.

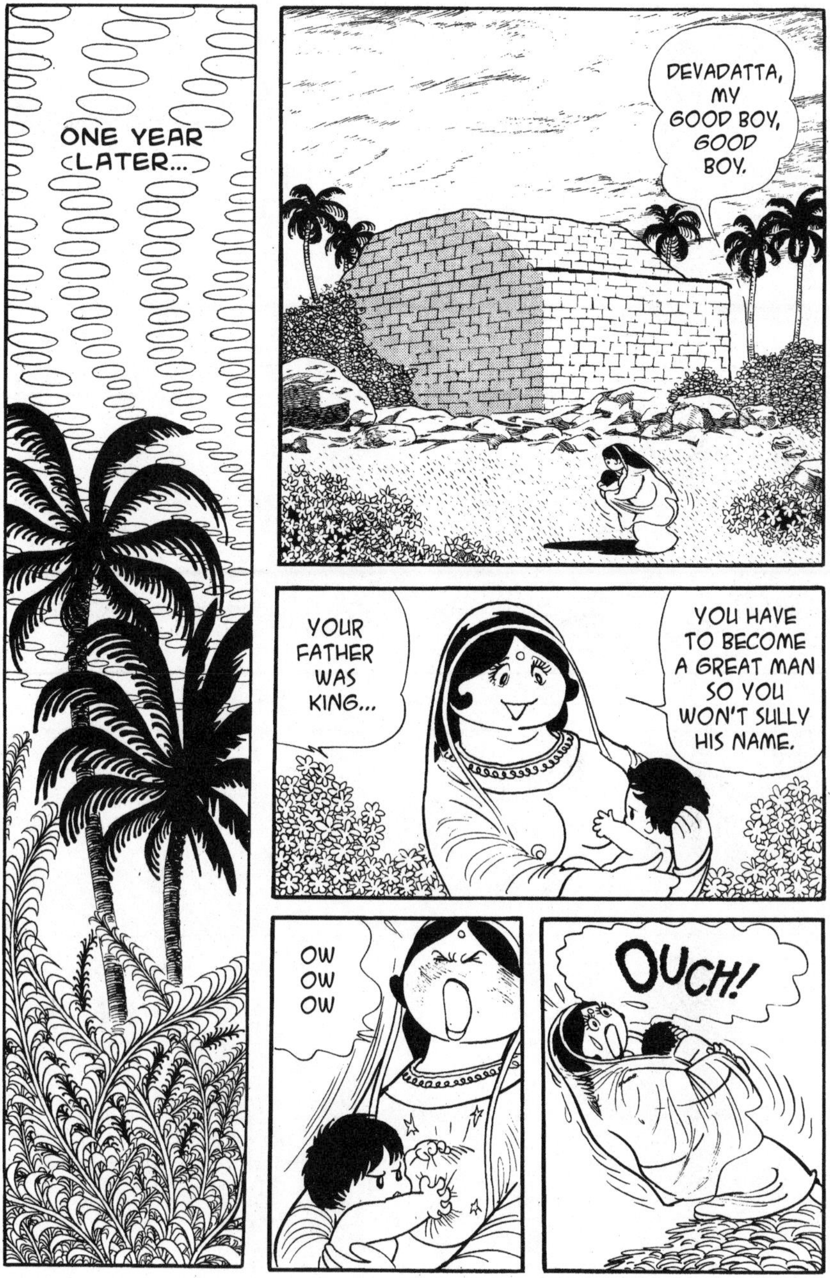
ONE YEAR LATER...
DEVADATTA, MY GOOD BOY, GOOD BOY.
YOUR FATHER WAS KING...
YOU HAVE TO BECOME A GREAT MAN SO YOU WON'T SULLY HIS NAME.
OW OW OW
OUCH!

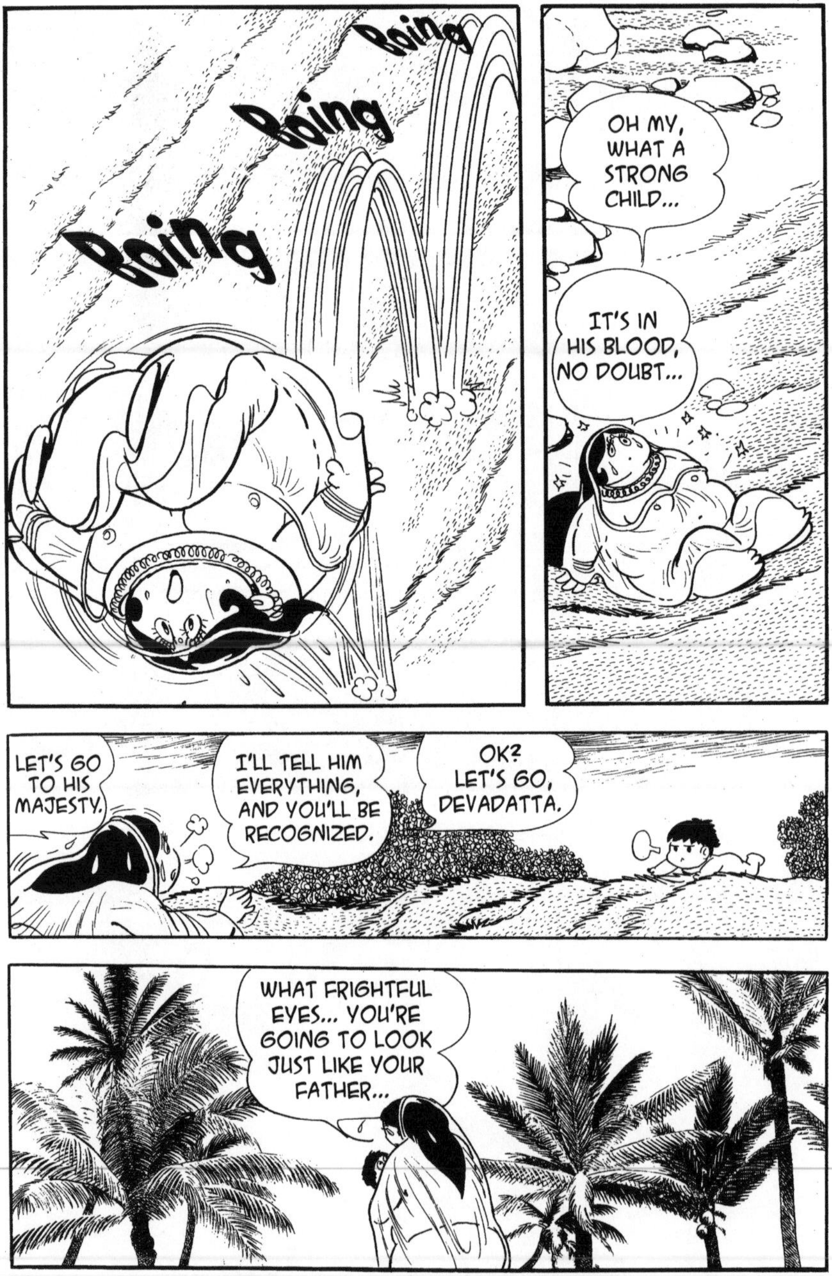
Boing
Boing
Boing
OH MY, WHAT A STRONG CHILD...
IT'S IN HIS BLOOD, NO DOUBT...
LET'S GO TO HIS MAJESTY.
I'LL TELL HIM EVERYTHING, AND YOU'LL BE RECOGNIZED.
OK? LET'S GO, DEVADATTA.
WHAT FRIGHTFUL EYES... YOU'RE GOING TO LOOK JUST LIKE YOUR FATHER...

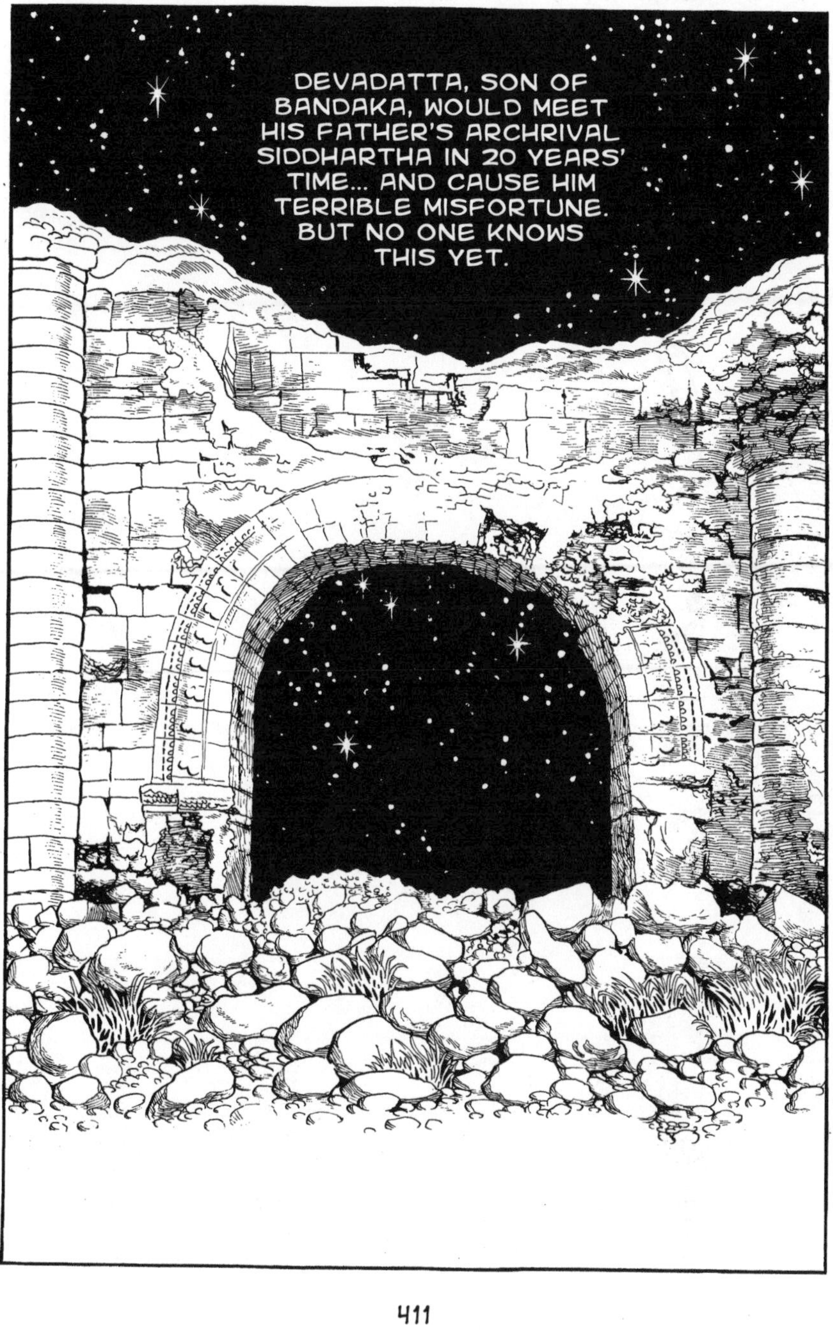
DEVADATTA, SON OF BANDAKA, WOULD MEET HIS FATHER'S ARCHRIVAL SIDDHARTHA IN 20 YEARS' TIME... AND CAUSE HIM TERRIBLE MISFORTUNE. BUT NO ONE KNOWS THIS YET.

TO BE CONTINUED...

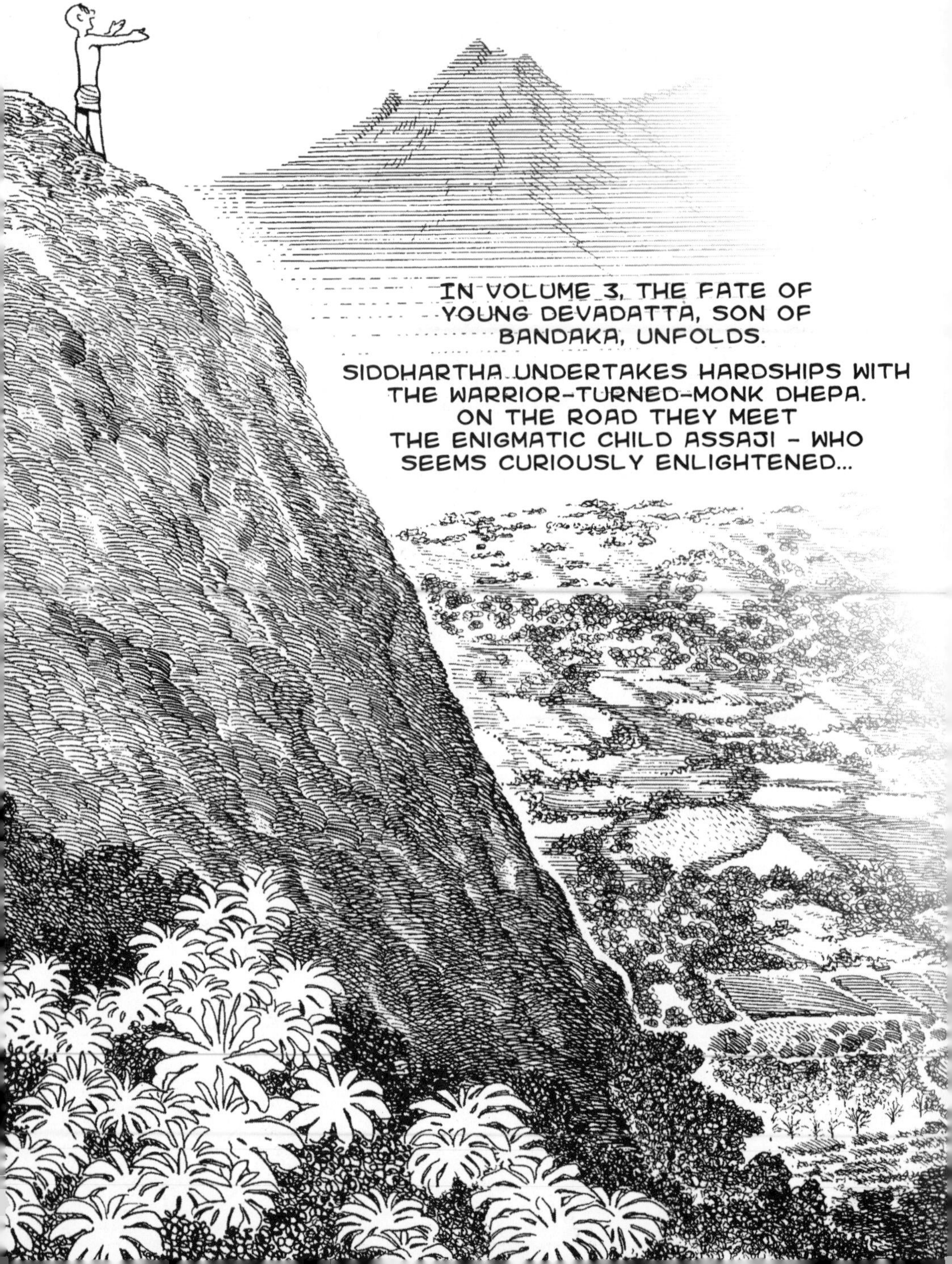
IN VOLUME 3, THE FATE OF YOUNG DEVADATTA, SON OF BANDAKA, UNFOLDS.
SIDDHARTHA UNDERTAKES HARDSHIPS WITH THE WARRIOR-TURNED-MONK DHEPA. ON THE ROAD THEY MEET THE ENIGMATIC CHILD ASSAJI - WHO SEEMS CURIOUSLY ENLIGHTENED...

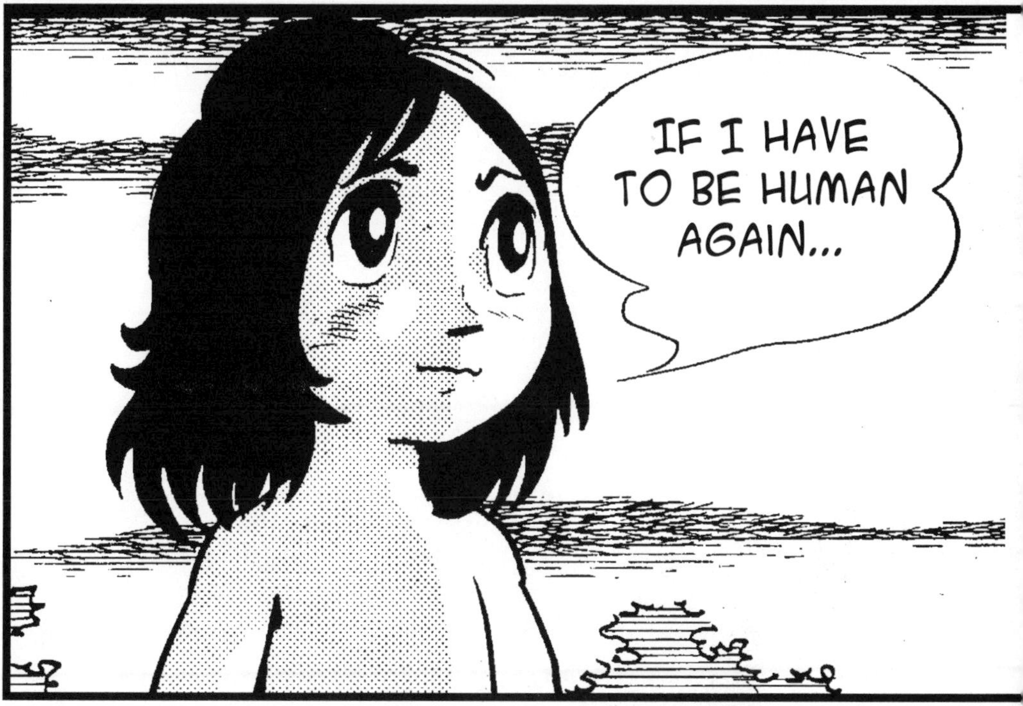
IF I HAVE TO BE HUMAN AGAIN...

BUDDHA

OSAMU TEZUKA

VOLUME 3: *Devadatta*

September 2006

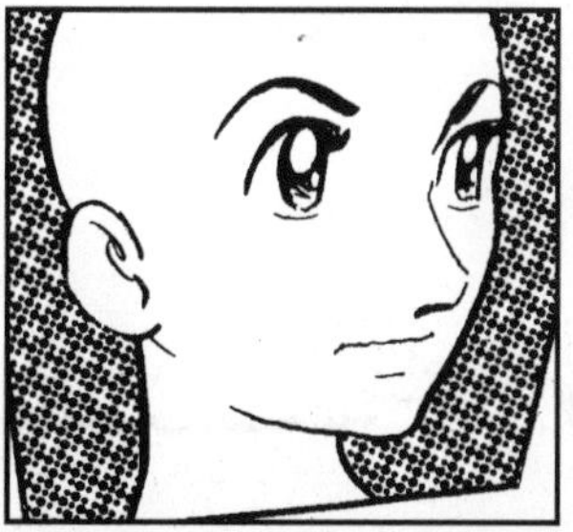

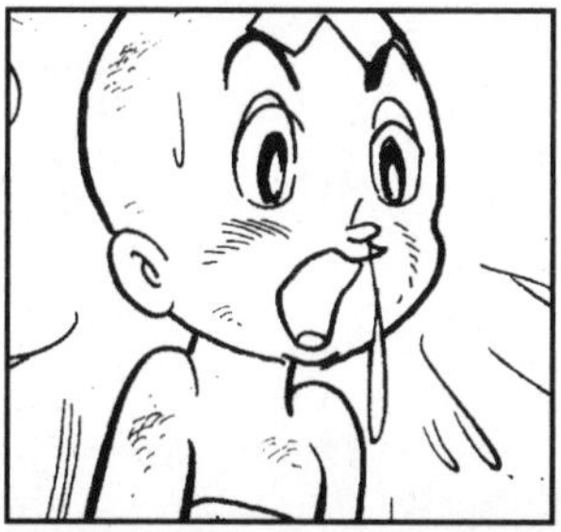

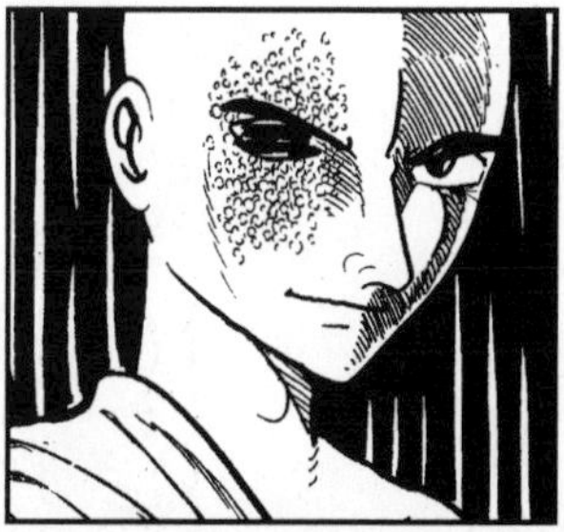